PUBLISHED IN COLLABORATION WITH WIKILEAKS, THIS IS THE ESSENTIAL BOOK FOR ANYONE INTERESTED IN AMERICA'S ROLE IN THE WORLD AND THE UNFOLDING HISTORY OF THE TWENTY-FIRST CENTURY.

WikiLeaks came to prominence in 2010 with the release of 251,287 top-secret State Department cables, which revealed to the world what the US government really thinks about national leaders, friendly dictators, and supposed allies. It brought to the surface the dark truths of crimes committed in our name: human rights violations, covert operations, and cover-ups.

The WikiLeaks Files presents expert analysis on the most important cables and outlines their historical importance. In a series of chapters dedicated to the various regions of the world, the book explores the machinations of the United States as it imposes its agenda on other nations: a new form of imperialism founded on varied tactics from torture to military action, to trade deals and "soft power," in the perpetual pursuit of expanding influence. It illustrates the close relationship between government and big business in promoting US trade.

An introduction by Julian Assange—writing on the subject for the first time—exposes the ongoing debates about freedom of information, international surveillance, and justice.

* *

"From government to big business, if you have a dirty secret, WikiLeaks is your nightmare." GUARDIAN

"WikiLeaks is the absolute most important project on the globe."
JACOB APPELBAUM

""Reveals a profound hatred of democracy on the part of our political leadership." NOAM CHOMSKY

* *

The WikiLeaks Files

The WikiLeaks Files
The World According to US Empire

Introduction by Julian Assange

VERSO
London • New York

First published by Verso 2015
The collection © Verso 2015
Contributions © The contributors 2015
Introduction © Julian Assange 2015

3 5 7 9 10 8 6 4 2

Verso
UK: 6 Meard Street, London W1F 0EG
US: 20 Jay Street, Suite 1010, Brooklyn, NY 11201
www.versobooks.com

Verso is the imprint of New Left Books

ISBN-13: 978-1-78168-874-8 (HB)
ISBN-13: 978-1-78478-271-9 (EXPORT)
eISBN-13: 978-1-78168-875-5 (UK)
eISBN-13: 978-1-78168-944-8 (US)

British Library Cataloguing in Publication Data
A catalogue record for this book is available from the British Library

Library of Congress Cataloging-in-Publication Data
A catalog record for this book is available from the Library of Congress

Typeset in Sabon by MJ & N Gavan, Truro, Cornwall
Printed in the US by Maple Press

Contents

Introduction:
WikiLeaks and Empire

Julian Assange

One day, a monk and two novices found a heavy stone in their path. "We will throw it away," said the novices. But before they could do so, the monk took his ax and cleaved the stone in half. After seeking his approval, the novices then threw the halves away. "Why did you cleave the stone only to have us throw it away?" they asked. The monk pointed to the distance the half stones had traveled. Growing excited, one of the novices took the monk's ax and rushed to where one half of the stone had landed. Cleaving it, he threw the quarter, whereupon the other novice grabbed the ax from him and rushed after it. He too cleaved the stone fragment and threw it afield. The novices continued on in this fashion, laughing and gasping, until the halves were so small they traveled not at all and drifted into their eyes like dust. The novices blinked in bewilderment. "Every stone has its size," said the monk.

At the time of writing, WikiLeaks has published 2,325,961 diplomatic cables and other US State Department records, comprising some two billion words. This stupendous and seemingly insurmountable body of internal state literature, which if printed would amount to some 30,000 volumes, represents something new. Like the State Department, it cannot be grasped without breaking it open and considering its parts. But to randomly pick up isolated diplomatic records that intersect with known entities and disputes, as some daily newspapers have done, is to miss "the empire" for its cables.

Each corpus has its size.

To obtain the right level of abstraction, one which considers the relationships between most of the cables for a region or country rather than considering cables in isolation, a more scholarly approach is needed. This approach is so natural that it seems odd that it has not been tried before.

The study of empires has long been the study of their communications. Carved into stone or inked into parchment, empires from Babylon to the Ming dynasty left records of the organizational center communicating with its peripheries. However, by the 1950s students of historical empires realized that somehow the communications medium *was* the empire. Its methods for organizing the inscription, transportation, indexing and storage of its communications, and for designating who was authorized to read and write them, in a real sense *constituted* the empire. When the methods an empire used to communicate changed, the empire also changed.[1]

Speech has a short temporal range, but stone has a long one. Some writing methods, such as engraving into stone, suited the transmission of compressed institutional rules that needed to be safely communicated into future months and years. But these methods did not allow for rapidly unfolding events, or for official nuance or discretion: they were set in stone. To address the gaps, empires with slow writing systems still had to rely heavily on humanity's oldest and yet most ephemeral communications medium: oral conventions, speech.

Other methods, such as papyrus, were light and fast to create, but fragile. Such communications materials had the advantage of being easy to construct and transport, unifying occupied regions through rapid information flow that in turn could feed a reactive central management. Such a well-connected center could integrate the streams of intelligence coming in and swiftly project its resulting decisions outwards, albeit with resulting tendencies toward short-termism and micromanagement. While a sea, desert, or mountain could be crossed or bypassed at some expense, and energy resources discovered or stolen, the ability to project an empire's desires, structure, and knowledge across space and time forms an absolute boundary to its existence.

Cultures and economies communicate using all manner of techniques across the regions and years of their existence, from the evolution of jokes shared virally between friends to the diffusion of prices across trade routes. This does not by itself make an empire. The structured attempt at managing an extended cultural and economic system using communications is the hallmark of empire. And it is the records of these communications, never intended to be dissected, and so especially vulnerable to dissection, that form the basis for understanding the nature of the world's sole remaining "empire."

ANATOMY OF THE US EMPIRE

And where is this empire?[2]

Each working day, 71,000 people across 191 countries representing twenty-seven different US government agencies wake and make their way past flags, steel fences, and armed guards into one of the 276 fortified buildings that comprise the 169 embassies and other missions of the US Department of State. They are joined in their march by representatives and operatives from twenty-seven other US government departments and agencies, including the Central Intelligence Agency, the National Security Agency, the Federal Bureau of Investigation, and the various branches of the US military.

Inside each embassy is an ambassador who is usually close to domestic US political, business or intelligence power; career diplomats who specialize in the politics, economy, and public diplomacy of their host state; managers, researchers, military attachés, spies under foreign-service cover, personnel from other US government agencies (for some embassies this goes as far as overt armed military or covert special operations forces); contractors, security personnel, technicians, locally hired translators, cleaners, and other service personnel.[3]

Above them, radio and satellite antennas scrape the air, some reaching back home to receive or disgorge diplomatic and CIA cables, some to relay the communications of US military ships and planes, others emplaced by the National Security Agency in order to mass-intercept the mobile phones and other wireless traffic of the host population.

The US diplomatic service dates back to the revolution, but it was in the post–World War II environment that the modern State Department came to be. Its origins coincided with the appointment of Henry Kissinger as secretary of state, in 1973. Kissinger's appointment was unusual in several respects. Kissinger did not just head up the State Department; he was also concurrently appointed national security advisor, facilitating a tighter integration between the foreign relations and military and intelligence arms of the US government. While the State Department had long had a cable system, the appointment of Kissinger led to logistical changes in how cables were written, indexed, and stored. For the first time, the bulk of cables were transmitted electronically. This period of major innovation is still present in the way the department operates today.

The US Department of State is unique among the formal bureaucracies of the United States. Other agencies aspire to administrate one function or another, but the State Department represents, and even houses, all major elements of US national power. It provides cover for the CIA, buildings for the NSA mass-interception equipment, office space and communications facilities for the FBI, the military, and other government agencies, and staff to act as sales agents and political advisors for the largest US corporations.[4]

One cannot properly understand an institution like the State

Department from the outside, any more than Renaissance artists could discover how animals worked without opening them up and poking about inside. As the diplomatic apparatus of the United States, the State Department is directly involved in putting a friendly face on empire, concealing its underlying mechanics. Every year, more than $1 billion is budgeted for "public diplomacy," a circumlocutory term for outward-facing propaganda. Public diplomacy explicitly aims to influence journalists and civil society, so that they serve as conduits for State Department messaging.

While national archives have produced impressive collections of internal state communications, their material is intentionally withheld or made difficult to access for decades, until it is stripped of potency. This is inevitable, as national archives are not structured to resist the blowback (in the form of withdrawn funding or termination of officials) that timely, accessible archives of international significance would produce. What makes the revelation of secret communications potent is that we were not supposed to read them. The internal communications of the US Department of State are the logistical by-product of its activities: their publication is the vivisection of a living empire, showing what substance flowed from which state organ and when.

Diplomatic cables are not produced in order to manipulate the public, but are aimed at elements of the rest of the US state apparatus, and are therefore relatively free from the distorting influence of public relations. Reading them is a much more effective way of understanding an institution like the State Department than reading reports by journalists on the public pronouncements of Hillary Clinton, or Jen Psaki.

While in their internal communications State Department officials must match their pens to the latest DC orthodoxies should they wish to stand out in Washington for the "right" reasons and not the "wrong" ones, these elements of political correctness are themselves noteworthy and visible to outsiders who are not sufficiently indoctrinated. Many cables are deliberative or logistical, and their causal relationships across time and space with other cables and with externally documented events create a web of interpretive constraints that reliably show how the US Department of State and the agencies that inter-operate with its cable system understand their place in the world.

Only by approaching this corpus holistically—over and above the documentation of each individual abuse, each localized atrocity—does the true human cost of empire heave into view.

NATIONAL SECURITY RELIGIOSITY AND THE INTERNATIONAL STUDIES ASSOCIATION

While there exists a large literature in the structural or realpolitik analysis of key institutions of US power, a range of ritualistic and even quasi-religious phenomena surrounding the national security sector in the United States suggests that these approaches alone lack explanatory power. These phenomena are familiar in the ritual of flag-folding, the veneration of orders, and elaborate genuflection to rank, but they can be seen also in the extraordinary reaction to WikiLeaks' disclosures, where it is possible to observe some of their more interesting features.

When WikiLeaks publishes US government documents with classification markings—a type of national-security "holy seal," if you will—two parallel campaigns begin: first, the public campaign of downplaying, diverting attention from, and reframing any revelations that are a threat to the prestige of the national security class; and, second, an internal campaign within the national security state itself to digest what has happened. When documents carrying such seals are made public, they are transubstantiated into forbidden objects that become toxic to the "state within a state"—the more than 5.1 million Americans (as of 2014) with active security clearances, and those on its extended periphery who aspire to its economic or social patronage.[5] There is a level of hysteria and non-corporeality exhibited in this reaction to WikiLeaks' disclosures that is not easily captured by traditional theories of power. Many religions and cults imbue their priestly class with additional scarcity value by keeping their religious texts secret from the public or the lower orders of the devoted. This technique also permits the priestly class to adopt different psychological strategies for different levels of indoctrination. What is laughable, hypocritical, or Machiavellian to the public or lower levels of "clearance" is embraced by those who have become sufficiently indoctrinated or co-opted into feeling that their economic or social advantage lies in accepting that which they would normally reject. Publicly, the US government has claimed, falsely, that anyone without a security clearance distributing "classified" documents is violating the Espionage Act of 1917. But the claims of the interior "state within a state" campaign work in the opposite direction. There, it orders the very people it publicly claims are the only ones who can legally read classified documents to refrain from reading documents WikiLeaks and associated media have published with classification markings on them, lest they be "contaminated" by them. While a given document can be read by cleared staff when it issues from classified government repositories, it is forbidden for the same staff to set eyes on the exact same document when it emerges from a public source. Should cleared employees of the national security state read such documents in the public domain, they are expected to self-report their contact with the newly profaned object, and destroy all traces of it.

This response is, of course, irrational. The classified cables and other documents published by WikiLeaks and associated media are completely identical to the original versions officially available to those with the necessary security clearance, since this is where they originated. They are electronic copies. Not only are they indistinguishable—there is literally no difference at all between them. Not a word. Not a letter. Not a single bit.

The implication is that there is a non-physical property that inhabits documents once they receive their classification markings, and that this magical property is extinguished, not by copying the document, but by making the copy public. The now public document has, to devotees of the national security state, not merely become devoid of this magical property and reverted to a mundane object, it has been inhabited by another non-physical property: an evil one.

This kind of religious thinking has consequences. Not only is it the excuse used by the US government to block millions of people working for the "state within a state" from reading more than thirty different WikiLeaks domains—the same excuse that was used to block the *New York Times*, *Guardian*, *Der Spiegel*, *Le Monde*, *El País*, and other outlets publishing WikiLeaks materials.[6]

In fact, in 2011 the US government sent what might be called a "WikiLeaks fatwa" to every federal government agency, every federal government employee, and every federal government security contractor:

> The recent disclosure of US Government documents
> by WikiLeaks has caused damage to our national
> security ... Classified information, whether or not
> already posted on public websites, disclosed to
> the media, or otherwise in the public domain
> remains classified and must be treated as
> such until such time it is declassified by an
> appropriate US government authority ... Contractors
> who inadvertently discover potentially classified
> information in the public domain shall report its
> existence immediately to their Facility Security
> Officers. Companies are instructed to delete the
> offending material by holding down the SHIFT key
> while pressing the DELETE key for Windows-based
> systems and clearing of the internet browser
> cache.[7]

After being contacted by an officer of the US Department of State, Columbia University's School of International and Public

Affairs warned its students to "not post links to these documents nor make comments on social media sites such as Facebook or through Twitter. Engaging in these activities would call into question your ability to deal with confidential information, which is part of most positions with the federal government."

A swathe of government departments and other entities, including even the Library of Congress, blocked internet access to WikiLeaks.[8] The US National Archives even blocked searches of its own database for the phrase "WikiLeaks."[9] So absurd did the taboo become that, like a dog snapping mindlessly at everything, eventually it found its mark—its own tail. By March 2012, the Pentagon had gone so far as to create an automatic filter to block any emails, including inbound emails to the Pentagon, containing the word "WikiLeaks." As a result, Pentagon prosecutors preparing the case against US intelligence analyst PFC Manning, the alleged source of the *Cablegate* cables, found that they were not receiving important emails from either the judge or the defense.[10] But the Pentagon did not remove the filter—instead, chief prosecutor Major Ashden Fein told the court that a new procedure had been introduced to check the filter daily for blocked WikiLeaks-related emails. Military judge Col. Denise Lind said that special alternative email addresses would be set up for the prosecution.[11]

While such religious hysteria seems laughable to those outside the US national security sector, it has resulted in a serious poverty of analysis of WikiLeaks publications in American international relations journals. However, scholars in disciplines as varied as law, linguistics, applied statistics, health, and economics have not been so shy. For instance, in their 2013 paper for the statistics journal *Entropy*, DeDeo et al.—all US or UK nationals—write that WikiLeaks' *Afghan War Diary* "is likely to become a standard set for both the analysis of human conflict and the study of empirical methods for the analysis of complex, multi-modal data."[12]

There is even an extensive use of WikiLeaks materials, particularly cables, in courts, including domestic courts, from the

United Kingdom to Pakistan, and in international tribunals from the European Court of Human Rights to the International Criminal Tribunal for the former Yugoslavia.

Set against the thousands of citations in the courts and in other academic areas, the poverty of coverage in American international relations journals appears not merely odd, but suspicious. These journals, which dominate the study of international relations globally, should be a natural home for the proper analysis of WikiLeaks' two-billion-word diplomatic corpus. The US-based *International Studies Quarterly* (*ISQ*), a major international relations journal, adopted a policy against accepting manuscripts based on WikiLeaks material—even where it consists of quotes or derived analysis. According to a forthcoming paper, "Who's Afraid of WikiLeaks? Missed Opportunities in Political Science Research," the editor of *ISQ* stated that the journal is currently "in an untenable position," and that this will remain the case until there is a change in policy from the influential International Studies Association (ISA). The ISA has over 6,500 members worldwide and is the dominant scholarly association in the field. The ISA also publishes *Foreign Policy Analysis*, *International Political Sociology*, *International Interactions*, *International Studies Review*, and *International Studies Perspectives*.

The ISA's 2014–15 president is Amitav Acharya, a professor at the School of International Service at the American University in Washington, DC. Nearly half of the fifty-six members on its governing council are professors at similar academic departments across the United States, many of which also operate as feeder schools for the US Department of State and other internationally-oriented areas of government.

That the ISA has banned the single most significant US foreign policy archive from appearing in its academic papers—something that must otherwise work against its institutional and academic ambitions—calls into question its entire output, an output that has significantly influenced how the world has come to understand the role of the United States in the international order.

This closing of ranks within the scholar class around the interests of the Pentagon and the State Department is, in itself, worthy of analysis. The censorship of cables from international relations journals is a type of academic fraud. To quietly exclude primary sources for non-academic reasons is to lie by omission. But it points to a larger insight: the distortion of the field of international relations and related disciplines by the proximity of its academic structures to the US government. Its structures do not even have the independence of the frequently deferent *New York Times*, which, while it engaged in various forms of cable censorship, at least managed to publish over a hundred.[13]

These journals' distortion of the study of international relations and censorship of WikiLeaks are clear examples of a problem. But its identification also presents a significant opportunity: to present an analysis of international relations that has not been hobbled by the censorship of classified materials.

THE WORLD ACCORDING TO US EMPIRE

This book begins to address the need for scholarly analysis of what the millions of documents published by WikiLeaks say about international geopolitics. The chapters use a constellation approach to these documents to reveal how the United States deals with various regional and international power dynamics. It is impossible to cover the wealth of material or relationships in this first volume, but I hope that this work will stimulate long-form journalists and academics to eclipse it.

Chapter 1 reflects on America's status as an "empire," and considers what this means, seeking to characterize US economic, military, administrative, and diplomatic power with reference to the long sweep of global history over the last century. The chapter establishes the "imperialism of free trade" framework that the rest of Part II then develops—a framework wherein American military might is used, not for territorial expansion, but to perpetuate American economic preeminence. Both themes are considered in more detail in Chapter 2 and Chapter 3. Chapter 1 also situates WikiLeaks in the context of an unprecedented growth in American official secrecy, and the evolution of US power following the commencement of the "war on terror."

Chapter 2 examines the WikiLeaks materials on the so-called "war on terror." Besides providing a keen summary of the war crimes and human rights abuses documented in WikiLeaks publications, along with a detailed historical overview of the US invasion and occupation of Iraq and the consequent unfolding disaster there, the chapter also draws conclusions about the ideological and conceptual substructure of America's "war on terror," and investigates how an aspect of the imperial prerogative of the United States is to exercise decisive power to ensure that terms like "just war," "torture," "terrorism," and "civilian" are defined in its own favor. The argument adduces evidence from the full range of WikiLeaks publications, along with other sources, such as the recent CIA torture report. In the process, the chapter also examines the double standards and problems arising from the misuse of these concepts (including the attempt to delegitimize and marginalize WikiLeaks itself).

Chapter 3 embarks on a thoroughgoing discussion of the "empire of free trade"—the relationship of the American form of empire with the worldwide promotion of neoliberal economic reform, providing American corporations with access to "global markets." The chapter draws on State Department cables published by WikiLeaks, as well as WikiLeaks publications dating back to 2007 concerning the "private sector," including material on banks and global multilateral treaty negotiations. The chapter provides luminous examples of how the drive toward economic integration buttresses the position of the United States as an arms-length empire, and provides the underlying rationale for the patterns of intervention, military or otherwise, pursued in Latin America and beyond.

Chapter 4 is a do-it-yourself guide on how to use WikiLeaks' Public Library of US Diplomacy (PlusD), written by investigations editor Sarah Harrison. At the time of writing, PlusD contains 2,325,961 cables and other diplomatic records. The State Department uses its own logic to create, transmit and index these records, the totality of which form its primary institutional memory. Harrison explains how to get started searching, reading and interpreting cable metadata and content, from the infamous CHEROKEE restriction to the use of State Department euphemisms such as "opposing resource nationalism."

The history of US policy regarding the International Criminal Court (ICC) is a rich case study in the use of diplomacy in a concerted effort to undermine an international institution. In Chapter 5, Linda Pearson documents what the cables reveal about the efforts of successive US administrations to limit the ICC's jurisdiction. These include the use of both bribes and threats by the George W. Bush administration to corral states signed up to the ICC into providing immunity from war crimes prosecutions for US persons—and, under the Obama administration, more subtle efforts to shape the ICC into an adjunct of US foreign policy.

Japan and South Korea have been epicenters of US influence within East Asia for decades. The cables document nearly a decade of US efforts to affect domestic political outcomes within these two countries in line with its own long-term interests. In Chapter 14, investigative journalist Tim Shorrock examines the geopolitical triangle created by US relations with both countries, including its attempts to play one off against the other, as part of long-term efforts to undermine left-wing governments and policies within the region.

Of global GDP growth over the last decade, over 50 percent has been in Southeast Asia. This understanding has led to an explicit reassignment of military, diplomatic, and surveillance assets to Southeast Asia, epitomized by Secretary of State Hillary Clinton as a strategy of "forward deployed diplomacy."[14] In Chapter 15, Richard Heydarian examines the cables on Southeast Asia and situates his findings within a broader historical critique of US influence in the region.

The critique of Western imperialism is most contentious in regions of the world that have historically been US protectorates, such as western Europe. So indoctrinated are European liberals in modern imperialist ideology that even the idea that the United States might be administering a global empire is routinely dismissed with references to concepts like "right to protect," demonstrating a willful deafness not only to the structure of US power around the world, but also to how it increasingly talks about itself as an "empire." In Chapter 6, Michael Busch examines the broad patterns of influence and subversion pursued by the global superpower on the political systems of Europe and its member states. Themes include European government collusion with the CIA's rendition and torture programs, the subversion of European criminal justice and judicial systems to rescue alleged US government torturers from prosecution, and the use of US diplomacy to open up European markets to US aerospace companies, or to invasive, monopolistic technologies and patents, such as Monsanto's genetically modified organisms.

In Chapter 13, Phyllis Bennis opts for a broad overview of WikiLeaks' publications on Afghanistan—including not just the State Department cables, but also the Significant Action Reports (SIGACTs) published by WikiLeaks as the *Afghan War Diary*, and Congressional Research Reports and other documents on Afghanistan published by WikiLeaks prior to 2010. What emerges is a stark assessment of the folly of US military involvement in Afghanistan since 2001 and its cost in terms of human life and societal well-being.

Geopolitics is complicated, and all the more so in relation to a country like Israel. Israel's military dominance in the Middle East; its diplomatic relations with other regional players such as Egypt, Syria, Iran, Lebanon, and Turkey; its role as an avatar for US imperial policy within the area; its wayward exploitation of its protected status in pursuing its own genocidal policies toward the Palestinian people—all of these themes are brought to the fore in Chapter 9, by Peter Certo and Stephen Zunes, which carefully interrogates the relevant State Department cables.

In Chapter 11, on Iran, Gareth Porter provides an excellent companion to the chapter on Israel, choosing to focus on what the cables reveal about the tripartite geopolitical standoff between the US, Israel, and Iran, and the shadow this structure casts on the rest of the Middle East. In particular, Porter focuses on the P5+1 talks about Iran's nuclear enrichment program, on US efforts to misrepresent intelligence in order to tip the international consensus against Iran, and on the role of Israel as both a catalyst for and an agent of US policy in the Middle East.

The conflict in Iraq is the focus of Chapter 12, by journalist Dahr Jamail, which draws on a wide range of WikiLeaks materials to argue that the United States had a deliberate policy of exacerbating sectarian divisions in Iraq following its invasion and occupation, in the belief that the country would be easier to dominate in such circumstances. The consequent devastation is documented in painstaking detail using WikiLeaks materials, including US cables, Congressional Research Reports dating between 2005 and 2008, and the *Iraq War Logs* from 2010. Jamail pays specific attention to the "Sahwa" movement—the US-sponsored program of counter-insurgency that was implemented to respond to the growing influence of al-Qaeda affiliates among Sunni Iraqis disaffected by the Shia-dominated US-client government of Nouri al-Maliki. The United States paid large numbers of Iraqis to defect from the Sunni insurgency and instead fight against al-Qaeda, on the promise of receiving regular employment through integration into the Iraqi military. As Jamail argues, the failure of the Maliki government to honor this promise saw huge numbers of US-trained, US-armed, and US-financed—but now unemployed—Sunni militants return to the insurgency, eventually swelling the ranks of the former al-Qaeda affiliate in Iraq, which in 2014 became known as ISIS, or the "Islamic State."

Across Iraq's northeastern border, in Syria, the cables also describe how the scene was set for the emergence of ISIS. Since the outbreak of the Syrian civil war in 2011, warmongers in the media have demanded the Western military pounding of Syria to depose Bashar Al-Assad—presented, in typical liberal-interventionist fashion, as a "new Hitler." The emergence of the Islamic State, to which the Assad government is the only viable counterweight within Syria, has thrown this propagandistic consensus into disarray. But US government designs on Syrian regime change, and its devotion to regional instability, long pre-date the Syrian civil war, as is demonstrated in the cables. Chapter 10, by Robert Naiman, offers a careful reading of the Damascus cables, pointing out important historical presentiments of the current situation in Syria, and unpicking the benign-sounding human rights constructions of US diplomats to bring into focus the imperialist inflection of US foreign policy and rhetoric toward Syria—including concrete efforts within the country to undermine the government and bring about the chaos of recent months during the entire decade preceding 2011.

Clichés abound about Turkey being a "bridge between East and West," but it cannot be denied that this country of some seventy-five million people occupies an important position— both as a regional player within Middle Eastern geopolitics and as a large and economically powerful nominal democracy on the fringes of Europe. As Conn Hallinan argues in Chapter 8, State Department cables illustrate US efforts to exploit the rich geopolitical significance of Turkey. Hallinan uses the cables as a pretext to provide a tour of Turkey's regional alliances, strategic concerns, and internal affairs. Among the topics he covers are the complex strategic energy calculations that necessitate Turkey's delicate relations with Iran and Russia, even as it cultivates the United States, Europe, and Israel in its efforts to gain access to Western markets. The chapter also examines Turkey's bargaining power, demonstrated in its use of a veto against the election of former Danish prime minister Anders Rasmussen as the head of NATO, in order to force the United States to pressure the Danish government into suppressing a Denmark-based Kurdish television channel. The essay also deals with Turkey's internal issues, such as government policy toward Kurdish separatist groups, and the extraordinary underground political conflict and intrigue between Recep Tayyip Erdoğan and the expatriate political figure Fethullah Gülen.

Since the end of the Cold War, and especially during the so-called "war on terror," US diplomacy has leaned toward South, Central, and East Asia. Except in the case of one or two flare-ups, US-Russian relations receded from the popular consciousness as the main geopolitical dynamic. This of course has changed as a result of the conflict in the Ukraine. But popular consciousness is not reality. As Russ Wellen shows in Chapter 7, in the decade following the century's turn the US has pursued a policy of aggressive NATO expansion, challenging Russia's regional hegemony within Eastern Europe and the former Soviet area and seeking to subvert nuclear treaties to maintain its strategic advantage. As the cables show, these efforts have not gone unnoticed by Russia, and are recurring points of conflict in US-Russian diplomatic relations, even during the most cordial of periods. The chapter provides the necessary context for recent East-West tensions centering around Syria, Ukraine, and the granting of asylum to Edward Snowden, and yields critical insight into a geopolitical relationship that, if mishandled, threatens the survival of our civilization and even of our species.

Perhaps no region of the world demonstrates the full spectrum of US imperial interference as vividly as Latin America. Since the 1950s, US policy in Central and South America has popularized the concept of the CIA coup d'état, deposing democratically elected left-wing governments and installing US-friendly right-wing dictatorships; inaugurating legacies of brutal civil war, death squads, torture, and disappearances; and immiserating millions to the benefit of the American ruling class. As Alexander Main, Jake Johnston, and Dan Beeton note in the first of their chapters on Latin America, Chapter 17, the English-speaking press saw no evil in the State Department cables, concluding that they did not fit "the stereotype of America plotting coups and caring only about business interests and consorting with only the right wing." The exact opposite is true: the cables demonstrate a smooth continuity between the brutal US policy in Latin America during the Cold War and the more sophisticated plays at toppling governments that have taken place in recent years. Chapter 17 offers a broad overview of the use of USAID and "civil society" astroturfing, as well as other, more direct methods of pursuing "regime change" in El Salvador, Nicaragua, Bolivia, Ecuador, and Haiti. Chapter 18, by the same authors, focuses on Venezuela, the socialist enemy of the day, and specifically on US efforts to undermine the country as a regional left-wing bulwark in the wake of the failed US-backed coup against the Chávez government in 2002.

The response of the United States to the release of the WikiLeaks materials betrays a belief that its power resides in a disparity of information: ever more knowledge for the empire, ever less for its subjects.

In 1969, Daniel Ellsberg—later famous for leaking the Pentagon Papers—had a top-secret security clearance. Henry Kissinger had applied for his own top-secret clearance. Ellsberg warned him of its dangers:

[I]t will ... become very hard for you to learn
from anybody who doesn't have these clearances.
Because you'll be thinking as you listen to
them: "What would this man be telling me if
he knew what I know? Would he be giving me the
same advice, or would it totally change his
predictions and recommendations?" You will deal
with a person who doesn't have those clearances
only from the point of view of what you want him
to believe and what impression you want him to

go away with, since you'll have to lie carefully
to him about what you know. In effect, you will
have to manipulate him. You'll give up trying to
assess what he has to say. The danger is, you'll
become something like a moron. You'll become
incapable of learning from most people in the
world, no matter how much experience they may
have in their particular areas that may be much
greater than yours.[15]

Freed from their classified seals, the WikiLeaks materials bridge the gulf between the "morons" with security clearances and nothing to learn, and us, their readers.

Part I

1. America and the Dictators*

WHAT IS IT WITH AMERICA AND DICTATORSHIPS?

The United States government very publicly and valiantly denounces autocratic regimes all the time: currently the targets of Washington's ire include North Korea, Iran, and Syria. At the same time it selectively wages war on autocratic regimes, from Panama to Iraq, as the situation requires. In private, the WikiLeaks cables, gathered since 2009, show that US diplomats are often very scathing about foreign leaders and overseas governments. And yet, the US has maintained networks of sympathetic authoritarian regimes in large parts of the world where it wields influence. The very same regimes it goes to war with have, at some point, once been American allies. This is an irony that can hardly have been lost on Noriega or Saddam Hussein as they were ousted and tried in kangaroo courts for crimes carried out with US support.

In contrast, Washington stands by other regimes to the bitter end. Consider the relatively minor example of Turkmenistan. In 2009, a cable sent from the US embassy in Ashgabat contained a poison-pen thumbnail description of the country's dictator, Gurbanguly Berdimuhamedow. Written by the US chargé d'affaires, it acidly depicted the dictator as "vain, suspicious, guarded, strict, very conservative, a practiced liar, 'a good actor,'

---

* The author of Chapters 1 through 3 has chosen to remain anonymous.

and vindictive." Perhaps most damning was the observation that, apart from being a vicious tinpot dictator, he was "not a very bright guy."[1]

None of this was exactly news. Berdimuhamedow had continued the despotic pattern established by his predecessor, the former Communist Party leader Saparmyrat Niyazov, when he had taken control in 2006. The US certainly knew all his methods before he was allowed to take command. But Turkmenistan provided a crucial corridor of access to Afghanistan for the US, as well as being strategically central to an energy-rich area circling the Caspian Sea.

So, if chargé d'affaires Curran's report was intended to make officials think twice about dealing with the dictator, it did not work. Hillary Clinton stopped in for a photo op with the dictator in the year the cable was sent, at which it was reported that human rights was not very high on the agenda. The next year, US military aid to the dictatorship increased from $150,000 to $2 million.[2] This aid, it should be noted, is being put to sterling work funding the regime's military exercises in the region. Berdimuhamedow was "re-elected" with 97 percent of the vote in 2012, and the US continues its warm relationship with the regime.

And there it is in black and white. The planners and strategists in Washington, DC—leaders of the Free World, as they once fondly styled themselves—think the blood-caked dictator of Turkmenistan is not just nasty but an utter dolt, and yet this personality flaw is offset by the observation that if he is good enough to sustain America's war, he is good enough for Turkmenistan, and well worth a couple of million dollars.

This kind of realpolitik looks bad for the US, but support for this cynical axis of repression is far down the list of such instances catalogued in the WikiLeaks documents. From east to central Asia to the Middle East to Latin America, the US has cultivated, funded, armed, and coddled authoritarian states in both hemispheres. Nonetheless, if this behavior seems staggeringly at odds with the spaniel-eyed, apple-pie rhetoric of the Obama administration, it is clear that there is more to this posture than rhetoric.

At the heart of postwar US policy-making is the doctrine of liberal internationalism. Pioneered by Woodrow Wilson, and embellished by Franklin D. Roosevelt and Harry Truman, this doctrine is generally understood as the justification of military and other interventions by the US if they help produce a liberal world order: a global system consisting of liberal-democratic nation-states, connected by more or less free markets and ruled by international law. In this world-view, the goal of achieving a liberal world system trumps the commitment to state sovereignty. The US sees itself as the natural vanguard of such a global order, as well as the chief bearer of any right to suppress state sovereignty in the pursuit of liberal goals.

As we see from the cables, this doctrine is taken seriously by state personnel of every hue. Their criticisms of undemocratic regimes, nepotism, and human rights abuses make no sense otherwise. However, there is an aspect of liberal internationalism that is not typically explicated by its adherents, but which is visible both in its origins and its practice.

As Domenico Losurdo, the eminent historian, has written, liberalism in this broad sense has historically been subject to a series of exclusions—working-class people, women, black people, and colonial subjects have all at various points been excluded from the citizenship rights, such as voting, granted to white, propertied men.[3] The logic of such exclusions in the international system is visible in the colonial origin of international law, which initially ratified the behavior of colonial states while leaving colonial peoples without rights in the emerging world system.[4]

The right of self-determination in the form of statehood was thus, for a long time, a right reserved by the overwhelmingly white citizens of Euro-American states—a fact that would become a source of anticolonial rebellion in the early twentieth century. As the American empire rose to world dominance, it met this state of affairs with a mixture of caution and sympathy for the colonial powers. Even as it gradually worked out a strategic perspective according to which territorial control was no longer an advantage, it was reluctant to see this crucial right extended to non-white peoples.

Woodrow Wilson, president of the United States from 1912 to 1920, was the austere poster boy for liberal internationalism, and the first president seriously to confront the dilemmas posed by the new anticolonial movements. Having championed American efforts to get in on the imperial racket, he witnessed the difficulties that US colonial policy experienced in the Philippines, while at the same time observing with horror the rise of global anticolonial movements. By breaking his 1916 electoral promise and leading the US into World War I, he facilitated a first attempt to construct a new world order.

Wilson did not eschew the occupation of foreign territories when it suited US interests; he was not only a champion of the US occupation of the Philippines, but himself sent troops into Haiti (1915), Nicaragua (1912), and Cuba (1912), as well as intervening in the Mexican Revolution (1914). Nonetheless, the scale of the Great War acted as a warning against unnecessary military campaigns. In addition, there was a growing idea among US planners suggesting that territorial control was less important than the control of markets in capital, labor, and resources.

In a global market dominated by the US, supporting national governments in place that were open to US investment was more important than becoming a colonial overlord. Profits could flow back to Wall Street without the debilitating costs of occupation. To achieve this world order, however, the US would need to prize open the colonial empires. One manifestation of this new strategic perspective was the Wilson administration's discovery of the language of "national self-determination." This has assumed a central place in the mythology of liberal internationalism, even though Wilson at first purloined the language from the Bolsheviks, the better to steal their thunder. He certainly had no intention of fulfilling the implied promise to anticolonial movements, which he regarded as having no capacity for self-government. Thus, while US propagandists enlisted the support of anticolonial forces in India for the Entente powers in World War I on the basis of Wilsonian doctrine, the ensuing negotiations at Versailles saw the US oppose a "racial equality" motion, and "self-determination" was denied to colonized nations. The result was that the anticolonial movements gravitated to the Left, with many looking to Russia as a model of successful modernization.[5]

Later, the US took the opportunity of World War II to relieve Britain of many of its colonial possessions in exchange for participation in the war on the Allied side. However, in the immediate aftermath, the US declined to push its tremendous strategic advantage home at the expense of the former colonial powers. The British were left with strategic control of South Asia, and the French maintained sovereignty in Indochina, while appeals for recognition from Sukarno in Indonesia and Ho Chi Minh in Vietnam were ignored. In general, the US only lent its tacit support to anticolonial ruptures—such as the Nasserite revolt in Egypt—where there was little risk of conflict.

The chief concern of US officials during this period was that "premature independence" might lead to a new freedom for people as yet unfit to govern themselves. Given this unfitness, they might not commit to building liberal capitalist states integrated into a US-led world market, instead preferring politically immature "populist" or radical solutions. They might even, in some cases, "go communist."

As a leading American expert on African politics, William J. Foltz, wrote in 1966, it would take more than a few generations to teach the majority of black Africans "the skills necessary to participate meaningfully and effectively in politics."[6] Therefore, if a further period of tutelage at the hands of white colonial masters was not possible, the "modernization theory" of US state mandarins held that these people would require a period of authoritarian rule under enlightened military regimes.[7]

The US thus responded to independence in the Congo by engineering the imposition of the kleptocratic Mobutu regime to prevent radicalism. The same policy supported a succession of dictators in South Vietnam to avert Viet Minh rule, and drove an extraordinarily bloody war to defend an allied dictatorship in South Korea. It supported the overthrow of Sukarno by the Indonesian general Suharto in a coup that killed up to a million people, but subsequently opened up the country's markets and resources to US investors.

In the Middle East, the US took over the British role, particularly after the latter's "East of Suez" commitments were finally abandoned in 1971. US administrators and oilmen had already co-engineered the rule of the House of Saud by this point. The CIA had helped overthrow the Iran's Mossadegh government in 1953, replacing it with the hated shah, and later played a role in supporting the Ba'athist coup in Iraq as part of its general offensive against radical Arab nationalism. Israel—neither strictly a dictatorship nor a normal democracy—had become the major US regional client, particularly after the 1967 war, in which it had dealt a lethal blow to Arab nationalism. Later, with the Camp David accords securing peace with Israel, the Egyptian dictatorship became the second major regional client. All the while, of course, the US supported a network of right-wing dictatorships in its "backyard"—Latin America—with the aim of suppressing leftist movements hostile to American business.

The traditional Cold War justification for these imperial interventions was that it was a nasty, brutal old world out there, and that, to protect freedom against a totalitarian menace, certain unpleasant things had to be tolerated. Perhaps the most eloquent exponent of this idea was the neoconservative guru Jeane Kirkpatrick, who would become Reagan's ambassador to the United Nations. Kirkpatrick argued forcefully in defense of right-wing dictatorships in Latin America, on the grounds that the workers, peasants, and nuns they were slaughtering represented a form of totalitarianism that was far worse than authoritarianism.

Kirkpatrick also offered a defense of the US alliance with El Salvador's death squads, writing for the hallowed papers of the American Enterprise Institute that these institutions were authentically rooted organizations of the Salvadoran people, representing the organized self-defense of civil society against communism, and would be much more civilized if harnessed to legitimate state power.[8]

By this point, however, Kirkpatrick was already swimming against the tide. In the post-Vietnam era, US state elites began to articulate their policy goals much more in terms of human rights and democracy. Kirkpatrick mocked the Carter administration for its human rights rhetoric, but even during Reagan's proxy battles with "communism" in Central America, the old anticommunist battle wagons were being carefully spruced up and re-sold as vehicles for progressive, democratic change, albeit within terms favorable to long-term US interests.

As a result, an apparatus of "democracy promotion" sprang up, linked to the International Republican Institute (IRI), the National Endowment for Democracy (NED), and a series of institutions through which funding could be allocated to support US-aligned civil society forces in various countries.[9] As a Reagan-era official put it:

```
The incoming Reagan administration sought to
turn the clock back on US foreign policy to
the pre-Vietnam era, to an old-fashioned cold
war approach in which the United States would
accept the need to support unsavory dictators
as an inevitable component of the global
struggle against Soviet communism. The Reagan
administration discovered fairly quickly,
however, that it was not possible to forge a
bipartisan foreign policy on this basis; a
concern for human rights and democracy also had
to be factored into the policy.[10]
```

In fact, the "concern" was hypocritical. The US was not doing anything very new. Allen Weinstein, a founder and first acting president of the NED, observed in 1991 that its existence meant that activities the CIA had performed covertly twenty-five years before could now be performed openly.[11] Nor did it signal a change of policy priorities. In El Salvador, for instance, the US was fully aware that the country's ruling class was engaged in a bitter war of annihilation against leftist peasants and workers, and was disposed toward a genocidal solution, favoring the "cleansing" of up to half a million people. And while the CIA continued to train Salvadoran death squads, and US money continued to pour in, the United States began to prepare a series of "democracy promotion" programs that in fact bolstered civil society forces close to the ruling ARENA party.[12]

This pattern continues. In recent years the NED has been directly involved in funding groups and individuals involved in the coup against Haiti's elected president, Jean-Bertrand Aristide, in 2004, and several of those involved in the attempted coup against Venezuela's Hugo Chávez in 2002. In short, while the language of cynical anticommunist realpolitik was being replaced with a focus on human rights, the apparatus of "human rights" was still being deployed against America's leftist enemies. In Egypt, the United States allocated an average of $20 million per year to "democracy assistance" in the years running up to the overthrow of Hosni Mubarak—while supporting the regime itself to the tune of $2 billion per year.[13]

But the advantage of the "human rights" policy was clear. While the United States could continue to rely on a series of dictatorships where it did not trust democracies to produces pro-US policies, it could simultaneously foster a pro-US bulwark in the opposition by funding and building relations with groups it trusted.

This was more than just hypocrisy. US elites may not have much sympathy for the poor and oppressed of the global South, but dictatorships lack legitimacy and have a worrying tendency to be consumed in sudden explosions of popular anger. Support for dictatorships, however essential to US grand strategy, also brings "blowback" of various types. The United States has every reason to prefer that the dictatorships it does support contain their worst tendencies in times of peace. There is therefore a strategic basis for the criticism of abuses of human rights that US diplomats sometimes direct at their overseas hosts in secret cables.

The WikiLeaks revelations are an unprecedented resource in exploring how the US government's relationship to dictatorships has evolved in practice, and how it has reconciled this practice with its normative commitment to liberal internationalism.

THE MIDDLE EAST: THE "GREATEST PRIZE IN HISTORY"

In his poem "September 1, 1939," W. H. Auden invoked the "elderly rubbish" spoken by dictators. It could have been written in 2011. In Libya, Muammar Qaddafi, menaced by a civil society movement that ultimately became an armed uprising, blamed drug-takers and WikiLeaks for his predicament. The president of Syria, Bashar al-Assad, blamed a "foreign conspiracy" for his dilemma, as he began bombing liberated territories. Later, Turkish president Recep Tayyip Erdoğan—an elected leader, but an increasingly erratic, authoritarian one—would blame drunks, Twitter users, and terrorists.

But these men were hardly the only ones inconvenienced by the turmoil. It had begun with a popular movement in Tunisia, precipitated by the self-immolation of Tunisian street vendor Mohamed Bouazizi on December 18, 2010. Bouazizi was protesting at the confiscation of his wares and the routine harassment he suffered at the hands of the authorities. His complaints resonated with the experiences and dissatisfactions of a wide layer of the population, who began to mount regular, sustained protests. These grew in scale, leading ultimately to the overthrow of the country's dictator, Zine El Abidine Ben Ali, on January 14, 2011.

This inspired Egypt's opposition, who had been gradually building up steam for over a decade, to mount a popular uprising against the dictator Hosni Mubarak. Beginning on January 25, 2011, with a series of mass protests, acts of civil disobedience, and strikes, it grew into a sustained frontal confrontation with the regime, until, on February 11, Mubarak was finally forced to resign.

At this point a whole network of regional autocracies became endangered, as popular movements risked rebellion in Libya, Syria, Bahrain, and to a lesser extent in Yemen, Algeria, Saudi Arabia, and later Turkey. This was all the more significant globally because most of these regimes were allies of the United States. Apart from Israel, the crux of American power in the region was formed by Egypt, the Gulf regimes, and the North African dictatorships.

This is where WikiLeaks comes in. WikiLeaks has justifiably gained much credit for helping to ignite the Middle East rebellion. One explanation for this was that, while the space of "civil society" was highly restricted, the remarkable upsurge in internet use created a virtual space in which information could be shared, discussed, and used as a basis for organization.

For example, as will be shown below, the cables released by WikiLeaks exposed the extent of corruption on the part of Tunisia's ruling oligarchs, and revealed the enervation of Egypt's military even as it carved itself larger slices of the economic pie. The cables also did Erdoğan the immense discourtesy of disclosing that, according to the US ambassador, he was known to have at least eight Swiss bank accounts—thus implying corrupt finances (see Chapter 8, below).[14]

The information disseminated through WikiLeaks gave form and substance to many lingering popular grievances. As Ibrahim Saleh notes,

The WikiLeaks releases played an influential role in fuelling public anger in the region and in

shaping global audiences' understanding of the
causes of what became known as the Arab Spring.
By exposing hidden secrets, double standards,
and hypocrisy of the Arab leaders, they provided
new perspectives on Arab politics, as well as
confirming widespread suspicions, and thus put
angry publics in direct confrontation with
autocratic governments.[15]

The predictable fall of Ben Ali

In January 2011, the Tunisian dictatorship of Zine El Abidine
Ben Ali was overthrown. One of the immediate triggers for the
movement that led to his downfall was the disclosures made by
WikiLeaks. In particular, two key cables—one written in June
2008, and one in July 2009—were sent by Ambassador Robert
Godec, each describing the Tunisian dictatorship of Ben Ali in
withering terms. The 2008 cable focuses on corruption. Tunisia
was ruled not just with an iron fist, but with a grasping hand:

Whether it's cash, services, land, property, or
yes, even your yacht, President Ben Ali's family
is rumored to covet it and reportedly gets what
it wants … Seemingly half the Tunisian business
community can claim a Ben Ali connection through
marriage … With Tunisians facing rising inflation
and high unemployment, the conspicuous displays
of wealth and persistent rumors of corruption
have added fuel to the fire.[16]

On the other hand, the 2009 cable is concerned with human
rights. The regime was "a police state, with little freedom of
expression or association, and serious human rights problems."[17]
The ambassador believed the state to be "in trouble." The cable
complained of the regime's restrictions on various US programs,

and of the hostility of the government press toward pro-American civil society figures. But, most problematically, the "risks to the regime's long-term stability [were] increasing" due to its corruption and narrow social base, as well as the lack of a clear successor.

The repressive nature of the Ben Ali regime was hardly news to the United States. He had persecuted all opposition groups since taking power in the "bloodless coup" of 1987. But Tunisia was a regional ally, and had been so since attaining independence from French colonial rule. The state provided crucial support in the "war on terror," and as a result it was a priority recipient of US military aid. As the "fact sheet" on the website of the US embassy in Tunisia still boasts, "Tunisia has been one of the top twenty recipients of US International Military Education and Training funding since 1994; and since 2003 has ranked tenth in overall funding."[18]

Tunisia's armed forces do not exist primarily to project military power abroad.[19] Rather, the regular army exists as the last line of civil defense protecting the secular, republican state. But, within the army itself, paramilitary units were created to intervene directly in political and civil affairs, in order to suppress opposition to the regime. Military aid, in this context, was support for the regime.

What Godec's broad-ranging cables suggested was that the US was in danger of being tied to a regime that was on a downward spiral. And this was not the first hint that US diplomatic staff had made regarding the potential vulnerability of the regime. As early as 2006, Ambassador William Hudson's cable had noted that "an increasing number of Tunisians" were already talking about the possible "succession and end of the Ben Ali era."[20] In the early flush of enthusiasm following President Obama's victory, however, Ambassador Godec suggested that the US needed to repair its image in the Middle East, and that military aid to the regime should therefore be cut.

When these cables were leaked, they became widely available

across Tunisia and caused quite a stir. For Tunisians reading them, the surprise was not the revelation of corruption, but the bluntness of the US assessment of the regime. Upon spotting the leaks, the regime went into panic mode. In December 2010 it tried to block access to websites carrying the cables, focusing specifically on the popular, progressive Beirut newspaper *Al-Akhbar*.[21]

Within a matter of days of this intervention, the street trader Mohamed Bouazizi set fire to himself in protest at the brutal and unjust treatment he had received at the hands of police. Bouazizi's complaints were not just about intolerable state abuse, however, but also invoked the declining standard of living that he, like many Tunisians, had suffered since the global financial crash, symbolized by soaring food prices and high unemployment. Finally, the corruption of the regime epitomized its increasingly narrow social base. While the postcolonial regime of Habib Bourguiba had rested on a broad basis of support among all social classes, Ben Ali's rested increasingly on a small number of business families with links to the state.[22] Bouazizi's protest dramatically symbolized the suffering of the populace, and the nepotism, corruption, and complacency of the elites disclosed in the cables. This was the spark that was needed for the accumulating dissent and anger against the regime, described by Godec and Hudson, to break out into a mass protest movement. In the course of the ensuing weeks, protesters often referred to the WikiLeaks exposures.[23]

Ironically, the leak of these cables did not persuade the Obama administration to back away from the regime or stop sending military aid, but they did help precipitate precisely the upheaval they anticipated. In another twist of irony, many of the protesters looked to the United States to furnish its slogans—"Yes, we can" was a popular chant. Yet Obama did not even make a bloodless statement half-heartedly supporting the overthrow until after Ben Ali had safely reached exile in Saudi Arabia.[24] This was a pattern that was replicated as the Egyptian opposition took the baton from Tunisia, challenging the Mubarak regime.

Downfall in Cairo

In 2009, a cable from the US embassy in Cairo reported a conversation with a leading regime figure. It discussed the upcoming parliamentary and presidential elections, as well as the regime's attitude to the opposition. There had been "bread riots," but the dictatorship saw little prospect of a popular challenge—and certainly not "widespread politically-motivated unrest" because it was "not part of the 'Egyptian mentality.' Threats to daily survival, not politics," the report continued, "were the only thing to bring Egyptians to the streets en masse."[25] The opposition parties were too weak to challenge for power, much less run the country, the regime held, and the only viable alternative, the Muslim Brotherhood, had no legitimate role. The "common sense" of the regime therefore seemed to be that the only way in which president-for-life Hosni Mubarak would be succeeded would be through an orderly transition organized by the Egyptian military —which would most likely ease the president's son, Gamal, into the role.[26]

What was the basis of this somnolent complacency? US cables depicted a military elite in "intellectual and social decline," increasingly narrow in its social basis, yet still essential to regime stability and in control of "a large network of commercial enterprises" in the "water, olive oil, cement, construction, hotel and gasoline industries."[27] On the other hand, the regime had demonstrated considerable staying power, partly due to its viciousness toward enemies, or even moderate critics.

A cable sent by Ambassador Margaret Scobey took note of Mubarak's severe brutality toward "individuals and groups." But this, the ambassador seemed to think, was an immense strength, as it had helped maintain domestic stability through two major regional wars, and marked the dictator out as a "tried and true realist" who was willing to inflict suffering on some rather than "risk chaos for society as a whole."[28] The same cable identified the gains of America's long-standing support for the Mubarak regime: "The tangible benefits to our mil-mil relationship are clear: Egypt remains at peace with Israel, and the US military enjoys priority access to the Suez canal and Egyptian airspace."

These messages from Cairo ooze with confidence in the dictator, and with gratitude for his services to empire. The back-slapping did not last long. The WikiLeaks documents pertaining to Egypt were released on November 28, 2010, as part of a cache of classified diplomatic cables allegedly leaked by a former private in the US army, Bradley (now Chelsea) Manning. They were leaked alongside the disclosures about Tunisia that led to Ben Ali's downfall.

The WikiLeaks cables had a complex series of effects inside Egypt. This was less because of the disclosures themselves than because of the processes they had already helped to instigate. The evidence of the brutality of the regime was hardly news, and some of the potentially explosive revelations—for example, that Israel preferred former spy chief Omar Suleiman as Mubarak's successor—were never translated in Egypt. Nor was the opposition particularly dependent on the internet or social media, through which the cables could be communicated—phone conversations and face-to-face contact were far more important.[29] Nevertheless, they had helped trigger the Tunisian uprising that gave confidence to the democratic opposition. They also confirmed and validated the analysis of Mubarak's opponents, and raised international awareness so that, when Egyptian protesters took to the streets, groups such as Anonymous were willing to offer assistance.[30]

Even if WikiLeaks had played a more direct role in inciting the Egyptian revolution, the Tunisian example would not have caught on had it not been for the presence of similar characteristics. Poverty and job insecurity preceded the global economic crisis, but by late 2010, 40 percent of Egyptians were living on less than $2 per day.[31] Also reminiscent of the Tunisian case was the narrowness and corruption of the regime—albeit that, in Egypt, the cables show that the military was directly inculpated in that corruption. Mubarak had concentrated tremendous power and patronage in the Interior Ministry, as well as accumulating up to $70 billion for his family.[32] Finally, as documented in Scobey's embassy cable, there were hundreds of firsthand accounts of police brutality, some of them recorded on video. These were the grievances that, prompted by the Tunisian uprising, galvanized support for the movement that began on July 25, 2011.

Initially, opposition groups such as the April 6 Youth Movement planned a protest outside the Interior Ministry to coincide with National Police Day, as a means of protesting police brutality. However, in the afterglow of Ben Ali's overthrow, the protest had much wider significance, and gained the support of a broad coalition of organizations such as the Muslim Brotherhood, and celebrities such as actor Amr Waked. In the event, the protest attracted tens of thousands of participants, including 20,000 in Alexandria and 15,000 in Cairo's Tahrir Square. The violent reaction of the authorities, far from causing the crowds to retreat, led to days of riots and growing protests, so that by Friday, January 28, the regime had decided to deploy the army, and was in regular meetings with the US military leadership.[33]

This proved a huge inconvenience for the American empire. When Vice President Joe Biden suggested on television, as Egyptian protesters turned Tahrir Square into a thriving mini-metropolis, that President Mubarak was not a dictator, should not step down, and was in fact "an ally of ours," he undiplomatically made public the attitude of US authorities to the regime it had been funding.[34] Former British prime minister Tony Blair put matters just as starkly, warning that overthrowing Mubarak would create a vacuum in which "extremism" would prosper. The Egyptian elite was "out of touch with public opinion," but it also had "an open-minded attitude," whereas public opinion had "the wrong idea and a closed idea."[35]

Mubarak, both the British and US administrations contended, should remain in power, but should make sufficient reforms to placate the crowds. When President Obama sent businessman and former diplomat Frank G. Wisner to Egypt to negotiate a settlement of the issues causing mass unrest, Wisner made it clear that Mubarak was an "old friend" of the United States, arguing that there should be reforms, but that he "must stay in office in order to steer those changes through."[36]

What was the "closed idea" that Blair was frightened of? What did Mubarak offer that was so valuable to Biden and Wisner? One issue was the concord with Israel negotiated at the Camp David talks in 1978, since when the Egyptian dictatorship had been a reliable and crucial ally of the Israeli government against the Palestinians. Undoubtedly, the US was concerned that a popular government in Egypt would take a more critical attitude toward Israel, cease enforcing the Gaza blockade, and even provide material aid to the Palestinians. Another issue of concern for Washington and London was the opening of Egypt's markets to overseas investment, the deregulation of its economy, and the privatization of its industries. Here, the pro-market attitude of the Muslim Brotherhood might have reassured them, but democratic processes are difficult to manage—particularly if the public has "the wrong idea and a closed idea."

The more far-sighted elements of the American state, however, had been preparing for the day when the dictatorship would no longer be the best means of achieving those goals. US institutions such as the NED had not been totally oblivious as the Egyptian opposition developed—first in response to the second Palestinian intifada in 2002,[37] and then in opposition to the second Iraq war. They had taken an interest in the emergence of a labor movement independent of the state-controlled unions, centered on textile workers.[38] Indeed, the WikiLeaks cables show the NED and affiliated institutions to have played a key role in coordinating with select groups of activists.[39]

These developments were linked to President Bush's aggressive military drive in the Middle East. An important complementary strategy to the projection of military power was the so-called "Freedom Agenda," by which funds for "democracy promotion" were linked to the expansion of free trade. The dictatorships had been useful allies in vigorous "counter-terrorism" policies, and partners in the implementation of free trade; but there were those in the US state bureaucracy who felt that they were ultimately unreliable allies.[40] Money had been dispersed from the NED and the IRI to the US trade union federation, the AFL-CIO, whose Solidarity Center played a crucial role in maintaining the anticommunist line during the Cold War. Through the Solidarity Center, the US sought to build links with Egypt's workers.[41]

In addition, as the WikiLeaks cables demonstrate, the United States made an effort to involve itself in the growing April 6 Youth Movement, thereby creating tensions in its otherwise close relationship with Mubarak.[42] The assistance offered was far from decisive. For example, US-funded seminars offered training in the use of social networking sites and mobile technologies in order to promote democratic change, as well as counseling non-violent strategies for achieving social change.[43]

The small change that the US threw into the hat of the Egyptian opposition was not enough to guarantee influence. When Secretary of State Hillary Clinton visited Egypt in March 2011, she was snubbed by a coalition of youth groups that refused to meet her on the perfectly reasonable ground that the United States had supported the Mubarak regime.[44] One of Obama's former advisers, Anne-Marie Slaughter, cited this rebuff as a key pragmatic reason why the United States had to be seen to side with the aspirations of Egypt's young people, who happened to make up 60 percent of the Middle East's population, and not with the decrepit dictators.[45]

In practice, however, this meant a series of repressive policies, such as continuing to assist the Yemeni regime in crushing its opposition. The cables from 2010 show that the United States had collaborated with Yemen's ruler, Ali Abdullah Saleh, in organizing air strikes against targets on Yemeni soil deemed to be bases for al-Qaeda in the Arabian Peninsula. Saleh offered the United States an "open door," the cables show, while he and his subordinates joked in meetings with General David Petraeus that he had lied to the public by claiming that the strikes were exclusively the work of the Yemeni government. In reality, the popular opposition to Saleh's regime, which it described as "terrorist," was broad and diverse, and partly based on tribal opposition to the centralized nature of his rule, while US strikes routinely caused harm way beyond their al-Qaeda target. And as the Yemeni struggle against the regime intensified, so did the drone strikes. For example, in June 2011 alone, a major upsurge in the rate of air strikes in the province of Abyan killed over 130 people and created 40,000 refugees.[46]

Among Washington's other repressive responses to the Arab Spring was the support it gave to Saudi Arabia's invasion of Bahrain to suppress democratic dissidents. While public statements from Hillary Clinton and Barack Obama called for "restraint" as the Bahraini ruling monarchy initiated the bloodshed, private briefings suggested that they were more concerned with stability than democracy. Moreover, Defense Secretary Robert Gates leaped to the defense of the regime, claiming that it was serious about democratic reform but had to worry about the possibility of Iran exploiting the protests to stir trouble.[47] Despite the promises of democratic reform, after the Saudi invasion to protect the regime, evidence has been produced by WikiLeaks showing that the US continues to assist the regime's security forces.[48]

But perhaps most egregiously, from the point of view of America's ostensible democratic principles, in 2013 the US government supported a military coup against the elected Muslim Brotherhood government in Egypt—a coup that resulted in several bloody massacres.[49] This inevitably inaugurated a period of ferocious authoritarian dictatorship[50] and wiped out the gains of the Arab Spring. All of this suggested that any tilt that the US might make toward supporting democracy in the Middle East would be extremely limited.

Despite America's oft-proclaimed ideals, and the post–Cold War triumphalism according to which all roads led to freedom, despotism was too valuable to forsake. To understand why, it is necessary to say something about the long-standing relationships between the United States and the region's dictatorships.

AMERICAN EMPIRE AND THE MIDDLE EAST DICTATORS

America's grand accession to the status of global hegemon happened as a result of the decisive blow dealt by World War II to the colonial powers of Europe. After 1945, Britain and France still retained most of their possessions in the Middle East and North Africa, but, one after another, anticolonial movements that had been in the ascent since the 1920s began to shake their colonial masters loose. In 1952, a pro-British monarch was deposed by Nasser and the Free Officers movement in Egypt. Between 1954 and 1962, Algeria was in revolt against the French. In 1956, the French ceded control of Morocco and Tunisia. In 1958, the pro-British king of Iraq was overthrown by Qassem, another modernizing military leader. In the case of Palestine, liberation was delayed by the inauguration of a new colonial master in the form of the State of Israel. Gradually, however, the colonial grip on the region was being prized open.

This development was particularly essential for the United States, as the Middle East had proved through a series of discoveries in the interwar period to have a vast supply of cheap and accessible oil. In a 1945 US Department of State document, Saudi Arabia—a nation effectively constructed through the decisive intervention of the British Empire, US politicians, and oil companies—was deemed "a stupendous source of strategic power, and one of the greatest material prizes in world history."[51]

Initially, the US strategic posture was to allow the empires to fold at their own pace, thus leaving them responsible for the deployment of military power and the maintenance of political order, while encouraging newly independent societies to adopt development strategies predicated on import substitution, in which countries would try to overcome their dependency on foreign imports by developing their own industrial base. As long as US capital was able to invest, the United States could gain access to these markets by other means than the "Open Door" that had been orthodoxy since the late nineteenth century.[52] Within a developing global financial infrastructure underpinned by Bretton Woods, states were thus encouraged to develop markets that could be incorporated into a US-dominated world system.

As more regional states won independence, the US gradually took more responsibility for military deployment. For example, a major asset to the United States was the development of the "Baghdad Pact"—a treaty organization linking a series of regimes to the United Kingdom in a strategic military alliance. The United States had not participated directly, but had applied pressure to make the alliance come about, and offered funding. But a growing wave of Arab nationalism represented a threat to the alliance. The essential premise of Arab nationalism was that the national divisions in the Middle East were an artifice of colonialism, and should be replaced with a state unifying all Arabs, independent of the colonial powers, the United States, and the USSR. The region's material resources would be subordinated to its own development, rather than the interests of international investors. This type of crazy thinking was exactly what had led Mossadegh, the elected prime minister of Iran, to attempt to nationalize the oil industry, thus leading to the joint CIA-MI6 enterprise to overthrow him and replace him with the shah, Mohammad Reza Pahlavi.

So it was that, when the Nasser government in Egypt nationalized the Suez Canal, an alliance of Israel, France, and Britain invaded the country to overthrow him. But the US government, whatever its worries about Arab nationalism, thought that this was a catastrophic miscalculation that might send Arab states rushing into the orbit of the USSR. Furthermore, its legitimacy in the world system would be harmed if it was seen to support aggression of the type Russia had just carried out in Hungary.

The following year, however, the Iraqi monarch was overthrown by Abd al-Karim Qasim and the Free Officers. It soon became clear that the new government was planning to withdraw from the Baghdad Pact, sending shockwaves through the region. President Camille Chamoun of Lebanon, who was supportive of the Baghdad Pact, was seen as particularly vulnerable. So US troops arrived in Lebanon in 1958 to secure the regime against internal opposition, as well as possible hostility from Egypt and Syria, in the first application of the "Eisenhower Doctrine," according to which US troops would protect regimes deemed vulnerable to "international Communism."[53]

Indeed, the specter of radical Arab nationalism—conflated with "international Communism"—led to a US tilt in favor of the old autocracies. So while the US had quietly backed the overthrow of King Farouk in Egypt by Nasser and the Free Officers movement, it supported King Hussein of Jordan in imposing martial law in 1957, the better to halt the government's alliance with Egypt, and more broadly its shift of allegiance toward Russia and China. The US also backed King Idris of Libya against opposition, until his overthrow by Colonel Qaddafi and the Free Officers of the Royal Libyan Army in 1969.

The withdrawal of the British navy from the Gulf region in 1971, as part of Britain's abandonment of its "East of Suez" commitments, left the United States to take up the slack. At the height of the Vietnam War, when military spending was bleeding the US Treasury dry, this was an unwelcome development. Nonetheless, the United States deployed its Middle East Force and replaced sterling patronage with dollar diplomacy. By this point, there was already a network of dictators in place who were aligned with the United States, while Israel had inflicted a consummate defeat on the forces of Arab nationalism in the Six Day War—thus becoming the major US client in the region, alongside Saudi Arabia and the shah of Iran. These regimes together helped stymie the tide of Arab nationalism, while their military dependence on the United States locked them into an international framework favorable to US investors. The decisive military defeats inflicted on Egypt, coupled with a growing economic crisis, led Egypt's rulers to realign their regime with the United States, inaugurating a relationship consecrated in the Camp David accords of 1978.

US economic aid and IMF loans were used as levers to win support for opening up these economies to global markets, superseding the import-substitution model of industrial development. They therefore became dependent on imports, and repeated balance-of-payments crises only deepened their dependence on IMF-organized loans, and thus their acceptance of their associated conditions—including the whole package of neoliberal reform dubbed "structural adjustment."

The ability of regimes such as Mubarak's in Egypt, and later Ben Ali's in Tunisia, to implement these programs while containing the resulting social turmoil was, indeed, a major factor in their usefulness to Washington. The collapse of the USSR and the end of Cold War rivalries also shut down a space for other regimes to pursue a different course of national development.

The dictatorship of Saddam Hussein in Iraq had been strongly supported by the United States in its invasion of Iran after the overthrow of the shah, and facilitated in its brutal war against the Kurds. But the regime was still predicated partly on Arab nationalism and heavy state involvement in the economy, and the moderation of hostilities with Iran meant that Iraq's usefulness was drawing to an end. Its invasion of Kuwait in 1991, in what was partly an attempt to resolve its growing debt crisis, demonstrated the unreliability of the regime.

By contrast, America's loyal dictatorships, led by Saudi Arabia and Egypt, looked to US intervention—and were rewarded in their support for the subsequent US-led war with major debt cancellations.

STRONG STATES, STRONG MARKETS

The 1991 Gulf War was a pivotal moment in the development of US policy. There would be no further tolerance of the remnants of Arab nationalism, or of the statist economic policies linked to it. In the aftermath of the short war, Iraq was caged and depleted by a UN-authorized sanctions regime. The "New World Order," as George H. W. Bush called it, was one in which the major global battles were no longer those of Cold War ideology, but rather the new struggle to incorporate the Third World into world markets and defeat sources of instability, such as "Islamic terrorism" or the drug trade.

At the same time, international economic institutions such as the G7 were expanded, and the vast markets of Russia were opened up.[54] In the Middle East, trade agreements bolstered political alliances, as when the United States encouraged the development of so-called Qualifying Industrial Zones in Jordan and Egypt, the products of which would be given free access to US markets, provided a proportion of the inputs came from Israel.[55]

The Bush administration's 2003 war on Iraq was sold, among other things, as a death-blow to dictatorship in the region. A "free market" state built on the ashes of the Ba'ath regime would be linked to the spread of free trade in the region through the Middle East Free Trade Area. By opening up its markets, the Middle East could enjoy the benefits of globalization, while the eradication of poverty would extinguish the sources of terrorism and other regional problems.[56] With such strong growth, social peace would follow and governments could relent in their use of repression and wind down their overly centralized bureaucracies.

This vision was just as much of a mirage as the infamous weapons of mass destruction: strong markets, experience might have taught US planners, require strong states. Nonetheless, the administration invested hundreds of millions of dollars in the apparatus of "democracy promotion," which linked the liberalization of the state to the liberalization of the economy. Even as the

US government cultivated its valued relationships with regional dictators, it sought to plant a foot gingerly in the civil societies that might one day challenge these despotisms, and guide them in a pro-market direction. Such was the basis upon which the Obama administration attempted to respond to the Arab Spring.

President Obama's speech to the United Nations in May 2011 stressed that the US would mobilize funding for Arab states to help both their economic and political reforms along these lines.[57] British prime minister David Cameron's notable speech to the Kuwaiti national assembly in February of that year had also invoked just this coupling of "political and economic reform."[58] And money spoke, too. The Institute of International Finance, representing the world's major financial institutions, declared in May 2011 that the priority of the post-Mubarak and post-Ben Ali regimes in Egypt and Tunisia should be "deepening and accelerating structural economic reforms ... fostering entrepreneurship, investment, and market-driven growth."[59]

In cooperation with allied governments and international financial institutions, therefore, the United States developed the Deauville Partnership with Arab Countries in Transition, launched at the G8 summit in May 2011, through which loan packages are offered to incoming Arab governments if they accept privatization, subsidy cuts, public-sector wage freezes, and deregulation.[60] This package has been implemented in a range of countries, from Tunisia and Egypt to Yemen and Libya. In Tunisia, for example, where a parliamentary democracy has been stabilized, the resulting government, headed by a moderate Islamist Ennahda party, worked to implement the Deauville agenda against considerable institutional resistance in Tunisia—even at the cost of losing its popular base and allowing the former regime party to gain office.[61]

In Egypt, the Muslim Brotherhood–linked Freedom and Justice Party, which won the 2011 parliamentary elections, also attempted to implement the program and access the associated loans. This was highly controversial within the country, since the military-led government that took over immediately after Mubarak's downfall rejected the package on the ground that the conditions attached represented an abridgement of Egyptian sovereignty. Further, the Muslim Brothers had seemed to be critical of such measures before attaining office. Before Mohamed Morsi won the presidency in 2011, they had criticized the interim government's budget, which had imposed cuts. On taking office, however, they retained the officials behind the budget and attempted to implement the same reforms, cutting fuel subsidies and other budgets in the face of strikes and protests.[62]

Ultimately, these protests fused with a growing rebellion against the authoritarianism of the new system, in which the armed forces continued to be unleashed on protesters, generating a secularist backlash against the Islamists and a broader pro-military reaction. This was the context in which the Egyptian military launched its coup, putting General Abdel Fattah el-Sisi in charge, and beginning a concerted killing spree and judicial roundup of activists.[63]

General el-Sisi's government was welcomed in Washington and offered some relief to worried financial institutions. It began to implement many of the measures that the IMF wanted, including slashing fuel subsidies, which caused petrol and natural gas prices to rise by 70 percent. In an article headlined, "IMF Cozies Up to Egypt amid Economic Reform," the *Wall Street Journal* reported that the reform package "was a major political risk because it dramatically increased living costs for the poor." Nonetheless, with a series of massacres under the regime's belt, "the changes went into effect without causing serious unrest."[64]

The American empire had promised the Middle East a "new partnership," drawing on the longstanding idiom of universal rights linked to free markets. Arguably, it would have been strengthened from a certain perspective, its international legitimacy boosted, had it chosen to support the democratizing processes. But the economic reforms that it sought—opening up service industries to international investors while attacking the living standards of the poor—proved to be fundamentally incompatible with popular rule. The dictatorship of "open-minded" elites remained indispensable.

LATIN AMERICA: THE THREE PHASES OF EMPIRE

Among the mass of material released by WikiLeaks since 2010 is a series of documents that provide jarring insights into US foreign policy in Latin America. From Honduras to Venezuela, Haiti to Ecuador, the United States appears to have an inbuilt predilection for dictators—and a distaste for democratic government—in its own "backyard." The documents both collectively and, at times, individually, illuminate the strategic reasoning behind such preferences.

Yet, in Latin America at least, US support for dictatorship is far from being as common as it was in previous phases of the empire. Where once dictators were the bulwark of regional stability, they now emerge chiefly as a mode of crisis management. They are the exception rather than the rule for American strategy in the region. This is partly because the old oligarchies that the US used to rely on as allies have been transformed or replaced through neoliberal modernization. This transition is worthy of some consideration.

US support for dictatorships in Latin America is vividly illustrated by the WikiLeaks cables relating to three countries in particular: Haiti, Chile, and Honduras. They enable an understanding of the historical context that has motivated changing US strategies.

The history of US empire and its relationship to dictatorships in Latin America falls into three broad phases, each corresponding to its own imperial moment. The first is that signaled by the "Monroe Doctrine," whereby the United States claimed a strategic preeminence against colonial rivals in South America—a period reaching its zenith with the colonial turn of 1898, in which the United States first claimed formal colonies in its battle with

Spain. The United States was still an up-and-coming economic power and, for much of the period, still expanding its territorial claims in North America. By the 1890s, it had defeated Native American opposition and closed the frontier, and was undertaking a longing look abroad for new territories, just as it developed a serious naval capacity. In this period, the US Marines were the main body used to impose American political authority on countries such as Cuba, Haiti, and Nicaragua. Once in control, they developed national security apparatuses to protect friendly client regimes. This lasted effectively until the "Good Neighbor" doctrine outlined by President Franklin Roosevelt, in which the US foreswore military intervention in Latin American states.

A new phase was opened up by the Cold War, in which the United States sought to encourage regimes to develop an industrial base and a prosperous middle class that could sustain stable political authority without creating an opening for leftist movements. This was linked to the development of a global series of institutions known collectively by the name Bretton Woods, after the location of the conference at which they were launched. These included a global monetary system in which currencies were pegged to the gold standard, and institutions such as the International Monetary Fund, set up to enable the development of world trade. The prevailing orthodoxy was that national states could intervene extensively in economic affairs to support and develop productive industry. In this period, the US intervened frequently in Latin American affairs, but much less through the traditional military means than through covert CIA-coordinated interventions to bolster the national security apparatuses of friendly governments, and to sabotage movements and governments that threatened US interests.

The third phase was signaled by the collapse of the Bretton Woods system amid a global economic crisis, and the American adaptation to defeat in Vietnam and a series of related crises in its rule. The outcome, following a protracted and violent process of reorganization, was a form of rule predicated on the liberalization of markets, capital controls, and regulations on finance and labor. Rather than encouraging the state-coordinated development of industry, the IMF pursued "structural adjustment," using debt as a mechanism to incorporate Latin American states into the global economy. Market dependency would exert its own disciplinary mechanisms, as unfriendly policies could be "punished" by capital flight, or ruled out of bounds by global institutions. This involved reorganizing national elites, reducing the power of protectionist oligarchies, and—once leftist movements had been defeated by a tornado of CIA-orchestrated violence—encouraging them to rule through parliamentary institutions. With some outstanding exceptions, such as Plan Colombia and the Venezuelan coup, the United States was largely able to withdraw from military and paramilitary interventions, and let markets do the talking.

Phase I: The "Monroe Doctrine"

The Latin American continent and the Caribbean islands had long been regarded as America's "backyard"—a colloquial expression of the doctrine outlined by US president James Monroe in 1823, which stated that any European intervention in these territories would be regarded by the US as an "unfriendly act."

This was arguably hubristic, given that the United States lacked the naval capacity to enforce the doctrine at this point. But it expressed the proprietorial attitude to South America that would define US policy. Just as the United States was expanding westward, it hoped to expand to its south—and to do so, it would have to break the grip of the European colonial empires. In the meantime, American capital penetrated markets in Cuba, Brazil, Nicaragua, and beyond. And by 1890, with westward overland expansion almost completed, it began to construct a much larger navy for overseas gains. A victorious war with the Spanish Empire in 1898 won it control of Cuba and inaugurated a period of frantic military activism, saber-rattling, invasions, and occupations in Honduras, Cuba, and Nicaragua. Thus was the "backyard" initially secured.[65]

The administration of Woodrow Wilson, over two terms from 1913 to 1921, was the most belligerent in establishing a "right" of US military intervention in Latin America, occupying both Nicaragua and Haiti. Haiti had always troubled the United States. Its revolutionary victory over colonial France in 1804 rattled slave-owners, terrified that the example of free black men would ignite a struggle in the south to break the spine of America's race system. Washington refused to acknowledge the country's independence, and even considered annexing the island. Like so much in the hemisphere, Haiti was chiefly of interest to the United States as potential property. It menaced Haiti repeatedly, with the deployment of its navy to "protect American lives and property," while Haitians could only dread the victory of an expansionist slave state behemoth to the north. But it was the occupation of 1915 that decisively involved the US in the government, politics, and economy of Haiti. This was just one of many regional exertions of power that President Woodrow Wilson, a reforming Democrat elected in 1912, would undertake. The US had already occupied Nicaragua in 1912, and after Wilson took office in 1913, he began a campaign of intervention in the Mexican Revolution. Later, against his re-election promises, he would lead the United States into participation in the charnel house of World War I. Wilson was acting in a context of rising US power, already signified by its success in the Spanish-American War and its acquisition of formal colonies in Central America and the Philippines—a venture he fervently supported. US troops had been sent to Panama and Honduras, and Cuba had been repeatedly occupied since being won from Spain in 1898. As a Southern patrician and white supremacist, Wilson strongly believed both in segregation and in America's destiny as a global empire, which he believed should take up its share of what Kipling would call the "white man's burden."

The immediate purpose of the 1915 intervention was to put

down a popular revolution that had ousted and executed the pro-American dictator Jean Vilbrun Guillaume Sam. The justification for the mission was that order had to be restored so that the situation would not destabilize the world system. This might have been a concern, although there were others. US investments were at risk if the revolution began to expropriate property owners. But the larger picture was that the United States faced growing competition from European powers for influence in the island—and US policy since the Monroe Doctrine in 1823 had been to treat the Caribbean islands as American property, to be shielded from European penetration. The United States regarded Haitians as children, just as they had Cubans and Filipinos when they had won those territories from Spain in the Spanish-American War of 1898. It was therefore quite normal for General Smedley Butler to claim that the people of Haiti were American "wards," who would benefit from a period of tutelage—even if some 11,500 had been killed as a result of the invasion and occupation.[66] The United States "stabilized" the country by engaging in ruthless "hunt-and-kill" expeditions and decimating the opposition, and subsequently began to restructure the country. A new gendarmerie was constructed, modeled on the US Marine Corps, and the population conscripted into forced labor. By the time the US had left the country in 1934, under the rubric of Roosevelt's "Good Neighbor" policy, a brutal pro-business, pro-US regime had been successfully pioneered. From this point on, the United States was able to satisfy its interests by supporting a succession of dictatorships, most notably that of the notorious François "Papa Doc" Duvalier, and his son Jean-Claude ("Baby Doc").

Other interventions were less intensive but equally presumptuous. For example, when US interests were threatened by the Mexican Revolution[67] against the gerontocratic dictatorship of Porfirio Díaz, Wilson intervened twice. The bulk of American foreign direct investments were held in Mexico, and the US investors had a big stake in Mexican timber yards, mines, and farms. More generally, the United States preferred a business-friendly

Mexico to one driven in a populist or radical direction. Hence, when Wilson decided that the revolution had run "out of control," he decided to intervene, ostensibly to support the moderate, liberal wing of the revolution. This faction, far from being delighted with US backing, denounced it as a manifestation of *yanqui* imperialism.[68]

Phase II: From Good Neighbors to the Cold War

This policy of occupying Latin American countries, giving the Monroe Doctrine a substance it had not acquired during the incumbency of the president whose name it bore, was successful enough in creating reliable client regimes for the United States to be able to withdraw from many of its commitments during the administration of Franklin D. Roosevelt, under the auspices of his "Good Neighbor" policy. At any rate, as the US was gradually learning, indirect control through friendly regimes and market access was preferable in most cases to direct occupation. As Walter LaFeber argued: "The United States had hit upon a solution to its traditional dilemma of how to inject force to stop revolutions without having a long-term commitment of US troops. The answer seemed to be to use native, US-trained forces that could both pacify and protect the country."[69]

US domination in the postwar era thus tended to take the form of shoring up a network of authoritarian regimes aligned to US interests, or overthrowing governments that were not so aligned. In place of direct occupation, they negotiated with regimes to establish military bases where there was a strategic interest for the United States. In the Caribbean, the slow diminution of British rule opened opportunities for US penetration. The region was rich with resources, had abundant cheap labor, and was geographically adjacent to the Panama Canal—built with US capital, under conditions of social and racial segregation, to facilitate imports to the United States. US planners could hardly wait to nudge the limeys out of the way and start planting bases in these islands. Where they could, they co-opted anticolonial leaders; where that was not possible, they applied relentless pressure. The Monroe Doctrine had reached the zenith of its influence.

From the point of view of US capital, this was ideal. US investors had brought industrial expertise that had transformed the production of fruit and sugar and the extraction of raw materials into immense, centralized productive enterprises. One effect of this was to drive small farmers and peasants off the land, filling the urban centers with willing employees. Combined with the powerful security apparatuses built by the US Marines, this centralization of economic power consolidated an economic oligarchy that had little incentive to respond to popular demands. And if the urban working and middle classes combined with peasants to pursue reforms, the United States had the means to obstruct them. In a global context of Cold War antagonism between the United States and the USSR, the former could defend renewed intervention as a means of resisting the aggressive, imperialist Soviet expansion.

Events in Guatemala in 1954 vividly illustrate this dynamic. The country's ruling class had long depended on an essentially feudal system of control over its workforce, with labor and vagrancy laws empowering the narrow oligarchy that owned most of the land. The system was close to slavery. A postwar wave of revolt and reform began to enfranchise labor, and the 1950 elections delivered power to the left-wing Jacobo Árbenz. It would be hard to overstate Washington's panicked reaction. A group of senators led by Lyndon B. Johnson fulminated about "international Communism"—a "new type of imperialism." It was alleged in a House resolution that the Russians had violated the Monroe Doctrine, to which there could only be one response: war. In due course, US bombs brought down the elected government and imposed the anticommunist dictator Colonel Carlos Castillo Armas as president. The profits of the United Fruit Company, as well as the position of the country's ruling class, were thereby protected.[70]

In principle, the United States favored liberal democratic governance against the reactionary oligarchies. In principle, it was on the side of progress. And in a long-term view of US interests, it could be argued that developing local industries, breaking the oligarchies, and consolidating a broad middle class as a basis for stable democracy and consumer markets was a good idea. In practice, whatever mild steps the empire took in this direction were almost always subverted by its deeper commitment to profitable investment conditions. Consider Kennedy's "Alliance for Progress." This was supposed to open an era of liberal magnanimity in which a Democratic administration furnished Latin American states with vital aid in exchange for benign reform, such as the redistribution of land, the break-up of monopolies, and the mitigation of poverty. In fact, pro-US oligarchies and US firms preferred to use the money to intensify the productivity of their land, invest in updating their technologies, and leave the challenge of poverty-reduction to the miraculous powers of the economic growth that would ensue.

Where Kennedy did support reformers, he usually came to regret it. For example, in the Dominican Republic, the United States had long supported the dictatorship of Rafael Trujillo—an extreme kleptocrat who took control of most of the country's resources but preserved the political stability desired by American governments. After his assassination, elections were held in which Juan Bosch ran as a reformist candidate. The United States backed him, assuming that he would privatize the former dictator's immense possessions. Instead, he preserved them as a public asset, and incurred the mobilization first of the oligarchs and their military supporters, then of the United States. The ensuing period of coup and counter-coup, backed by US troops, took thousands of lives and was finally concluded only when the Johnson administration engineered the accession of Trujillo's former vice president, who duly privatized the country's wealth and opened the economy to US investors.[71]

Coterminously, the United States invested in a program of

military training intended to bolster the internal security apparatuses of Latin American dictatorships. This was a necessary counter-strike against the wave of radicalization already evident in Guatemala, and given extra force when the Cuban Revolution of 1959 removed the major local prize of the Spanish-American war from the American sphere of influence. A wave of right-wing military coups began, starting with Brazil in 1964 and concluding with Argentina in 1976. The apex of this reactionary wave was Augusto Pinochet's coup in Chile, which essentially converted the country into a laboratory of neoliberalism under the guidance of experts from the University of Chicago. A range of institutions, from the State Department to the CIA, worked on the program, out of which emerged the notorious death squads whose cumulative body-count reached such staggering proportions throughout the 1970s and 1980s.[72]

This was particularly important in the context of defeat for the US in Vietnam, which made direct military intervention in most circumstances impossible. Only in Grenada in 1982 was a direct invasion attempted, to overthrow the leftist government of Maurice Bishop. This tiny Caribbean island represented no vital interests of the United States, let alone posing the "communist" threat that was invoked. But Reagan's intervention sent a clear message: a "New Right" administration had taken power in Washington and was openly at war with leftist movements in Latin America. In Nicaragua, the US-aligned Somoza dictatorship, despite controlling a security apparatus created and sustained over decades by its US patron, was overthrown by the popular Sandinista movement. In El Salvador, a similar popular movement of peasants and workers was poised to overthrow the country's oligarchs. The Reagan administration characterized this as outright Soviet aggression and embarked on an extensive program of recruiting, training, and arming death squads from bases in Honduras. The CIA supplied centralized intelligence systems based in both Honduras and Panama, providing crucial information to the killers. In Nicaragua, the Contras—as the death squads were collectively known—killed approximately 50,000 people in their offensive. In El Salvador, the civil war killed up to 80,000, although the evidence suggests that the country's oligarchs were prepared for an all-out "cleansing" operation that would have annihilated up to half a million people.

Phase III: Human rights and neoliberal reform

It was in this bleak and bloody period that the old anticommunist saws of the Cold War began to be displaced by the language of human rights. The Reagan administration claimed that its concern in Latin America was precisely to establish regimes that respected universal rights. In El Salvador, it declared that it was backing the Christian Democrats as an anticommunist alternative to the fascist ARENA party, which would go on to attain civilian rule. In Haiti, it declared that its support for the dictatorship of Jean-Claude Duvalier was at an end and that it would favor free elections. In Nicaragua, after years of Contra violence, it eventually turned to Violeta Chamorro to defeat the Sandinistas in the 1990 elections, with substantial US assistance—and the threat of economic blockade had she lost. Taken alongside its decision to ditch the Marcos regime in the Philippines, *Foreign Affairs* hailed such developments as a "turnaround on human rights."[73] Nevertheless, in both Nicaragua and El Salvador it was the death squads that won the day, ensuring the continued dominance of the old ruling classes. In Haiti, the eventual success of the popular candidate, Jean-Bertrand Aristide, in the 1990 elections was quickly overturned by *génocidaires* in a US-supported coup the following year. Aristide was not allowed to return to office until 1994, when he had agreed to implement the agenda of the opponent he had defeated in the elections. In each case, the US was able to accept some form of democratic rule only after the old dictatorships had proved unfit for their purpose—and only once popular forces opposed to the business classes supported by the United States had been brutally defeated.

The wave of violence in the 1980s coincided with the drastic economic restructuring of Latin American societies, for which the first major stimulus was the so-called "Volcker Shock." International banks had lent copiously to South American dictatorships during the 1970s, leaving them vulnerable to US Federal Reserve chairman Paul Volcker's decision to drive up interest rates. Very soon, most Latin American export income was consumed by debt repayments, leaving the region dependent on bailouts from the IMF. The conditions attached to these bailouts included drastic "structural adjustments," along the lines implemented in Chile under the guidance of the "Chicago Boys." The prescriptions of the IMF involved the by now familiar mix of privatization, subsidy cuts, wage restraint, and consummation of the long-term transition to "export-led growth," in which domestic consumption was suppressed so that goods could be produced for export. In key dictatorships like Haiti, aid and loans were similarly used to open up agricultural and industrial production to US capital. Amy Wilentz summarizes the strategic goals of the United States in Haiti as, "one, a restructured and dependent agriculture that exports to US markets and is open to American exploitation, and the other, a displaced rural population that not only can be employed in offshore US industries in the towns, but is more susceptible to army control."[74]

Despite the successes of neoliberal reform and the defeats suffered by the Left, the mitigation of Reagan-era violence, the normalization of parliamentary democracy, and the slow displacement of the power of the old oligarchies gradually created opportunities for new popular forces. In the context of the "war on terror," the United States focused its energies on expanding its dominion in the Middle East, and several Latin American countries were able to begin the slow process of extricating themselves from US domination. Under Hugo Chávez, Venezuela defeated a US-backed coup d'état and embarked on an agenda of social reform funded by energy revenues. He was soon joined by a raft of other leftist leaders, who consolidated their regional strength through the Bolivarian Alliance for the Peoples of Our America (ALBA). The United States, whatever it attempted to do in Venezuela, generally refrained from sustained military or proxy intervention in the continent—with the singular exception of Colombia—preferring instead to use the "democracy promotion" institutions that it had been refining since the 1980s to support pro-US currents.[75] But where it did intervene decisively, in Haiti, it was careful to use a multilateral agency and a UN mandate to legalize the post-coup situation. As violent as the post-Aristide regime frequently was, the US was anxious to normalize an electoral politics without Aristide, his Fanmi Lavalas party, and the popular politics they represented. This approach was authoritarian, undemocratic, and brutal—but it was a far cry from the near-genocidal "low-intensity warfare" of the 1980s.

HAITI: DICTATORSHIP, DEATH SQUADS, AND SWEATSHOPS

During the Cold War, an apocryphal remark attributed to Franklin D. Roosevelt about America's client dictatorship in Nicaragua was assumed to sum up America's attitude to despotism in its "backyard": "Somoza may be a son of a bitch, but he's our son of a bitch."[76] This off-the-cuff quip went to prove that if a dictatorship could be relied upon in the struggle against communism, it could enjoy the protection of the leader of the "Free World." In fact, the story goes deeper—as the example of Haiti shows.

Among the 2011 leaks of State Department cables was a bundle of documents relating to the Caribbean island-state and American diplomacy there. The documents show the United States frantically trying to protect the interests of US corporations, anxious to prevent the return of the democratically elected leader ousted in a US-backed coup, and in league with sweatshop elites who used the police as their own private mercenary force.

One batch of cables shows that the US worked overtime to prevent the return to Haiti of the "turbulent priest" Jean-Bertrand Aristide, the elected president who had been deposed in 2004 by a US-backed coup d'état.[77] During that operation, Aristide had been "escorted" out of the country by US Navy Seals in what he described as a "modern-day kidnapping." In its aftermath, a UN occupation force—the United Nations Stabilisation Mission in Haiti (MINUSTAH)—was quickly assembled and the coup regime consecrated in power.

In the following years, US officials were worried that Aristide might gain popular "traction" and return, thus threatening the "democratic consolidation" resulting from the coup. The United States was particularly worried by the "resurgent populist and anti-market economy political forces" that might be unleashed if Aristide were able to return. It therefore applied pressure for MINUSTAH to stay and help realize "core [US government] interests in Haiti." In turn, the head of the MINUSTAH mission, Edmond Mulet, asked the US government to press legal charges against Aristide to prevent him from returning to Haiti.[78]

Another batch of documents shows that the US embassy was complicit with major US companies in lobbying the Haitian government against an increase in the minimum wage.[79] Haitian wages being among the lowest in the world, there was a political movement of the low-paid and unemployed to legislate for a higher wage. US diplomats pressured President René Préval to intervene and prevent the political situation from spiraling out of control. But Préval's intervention, agreeing a staged increase in the minimum wage, was then scorned by the US embassy as not reflecting "economic reality"—the reality in question presumably being that Haiti's growth and export strategy depended upon an abundance of extremely cheap labor.

Other revelations disclosed the nature of the elites supported by the United States, and the brutal methods of repression they used after the 2004 coup in order to break the political spine of Aristide's popular supporters and the Fanmi Lavalas party. Despite killing thousands through the use of its own paramilitaries—successors to the death squads that had tormented Haiti in 1991—the post-coup government could not be sure of maintaining political order. Business elites therefore supplied lethal weapons to units of the Haitian National Police force and effectively deployed them as a private army to suppress political opposition.[80]

All of these facts—America's support for an anti-democratic coup, its alliance with sweatshop owners and murderous elites, its efforts to stop Haiti's elected leader returning—can only be made sense of in light of America's evolving strategy in its "back-yard." For the history of US-backed dictators covers all of the three phases outlined at the beginning of this chapter. As we have seen, this history was initiated by the intervention of US forces in 1915, whose first task was to build a new client regime. At this stage, the US still prioritized direct territorial rule. It continued through a new phase in the Cold War, as the US sought stable regimes that could "modernize" while preventing the Left from taking power. Thus, while the US no longer needed to rule Haiti through direct military control, since it had already constructed a national security apparatus, it indulged, armed, and supported regimes such as that of "Papa Doc" Duvalier and then that of his son "Baby Doc." In the case of the former, this extended to direct military intervention to protect the dictatorship.

US support for the conservative "Papa Doc" Duvalier had begun in the elections of 1957, when he stood against the wealthy French-backed candidate Louis Déjoie. Duvalier won the elections convincingly, but quickly established a brutal regime based on the deployment of his own paramilitaries, the Tontons Macoutes. And within two years, as Déjoie stood ready to organize an insurgency against the dictatorship, US Marines teamed up with Duvalier's forces to crush the rebellion, as Duvalier's Macoutes began rounding up suspects. US actions were justified by claims that the uprising had been organized by the Castro regime, but there was little evidence of this: Duvalier had simply proved his mastery for manipulating the US obsession with communism to reinforce the support America was already inclined to give him.[81] In the aftermath, Duvalier disbanded all other law

enforcement apparatuses and invested their authority in the paramilitaries, which subsequently terrorized the population with
rape and massacres.

For a brief period during the Kennedy administration,
Duvalier's lavish way of spending US-supplied money, and his
decision to "re-inaugurate" himself as Haiti's ruler in 1961, led
the US government to consider him an unreliable ally. As Edwin
Martin, assistant secretary of state for inter-American affairs,
put it, Duvalier "would move in whatever direction [suited] his
purpose in maintaining himself in power."[82] Kennedy debated military intervention to remove him. Indeed, plans were developed to
bring Déjoie into contact with leading New York business circles
who would provide funding for a coup, in exchange for access
to Haitian markets and government contracts.[83] By this time,
however, Duvalier had entrenched his power through the very
bloody actions that US aid had paid for. No action was taken,
and while aid was reduced, it was not eliminated. The Johnson
administration resumed normal relations and increased aid.

A new phase was inaugurated by the overthrow of "Baby Doc"
Duvalier in 1986, and consolidated when Aristide was allowed
to take power in 1994. The Reagan administration had continued the policy of Nixon and Carter in supporting the younger
Duvalier, on the pretext that he was an anticommunist regional
presence. In fact, by this time the "red menace" had some substance, in that there was a strong leftist movement in Haiti. The
Lavalas movement—a populist alliance growing out of the slums
of Port-au-Prince—aimed to uproot the system of paramilitary
rule, as well as the economic policies benefiting the country's elite
of sweatshop owners. This movement responded particularly to
the passionate speeches of a priest named Jean-Bertrand Aristide.

Lavalas evidently inspired panic in the Reagan administration. It sought to adjust its posture toward Haiti, sporadically
withholding aid and offering mealy-mouthed opposition to government violence. However, this was not to be a case where the
United States could tolerate a democratic transition. The younger

Duvalier had been making efforts to incorporate Haiti into global markets along the neoliberal lines advanced by Washington, but Aristide's movement was threatening to undo it all. Thus, when Aristide won office in 1990 with 67 percent of the vote, compared to just 14 percent for the World Bank economist and US favorite Marc Bazin, CIA-trained death squads descended on the country and initiated three years of terror that only ended when the US government persuaded Aristide to accept the political agenda of his opponent and govern along the lines prescribed by the IMF and World Bank. He was compelled to accept a structural adjustment program that included further cuts to the wages of Haiti's already extremely poor workers. As UN envoy Lakhdar Brahimi told Haitian radio in 1996, the US would accept that political change was necessary, but when it came to economic power, the elites should know "they have the sympathy of Big Brother, capitalism."[84]

But Aristide's reluctant acquiescence was not sufficient, and the attempt to implement structural adjustment created divisions in the Lavalas movement between a "moderate" wing close to Washington and those aligned with Aristide, who tried to dilute the program. Aristide's wing of the Lavalas movement had not sufficiently adjusted to the political defeat wrought by death squads, nor satisfactorily internalized the new "free market" dispensation. Its ongoing failure to do so was, as had become standard US practice by this point, linked to a critique of the regime based on its human rights record. The journalist Amy Wilentz, observing the development of this line of attack, remarked on how extraordinary it was that the United States had suddenly developed a concern for Haitian human rights that had eluded them for practically the entire period of dictatorship. Nevertheless, the growing movements against the sweatshop owners and backlash against structural adjustment were, to some extent, channeled by Aristide. After he was re-elected as president in 2000, business groups began to organize a political opposition alliance called the "Group of 184," which presented itself as a broad civil society coalition. Together with groups such as Convergence Démocratique, they attempted to annul the election results. By 2004, with the support of the Bush administration, a coup against Aristide had begun. He was soon being told by French and American leaders to resign and was escorted at gunpoint out of the country as American, Canadian, and French troops occupied the country.[85]

This did not mean that the United States was intent on another period of outright dictatorship. Under a multilateral occupation that bore the seal of the United Nations, they instead imposed an emergency government, followed by elections, and relied upon UN forces to suppress the Lavalas movement—demonized as "gangs." As long as Aristide was out of the country, and his political movement neutralized and kept under control, carefully managed elections could be allowed to take place. The meaning of ongoing US intervention in Haiti was not that it required the political rule of a dictatorship, but simply that sufficient violence had not yet been inflicted on the population to discipline them into voting for the new market regime.

CHILE: THE KISSINGER CABLES

In April 2013, Wikileaks published 1.7 million US Department of State diplomatic and intelligence records from a period when Henry Kissinger was US secretary of state: the "Kissinger cables."[86] These cables provide a unique insight into the role of the State Department in managing the difficulties of the US empire in this period. Kissinger's singularly cynical style of operating aside, this was clearly a period of crisis and transition, and the extraordinarily violent US interventions in this period can be understood in this context.

The immediate harvest from a first appraisal of these documents included a number of juicy, headline-grabbing morsels. These include, for example, Kissinger's meeting with the Turkish foreign minister in 1975. The US Congress had just imposed an arms embargo on Turkey in response to the latter's bloody invasion of Cyprus. Yet the cables show that Kissinger proposed various means of circumventing the embargo. Told that his proposals were illegal, he remarked: "Before the Freedom of Information Act, I used to say at meetings, 'The illegal we do immediately; the unconstitutional takes a little longer.'"[87] A cynical witticism of this kind might hardly merit attention were it not for the evidence that Kissinger and the administration had already worked to instigate and enable Turkey's invasion, and did indeed subsequently work to circumvent the arms embargo.[88]

In 1973, a CIA-backed coup overthrew the elected government of Salvador Allende and installed in power the military dictator General Pinochet. The most cynical documents relate to the US government's secret response to the coup that complement previous waves of declassified cables accumulated by the National Security Archive at George Washington University[89] as well as the findings of the Hinchey Report on the CIA's activities in the coup conducted by the National Intelligence Council in 2000.[90] The facts show that the United States played a consistent role in sabotaging the administration of the elected leftist Salvador Allende, and in its ultimate overthrow.

Until 1970, Chile was a relatively stable and conservative society, where the Left was comfortably excluded from power. Yet, in the face of a rigid oligarchy that refused to accede to reforms, the Left gained a slight plurality in 1970 and secured the support of some traditionally centrist political groups. Allende thus gained a mandate to govern and implement his reform agenda. He spoke in Marxist language, in a continent where paranoid anticommunism furnished the language of the entrenched oligarchies and their justification for repression.

The immediate response of the Nixon administration was to begin looking at possibilities for a coup against the government. Kissinger instructed the CIA to keep the pressure on "every Allende weak spot in sight." Nixon, in a meeting with CIA director Richard Helms, authorized a program of sabotage against the regime: "Make the economy scream."[91] Kissinger then embarked on a plan to kidnap and dispose of the leader of the Chilean military, who was known to oppose army meddling in electoral politics. The hope was that it would panic the Chilean parliament into denying Allende his right to take office.

Plan B—"Track II," as it was called—was to engineer a coup against Allende then re-stage elections, in which he would be defeated. It was "firm and continuing policy that Allende be overthrown by a coup," as the CIA wrote to the Track II group in Santiago. Weapons were ferried to the country in the hope that factions of the military could be signed up to such a coup effort.[92] American companies with holdings in Chile, such as ITT and Pepsi-Cola, were drafted to the government's aid—ITT helping to route US aid to anti-Allende factions. Meanwhile, international financial institutions were encouraged to boycott Chile, and traditional aid to US corporations investing in the country was suspended—and thus, indeed, was the economy made to scream.

Had it been up to the Nixon administration, the Chilean military would have been settling Chile's political affairs long before 1973. However, even with such extensive interference, a coup might not have materialized had it not been for the fact that Allende's agenda met ferocious opposition from Chile's business community and sections of its middle class. Allende may have increased his vote from 36 percent of electors in 1970 to 44 percent in 1973, but the centrist parties that his coalition depended on had shifted back to supporting the Right.

On September 11, 1973, forces led by General Augusto Pinochet overthrew the government, bombed the presidential palace, and began rounding up members of the opposition, who were then tortured and executed en masse. On September 12, General Pinochet contacted the US government—using a proxy "in view of delicacy of matter of contact at this moment in time"—and informed them that the new regime would break relations with "communist bloc" countries, and sought to "strengthen and add to traditional friendly ties with the US."[93]

The next day, the American reply welcomed "General Pinochet's expression of junta desire for strengthened ties between Chile and US ... the USG wishes make clear [*sic*] its desire to cooperate with the military junta and to assist in any appropriate way. We agree that it is best initially to avoid too much public identification between us."[94] On September 20, the US received a message from the junta requesting special forces training for the following objectives:

    A. Psychological warfare.
    B. Organization and operations of special forces.
    C. Organization and operations of civil affairs.[95]

In the circumstances, the chief goal of the Chilean military was to suppress and control the civilian population. The response from Washington, after a few weeks of pondering, was a provisional "no," due to the potential for negative publicity—but note the implied approval of the regime's ends: "[I]t would be better for us if [the Chilean government] would meet these requirements at this time through other channels."[96] Pinochet, in a subsequent conversation with State Department officials, conveyed his understanding and sensitivity toward the need for "caution in development of overly close identification." Publicity on US involvement in delivering humanitarian supplies was welcome, but they should keep "pretty quiet" about "any cooperation in other fields." The State Department agreed, mentioning military assistance such as "mine detector gear" as an "example of the other kind of thing." In fact, the State Department continued to lobby the Senate for extensive military assistance for the Chilean regime.[97]

Further cables demonstrate the efforts of diplomats to reconcile the US government's support for the regime with the global criticism the regime was incurring, particularly from the UN Human Rights Commission. "Pinochet is of course quite right about the inequity of the double standard as applied to Chile on the one hand and Cuba on the other," stated a March 1975 telegram from Ambassador Popper in Santiago. The problem was that the Chilean image had been "tarnished in the outside world." Pinochet may have "made a case for the need to restrict human rights temporarily" in light of the "emergency civil war situation" that had prevailed under Allende, but Chile had to "convince the doubting" with a "strong reply" to the UN Human Rights Commission.[98] For cavils such as these, Ambassador Popper was seen as a "wet" by the administration. Kissinger once sent a cable to Santiago reading: "Tell Popper to cut out the political science lectures."[99]

This was, however, only the prelude to a wave of terror conducted by the regime, the most notorious phase of which was Operation Condor, carried out by a team "structured much like a US Special Forces Team,"[100] and involving the dictatorship in a network of military regimes across Latin America in an international program of terror, torture, and killings aimed at eliminating leftist movements and leaders wherever they lay. The head of the Chilean secret police who organized Condor was a CIA agent during the same period.[101]

Just as important as the apparatus of terror linked to the regime, though, were its economic reforms. The role of Milton Friedman's "Chicago Boys" in advising the Chilean government on how to reform the economy has been well documented.[102] The privatization of the industries nationalized by Allende, the privatization of social security, and the opening up of the country's assets to US investors were all recommended and implemented. More than this, however, the disruption to the old oligarchic rule represented by Allende, and the Pinochet regime's relative autonomy from the business class, enabled the dictatorship to restructure industry in such a way as to displace the dominance of old mining and industrial capital. This was part of a global trend, as investors everywhere felt shackled by the old statist models of development. They demanded the reorganization of industry, the freeing up of the financial sector, and the opening of international markets. In place of the old economic model of "import substitution," protecting and developing the nation's industries to overcome dependence on imports, a new model of "export-led growth" was implemented, in which domestic consumption was suppressed so that goods could be more profitably exported abroad.[103]

The WikiLeaks documents, taken together with previous historical findings, show us a US government immensely relieved by the Pinochet coup, and desperate to work with the new regime. The cables display the State Department's cavalier attitude toward the junta's program of mass torture and executions, while they evince an anxiety to correct any movement to the left on the dictatorship's part.[104] The US was clearly prepared to collaborate with the military dictatorship in a new region-wide wave of terror, and at the very beginning of a new framework of economic power underpinning the American empire.

HONDURAS: HILLARY CLINTON AND THE DRUG LORD

the richest man in Honduras today is Miguel Facussé Barjum, a landowner, bio-fuels businessman, and major cocaine trafficker whose private security apparatus has killed dozens of rural activists—campesinos—in recent years.[105] Facussé and his wealthy family are a textbook instance of the kinds of oligarch who benefited most from the June 2009 military coup against the elected government of Manuel Zelaya. Since then, with the backing of the coup regime, he has escalated his bloody battle against the campesinos.

The United States, of course, has declared itself on the side of democracy in Honduras. Courtesy of the State Department cables, we know that Washington was in no doubt that a coup had taken place from the moment it happened. The US embassy in Tegucigalpa sent a cable home declaring the matter an "open and shut" case.[106] The arguments of the coup-mongers were efficiently taken apart in this cable, which noted that all of the allegations against Zelaya that had been used to justify his overthrow were either falsehoods, speculation, or unproven allegations, and that none of them had any "substantive validity."

Yet the public response from US officials was strangely unclear. On the day of the coup, June 28, 2009, the United States declined to condemn what had happened, instead evasively calling on Hondurans to respect democracy. The following day, even after President Obama admitted that an "illegal" and "unconstitutional" coup had taken place, setting what he called a "terrible precedent," Secretary of State Hillary Clinton refused to comment when asked whether Zelaya should be returned to office. The State Department, when challenged, declined to refer to what had happened as a coup.[107] Even in late August 2009, the State Department was still pretending in its press briefings not to know that a coup had taken place.[108]

The reason for this prevarication later became clear: the United States was going to support the new regime. The State Department had conceded that, under US law, it would not be permitted to continue to send aid to the regime if it had taken power in a military coup. But the aid continued to flow. The United States funded the Honduran military and police while they acted as death squads for the elites, despite a request from Congress to stop doing so. These forces worked side by side with Facussé's assassins, providing him with the crucial support of a US-backed state apparatus as he went about his private, often illegal, business. WikiLeaks documents showed that the State Department had known since at least 2004 of Facussé's cocaine profiteering, and that on at least two occasions US officials had had high-level meetings with him. One of those occasions was in 2009, while the coup was ongoing.[109]

Moreover, the United States continued to oppose any attempt to restore genuine democratic government in Honduras. A month after the coup, Clinton expressed her ire at the former president for trying to return to his country, deeming it a "provocative" action. Subsequently, the United States blocked a resolution at the Organization of American States refusing to recognize the neutered elections organized by the coup regime.[110] The echoes of Haiti were palpable.

What did the Obama administration dislike so much about Manuel Zelaya's elected government that it effectively embraced what Obama had publicly decried as an "unconstitutional" coup? There were a number of things that identified him as a trouble-maker. First, he had formed a close alliance with Venezuela's Hugo Chávez, who had already embarrassed the United States by defeating a US-supported coup attempt against him in 2002, before embarking on a process of radical reform. By incorporat-ing the country into Chávez's Bolivarian regional alliance, ALBA, Zeleya threatened opportunities for US investors. Second, he pro-posed an agenda of constitutional reform that was popular with labor and grassroots constituencies, and was in danger of gaining support in a national consultation.

The existing constitution had been drafted during a period of crisis in the Central American region, when the country had been used as a base for the CIA-sponsored death squads ravaging Nicaragua and El Salvador. Honduras had avoided the catastro-phes of its neighbors in the 1980s because its weaker oligarchy and more plentiful land enabled it to deliver reforms demanded by the poor. This was assisted by US economic and military aid, offered in exchange for Honduras's hosting of the death squads.

Nonetheless, the constitution adopted in this era was seen by most of the political class as deeply flawed—particularly the rule against presidential candidates seeking re-election, a holdover from the period when the military had more political authority. What rankled the powerful about Zelaya's proposals for reform was who was behind them, and the nature of his project. It was clear that Zelaya saw the executive branch of government as his best bulwark against the powerful forces opposing him in the Supreme Court, Congress, and the military, as well as much of the business community. By changing the constitution, he could ensure his re-election and thereby gain time to bring Honduras into ALBA, as well as pursuing other reforms.[111]

But it is also important to register what the WikiLeaks cables do not show. The US alliance with the Honduran coup was not an enthusiastic one. Nor is there evidence that the US either planned or instigated the coup, even if those who did had benefited from US funding and training. What seems to have happened is that, after an evaluation of the options, and some internal argument, the US government resolved that restoring Zelaya would be a greater evil than accepting a regime that America's partners—the Honduran elites—evidently wanted. Further, the coup regime was careful to legitimize itself by staging new elections and giving itself a constitutional gloss, rather than simply declaring emergency military rule. The scale of violence, though not negligible, was much less than in previous coups in the region.

It also seems probable that Obama's worry about setting a "terrible precedent" was not mere dissimulation. Any return to routine coups and military rule in Latin America would upset the relatively stable political and economic climate that the United States had been able to achieve in its hemisphere. It would threaten to reanimate revolutionary political movements in an era when the threat had largely been killed off, and poison any future resurrection of the Free Trade Area of the Americas.

The WikiLeaks cables relating to Latin American dictatorships and human rights abuses thus disclose a pattern that is quite different from that of other regions, such as the Middle East, where the US has clung tenaciously to dictatorship as its favored political form. Gradually, the phase during which the American empire required direct military rule was replaced by a phase of rule-by-proxy, bolstered by constant military and paramilitary interventions. At the time of writing, after a wave of transitional violence has enabled a process of structural adjustment and the institutionalization of free trade, there is a gradually emerging regional order in which US interventions have been rarer, usually more subtle, and ultimately supplementary to the disciplinary rule of markets.

2. Dictators and Human Rights

With a heavy dose of fear and violence, and a lot of money for projects, I think we can convince these people that we are here to help them.

Colonel Nathan Sassaman[1]

"OUR" VIOLENCE ...

Talal Asad, summarizing the elements of a just war, argues that such a conflict is one waged by people of good character, for benign motives, after all possible alternatives have been exhausted, and under the civilizing restraints of morality and law.[2] For the American empire, all wars waged by its leaders are just wars, launched only in the face of overwhelming provocation, to achieve liberal and humane objectives. With this hollow self-justification in mind, can the "higher ground" posited by Asad ever exist?

Consider some of the acts that the empire has afforded itself in its recent, supposedly just, wars. From the WikiLeaks cables we have learned that the United States has bombed civilian targets; carried out raids in which children were handcuffed and shot in the head, then summoned an air strike to conceal the deed;[3] gunned down civilians and journalists;[4] deployed "black" units of special forces to carry out extrajudicial captures and killings;[5] side-stepped an international ban on cluster bombs;[6]

strong-armed the Italian judiciary over the indictment of CIA agents involved in extraordinary rendition;[7] engaged in an undeclared ground war in Pakistan;[8] and tortured detainees at Guantánamo Bay, few of whom have ever been charged with any crime.[9] This is but a sample of the grueling realities of America's wars in the last decade or so—and yet, they would appear to represent a strong prima facie case that the United States knows no law, no morality, and no restraint in its pursuit of war.

Many commentators consider these actions to be war crimes.[10] Indeed, some of the most informed international legal commentators have produced devastating indictments of what they say is the Bush administration's reckless disregard for the law.[11] However, in the cases where the US authorities have acknowledged these actions, they are justified as a response to terrorism. Terrorism, it is suggested, is the opposite of the just war, both describing an illegitimate form of political violence and providing a primary justification for war. It is not limited by restraint, morality, or law. And of course, as every right-thinking person knows by now, terrorists cannot be negotiated with.

But the WikiLeaks documents give us plenty of reason to doubt this rationale. For example, with regard to Guantánamo, we were told that those detained there were the worst of the worst—terrorists who posed a clear and present danger to the safety of Americans and others. The *Guantánamo Files*,[12] however, show this not to be the case. Many prisoners were knowingly held despite posing no risk. A tiny proportion were ever charged, despite the obvious advantage that interrogators would have in eliciting a confession.

Often, "high value" detainees had little or no evidence against them. For example, Sami al-Hajj was referred to as being of "HIGH intelligence value" and also a "HIGH risk, as he is likely to pose a threat to the US, its interests, and allies." This would seem to be precisely the sort of person the Bush administration had told us should be in Guantánamo. The detainee assessment, however, cited no positive evidence of its claims that he was "a member of al-Qaida and logistics expert with direct ties to al-Qaida ... and the Taliban leadership." Rather, in its description of the evidence under "recruitment" and "training and activities," it describes his work as an Al Jazeera journalist and, prior to that, as an employee of a beverage company.

Nothing in the list of charges does more than raise an eyebrow. Further, the assessment makes it clear that at least part of the reason that al-Hajj was being detained was so that he could be grilled for information about Al Jazeera. Indeed, al-Hajj's solicitor states that interrogators constantly attempted to make him say that there was a link between Al Jazeera and al-Qaeda. Eventually, Sami al-Hajj was released with no charges against him, after the Sudanese government assured the US that he was an ordinary citizen and posed no security threat. This, according to his solicitor,[13] was not before he had been beaten and sexually assaulted.

Other WikiLeaks cables show either a reckless disregard for civilian life or the knowing perpetration of atrocities against civilians. For example, alongside investigative journalism inspired by WikiLeaks, the "FRAGO 242"[14] protocol was discovered, in which the Pentagon ordered military personnel not to investigate claims of torture against Iraqi soldiers and paramilitaries. It was partly explained by the fact that the United States was training these forces in the use of torture. As we shall see, this was deployed in a ruthless civil war and counter-insurgency strategy in which civilians were terrorized, brutalized, and killed.

We still do not have access to the most incriminating records concerning the use of torture in Iraq by US troops. As the Abu Ghraib revelations were emerging, the journalist Seymour Hersh discovered that the Pentagon had a tape of a grotesque incident at the prison, in which "[t]he women were passing messages out saying 'Please come and kill me, because of what's happened.'" The women had been detained alongside a group of young boys. The boys had been sodomized, with the cameras rolling. There was also an audio track of the boys' shrieking.[15]

... AND "THEIRS"

The state leaders who waged this war seem unperturbed by any of these brutalities. Former vice president Dick Cheney, when quizzed about the Bush administration's role in torture, said: "I have no problem as long as we achieve our objective. And our objective is to get the guys who did 9/11 and it is to avoid another attack against the United States." When told of an example of a man who was chained to the wall of a cell, doused with cold water, and frozen to death, only for it to turn out that he was entirely innocent, Cheney was intransigent: "I'm more concerned with bad guys who got out and released than I am with a few that in fact were innocent."[16]

This was a recurring theme. As long as it was happening to "bad guys," then implicitly any brutality was permissible. Rarely has the relationship between demonization and terrorism been so concisely articulated.

During his time as chief executive, President Bush repeatedly characterized the Iraqi insurgency as "terrorist" and described its "strategic goal" as being to "shake the will of the civilized world": "Two years ago, I told the Congress and the country that the war on terror would be a lengthy war, a different kind of war, fought on many fronts in many places. Iraq is now the central front. Enemies of freedom are making a desperate stand there—and there they must be defeated."[17] The problem was that his own intelligence did not support his claims. The argument was that al-Qaeda had reappeared in Iraq as "foreign fighters" after a thorough routing in Afghanistan, but US intelligence estimated that only 5 percent of the insurgent force comprised "foreign fighters." The penetration of al-Qaeda into Iraq was supposed to be felt through the person of Abu Musab al-Zarqawi, but his influence was small, and his forces were under attack from the mainstream of the insurgency from early on in the occupation.[18]

The view of US intelligence was that the insurgency was driven chiefly by nationalist opposition to the occupation rather than by al-Qaeda-style jihadism. The tactics of the insurgency, moreover, failed an essential condition for being defined as "terrorist": most of their actions, according to the quarterly studies conducted by the US Department of Defense, were directed against occupying troops rather than civilians.[19]

A similar pattern was found in Afghanistan, where larger numbers of people joined a revived Taliban movement as a result of the occupation's brutalities, until almost 80 percent of the country had a heavy Taliban presence. A former employee of the UN mission in Afghanistan suggested that, while Taliban tactics inflicted a grueling toll on civilians, this was—to use the American idiom—"collateral damage," a result of "technical shortcomings." The aim was "not to terrorize the population," but to "inflict casualties on the enemy."[20]

This tendency to demonize opponents in order to justify the administration's policy—a deliberate military goal, as the *Washington Post* revealed in 2006[21]—at times left America's allies rather frustrated. General Sir Richard Dannatt, then head of the British Army, gave an important speech in 2007 rejecting the main arguments of the "war on terror." Reflecting on the characterization of the Iraqi insurgency as "terrorists," he said: "By motivation ... our opponents are Iraqi Nationalists, and are most concerned with their own needs—jobs, money, security—and the majority are not bad people." He went on to make similar remarks about the insurgency in Afghanistan, regretting its lazy characterization as "Taliban."[22]

THE POWER OF LABELS

It is extraordinary to think that the empire deploys such awesome force with such catastrophic results. Yet how does it successfully moralize its own actions and villainize those of its opponents? The WikiLeaks cables give us some clues. In them we find, again and again, the careful use of a legal, bureaucratic, and political language that is all about providing a normative frame for US government actions.

Returning to the case of Sami al-Hajj, the documents display the fruits of careful rituals of military-legal process, jurisprudence, and categorization that allowed him to be detained as if he had been a high-risk terrorist. These labels provided the basis for the Bush administration to claim that the people in its captivity were all or mostly "bad guys." Yet they in turn depended upon the decisions of the Justice Department and the Bush White House in interpreting the relevant application of international and domestic law, and deciding the status of detainees. Between a captive and the entire power and authority of the US state, it was the state that had the power to apply labels and make them stick: and it was Sami al-Hajj who had to beg for his freedom despite there being no evidence against him.

This theme recurs too often. Between the armed might of the United States and its allies, on one hand, and that of loose militias gathered to repel occupying forces in Iraq and Afghanistan, on the other, it is the United States that has the power to determine what the war is about, who is a "terrorist," and who is fighting a "just war."

These verbal manipulations highlight the power of classifications, and the classifications of power. Whether the subject is "just war" or "terrorism," "torture" or "enhanced interrogation techniques," "enemy combatants" or "political prisoners," we find that the ability to assert a definition and to back it up with force are essential elements of imperial rule. Defining and classifying are part of what states do: they define the social categories that make sense of everyday life—married, single, criminal, cop, black, white, terrorist, soldier, hero, villain. And they do this through language, law, and culture. An empire, it turns out—even amid the resort to extreme violence—cannot do without the power of ideas.

WHAT IS A TERRORIST?

"Worse than a military attack," the Republican congressman Peter King expostulated in November 2010, urging that WikiLeaks be categorized as a "terrorist organization."[23] Vice President Joe Biden accused Julian Assange of being a "high-tech terrorist." Hunt him down like bin Laden, exhorted Sarah Palin.[24] "Yes, WikiLeaks is a terrorist organization," said Fox News.[25]

The basis of this overblown charge was that WikiLeaks was waging a "cyber-war" on the United States that placed "vital interests" at risk—particularly the flows of information necessary to track down and capture "terrorists"—thus putting American lives in danger. When WikiLeaks invited the US government to name a single cable whose publication put anyone at significant risk of harm, the State Department's legal advisor wrote back formally declining to name a specific danger, but nonetheless ordered WikiLeaks to shut down its websites, cease publication, and destroy all the information it held.[26]

This charge of "terrorism" was not merely lazy or over-excited: there was real power behind it. The 2013 prosecution of Chelsea—then Bradley—Manning, the soldier who had leaked the cables to the website, depended upon the claim that she had "aided the enemy"—a charge that is close to treason and carries the death penalty. Manning had joined the armed forces in 2007 and, despite suffering bullying from other soldiers related to his homosexuality and gender identity dysphoria, excelled sufficiently to be promoted and gain a services medal. He was then deployed as an intelligence analyst in Baghdad, and it was there that he discovered "the true nature of twenty-first-century asymmetric warfare."[27] By 2010, Manning had discovered WikiLeaks, and over time developed a relationship with them that led to his disclosure of hundreds of thousands of documents, including what became known as the *Iraq War Logs*, *Cablegate*, and the *Guantánamo Files*, including footage of a Baghdad air strike that was subsequently criticized as a war crime. The "enemy" who

Manning had supposedly aided by releasing this information was al-Qaeda. When Manning was captured, he was subject to cruel, degrading, and inhumane treatment of the sort generally inflicted on those the US government deems "terrorists."[28] This raises an obvious question: What is a terrorist?

There appears to be no agreed definition.[29] Leaking secret materials is hardly a qualification in itself: US officials do it all the time as part of their public relations strategies. Apparently, the standard is: when you leak, that is terrorism; when we leak, that is fine. And perhaps one of WikiLeaks' sins, in the view of the US government and its defenders, is precisely to have exposed how unstable the category is, and how porous is the distinction between what the US government does and what its enemies do.

JUST WAR AND TERROR

A pivotal moral justification for Western political violence is that it operates within constraints that respect civilian life. It is a standard refrain of Western military sources that "we do not target civilians." This claim, central to the US Department of State's overseas public relations strategy,[30] is made with apodictic solemnity. It is what is held to separate "terrorism" from the actions of those claiming to wage war against "terrorism." As George W. Bush explained, "Every life is precious. That's what distinguishes us from the enemy."[31] Terrorism is the opposite of the just war—both an illegitimate form of political violence and a justification for legitimate political violence.

The difficulty is that there appears to be no commonly agreed definition of terrorism. For example, one current US government definition claims that terrorism "is premeditated, politically-motivated violence perpetrated against non-combatant targets by sub-national groups or clandestine agents."[32] This definition leads us to an immediate problem. Aside from the fact that the exclusion of state institutions as potential agents of terrorism is arbitrary and unfounded, this definition seems to exclude the bombing of US military bases, which are staffed by combatants.

The State Department caught up with this in 2003: "We also consider as acts of terrorism attacks on military installations or on armed military personnel when a state of military hostilities does not exist at the site, such as bombings against US bases."[33] Yet even this refinement left a problem, by excluding those forces whom the US routinely characterized as terrorist for attacks on US soldiers while on combat duty in Iraq and Afghanistan.

Perhaps a solution could be found by invoking the broader definition used in a US army manual, where terrorism is understood as "the calculated use of violence or threat of violence to attain goals that are political, religious, or ideological in nature. This is done through intimidation, coercion, or instilling fear."[34] But this leads to an even worse conundrum. Looking at the range of options that occupying forces have permitted themselves in Iraq and Afghanistan, one would have to ask what exactly distinguishes US actions from those of terrorists? Examining just one batch of WikiLeaks materials, the *Iraq War Logs*,[35] comprising 391,902 US Army field reports from Iraq, tells us several things: that the US government was aware of many more civilian casualties in its occupation than it publicly admitted;[36] that it had received hundreds of reports of civilians, including pregnant women and the mentally ill, being brutally gunned down for coming too close to occupation checkpoints;[37] that US soldiers knowingly opened fire on surrendering Iraqi insurgents;[38] that its practice of torture continued after the revelations about Abu Ghraib; and that it had failed to investigate hundreds of reports of torture, rape, and murder by Iraqi police and troops under its command.[39]

Similar revelations emerged the *Afghan War Diary*[40]—a collection of 91,731 US military logs pertaining to the combat in Afghanistan. They disclose the gunning down of civilians at checkpoints;[41] a "revenge" mortar attack on an Afghan village, killing five civilians, after a group of occupying troops experienced an

IED explosion nearby;[42] CIA paramilitaries gunning down a deaf, mute civilian who was running away from them;[43] US Marines opening fire on civilians in Shinwar, killing nineteen and wounding fifty.[44]

This archive—only a small sample of what has taken place—is a record of breathtaking atrocity and cruelty. Moreover, as Dahr Jamail demonstrates in Chapter 12, below, these events were not incidental to the "mission." Their origins can in fact be traced to the beginning of the war itself.

One of the defining elements of American empire is that it has no colonial aspirations. Territorial land-grabs are superfluous: the point is to have access to markets and resources under stable political regimes. Ideally, these regimes are acolytes of the "free market," willing to integrate their economies into a globalizing, US-led system. Saddam Hussein had been an ally of the United States during the period of his war with Iran, but by 1990–91 his regime was considered an unreliable outpost of senescent Arab nationalism. The Bush administration thus made the conquest of Iraq the lynchpin of its global strategy.

The new regime was to be, as the *Economist* phrased it, a "capitalist dream." The occupying authority passed a law, Order 39, which "announced that 200 Iraqi state companies would be privatised; decreed that foreign firms can retain 100 percent ownership of Iraqi banks, mines and factories; and allowed these firms to move 100 percent of their profits out of Iraq."[45] But in order to build a new, "free market" state on the rubble of the Ba'athist state, with unemployment rising to 70 percent[46] on some estimates and no Ba'athist army to keep control, the US would need political allies and an armed force capable of maintaining order once the old state was dismantled.

This is where the input of Iraqi exiles such as Ahmed Chalabi and, to a lesser extent, Kanan Makiya, proved useful.[47] One of Chalabi's strategic inputs was to persuade the US to forge an alliance with the Iran-backed Shi'ite movement, the Supreme Council for the Islamic Revolution in Iraq (SCIRI), later known as the Supreme Iraqi Islamic Council (SIIC).[48] This movement, founded in Tehran under the leadership of Muhammad Baqir al-Hakim, was initially sponsored by the Islamic Republic as part of a project to promote pan-Shi'ite unification.

SCIRI had little support in Iraqi society, but it did have an established intelligence and military apparatus. Its militia, the Badr Army, was built and encouraged by the Iranian government during its war with Iraq, and mandated to run Basra in the event that Iranian forces took control. In effect, it had been designed as an occupying government. The US was therefore persuaded to integrate it into the new post-Ba'ath security apparatus. It took over several southern Iraqi cities, including Basra, replaced local police commanders with its own personnel by fiat, and quickly became known for its brutality in countering opposition.[49] It became a virulent source of anti-Sunni sectarianism in the Iraqi state, a key enforcer of the new regime (often controlling the torture chambers that, so the UN told us, were "worse than under Saddam"[50]), and a decisive force in the civil war that gripped Iraq in 2006.

But the Badr militia could not control Iraq by itself. Its influence was limited at first to cities and towns in the predominantly Shi'ite south. Gradually, the US began to build up a new Iraqi army and police force, as well as a paramilitary agency trained under General David Petraeus, known as the Special Police Commandos (SPC). Petraeus explained his role in forming these "paramilitary units," first revealed to the public in September 2004, with some pride. Initially led by former Ba'athist General Adnan Thabit, the commandos were under the control of the Ministry of Interior and trained by the US military, as well as by the Virginia-based contractor USIS, which was alleged to have been directly involved in some killings by the commandos.[51] The paramilitary strategy was coordinated under John Negroponte, the US ambassador to Iraq, whose salient previous experience involved organizing counter-insurgency death squads in El Salvador. A US military official explaining the logic of the program to *Newsweek* suggested that it was about punishing Sunnis for their opposition to the occupation: "The Sunni population is paying no price for the support it is giving to the terrorists ... From their point of view, it is cost-free. We have to change that equation." This would seem, on its face, a straightforward declaration of terrorist intent. *Newsweek* aptly dubbed this operation "the Salvador Option."[52]

The kinds of activities attributed to the SPC, subsequently dubbed the National Police, include torture, mutilation, and murder. A fearsome unit attached to the SPC, known as the Wolf Brigade, comprised Badr Organization members. It launched notable counter-insurgency operations in cities such as Mosul, with the backing of US troops, and its leader Abul Walid became notorious for his interrogation of captured, and obviously beaten, "terrorist" suspects on the television program "Terrorism in the Grip of Justice." Broadcast on the Pentagon-funded Al Iraqiya network, the program augmented the terror that Walid's paramilitaries were promulgating in the streets.

The Wolf Brigade was also held responsible for a detention center discovered in the Iraqi Ministry of Interior, in which bodies were found with signs of horrendous torture: burn marks, bruises from severe beating, and drilling around the kneecaps.[53] In one astounding incident, commandos contacted a Baghdad morgue demanding that the metal handcuffs found on the corpse of a tortured and murdered man be returned on the grounds that they were too expensive to replace.[54]

Even if one were to accept that counter-insurgency was categorically distinct from terrorism, any boundary between counter-insurgency and sectarian terror in this context was decidedly murky and porous. And this was not an accident, but a logical outcome of the American strategy. To construct an Iraqi "free market," a strong state was needed—not only to suppress the opposition but to promote the development of markets where public provision had once existed. Sectarianism provided not only a technique of control, modeled on the old colonial principle of "divide and rule," but also the political forces capable of implementing it.

ATTACKING CIVILIANS, REDEFINING "CIVILIAN"

Another reason for the very high number of civilian casualties arising from the Bush-era wars—whether one believes the lowest estimates acknowledged in the leaked US documents (66,000 civilian deaths),[55] or the *Lancet's* findings (600,000 deaths, mostly civilian)[56]—might be that US military rules in the "war on terror" permitted the killing of civilians during air strikes. As former Pentagon advisor Marc Garlasco explained, "[I]f you hit 30 as the anticipated number of civilians killed, the airstrike had to go to Rumsfeld or Bush personally to sign off," but otherwise no one need be told.[57]

This standard authorizes a certain level of civilian killing, thus belying the claim that "every life is precious" to war planners. Further, "anticipation" is at least partially a subjective response, and allows a degree of latitude on the part of military tacticians: there is no reason in principle why many more than thirty might not be killed in a single strike, without the need to trouble the president. The practice of the US military in many such cases was to insist that those killed were "insurgents." Chief Warrant Officer Dave Diaz, heading Special Forces A-Team in Afghanistan, put the point bluntly: "Yes, it is a civilian village, mud hut, like everything else in this country. But don't say that. Say it's a military compound. It's a built-up area, barracks, command and control. Just like with the convoys: If it really was a convoy with civilian vehicles they were using for transport, we would just say hey, military convoy, troop transport."[58]

There is evidence that this approach was institutionalized. Consider the case of the footage from a massacre in Baghdad, released by WikiLeaks under the heading "Collateral Murder."[59] The thirty-nine-minute video, consisting of footage shot from a US Apache helicopter, shows a sequence of three incidents in

Baghdad in 2007, during Bush's so-called "troop surge." It begins with an attack initiated by the helicopter pilot on a group of Iraqis, among whom were two agency journalists. The pilot is heard to report that some of the men appear to be carrying weapons, then asking permission to "engage." He is told there are no US personnel in the area and that he has permission. Soon, he is told to "shoot," "light 'em all up," and, as he does so, is repeatedly told, "keep shootin' … keep shootin' … keep shootin'." Eventually, as the camera alights on eight dead people, including a Reuters journalist who had tried to escape, the voice of someone identified as Hotel Two Six says to the pilot, "Oh, yeah, look at those dead bastards. Nice. Nice. Good shootin'." "Thank you," the pilot replies.

This is but the first of a series of three incidents recorded in the footage. The US military argued that it had good grounds for making a positive identification of those attacked and reasonable certainty of hostile intent. It claims that the grainy images taken from the footage show at least two men carrying weapons. In fact, the shapes indicated are every bit as much a Rorschach nightmare as those grayish blobs on satellite images that Colin Powell's infamous UN speech of February 2003 referred to as WMD production plants. As if to satirize their own claim, the military also suggested that the two Reuters journalists killed were holding cameras that "could easily be mistaken for slung AK-47 or AKM rifles."[60] The army's investigation also referred to the "furtive nature" of movements made by the cameramen, giving "every appearance of preparing to fire an RPG on US soldiers." Just as importantly, the military claimed that the individuals killed were legitimately attacked because they were a group of "military-age men," and thus represented a danger. The war logs record all deaths from the incident as "enem[ies] killed in action,"[61] despite only two men being positively identified as bearing weapons.

The army's report into this incident naturally emphasizes the perspective of the soldiers who took the decision to kill, citing all the possible operational factors demanding a subjective judgment call and favoring the use of deadly force. In a way, this is reasonable: occupation soldiers are acting according to the training they have been given and the mission goals they have been set—and within an occupation context that often necessitates violence against civilians as a condition of success. But there are two crucial classifications being used to frame the killings and justify them: "military-age men" and "enem[ies] killed in action." These are common ways in which the category of "civilian" is modified. The classification of "enemy killed in action" is the most commonly used in the *Iraq War Logs* to describe those killed by US campaigns. For example, the US military counted 1,723 killed in the Fallujah area in 2004, during its most determined assault. Of these, 1,339 were deemed "enem[ies] killed in action."[62] This would leave 384 potential civilians killed. But during the two major battles, in April and November, the most conservative estimates suggested that approximately 600 civilians had died in April, then 800 in November.[63] Given this, it is plausible that a large number of those classified as "enem[ies] killed in action" were in fact civilians.

As for the classification of "military-age men," this typically refers to males aged between fifteen and fifty-five, so includes most male civilians. When the US launched its assault on Fallujah in November 2004, it encouraged Iraqi civilians to flee before the bombing began—but prohibited all males estimated to be in this age range from escaping. *Newsweek* reported in 2006 that it had become common for US troops to treat all "military-age men" in Iraq as enemies. Later it emerged that soldiers charged with committing war crimes in Baghdad alleged that they had been given orders to "kill all military-age men."[64] More recently, the Obama administration used this category adroitly to misrepresent its drone strikes as attacks largely on "militants." In an extraordinary, lengthy article in the *New York Times*, based on interviews with dozens of Obama's advisers, it was revealed that Obama

embraced a disputed method for counting civilian
casualties that did little to box him in. It
in effect counts all military-age males in a
strike zone as combatants, according to several
administration officials, unless there is explicit
intelligence posthumously proving them innocent.
Counterterrorism officials insist this approach is
one of simple logic: people in an area of known
terrorist activity, or found with a top Qaeda
operative, are probably up to no good.[65]

This might explain why, despite only forty-one individuals allegedly having been targeted for drone assassination by the Obama administration, the human rights organization Reprieve has counted a total of 1,147 civilians killed in various attacks. In Pakistan, for example, this meant that, in strikes aimed at twenty-four individuals, 874 people died, 142 of them children. One remarkable fact arising from this is that many of the "high value targets" identified by the administration have been reported to have been killed several times over. As Reprieve pointed out: "These 'high value targets' appear to be doing the impossible—dying not once, not twice, but as many as six times."[66]

However, the tendency to identify "military-age men" as enemies only partially explains the high civilian body count. For, as a study based on the Iraq Body Count figures suggests, 46 percent of those killed by US air attacks in Iraq were women, and 39 percent were children.[67] The evidence is that, from checkpoints to air strikes, house raids to street battles, the methods adopted in the course of occupation necessitated a heavy death toll of civilians.

CIVILIAN TARGETS

It may be argued that this is all very well, but these points mainly pertain to the collateral killing of civilians. Civilians are not the main target; their deaths are an unfortunate by-product of a difficult war. Before testing this claim, it is worth pointing out how far we are drifting into the logic of al-Qaeda. This is what Osama bin Laden said of the World Trade Center attacks in a recording from October 20, 2001:

> The men that God helped [attack, on September 11] did not intend to kill babies; they intended to destroy the strongest military power in the world, to attack the Pentagon that houses more than sixty-four thousand employees, a military centre that houses the strength and the military intelligence. The [twin] towers [were] an economic power and not a children's school or a residence. The general consensus is that those that were there were men that supported the biggest economic power in the world.[68]

So, bin Laden first declared that the deaths of those whom he classified as "innocent" and "civilians" were unintended, a collateral effect of a just war, and secondly defined "civilian" in a way that suited his political purpose. To claim that one "did not intend" to kill civilians when one chooses methods and targets that are likely to do little else rings hollow.

In that light, let us look again at how the United States waged its war in Iraq. The battleground was chiefly urban, a matter of winning cities one by one. The twin assaults on the "Sunni triangle" city of Fallujah in April and November of 2004 quickly became emblematic of the occupation. It had been one of the most peaceful cities in the early months of the occupation, but the first violent scenes broke out when US forces shot at a peaceful demonstration against the American decision to occupy a local school, on April 28, 2003. Twenty people were killed, while shots were fired at those trying to recover the bodies, and even ambulance crews came under fire. An attempt was made to capture the city in April 2004, after the killing of four mercenary contractors by Iraqi crowds. The operation, known as Vigilant Resolve, saw 600 Iraqis killed—but US troops were obliged to make a temporary retreat.

In 2007, WikiLeaks released a remarkable document that shed some light on all of this: a classified US government report into the April 2004 siege of Fallujah.[69] One of the justifications for the US-led assault was that the place was teeming with al-Qaeda operatives. The classified report, on the other hand, suggested that it was more to do with the fact that the place had become a "a symbol of resistance" to the occupation, which had "dominated international headlines." The report described the loose cooperation between opponents of the US as resembling an "evil Rotary club" rather than a centralized al-Qaeda hub.

"Enemy combatants," the report said, "came from several broad categories including former Ba'athists and soldiers of the Saddam regime, nationalists, local Islamic extremists, foreign fighters, and criminals." This was roughly what good reporting and intelligence had been saying about the character of the Iraqi insurgency as a whole, though the picture was denied by military leaders. The report suggested that the opposition would have been easy for US forces to defeat, but that the operation was brought to an end for political reasons partly related to the Abu Ghraib torture scandal—a decision that left Paul Bremer, who had somehow ended up as the head of the Iraqi state, "furious."

Bremer's fury was understandable: the settlement looked like a defeat for US forces in a city that had become a symbol of resistance. At any rate, unable to let that stand, the United States subjected the city to repeated raids and assaults. For three weeks after the ceasefire was announced, the bombing continued, thus rendering it—as the report acknowledged—"a misnomer."

In November 2004, the US launched its most fearsome assault yet, known as Operation Phantom Fury. In the prelude to the attack, the US bombed the city to "encourage" those inhabitants who could to flee—barring "military-age males," who were prevented from leaving—then sealed the city off to prevent those remaining from escaping. War crimes such as the bombing of one hospital and the military take-over of another were openly reported, but less well reported were the beatings carried out against doctors and the attacks on ambulances. It later emerged that the US had used white phosphorus, a chemical that burns the flesh and melts right down to the bone.

NGO estimates maintained that between 4,000 and 6,000 were killed in the assault, and that 36,000 houses, 9,000 shops, sixty-five mosques and sixty schools were demolished. While the operation had been justified by the need to evict an al-Qaeda cell said to be operating in the city, the leaders of the resistance there were found to be local. Some 350,000 dispossessed refugees were eventually filtered back into the city, subjected to biometric scanning, and coerced into military-style battalions carrying out forced labor to reconstruct the city.

The assault on Fallujah stood out for the brutality of the methods deployed, but the same techniques were used to conquer other Iraqi cities. In mid 2007, a detailed report by thirty NGOs for the Global Policy Forum analyzed the modus operandi of the occupiers when assailing major towns and cities. The report discussed the main techniques for subduing major population centers in Iraq, citing seven that were of particular importance:

    1) encircle and close off the city, as in
    Fallujah and Tal Afar, where the occupiers built
    an eight-foot-high wall around the entire city
    before launching an attack;
    2) forcefully evacuate those who remain, as in
    Fallujah and Ramadi;
    3) cut off food, water and electricity, as in
    Fallujah, Tal Afar and Samarra;
    4) confine reporters and block media coverage,
    with the systematic exclusion of all non-embedded
    reporters during such assaults;

5) conduct intense bombardment, usually targeting the infrastructure;

6) conduct a massive urban assault, using sniper fire, and put survivors through violent searches;

7) attack hospitals, ambulances and other medical facilities.[70]

WHEN TERROR IS THE NORM

It may finally be argued that all of this is lamentable but nonetheless represents a regrettable deviation from normal American conduct that will quickly be corrected. The Bush administration was an extreme one, it might be argued, which abandoned the precepts of multilateralism and law and order to wage a profoundly unpragmatic war. There may be elements of truth to this. However, the brutalities exposed by WikiLeaks are not aberrations. From the conquest of the Philippines to the occupation of Haiti, the methods of American war-making have depended upon terrorizing civilians. The scale of violence seems to be far more determined by the context in which war is conducted than by the ideology of a given administration waging war.

It has been argued that the slide into attacking civilians is built into modern war: what begins with tactics that transfer the risk of war to civilians ends with tactics that treat civilians as the bedrock of opposition and a legitimate target.[71] One could, on the basis of the foregoing, take this point further. Terror is a quintessential element of the American empire, as important as soft power and hard cash. If the American way of empire depends upon maintaining a global plexus of national states aligned to US interests and in favor of "free markets," civilian populations must be deterred from pursuing alternatives every bit as much as armed states.

Yet, as we have seen with the pursuit of WikiLeaks backed by courts and politicians, justified by the label of "terrorism," part of being an empire means having the power to assign classifications,

and to make them stick. As a result, "terrorism" is always something the enemy does.

WHAT IS TORTURE?

Among the practices exposed in the WikiLeaks documents are
those taking place within the extensive US network of detention
and torture. The *Guantánamo Files*, in particular, identify how
the system of torture became a feedback loop, in that the inherently unreliable information extracted through torture was used
to identify detainees who could in turn be tortured. They show
that many detainees were held despite the knowledge that they
had no association with the Taliban or al-Qaeda.[72]

In a stroke of grim irony, the United States responded to
the cascade of revelations through WikiLeaks by capturing
one of the people accused of leaking the original cables from
the State Department, US army private Bradley (now Chelsea)
Manning, and torturing him. A State Department spokesperson
who criticized this practice was forced to resign. Yet it appears
that none of those responsible for the torture program have lost
employment as a result, nor will they be charged—much less
stripped naked and thrown into solitary confinement for almost
a year.[73]

All of this goes on while the soothing bromide "We do not
torture" is ceaselessly repeated.[74] For, while US politicians have
never seemed to be in much doubt about what "terrorism" is,
when the subject of "torture" arises a strange epistemological
relativism intervenes. Victims may be waterboarded, so that they
involuntarily inhale lungfuls of water and are almost drowned.
They may be given the strappado, with their hands bound behind
their back, and suspended from the ceiling so that the pressure
crushes their chest until they die. They may be kept in coffins
filled with insects, raped with chemical light sticks, and forced to
masturbate or simulate sex acts. But, the politicians query, is this
really "torture"?

What are the laws concerning torture in the United States? The government ratified the UN Convention Against Torture in 1994, a decade after it was adopted by the UN General Assembly. Article 1 of the convention defined torture as

```
any act by which severe pain or suffering,
whether physical or mental, is intentionally
inflicted on a person for such purposes as
obtaining from him or a third person information
or a confession, punishing him for an act he or
a third person has committed or is suspected of
having committed, or intimidating or coercing
him or a third person, or for any reason based
on discrimination of any kind, when such pain or
suffering is inflicted by or at the instigation of
or with the consent or acquiescence of a public
official or other person acting in an official
capacity. It does not include pain or suffering
arising only from, inherent in or incidental to
lawful sanctions.
```

This seems fairly precise, going into some detail about who can be guilty of torture, to what end, and under what circumstance. The convention also makes the following categorical statement: "No exceptional circumstances whatsoever, whether a state of war, or a threat of war, internal political instability or any other public emergency, may be invoked as a justification for torture." As the National Lawyers Guild argues, this seems to provide an unequivocal argument in favor of prosecuting the perpetrators of torture.[75] But there are three problems that throw this definition into some obscurity. First, it is not clear what qualifies as "severe." It does not seem to be possible to quantify pain in an objective way, as it is a subjective response.

The infamous "torture memos"—a set of legal memoranda drafted by Deputy Assistant Attorney General John Yoo in

August 2002 that carefully defined torture so that anything short of serious injury or organ failure would be permissible—played on precisely this necessary ambiguity. Second, the insistence that torture must be "intentionally" inflicted makes it almost impossible to verify that torture has been inflicted, short of a confession. Third, by excluding pain or suffering arising from "lawful sanctions," the convention opens up significant leeway for states to legitimize forms of torture as legal penalties.

The vagueness of this definition of torture is not simply a matter of unfortunate phrasing in the convention, but derives from two facts external to the text. The first is that "torture" is inherently a prescriptive, normative term and, like any term in political language, is contested. The second is to do with the legal system itself. The US empire is based on a liberal world order under law. But these norms pull in opposing directions. The right to be free from torture comes into conflict here with the right of states to punish. This partially explains why, even though the American empire has always tortured, it has never had a coherent position on torture—those who torture have always had to confront those for whom torture is anathema by America's own standards.

Many polls find that most Americans view torture as an acceptable way of treating "those people," believing that it generates actionable intelligence—a fact that the historian Greg Grandin relates to the long tradition of demonology that begins with the origins of the United States as a settler-colonial state based on slavery, always threatened by racial "others."[76]

But even in the highly charged atmosphere of the "war on terror," many CIA staff found the infliction of torture intolerable. Those who witnessed the punishments inflicted on Abu Zubaydah, a Saudi national and Islamist fighter whom the United States tortured in Guantánamo under the erroneous pretext that he was connected to al-Qaeda, were said in internal documents to be "very uncomfortable ... to the point of tears and choking up."[77]

It is these moral and political differences that are given expression in the form of legal arguments. In almost all legal situations, there will be more than two relevant legal concepts that enter into the argument, thus opening up a surfeit of possible legal interpretations. When it comes to applying these laws, there is nothing but superiority of power to decide between rival interpretations.[78]

This has been particularly useful for the US government since the CIA alighted on the advantages of psychological torture during its "mind-control" experiments between 1950 and 1962. The result of this intense human experimentation was a dark scientific breakthrough: the CIA learned that torture methods involving psychological manipulation and no physical contact were far more effective than physical torture. Having spent so much time looking for the frailties and vulnerabilities of the human organism, they developed a sophisticated system of torture that left psychological wreckage, but no physical evidence. The two key elements were "sensory deprivation," such as hooding or masking, and "self-inflicted pain," such as stress positions. These are the types of methods that the CIA classifies as "enhanced interrogation techniques," and thus were perfectly congruent with America's international legal obligations.[79] Once again, the power to classify is an immense, indispensable asset for the empire.[80]

The WikiLeaks cables tell us much about America's torture programs, alongside the evidence from the Taguba Report, the Senate Intelligence Committee, and investigative journalism. The examples that follow will show how the US developed its torture complex, building on past practices and developing a series of legal and moral justifications as it did so.

THE GUANTÁNAMO FILES

Before Abu Ghraib, there was Guantánamo. In January 2002, brandishing photographs of shackled, blindfolded prisoners in orange jumpsuits, the US government proudly announced that it had opened a new military prison in its forty-five-square-mile colony in Guantánamo Bay, Cuba.

The history of the naval base in Guantánamo Bay explains a lot about the peculiar nature of the American empire. From the earliest days of the nation's foundation, US elites had nurtured the goal of possessing Cuba, then under the control of the Spanish Empire. They had even tried purchasing the island, all to no avail. It was the appearance of a vigorous anti-Spanish revolt in Cuba from 1895 that opened the door to an American subvention. The Spanish were unable to defeat the insurgents, and the United States quickly moved to take control of the situation. Deeming the Cuban population "incompetent" to "maintain self-government,"[81] they intervened ostensibly on behalf of the rebels, in the name of liberty, defeated the Spanish, and occupied the island. The structures of segregation, mafia capitalism, and dictatorship that emerged in the ensuing period were installed by the United States. This was the same model of using military power to create client regimes in lieu of direct political rule that would be deployed by the United States across other parts of Latin America in the following century.[82]

It was in 1903 that the US first "negotiated" control of forty-five square miles around Guantánamo Bay as a base for US Navy ships, which stood firm until 1959—and even after that the Castro government that overthrew the regime was unable to compel the US to leave the territory. Following Kennedy's futile attempts to crush the Cuban revolution during the Bay of Pigs fiasco, and the near-miss of the Cuban Missile Crisis of 1962, the United States decided to create a permanent Marine base in Guantánamo, ostensibly to protect the United States against a Cuban attack. Here it sat, almost forgotten, until 2001.

The "war on terror" was launched with the specific intention of accumulating thousands of captives and interrogating them over a long period. And since the interrogation had to take place offshore, where—so the rationale went—detainees would not be protected by the US legal system, Guantánamo Bay provided an ideal location.[83] In January 2002, a military prison was opened in the base, consisting of three distinct areas, known as Camp Delta, Camp Iguana, and Camp X-Ray.

By 2005, there were 540 prisoners known to be in the Guantánamo Bay prison camp. Of these, only four had been charged with a crime. The Bush administration nonetheless defended the camp on the grounds that prisoners were "well-treated," and there was "total transparency."[84] This was unpersuasive: anyone who knew that prisoners had been tortured at the camp owed such knowledge to leaks. Among the raft of public testimony available on this was that of a US soldier, Erik Saar, who worked as a translator in interrogation sessions. Saar detailed practices of physical assault and sexual torture. Even the official probe into the camp acknowledged that Guantánamo had pioneered the practices later used against Iraqi prisoners in Abu Ghraib.[85]

But the rationale for the prison, and thus implicitly for any unpleasant treatment visited upon detainees, was that the people locked up there, despite having gone through no judicial process, were certainly "terrorists" on a mission to attack the United States. As Bush put it in his State of the Union address in 2002, "Terrorists who once occupied Afghanistan now occupy cells at Guantánamo Bay."[86] Dick Cheney, out of office but not out of mind, repeated in 2009 that the prison contained "the worst of the worst."[87]

The WikiLeaks documents allow us to see how such labels relate to reality. The *Guantánamo Files*, leaked in April 2011, detailed the cases of almost all of the 779 prisoners held at Guantánamo.[88] Consisting centrally of memoranda signed by the commander at Guantánamo, they show that the majority of detainees were known by their captors to be unconnected to al-Qaeda, and they identify at least 150 men known to be civilians seized by mistake, who were then detained for years without trial.

The files, discussed on the WikiLeaks site by the journalist Andy Worthington, corroborated the details obtained through previous campaigns, including the release of documents pertaining to prisoners who had been through the Combatant Status Review Tribunals won in a lawsuit filed by media organizations.[89] As a result of this work, it was already clear that hundreds were held for no good reason, some 600 prisoners having been eventually released for lack of evidence.[90] The new documents, Worthington explained, show

> why it was that Major General Dunlavey, who was the commander of Guantánamo in 2002, complained about the "Mickey Mouse" prisoners, the number of "Mickey Mouse" prisoners, as he described them, that he was being sent from Afghanistan. Here they are. Here are the farmers and the cooks and the taxi drivers and all these people who should never have been rounded up in the first place and who ended up in Guantánamo because there was no screening process.[91]

Aside from those who were manifestly civilians snatched in an indiscriminate way by US forces, there are others who are held on the basis of accusations made by supposedly "high value" detainees. These include people who were tortured for information, prisoners who were mentally unstable, others who would have good reason to fabricate accusations in order to gain preferential treatment, and notorious liars.[92]

In effect, what the US seems to have created is a global apparatus that does not so much catch "terrorists" in order to put them on trial as capture hundreds of people in order to find ways to label them as "terrorists." The machinery is, in its way, an impressive attempt to substantiate the US government's claim that its opponents in Afghanistan and Iraq were all, in fact, "terrorists."

The singular failure of the facilities to turn over many "terrorists" led to both public and Congressional opposition, and was expressed in Barack Obama's presidential campaign in 2008. But Obama kept the facilities open. In March 2011, just a month before the WikiLeaks revelations hit, President Obama had signed an executive order mandating the ongoing indefinite detention of prisoners at Guantánamo.[93]

This was almost certainly an embarrassment. The US media, however, rushed to the president's aid. While the overseas press noted the revelations of brutal and unjust behavior by US forces, the American media systematically downplayed this fact. While publishing the leaks, they stressed the light thrown on "al-Qaeda" and its activities—thus validating the camp's supposed "intelligence-gathering" function.[94]

FROM VIETNAM TO IRAQ

The historical origins of this practice can be traced to the CIA's postwar development of torture techniques and apparatuses, as it sought to prop up a network of dictatorships and states aligned to the US. The surreal investment in "mind-control" research on the part of the Agency was initially justified as a legitimate defensive response to communist "brainwashing," but quickly assumed an offensive purpose. This also drew in leading psychologists, such as the behaviorist Donald Hebb, in a series of human experiments.[95]

This research constituted the first attempt to rationalize and modernize the practice of torture, making it subtler than traditional "rack" methods. Nonetheless, the CIA did not abandon those older means. The main institutional framework for the dissemination of torture was, at first, the Office of Public Safety (OPS), a division of USAID. As part of this offensive, the OPS trained over a million police officers in forty-seven nations and taught them the interrogation techniques that the CIA had been developing. The justification for this was the need to break the spine of "communist subversion" in these countries. A major theater of these operations was South Vietnam, where the US had struggled to preserve French colonial power, and then to uphold a dictator allied to the French and the United States.

From 1965, the CIA launched a "counter terror" program whose remit was, ironically enough, to deploy the "techniques of terror—assassination, abuses, kidnappings and intimidation—against the [Viet Minh] leadership." Out of this program was developed Operation Phoenix—a dirty war in South Vietnam to destroy Viet Minh "infrastructure" by killing or capturing leading fighters, with those captured subjected to imaginative forms of torture. The program eventually accounted for "82.9 percent of [Viet Minh] killed or captured." In truth, however, only a minority of those were senior Viet Minh members, and over half were not members at all. In addition, rather than imposing a colonial policy of territorial ownership, these methods were useful in creating a loyal dictatorship that would run Vietnamese affairs on behalf of the US empire. As part of a wider process known as "Vietnamization," the program was therefore gradually turned over to the control of the South Vietnamese bureaucracy.[96]

The CIA was thus freed, with this experience under its belt, to turn its attention to other global frontiers. The lessons of Phoenix were applied in Latin America, in a program known as "Project X," in which the CIA and military intelligence trained officers from Latin American societies in the techniques of torture. The training manuals developed for these conflicts schooled recruits in the use of interrogation techniques such as the abduction of family members of the detainee, and in how to assess targets "for possible abduction, exile, physical beatings and execution." These were the hallmarks of Phoenix tactics.

Alongside these techniques, however, the CIA continued to develop its psychological torture repertoire, using "psychological distress" and "intolerable situations," "isolation, both physical and psychological," and a series of subtle techniques designed to "induce regression." The threat of pain, or "self-inflicted" pain, "usually weakens or destroys resistance more effectively" than pain inflicted by the interrogator, which may only "intensify" the detainee's "will to resist." The use of these more sophisticated techniques always involved, from the beginning of the CIA's "mind-control" experiments, the participation of professional psychologists. These techniques were disseminated throughout the military elites of ten Latin American states allied to the US government and were instrumental in securing the Reaganite victory over leftist and popular movements in Central America.[97]

These were the methods revived at the inception of the "war on terror," institutionalized at Guantánamo and Bagram, and transferred to Iraq. Many familiar methods, blending both physical and psychological elements—including hooding, beating with hard objects, threats against family members, stress positions, being stripped naked and kept for days in solitary confinement, rape, laceration, and the use of the horrible medieval torture technique called the strappado—were found to have been used by US forces themselves.

Nor was this just an Abu Ghraib phenomenon. At Camp Mercury, for instance, a military prison set up on the outskirts of Fallujah, prisoners continued to be detained and subjected to brutal torture—a process known to the 82nd Airborne Division troops guarding the prisoners (who referred to themselves as "Murderous Maniacs") as "fucking" them. The ACLU gained sworn testimony that soldiers regularly "beat the fuck out of" detainees. This was systematic and widespread, and many of the techniques, as leading torturers including the military intelligence chief at Abu Ghraib attested, had been directly learned from CIA operatives in Guantánamo Bay and Afghanistan.[98]

But, just as in Vietnam, the US did not intend to stay forever in Iraq. Its goal was to generate a reliable Iraqi state, ideally with some democratic legitimacy, able to take on the responsibilities of government in broad alignment with US interests.

One of the revelations contained in the *Iraq War Logs* was that US troops refused to investigate hundreds of reports of brutal torture carried out by the Iraqi forces under their command. This was a result of an edict issued by Donald Rumsfeld known as "Frago 242," disclosed in the *Iraq War Logs*.[99] "Frago 242" was a "fragmentary order" that obliged US personnel occupying Iraq not to investigate any breach of the laws of war pertaining to torture unless occupying personnel themselves were directly involved. Iraqi forces, trained and supervised by the US military, were thus enabled to practice the most egregious forms of torture:

> A man who was detained by Iraqi soldiers in an underground bunker reported that he had been subjected to the notoriously painful strappado position: with his hands tied behind his back, he was suspended from the ceiling by his wrists. The soldiers had then whipped him with plastic piping and used electric drills on him. The log records that the man was treated by US medics; the paperwork was sent through the necessary channels; but yet again, no investigation was required.
>
> …
>
> [T]he entirely helpless victim—bound, gagged, blindfolded and isolated—[is] whipped by men in uniforms using wire cables, metal rods, rubber hoses, wooden stakes, TV antennae, plastic water pipes, engine fan belts or chains. At the torturer's whim, the logs reveal, the victim can be hung by his wrists or by his ankles; knotted up in stress positions; sexually molested or raped; tormented with hot peppers, cigarettes, acid, pliers or boiling water—and always with little fear of retribution since, far more often than not, if the Iraqi official is assaulting an Iraqi civilian, no further investigation will be required.

> Most of the victims are young men, but there
> are also logs which record serious and sexual
> assaults on women; on young people, including
> a boy of 16 who was hung from the ceiling and
> beaten; the old and vulnerable, including a
> disabled man whose damaged leg was deliberately
> attacked. The logs identify perpetrators from
> every corner of the Iraqi security apparatus—
> soldiers, police officers, prison guards, border
> enforcement patrols.[100]

Surveying the WikiLeaks documents, the Bureau of Investigative Journalism noted that, for the 180,000 people held captive in Iraqi prisons from 2004 to 2009, the US military received 1,365 reports of torture. Nevertheless, the US authorities in Iraq continued to inspect the prisons and find "no abuse, no evidence of torture in those facilities."[101] It later transpired in a *Guardian* investigation that the US was closely involved in the torture centers through the Special Police Commandos, who were trained by a special forces veteran from the Reagan-era death squad wars in Central America, Colonel James Steele.

US advisors were directly involved, according to both American and Iraqi witnesses, in the use of torture.[102] This showed the policy of "Iraqization" in motion. As in previous wars, the US took initial responsibility for violence on all fronts and gradually built a little local epigone to take up its mantle.

THE CIA BUST

In December 2014, an avalanche hit the CIA. The US Senate released an investigation into the CIA's use of torture[103] in the context of the "war on terror." The report had been circulated among state personnel for two years, and subsequently "updated," before being released to the public. The "update" actually redacted 93 percent of the content. But even the pared-down public version was damning, and complements with copious detail and documentation much that is revealed in the WikiLeaks sources.

The report slammed the agency for deploying methods that were both "brutal" and "ineffective," neither contributing to significant capture nor disrupting a single authentic "plot." The methods disclosed in the CIA's documents included forcing water into detainees' rectums; waterboarding a detainee until he became totally unresponsive and bubbles gurgled out of his open mouth; forcing detainees with broken hands or feet to stand in the stress position for hours; playing "Russian Roulette" with a detainee; threatening to rape a detainee's mother and slit her throat; and causing a detainee to die of hypothermia after beating and punching him for extended periods.

Some of the worst torments were inflicted on Abu Zubaydah, a Saudi national captured in Pakistan, alleged to be associated with al-Qaeda. His capture was touted by the CIA as its biggest success until the capture of a leading associate of Osama bin Laden, Khalid Sheikh Mohammed. Zubaydah's file at Guantánamo shows that, while he admitted involvement with several armed jihadi groups, he persistently denied involvement with al-Qaeda. It seems that he was telling the truth.[104] But interrogators were so desperate for solid information that they began to subject him to a regime of torture. He spent approximately two weeks inside a coffin-sized box and was subject to sleep deprivation, stress positions, and slaps. At one point, insects were placed inside the coffin to add to his terror. Much of the interrogation took place while a bullet wound he incurred during capture was allowed to fester and rot without treatment. As much of this went on, the US decided to "disappear" Zubaydah, deciding that he should no longer be accessible to the International Red Cross.[105] The US government never charged Zubaydah with any crime.

As with previous CIA torture practice, for the program to be effective there had to be a range of professionals willing to assist. These included the two psychologists who helped devise the torture program over a period of seven years and were paid $81 million for their services.[106] On one occasion they were escorted to Thailand, where Abu Zubaydah was being held, and given the opportunity to use the detainee as an experimental subject on whom to perfect the techniques they were developing, which directly drew on past CIA expertise in the field. In bidding for the contract, the psychologists recommended such techniques as "The attention grasp, walling, facial hold, facial slap, cramped confinement, standing, stress positions, sleep deprivation, waterboard, use of diapers, use of insects, and mock burial."

The CIA had been given time before the release of the report to prepare its defense, whose first component was summarized by George Tenet, director of the CIA while the torture program was being rolled out: "We don't torture people," he asserted, insisting that the CIA's methods "saved lives."[107] Tenet refused to substantiate his claim that the CIA's methods did not constitute torture, simply stating that he would not discuss specific methods. Nor is there any single case where it can be shown that the use of these methods saved any lives.

The second component of the CIA's defense was to try to undermine the self-righteousness of Congress by producing a document "for official use only" (eventually released via WikiLeaks) that listed all the occasions on which leading members of Congress had been briefed by the CIA on the interrogation methods used.[108] This may be true, and such hypocrisy on the part of official Washington can hardly be surprising. But it is impossible to establish exactly how much the CIA told its congressional audiences. And there are reasons to be skeptical, particularly given the report's finding that even President Bush was kept in the dark about a lot of what was taking place.

The third part of the defense was to stress the legality of what the CIA had done. A veritable phalanx of CIA ghouls and Republican Party apologists lined up to assure a concerned public that what the CIA had done had been legally sanctioned by the Justice Department, and thus did not constitute torture.[109] Here, the CIA is on more solid ground. When it initially requested a legal endorsement of what it was doing, it was told in a memo sent by Assistant Attorney General Jay Bybee to Counsel to the President Alberto R. Gonzales that the president was able in times of war to consider certain laws inapplicable. In particular, the Geneva conventions giving certain groups prisoner-of-war status, the memo argued, clearly did not apply in Afghanistan. The memo cites ample precedents from US history in which the government went to war and did not consider itself legally bound by these conventions, even if it chose to defer to them anyway. Further, the memo offers some latitude to implement torture: "If the President were to find that Taliban prisoners did not constitute POWs under article 4, they would no longer be persons protected by the Convention."

Thus, the US could define torture in such a way as to exclude most of their measures from the definition. For something to be torture, the resulting distress had to be "equivalent in intensity to the pain accompanying serious physical injury, such as organ failure, impairment of bodily function, or even death."[110] As I have suggested, this interpretation—as innovative as it is— appears to be inherently plausible within the framework of the UN Convention Against Torture, which defines the pain associated with torture only as "severe," without further stipulations.

This extraordinary memo, chiefly written by Deputy Assistant Attorney General John Yoo, was Schmittian[111] in its legal doctrine of almost limitless executive power. Critics of the memo describe many of its interpretations of law as "unconventional." In particular, its statement that the Geneva Conventions can be suspended in regard to Afghanistan, al-Qaeda, and the Taliban has generated the most forceful denunciation among legal scholars, leading to calls for its authors to be prosecuted.[112]

But the Bybee memo—whatever its moral status—is an example of impressive legal virtuosity. It relies on a rigorous reading of the logic of the legal axioms and of precedent. Yet the Bush administration could not wholeheartedly embrace its hegemonic considerations. While Defense Secretary Donald Rumsfeld argued that this was a new type of war, unimagined by the framers of the Geneva Conventions, Secretary of State Colin Powell considered that denying prisoner-of-war status to captives would "have a high cost in terms of negative international reaction" and "undermine public support among critical allies."[113]

The Bush administration's compromise between the two pressures was to say that prisoner-of-war status would apply to captives in Afghanistan, but not to Taliban or al-Qaeda suspects: they were "enemy combatants," and thus excluded from protection under the Geneva Conventions. Indeed, this continued to be the basis of US policy in Guantánamo, as when State Department legal adviser John Bellinger invoked the "typical laws of war," including the Geneva Conventions, as providing justification for detaining people "captured on the battlefield" but who have forfeited their right to communication with the outside world.[114] The United States, of course, was still a signatory to the UN Convention Against Torture, but it applied the definition of torture identified by Bybee—until the Abu Ghraib scandal forced the Office of Legal Counsel to abandon it.

The CIA could thus say that it did not torture, and had not tortured, precisely because the American empire had the power to define torture legally and to impose that definition through force.[115]

HOW TORTURE WORKS

One of the most important criticisms of torture, made by Obama and by the Senate Intelligence Committee, is that it does not work. It is ineffective at generating actionable intelligence leads that result in lives being saved. Insofar as this is the justification for torture—that it is a defensive measure against ruthless terrorism—the critique is accurate. However, what we see in the WikiLeaks documents, and in the history of the American government's practice of torture, is that this is not necessarily what torture is for.

It is true that interrogation is a key purpose of the torture: the desire to elicit statements, confessions, and background information. But much of this had no relevance to the Taliban or al-Qaeda, and many captives had nothing to do with these groups either. At least one detainee was interrogated for information about Al Jazeera's journalism practices. This was partly because the United States considered Al Jazeera a hostile broadcaster. Further, even if much of the information gained from the interrogation could not be verified, it nonetheless provided the US with confessions that supported its narrative and underpinned prosecutions.

Consider, for example, the case of Khalid Sheikh Mohammed, a leading al-Qaeda member whose capture was celebrated by the CIA as a major victory. He was among a number of prisoners tortured "to the point of death," waterboarded until he almost drowned.[116] This sustained torture produced a confession so elaborate, sweeping, and implausible that it led a prominent legal expert to declare it akin to the confessions in Stalin's show trials. Mohammed confessed to everything from the 1993 World Trade Center attack to bombings in Bali, the beheading of Daniel Pearl, and a series of plots to blow up NATO headquarters, New York suspension bridges, the Empire State building, the Sears Tower in Chicago, and London's Heathrow Airport: thirty-one confessions in total.[117]

Another purpose of torture is to punish and intimidate enemies. The United States was directly involved in training the Special Police Commandos in torture techniques, and the commandos played a key role in the unfolding of the Iraqi civil war—especially the suppression of anti-occupation activity. Torture, in this case, was meant to terrorize the opposition. And this is consistent with the uses of torture by the CIA and affiliated military and paramilitary cohorts on previous fronts, such as in Vietnam, the Philippines, and Latin America.

The fact that torture "works" in this sense does not mean

that it is necessarily always a good idea for the empire to engage in such practices. America's empire has always consisted in the expansion of its dominion through the opening of markets and global trade institutions. In this, even more than in war, it needs allies. If the torture disclosures show anything, it is that there were considerable pressures from within the Bush administration and beyond not to resort to torture, as this would alienate key allies and undermine the legitimacy and long-term interests of the United States. Indeed, one of the reasons why so much information has been disclosed is a struggle between factions of the US state, in which many argued that torture was counterproductive.

But there has been no final resolution of this struggle, and the United States has still not ceased to torture: it seems likely that, as long as America is an empire, it will torture again.[118] But that bind, between the normative claims attached to America's stewardship of a liberal world order and the harsh realities of military domination, is one that has repeatedly caught its leaders out. Even as they authorize torture, they must seek to define it out of existence.

3. War and Terrorism

Armies march, but they must have a destination. Empires go to war, but they must have a purpose. It is natural that when we think of empire, we think blood. The aspect of the American empire that is involved in war, torture, subversion, and espionage attracts the greatest share of critical attention. Yet, this is not the point of empire, and—as with torture, or terror—we must not forget the relationship between means and ends.

When the billionaire *New York Times* journalist Thomas Friedman spoke of the "hidden fist" of the US military making the world safe for Silicon Valley and McDonald's,[1] what was most arresting about his claim was not the assertion of America's overpowering military dominance, but the connection he drew between politico-military power and economic power.

Pre-modern empires tended to be about the acquisition of fertile or resource-rich territory for landed oligarchies, the enslavement of populations for exploitation, and the conquest of trade routes. The Roman Empire annexed land for its rich landowners. The Dutch Empire used piracy to take control of trade routes. And the Spanish Empire's colonization of Southern America, put crudely, turned the continent into vast gold- and silver-mining enterprise, and its population into slave labor.

The modern American empire is a different beast. Its network of military bases from Greenland to Australia is not part of a system of territorial occupation or annexation, but rather serves to localize American military power in convenient ways, so that it can maintain a system of states whose features suit its interests. In general, the United States wants access to trade routes, and can back up its claims with impressive naval power, but does not need to control them directly. And it has learned, by and large, to do without slavery since 1865, as waged labor has proved adequate. In the modern era, we have trade agreements, debt bondage, and structural adjustment. What the United States wants is to expand the domain of markets. In any national state, business classes derive an overwhelming advantage from their strategic control of markets. This is also true on a global level, so that US corporations stand to benefit most from the progressive opening of markets and trade.

The grinding, crashing halt of world markets in 2008, just as the Iraq "surge" was winding down and a lame-duck President Bush was on his way out, served as a sharp reminder of what the empire is all about. The crisis of the US banking system quickly caused havoc in the world system, illustrating how far American finance had penetrated the economies of allied states, and how far overseas banks were invested in the US economy. The subsequent response of governments to the banking crisis illustrated just how much American political leadership set the pace for the rest of the world.

It is highly appropriate, therefore, that WikiLeaks, in the same moment as it exposes the doings of governments, discloses reams of documents about corporate corruption and the links between governments and business.

EXPOSING BUSINESS

"Be afraid," the *Economist* warned in 2010 when WikiLeaks announced it would release five gigabytes of secret files from a prominent financial institution.

Having gone after states, it would now be targeting corporations. In the future, business would no longer be able to depend on secrecy. "Employees increasingly bring their own devices to work. Even the simplest can store the equivalent of several tonnes of paper. And more and more people use social networks at work, which thrive on exchanging information."[2] *Forbes* magazine, an American counterpart to the *Economist*, was similarly worried. WikiLeaks "wants to spill your corporate secrets," it announced. And it might succeed, because it "offers the conscience-stricken and vindictive alike a chance to publish documents largely unfiltered, without censors or personal repercussions, thanks to privacy and encryption technologies that make anonymity easier than ever before."[3]

This fear was well placed. The year before these worries were aired, WikiLeaks had caused the giant multinational commodities- and oil-trading firm Trafigura considerable embarrassment by leaking the contents of an internal report on a toxic dumping incident in the Ivory Coast. The "Minton Report," named after the consultant who was its chief author, told of how the company had broken EU regulations in what WikiLeaks called "possibly [the] most culpable mass contamination incident since Bhopal."[4]

The reason for Trafigura's culpability was clear. It had spotted an opportunity to make a swift, extraordinary profit margin by purchasing cheap, dirty fuel being sold off the coast of Mexico. In order to clean up the fuel, it would use a process banned in most Western countries, which resulted in the production of a toxic by-product that internal company emails cheerfully referred to as "crap" and "shit." The issue, then, was what to do with the "crap." Eventually, a local contractor was found in the Ivory Coast who would dump the waste for a fee, either unaware or unconcerned about the grim effects of the substance on human beings, including—according to the Minton Report—"burns to the skin, eyes and lungs, vomiting, diarrhea, loss of consciousness and death."[5]

The company went all-out to prevent the disclosure of the document's contents, securing a legal ruling with the assistance of the distinguished law firm Carter Ruck that prevented British newspapers from directing readers to the location of the report, or giving them any information as to how they could access it. When it later emerged that a member of parliament could use his parliamentary privilege to ask the secretary of state for justice a question about the matter, Trafigura went so far as to seek a "super-injunction" against the *Guardian* newspaper, again with the help of Carter Ruck, which prevented the paper from reporting on the parliamentary exchange.[6]

The previous year, the Swiss bank Julius Baer had suffered a similar squirming fit after WikiLeaks began releasing documents about the company's operations that alleged its involvement in the concealment of assets for influential political figures, money laundering, and tax evasion. The company overreached in its response to the WikiLeaks revelations. It obtained an injunction against WikiLeaks, obstructing the circulation of the documents it found embarrassing, but this was not enough. It felt compelled to try to shut down WikiLeaks entirely, suing both the organization and its online domain registrar.

It initially gained an injunction but, after a furious public backlash and a series of counter-actions filed by WikiLeaks supporters, was forced to back down. The negative publicity was even more damaging for the company when a former employee who had supplied the incriminating information came forward in 2011 with thousands more documents pertaining to high-net-worth clients, which he said would shed more light on the company's practices[7] and on the wealthy individuals avoiding tax.

Among the other corporate targets of WikiLeaks over the years have been Kaupthing Bank, Peruvian oil dealers, Northern Rock, and Barclays Bank. WikiLeaks was also passed information on Bank of America and British Petroleum that it was unable to publish, partly because it lacked the resources to carry out a thorough fact-check. All of this by itself may simply constitute some good old-fashioned muck-raking journalism, exposing corporate malpractice and its almost inevitable corollaries of political corruption and repression. Indeed, the ramifications of

WikiLeaks for investigative reporting and the future of the Fourth Estate have been the source of much academic hair-splitting and journalistic soul-searching.[8] But what does it tell us, if anything, about the American empire?

We have learned from the bank bailouts that, when business cries out for help, it is the state that answers. The United States, in particular, had to take over the central global role in shoring up the private banking industry, saving capitalism from itself in 2008. This seems contrary to the "free market" doctrine according to which individuals and enterprises must bear the consequences of their bad investment decisions, or else those bad decisions will be repeated. This is a "thin Darwinism" that does not necessarily describe how markets really work, but the belief that "free market" orthodoxy had been undermined so scandalized American politicians that it produced a congressional revolt that almost prevented the bailouts from taking place.

But what we discover from the WikiLeaks documents is that there is no such thing as "free markets" without strong states— that nowhere does the "invisible hand" work without the mailed fist of government. For example, one batch of documents depicts the US government's attempt to support its GM technology giants in overseas markets. The US ambassador to France went so far as to urge the Bush administration to embark on a "trade war" with the country in order to penalize it if it did not support the use of GM crops. Other leaked cables showed that US ambassadors across the world had taken up the promotion of GM crops as a vital strategic and commercial interest, including lobbying the pope to express his support for the technology, and thus undermine opposition in Catholic countries.[9]

In fact, research after the boom years of the 1990s showed that, of the Fortune 100 best companies, at least twenty would not exist at all were it not for state intervention. Corporations are notoriously bad at managing their international operations, and rely on government agents to open doors for them. An example would be Apple, whose immensely profitable iPhones and iPads rely on technology developed in the public sector and passed on to private capital. The company's access to East Asian labor markets, which keep the costs of production low, depends crucially on the role of the US government in negotiating the opening of those markets to American investors.[10] Again and again, wherever American officials carol the virtues of "free trade," we find that it is political power that makes it possible for the US to dominate world markets and enjoy the benefits of trade.

A key part of this story, discussed below, is the emerging Trans-Pacific Partnership (TPP) free trade agreement. WikiLeaks published the fruits of some of the negotiations on establishing the TPP—negotiations that were still ongoing in 2014—drawing attention to a grave threat to freedom of information, civil rights, and access to healthcare contained in the proposed new laws. The agreement would, WikiLeaks noted, amount to "the world's largest economic trade agreement that will, if it comes into force, encompass more than 40 per cent of the world's GDP."[11] In fact, this agreement is two things: first, it is a corporations' charter, assigning a variety of rights and powers to corporations in the name of free trade; and second, it is a result of President Obama's "pivot to Asia"—his attempt to incorporate East Asian national economies into a trading bloc with the US excluding China. This is where the lion's share of future economic dynamism will be focused, and the US is using its considerable political influence to ensure continued access to its benefits. It is, in other words, a fitting exemplar of the "imperialism of free trade."

THE DIRTY SECRETS OF "FREE TRADE" IMPERIALISM

To understand the WikiLeaks revelations, and all that lies behind the violence and brutality outlined in previous chapters, it is necessary to understand the political-economic basis of this "free trade" empire. The American empire is of a new type, in that its mission—its "manifest destiny" as it were—is the global spread and institutionalization of capitalism.

The process that we now call "globalization" is often spoken of as if it were a natural, almost climactic process: a flourishing of "the market" that moves ahead in leaps and bounds as long as it is not impeded by state-imposed rigidities or artificial monopolies. This is rather akin to the way in which news media talk of "the market" as if it was an angry god whenever a recession strikes or a bank collapses, and the image is profoundly misleading. There are markets, each leavened in its own way by cultural and political structures, but there is no "the market." It requires political leadership and initiative to bring markets into existence, make them socially and economically sustainable, and develop rules and institutions that maintain them. It requires time and planning to incorporate populations into markets. The United States has been able to use its political dominance since World War II to develop, in an often haphazard or self-defeating way, a globally integrated economy in which its businesses are dominant and have privileged access to key markets and resources.

Schematically, in the postwar era we can see that the American empire has ruled through two international regimes: the Bretton Woods system, and what Peter Gowan calls the "Dollar–Wall Street regime."[12] Bretton Woods fixed international currencies to the gold standard in order to prevent destabilizing price fluctuations and enable an international economy to develop. The International Monetary Fund was the key institution set up to manage this global system and adjust currency prices based on a cooperative arrangement. Of course, the United States dominated, but it ruled in what might be called a collegiate fashion, taking the bulk of responsibility for the world system while expecting allied states also to participate in the global administration of markets, currencies, contracts, and property. This was linked to a series of controls on the operations of banks and on the movement of capital in and out of countries, in order to ensure that capital was directed primarily toward productive investment and industrial development. It gave national states a degree of freedom in broadly planning the pattern of economic development.

This was not yet an era of global "free trade," but that—as the editors of *Fortune*, *Time*, and *Life* magazines pointed out in 1942—was ruled out by the "uprising" of the "international proletariat." In order to satisfy this political "uprising," it would be necessary to have some controls on capital for a while. "Third World" countries were encouraged to develop their national economies using import-substitution strategies, so that stable business classes could take root. Meanwhile, trade with Britain and Europe would be the "strategic pivot" on which "the area of freedom would spread," eventually creating the opportunity for "universal free trade."[13]

In fact, there was no guarantee that "free trade" would ever be universalized. Certainly, the postwar system boomed. Between 1945 and 1970, world GDP grew by an average of 4.8 percent a year—although this figure concealed the enormous "catching up" of defeated World War II powers. And with growth came an expansion of global trade, the total volume of exports rising 290 percent between 1948 and 1968.[14] And yet, by the late 1960s, the US economy was weakening, and in relative decline compared to Japan and West Germany—the two powers it had helped defeat, then helped to reconstruct. The war in Vietnam and the armaments spending it demanded was sapping the Treasury and the productive economy of vital investment funds. Relative domestic peace had given way to turbulence and the breakdown of "law and order." And it soon became clear that the global economy, which had boomed under US tutelage since 1945, was entering a serious crisis. America's global dominion might well have begun an irreversible slide at this point.

Under the Nixon administration, a series of decisions that were largely fortuitous from the US point of view enabled a remarkable re-pivoting of the entire world system on a new basis. US dominance entered a new phase. What Nixon did first was to abandon the gold standard, ending fixed exchange rates.

The dollar was still the major international currency, the one in which most trade was conducted, but now its value could swing wildly, depending on what the US Treasury decided. The next move compounded the impact of the first. The Nixon administration downgraded the role of central banks in the organization of international finance, empowered private banks to lend, and sought a new regulatory structure that would liberate financial investors. The "cold" flows of money investment in production were quickly overtaken by "hot" flows of cash moving across borders, reacting sharply to the slightest international stimulus.[15] None of this amounted to a master plan for world domination, and indeed the changes were effected initially against considerable resistance within the state, and even from the banks.

But the effect was to empower finance, which also helped to solve growing domestic problems. American businesses, by the late 1970s, were convinced that wage-driven inflation and union militancy were the major problems holding back a revival of profitability. The Carter administration looked to Paul Volcker, chair of the Federal Reserve, to address the problem. He reasoned that, to provide stable investment conditions, it was necessary to anchor the expectations of workers and consumers to a fixed criterion. Whereas the "gold standard" and fixed exchange rates had created some stability in the postwar system, the new criterion of stability was counter-inflation. This was to take precedence over traditional postwar objectives such as full employment or managing consumer demand through incomes policies.

The Federal Reserve therefore embarked on a strategy of driving up interest rates to punishingly high levels—the so-called "Volcker shock"—in order to break the inflationary expectations of wage-earners. Soaring unemployment was an acceptable political price in order to establish the objective of counter-inflation. This was exactly the monetary policy that Wall Street had wanted for some time, and to some extent it was possible because of Wall Street's frenetic expansion after the abolition of exchange controls in 1974. But, more importantly, it was possible because businesses in other sectors, such as industry, had come to accept that empowering Wall Street was a necessary condition for their problems to be resolved.[16]

With the freeing and expansion of international financial markets, the importance of the dollar was magnified, and with it the impact of any changes in the dollar's value. This was a tremendous source of political strength, enhancing the global role of the US Treasury. And it landed other countries with a restriction that the United States did not face: they had to worry about their balance of payments and ensure they had enough international currency to cover the goods purchased from overseas, while the United States could always just print more of its own currency. Wall Street and its less regulated sidekick, the City of London, dominated the new international financial system, and a series of international agreements—most notably the financial services agreement arising from the Uruguay Round of the GATT negotiations, lasting from 1986 to 1994—consolidated a new global regulatory structure that favored financial "innovation" (the freedom of financiers to develop ever more intricate instruments for maximizing royalties, however risky). The IMF, meanwhile, came to play a key role in using debt to open the markets of the global South and force the "structural adjustment" of their economies so that they would become more tightly integrated into the Dollar–Wall Street regime. Finally, a flurry of new international treaties, regional trading blocs, and multilateral organizations developed: the euro was born, the North American Free Trade Agreement (NAFTA) was signed, and the World Trade Organization (WTO) was launched. IMF "shock therapy," previously a treatment chiefly reserved for the Third World, was rolled out in Russia and eastern Europe.

This sequence of outstanding successes was linked to another change in the mode of American domination. In the postwar period, US attempts to manage the world system had necessitated reliance on a string of right-wing dictatorships that were relied on to modernize their national economies, creating an indigenous business class while averting the influence of communism. In the early, transitional phase of the Dollar–Wall Street regime, a wave of extraordinary violence was unleashed in America's old "backyard," beginning with the coup in Chile and culminating with the long war of attrition in Nicaragua. This was partly a counterinsurgency thrust against rising leftist movements that threatened the position of local business classes. But it was also linked to a series of reforms—economic liberalization that strengthened business elites with an international orientation, and later, as the wars were won, political liberalization tied to human-rights discourse.

In the post–Cold War world, the reigning world-view was that liberal capitalist democracy was the ultimate terminus of history, the endgame to which all states tended. And the more America's "backyard" was integrated into the world system, the more it opened its markets, allowed public goods to be privatized and run by US firms, and the more it signed up to global and regional trade treaties, the less need there was for direct violent interventions. The political form of dictatorship often became more of an impediment than an asset, and the United States was even willing to offer limited support to some pro-democracy movements, provided they were congruent with the overall goal of expanding "free markets" under the direction of strong states.

But this was only a tendency. As we have seen, the United States cannot entirely dispense with the old, crude techniques of coups, puppet regimes, and wars. The world system, even were it not structured by inequities that propel conflict, can never attain perfect and perpetual coherence and thus ascend to the Kantian paradise of eternal peace. The "hidden fist," as Milton Friedman called it, is ever present. But the "hidden hand" works wonders too.

WHERE ARMIES FAIL, MARKETS SUCCEED

Winning without fighting

Why does the American empire bother to support coups in Haiti or Ecuador? Why have repeated governments sent troops into the Dominican Republic? Why did Reagan go to war for the tiny island-state of Grenada? In many cases, it is difficult to discern a material interest commensurate with the outlay of American force. Surely, for example, Grenada was not invaded for the sake of the nutmeg trade? Could it be that, as Oxfam suggested of US policy in Nicaragua, they are worried by "the threat of a good example"?[17] This would imply, at least, that "interests" could be interpreted more broadly than the usual assumption that wars are waged for oil companies, or Pepsi, or United Fruit. Of course, such narrowly self-interested interventions have been waged from time to time. But an empire in rude health has what might be termed higher aspirations. Its higher purpose can be summed up as the universalization of "free markets," and the institutions and laws sustaining them.

One of the long-term benefits of achieving the subsumption of ever larger areas of the world under the law of the market is that, once institutionalized, it does its work almost automatically. In fact, the market can often succeed where military efforts might fail. Take Vietnam. Through the 2000s, over a quarter of a century after US defeat to the Viet Minh, WikiLeaks' disclosures show the US embassy in Hanoi charting with some satisfaction the Vietnamese government's incorporation into US-led globalization. This included laying the foundations for accession to the WTO, engaging in market-led reforms and privatization programs, and willing submission to IMF orthodoxy and compliance with all necessary prerequisites for participation in IMF structural adjustment programs.[18] Such programs are notorious for the effects they have on national economies and for the ignominious nature of dependency they generate between debtors and creditors: in short, debt bondage. On the other hand, they are extremely useful tools for the United States, in that the loans can be selectively deployed to help countries more indebted to American corporations, or those that are politically close to the US government.[19]

Why did the Vietnamese government, nominally a socialist one that had defeated the American empire in a horrifying war, accede to this? The short answer is that the new Politburo's attempt to reconstruct the economy of a unified Vietnam on a statist basis after the devastation of war was simply untenable in an increasingly integrated and competitive world economy. The attempt to make a rational allocation of economic resources and to plan efficiently turned out to be too difficult. In a global economy in which the price fluctuations of almost all goods and services were under no one's control, and in which Vietnam was often isolated, it was practically impossible.

The Politburo's eventual conclusion was that its problems were caused by a failure to obey the "objective laws" that guide economic affairs everywhere. The discovery of such "objective laws" was to an extent an evasion of responsibility. As US planners had learned, real-world economies do not behave according to such abstractions, which take no account of the complex relationships between political structures, law, property, and markets. It was nonetheless highly convenient, inasmuch as it allowed the Politburo to follow the Gorbachev administration in embracing privatization and pro-market policies. And in short order, since Vietnam owed over $1 billion in debt, the IMF offered its services and, of course, recommended the same policy mix as it recommends to all would-be debtors: cut subsidies, remove price controls, remove exchange and capital controls, privatize and let the market rip.

The classic debt trap was initiated. The more Vietnam borrowed from the IMF, the more it needed to borrow, and its rate of indebtedness soared. The more it adopted "free market" policies, the more dependent it was on markets and the less able it was to apply controls. The United States had visited an apocalypse on

Vietnam to avert the danger of "communism," and failed. But where it failed, debt, finance, and the institutions of global capitalism succeeded.[20] And this, as the case of Ecuador illustrates, is a problem that still dogs attempts to revive socialism in the current century.

The Dollar–Wall Street regime

Ecuador's Rafael Correa had frightened Washington badly with his promise to implement "twenty-first century socialism." Studying the WikiLeaks cables, it is obvious that, from early on, the embassy in Quito was concerned about the appearance of this "dark horse populist, anti-American candidate."[21] As in the case of Haiti's Jean-Bertrand Aristide, "populism" is troublesome to the United States because it is linked with anti-market politics. And yet here the US approach has been consistently far more subtle and relaxed than in Venezuela, Haiti, or Honduras. Its interventions were limited, selective, and free of the traditional sabotage, coup-plotting or military interventions—leaving aside the vexed matter of Colombia's violations of Ecuadoran sovereignty in its US-backed war with FARC, which incursions the US does not seem to have supported.

Correa emerged as a leading figure in Ecuadoran politics in the period when the Bush administration was attempting to win Latin American support for a Free Trade Area of the Americas (FTA). Venezuela's Hugo Chávez had already successfully blocked a US-supported coup attempt, and was implementing a left-populist agenda of redistribution and public spending. He had launched the Bolivarian Alliance for the Peoples of Our America (ALBA), an alliance with Cuba that would go on to incorporate Bolivia, Nicaragua, and Ecuador. More than a trading agreement, it aimed to integrate member states around a common leftist political and social agenda. Related agreements included an inter-government energy company called PETROSUR, which would fund social programs, and the regional media conglomerate TeleSUR, considered a hostile entity by the US government.

At the turn of the millennium, Ecuador had been a fully signed-up partner of the United States in its neoliberal "free market" project. It had participated in the drug wars by allowing US surveillance aircraft to use its airbase in Manta. It had undergone dollarization in January 2000, using the US currency in place of its own. This was the result of a policy turn initiated by the United States in 1999, at the tail end of the Clinton era. The United States had last engaged in "dollar diplomacy," attempting to export the dollar to Latin American countries, at the beginning of the twentieth century. But this had been far more limited in the past, as US diplomacy had simply sought to encourage Latin America to adopt the dollar alongside its national currency.

This had its advantages, particularly in countries or economies that were only partially independent and where large numbers of American workers were based. In these cases, the dual currency could be used to maintain a Jim Crow structure, with US workers paid at dollar rates and indigenous workers paid at local rates. But in the Cold War era, under the reign of Bretton Woods, the US expressly preferred that Latin American governments de-dollarize and maintain their own stable currencies. This was partly because US policy-makers recognized the major lesson of the interwar period, which was that a monetary system where currencies were pegged to a single value could actually exacerbate international instability. It also constituted a recognition that, in order for these countries to develop a solid industrial base, they would need to make use of capital controls and deploy monetary policy to encourage economic growth.

The millennial turn to aggressive "full dollarization"—in which the dollar replaced the local currency entirely, at the high point of neoliberal transformation—was a significant moment. It meant national governments giving up control of monetary and exchange policy—important instruments for democratic intervention in market economies—in the interests of countering inflation, which had ravaged the Ecuadoran economy in the 1990s, and maintaining stable investment conditions for finance.

US government publications noted that this transformation would open new opportunities for US financial institutions, and also provide a vital material basis for a new Free Trade Area. Meanwhile, currency devaluations were no longer in the gift of the national government, but were now controlled by the US Federal Reserve.[22] This helped local elites allied to Washington to lock neoliberal policies in place. This was hugely controversial in Ecuador partly because of the conditions that came with it: wage cuts, public-sector job losses, and gas price increases. The protests over the measure converged with a rising arc of mobilization by the country's indigenous population and formed part of the basis for the popular movements that later brought Correa to power.

Already in 2005, when Correa was minister for the economy in a populist administration, the US embassy in Quito had noted that he was "a strong critic of the FTA negotiations." Correa favored abandoning the tight fiscal policy of the former administration that had aligned closely with the US and using oil revenues to invest in public-sector wages and development. He was critical of "trade liberalization in general ... of the IMF, and of any orthodox economic reform."[23] A further cable noted that "Correa made public statements on April 21 that foreign debt needed to be renegotiated, that Ecuador's oil revenue needed to be spent on social programs, that Ecuador would be completely sovereign in its relations with the IMF, and that any free trade agreement would be submitted to a referendum (where it would most likely be voted down)." The cable went on to report concerns expressed by the central bank president that Correa's statements might lead to "serious financial damage."[24] The next cable expressed even more alarm: "Of critical concern are early indications that brash young Economy Minister Rafael Correa is considering a debt moratorium."[25] This indicated the real source of US worries. On the one hand, the US should not be overly worried if a government in its sphere of influence made some concessions to a popular movement by raising public spending a little. Such measures can be temporary. But in the thirty-three years since Ecuador's military dictator General Rodríguez Lara had promised that exploiting the country's oil resources would help alleviate pauperism, the country was still blighted by poverty. Taking control of the oil and diverting oil revenues from debt repayment were essential if social spending was to increase, and the country's debt was both a key component of the country's financial interests and a critical lever by which successive governments could be encouraged to implement the Washington Model. Thus, the government was abandoning "fiscal responsibility."

On top of this, Correa was a vocal opponent of dollarization,[26] which he would reverse if he thought it practicable. He supported state control of the oil fields and had committed to ending the agreement with the US military. International financial institutions, unsurprisingly, did not like Correa's ideas, which they found "naive and outdated," and they were "reaching out" to key officials to frustrate this agenda.[27]

Nevertheless, any sense that the country's business class would put up determined resistance turned out to be misplaced. Business murmured private "concern," but there were "few signs of capital flight." The US government, despite its worries, was tactically cautious, looking to the Organization of American States to keep watch over the situation. A visit by the OAS would be "viewed skeptically" by the Ecuadoran government, "its more nationalist backers, and by the protest movement which brought them to power." The embassy recommended, in order to "blunt local resistance to foriegn [sic] oversight of the internal political situation [that] the OAS mission be encouraged to strike forward-looking themes, and deflect attention from recognition or judgment of the change in government per se."[28]

Later, as Correa looked likely to win the 2006 presidential elections, the United States invested in an "elections working group" to try to ward off support for "populist politicians who promise magic solutions that haven't worked anywhere." The embassy noted: "[W]e have warned our political, economic, and media contacts of the threat Correa represents to Ecuador's future." As it turned out, the National Endowment for Democracy, an organization set up in the 1980s to take over some of the covert functions of the CIA, also invested $1 million in Ecuador that year, a large chunk of it being deployed to assist the major opposition to Correa. Even so, the embassy noted that it was keeping dialogue open with Correa to "avoid estrangement."[29]

Despite US subventions, Correa won. Indeed, he rapidly had what the United States called—not without a certain admiration—"the strongest political organization that the country has seen since returning to democracy in 1979." More importantly, its profile represented a profound generational change, with its representation in the National Assembly "relatively young and well-educated, with women, Afro-Ecuadorians, and the indigenous well-represented."[30] His program, the embassy noted, was a relatively "moderate" version of what Chávez and Morales called "twenty-first-century socialism."[31] And in fact, given the bogey alternative of full-blooded Chavismo, the US seems to have been pleasantly surprised by just how convivial Correa's government was. Even the radical constitutional reform of 2008 generated little response from the embassy other than interest.[32] The IMF, for its part, indicated that "a high level of anxiety is not merited."[33]

Among the positive signs coming from Ecuador was that Correa was prepared to combat the social movements that had brought him to power, as when protests caused a petroleum shutdown: "In contrast to the previous administration that sent [Government of Ecuador] teams to negotiate with communities on additional benefits, Correa is sending a strong signal that he is not going to stand for protests that affect the country's key petroleum revenues."[34]

Certainly, Correa's "tendency toward market interventions" was irritating. Citing the case of the cap placed on the price of milk, the ambassador noted that, while it was hardly an extreme policy, "it is not a good sign if this type of control ends up being used more widely."[35] The administration's tax reforms were "breath taking" in their ambition and suddenness, but "probably more good than bad." The embassy echoed the views of the Ecuadoran business class who, it said, were strongly critical of the imposition of a tax on capital movements, as it would lead to capital flight. But also, citing the IMF, suggested that the decision to freeze VAT rather than cut it suggested that the government was relatively pragmatic.[36] Even as public spending rose dramatically, reaching 44 percent of GDP in 2013, the IMF was relatively gracious in its advice to the Ecuadoran government, acknowledging the important role of the public sector in driving growth while still championing private-sector investment.[37]

What the US government found consistently problematic were the administration's measures aimed at strengthening national sovereignty against its incorporation into a neoliberal development model. As a result, Ecuador withdrew from several bilateral treaties,[38] including with the United States; abandoned the International Centre for Settlement of Investment Disputes,[39] a World Bank court formed in 1965 to arbitrate in disputes between states and private capital; rejected pleas from major firms such as Apple and RIM to abolish tariffs;[40] and reformed intellectual property law to support access to medicine—including HIV drugs—as a vital public interest.[41] Importantly, reflecting the administration's support for a return to import-substitution, the production of drugs was to favor local producers rather than multinationals.

What the US government therefore did in Ecuador, rather than demonize the government and throw its support behind a military putsch, was to gripe. There is some evidence in the cables of lobbying, secretive maneuvering, and, in the case of drug patents, coordination with pharmaceutical business interests—albeit to little overall effect. But, for the most part, the embassy appears to have confined itself to grumbling. In regard to the rebuff to Apple and RIM, the US embassy petulantly complained that these companies, among the "most iconic" in the world, were not welcomed "with open arms," and lamented that Ecuador's leaders were evidently "not interested in unleashing the entrepreneurial spirit," but instead had a "short-term" focus on "leveling society, protecting what they have, and allowing foreign companies into Ecuador on their terms."[42]

Ultimately, for all these histrionics, and for all the warnings about the Correan "dark horse" and his "magic solutions" representing a "disaster" for Ecuadoran development, the US even found itself grudgingly acknowledging the success of the government as—far from fleeing—capital was attracted to Ecuador.[43] The response of ambassadors and other diplomatic staff to Correa was certainly rich with bombast and self-righteousness, but when they remarked that the government's policies were more "practical" than its rhetoric, they were shrewd. They saw that, if the administration genuinely aimed to develop in a world economy integrated under US dominance, it had limited room for maneuver. Capital flight was constantly invoked as a danger—and it would be perilous indeed for the government to challenge the rights of capital fundamentally.

As it is, the reforms reflected the moderate, progressive aspirations tied to what the embassy, also shrewdly, regarded as a generational shift in Ecuadoran politics. However much Correa's nationalism and mild reformism grated against the preferences of American diplomats schooled in the US doctrine of "free enterprise," the position of the country's business class was not seriously threatened. At the time of writing, Ecuador's participation in global institutions like the WTO and close work with the IMF continues. It is unlikely to abandon dollarization, which has offered the counter-inflationary bulwark that financial investors have sought. The long-term prospects for US investors might even be improved by the development of an autonomous Ecuadoran industrial base.

The previous chapter examined how torture had evolved as a tool of imperial discipline, and how the CIA had invested in decades of work trying to find more subtle and effective modes of torture, rendering the rack unnecessary. Analogously, the American empire is developing a far more subtle science of domination than its predecessors. The case of Ecuador shows that, once market-dependency has been cultivated and global capitalism thoroughly institutionalized under US dominance, what Marx once called the "dull compulsion of economic relations" will do much of the work by itself.

THE IMPERIALISM OF FREE TRADE

When sheep eat people: Enclosure in the twenty-first century

Thomas More complained in his fiction *Utopia* that sheep had begun to eat people. How had such notably mild creatures, "that were wont to be so meke and tame, and so smal eaters," turned savage? More blamed the enclosures. These were a process by which lords, seeking to make money through the production of sheep wool, kicked peasants off the land they had customarily inhabited. The result was human starvation, while sheep passively grazed.

From the fifteenth to the eighteenth centuries, vast tracts of land were converted into private property. As the economist Karl Polanyi pointed out, were it not for the intervention of the Tudor and Stuart states to manage the fall-out, the resulting social catastrophe might have been enough to wipe out large swathes of humanity.[44] This process was then repeated in one domain after another, as more and more areas of life previously held in common were commodified. First sheep ate people, then machines dominated humanity. Now, increasingly, information is our master.

In 2014, WikiLeaks revealed drafts of two obscure "free trade" treaties, one called the Trade in Services Agreement (TISA)[45]—being pushed through the WTO—and the other called the Trans-Pacific Partnership (TPP).[46] As usual, it is a misnomer to refer to these as "free trade" treaties, since the scope of their action extends well beyond issues of trade. The central issue in these drafts is not trade but property, and the circumstances under which information can be held as property.

The origins of the idea of intellectual property extend back to the seventeenth century, but only with the rise of advanced information and communications technology did it begin to become the major global concern that it is today. The emergence of these technologies coincided with the globalization of finance and commerce, the emergence of transnational corporations as major global actors, and the spread and development of international commercial and property law. These are the forces that have made intellectual property in its present form possible.

Intellectual property rights in the era of the internet have become the modern legal form of enclosure—the means by which the status of valuable knowledge is settled at the expense of the majority who have no property in knowledge. It has been institutionalized through successive rounds of trade talks and recognized in global bodies such as the UN World Intellectual Property Organization (WIPO), the WTO (with its Trade-Related Intellectual Property agreements, or TRIPs), and the EU and OECD. This state of affairs is neither inevitable nor "natural,"[47] but the discussions at the level of global institutions are largely predicated on agreement among the parties as to the naturalness and ineluctability of intellectual property, with differences largely confined to questions of application.

It is clear from the leaked documents that the American empire, in the person of the US trade representative, is pressing for the globalization of the most severe current interpretations of copyright law. The portion of the TPP draft leaked via WikiLeaks centrally involves a chapter on intellectual property rights, which demands laws punishing the circumvention of Digital Rights Management technology (DRM), lengthens copyright terms, and treats the breach of trade secrets as a criminal act (which could potentially penalize journalists). In addition to such measures,

WikiLeaks highlighted the threat to healthcare, as the United States cited intellectual property rights to defend the creation in law of artificial monopolies in the production and retail of life-saving drugs, including cancer treatments.[48]

The draft TPP agreement is not, of course, lacking in sophistication. It recognizes that the commitment to TRIPS will have to be modified in each member state by a recognition of its legal traditions, and by flexibility as to the methods and tactics needed to implement such laws. It acknowledges that member states will need to implement certain protections for access to affordable medicine and healthcare, without which the agreement might be democratically untenable. In some versions of the agreement, this could mean granting limited exceptions to patents so that governments could—in a narrow range of cases—authorize the production of low-price drugs in return for royalties to the patent holder. However, in the course of negotiations the availability of even this option was restricted.[49]

TISA, driven by a coalition of member states of the WTO led by the United States, has similar provisions, seeking, for example, to prevent national governments from enforcing their own privacy laws.[50] It also supports the privatization of public services—another form of modern enclosure—and promotes the lifting of regulations that protect environmental or labor standards. Countries signing up to TISA would be locked into their existing liberalization commitments and pushed to extend them, thus narrowing the scope for democratic policy-making.

As with previous processes of enclosure, however, the promised rewards are considerable. The US Chamber of Commerce supposes that the "payoff ... could be huge" and "a once-in-a-generation opportunity" for American services firms:[51] "Eliminating barriers to trade in services could boost US services exports by as much as $860 billion—up from 2012's record $632 billion—to as much as $1.4 trillion," the Chamber drooled. And indeed, with transnational firms given monopoly control over the development and sale of crucial medicines, technology, and content in the name of intellectual property, and with US companies invited to profit from the provision of what had been public services, it is difficult to deny their right to such hand-rubbing glee.

Like almost all such documents, these treaties are obscure. Negotiated in relative secrecy by national governments, they are implemented without consultation. We find ourselves being governed according to these laws despite never knowing how or why they were imposed. This is partly because such treaties are a convenient way of bypassing democratic processes. For example, when the US Commerce Department wanted to implement harsh laws criminalizing the circumvention of DRM in the late 1990s and was unsure of the congressional response to such proposals, it lobbied the US trade representative to propose them at the WIPO. With the rules thus included in a binding global treaty, Congress could then be instructed that it was required to implement them in law.[52] The result was the Digital Millennium Copyright Act, which has played a key role in protecting intellectual property online.[53]

Were it not for the existence of Wikileaks, we would not even have at our disposal the scant information about these reforms that we do, and thus would not have the opportunity to protest, as hundreds of global organizations did when the disclosures were made. As these examples show, however, secrecy does not necessarily equal conspiracy. On the contrary, there are deep divisions within and between national governments over how to proceed, and over the correct institutional locus for action. The leaked TPP content demonstrates that the US is finding it difficult to mobilize agreement on its preferred copyright laws.[54] In a similar way, while many of the policies pursued in international agreements are driven by powerful business coalitions—TRIPs being a case in point[55]—there is no simple translation between a business consensus and government policy. The TPP provisions are controversial with some elements of the pharmaceutical industry, while, as a whole, it could expect to profit from them: the producers of generic drugs derive their incomes largely from the production and retail of unbranded versions of brand-name drugs, and are directly threatened by the expansion of monopoly rights for the big drug firms.[56]

Nor is there necessarily a seamless fit between the components of this emerging global architecture. For example, one of the reasons why American politicians are pushing the TPP is because the WTO is deemed too resistant to certain agendas favored by US investors.[57] These draft agreements, moreover, stand in a long line of failed agreements and collapsed negotiations, from the Multilateral Agreement on Investment (which was dropped after public protests led to France bailing out in 1998) to the Anti-Counterfeiting Trade Agreement Act (which fell apart in 2012 after the European Parliament rejected it). There is nothing inexorable about their success.

Bailing out the banks, globalizing finance

One of the most shocking aspects of the financial services annex to TISA, distributed by WikiLeaks, is that it shows that the world's deepest economic crisis since the Great Depression has done nothing to alter the financial orthodoxy of the world's leading states. The American empire is still evidently committed to the same financial regulatory model as it was in the days of the "goldilocks economy," when Wall Street was booming and the internet was still on dial-up. How extraordinary this is: the banks were briefly panicked and, like the vessels of the Danaides, hemorrhaging public money as fast as it was poured in. Now, helped to their feet by aggressive state intervention, they are back in charge. As the general secretary of the International Trade Union Confederation lamented: "Governments are negotiating away financial regulation in secret, instead of tackling the unfinished regulation task that triggered the current global economic crisis in 2007. It defies belief that they are actually planning to help the already 'too big to fail' banks and other financial conglomerates to expand."[58]

In TISA, the US and its allies are attempting to build an agreement on the model that had earlier been enshrined in the annex to the 1994 General Agreement on Tariffs and Services in 1994, and in the 1999 Financial Services Agreement: the GATS model of financial regulation. These are, as Jane Kelsey pointed out in an analysis for WikiLeaks, the same states that developed the pro-banker regulations that were essential in enabling the global financial crash—and the same states who blocked attempts to review the global rules on finance at the WTO after it occurred. They call themselves Really Good Friends of Services—in this case, "services" means financial firms. And their friendship has served the financial industry well, helping to ensure that Wall Street remains as dominant today as it was when it lobbied states to adopt the WTO financial services agreement in 1999.[59]

The basis of the earlier agreement was to "lock in" the liberalization of financial markets, thus compelling signatories progressively to remove laws and restrictions protecting their banking and industrial sectors. The GATS model required member states, in a pragmatic way that was sensible of the domestic context, to roll back all restrictions on financial investment that could reasonably be dispensed with. Covering some 90 percent of global finance by revenue, its job was mainly to integrate economies of the global South—there being relatively few trade barriers between the US and EU. Given that it was signed shortly after a major financial crash in Southeast Asia, this agreement took some selling. But a crucial ingredient of the elite debacle that led to the "credit crunch" and global depression was the extraordinary cultural success of capitalism in the era of neoliberalism.

Finance came to be understood as the true epitome of capitalism and was linked to the virtues of innovation, dynamism, and the allure of testosterone-driven aggression and risk-taking. With great risks, after all, came great rewards. And countries of the South were told that, if they opened their financial markets, the flows of "hot" cash would kick-start their slow economies.

Such claims were pure myth-making: most of the movements of money in financial markets have nothing to do with kick-starting investment in the productive sector. They are bets—increasingly elaborate and risky gambling instruments, through which investors hope to make a royalty. And since that money does not materialize from nothing, by magic, it must come out of the revenues driven by productive investment. The profits of investment in, for example, capital markets, are essentially a drain on productive investment. There is certainly little empirical evidence of a link between financial "innovation" and enhanced growth.[60] But the promises of growth were highly seductive.

Nevertheless, there was more going on here than just seduction. Significant groups of businesses in the global South stood to benefit from liberalization. They had felt constrained by protected domestic markets and capital controls, and limited by decreasing returns on industrial investment. The liberation and growth of finance, like privatization, offered unprecedented windfalls to investors able to take advantage of it. This had already been a significant factor in the "structural adjustment" of countries in the South. It was not merely a question of the IMF using debt to manipulate weak governments. The same Third World states that had pushed the Charter of Economic Rights and Duties of States through the UN General Assembly in 1974, mandating the use of nationalizations and expropriations to solve economic dysfunctions and social inequities, had already abandoned these strategies by the mid 1980s.

From then on, the debate concerned the speed and timing of reforms intended to open markets, remove obstacles such as financial restrictions and labor productions, and permit the access of foreign capital to national resources.[61] The reversal of these measures would constitute a considerable loss for investors in these economies, leading to capital flight and currency panics. This in itself represents a significant incentive and disciplinary mechanism keeping most countries on the same trajectory toward ever greater liberalization and integration into the world economy.

There is also the changing position of the banks to take into account. A product of financialization is that the creditworthiness of states is now entirely determined by financial markets, and particularly by credit ratings agencies. The "big three" agencies—Standard & Poor's, Moody's, and Fitch—make up about 90 percent of the global ratings market. The government's Financial Crisis Inquiry Commission deemed their pre-crash activities to be "key enablers of the financial meltdown," "essential cogs in the wheels of destruction"[62]—due largely to their positive ratings of the mortgage-backed securities whose fundamental precariousness had precipitated the crash. Yet these agencies functioned, and still function, as a key regulatory mechanism in global finance. Moreover, as they are based in New York, they are answerable to the US government. Like all financial institutions, their functions and capabilities are a product of regulation and political authority.

Alongside these agencies, Wall Street banks have become the strategic nerve centers not only of financial capital, but of the world economy as such. In the United States, between 1973 and 2007, as a result of politically driven changes to the domestic and global economy, financial profits rose from 16 percent to 41 percent of total profits in the US economy.[63] Wall Street accounts for just over a third of total global financial transactions. And with economic weight comes intellectual clout. Banks provide the technical expertise, training, legal knowledge, and professional discourses that financial communities organize themselves around. They assemble the economic advice that governments follow and distribute the information that determines media reporting. At the apex of the US banking system, of course, is the Federal Reserve, which has become a locus of high-end economic research.[64] American finance is thus extremely well placed to conserve its position in the world system, defend its interests against democratic curtailments, and drive forward the integration and institutionalization of international markets from which it profits.

The durability of the GATS model is therefore less surprising than it would appear. In the context of the overall response to the crash by the US government and its allies, it is clear that the major goal of post-crash legislation is to conserve the system as much as possible. One of the first steps taken by the US government was to convene the G20 economies and win from them commitments not to enact the kind of restrictions on trade and capital flows that national economies had undertaken in response to the Great Depression. The state's arrogation of considerable powers to intervene in markets, far from contravening this general tendency, reinforced it. Banks were bailed out in exchange for remarkably little change on their part. The government assumed all the risk of "toxic debt," laid out all the finance, and allowed the private sector to price assets. As government officials repeatedly insisted, any reforms had to be implemented with the cooperation of the bankers, thus placing a limit on what could realistically be done. Those financial institutions that were nationalized were allowed to operate as commercial entities at arm's length from the government, and mainly returned to the private sector when they became profitable. New regulations were modest, aimed at greater transparency and some limited consumer protections, but there were no new restrictions on the size of bank holdings, there was to be no reform of the ratings agencies, and there was no attempt to go back to the sorts of tougher regulatory structures represented by Glass-Steagall in the United States.[65]

The centrality of the dollar and Wall Street to the global system furnishes far too much political leverage to Washington for there to be any appetite to relinquish it—which would imply not bringing the banks to heel, but also reforming global trade institutions and the US state itself. Yet the nature of the global financial crash and its reverberations suggests a more unsettling truth about the empire.

The crisis arising from the US banking crash was global. It did not merely hit the City of London, with which US banks have strong transatlantic connections, and which effectively acts as an offshore haven for US investors—sometimes dubbed "Guantánamo" because one could get away with things there that were not permissible on the American mainland.[66] It hit the Eurozone badly and precipitated a series of "sovereign debt" crises that almost sank the single currency. It also hit East Asia, despite hopes that the region would be able to ride out the storm.

This is a testament to the extent of economic interpenetration that has already developed, and the extent to which the rest of the world depends upon the US economy. It is also a very good reason why, after the worst economic crisis since the 1930s, the US can still lead a wide coalition of states as it presses for further entrenchment of the "Washington Consensus."

The dominance of Wall Street is reminiscent of British domination of world trade in the nineteenth century, in that US interests have in a way become synonymous with those of the world. If it goes down, we all go down.

Part II

4. Indexing the Empire

Sarah Harrison

WHAT IS PLUSD?

"The Public Library of US Diplomacy," or "PlusD," is a very large and constantly expanding collection of internal documents from the US Department of State, published by WikiLeaks in a searchable archive. The library began in 2010 and at the time of writing contains 2,325,961 individual documents made up of about 2 billion words, spread over three collections of cables: *Cablegate*, the Kissinger Cables, and the Carter Cables. The State Department is the foreign affairs department of the US government and oversees the embassies and consulates of the United States all over the world. Each embassy or consulate corresponds with the State Department in Washington, DC, by sending daily telegram reports, or "cables," between them, using a special electronic communications system.

PlusD contains within it the WikiLeaks publication known as *Cablegate*: the collection of State Department cables published by WikiLeaks in 2010 and 2011. *Cablegate* itself consists of 251,287 cables, accounting for 261,276,536 words in total. If printed out in a standard-sized font, *Cablegate* alone would form a single line over 6,000 kilometers long—the distance to the center of the Earth. The cables are an average of 1,039 words long, revealing detailed internal information about the operation of 274 US embassies and consulates, and their activity within their host country.

WikiLeaks specializes in publishing, curating, and ensuring easy access to full online archives of information that has been censored or suppressed, or is likely to be lost. An understanding of our historical record enables self-determination; publishing and ensuring easy access to full archives, rather than just individual documents, is central to preserving this historical record. Since publishing *Cablegate*, WikiLeaks has continued to work to make PlusD the most complete online archive of US Department of State documents, adding to the library each year with newly available cables and other documents from the State Department communications system. It can be accessed through a set of specially developed search interfaces at https://**wikileaks.org/plusd**.

HOW TO READ THE CABLES

Probably the first question for anyone researching a serious topic in the cables is: Where do I start? Experience has shown that the answer is: Don't start by searching for specific things.

Because of what it is—the archive of a foreign ministry—PlusD is a rich repository of information on countries, major international and domestic figures, political parties, events, policies, processes, trends, and developments. There is a natural temptation to "mine" PlusD: to think of particularly notable topics from the news, then to dig a narrow shaft down through the huge amount of information to find the cables where only that topic is mentioned, treating those cables as an authority on the subject. Much of the early reportage on the cables in the mainstream media was done this way.

This approach is not necessarily a misuse of the cables—there is plenty of information in them that is responsive to this kind of query. But, in general, reading the cables this way will result in a superficial understanding of them, and of the subject of the research. Because there is so much information in PlusD, it is easy to find information that confirms your biases as a researcher, with the result that you will see only what you want to see. If these pitfalls are to be avoided, you must think about your reading strategy from the outset.

First, try to get a good feel for what kind of material you are handling. The cables were not written to provide instant information on a range of discrete topics to a general readership. Instead, they are the means the State Department uses to communicate with itself—the by-product of the daily operation of embassies all over the world. The original way they were read was as updates on preceding documents, in a continuous succession.

This gives the documents features which must be kept in mind if they are to be understood properly. First, the people who wrote the cables are diplomats: they are specialists in communicating with each other, and this means they assume a lot of prior knowledge. Often, to understand a cable it is necessary to understand what is *not* said in the cable but left implicit; in order to do this it is necessary to read other cables to get a more general picture.

Second, the cables are episodic. Each of them is part of a succession of cables over time, reporting how—to the best of the knowledge of the authors—situations are unfolding in the country in question. Without appreciating the dynamic nature of the subject-matter of the cables, and the fact that the authors are often working with incomplete knowledge of that subject-matter, it is easy to miss out on the rich historical insight the documents offer.

The obvious remedy to this is to read widely around the topic you wish to research, and to become as familiar as possible with the documentary context of your topic. If your research focuses on a particular country, a good way to do this is to take the highest classification level for that country (which will be a small subset) and read all of the cables in it, chronologically. If you are reading about a particular event, make sure to define a period covering that event, and read all of the cables from the same embassy within that time period. If your topic centers on a few keywords, such as a particular figure, or a hot issue within the cables, such as "extraordinary rendition" or "genetically modified organisms," make sure that, once you have located cables responsive to your search queries, you also scan the cables for related issues and topics—reading widely within those searches too. Try also to read other cables sent around the same time. Understanding that the US government actively lobbies foreign governments to encourage deregulation of GMOs is, in isolation, a narrow insight; understanding how this policy evolves over time, and how it interrelates with Washington's other long-term diplomatic goals in that country, furnishes a broader understanding, and it will inform any reading about similar topics.

Make sure at all times to maintain a critical distance from the documents. When the *New York Times* offered an overview of the cables, it remarked that the cables broadly confirmed the dominant view of the US as a benevolent superpower, upholding American values and advocating for human rights abroad. This is unsurprising, if you consider that the *New York Times* shares the same ideology of US exceptionalism that is compulsory in the State Department. As the output of the US diplomatic community, the cables will reflect the biases and ideology of the US government and establishment, and its aspirations in the wider world. It is important always to be on the lookout for how ideology is shaping the content: the euphemisms and clichés, and the way in which contentious issues are hidden in plain sight, or left out entirely.

For example, the concept that US oil corporations are entitled to extract and export the natural resources of Venezuela and Libya would be too brazen a concept for US diplomats to endorse explicitly. Hence, it is reframed in the cables as "resource nationalism," to make it seem as if it is a bad thing when the government of Venezuela decides that the natural resources of Venezuela should principally benefit Venezuelans. It is only by reading widely that it is possible to understand the full implications of a concept like "resource nationalism," and how it is involved with US foreign policy, and thereby to be able to read it against the grain.

Bias in the US diplomatic corps is not monolithic, either. Policies and orthodoxies change over time, and in the cables you can see diplomats amending their language as perspectives change—choosing to observe institutional taboos, or to pander to new policy obsessions coming from Washington. Different administrations—the Bush and Obama presidencies are very well covered in the documents—also usher in different priorities and emphases.

Besides bias and ideology, it is important to remember that specific information in a cable can be inaccurate. Sometimes reports will reflect incomplete information; sometimes diplomats will engage in speculation that turns out, in hindsight, to have been unfounded; and, sometimes, what they report will be simply wrong. But these cables are still important, as they provide a genuine record of what information was being sent to or from an embassy at that time.

KNOWING YOUR WAY AROUND A CABLE

As with any specialized document, there are some things it is important to understand about the cables in order to read them properly.

First, metadata. This is what the cable tells you about itself: its unique reference number, its date, where it comes from, where it was sent, what kind of subjects it touches on, which other cables it references, its classification level and handling restrictions, and other specific information about each cable. In the PlusD archive we have processed the metadata of each document, presenting it in a special box at the top of each cable. For each class of metadata, you can click on the metadata field to see more information. You can, for example, click on the classification for more information about the classification scheme and how it applies to the cable you are reading. You can also choose to view the "raw header"—the metadata as it was before we processed it. All these fields are individually searchable in the PlusD search interface.

Each cable also has a text title—for example, "EGYPT: GAZA ROUND-UP: DECEMBER 31"—and a date that is exact to the minute—for example "2009 January 1, 02:45 (Thursday)." Each cable also has an official reference ID given to it by the State Department—a unique reference number that is meant to refer only to that cable. This is typically of the form "09CAIRO1." The first two digits, "09," denote the year the cable was sent: 2009; the middle of the cable ID indicates the origin (the US embassy in Cairo); and the final digits indicate the sequential number of the cable that year (in this case, it is the first cable of the year 2009: "1"). In some cases, the State Department's reference ID system breaks down and cables are given duplicate names. In PlusD, we have created a canonical ID which ensures that all cables have a unique identifier across all datasets, rectifying any mistaken duplications by the State Department. This canonical ID is created by taking the original document ID and adding a "_" at the end, followed by WikiLeaks' annotation for different datasets: *Cablegate* = a, the Kissinger Cables = b, and so on. For document IDs that were duplicated in the original datasets, we number each duplicate—for example, 1976WARSAW05657_b2 is the second document with that State Department ID in the Kissinger Cables.

Like most government agencies, the State Department uses classification to restrict access to information on a "need to know" basis. Cables are assigned a classification level depending on how sensitive they are, and only people with the corresponding "clearance" can read those cables. The higher the classification, the smaller the set of people who are allowed official access. Some

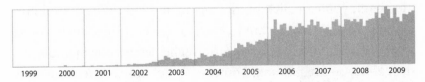

Figure 1: Frequency of US Department of State Cables between 1999 and 2009

cables also have handling restrictions, such as "NOFORN," meaning the cable cannot be shown to any non-US nationals, or "FOR OFFICIAL USE ONLY." The *Cablegate* set, for example, does not contain any cables with the highest classification level ("TOP SECRET"), but does contain cables with every classification beneath this. There are 4,330 cables classified as SECRET// NOFORN. There are 11,322 classified as SECRET. Some 4,678 cables are classified as CONFIDENTIAL//NOFORN, and 97,070 as CONFIDENTIAL. Furthermore, 58,095 cables are marked UNCLASSIFIED//FOR OFFICIAL USE ONLY, and 75,792 are marked UNCLASSIFIED. Most embassies will have some cables within each classification.

Classification level does not necessarily equate with significance or "newsworthiness." Even if a cable is marked "SECRET// NOFORN," this does not mean that the information contained within it will be more sensational or interesting for your purposes than information contained in a document with a lower classification level. The reason is normally given for why a particular cable has been given its classification, and reasons often include the fact that a cable deals with a past operation, or communications security, or contains information that would be embarrassing, either to the US government or to the host government, if disclosed. The content of these cables can sometimes seem quite pedestrian, and the classification might have been given to it simply because it was formally required. But there will often be other cables from that period, possibly at a lower classification level—or even unclassified—that contain important comments by a senior diplomat shedding light on a US perspective on a national issue, or in aggregate disclosing an historically significant or important insight. It is therefore important not to assume that the lowest-level security classification denotes the lowest level of political significance.

Sometimes the classification schemes are not rigorously adhered to by the diplomats. Particularly with some of the smaller embassies, there is either no facility for TOP SECRET ciphers, or it is used so infrequently that the opportunity costs involved with using it encourage diplomats to take shortcuts. The result is that information that by all rights should be highly classified is sometimes given in cables with a lower classification level.

Each cable is normally marked with one or more "TAGS." "TAGS" refers to "Traffic Analysis by Geography and Subject"—a categorization system implemented by the State Department in 1973 to group cables more effectively according to their subject matter and geographical relevance. TAGS range from country codes ("GR" for Germany, "IZ" for Iraq, and so on) to organization codes ("AEC" for Atomic Energy Commission, "DOD" for Department of Defense, and so on), program codes ("KCIP" for Critical Infrastructure Protection, "KMPI" for Middle East Partnership Initiative, and so on), and subject codes ("PROP" for Political Affairs—Propaganda and Psychological Operations, "PREL" for Political Affairs: External Political Relations, and so on). WikiLeaks has researched the acronyms and expanded all of them so that they can be read without having to consult a key. You can now click each tag to see other cables to which it is attached. A full list of the TAGS acronyms can be found at http://wikileaks.org/plusd/about-ta.

Watch out for "reftel," which is the internal citation system for the cables. If the cable you are reading uses the word "reftel," this is a reference to a previous cable in which the topic is expanded upon. Normally, reftels are listed at the top of the body of the cable. If the reftel is one of the cables contained in the PlusD dataset, it should be hyperlinked, and you should be able to read the reftel simply by clicking on it. Following the thread of reftels is often a useful way of getting a full impression of the events or topic dealt with across a succession of cables.

The body of each cable is more straightforward. Cables are divided into numbered paragraphs. The cables will typically take the form of a report on a meeting or discussion that has taken place within the diplomatic premises, or as part of the official business of the diplomatic mission. Commentary is often included in brackets around the main report. The first paragraph is normally a summary of the cable. The rest of the cable goes into more detail. Cables are normally signed off by one of the senior officials within the diplomatic mission: the ambassador, the chargé d'affaires, the political officer, the consul, or another official who is made responsible for a specific set of duties. But this is a formality, and an individual's signature does not mean that that person actually read the cable. Many cables begin with a brief note explaining which official within the embassy or consulate classified the cable, and for what reason.

Reading the cables will turn up some unfamiliar terms and acronyms, such as "POLOFF" (political officer) and "SIPDIS" (SIPRNet Distribution). WikiLeaks has assembled a comprehensive explanatory database of known terms at https://wikileaks.org/plusd/tags to aid researchers in understanding the information in context.

HOW TO ACCESS PLUSD

The best way to read State Department cables published by WikiLeaks is through our special search interface at https://wikileaks.org/plusd. It is impossible to provide a comprehensive summary of the research tools available on PlusD here, but full instructions are available on the website. Researchers can choose which collection to search (*Cablegate*, Kissinger Cables, and so on, or several at once) and can choose to search within specific date ranges, specific geographical regions, specific embassies or consulates, and within specific classification levels, among many other fields and tools available for precise searching and research. For example, PlusD will generate a graph from any search term, showing you the frequency of the occurrence of that search term within the whole of the PlusD database.

PlusD allows users to limit their searches with reference to fields from the cable metadata. Some of the most interesting of these are the lesser-known ones. The office field refers to the particular office or bureau within the State Department that the cable was to or from, and whether it was regarding an "action" by the State Department ("to"), or originated in the State Department ("from"). This field allows researchers either to narrow their search results for a certain field (for example, narrowing a search to documents to or from the Committee on Oceans and Atmosphere for someone researching DOS communications on fisheries), or to gain a better understanding of how the State Department is dealing with a certain topic (for example, if researching a topic that is discussed in cables copied specifically to the Bureau of Intelligence and Research, it allows for a more nuanced understanding of how the United States views this topic).

There are some fields searchable in PlusD that the *Cablegate* collection does not record—for example, Handling Restrictions. The Handling Restrictions field provides for a more detailed understanding of who was and was not allowed to see each document, over and above the classification level a person would need to hold, by stating the allowed range of distribution—for example, Exclusive Distribution Only (EXDIS), which indicates "extremely limited dissemination." To prepare this field for PlusD, WikiLeaks not only extracted the field from the metadata of the document, but searched in the raw data of the cable for the word "Cherokee," which appears 2,208 times in the Kissinger Cables and 1,263 times in the Carter Cables, and extracted this as one of the searchable handling restrictions possible. The word "Cherokee" is reserved for messages involving the Secretary of State and senior White House officials only. The term originated during the 1960s, when Secretary of State Dean Rusk named it after Cherokee County, Georgia, where he was born. Due to the limited distribution of cables carrying this handling restriction, it is a rare and important addition to the possible entries in this field, only specifically searchable in PlusD.

The PlusD text- and field-search interface facilitates searching and search refinement across seventeen different fields, including additional explanations of what abbreviated entries in each field mean. Other interfaces available in PlusD to search the archive include mapping occurrences of certain words over time and browsing frequencies of TAGS used in the documents. This variety of tools allows all types of researchers to access the full PlusD archive for searches both broad and narrow.

WikiLeaks has been publishing classified or otherwise suppressed documents and archives since 2006. These are not just cables, but include a diverse range of documents—from internal military reports and government documents to suppressed studies and investigative work, internet filter lists, and internal bank documents. A dedicated global search engine for every single document WikiLeaks has published can be found at https://**search.wikileaks.org**. A guide to using the global search engine can be found at https://**search.wikileaks.org/info**.

Since late 2012, we have included a tool that allows readers to highlight the parts of the cable they find most interesting and link other internet users directly to that material. The highlighter can be found at the bottom-right of the screen on the PlusD reader.

A full overview of how PlusD was prepared by WikiLeaks, providing insight into the structure of the cables, can be found at http://**wikileaks.org/plusd/about**.

PUBLISHING PLUSD

The first collection in PlusD was *Cablegate*, which was originally published in 2010 as part of a partnership of international newspapers and media organizations globally, coordinated by WikiLeaks. We designed and implemented a system that allowed us to coordinate a publication schedule between over a hundred global mainstream media partners. Whenever the media partners were to publish a story, they would enter into this system the cables they were going to use in their story, so that WikiLeaks would publish the cable at the same time. These partnerships ran for almost a year, after which—because WikiLeaks holds fast to the principle that full archives should be published—we ensured that every single cable was published in full. All of them can now be read online.

Through the partnerships, WikiLeaks' media partners were under a memorandum of understanding (MOU) to publish the full text of the cables (initially redactions were permitted in a few very specific circumstances outlined in the MOU) when their story went live, but this did not always happen. The redactions, according to the MOU, were to be made only if a specified and identifiable individual would be at real risk of death or punishment with no judicial process. However, the press often abused this agreement, and in many cases redacted for entirely different reasons—for example, political bias. In addition, many media published only extracts from selected cables, or did not publish the cable at all. Since WikiLeaks published the full unredacted archive, the public has had unhindered access to the record. This has resulted in the exposure of journalistic error and bias, and has enabled the global readership of *Cablegate* to become active participants in the interrogation of our historical record.

There are nearly a quarter of a million cables in *Cablegate*, from as early as 1966, although there is a thinner distribution of cables over the earlier decades than there is for recent years. The bulk of the cables in *Cablegate* are from the State Department under the George W. Bush and Barack Obama administrations, thus relating to the decade beginning around the year 2000. The most recent cables in the collection are from early 2010. PlusD also contains collections of cables that originally became available through US Government declassification procedures. In order to ensure that these cables could not be unpublished or reclassified by the government (a common occurrence), and in order to make the documents more visible and searchable, WikiLeaks incorporated them into PlusD in two collections, depending on the date of their release by the US Government: at the time of writing, this meant that there were three individual collections of cables in the PlusD archive. In early 2013, we published the "Kissinger Files"—that is, 1,707,500 diplomatic documents originating between the years 1973 and 1976, the Kissinger years; and in April 2014, we published the "Carter Cables"—367,174 diplomatic cables from the year 1977.

The creation of PlusD involved complex data journalism and archival processes, which included manually processing each cable and correcting spelling errors introduced by the State Department in indexing information. Thanks to our work, cables tagged by the State Department as, for example, "Brasil" and "Brazil" are now indexed as referring to the same country in PlusD. In some cases, our journalistic partners were able to discover twice as many cables in response to a single search term as a consequence of our work. PlusD is consequently the most comprehensive and powerful database of US diplomatic cables in existence. As more State Department cables become available, whether through declassification or the brave actions of whistleblowers, we will continue to grow the PlusD database.

One of WikiLeaks' principles is to provide the public with the resources to inform itself, and this means ensuring the data are presented in a manner that ensures easy interaction and research for all. Some of our hardest work goes toward adding value to datasets and making our publications more accessible and usable. This involves researching the structure of the data, designing and implementing search engines, optimizing metadata, and adding a large number of features to make the data easier to navigate and explore for researchers, journalists, human rights groups, historians, students, and others.

Over the years, we have improved our search interface and sought to contextualize the cables, making them more accessible and navigable. Our efforts have been reflected in the continued use of our publications by the media and the public alike. PlusD continues to be an invaluable resource for investigative journalists looking for context and background for developing stories. Every day, new stories are published in mainstream news publications that explicitly reference the *Cablegate* archive. There is not a significant geopolitical event in the world that cannot be illuminated with material published by WikiLeaks. We expect PlusD to continue to yield crucial historical insight long into the future.

USE OUR WORK

WikiLeaks undertakes to publish information of diplomatic, ethical, or historical significance that has been censored, suppressed, or is under threat of being lost to history. This information is frequently available only through the actions of courageous individuals within secretive organizations: whistleblowers. Commensurate with the risks taken by such individuals, WikiLeaks undertakes to protect our journalistic sources with the best, most advanced techniques available. We promise our sources that we will publish in such a way as to produce the maximum impact possible. We promise to publish in full, and that once something has been published it will never be unpublished.

Our work is dedicated to making sure history belongs to everyone, not just to elite organizations and their counterparts in the news industry. By publishing source documents, WikiLeaks helps to ensure accountability on the part of not only those with executive power, but also the media. If you use our publications in your research and writing, make sure to link to the source document, publicize your discoveries widely, and demand of every other news organization that it does not hold back or suppress the common history of humanity.

Donations to WikiLeaks are welcome, at https://**wikiLeaks.org/ donate**.

5. US War Crimes and the ICC

Linda Pearson

The WikiLeaks cables reveal evidence of war crimes and human rights abuses carried out at the behest of the US government. They also show the lengths to which the administration of George W. Bush was prepared to go to ensure that those responsible for such crimes would remain unreachable under international law.

The US government has for decades demanded that US military personnel be tried in the US, under US law, for any crimes committed overseas. "Status of forces" agreements between the US and other nations generally include such provisions.

When the Iraqi government refused to sign an agreement granting US forces immunity from Iraqi law in 2011, US forces were withdrawn. Immunity from Afghan law was also the main sticking point in negotiations between the US and the government of Hamid Karzai on an agreement to keep US forces in Afghanistan beyond the original 2014 deadline for withdrawal.[1]

Immunity from local laws usually means impunity, as the US has a poor record of prosecuting its citizens for crimes committed during military engagement overseas. There have been some prosecutions of low-ranking troops in relation to war crimes committed in Iraq, but, as Iraq Body Count has reported, "no soldier or official involved in the Iraq war has faced the level of vindictive punishment that US prosecutors have sought to impose on [Chelsea] Manning."[2] Journalist Glenn Greenwald has documented extensively how "elite immunity" works to protect the rich and powerful from prosecution in the US, including those responsible for grave human rights abuses carried out during the "global war on terror."[3]

After taking office in 2009, President Barack Obama authorized the publication of US Department of Justice memos detailing the "enhanced interrogation techniques" that had been employed at the behest of the Bush administration. At the same time, however, Obama declared that those responsible for the torture program would not be prosecuted, insisting: "This is a time for reflection, not retribution."[4]

In December 2014, the publication of a largely redacted summary of the US Senate Intelligence Committee's report on CIA torture prompted renewed calls for prosecutions. But Obama immediately invoked the doctrine of elite immunity again, saying that the report should not provide "another reason to refight old arguments."[5]

THE INTERNATIONAL CRIMINAL COURT

When states are "unwilling or unable" to prosecute individuals alleged to have committed such crimes, the International Criminal Court (ICC) can offer another avenue for justice. The court was established in 2002 by the Rome Statute, an international treaty that has been ratified by 122 countries. It has jurisdiction to investigate individuals for war crimes, crimes against humanity, and the crime of genocide.

During the 1998 conference of 160 nations that formulated the Rome Statute, US negotiators sought to limit the ICC's jurisdiction and its independence. A large number of states wanted the court to have "universal jurisdiction"—that is, the power to prosecute crimes committed anywhere. But US opposition forced a compromise: the ICC only has jurisdiction over crimes committed by an individual of a state, or on the territory of a state, which is a party to the Rome Statute.

The US also wanted the United Nations Security Council (UNSC) to have the power to veto prosecutions, effectively giving the US the power to prevent cases proceeding against its citizens. This was rejected by other nations at the Rome conference. Instead, the ICC's prosecutor, who is elected by the member states, has the final say on which cases will be prosecuted.

US OPPOSITION AND ICC-RELATED SANCTIONS

Unhappy with the outcome of the negotiations, the US president at the time, Bill Clinton, signed the Rome Statute in 2000, but only so that the United States would be "in a position to influence the evolution of the court."

In May 2002, Clinton's successor, George W. Bush, formally "unsigned" the treaty. His under secretary of state for arms control and international security, John Bolton, summed up the Bush administration's opposition to the court when he said in 2003: "Whether it is removing a rogue Iraqi regime and replacing it, preventing WMD proliferation, or protecting Americans against an unaccountable Court, the United States will ... follow its values when measuring the legitimacy of its actions."[6] In other words, the United States will not subject its actions to the constraints of international law, nor the jurisdiction of a court it cannot control through the UNSC.

The effect of Bush's "unsigning" was to exclude US nationals from the jurisdiction of the ICC unless their alleged crimes were committed on the territory of a state that was a party to the Rome Statute. Even where it has jurisdiction, the chances that the ICC would ever indict a US national are remote, as the court depends on the financial and political support of the West. In its thirteen-year history, the court has indicted only Africans. Moreover, without its own police force, the court depends on the cooperation of governments to detain and extradite individuals who it indicts. It is unthinkable that any US government would surrender one of its nationals to the ICC.

Nevertheless, members of the Bush administration wanted to eliminate any possibility that they might one day find themselves at The Hague. In August 2002, Bush enacted the American Service-Members' Protection Act (ASPA), which authorized the US president to use "all means necessary" to free a US national detained by the ICC. ASPA—or the "Hague Invasion Act," as it become known—also banned military aid to countries that had ratified the Rome Statute.

Further measures passed in 2004, known as the "Nethercutt Amendment," extended the scope of the sanctions to Economic Support Funds (ESF) assistance. ESF funds are provided to "countries of strategic interest to US foreign policy" for a variety of programs, including peacekeeping, "democracy promotion," and "counter-narcotics" initiatives. NATO countries and designated "major non-NATO allies" were exempted from these measures. The restrictions could be waived for other countries if the president deemed it "important to the national interest of the United States."

For other states that had signed the Rome Statute, the only way to avoid the sanctions was to sign an "Article 98," or bilateral immunity agreement with the US, by which they agreed not to surrender Americans to the ICC without the consent of the US government.

THE WIKILEAKS CABLES ON THE GLOBAL
PURSUIT OF ARTICLE 98 AGREEMENTS

Hundreds of diplomatic cables published by WikiLeaks show how the Bush administration used the threat of sanctions and the promise of rewards to coerce weaker states into signing Article 98 agreements. By this "carrot and stick" approach, as a cable from Honduras put it, the United States would "help those countries that sign Article 98 agreements and cut aid to those that do not."[7]

However, the "carrots" on offer often amounted to no more

than vague promises of favorable treatment. US diplomats told the Sri Lankan prime minister in 2002 that "[s]igning soon would win [the government of Sri Lanka] valuable positive attention among Washington decision-makers; waiting too long could result in other countries stealing Sri Lanka's thunder."[8] The Maldives was promised that it would "gain significant credit with the US the sooner it joined with us on this vital issue."[9] Lesotho, which was struggling to cope with an AIDS epidemic, was told in June 2006 that its "high profile" status as a non-signatory of an Article 98 agreement had led to a request for aid from the US being denied.[10] However, if Lesotho signed, the US ambassador told the prime minister that he would "receive a warmer welcome whenever he travelled to the US." As the cables show, governments were subjected to sustained pressure. After Romania capitulated and became the first European country to sign, foreign minister Mircea Geoană said: "I can't remember anything they put so much weight or interest into."[11]

The bullying tactics of the United States attracted global condemnation, particularly from the European Union, where support for the ICC was strong. In September 2002, the EU Council published Guiding Principles for its members, which stated: "Entering into [Article 98] agreements—as presently drafted— would be inconsistent with ICC States Parties' obligations with regard to the ICC Statute."[12]

Several EU candidate countries told the US that they could not sign Article 98 agreements because of EU opposition, but US diplomats gave short shrift to these objections. The US told Croatia that it should not be concerned about offending EU states, which had less to lose than Croatia from refusing to sign an Article 98 agreement. According to an April 2003 cable, the US embassy in Zagreb told the Croatian government that it "should begin negotiating with us in earnest: because the ASPA exempts NATO members from the military assistance cutoff, key EU states do not feel a sense of urgency."[13]

When the Moldovan justice minister raised concerns about "negative reactions from EU countries that could hinder Moldova's chances of integration," the US ambassador told him that "European governments would be upset for no more than a week."[14]

Other governments told the US that, while they were willing to sign, they would not be able to secure parliamentary approval for an Article 98 agreement because of the ongoing war in Iraq— particularly after the 2004 publication of photographs of US soldiers abusing Iraqis at Abu Ghraib prison.

Needless to say, it was difficult to sell the idea that the United States should not be subject to the dictates of international law at a time when it was waging an illegal war of aggression and its soldiers were committing war crimes. Reflecting the double-standard inherent in the US attitude toward international law, the same cable reported that the US ambassador "urged the [government of Honduras] to make stronger public statements on Iraq, including on Iraqi war crimes."

A June 2004 cable reported that the Guatemalan government also told US diplomats that its congress would not pass its Article 98 agreement, partly because "events at Abu Ghraib have given powerful ammunition to Article 98 critics."[15] The cable said the Guatemalan government had "requested that [the United States] keep the agreement confidential while it devises a strategy for Congressional approval."

And a similar story unfolded in Yemen, which had signed a secret agreement in 2003 via an exchange of diplomatic notes.[16] When US diplomats brought up the "importance of Article 98 ratification" the following year, a cable reported that the Yemeni deputy foreign minister noted, "[i]n an obvious reference to Abu Ghraib ... that the timing for Article discussions was 'difficult' and 'not good for the US.'"[17]

As cables from Bahrain and Paraguay illustrate, the relentless push for Article 98 agreements threatened to undermine the broader strategic objectives of the United States, leading some diplomats to advise that Washington reconsider the policy.

Bahrain

The government of Bahrain had signed a secret Article 98 agreement with the United States in February 2003. In May 2004, a cable from the US embassy in Manama reported that only five officials at the Bahraini Foreign Ministry knew of the agreement's existence.[18] Both the US embassy and the Bahraini government judged that the agreement would be rejected by Bahrain's parliament if submitted for ratification. The Bahraini government was facing increasing opposition to its pro-US policies—and the publication of the Abu Ghraib pictures made news of a secret immunity agreement all the more incendiary.

The May 2004 cable reported that a Bahraini government official had told the US: "Given the Abu Ghraib revelations in Iraq ... the [government of Bahrain] has no desire whatsoever to notify parliament or the public of the existence of the article 98 agreement." A cable from June 2004 said the king of Bahrain had promised to bring the agreement into force, but that Bahrain's foreign minister was "struggling to find a way to carry this out without causing a political explosion."[19] The United States therefore pushed for the agreement to be brought into force "through a secret exchange of notes"—an executive agreement that would not seek parliamentary approval.

Cables from other countries show that this tactic was the standard US response to concerns about parliamentary opposition. A 2005 cable reported comments by John Bolton that "two-thirds of all the Article 98 agreements had entered into force via diplomatic notes."[20] But some members of Bahrain's government argued that this method was not legal, and negotiations stalled. The United States kept up the pressure, refusing to rule out sanctions on military aid if Bahrain failed to ratify the agreement.[21]

The deputy chief of mission at the US embassy in Bahrain, Robert Stephen Ford, cautioned Washington that such measures could damage the country's close military and political ties with Bahrain. Ford wrote in a March 2004 cable that the programs that would be affected by the sanctions—the International Military Education Training (IMET) and Foreign Military Financing assistance programs—were "key to boosting Bahraini forces' interoperability with our own in such operations."[22] In a subsequent cable, the US ambassador, Ronald E. Neumann, went further, writing that Washington's pressure for formal ratification "ought to be reconsidered."[23] Neumann wrote: "I believe I have a responsibility to tell you that in my judgment pressuring formal ratification has large potential political pain for infinitesimal gains." The ambassador wrote Bahrain could be trusted not to transfer an American to the ICC, because "[t]o do so would be contrary to the fundamental strategic relationship that underpins Bahrain's security and survival." By pursuing ratification, the US would only achieve "a legal formula without any real substantive change." Yet public knowledge of the agreement "could touch off a major political problem, pulling Bahrain's support for our military into the middle of a domestic firestorm." Neumann further warned that the "abuse of Iraqi prisoners in Abu Ghraib [had] made the whole issue of American 'criminal' behavior a white hot issue in Bahrain ... A leak of a concluded Article 98 agreement at this time and in these circumstances would be an issue tailor made for the opposition to take to the streets."

This was something neither the repressive Bahraini regime nor its powerful US backer wanted to see. Neumann expressed concern that "all of this focus on the security relationship would tempt political opponents to try to expand the debate to other 'surrenders' of Bahrain rights, in such matters as the Defense

Cooperation Agreement." This agreement, signed by the United States and Bahrain in 1991, gives the US military access to Bahrain's military bases. The US Navy's Fifth Fleet has been stationed in Bahrain since 1995, and Bahrain is home to the US Naval Forces Central Command. In 2002, the Defense Cooperation Agreement was secretly extended by the Bush administration until 2016.[24] The risk, from the ambassador's point of view, was that news of the secret Article 98 agreement could bring unwelcome attention to the secretly extended Defense Cooperation Agreement.

The experience of other US allies in the region showed that Article 98 agreements would not pass easily. When Kuwait's agreement was submitted for ratification in April 2007, a cable reported that "parliamentarians objected strongly."[25] The cable reported that opponents of the agreement had said it was in violation of Kuwait's ICC obligations, and would place the United States "above the law." Others compared the treatment of US nationals under the agreement to the detention and alleged torture of Kuwaiti citizens held at Guantánamo prison, and argued that Kuwait should not bow to US bullying.

When Jordan's government submitted its agreement for parliamentary ratification in July 2005, a cable from the US embassy in Amman reported: "The Lower House voted overwhelmingly to exclude the Article 98 agreement from its agenda."[26] The agreement was not ratified until the next year, after the king of Jordan had "read the riot act" to parliamentarians, the embassy reported.[27]

Despite Neumann's recommendations, pressure on Bahrain to ratify continued for at least another two years. It is unclear from the cables whether an Article 98 agreement was ever brought into force in Bahrain or Kuwait.[28]

Paraguay

US diplomats faced a similar dilemma in Paraguay. They believed the pursuit of an Article 98 agreement threatened the "permissive environment" that Paraguay offered for US military exercises. Like Bahrain, Paraguay's government told the United States that its congress would not pass an Article 98 agreement.

The US agreed with this assessment, and the US embassy in Asunción instead advocated an exchange of notes "which would both give us Article 98 protections and allow the [government of Paraguay] to continue to say it had not/not signed an Article 98 agreement; we are seeking a 'non-agreement' 'arrangement' open to diverse interpretations."[29]

In June 2005, Paraguay's government came under criticism from local media and neighboring countries for granting immunities to US soldiers taking part in joint US-Paraguay military exercises over an eighteen-month period. As a result, Argentina, Brazil, Paraguay, and Uruguay agreed to a declaration at the 2005 Common Market of the South (Mercosur) summit, which committed them not to sign any agreements that would undermine the jurisdictional basis of the ICC. By this stage, Article 98 negotiations between the US and Paraguay had been ongoing for two years. Cables show that while the president at the time, Óscar Nicanor Duarte, publicly said that Paraguay would not sign an Article 98 agreement, his government told the United States that it would seek ways to provide the immunities it was seeking.[30]

A cable from the US embassy sent shortly after the Mercosur summit reported that "Paraguay's lawyer for Article 98 negotiations with the US conveyed concern that [the Mercosur] declaration could pose a further obstacle to concluding an agreement."[31]

A July 7 cable warned the commander general of US Southern Command (responsible for US military contingency plans for Central and South America) "to avoid discussion of the ICC with Paraguayan interlocutors" during an upcoming visit.[32] The cable said: "You come at a particularly sensitive time, with press and political activity calling into question important aspects of our military to military relationship. The open and permissive environment for exercises and other military activities here is both extremely valuable and potentially vulnerable to local and regional pressures." The cable reiterated the embassy's concern that pushing Paraguay on Article 98 negotiations in the wake of the "flap" over immunities could jeopardize "the most permissive environment for exercises in the region." The cable said, "We may need to wait until current unfavorable press coverage blows over to get a good sense of how best to proceed."

Paraguay was subject to sanctions for failing to sign an Article 98 agreement, but in 2006 President Bush waived the restrictions on the grounds that it was "important to the national interest of the United States" to do so.

UNINTENDED CONSEQUENCES OF ICC-RELATED SANCTIONS

By May 2005, one hundred states had signed Article 98 agreements. Twenty states were subject to ASPA sanctions, and seven to Nethercutt measures, for failing to sign.[33]

Support for these measures waned during Bush's second term, but not because the administration's hostility toward international law had diminished. Rather, as documents published by WikiLeaks show, some US politicians and diplomats were worried that the sanctions were having "unintended negative effects" on US policy objectives—and were undermining US power in countries of strategic importance. A 2007 US Congressional Research Service (CRS) report, made publicly available by WikiLeaks, outlined the "evolving policy debate in the US government" in the context of the effect of ICC-related sanctions in Latin American countries.[34]

The CRS report noted Secretary of State Condoleezza Rice's March 2006 comment that implementing ASPA sanctions against US allies in the "war on terror" and the "war on drugs" was "sort of the same as shooting ourselves in the foot," also noting the concern of some US policy-makers that the sanctions were reducing US influence in the region, as affected states looked to other countries—such as China and Russia—for military training and assistance. This conflict of interests is further detailed in US diplomatic cables.

Costa Rica

Costa Rica was one of twelve Latin American countries that refused to sign an Article 98 agreement, and was therefore subject to ASPA and Nethercutt sanctions. In 2005, the US ambassador to San José wrote that the "unavailability of US military assistance and ESF unavoidably contributes to a decline in US influence in Costa Rica and makes it more difficult to achieve our objectives in the areas of counternarcotics, counterterrorism, and, to a lesser extent, free trade."[35] The ambassador noted that the withdrawal of funds had led to a "noticeable deterioration of the seaworthiness of the Costa Rican Coast Guard fleet and degradation of the operational readiness of other law enforcement units such as the SWAT team." "More worrisome," the ambassador wrote, was that "the absence of training and other US military assistance may eventually cause Costa Ricans to call into question the value to them of the Bilateral Maritime Agreement." This 1999 agreement allows US Coast Guard ships to patrol in Costa Rican waters and US aircraft to fly into Costa Rican airspace. In 2010 it was controversially extended to allow US warships carrying Black Hawk helicopters and other aircraft into Costa Rican waters.[36] The ambassador wrote: "Our task is to find a way out of the dilemma faced by the [Government of Costa Rica] because it is in reality also a dilemma for the United States as we strive to stem the flow of illegal drugs, stop terrorists, and foster an ever-growing trade relationship with Costa Rica."

In October 2006, Bush deemed it in the national interest of the United States to waive IMET restrictions for Costa Rica. The US ambassador to San José welcomed the resumption of US military training, which had previously "provided the US with access and influence among key Costa Rican officials."

Brazil

In Brazil, the US embassy was concerned that IMET restrictions had meant that the country's Ministry of Defence was "shifting to other countries for training and exchanges previously done with the US." A March 2004 cable reported: "While France and the United Kingdom have picked up much of the slack, Brazilian officers, according to military sources, are now being sent also to training programs in China, India, and South Africa."[37] As well as weakening "traditionally close ties between our two armed forces," the cable reported that the sanctions were prejudicing US weapons manufacturer Lockheed Martin's prospects of winning a contract from Brazil for new F-16 fighter jets worth $700 million. The cable noted: "When a decision on purchase of Brazil's next generation fighter jet ... is finally taken, training for pilots will likely be in the country of origin of the new aircraft." With such training prohibited in the US, Brazil might look to buy the jets from another country.

Brazil subsequently abandoned its plan to purchase new jets because of budgetary constraints. But a cable from December 22, 2004, reported that the government of Brazil instead "may review whether to purchase less costly used aircraft," and said: "In this regard, the Lockheed Martin F-16 would have the inside track."[38] The cable suggested that US diplomats had had some success in convincing generals in the Brazilian air force that buying used F-16s was "the most logical way forward both tactically and economically." However, in the embassy's view, the Brazilian government might not be so easily won over because, "[a]s Brazil observes the bite that ASPA is taking on countries that do not sign Article 98 agreements, it [*sic*] questions about the reliability of the US as a supplier/strategic partner will continue."

In 2006, Bush also waived IMET restrictions against Brazil on national interest grounds.

Chile

It was a different story in Chile, where the US embassy in Santiago reported in 2006 that it was pleased that the pursuit of an Article 98 agreement "has yet to interfere with future military sales, bilateral relations, or exchanges or humanitarian operations between our countries' armed forces."

Chile had signed a deal to purchase ten F-16s for $500 million in 2002, the first of which were delivered by Lockheed Martin in January 2006. Unlike Costa Rica and Brazil, Chile had not ratified the Rome Statute and was therefore not subject to sanctions. The cables report that the Chilean government told the US that it would eventually ratify the treaty because of strong domestic and regional support for the ICC, and that signing an Article 98 agreement "would not be politically possible."[39]

The Chilean government was concerned that joining the ICC without signing an immunity agreement would jeopardize the "strong US-Chile relationship." According to a December 2005 cable, Chilean foreign minister Ignacio Walker told the US ambassador that this relationship was "more important now than ever, given the recent troubling developments in the region."[40] Specifically, the cable said, "Walker cited Evo Morales' recent election in Bolivia, the Chávez-Morales axis, and increasing ties between Venezuela and Argentina as reasons why 'like-minded countries' like the US and Chile need to remain close."

A January 2006 cable reported that Stephen Rademaker, the US international security and nonproliferation assistant secretary, had told Chilean officials that "Chile should not count on a Presidential waiver of ASPA sanctions" if it went ahead with ratification.[41] According to the cable, Rademaker said: "Several other countries, notably Colombia in the hemisphere, have faced political difficulties in deciding to enter into an Article 98 agreement with the US. Granting a national interest waiver for Chile now could harm our relations with those countries."

In the end, Chile avoided ICC-related sanctions by delaying

ratification of the Rome Statute until 2009, by which time the Bush administration had abandoned the measures.

Ecuador

Ecuador's refusal to sign an Article 98 agreement rendered it subject to sanctions. Cables from Quito detail the variety of underhanded tactics employed by the US embassy to persuade Ecuador to sign. They also show that the embassy was concerned about the "unintended consequences" of ICC-related sanctions for other US policy objectives in Ecuador.

A cable sent on November 17, 2004, from the US embassy in Quito alluded to the Bush administration's fear that US leaders and military personnel could find themselves on trial at The Hague for crimes carried out during the "global war on terror." The US ambassador complained that Article 98 negotiations with Ecuador had "stagnated" and wrote: "Cognizant that increasing deployments of US forces worldwide makes inking an Article 98 with Ecuador imperative, we are conducting another offensive."[42] This "offensive" included urging the Ecuadorian military to lobby the Ecuadorian government for an Article 98 agreement, so that it could regain access US military assistance: "[W]e are not missing any opportunities to flog the military over the need for Article 98." "Big-ticket items," the cable reported, "such as A-37 upgrades for [air base defense] and additional helicopters ... are non-starters until we get an agreement." According to the cable, the embassy hoped that a "joint special forces counter-terrorism operation featuring Blackhawk helos," which was taking place near Quito, would lead "battalion- and brigade-level officers to push their HQ superiors for similar goodies." The cable said: "The [Foreign Affairs Ministry] continues to believe it can wait us out. It cannot. We are helped by Washington re-opening the second front, calling in Ecuadorian Ambassador Raul Gangotena for meetings with Assistant Secretaries Roger Noriega and Steven Rademaker."

Another cable, sent on November 26, 2004, detailed the embassy's "game plan" for persuading Ecuador to sign an Article 98 agreement.[43] This plan was described as "heavy on personal diplomacy and media education," and included hosting "a series of roundtables with interested journalists, hoping to correct Article 98 misperceptions." It also featured "a possible International Visitor program for Ecuadorian think-tankers and talking heads, whose support will be vital come ratification time (and who are bashing us now)."

The cable went on to note that Ecuadorian president at the time, Lucio Gutiérrez, had told the US defense secretary Donald Rumsfeld that he agreed in principle to signing an Article 98 agreement, but that "it was a hard sell, especially with the left-leaning legislature," and that he "would need serious quid pro quo to go forward." The embassy was therefore considering implementing "Plan Ecuador," described in the cable as a "mostly PR effort to recast existing [US government] assistance efforts as political 'payback' for Article 98 … Believing our aid package already robust but seeing utility in providing deliverables, we deliberated in-house how best to recast and repackage existing programs for maximum political benefit."

By March 2005, the cables reported, Ecuador was no closer to signing an Article 98 agreement. The US ambassador to Ecuador, Kristie Kenney, wrote that she was hopeful that imminent ESF cutbacks "might spur the [government of Ecuador] to reconsider their 'ignore them, they'll go away' strategies."[44] The ambassador saw the appointment of a new Ecuadorian ambassador to Washington, Mauricio Pozo, as another opportunity to leverage the Ecuadorian military's interest in US aid in favor of an Article 98 agreement: "I have suggested to Ecuador's military leaders that they concurrently lobby their newest envoy for movement on Article 98." Further, Kenney wrote, "a 'deliverable' or two might help also in the fight for 98." She suggested the US government consider the extradition from the US of one of a number of corrupt bankers suspected of embezzling millions from Ecuadorian banks, as a quid pro quo for signing an Article 98 agreement. But the cable also reported the embassy's concerns about the unintended consequences of the Bush administration's policy on Article 98 agreements. ICC-related sanctions had mandated a suspension of IMET assistance to Ecuador which, the cable said, "represents perhaps the most cost-effective manner to influence Ecuador's armed forces." Moreover, the embassy was concerned that "other nations, especially China, have rushed to fill the gap."

A subsequent cable reiterated this concern: "ASPA sanctions, especially those restricting US training opportunities (IMET), are costing us influence with the Ecuadorian military."[45] In April 2005, Gutiérrez was forced out of office after Ecuadorians took to the streets in their thousands to protest his government's economic policies. Gutiérrez had been elected on the promise that he would break with the neoliberalism of his predecessors, but quickly reneged on this after taking office. While Gutiérrez's economic policies were unpopular with the Ecuadorian people, they gained him favor in Washington, as did his support of the US-backed Free Trade Area of the Americas (FTAA) and its "war on drugs." Moreover, Gutiérrez had allowed the US considerable influence in Ecuadorian affairs, and the US embassy in Quito was sorry to see him go.[46]

When the government of Alfredo Palacio took over from Gutiérrez, Kenney wrote that "Article 98's chances in Ecuador sunk from bad to worse."[47] Ecuadorian minister of government, Mauricio Gándara, described by the ambassador as "the quintessential gringo-basher," announced publicly that Ecuador would not sign an Article 98 agreement with the US. But the ambassador saw some hope in new Ecuadorian foreign minister Antonio Parra, who, she said, "appeared less ideological and more approachable than Gándara and company" and therefore "merited cultivation." The ambassador wrote: "Rather than hit Parra with Article 98, perhaps the hottest bilateral potato he'll encounter, we favor an early campaign to educate him on 'softer'

US assistance and shared interests ... As Parra grows to realize that close US relations benefit Ecuador, he should become less apt to dismiss Article 98 out-of-hand."

In September 2005, the new US ambassador to Ecuador, Linda Jewell, reiterated the embassy's concerns about an unintended loss of US influence in Ecuador, in a cable titled: "Democracy Promotion Strategies for Ecuador."[48] As this cable illustrates, so-called "democracy promotion" is a strategy by which Western governments seek to influence and contain political and economic change in countries of strategic importance.

In Ecuador, the US wanted to counteract the influence of Latin America's burgeoning social movements. Demanding democratic reforms and an economic alternative to the Washington consensus, these movements had brought left-wing leaders to power in Venezuela, Bolivia, and Uruguay. The embassy feared that the "pink tide" would engulf Ecuador, damaging US business interests in the country and dashing any hopes of negotiating a free-trade agreement. Moreover, the Ecuadorians who had mobilized against Gutiérrez were calling for an end to US interference in Ecuador and closure of the US Forward Operating Base at Manta.

Under the heading "Democracy is broken here," Ambassador Jewell warned that "the danger of democratic backsliding is very real, whether in the form of a tradition of [sic] strongman military or civilian solution or a more populist Bolivarian movement ... Nethercutt/Article 98 restrictions that prohibit support to the [government of Ecuador] greatly hinder USG ability to effect change [and are] putting at risk our influence over an entire generation of [military] officers." ESF restrictions would also "undermine USG democracy building efforts with local governments and hamper policy reform efforts with a wide array of Central Government institutions, including the Electoral Tribunal, other courts, and the Trade and Environment Ministries."

The embassy was particularly concerned about Palacio's proposal for a referendum on whether to convoke a constituent assembly to reform Ecuador's political system and rewrite its constitution. "The contents of the referendum will be determined through negotiations with Congress," wrote Jewell, "which presents some risk to [US government] interests." The cable said that one of the tasks of the embassy's "democracy promotion" working group would be to "[e]ncourage informed debate on electoral and political reforms being considered for inclusion in the referendum, while shielding [US government] security and trade interests from inclusion." Specifically, Jewell wanted US "interests in [a Free-Trade Agreement], the Forward Operating Location at Manta, and security cooperation protected from inclusion in any popular referendum."

In late 2006, Bush waived the military and economic sanctions against Ecuador on national-interest grounds. But the embassy's "democracy promotion" efforts failed to prevent the election that year of "dark horse populist, anti-American candidate"[49] Raphael Correa, who has taken Ecuador in a very different direction to the one preferred by the US.

A NEW ERA OF ENGAGEMENT WITH THE ICC?

ICC-related sanctions were impeding cooperation between the United States and other states in the "war on terror" and the "war on drugs," and costing the US military and political influence. As the Congressional Research Service reported in 2007,[50] these unintended consequence had led the Bush administration to rethink the policy, and the sanctions were gradually abandoned. By January 2008, all the provisions prohibiting military aid to countries that had refused to sign Article 98 agreements had been removed from ASPA Act. The Nethercutt Amendment was dropped in 2009, so that ESF assistance could be restored to countries that had failed to sign.

Actions taken by the Obama administration have led to hopes that the US is embarking on a new era of engagement with the ICC. The US began sending delegations of observers to sessions of the Rome Statute's Assembly of States Parties in 2009. In 2011, it voted in favor of a UNSC resolution referring the situation in Libya to the ICC—the first time it had approved a UNSC referral to the Court.

In 2013, when ICC indictee and M23 leader Bosco Ntaganda surrendered to the US embassy in Kigali, the United States arranged for him to be extradited to The Hague, even though it was not legally obligated to do so. In the same year, the US Congress voted to extend the US Rewards for Justice program, which offers substantial cash rewards for information leading to the arrest of terrorism suspects, to individuals indicted by the ICC.

While these developments and other instances of cooperation between the United States and the ICC suggest a greater acceptance of the role of the court in bringing war criminals to justice, the likelihood that the US will ratify the Rome Statute has remained remote during Obama's terms of office. Moreover, rather than offering principled support for the Court, cooperation with the ICC has been selectively undertaken when the administration has believed that it will further US interests.

The administration chose to support the UNSC referral of Libya to the ICC in the hope that it would help to expedite Muammar Qaddafi's removal from power. At the insistence of the United States, a provision was included in the resolution stating that nationals of non-signatories to the Rome Statute would not be subject to the jurisdiction of the ICC. As Glenn Greenwald reported, the Obama administration was worried that without this provision the resolution would set a precedent, potentially paving the way for ICC indictments of US nationals. According to Greenwald, the resolution was therefore "yet another episode where the US exempts itself from standards it purports to impose on the rest of the world."[51]

The Obama administration has also worked consistently to try to ensure that the actions of its key Middle East ally, Israel, remain outside the ICC's jurisdiction. In May 2014, the US supported a UNSC resolution referring alleged war crimes committed in Syria to the ICC—but only on the condition that the Court would not have jurisdiction to investigate alleged crimes committed by Israelis in the occupied Syrian Golan Heights.[52]

The greatest threat to Israel, however, has been the prospect of a Palestinian referral of alleged Israeli war crimes to the ICC. Until recently, neither Israel nor Palestine was party to the Rome Statute, so such crimes did not fall under the Court's jurisdiction. Knowing that Palestinian membership of the ICC would change this, the Obama administration has fought publicly and privately with Israel against Palestinian attempts to join. According to a February 2010 cable from the US embassy in Tel Aviv, the IDF's military advocate, General Mandelblit, told the US ambassador to Israel that the ICC was "the most dangerous issue for Israel." The cable said that Palestinian justice minister Ali Kashan had met with ICC prosecutor Luis Moreno Ocampo to ask him to investigate alleged Israeli war crimes in the occupied territories. Mandelblit "warned that [Palestinian Authority] pursuit of Israel through the ICC would be viewed as war by the [government of Israel]" and urged the US ambassador to "help the PA understand the gravity of its actions." The ambassador reassured Mandelblit that "the US had consistently pressed the [Palestinian Authority] to cease such action."[53]

In the past, the Palestinian Authority (PA), led by President Mahmoud Abbas, has toed the US-Israeli line on war crimes investigations. In 2009, the PA agreed to support a postponement of the referral to the UNSC of the Goldstone Report into Operation Cast Lead. The United States and Israel feared that the referral would lead to an investigation into war crimes alleged to have been committed by Israel during the 2008–09 assault on Gaza. Leaked intelligence documents published by Al Jazeera and the *Guardian* in 2015, the "Spy Cables," suggest Abbas was concerned that the referral would "play into the hands of" his rivals, Hamas.[54]

However, in December 2014, after a resolution calling for the establishment of a Palestinian state failed at the UNSC, Abbas submitted an application for Palestinian membership of the ICC. In early January 2015, UN Secretary-General Ban Ki-moon announced that Palestine's membership would take effect from April 1, and alleged Israeli crimes committed after June 13, 2014, were thereby brought under the Court's jurisdiction.

The Obama administration condemned the Palestinian application as counterproductive, maintaining the US position that Palestine is not a sovereign state and is therefore not eligible to join the ICC. Israel retaliated by announcing that it would withhold $127 million in tax revenues due to the Palestinian Authority.

On January 16, 2015, ICC prosecutor Fatou Bensouda announced that the ICC would open a "preliminary examination" into Israel's 2014 military offensive against Gaza, which killed over 2,100 Gazans, including 500 children. The Israeli government has stated that it will not cooperate with the investigation, and Israeli foreign minister Avigdor Lieberman has warned that Israel will now "act to dissolve the ICC." The US Department of State issued a statement saying that it "strongly" disagreed with the ICC prosecutor's decision, and promised to "continue to oppose actions against Israel at the ICC as counterproductive to the cause of peace."[55] There have also been calls from US senators to block $440 million of US aid to Palestine if it pursues criminal proceedings against Israelis at the ICC.[56]

In short, while the Obama administration's limited cooperation with the ICC may have improved the international image of the United States, it does not represent a genuine embrace of the Court and its mandate. Taken as a whole, Obama's actions show that the US is still committed to the double-standard that US enemies should be subject to the dictates of international law, while the United States and its allies should not.

6. Europe

Michael Busch

In the nearly four years since WikiLeaks began publishing its massive US embassy document trove, the importance of *Cablegate* has become impossible to dispute. Early reactions, especially in liberal circles and on the right, varied from outrage at a perceived breach of American security to skeptical shrugs doubting the importance *Cablegate* held for posterity. These views were premature. Today, the WikiLeaked cables have become indispensable primary sources for journalists, academics, and students of history and international relations. What were initially surprising revelations concerning the nature and practice of American foreign policy have since become firmly embedded in mainstream understandings of world affairs.

On the face of it, the European cables are a tame bunch. To be sure, there's plenty of headline-grabbing stuff peppered throughout the reports that initially caught the media's eye. American diplomats were unabashedly critical and catty in their assessments of European leaders and personalities. Former French president Nicolas Sarkozy, according to American dispatches, is impatient, hyperactive, "thin-skinned and authoritarian"[1] [11PARIS4357 and 09PARIS1638]. German chancellor Angela Merkel is described as being "risk-averse and rarely creative."[2] Italy's former prime minister Silvio Berlusconi received unusually rough treatment for being "feckless, vain and ineffective as a modern European leader," "physically and politically weak," and Vladimir Putin's "unconditional spokesman in Europe."[3] In light of *Cablegate*'s more sensationalist revelations, however, the embassy documents from Europe may at first blush appear banal.

Beyond the bits of gossip embedded throughout the European cables, this chapter makes the case that the documents published by WikiLeaks also contain groundbreaking disclosures that, while not fundamentally changing our sense of US imperialism, provide valuable and unique insights into the nature of American power. Of all the regions around the world, Europe stands alone as the place where Washington's interests are most readily embraced and understood. The European experience with colonialism and its shared commitment to defending and expanding the capitalist sphere of influence during the Cold War and afterwards have bound the region tightly to Washington, especially since the end of World War II.

But Europe is also where Washington's coercive influence enjoys the least currency. Even during its weakest moments, European power has prevented the United States from exploiting the region to the same degree as other parts of the world.

This chapter focuses on two issues on which European states have been least willing to cooperate with Washington, and that US diplomats clearly deem critical to the maintenance of American hegemonic order—trade and the war on terror. These two issues dominate huge numbers of the WikiLeaks cables sent from Europe, and offer a rough roadmap for understanding where points of cooperation, acquiescence, and opposition to US interests lie throughout the region. Examined through this lens, the textures and complexity of US-European relations in the twenty-first century begin to emerge. So too does a sense of the power and limitations of American imperialism in the Global North.

At the core of US-European relations lies the American alliance with Great Britain. Not surprisingly, the cables reveal deep and intimate ties binding Washington and the United Kingdom. From the Kissinger Cables to the most recent embassy reports published by WikiLeaks, British governments consistently prove willing partners in securing American interests abroad. During the Cold War, and then again during the war on terror, the cables make clear that, while the United States came to expect London's friendship and support, American officials did not view the relationship as one between equals. Indeed, US diplomats are frequently condescending in assessing their counterparts—an attitude sometimes encouraged by Great Britain's eagerness to please.

In a particularly startling case of British zeal for assuring American officials of their undying loyalty and support, British foreign minister William Hague, then a member of the opposition, tried to persuade US embassy personnel that a future Conservative government would abide by its commitment to bolstering the transatlantic partnership enjoyed by London and Washington, and remain firm in its respect for American hegemony:

```
Hague said he, David Cameron and George Osborne
were "children of Thatcher" and staunch
Atlanticists … For his part, said Hague, he has a
sister who is American, spends his own vacations
in America, and, like many similar to him,
considers America the "other country to turn to."
Asking his Senior Advisor her views, [Arminka]
Helic (who is Bosnian), said, "America is the
essential country." Hague said whoever enters
10 Downing Street as Prime Minister soon learns
of the essential nature of the relationship
with America. He added, "we want a pro-American
regime. We need it. The world needs it."
[08LONDON930]
```

But the world, or at least the rest of Europe, does not seem so sure. Dozens of documents from the *Cablegate* trove point to moments of tension and conflict between the United States and governments across the continent. The area in which American and European officials clash most regularly, according to the WikiLeaks cables, is trade. This does not come as a surprise. The question of corporate power in world affairs has long been subject to debate. Are the world's powerful multinational firms little more than extensions of state power, as some contend, subject to the control and limitations imposed upon them by the economic policies and institutions of their home country? Or have corporations been loosed from these constraints, allowing them greater autonomy from state control, and influence over the decision-making authority of government actors? The documents made public by *Cablegate* cannot claim to resolve this debate, but they do offer a startling look at the intimate connections between corporate interests and state action.

In the months following the first leaks of *Cablegate* documents, much was made of the revelation that State Department diplomats served as sales agents around the world for Boeing aircraft. Particularly, the focus centered on the lengths to which Washington was willing to go to ensure that foreign leaders would choose Boeing, which were greater than generally understood. The *New York Times* reported,[4] for example, that Washington was willing to negotiate upgrades to the private plane of King Abdullah of Saudi Arabia—who was weighing the purchase of forty-three Boeing 777 airliners—that would approximate the technology available on Air Force One [06RIYADH8234]. In the case of Turkey, American officials were asked to put a Turkish astronaut in orbit to ensure the purchase of twenty aircraft [10ANKARA74]. While it is not clear how Washington answered this demand, the deal was eventually sealed. And in the case of Bahrain, the *Times* revealed that State Department officials, including the American ambassador, applied a full-court press to all levels of the national airline company, and also intensively lobbied the royal family to prevent the purchase of Airbus jets from France—Washington's main competitor in airliner manufacturing—in favor of Boeing models from the United

States [08MANAMA47]. Despite the additional $400 million the Boeing offer demanded of the emirate, Bahrain was convinced to buy American.

The Boeing-Airbus rivalry was on the minds of US officials in Europe, as well. In one cable issued by the consulate in Munich following an internal shakeup of high-ranking corporate personnel at Airbus, American diplomats take delight in reporting on problems experienced by the European aircraft manufacturer and the schism between the company's Franco-German leadership. The cable notes that "senior German officials" at Airbus "told the consulate that [former French CEO of Airbus] Noel Forgeard's departure was necessary for [Airbus] to move beyond its current mess, and the Forgeard affair was but one example of the challenges of dealing with spotlight-seeking French partners." The cable goes on to suggest that "Airbus was facing a tough year in its competition with Boeing," and had "not expected the remarkable reliability of the twin-engine Boeing 777, which had pulled customers from the less-efficient four engine airbus" [06MUNICH437]. Underscoring the brutal nature of the cut-throat competition between Boeing and Airbus, one German embassy contact from the European multinational "pointedly said that a mid-ocean failure of both engines on a 777 would bring customers back to the A340" [06MUNICH437 (July 13, 2006, 12:41)].

The European cables demonstrate that the State Department did not focus its efforts exclusively on selling state-of-the-art Boeing aircraft, however. A document from Bulgaria shows that American diplomats were not above playing the role of used car salesmen in ensuring that Europe's peripheral states chose older-issue military planes manufactured in the United States over newer models made in Europe. The cable, dating from October 2007, was written following the decision by the Bulgarian Council of Ministers to "revise [the country's] 'Plan 2015' military modernization roadmap" [07SOFIA1271]. According to American officials, this provided "an important opportunity for the United

States to influence the development of Bulgarian military capabilities over the medium and long-term," and make some money along the way.

At heart, the dispatch suggests that Bulgaria's challenge lay in building the capacity to deploy and sustain its military forces abroad, specifically in service to American wars in the Middle East and Central Asia. "The overwhelming majority of its currently deployed 727 service members," the cable notes,

> are drawn from the Bulgarian Land Force's four maneuver battalions, virtually all of which have been transported and are sustained by the United States. These realities represent the most basic limitations to increased Bulgarian commitments to Iraq and Afghanistan. The highest priority should be placed on encouraging Bulgaria to invest in the equipment, vehicles and weapons that will enable them to deploy and fight interoperably with US and NATO forces overseas. [07SOFIA1271]

American diplomats had a solution to Bulgaria's limited deployment capacity at the ready, of course—the purchase of American-made transport aircraft. In particular, US embassy staff in Sofia urged Bulgarian officials to purchase Lockheed Martin C-27J planes, and counseled Washington to steer the EU's newest member state "away from the purchase of additional Russian fighters, which are currently an obstacle to Bulgaria's transformation to a more operationally and tactically flexible organization as expected by NATO" [07SOFIA1271].

The Russians were not the primary concern of American diplomats, though. Outbidding European military equipment manufacturers was the bigger worry: "Bulgaria has been under intense pressure from France to sign a massive ship procurement deal worth over one billion dollars," as well as deals from European powers offering state-of-the-art fighter planes.

The cable reports that the embassy planned to "advocate against new, very expensive systems such as the Eurofighter, Swedish Gripen, and Joint Strike Fighters in favor of very capable older versions of the F-16 or F-18 as a bridge and catalyst for operational and tactical transformation" [07SOFIA1271]. It appears that the purchases did not come to pass. The worsening economic situation across Europe blocked Bulgaria from purchasing the fighter jets, and any decisions with respect to future purchases have been put off until 2015, at the earliest.[5] Even this may be an optimistic prognosis, however. As *Forbes* recently reported, defense spending in Europe's eastern regions has suffered "outright collapse" since 2008, though recent actions by Russia in Ukraine and Crimea may stimulate the market for military goods.[6] Whatever happens, the cable notes, when the Bulgarians begin "eyeing new combat aircraft," America manufacturers "will, of course, be in this hunt."

THE CASE OF MONSANTO AND GMOS

Initial attention paid to the State Department's part in pushing industrial manufactures on its allies obscured the even bigger role it played in assuring a place for genetically modified agricultural products (GMOs) in a region that largely wanted nothing to do with them. The American campaign promoting biotech products was a worldwide effort. In all, some 1,000 documents from the *Cablegate* cache address this effort, a significant number of which originate in Europe.[7] US diplomats on the continent gave considerable attention to insuring the interests of American biotech firms in Europe—whether through "education" programs, government lobbying, or outright coercion—as well as to stripping down European Union regulations designed to act as a buffer against them. Available cables published by WikiLeaks suggest that the United States invests considerable time, effort, and expense in its operations on behalf of the American biotech firms, and for good reason.

Resistance to the advent of genetically modified foods has been pronounced across Europe. The continent features some of the strictest regulations governing the use and cultivation of GMO products, and public skepticism about biotech goods is quite high—a fact not lost on American diplomats. In a lengthy report dating from late 2007, a cable issued by the State Department outlined its "Biotechnology Outreach Strategy," which, among other things, recognized the European Union's "negative views on biology" and committed as a national priority to limiting them [07STATE160639]. More locally in the region, the troubles with convincing European publics of the value of biotechnologies are mentioned in numerous WikiLeaked cables. In Austria, US officials observed that there existed "absolutely no demand from consumers or producers" for genetically modified foodstuffs [08VIENNA211], whereas in Budapest diplomats reported back to Washington that people there exhibit unwillingness "to chang[e] their minds about the ban on biotech corn" even in the face of American attempts to "eventually wear down Hungary's resistance" [09BUDAPEST210]. Indeed, the only country clearly ready to follow Washington's lead on the use of genetically modified crops in Europe was the United Kingdom, which pledged to loosen its own GMO regulations. The British environment secretary made clear the government's position, arguing that criticisms of genetically modified products were "complete nonsense."[8]

According to cables published by WikiLeaks, the State Department's efforts on behalf of Monsanto and other biotech firms took a number of different forms in Europe. Washington looked to soften the market for GMOs through publicity campaigns designed to improve the image of agricultural biotech products around the world. The fanciest of these endeavors took place in Italy in 2005. A cable from the Milanese consulate describes American officials pulling out all the stops. At the invitation of US diplomats there, Bruce Chassy, an American scientist, toured the country and spoke at a series of high-profile meetings and public events, including a "First World Conference on the Future of Science" which "received extensive national and international media coverage and brought together a comprehensive group of about 700 representatives of the world's scientific, economic and political community." The cable reported great successes for its labors. Among other "results," the cable noted that "The September 15 weekly issue of *L'Espresso* ... the Italian version of *Newsweek* carried a four-page interview of Prof. Chassy. As noted by our Economic Office 'it was the first time that the center-left weekly *L'Espresso* had ever written a positive article on a US interest." In addition, the "Venetian daily *Il Gazzettino* published a four-column article titled "With GMOs, We Defend Nature" [05MILAN532].

Romania

American diplomats also furiously urged governments across Europe to comply with EU regulations promoting the use of GMOs in member states. One of the most elaborate lobbying campaigns undertaken by American officials targeted Romania, the newest member state (alongside Bulgaria) admitted to the European Union. In early 2005, Thomas Delare, chargé d'affaires at the US embassy in Bucharest, wrote to Washington about the possibility of using Romania as an eastern ally of agribusiness in the EU. "A unique case in the region, Romania is a pioneer in biotechnology," Delare wrote. "It cultivates and promotes genetically modified soy, prohibited in the EU. The objective of the embassy is to help Romania enter the EU with a well-developed biotechnology sector and an educated population which understands the merits of biotechnology." Delare argued that by "intensifying its efforts in Romania, the US will have a strong European ally, with common interests and beliefs in fighting against the anti-GMO position in the EU." Delare encouraged Washington to act fast. "This initiative is now critical as Romania counts down to EU membership, while pressure from anti-GMO groups builds. With this in mind, Post is proposing a broad public education campaign, in order to disseminate scientifically sound information about modern biotechnology through workshops and forums" [05BUCHAREST133_a].

These initial efforts did not pay off. By early 2006, the Romanian government had fallen in line with demands from Brussels that the EU hopeful restrict the cultivation of genetically modified soy, and indicated that it would move toward banning the GMO outright in an effort to ease passage into the European Union. The American ambassador, Nicholas Taubman, wrote Washington that the Romanian "Biotech Farmers Association, a local non-governmental organization established last fall with the assistance of the Embassy," was prepared to plant the genetically modified soy "anyway" in the event the government banned it, to "create a political and legal crisis" [06BUCHAREST574_a]. The crisis did not come to pass, and Romania banned the cultivation of modified soy in its territory. It was admitted to the EU in 2007.

US officials did not give up, however. American diplomats in Bucharest kept up the pressure on Romania, as did Washington when Monsanto's interests came under threat. In 2008, Romania considered banning Monsanto's MON810, a genetically modified corn seed allowed for cultivation by the European Union. A cable sent to Washington by Deputy Chief of Mission Mark Taplin describes Romania's move to enact a provisional safeguard clause to ban MON180 as a political ploy to "curry favor with the young, urban, liberal voting bloc during the upcoming election cycle." Taplin worries openly in the cable that the "heretofore pro-biotech Ministry of Agriculture is wavering," and notes that the ambassador will be pressuring government ministries "to make commercially and scientifically sound policy decisions" [08BUCHAREST112].

A few months later, the United States sent backup to support these operations. In August, Senator Richard Lugar arrived in Bucharest, where he met with various officials on the issue. A cable reports that "highlighting his experience as a farmer ...

Lugar ... encouraged Minister of the Environment Attila Korodi to permit the use of more advanced agricultural methods in Romania, including biotechnology ... such as GMO seeds" [08BUCHAREST717]. Korodi received Lugar's arguments coolly, telling the senator that his government was still assessing the safety of MON810, an attitude in keeping with his general approach to US diplomats. The cable notes that the post's relationship with Korodi "has occasionally been difficult, due in part to perceptions at the ministry" that Romania and the United States have "little in common on issues of biotechnology and climate change." Still, the cable reports that Korodi signaled he could be swayed on the issue of MON180, concluding: "Post will work to expand on these openings with the Ministry in the coming months."

The WikiLeaks archive shows that they followed up. In April of the following year, the State Department's senior advisor for biotechnology, Jack Bobo, visited Romania to meet with the new government that had recently taken power to advocate on behalf of Monsanto and "educate" officials in Bucharest on biotech issues more broadly. A cable documenting Bobo's activities in the country describes the adviser lecturing Romanian officials on their history, encouraging them to be strong advocates for looser biotech regulations in the European Union, and reminding them of the huge economic losses the state had suffered since banning the cultivation of genetically modified soy a few years earlier. The cable also mentions Romanian officials complaining of problems with weeds and corn root worms on farms around the country, troubles that could not be "addressed by MON810, but could be addressed by varieties commercially available in the US" [09BUCHAREST232_a]. Frighteningly, the Romanians told Bobo they looked forward to the introduction into local markets of Monsanto's Roundup Corn—a product that has been demonstrated to stimulate the evolution of chemically resistant "superweeds" around the world.[9]

In 2013, American lobbying delivered a legislative win in

Romania for Monsanto. A bill that had been introduced by opposition politicians in 2010 proposing an all-encompassing ban on GMO products in Romania was resoundingly defeated by the same party, now in power, that had originally introduced it. Media analysts chalked the final vote tally up to American pressure and the economic interests of biotech firms. As one report reminded readers, "The stakes are high. Monsanto has invested around $150 million in its Romanian seed production units and is planning to spend another $40 million on its facility in Sinesti, Ialomita County, over the next two years."[10]

Poland

State Department officials also ran into trouble in Poland when attempting to convince government representatives there of biotech's many wonders. A notable dispatch from Warsaw in 2006 [06WARSAW1142] describes a difficult set of meetings between the State Department senior advisor for agricultural biotechnology, Madelyn Spirnak, and a variety of Polish government representatives. In one conversation with Polish parliamentarians,

```
Spirnak discussed the increased yield and
efficiencies gained through planting GM seed,
the need for a no trade barrier approach to GM
products, and the myths surrounding the dangers
of GMOs. The Senators were quick to refute
her arguments and pointed out that [Poland's]
negative stance on biotech is based on economic
and safety concerns. They first mentioned that
Poland does not have a food shortage and thus
does not need to produce more food … GMOs are
simply not of use to Polish farmers given current
realities in Poland. [The two senators] also
stated that [the government], as well as Polish
society, is not convinced of the safety of GMOs,
```

and is not ready to accept the notion without
well-crafted scientific studies. The Senators
also stated that thousands of agricultural
workers would lose their jobs if GM foods were
introduced and that no other sector of the Polish
economy could absorb them … thus canceling out
the potential efficiency gains from harvesting GM
products.

Conversation then turned to newly enacted
Polish legislation banning GMO seed sales
and registration in Poland. Spirnak asked the
Senators how the [Polish government] would
react if the legislation were to conflict with
existing EU and WTO regulations. Answering with
a question, Chroscikowski [one of the senators]
wondered aloud why the US is so concerned with
Poland's EU relations.

Later that day, Spirnak lunched with other Polish government representatives and "attempted to discuss the benefits that had been gained globally through GMO crops as well as the growing number of EU countries which were adopting the technology" [06WARSAW1142]. Things did not go well. As the cable reports, "In response, the parliamentarians gave unsophisticated arguments such as: US women are heavy because they eat GMO food; organic is 'healthy' because it is natural; confusing fertilizers with pesticides; and most importantly, nationalistic arguments about US and multinational companies coming to Poland and destroying the Polish farming system" [06WARSAW1142].

In the face of Poland's parliamentary resistance to the use of genetically modified agricultural products, Spirnak resorted to subtle threats, making clear to Polish officials that any regulations enacted by the government "that go beyond the stringent EU regulatory system could be harmful to joint US-Polish trade interests as well as US-EU relations on this sensitive issue" [06WARSAW1142]. In early 2013, Poland, apparently having decided to take its chances, banned the cultivation of certain GM strains of corn and potato, including Monsanto's MON810, even after the European Commission had given the go-ahead for their use throughout the EU.[11] Later that year, the European Commission hauled the Polish government in front of the European Court of Justice on charges that Poland had failed to comply properly with EU regulations governing the use of GMOs. The case was still pending at the time of publication.[12]

France

When soft-power approaches and intimidation tactics failed to yield the desired results, American diplomats considered applying more coercive tools of statecraft. After France moved to ban MON810 in 2007 following studies that concluded the crops threatened the environment, Craig Stapleton, former ambassador to France, counseled launching a trade war across Europe. "This is not just a bilateral concern," Stapleton wrote. "France will play a leading role in renewed European consideration of the acceptance of agricultural biotechnology and its approach toward environmental regulation more generally ... Our contacts have made clear that they will seek to expand French national policy to a EU-wide level and they believe that they are in the vanguard of European public opinion in turning back GMO's [sic]" [07PARIS4723_a]. Therefore, Stapleton wrote,

```
Country team Paris recommends that we calibrate
a target retaliation list that causes some
pain across the EU since this is a collective
responsibility, but that also focuses in part on
the worst culprits. The list should be measured
rather than vicious and must be sustainable over
the long term, since we should not expect an
```

```
early victory. Moving to retaliation will make
clear that the current path has real costs to EU
interests and could help strengthen European pro-
biotech voices. [07PARIS4723_a]
```

As it turned out, an all-out trade war was not necessary to ensure American interests. In mid 2013, the French high court annulled the country's ban on MON810 following the European Food Safety Authority's findings that France had banned the product in the absence of compelling evidence of its deleterious effects on the environment. And as in the case of Poland, the court found France in violation of EU law regarding GMO governance.[13]

Alongside promotion of the American biotechnology industry, the US war on terror features prominently in the *Cablegate* documents as a regular flashpoint between Washington and its European allies. The unwillingness of most European states to go along with the program reflected the extent to which European publics rejected the aims of American intervention in Iraq, not to mention the deep unease with which European governments viewed the methods and legality of US actions in both Afghanistan and the Middle East. If Europe had been broadly supportive of US actions following the attacks of September 11, 2011, the use of extraordinary rendition, torture, and Guantánamo Bay as tools for combating Islamic fundamentalism was a bridge too far for the major continental powers. When Washington made clear its plan to bring its war to Saddam Hussein, the stage was set in Europe for a regional diplomatic crisis.[14]

American arrogance in the face of European opposition to US intentions for Iraq exacerbated the situation. In the months before the American invasion of Iraq in 2003, French and German officials were particularly outspoken about the need to avoid war at all costs. Asked about this resistance to American designs on Baghdad, then secretary of state Donald Rumsfeld told reporters: "Germany has been a problem, and France has been a problem. But you look at vast numbers of other countries in Europe. They're not with France and Germany on this, they're with the United States."[15] Rumsfeld's divisive rhetoric soiled American relations with western Europe, and put eastern European states in the unenviable position of appearing to be Washington's lackeys on the continent's periphery. These strained relations are reflected consistently in the reporting of US diplomats stationed in Europe, and clearly complicated Washington's efforts to secure its interests on the continent and beyond. Long gone were the days immediately following September 11, when even the French proclaimed *"Nous sommes tous Américains."*[16]

US diplomats on the continent encountered a variety of problems related to Washington's prosecution of its wars abroad. Some of the episodes related in the cables are relatively minor, yet troubling. In Berlin, for example, US diplomats were confronted by angry German officials who were upset with Washington's financial malfeasance. In early February 2010, Berlin filed a demarche with NATO ambassador Ivo Daalder complaining that the United States was mishandling German contributions to the ANA Trust Fund and taking a cut from donations for itself. According to a cable sent by the US mission to NATO, German ambassador Ulrich Brandenburg contacted Daalder regarding a €50 million donation to the ANA Trust Fund in October 2009: "According to Brandenburg, this money had been earmarked for use in several specific projects—the ANS Logistics School in Kabul, an engineering school in Mazar-e Sharif, and an ANA Barracks in Feyzabad—but so far no money had been disbursed for these projects. He argued, for example, that construction of the logistics school had come to a halt" [10NATO052].

What really rankled the Germans, however, was the fact that not only were the Americans dragging their feet on disbursing the money, but also taxing the contributions, to boot. The cable relays German concerns "about a 15 percent administrative fee allegedly being charged by the US Army Corps of Engineers" on all donations to the fund. "Brandenburg said that this was more than a technical budget and project management issue," and that while the German Bundestag was willing to make future payments into the fund, "parliamentary questions and concerns about how the initial 50 million euro contribution was being handled could make this increasingly difficult."

In Daalder's view, the Germans had a point. "While there may be good reasons for the 15 percent fee—we understand it is a contingency fee not an administrative one," he wrote to Washington. "[T]he appearance that the US is charging Allies an excessive fee for the use of monies they have donated to the ANA Trust Fund may be difficult to explain away during a parliamentary debate ... We therefore urge Washington to look into this issue from a political, as well as a technical/financial, dimension and with as much transparency as possible." Despite Daalder's plea, the issue was not resolved in Berlin's favor. *Der Spiegel* reported that American officials claimed their hands were tied in overseeing the procurement and administration of funds in the ANA trust: "There was, however, at least one gesture of goodwill," the newspaper reported. "The Americans wired €3 million back to the Bundeswehr."[17]

Some cables reflected more serious concerns. In these situations, the *Cablegate* files reveal American diplomats were concerned where possible with frustrating European concerns about justice and accountability in the war on terror, while keeping the public in the dark. This was most clearly the case concerning the longstanding issues at the heart of the war on terror, such as Washington's worldwide program of extraordinary rendition. In late 2005, the BBC's *Newsnight* reported that Ireland's Shannon Airport was possibly serving as a pit stop for CIA-chartered aircraft rendering suspected terrorists to so-called black sites for interrogation and torture. Public outrage throughout Ireland flared, especially in Shannon. The airport continued to be a focal point of protest[18] following the American invasions of Afghanistan and Iraq, when it was revealed that the US military had used Shannon as a transit point for the US military aircraft making their way to and from the battlefields. For many Irish activists and politicians, American operations funneled through the airport constituted a violation of Irish neutrality in Iraq. A cable from 2004, however, reports that, in the face of this public dissent, "the state of US-Irish relations remains as strong as ever. Ireland continues to allow the US military to refuel at Shannon airport" [04DUBLIN867].

The BBC report changed all that. A 2010 cable notes that "in late 2005/early 2006, EU-wide debate on extraordinary renditions similarly galvanized" those members of the public opposed to the war "to question US military access to the airport." The cable goes on to suggest with some annoyance that public dissent had pushed the Irish government to "place limits on certain forms of US transits at Shannon," including the requirement that the American military clear all cargo transiting through the airport, including "non-lethal military articles ... Indications of this trend to constrain US operations at Shannon," the cable continues, "first arose ... in late 2005," when the "DFA informally denied a DHS deportation transit through Shannon of convicted foreign national from the United States out of apparent concern that the public would misread the transit as a rendition" [06DUBLIN1020].

Still, it could have been worse for the Americans:

```
Ambassador Foley thanked Ahern for his staunch
rejection of the Irish Human Rights Commission's
(IHRC) demand that the Irish Government inspect
aircraft landing in Ireland that are alleged to
have been involved in so-called extraordinary
rendition flights. Ahern declared that the IHRC
report contained no new information, but warned
that opposition parties Fine Gael and Labour
could be expected to continue to raise the issue
from time to time in efforts to politically
```

```
embarrass the Fianna Fail-run Government. Ahern
said that several alleged rendition flights had
been inspected during the past year and fully
cleared; the last flight, he wryly noted, was
carrying six touring golfers. [07DUBLIN916_a]
```

If the officials shared a laugh, it was short lived. Ahern told Foley that he "had 'put his neck on the chopping block' and would pay a severe political price if it ever turned out that rendition flights had entered Ireland or if one was discovered in the future." Ahern suggested to the Americans that routine searches of aircraft passing through the Shannon airport would serve both governments well "and provide cover if a rendition ever surfaced." Ahern, the cable notes,

```
seemed quite convinced that at least three
flights involving renditions had refueled at
Shannon Airport before or after conducting
rendition flights … While Ahern's public stance
on extraordinary renditions is rock-solid, his
musings during the meeting seem less assured.
This was the only issue during the meeting that
agitated him; he spent considerable time dwelling
on it. Ahern seemed to be fishing for renewed
assurances from the Ambassador that no rendition
flights have transited Ireland, or would transit
in the future. [07DUBLIN916_a]
```

The Americans could give Ahern no such assurances. In fact, rendition flights had transited through Shannon. One case, documented by Amnesty International, involved Binyam Mohammad, who had been detained in Pakistan and rendered to Morocco in 2002, and then later to Guantánamo Bay in 2004, where he was allegedly tortured. According to Amnesty, "The plane used to render him to Morocco in 2002 returned to the USA via Shannon, and the plane that rendered him from Morocco to Afghanistan in 2004 transited Shannon" on the way back.

State Department troubles with Europe were not limited to what transpired on European soil. In March 2005, an Italian intelligence officer was gunned down in Baghdad at a US security checkpoint. Though it was never clear what had led to Nicola Calipari's murder, Washington and Rome had differing accounts of what transpired. US officials were displeased by the findings of an Italian investigation into the killing, according to a cable from May that year, though they were reassured by politicians in Rome that the government there had no intention of acting on its conclusions:

> The Italians stressed that the GOI wanted to put
> the incident behind us, that it would not damage
> our strong friendship and alliance, and that
> it would not affect the Italian commitment in
> Iraq. The Italians said that while US cooperation
> with Italy in the joint investigation had been
> total and thoroughly professional, Italy had
> to stand by the Italian reconstruction of the
> March 4 incident. The Italian report, they said,
> concluded that the shooting was not intentional
> and that no individual responsibility could
> be assigned for the shooting, thus making
> the magistrate's criminal investigation less
> likely to develop into a full criminal case.
> [05ROME1506_a]

The cable goes on to note:

> While the Italian report quibbles with many
> findings and much of the methodology of the US
> AR 15-6 report on the incident, we will be best

```
served by resisting the temptation to attack
the Italian version point-by-point, and should
instead continue to let our report speak for
itself. While our instinct at Post is to defend
the US report and criticize the Italian one, we
realize the consequences of doing so could be
asymmetrical: while the criticism in the Italian
report is unlikely to have serious negative
consequences for the USG, if the GOI appears
to be disloyal to its public servants—or to be
rolling over to please the USG in this matter,
the consequences for Berlusconi's government and
Italy's commitment in Iraq could be severe.
```

Roughly a week later, a second cable reiterated this position, noting: "[W]e continue to urge Washington to discourage USG spokespeople from point-by-point refutation of the Italian report or Berlusconi's remarks. As much as possible, we should allow our report to speak for itself on our view of the incident. This will hasten the fading of the case from the political radar screen" [05ROME1593_a]. It did not. In 2007, an Italian judge ordered the American soldier responsible for Calipari's death to be tried on murder charges in Italy. Later that year, however, an Italian court threw out the case, arguing that it had no jurisdiction over the matter. Said the woman who had been in the car with Calipari when he was shot, "We've given up trying to find the truth about what happened to Nicola Calipari. The arrogance of America, which never wanted this trial, has won."[19]

The strong line held by Washington in such matters was not indicative of unflappable State Department confidence. Far from it. US diplomatic fears crop up in numerous cables, and are most pronounced in those relating to the case of Khaled El-Masri, a German national who was abducted while on vacation by security forces in Macedonia on New Year's Eve 2003. El-Masri was turned over by the Macedonians—who mistook him for a known al-Qaeda operative with the same name—to the CIA, which purportedly flew him to Afghanistan, where he was imprisoned and tortured. As El-Masri later wrote in the *Los Angeles Times*,

I was detained incommunicado for more than three
weeks. Then I was handed over to the American
Central Intelligence Agency and was stripped,
severely beaten, shackled, dressed in a diaper,
injected with drugs, chained to the floor of
a plane and flown to Afghanistan, where I was
imprisoned in a foul dungeon for more than four
months. Long after the American government
realized that I was an entirely innocent man, I
was blindfolded, put back on a plane, flown to
Europe and left on a hilltop in Albania—without
any explanation or apology for the nightmare that
I had endured.[20]

The United States would later chalk up El-Masri's suffering to a simple case of mistaken identity. Behind the scenes, however, American officials worked diligently to ensure that the CIA officers involved in El-Masri's rendition were kept shielded from European justice. In particular, they were concerned with the German judiciary's intention to arrest and prosecute thirteen CIA operatives involved with the case. In a cable dating from February 2, 2007, the Munich consulate reported back to Washington:

The Office of the Munich Prosecutor announced
January 31 the issuance of 13 arrest warrants
for the alleged kidnappers of Khaled El-Masri
… The Munich prosecutor's office told [the]
Consul General [of] Munich that there had been
intense media pressure to act and that they
will seek an international arrest warrant. The
[deputy chief of mission] spoke with State

```
Secretary Boomgaarden who said the German Federal
Government had not been warned in advance of
the arrest warrants. Boomgaarden called the
prosecutor's action "premature" in his personal
view. The Bavarian Chancellery called … to say it
was surprised and displeased by the prosecutor's
actions. [07BERLIN200]
```

The cable notes that the arrest warrants could not be issued without the permission of the Ministry of Foreign Affairs or the Ministry of Justice, and that the mission had been assured by State Secretary Boomgaarden that the former would "weigh foreign policy implications if the Munich prosecutor seeks an international arrest warrant. He stressed the need to stay in close contact with the USG as this situation unfolded" [07BERLIN200].

Meanwhile, in Madrid, American officials were writing back to Washington with news that the Spanish media were reporting connections between German actions in the El-Masri case and the Spanish military. On February 1, 2007, the American embassy issued a cable reporting on a Spanish judge's attempts to have secret government records declassified to determine Spanish complicity in US rendition operations on the continent. The judge, Ismael Moreno, asked his government

```
for a report on "whether Spanish airports were
used in the alleged events described in Council
of Europe Report 10957 of June 12, 2006" related
to the detentions of twelve alleged terrorists
… Judge Moreno denied motions by the plaintiffs
demanding that the 13 US persons accused by the
plaintiffs of abduction and torture be formally
named as suspects … He also denied a plaintiff's
motion requiring the testimony in the case of CNI
Director Alberto Saiz as well as his predecessor
Jorge Dezcallar (brother of MFA director general
```

for foreign policy Rafael Dezcallar). This
request by the plaintiffs stems from a November
28, 2001 meeting between President Bush and then-
President Aznar, after which Aznar reportedly
declared that "all of the mechanisms for
cooperation in intelligence operations" were in
place. Shortly thereafter, on December 11, the
first alleged CIA flight through Spanish territory
took place. [07MADRID173_a]

Curiously, American diplomats were not as worried about the
details of the Spanish case as they were that there appeared to be

coordination between Judge Moreno in Spain
and German investigators in the El Masri case.
Spanish media reported January 31 and February
1 that German investigators used information
from Spanish news sources and from the Spanish
Civil Guard in ordering the detention of thirteen
"CIA members" on charges of abduction and bodily
harm. The plaintiffs and extreme left political
parties will work together to keep this issue on
the front burner in Spain … The most worrisome
element of this episode is the joint timing of
the announcements by the German prosecutors and
Examining Magistrate in the Spanish CIA flights
investigation, timing that suggests that they
are coordinating to advance the cases in their
respective jurisdictions. This coordination
among independent investigators will complicate
our efforts to manage this case at a discreet
government-to-government level. [07MADRID173_a]

Back in Germany, a cable dated February 6, 2007, reports that
that day the deputy chief of mission John Koenig had met with

German deputy national security advisor Rolf Nikel to express Washington's

> strong concerns about the possible issuance of
> international arrest warrants in the al-Masri
> case. The DCM noted that the reports in the
> German media of the discussion on the issue
> between the Secretary and FM Steinmeier in
> Washington were not accurate, in that the
> media reports suggest the USG was not troubled
> by developments in the al-Masri case. The
> DCM emphasized that this was not the case and
> that issuance of international arrest warrants
> would have a negative impact on our bilateral
> relationship. [07BERLIN242]

Though the cable takes pains to make clear that the embassy's "intention was not to threaten Germany," it is hard to see how the American position could be interpreted in any other way. Koenig told German deputy national security advisor Rolf Nikel that Berlin ought to "weigh carefully at every step of the way the implications for relations with the US." Koenig also reminded Nikel that, while Washington respected the independent authority of the German courts, "a decision to issue international arrest warrants or extradition requests would require the concurrence of the German Federal Government, specifically the MFA and the Ministry of Justice."

What follows, however, betrays the panic behind Koenig's tough-guy tactics. While American authorities had previously assumed that "German federal authorities would not allow the warrants to be issued," Koenig confided to Nikel that "subsequent contacts led us to believe this was not the case." To his credit, Nikel did little to assuage Koenig's concerns. The cable reports that he "underscored the independence of the German judiciary ... From a judicial standpoint, the facts are clear, and

the Munich prosecutor has acted correctly." While Nikel conceded that "Germany would have to examine the implications
for relations with the US ... he noted our political differences
about how the global war on terrorism should be waged, for
example on the appropriateness of the Guantánamo facility
and the alleged use of renditions." Despite all this, it seems that
Washington ultimately got its way. Germany did not press for
the extradition of any Americans involved with the El-Masri
case. And while the European Court of Justice ruled in late 2012
that El-Masri had been tortured by the CIA while in detention,
it directed blame at Macedonia. The court ruled that the country
had violated the European Convention on Human Rights
and ordered Macedonia to pay out damages in the amount of
$78,000.[20]

El-Masri's case was not unique. In 2003, Abu Omar—a
radical cleric in Milan, Italy—was openly abducted by the CIA
and Italian intelligence figures, then, according to *Der Spiegel*,
"flown from Italy to Egypt via Germany. There, Omar claims
he was brutally mistreated by Egyptian intelligence officers."[21] A
few years later, following revelations on Omar's case, an Italian
high court brought charges against twenty-three CIA officers in
connection with Omar's rendition and torture. The case became
a matter of priority for American officials, who brought their
displeasure directly to the attention of the Italian government.
As early as 2006, when the court's intentions had become clear,
Ronald Spogli, then ambassador to Italy, made clear to the
under secretary to the prime minister, Gianni Letta, that the
fate of the US spies would have a direct impact on US-Italian
relations.

The trial of the twenty-three spooks went forward despite
American objections, and became the subject of the highest levels
of bilateral discussions between Washington and Rome. In 2010,
then secretary of defense Robert Gates met with Italian prime
minister Silvio Berlusconi to discuss a broad agenda of security
issues important to both countries. Before closing, Gates brought

up the Abu Omar case with Berlusconi, and pressed the Italian leader to keep American personnel involved with Omar's rendition safe from Italian justice. A WikiLeaked cable reports that Gates

> asked Berlusconi for his assistance in affirming
> US jurisdiction over Colonel Romano, one of
> the defendants in the Abu Omar case, under
> the NATO SOFA. Berlusconi and Cabinet Advisor
> Letta assured SecDef the GOI was working hard
> to resolve the situation. Berlusconi gave
> an extended rant about the Italian judicial
> system—which frequently targets him since it is
> "dominated by leftists," at the public prosecutor
> level. Berusconi predicted that the "courts will
> come down in our favour" upon appeal, noting that
> higher-level appellate courts are significantly
> less politicized than local courts. [10ROME174]

Gates also pressed his case with Italian defense minister Ignazio La Russa, thanking La Russa

> for his efforts to have the Italian Minister
> of Justice send letters to relevant judicial
> authorities affirming US jurisdiction over Colonel
> Romano … La Russa advised the US to be more
> present in the appeals process and not leave it
> solely to the Italian government to make the case
> for recognition of US jurisdiction. He noted that
> the assertion of jurisdiction late in the trial
> had given prosecutors a chance to politicize
> the issue. SecDef reminded La Russa that the US
> decision not to immediately assert jurisdiction
> was made at the advice of GOI and has not served
> US interests well. [10ROME172]

Berlusconi and his government's assurance aside, the court in Milan pressed ahead with its prosecution of the Americans involved in Omar's case. In 2009, the Milanese court convicted twenty of the Americans accused of illegal rendition and sentenced them in absentia. Three of the Americans, including the CIA station chief in Rome, were granted diplomatic immunity and acquitted of charges against them. Four years later, an appeals court overturned that acquittal and sentenced the three Americans in question to jail time. It also sentenced Italy's military intelligence chief to ten years in prison for his part in the Omar fiasco.[22] The twenty-three Americans all remain free, thanks to successful efforts by the Bush and Obama administrations to rebuff extradition requests from Italian courts.

Even as the United States avoided responsibility for the Omar and El-Masri affairs, its dealings with European courts continued. For the next several years, American diplomats in Madrid collaborated with members of the Spanish judiciary and government to prevent cases targeting US officials and military personnel from being prosecuted. Among other incidents reported in the cables, US officials succeeded in getting the Spanish government to throw out an investigation into the murder of a Spanish journalist killed in Iraq by American soldiers, and leaned heavily on Madrid to bury an investigation into the so-called "Bush Six"— which includes Alberto Gonzales, Jay Bybee, Douglas Feith, and John Yoo—for their role as the architects of a legal system that justified American practices of torture and other crimes in the war on terror. As late as 2009, the Obama administration was continuing to threaten and cajole Spanish authorities to make the case go away [09MADRID392].

The White House went as far as to send former Republican Party chairman Mel Martínez to Madrid, where he reminded the Foreign Ministry there that if the government allowed the case to move forward it would "have an enormous impact on the bilateral relationship." Why the Obama administration would be so concerned with the fate of the Bush Six is made plain in one cable dating from April 1, 2009: "The fact that this complaint targets former Administration legal officials may reflect a 'stepping-stone' strategy designed to pave the way for complaints against even more senior officials"—a frightening precedent for any state executive [09MADRID347]. The cable comments that the Spanish government, "whatever its disagreements with the Bush Administration, will find this case inconvenient ... That said, we do not know if the government would be willing to take the risky step of trying behind the scenes to influence the prosecutor's recommendation on this case or what their reaction would be." As of January 2015, the case is still making its way, albeit slowly, through the Spanish system.

American officials were especially concerned by the role played in this case and others by investigating magistrate Baltazar Garzón, who had achieved fame in the 1980s by issuing arrest warrants for Augusto Pinochet. Garzón was dogged in pursuing the United States, as well, for misdeeds in the war on terror. He clearly scared the State Department. According to one cable, Garzón "clearly has an anti-American streak (as evidenced by occasional scathing editorials in the Spanish press criticizing Guantánamo and aspects of what he calls the 'US-led war on terror'), and we are certainly under no illusions about the individual with whom we are dealing" [07MADRID2282]. Garzón pursued a number of different investigations against the United States even as he was coming under fire from within his own government for looking into crimes committed by Spanish authorities under the Franco regime. Washington was concerned that, were Garzón pushed out of the judiciary, he would not go quietly: "We also fear Garzon—far from being deterred by threats of disciplinary action—may welcome the chance for martyrdom, knowing the case will attract worldwide attention" [09MADRID440]. Garzón was finally removed from the bench in 2010, and in 2012 a Spanish court convicted him of improper conduct in another investigation. Later that year, Garzón agreed to serve as lead defense attorney for Julian Assange in the WikiLeaks founder's asylum case in Great Britain.[23]

Visiting Brussels during the 2014 crisis in Ukraine, President Obama gave a speech rallying his European allies to stand up to Russian aggression in Crimea. In his remarks, Obama conceded: "neither the United States nor Europe are perfect in adherence to our ideals. Nor do we claim to be the sole arbiter of what is right or wrong in the world." He continued, "We are human, after all, and we face difficult decisions about how to exercise our power. But part of what makes us different is that we welcome criticism, just as we welcome the responsibilities that come with global leadership."

The WikiLeaks cables demonstrate quite the opposite. In the documents pertaining to the war on terror, particularly, US diplomats strive to tamp down dissent from European governments critical of American actions, and seek wherever possible to evade accountability when Washington's behavior is clearly in breach of international law. Behind closed doors, State Department personnel use both carrots and the threat of sticks, according to the cables, to ensure that their European allies come to heel. The expectation is unmistakable—whenever powerful groups or individuals on the continent challenge Washington's authority to prosecute its war on terror with impunity, European governments are to make the problems go away or suffer serious damages in their bilateral relationships with the United States. For the most part, as a long parade of cables suggests, they fall in line.

American diplomats are similarly averse to respecting the opinions of foreign publics when they cut against the interests of American multinationals. Indeed, US insistence that Europe's opposition to GMOs is simply the product of their own ignorance suggests that the civilizing mission of colonial projects is alive and well in the era of American imperialism—even with regard to the former colonial powers in Europe. *Cablegate*'s documents consistently suggest that European publics lack the proper information and understanding that would allow them to make beneficial decisions for themselves. Washington, therefore, is tasked with the responsibility of leading them to higher states of awareness. When these efforts prove unproductive, however, US diplomats do not hesitate, from what is gathered in the cables, to consider applying a heavier hand. Just as the war on terror eschewed the strictures of international law, so too are American diplomats dismissive of European sovereignty when it comes to ensuring the interests of corporate power.

Yet for all this, American power on the continent is not without limits; American diplomats are not without their fears. The coercive successes of American hegemony outlined in this chapter are impossible to deny, to be sure, but they also reflect the power of people to resist the egregious excesses of imperial manipulation. The stiff resistance in Europe to genetically modified food, despite considerable investments of money and time, is one example of this resilience. The continuing pressure on the continent to hold Americans accountable for crimes committed in the name of the war on terror—and the anxieties it provokes in US officials—is another example of this strength. Indeed, the true value of the cable cache published by WikiLeaks is not its enormous size, or even its most explosive revelations. Instead, *Cablegate* is remarkable for revealing the internal machinery of US foreign policy, Washington's myriad messy entanglements, and—most vitally—those points of contact where challenges to American imperial interests are most effective.

7. Russia

Russ Wellen

Among the most significant cables that WikiLeaks divulged to the world are those obtained from the US embassy and its consulates in Russia. Covering the period from 2002 to 2010, they afford a peek under the hood of US-Russian relations during much of the first decade of the new millennium. Though tensions never reached a red line, as during the Cold War, conflicts were legion. For instance, the United States objected to Russia's rollback of democratic reforms: circumscribing journalists, murdering dissidents, and seizing radio stations, as well as Vladimir Putin's plan to abolish the election of governors and instead empower the Kremlin to appoint them.

Russia, meanwhile, objected to Nato's granting of membership to countries of the former Eastern Bloc—Bulgaria, Romania, Slovakia, and Slovenia, as well as the three Baltic states. After all, Mikhail Gorbachev believed that, in exchange for Russia accepting the reunification of Germany, NATO would not expand to the east, which would pose a geopolitical threat to Russia and lessen its sphere of influence. Nor was Russia pleased when President George W. Bush withdrew the United States from the Anti-Ballistic Missile Treaty to continue development of a US missile defense system, including deployment in the former Eastern Bloc territories of Poland and the Czech Republic. Add American support for the Rose Revolution in Georgia and the Orange Revolution in Ukraine, and one cannot help but understand Russian resistance to moves by the United States and NATO.[1]

Numerous cables will be explored that shed light on some of these issues, as well as satellite surveillance and nuclear-weapons treaties. First, though, we will briefly revisit the more sensational cables that gained notoriety when Western commentators zeroed in on them at the time of the leak. It is no surprise that they cast Russia in a bad light and failed to reflect Russian objections to United States policy.

Among these was a cable titled "Medvedev's Address and Tandem Politics." Classified by deputy chief of mission at the US embassy in Moscow, Eric Rubin, it is a summary of the opinions by contacts of the embassy eight months after Medvedev had been elected president. Some, it reads, argue that "Medvedev continues to play Robin to Putin's Batman, surrounded by a team loyal to the Premier and checked by Putin's dominance over the legislature and regional elites" [08MOSCOW3343]. (Though the office was dissolved along with the Soviet Union, the term "Premier" is sometimes interchangeable with "prime minister," Putin's office at the time.)

Another cable reflecting poorly on Russia, titled "SecDef Gates's Meeting With French Minister of Defense Herve Morin," was classified by Alexander Vershbow, the assistant secretary of defense for international security affairs (mostly NATO). On that occasion, Gates sought to convince Morin to refrain from selling an amphibious assault ship to Russia—a plan to which other NATO states, as well as Georgia, also objected. The cable reads: "Some allies, because of their past experiences, are still very concerned with Russia and are not sure how much to trust the West. SecDef [Gates] observed that Russian democracy has disappeared and the government was an oligarchy run by the security services"[10PARIS170].

A cable titled "Questioning Putin's Work Ethic" is sharply critical of Putin, though arguably of little more than prurient interest. Classified by the ambassador to Russia, John Beyrle, it presented the insights of two native Russia watchers. New Economic School director Sergey Guriev said Putin had been "distracted" and "disinterested," and the general director of the center for political information, Aleksey Mukhin, said, "the day-to-day operations of government [are] in the hands of the 'actual Prime Minister,'" by which he meant First Deputy Prime Minister Igor Shuvalov.

Though a poll showed that "most Russians continue to see Putin as 'running' the country … Eurasia Foundation Director Andrey Kortunov told us it is well known that Putin did not like coming to the Russian White House, where he was confronted with stacks of papers on issues of minuscule importance, on which he did not want to expend his energy" [09MOSCOW532].

Also attracting significant attention were those cables in which the embassy reported on how incorrigible it viewed corruption in Russia to be. A cable filed by Beyrle titled "The Luzkhov Dilemma" described Moscow and its mayor, Yury Luzkhov, who was soon to be dismissed from the post he had held since 1992, as his corruption had become too blatant even for the Kremlin. "Analysts identify a three-tiered structure in Moscow's criminal world," the cable reads, in which criminal elements "enjoy a 'krysha' (a term from the criminal/mafia world literally meaning 'roof' or protection) that runs through the police, the Federal Security Service (FSB), Ministry of Internal Affairs (MVD), and the prosecutor's office, as well as throughout the Moscow city government bureaucracy." To be more specific: "Luzhkov is at the top. The FSB, MVD, and militia are at the second level. Finally, ordinary criminals and corrupt inspectors are at the lowest level. This is an inefficient system in which criminal groups fill a void in some areas because the city is not providing some services" [10MOSCOW317].

The last cable that I will single out for attracting media attention is titled "Litvinenko Assassination: Reaction in Moscow." Classified by Ambassador William Burns, it itemized the various theories about the November 2006 poisoning death of former

FSB officer Alexander Litvinenko in London. In 1998, Litvinenko was one of a group of FSB officers who accused their superiors of attempting to assassinate Russian oligarch Boris Berezovsky in Great Britain, where he had been granted asylum. Litvinenko had also written a book in which he accused the FSB of staging the Russian apartment bombings in 1999 that killed almost 300 people, as well as other acts of terrorism, in order to secure Vladimir Putin's election.

The theories cited in the cable are all over the map, alternately blaming Putin and attempting to discredit him. For example, linking the murder of Litvinenko with that of journalist Anna Politkovskaya, a staunch opponent of Putin and his pursuit of the Second Chechen War, may have been only natural. But the rationale, as laid out by Aleksey Venediktov, the head of an independent radio station, was anything but. The cable reads:

> In his telling, both murders, with perhaps more
> to come, are part of an effort to force Putin
> to remain in office beyond 2008 by, in effect,
> making him persona non grata in the West. (Putin
> has repeatedly insisted he will leave when
> his term expires in 2008.) … Venediktov pegged
> the two assassinations to rogue or retired FSB
> or military intelligence agents controlled by
> forces either within or without the Kremlin.
> Putin, Venediktov thought, is well aware of
> the game being played, but is powerless to stop
> it; in part because he is not certain whom to
> hold responsible. Venediktov subscribed to the
> generally-held view here that Putin values his
> reputation in the West, and that sabotaging it is
> one path to having him reconsider his decision to
> leave the Kremlin in 2008. [06MOSCOW12751]

Apparently, the agents thought it would be beneficial to the FSB to keep in office a former lieutenant colonel of its predecessor, the KGB. Implicated in Litvinenko's death, Putin would seek to redeem his reputation. In the event, the cable reads, "the Carnegie Moscow Center's Masha Lipman cautioned against falling prey to conspiracy theories." She noted that recent violence may partly have reflected a sense, "at least in the Kremlin, that Putin no longer is fully in control as his power wanes with the approaching end of his term." The cable's crucial comment is that "Whatever the truth may ultimately be [about Litvinenko]—and it may never be known—the tendency here to almost automatically assume that someone in or close to Putin's inner-circle is the author of these deaths speaks volumes about expectations of Kremlin behavior" [06MOSCOW12751].

Before and during the *Cablegate* dump, many foreign-policy experts reflexively questioned whether it would hurt US-Russia relations. For instance, Fred Weir reported for the *Christian Science Monitor*:

> Russia's former ambassador to Belgium, Dmitry Ryurikov, says it is … going to roil the diplomatic waters, perhaps for years to come.
>
> "This is a ticklish issue, and it might cause damage to relations, scandal, refutations, and even lead to lawsuits … One group of people might read them and say, "We told you that [the Americans] can not [sic] be trusted," and another group might say, "[W]e always knew that these people [who talk privately with US diplomats] are rascals who are ready to sell out their country," he says.[2]

In the same vein, Heather Hurlburt wrote in the *New Republic*:

```
Russian leaders are likely to get skittish
about continuing the depth of intelligence-
sharing they've moved to under the current
Administration, as Sam Charap of the Center for
American Progress noted: "The ramifications for
US-Russia relations are difficult to overstate.
So much rests on trust between individuals in a
relationship like that where baggage of mutual
suspicion extends decades back."³
```

Whether those concerns have been realized is difficult to determine. Since Russia's support for separatists in Ukraine and its annexation of Crimea, US-Russia hostility may have eclipsed any distrust sown by *Cablegate*. But concern about damage done to relations between states is not the domain of WikiLeaks: let diplomats clean up their own messes. Ironically, though, what may have angered Russians more than any cable was a document described in a cable. Far from classified, it was open source.

Foreign Affairs is the organ of the Council on Foreign Relations. Steeped in the belief that elites must guide democracy, the Council has worked with the US government to ensure American hegemony. For example, the Rockefeller Foundation funded the War and Peace Studies Group, a secret Council project in collaboration with the US Department of State to develop a plan for US domination after World War II.⁴

In a 2006 *Foreign Affairs* article titled "The Rise of US Nuclear Primacy," the political scientist duo Keir A. Lieber and Darryl G. Press wrote: "If the United States launched a nuclear attack against Russia (or China), the targeted country would be left with only a tiny surviving arsenal—if any at all. At that point, even a relatively modest or inefficient missile defense system might well be enough to protect against any retaliatory strikes." In fact, Lieber and Press wrote, "It will probably soon be possible for the United States to destroy the long-range nuclear arsenals of

Russia or China with a first strike." Because of factors such as "a series of improvements in the United States' nuclear systems" and "the precipitous decline of Russia's arsenal," they concluded that, "for the first time in almost 50 years, the United States stands on the verge of attaining nuclear primacy."[5]

Shortly after publication of the article, the ambassador to Russia, William Burns, classified a cable titled "US Nuclear Primacy Article Hits a Nerve":

> Aleksey Arbatov, a former Duma Defense Committee
> Deputy Chairman, raised the article in a March 28
> meeting with us. He acknowledged that the authors
> were not well-known, but said the article's
> publication in *Foreign Affairs* nonetheless gave
> it the aura of a "semi-official statement."
> Arbatov, who chairs an advisory group on
> strategic issues at the Security Council, told us
> officials there were dismayed. He said some in the
> Kremlin saw the article as part of a series of
> salvos aimed at Russia and pointed to "demeaning"
> references to Russia in the US National Security
> Strategy, the accusation that Russia passed
> military information to Saddam, and the lack of
> US recognition for Russia's prerogatives in its
> neighborhood.

Former Prime Minister Yegor Gaidar also joined the chorus of lamentation in the March 29 *Financial Times*, noting that the *Foreign Affairs* article had had "an explosive effect … Even Russian journalists and analysts not inclined to hysteria or anti-Americanism have viewed the article as an expression of the US official stance." Gaidar argued that "if someone had wanted to provoke Russia and China into close cooperation over missile and nuclear technologies, it would have been difficult to find a more skillful and elegant way of doing so."

Anger over the article may have spurred another Russian to an act of bravado—instead of his usual expressions of anxiety—about missile defense:

```
Colonel General Nikolai Solovstov, Commander of
Russia's strategic rocket forces, focused on the
article's assertion that BMD [ballistic missile
defense] technology could give the US a shield
for a first strike. He stated in an interview:
"We have always managed to find resources for
preserving and renewing our strategic nucleaer
[sic] potential. Current technologies make it
possible to develop new missiles and other
weapons for outsmarting even the most effective
ABM system."
```

Burns concludes: "The article's forecast of US nuclear primacy plays to deep-seated Russian fears and undermines efforts to build confidence that our BMD efforts do not come at the expense of Russian security" [06MOSCOW3333].

The conviction held by Russians that US missile defense in Europe is directed not at Iran, as the United States maintains, but at Russia, will be examined in a later section.

Bordering Russia to the north, South Ossetia, site of the nine-day Russo-Georgian War of 2008, is for all practical purposes an autonomous ethnic region of Georgia. At the same time that Georgia declared its independence from Russia, in 1991, South Ossetian leaders sought to secede from Georgia. In response, Georgia mounted a military offensive, but was defeated by South Ossetian secessionists, backed up by Russians fighting unofficially. In 1993, Georgia struck South Ossetia again, as well as Abkhazia, another ethnic enclave in the northwest of Georgia, to prevent it, too, from seceding. Again, Georgia lost, and both provinces retained their autonomy.[6]

In 2003, thousands convened to protest the results of a parliamentary election and to call for the resignation of President Eduard Shevardnadze, a holdover from the Soviet era. When he dispatched armed forces into the streets, demonstrators offered them red roses, in response to which many soldiers disarmed. Demonstrators then stormed the parliament, where Shevardnadze was giving a speech. Their leader, Mikhail Saakashvili, waved a rose in front of his face, and the Rose Revolution was on the verge of success. The following year, the pro-Washington, pro-NATO Saakashvili was elected president, and his party swept parliamentary elections.[7]

When Georgia intensified its military presence at its border with South Ossetia in August 2008, the secessionists saw it as a provocation and attacked. At around 6:00 p.m. on August 7, Georgia declared a ceasefire, but less than five hours later it mounted a sneak attack on Tskhinvali, South Ossetia's capital, with rockets and artillery, then invaded with 1,500 troops. In the end, the Georgian assault on South Ossetia killed an estimated 160 South Ossetians, as well as forty-eight Russian troops.

The European Union's Independent International Fact-Finding Mission on the Conflict in Georgia, headed by Swiss diplomat Heidi Tagliavini, later reported: "None of the explanations given by the Georgian authorities in order to provide some form of legal justification for the attack" were legitimate. Nor was it "possible to accept that the shelling of Tskhinvali with Grad multiple rocket launchers and heavy artillery would satisfy the requirements of having been necessary and proportionate." In support of the secessionists, Russia launched air strikes and sent troops into South Ossetia, as well as Abkhazia. Still, Tagliavini herself said, "In particular, there was no massive Russian military invasion under way, which had to be stopped by Georgian military forces."[8]

Meanwhile, in hopes of diminishing Russia's influence and reinforcing the sovereignty of an independent former Soviet state, the United States seemed to take Saakashvili at his word.

A cable titled "South Ossetia Sitrep 1: Fighting in South Ossetia Escalates," classified by Ambassador John Tefft, comments on the initiation of hostilities on August 7:

> From evidence available to us it appears the South Ossetians started today's fighting. The Georgians are now reacting by calling up more forces and assessing their next move … Deputy Minister of Defense Batu Kutelia told Ambassador at mid-day August 7 that Georgian military troops are on higher alert, but will not be deploying in response to Wednesday's events. [08TBILISI1337]

A cable the next day, classified by Tefft and titled "South Ossetia Sitrep 2: Georgia Claims to Control Much of South Ossetia, Fighting Continues," showed the US embassy again accepting the account of Saakashvili, who, according to the cable,

> has said that Georgia had no intention of getting into this fight, but was provoked by the South Ossetians and had to respond to protect Georgian citizens and territory … [He] confirmed that the Georgians had not decided to move ahead until the shelling intensified and the Russians were seen to be amassing forces on the northern side of the Roki Tunnel.

Worse, Tefft's cable reads, in a tacit admission that the embassy was ignoring evidence out of deference to Washington, "All the evidence available to the country team supports Saakashvili's statement that this fight was not Georgia's original intention." Among that evidence:

> Key Georgian officials who would have had responsibility for an attack on South Ossetia

```
have been on leave, and the Georgians only began
mobilizing August 7 once the attack was well
underway. As late as 2230 last night Georgian
MOD and MFA officials were still hopeful that
the unilateral cease-fire announced by President
Saakashvili would hold … Only when the South
Ossetians opened up with artillery on Georgian
villages, did the offensive to take Tskhinvali
begin. [08TBILISI1341]
```

In fact, OSCE observers at the scene neither saw nor heard evidence of South Ossetian artillery attacks prior to Georgia attacking Tskhinvali. They claimed that "the Georgian attack on Tskhinvali began at 2335 on Aug. 7 despite the ceasefire."[9]

In 2007, Russia caught the US embassy off-guard by raising the issue of Google Maps. A cable classified by the deputy chief of mission, Daniel A. Russell, titled "US-Russia Security Talks," states that the United States assistant secretary of state for verification, compliance, and implementation, Paula De Sutter, and the director of the Russian Foreign Ministry's Department of Security and Disarmament Issues, Anatoliy Antonov

```
had begun a dialogue on outer space issues
at their meeting in Paris on January 25 … De
Sutter offered a proposed joint Presidential
Statement on the free access to and use of
outer space for peaceful purposes … [Russian
deputy foreign minister Sergey] Kislyak segued
from space cooperation to concern over Google
satellite maps available on the Internet. He
clothed his comments as repeating reactions from
various other governments which objected to the
precise identification of their industrial and
military assets. He noted that Google Map [sic]
```

```
covered all areas of the world except the United
States [at the time]. In his view the exact
coordinates created a handbook for terrorists
to plan strikes. He claimed three dimensional
representation raised a serious question that
should be addressed by the United Nations.
The [Government of Russia] was planning an
international meeting to discuss all aspects of
outer space, security and terrorism.
```

Perhaps blindsided, the assistant secretary of state for international security and nonproliferation, John Rood, "acknowledged that Internet map availability was a new topic. He urged examination of the topic in future discussions. Kislyak responded that there were legal and practical concerns for both military and civil areas [07MOSCOW1877_a].

Russia raised objections that were obviously legitimate. Alas, no further cables document whether or not the United States addressed its concerns. Furthermore, US inability to anticipate the depth of, or its blithe lack of concern for, Russia's reactions to satellite surveillance also applied to US deployment of missile defense in Europe. From the beginning, missile defense—basically anti-aircraft on steroids—has long been a powder keg of controversy between the United States and Russia. Before exploring cables detailing US-Russian discussions on the subject, some background is required on why missile defense both rattles Russia and is considered destabilizing to the nuclear-weapons balance.

In 1983 President Ronald Reagan introduced the Strategic Defense Initiative, presciently ridiculed as "Star Wars" at the time because it sounded like as much of a fantasy as it does to this day. Patriot missiles were deployed in the Middle East during the first Gulf War and, while they achieved little success, the idea of missile defense, at least against smaller nuclear arsenals, caught on.

At the Reykjavík summit in 1986, Soviet leader Mikhail Gorbachev proposed eliminating half of all strategic (as opposed to tactical, or battlefield) nuclear weapons. In exchange, he asked that Reagan refrain from implementing missile defense for the next ten years. Reagan's team responded with an offer to eliminate all ballistic missiles within the same time span, while retaining the right to missile defense thereafter.

That is when Gorbachev made the game-changing proposal that both sides abolish all nuclear weapons within ten years. Swept up in the moment, Reagan and Secretary of State George Schultz agreed, but they could not abide Gorbachev's condition that missile defense research be confined to laboratories for that period. Ultimately, Reagan, Schultz, and their team were unable to set aside their deeply ingrained distrust of Russians and agree to that condition. The irony is that missile defense lacked the ability to close any windows of vulnerability in US national security that might be left ajar while the United States and Russia disarmed. Its powerlessness to block a major nuclear attack lingers to this day and, along with its destabilizing component, makes a formidable case for discontinuing its development.

But the Reykjavík summit did pave the way for the Intermediate-Range Nuclear Forces Treaty, which banned weapons suitable for Russia to launch at Europe and for the United Sates to launch at the Soviet Union from Europe. However, since 2012 the United States has complained that Russia is violating the treaty, and in 2014 it formally notified Russia of a breach. Also, not long after his inauguration, President George W. Bush withdrew from the Anti-Ballistic Missile Treaty, which limited the number of anti-ballistic missiles that could be used against a ballistic missile attack, in order to develop missile defense further.[10]

One might be forgiven for wondering how a defense system can be destabilizing. Why exactly does simply fending off—not even retaliating against—a nuclear attack constitute an "existential threat" in its own right? But, counterintuitive as it may seem, missile defense is provocative. To begin with, it prompts the state with negligible or no missile defense to think that it needs to mount a nuclear attack before the other state's more advanced missile defense system becomes operational. Never mind that no system is of much use against a massive attack. Perhaps most frighteningly of all, the state with the more advanced—or, more accurately, less rudimentary—missile defense system is prompted to engage in a first strike against the nuclear weapons of the state with the less advanced system in order to keep that state's attack from overwhelming the missile defense of the first state. Finally, the state with the less advanced system feels compelled to build more nuclear weapons, both to make up for those it might lose in a first strike and also to overwhelm missile defense. Destabilizing enough for you?

As if missile defense were not provocative enough already, tensions ratcheted up when the Bush administration decided to expand missile defense to Europe in the form of ground-based midcourse interceptors and radar in, respectively, Poland and the Czech Republic. The Obama administration continued with what it called a "phased adaptive approach," consisting of the Aegis Ballistic Missile Defense system (currently sea-based, but eventually intended to move onto Polish and Romanian soil) against short- and intermediate-range ballistic missiles.[11]

According to the United States, the purpose of missile defense in Europe is to provide protection from the ballistic missile arsenal that Iran obtained from North Korea. But the range of most of Iran's ballistic missiles, not very accurate to begin with, is 500 kilometers. Reaching Europe would require them to be fired from Iran's Persian Gulf coastline, and leave them vulnerable to attack. Some of Iran's missiles are longer-range and capable of reaching Israel, but are at least as inaccurate.[12]

In 2013 the United States canceled the fourth, last, and most controversial phase of the Phased Adaptive Approach—long-range interceptors theoretically capable of stopping Russia's intercontinental ballistic missiles.[13] Nevertheless, in 2014, the United States reiterated that, despite budget problems, it still planned to deploy those land-based Aegis Ashore sites in Romania and Poland.[14]

The lack of a genuine threat to Europe from Iran's missiles is foremost among the reasons that Russia claims that US missile defense is directed against its missiles. Also, the proximity of US missile defense to Russia is of a piece with its sense of US and NATO encroachment on its homeland, which also threatens to shrink its sphere of influence on former Soviet and Eastern Bloc states. The United States, meanwhile, maintains that Russia's objections are just a diplomatic ploy: Russia cannot possibly believe that missile defense is directed against Russia, because Russia's missiles, as everyone knows, would overwhelm it. Besides, the United States seeks Russian cooperation with its program. Or you can look at it like Jeffrey Lewis of the James Martin Center for Nonproliferation Studies, who wrote in *Foreign Policy* that, fundamentally, most of Russia's concern "is probably sheer terror at the persistent technological advantage held by the United States in light of Russian vulnerabilities."[15]

Some of the cables illustrate Russian objections to US missile defense in Europe, none more so than a 2007 cable classified by Deputy Chief of Mission Daniel A. Russell titled "US-Russia Strategic Security Talks." A representative of the Russian Ministry of Defense named Col. Ilian presented Russian reactions to missile defense in Europe by means of a PowerPoint presentation. The bullet-points included:

- The Russians disputed or disagreed with
  most US assumptions and decisions regarding
  threats posed by North Korean or Iranian
  ICBM development. US forecasts, such as the
  1998 "Rumsfeld Commission" and 1999 "National
  Intelligence Estimate," had proven incorrect.
  At best, Iran and North Korea currently
  have missiles with a maximum range of 2,500
  kilometers, which presents no threat to the
  US and essentially no threat to Europe. The
  Russians predict the range of Iranian BMs would

increase to no more than 3,500 kilometers by 2015. Even this range poses a threat only to the eastern portion of the European continent.

- The Russians said the MD sites in Poland and Czech Republic, if effective against Iranian BM threats, would also be effective against Russian ICBMs. The direction of flight of Iranian missiles practically coincides with Russian missiles based at Kozelsk and Tatishevo …

- The Russians contend that to better protect Europe from Iran, the proposed MD sites should be located in Turkey, France and Italy. If located there, they would not threaten Russian ICBMs.

- Radar coverage from the Czech Republic would provide early detection and would lead to MD interception of Russian ICBMs, in addition to Iranian missiles. The Russians contend that radar-based elements of MD in Czech Republic could be rapidly reoriented from the south to the east …

- The Russians believe that 10 interceptors is only the beginning of a MD in Europe and that the site could be enhanced by increasing the number of interceptor missiles, increasing interceptor missile velocity, and using separating warheads for BM destruction.

- The Russians also expressed concerns that MD interceptors in Europe could have anti-satellite (ASAT) capabilities.

- Based on Russian calculations, US interceptor missiles in Europe could "catch-up" and destroy Russian ICBMs.

- The Russians said debris caused by an interception posed a far greater risk of danger than the US has briefed. A 100 gram fragment would be enough to pierce through a five-floor building from rooftop to ground floor. If the BM had chemical, biological, or radiological agents, the payload could be spread over a great area in the atmosphere.

[07MOSCOW1877_a]

In a 2009 cable classified by Ambassador Beyrle titled "Missile Defense, JDEC, Non-Proliferation Negotiations," another feature of missile defense alarmed Deputy Foreign Minister Ryabkov, who

pointed to one of the briefing slides showing … how a radar in the Czech Republic would track across Russian territory and that it would be difficult—or almost impossible … to intercept missiles along such a track. A radar in the Czech Republic would not be able to ensure the necessary data flow for interception of a missile from Iran, it could only enable the US to distinguish between real and decoy launches originating in Russia. [09MOSCOW1491_a]

Clearly, Russia's grievances, seldom expressed in the West, are convincing. In the "US-Russia Strategic Security Talks" cable, ISN Assistant Secretary John Rood presented US justifications for missile defense in Europe:

North Korea's launches of the Taepo-Dong missile
in 1998 and last year's July 4 launch of the
Taepo Dong-2, even if not completely successful,
clearly indicated that North Korea was already
a threat … Regarding Iran, Rood said that
relations between the US and Iran are poor and
that President Ahmadinejad's public remarks
on wiping Israel "off the map" and achieving
"a world without America," as well as regular
demonstrations where "Death to America" is
commonly heard, are all representative of a
threatening view. He noted that when Iran paraded
its Shahab-3 missile a few years ago, it carried
a sign saying "USA can do nothing," clearly
indicating that the absence of missile defenses
at that time was clearly a factor in Iran's
interest in ballistic missiles. The US, Rood
said, perceived the BM threat from both North
Korea and Iran as serious. [07MOSCOW1877_a]

Rood's response befits a hard-right commentator more than a
representative of the US government. Deputy Foreign Minister
Kislyak responded that he

agreed that Russian and American threat
assessments were different. He said North Korea
was not in ICBM production, let alone Iran. To
reach the US, he said, any missile from either
of those two countries would need to travel at
least 8000 kilometers. Iran's capabilities in
liquid and/or solid fuel are limited, and Russia
would know if Iran was preparing to expand
research. He agreed that the Iranian President
Ahmadinejad's remarks were unacceptable but
asked, rhetorically, if such statements reflected
the country's capabilities. [07MOSCOW1877_a]

That last sentence, especially, is difficult to refute. A later cable, titled "Russia-US Missile Defense Negotiations, Part 2: Assessing Qabala, The Iranian Threat, and Czech Radar Capabilities," describes Russian objections in more detail. Classified in 2009 by the ambassador to Russia, William Burns, it reads: "[R]egarding the need to stop Iranian missiles as the rationale for stationing missile defense in Europe: 'Russia's assessment was that the US exaggerated the state of Iranian R&D, the technical level of its rocket and missile sectors, and the capabilities of its scientists.'"

In fact, according to the cable, Russia objected to the very assumption on the part of the United States that "Iran was strategically committed to the development of ICBMs, with [Vladimir Venevtsev of the SVR (the Russian foreign intelligence service)] concluding that it was not in Iran's doctrine." As paraphrased in the cable, Venevtsev said, "The level of sophistication of North Korea's ICBM technology for long range missiles [which it provided Iran] was inflated," as was "the track record of [Russia's] transfers to Iran." Venevtsev also noted: "The US failed to take into account the limits on the development of the Shahab-3 system, caused by the lack of test range equipment, with Russia maintaining that the Shahab was simply the [North Korean] No Dong, but renamed."

Venevtsev further maintained that "Iran did not enjoy technical mastery of the design process, but upgraded and reverse-engineered others' systems; its engineers were insufficient in number and not highly skilled; and, consequently, Iran was still dependent upon North Korean engines." Then "Venevtsev concluded that given the weakness of the Iranian program, the US and Russia had the opportunity to monitor its development and undertake joint measures over time" [07MOSCOW5106].

Returning to the 2007 "US-Russia Strategic Security Talks" cable, Deputy Foreign Minister Kislyak also "stressed that Russian concerns about the dangers of a false alert and possible miscalculation remained."[16]

The [Government of Russia] had not come up with
a mechanism that could adequately discriminate
between a nuclear-tipped SLBM and one with a
conventional warhead. The US had not offered
any information that allayed these concerns.
Rood agreed that we needed to continue to
discuss this issue, but stressed that the risk
of a misinterpretation of a hostile launch was
low. DASD [Deputy Assistant of Defense Brian]
Green explained that the number of SLBMs with
conventional warheads would be limited and
pointed out that CBMs could be put in place that
would reduce the chances for error. The US was
waiting on a Russian response to our non-paper
on the subject. [Lt. Gen. Evgeniy Buzhinskiy,
deputy chief of the Russian Defense Ministry's
Main Administration for International Military
Cooperation] highlighted the possibility for
error given the limited time the Russians would
have to respond once a launch was detected and
certain "automatic" features of the Russian
launch warning system. [07MOSCOW1877_a]

Differentiating between the varieties of launches also played a
central role in the New START Treaty negotiations. Instead of
being concerned with the distinction between real and decoy,
however, this time Russians were concerned with separating
nuclear from conventional strikes. New START is a replacement for the START I Treaty, which expired in 2009. Signed by
President George H. W. Bush and Soviet president Gorbachev
in 1991, START I was the most drastic arms control treaty in
history. For the United States it represented a decrease of about
80 percent of its nuclear-weapon arsenal from its peak during the
Cold War.[17]

Once in force, New START reduced the maximum number

of deployed US and Russian strategic nuclear warheads to 1,550 each (not including the inactive warhead stockpile). But, because the Russians held that warheads were nothing without their delivery systems, a unique system for adding up warheads was implemented in which, no matter how many warheads it carries, a bomber counts as only one.

In a cable titled "START Follow-on Negotiations," lead US New START negotiator Rose E. Gottemoeller (the Department of State's assistant secretary for arms control, verification, and compliance) shed light on the dispute over distinguishing between types of strikes, on the way in which the method of tabulating the number of warheads was adopted, and the bearing each issue had on the other. Ambassador Mikhail Streltsov of the Russian Ministry of Foreign Affairs

> noted that in her statement on the previous
> day,[18] the US Secretary of State referred to the
> title of the new treaty as bearing on strategic
> "nuclear" arms. In this context, it was necessary
> to consider whether non-nuclear-armed ICBMs and
> SLBMs should be considered START items. There
> is a further question, he added, of whether new
> types of non-nuclear missiles will be considered
> ICBMs and SLBMs. What should be counted? Warheads
> or "nuclear" warheads? The Joint Understanding
> signed in Moscow by the two Presidents, he
> reminded the group, referred to strategic
> delivery vehicles and their associated warheads,
> not associated "nuclear" warheads.

Meanwhile, deputy head of the US delegation Dr. Ted Warner (secretary of defense representative to the New START negotiations)

commented that, since the beginning of their
discussions, the US and Russian sides have
had a markedly different view of how to treat
conventionally-armed ICBMs and SLBMs. The Russian
side has proposed that the deployment of such
systems should be banned, while the US side
proposes that new types developed and tested
solely for non-nuclear warheads should not be
subject to the limitations of the SFO [START
Follow-on] Treaty.

In the summary at the start of the cable, Gottemoeller had
explained:

The Russian side commented extensively on
issues related to counting rules, but returned
repeatedly to the question of conventional
warheads on ICBMs and SLBMs. Amb Streltsov
used a lengthy commentary on "what should be
counted" in an attempt to demonstrate that there
were ambiguities and inconsistencies in the US
approach, arguing the nuclear or non-nuclear
status of deployed ICBMs and SLBMs would be
difficult to determine. He further questioned how
it would be possible to distinguish whether a
warhead was conventional or nuclear after it was
launched.

The Russians may have been referring to the Conventional
Trident Modification program—a plan to arm Trident II SLBMs
with conventional warheads that was killed by Congress in
2008.[19] Still, Congress provided funding for the research and
development of its successor, the conventional prompt global
strike (CPGS), which entails arming a ballistic missile, or a glider
that operates at hypersonic speed (at least five times the speed of

sound), with conventional weapons. It would thus emulate the ability of nuclear warhead-equipped ballistic missiles to strike anywhere in the world within one hour. To American military planners, this "niche capability," as it has been called, may have been the greatest leap in fine-tuning a first strike since the 1960s. At that time, President John F. Kennedy's secretary of defense, Robert McNamara, engineered a shift in nuclear policy from the Eisenhower era's massive retaliation, which called for an all-out response to even a minor nuclear attack, to a modulated response.

Russians, however, looked at it from another perspective. Streltsov asked how the United States was "going to prove/demonstrate its nuclear or non-nuclear character?" In other words, what was to stop Russia from responding to all ballistic missile attacks as if they were nuclear? Warner conceded "the point that Streltsov had made about 'nuclear ambiguity'—it would be extremely difficult to determine the payload, whether nuclear or non-nuclear, while a strategic missile was in flight. But he recalled that the US side had spoken in the past about possible steps to mitigate this problem, which might include advance notification" [09MOSCOW2607_a].

It is tough to expect Russia to take it on faith when the United States announces that it is about to launch conventional ballistic missiles, and that there is no need to respond with a nuclear strike. Russia may also be wondering what exactly qualifies a target for a strike by the United States with a conventional, instead of nuclear, warhead, unless it was, in fact, a nuclear installation.

The patronizing attempts that the United States made to allay Russian concerns about a conventional warhead mounted on an ICBM or SLBM parallel its assurances that missile defense stationed in Europe is not directed at Russia. As recently as December 2013, *RIA Novosti* reported:

```
Deputy Prime Minister Dmitry Rogozin said that
Russia was "preparing a response" to plans by
the United States to develop a new fast-strike
```

```
weapons platform capable of hitting high-priority
targets around the globe … "They may experiment
with conventional weapons on strategic delivery
platforms, but they must bear in mind, that if
we are attacked, in certain circumstances we will
of course respond with nuclear weapons," Rogozin
said.[20]
```

Nor is that the end of the risks posed by conflating conventional with nuclear strikes. In the cable's summary, Warner wrote:

```
Russian head of delegation Amb Antonov argued
there would be a negative impact globally
if conventionally-armed ICBMs and SLBMs were
deployed. He also alleged that failure to
constrain the development of such weapons would
pose a dilemma for both the United States and
Russia if third countries carried out missile
tests, claiming that they were conventional but
which the United States and Russia suspected
covered a nuclear program. He also commented that
there were already discussions in Non-Aligned
Movement (NAM) circles that US deployment of such
weapons could lead to an arms race in long-range
conventional ballistic missiles.
```

Warner's response was anemic. He "recognized the Russian side had not judged the US approach to the handling of missiles with conventional warheads as positive." But "he reminded the Russian side that the United States had not judged their proposal to ban the deployment of conventionally-armed strategic missiles as 'positive' either" [09MOSCOW2607].

The Cold War was a chronicle of misunderstanding. The United States consistently overestimated the size of Russia's nuclear-weapons arsenal. The Soviet Union concluded from US policies and deployments that the United States was seeking to launch a nuclear first strike. In the years since, as documented in the WikiLeaks collection of cables from the US consulates and the embassy in Moscow, the United States has refused to sufficiently acknowledge Russian concerns about US nuclear weapons and missile defense. It acts as if Russia is being obtuse, as if it were obvious that the United States has no interest in an offensive attack on Russia with ballistic missiles—nuclear or conventional—or in defending itself against Russia with a provocative missile defense system. Russia cannot help but feel, at best, patronized—and, at worst, threatened.

Instead of wasting time and resources lamenting the effects of the cables on international relations and harassing WikiLeaks, the United States needs to overhaul its foreign policy. Continuing to view a state such as Russia as a rival in a zero-sum game, as well as an energy resource and an emerging market, instead of as representing a people, only perpetuates conflict. The source of other states' mistrust of the United States is much deeper than the revelations of the minutes of US diplomats' meetings with the diplomats of those states.

8. Turkey

Conn Hallinan

We have no eternal allies and we have no eternal enemies. Our interests are eternal and perpetual, and these interests it is our duty to follow.

—3rd Viscount Palmerston, 1848

Reading through the WikiLeaks cables and documents on Turkey brings to mind Lord Palmerston—prime minister, foreign secretary, and Britain's hammer of empire. The same whiff of cold calculation comes through time and again as US diplomats—at times insightful, at times not—analyze governments, pressure regimes, and quietly double-cross allies.

What WikiLeaks has uncovered cuts across thematic areas: "commitment to democracy" and "rule of law"—even the so-called war on terrorism—and reveals the real aims of US foreign policy: punishing perceived enemies—Russia, Syria, and Iran—and lobbying for US arms and energy companies.

German chancellor Otto Von Bismarck once commented that people who like politics and sausages should not watch them being made. Reading through the WikiLeaks cables feels a lot like watching sausage-making: it takes a strong stomach.

US foreign policy in the Middle East has generally rested on four pillars: Turkey, Egypt, the Persian Gulf monarchies, and Israel. That combination of strategic placement, wealth, and military power has successfully kept the region divided and powerless for more than a half century. American strategy has largely revolved around close ties with those four pillars through military aid and political support. To that end, the US has backed feudal monarchies in the Gulf, authoritarian governments in Egypt and Turkey, and several wars of expansion and occupation by Israel.

For American policy-makers, the only flies in that Middle East ointment have been Libya, Iraq, Syria, and Iran. The first two have been removed from the chessboard by American military power, and Syria is currently imploding in a civil war in which the US and its allies are playing a leading role. In a sense, Iran is the last man standing, although it has been badly weakened by US-led economic sanctions.

The "Turkish pillar" has been a mainstay since the end of World War II. As one cable notes, "A stable Turkey is important to the United States mainly for geostrategic reasons. Turkey is situated amid the troubled Balkans, the Caucasus, and the Middle East regions, and is a critical energy transit hub between Central Asia/the Caucasus and Europe" [CRS-RL34642]. Turkey fields the largest army in NATO and bolsters the alliance's southern border with Russia. For several years, US Jupiter medium-range missiles carrying nuclear warheads fifty times as powerful as the Hiroshima bomb were deployed in the country. According to one cable, Turkey still hosts between fifty and ninety nuclear weapons. The Ankara government has long played a key role for US interests, both locally and worldwide. As one cable puts it, Turkey has been a "tough combat partner in Korea, major NATO ally, US anchor in the Middle East" [10ANKARA87].

At the same time, the Americans are well aware of the fact that NATO membership is by no means popular with the average Turk, and the US has a glass-half-full way of looking at that sentiment:

```
NATO is essential to and much respected by
Turkey. The fact that, on one poll, "only"
```

```
about one-third of the Turkish population
sees NATO as important to Turkey's security is
actually a plus. On any poll, Turks are usually
overwhelmingly negative about any foreign
engagement or relationship. But we should not be
too sanguine since support for NATO has halved
over the past decade. The military is armed by
the US, and Turkey recognizes that many fires
in its backyard—from Iraq to Afghanistan to
Pakistan—can only be solved by close cooperation
with and acceptance of US and NATO leadership.
[10ANKARA87]
```

Of course the average Turk's tepid view of NATO might be based on the fact that the Americans lit all three of those "fires," one of them quite literally in Turkey's backyard. Turkey's Incirlik Air Base serves as a land-based aircraft carrier for the Americans. The base was not only a key supply route for the US invasion of Iraq—58 percent of all supplies going to Iraq pass through the Turkish base—but also hosted rendition flights for the Central Intelligence Agency (CIA) moving suspected terrorists—many of whom were tortured—to prisons in Poland, and eventually Guantánamo prison in Cuba [04ANKARA003352].

Turkey has long denied the rendition charge, but in a June 8, 2006 cable, the US ambassador to Turkey, Ross Wilson, confirms that the

```
Turkish military … has allowed the US to
use Incirlik as the key transit point for
humanitarian and other forms of assistance
(including lethal munitions) to the Northern
Alliance and US Special Operation Forces in
Afghanistan; offered the use of additional
air bases in Turkey for OEF [Operation
Enduring Freedom, the US name for the war in
```

Afghanistan]-related operations; authorized
the use of Incirlik Air Base to transit Taliban
and al-Qaida detainees from Afghanistan to GTMO
[Guantánamo prison in Cuba]. [05ANKARA008305]

One confidential US Congressional report outlines the role of
Incirlik Air Base as the centerpiece in a long relationship:

Turkey's geostrategic importance for the United
States depends partly on Incirlik Air Base,
located about 7 miles east of Adana in southeast
Turkey. The United States constructed the base
and the US Air Force began using it during the
height of the Cold War in 1954. The Turkish
government transferred control of the base to its
military in 1975 in response to an arms embargo
that Congress imposed on Turkey in reaction to
Turkey's intervention/invasion of Cyprus in 1974.
The base continued to fulfill its NATO missions.
After the embargo ended, the US and Turkey signed
a bilateral Defense and Economic Cooperation
Agreement (DECA) in 1980 to govern US use of
the base and a DECA, under a NATO umbrella,
continues to allow US air force to use it for
training purposes. As an executive agreement, the
DECA does not require congressional or Turkish
parliamentary approval. US requests to use the
base for other purposes are made separately and
may require Turkish parliamentary authorization.
[CRS-RL34642]

Incirlik is an invaluable instrument for the execution of NATO
and US policies in Iraq, Afghanistan, and elsewhere in the Middle
East. It offers a 10,000-foot runway and a 9,000-foot alternative
runway able to service large cargo planes. Some 74 percent of all

air cargo into Iraq transits Incirlik. The US Air Force prizes the efficiency of the use of the base: six C-17 aircraft based at Incirlik move the same amount of cargo that nine or ten aircraft used to carry from Rhein-Main Air Base in Germany, saving about $160 million a year. In addition, thousands of US soldiers have rotated out of Iraq using Incirlik for transit. K-135 tankers operating out of Incirlik have delivered more than 35 million gallons of fuel to US fighter and transport aircraft on missions in Iraq and Afghanistan. "Added to Turkey's strategic importance to the United States is its willingness to house US nuclear weapons at Incirlik Air Base. According to a 2005 report, about 90 US nuclear weapons were stored there, although a different group estimated in 2008 that the number of weapons is 50 to 90—still the most at any base in Europe" [CRS-RL34642].

Ross Wilson, ambassador from 2005 to 2008, is an "old hand" in Central Asia. He previously served as ambassador to Azerbaijan and has extensive experience in Russia. In 2012 he told *Business Insider* that "NATO needs to pick up its game" by increasing its support for Turkey's involvement in the Syrian civil war.[1] NATO, he said, must "make clear that [Turkey's] security is an alliance concern" and that Turkey should be a NATO "platform" in case of "either intervention or some kind of operation" in Syria.

As a 2006 cable indicates, Turkey also serves as an entry for the Americans in Central Asia and the Caucasus:

```
As part of a continuing effort in the Caucasus,
the US and its allies continue to promote
collective assistance to Azerbaijan, Armenia
and Georgia. A recent proposal—the upgrade
of Nasosnaya Airfield located outside of Baku
[Azerbaijan]—has not taken hold with our Turkish
counterparts (at least not in Ankara). Over the
past 2-3 years, the idea of upgrading the airfield
has been briefed in several venues (the Caucasus
```

Working Group and the South Caucasus Clearing
House).

Additionally, the idea of a joint venture among
the allies to perform the upgrade has been
informally sent to the TGS J5 [Turkish General
Staff, similar to the US Joint Chiefs of Staff]
on several occasions. While the military has
not responded to our entreaties in Ankara,
the Turkish DATT (a one-star general) in Baku
recently told us that Turkey is enthusiastic
about working with us on Nasosnaya. A push at
the senior levels within the TGS might help
break this proposal loose. Any interest you can
promote during your visit would be beneficial.
[04ANKARA003352]

THE KURDS

Turkey has been helpful to the US in the Middle East, but this has
come with a price. One cost was a secret agreement to give the
Turks surveillance information on the Kurds, one of America's
key allies in Iraq, Syria, and Iran. Some 25 to 30 million Kurds
are scattered through those countries and eastern Turkey, and
have long been discriminated against by governments in Ankara,
Damascus, Baghdad, and Tehran. Kurds make up the largest
ethnic group in the world without a country of their own.

"Protecting" the Kurds was a major rationale for Washington's
pre-invasion embargo of Iraq, and from 1992 to the invasion
in 2003 the US enforced a "no-fly zone" over Kurdish areas in
Iraq's north. It is therefore unexpected to read that the US has
also actively aided the Turkish government's counter-insurgency
against the Kurds—a conflict that has killed more than 40,000
people:

The PKK [Kurdistan Workers Party], which seeks
to carve off the primarily Kurdish portion of
Eastern Turkey by force of arms has intensified
its terrorist campaign in Turkey: over 150
Turkish security forces have died so far in 2006,
a dozen in the past week alone. This violence has
increased pressure on the GOT to take decisive
measures to cope with the problem, including
attacking PKK strongholds in Northern Iraq, which
the organization uses as a command, control,
and logistics base to infiltrate Turkey and carry
out attacks. Turkey wants the new government in
Iraq to take immediate, concrete steps to limit
PKK freedom of action in the country. The PKK's
isolated location, the long list of priorities
facing the GOI [Government of Iraq], and the
attitudes of Kurdish authorities in northern Iraq
make this complicated.

[US secretary of state Condoleezza] Rice told GOT
leaders April 25 that the US would reinvigorate
trilateral (US-Turkey-Iraq) discussion on the
issue. While recognizing that the insurgency
prevents coalition troops from engaging the
PKK in Iraq, the GOT remains frustrated at its
inability, and US unwillingness, to stop attacks
by people coming from the other side of its
border.

If you are confronted with this issue, you
can point to significant efforts the USG [US
Government] is undertaking to ameliorate the PKK
threat

• Sharing of sensitive intelligence on PKK

activities within Turkey has led to successful
Turkish COIN [counter-insurgency] operations.

- MNF-1 surveillance flights over PKK camps in
  northern Iraq, which have also had a salutary
  effect in terms of psyops [psychological
  operations].

- An intelligence fusion cell, which meets weekly
  in Ankara to pass information to the Turkish
  military on PKK activities.

- A new initiative to work with Turkey on
  building law enforcement cases against PKK
  operatives in Europe.

[04ANKARA003352]

US intelligence is used by Turkish war planes to bomb Kurdish villages where the PKK has a strong presence, killing many civilians in the process. In 2007, as the Turkish Army massed on Iraq's northern border, US president George W. Bush met with Turkey's prime minister Recep Tayyip Erdoğan to try and head off an invasion, which, in the opinion of the Americans, would further destabilize Iraq:

The President promised to provide Turkey with
"actionable intelligence" to use against the PKK
and set up a tripartite consultation mechanism
among Gen. David Petraeus, then commander of
the Multinational Force in Iraq, General James
Wainwright, US Deputy Chief of Staff, and General
Ergin Saygun, then Deputy Chief of the Turkish
General Staff. Since that time, Turkish forces
have launched targeted air and ground strikes
against PKK camps and other facilities located

in the mountains of northern Iraq. They have
expressed satisfaction with their results.
[CRS-RL34642]

The cables reveal good old-fashioned horse dealing, like a deal
between US deputy secretary of state William Burns and Turkish
under secretary of foreign affairs Feridun Sinirlioğlu aimed at
persuading Turkey to drop its objections to appointing Andars
Fogh Rasmussen as NATO's general secretary. Rasmussen was
the prime minister of Denmark during an uproar over several
anti-Muslim cartoons printed in the Danish press that insulted the
Prophet Muhammad. Rasmussen angered Muslims by initially
being dismissive of the incident.

According to the cable, in exchange for Rasmussen getting
the post, Denmark agreed to close down a Kurdish TV station
Ankara objected to, which was broadcasting Kurdish programming into Turkey. Rasmussen got the job, but the Turks got stiffed
on silencing the station, which, as a 2002 cable reflects, they were
deeply unhappy about:

Burns inquired about Turkey's bilateral relations
with Europe. Sinirlioglu briefly recapped Turkey's
unhappiness with [French President Nicolas]
Sarkozy. He described his country's relationship
with Austria as infected by the latter's ethnic
prejudice. He complained Belgium and Denmark are
reluctant to suppress terrorist PKK-affiliated
organizations active in their countries. Tacan
Ildem [Turkish ambassador to the US] added that,
as part of the 2009 POTUS [President of the
United States]-brokered deal that had overcome
Turkish objections to the appointment of Andars
Fogh Rasmussen as NATO General Secretary, Denmark
had promised to clarify its legal requirements
prerequisite to acceding to Turkey's request for

the closure of Roj TV, a PKK mouthpiece. This
still needed to be done, Ildem said.

Picking up from Ildem, Sinirlioğlu recalled
POTUS-brokered deal had included an understanding
that a qualified Turk would be considered for
Assistant Secretary General, he said instead a
German of uncompelling merit was selected. "We
suspect a deal between Rasmussen and [German
Chancellor Angela] Merkel." Ildem complained
high-level positions should be part of NATO
reform. "We missed an opportunity with the
selection of an Assistant Secretary General."
Sinirlioğlu added: "We let Rasmussen have
Secretary General because we trusted you."
[05ANKARA000302]

IRAN

For the past several decades, Iran has been a key focus for US
policy in the region, and Turkish-Iranian relations loom large in
the cables.

Bilateral Turkish-Iranian relations have a strong
economic dimension. About 1.5 million Iranian
tourists visit Turkey annually. Trade is growing
with a volume of $8 billion in 2007 that is
expected to reach $10 billion by the end of 2008,
with a target of $20 billion within four years.
The balance is sharply in Iran's favor because
Turkey imports oil, oil products, and gas from
its neighbor.[2] Turkey is a net importer of oil and
gas and depends on Russia for 68 percent of its
gas supplies; it looks to Tehran to lessen that
dependence and sees the bilateral relationship as

in its vital national interest. The first Iranian-
Turkish gas pipeline went on stream in 2001, but
supplies have been sporadic during the winter as
Iran diverts them for its own use.

In July 2007, Turkey and Iran signed a memorandum
of understanding or preliminary agreement for the
Turkish Petroleum Company (TPAO) to be granted
the right to develop natural gas in South Pars
[Iran], to extract up to 20 billion cubic meters
(bcm) of gas, and to transport it via a new
pipeline from Tabriz in Iran to Erzurum in Turkey
and onto the planned 3,300-kilometer Nabucco
pipeline. Should the agreement be finalized,
Turkish investment would be approximately $3.5
billion. Nabucco is intended to carry natural
gas from Turkmenistan via Azerbaijan, Georgia,
and Turkey to a major natural gas terminus
in Austria, thereby bypassing and lessening
European dependence on Russia. It is scheduled
to be completed by 2013. Iranian gas would make
the pipeline more viable. Turkey's partners in
Nabucco (Hungary, Bulgaria, Romania, Germany and
Austria) maintain that "No Iranian gas will be
accepted unless the nuclear problem is solved."[3]
[CRS-RL34642]

Any Turkish activity in the South Pars field, however, runs counter
to US policy: "The state Department warned Turkey against
finalizing the South Pars energy agreement, asserting, 'such a deal
by Turkey with Iran would send the wrong message at a time
when the Iranian regime has repeatedly failed to comply with
its UN Security Council and IAEA [International Atomic Energy
Agency] obligations."

The deal was canceled.

The cables reflect Washington's nervousness about Turkish-Iranian ties, and the pressure from Washington on Ankara to assume a posture toward Tehran more congruent with those of the US, the Gulf States, and Israel. But because Turkey has very little energy resources of its own, it needs Iranian and Russian oil and gas. In an effort to undermine Moscow and Tehran, the US was trying to push Ankara away from Iran toward Central Asia—Azerbaijan in particular—to fulfill its energy needs. One cable says that energy needs and "certain domestic considerations" all "push Turkey in the wrong direction," concluding with the warning that eventually "Turkey will have to stand and be counted on Iran" [05ANKARA000302].

An important part of US energy strategy in the region is the yet-to-be-completed Nabucco pipeline. The Turks agree with the Americans that they would rather draw their energy resources from Azerbaijan. But the idea that Turkey might not have interests identical to Washington's simply does not seem to occur to US diplomats—or, if it does, they consider those interests irrelevant.

The American media is fond of ridiculing Iran's moniker for America of "The Great Satan," but the cables reflect a singular US enmity toward Iran that mirrors the demonization Tehran has hung upon Washington. But the Iran we hear about from Washington is not necessarily the Iran that emerges from reading these cables.

In a 2009 cable, assistant secretary of state Philip Gordon reports on a meeting with Turkish foreign minister Ahmet Davutoğlu, who had just gotten off the phone with Mohamed El-Baradei, director general of the IAEA, who he writes had had

```
two long "harsh" sessions with the Iranians in
Istanbul over a plan to ship low grade enriched
Iranian nuclear fuel to other countries in
exchange for other countries sending the Iranians
enriched fuel for their reactors and medical
```

industry. The purpose of the Peter-Paul exchange
was to shut down Iran's enrichment program.

The Iranians have said they are willing to meet
with [Javier] Solana [secretary general of the
Council of the European Union], but have told
the Turks that they have serious problems with
[Robert] Cooper [diplomatic advisor and member of
the European Council on Foreign Relations] and
the British. They have "more trust" in the US.
The Iranians would also prefer to get fuel from
the US rather than the Russians.

Davutoglu said the Iranians: a) are ready to send
a delegation to Vienna to work out the specifics
on this proposal; b) have given "full trust"
to Turkey; c) continue to face serious domestic
problems inside Iran. He said the Turks actually
see Ahmadinejad as "more flexible" than others who
are inside the Iranian government. Ahmadinejad
is facing "huge pressure" after statements from
some P5 members [the US, Britain, China, France,
the UK, and Germany] to the effect that a nuclear
deal would succeed in weakening Iran's nuclear
capability—which is interpreted by some circles
in Iran as a virtual defeat.

Given this context, the Turks had asked Ahmadinejad
if the core of the issue is psychological rather
than substance. Ahmadinejad had said "yes," that
the Iranians agree to the proposal but need to
manage the public perception. [02ANKARA001654]

The meeting between Gordon and Davutoğlu apparently got a
little heated.

Noting that Davutoglu had only addressed the
negative consequences of sanctions or the use
of military force [on Iran], Gordon pressed
Davutoglu on Ankara's assessment of the
consequences if Iran gets a nuclear weapon.
Davutoglu gave a spirited reply, that "of course"
Turkey was aware of this risk. This is precisely
why Turkey is working so hard with the Iranians.
President [Abdullah] Gul himself had spent two
hours Sunday with Ahmadinejad in Istanbul.

Gordon then pressed the Turks on how they view Iran, given that
the UK *Guardian* reported that Erdoğan had referred to Iran as a
"friend." Davutoğlu replied that if the prime minister

had said "no," that Turkey did not view Iran
as a friend, it would not have been possible
to convince Tehran to cooperate on this latest
proposal. Only Turkey can speak bluntly and
critically to the Iranians, Davutoglu contended,
but only because Ankara is showing public
messages of friendship for Iran.

Gordon pushed back that Ankara should give a
stern public message about the consequences if UN
resolutions are ignored. Davutoglu countered that
Erdoğan has given just such a statement in Tehran
when he visited. He emphasized that Turkey's
foreign policy is giving a "sense of justice"
and a "sense of vision" to the region. Turkey
has provided a "third option" in addition to
Iran and the Saudis (who he contended are viewed
as "puppets" of the US). The result is that we
"limit Iranian influence in the region."

OUR TERRORISTS

Other countries' views of Iran creep into the cables. One cable reflects an Israel so focused on regime change in Iran that it discusses supporting so-called "terrorist" groups [05TELAVIV2652].

In a 2007 meeting between Israeli Mossad chief Meir Dagan, US under secretary of state William Burns recorded the spy chief's "assessment of the Middle East Region." According to Burns, Dagan "stressed that Iran is economically vulnerable, and [he] pressed for more activity with Iran's minority groups aimed at regime change." The cable appears to implicate the US and Israel in aiding the Baluchistan Liberation Army in Baluchistan, and the Mojahedin-e-Khalq and the Kurdish Party for Free Life for Kurdistan in Iran. The latter group is associated with the PKK. All are considered to be "terrorist" organizations by Washington, and the US has helped Turkey target the PKK.

Dagan goes on to specify one of the "five pillars" of Israeli strategy in the region as Tel Aviv's policy to "Force Regime Change: Dagan said that more should be done to foment regime change in Iran, possibly with the support of student democracy movements, and ethnic groups (e.g. Azeris, Kurds, Baluchs) opposed to the ruling regime ... He added that Iran's minorities are 'raising their heads, and are tempted to resort to violence.'" The cable reflects that the US "war on terrorism" depends on whether they are "our" terrorists or "their" terrorists. As for the Kurds, while US intelligence on the PKK is being fed into the targeting computers of the Turks bombing Kurds in Iraq, the PKK's wing in Iran is being encouraged to try to overthrow the government in Tehran.

It is also somewhat disconcerting to hear how French diplomats characterize the Tehran regime:

```
[Jean-David] Levitte [former French ambassador to
the US and diplomatic advisor to French president
Nicolas Sarkozy] noted the Iranian response to
```

the overture of President Obama and the West was
a "farce," although Russia had received it as a
real initiative. The current Iranian regime is
effectively a fascist state and the time has come
to decide on next steps ... He noted that German
Chancellor Angela Merkel shares the view of the
French President and is willing to be firm on
sanctions, but that FM [foreign minister Frank-
Walter] Steinmeier was more cautious. The Iranian
regime must understand that it will be more
threatened by economic harm and the attendant
social unrest than it would be by negotiating
with the West. [09PARIS1254_a]

*   *   *

In general, the cables are fairly dismissive of Turkey's foreign
policy, which one 2010 cable says consists "mainly of popular
slogans, ceaseless trips, and innumerable signatures on MOUs
[Memorandums of Understanding] of little importance"
[10ANKARA87].

A 2010 cable from ambassador James Jeffrey notes: "Despite
their success and relative power, the Turks can't really compete
on equal terms with either the US or regional leaders (EU in the
Balkans, Russia in the Caucasus/Black Sea, Saudis, Egyptians and
even the Iranians in the ME [Middle East]). With Rolls Royce
ambition but Rover resources," the Turks "cheat" by finding
underdogs and taking up their cause. According to US diplomats,
little comes of it:

The AKP's new approach to international affairs
receives mixed reviews inside and outside of
Turkey.

It is not a major factor in the AKP's relative
popularity, but several elements of it

(unfortunately, those we are least happy with) do
appeal to voters. Criticism of Israel post-Gaza
is overwhelmingly popular, and the relatively
soft Turkish position on Iran—a country about
which many Turks are skeptical—is presumably
helpful with a narrow, but for Erdoğan's
electoral fate, important, more separate group of
Islamic voters associated with former PM Erbakan.
[10ANKARA87]

INTERNAL AFFAIRS

Because it is a major strategic ally, Turkey's internal politics are a major concern of the cables. But their central theme is clear: Does this aid American interests?

The analysis of Prime Minister Erdoğan—one cable describes him as lacking "vision" and "analytic depth"—and his Justice and Development Party (AKP) is accurate much of the time, and foreshadows some of the current turmoil in Turkey around government corruption [04ANKARA7211]. Erdoğan's authoritarian streak [04ANKARA348_a] and political deafness are recognized early on, as well as his stubbornness and demand for absolute loyalty [04ANKARA7211]:

Inside the [AKP] party, Erdogan's hunger for
power reveals itself in a sharp authoritarian
style and deep distrust of others: as a former
spiritual advisor to Erdogan and his wife Emine
put it, "Tayyip Bey believes in God … but doesn't
trust him." In surrounding himself with an iron
ring of sycophantic (but contemptuous) advisors,
Erdogan has isolated himself from a flow of
reliable information, which partially explains
his failure to understand the context—or the real
facts—of US operations in Tel Afar, Fallujah,

and elsewhere and his susceptibility to Islamic
theories. [04ANKARA348_a]

For US ambassador Eric Edelman to attribute Turkish discom-
fort with the bloody US sieges of Tel Afar and Fallujah during
the Iraq War—sieges that killed many civilians and destroyed
60 percent of Fallujah—as "a failure to understand the context"
suggests it is the embassy, not Erdoğan, who is out of touch.
But there is less concern for what this means vis-à-vis Turkish
democracy than for how it affects US interests: "[Prime Minister]
Erdoğan and his ruling AK Party seem to have a firm grip on
power ... Nevertheless, Erdoğan and his party face enormous
challenges if they are successfully to embrace core principles
of open society, carry out EU harmonization, and develop and
implement foreign policies in harmony with core US interests"
[04ANKARA7211].

As one cable puts it, in spite of an "imperfect, crabbed" Turkish
democracy that does not reach out to opponents, and the fact that
"AK appointees at the national and provincial level are incompetent and narrow-minded Islamists," still the US looks forward to
"continuing to work with Turkey on behalf of common interests
in Iraq, Afghanistan, the Caucasus, the Balkans, on terrorism,
on energy security, on the Cyprus problem and elsewhere in the
region and the world" [04ANKARA348_a].

A major interest for the US is the competition between the two
dominant Islamic political currents in Turkey—Erdoğan's AKP
and the Gülen Community. While many of the observations in
these cables are insightful, they also seem contradictory, a stance
that puzzles even some Turkish observers.[4]

Fethullah Gülen, who currently lives in self-imposed exile in
rural Pennsylvania, leads the Gülen Community. The movement
runs hundreds of secular schools, or "dershanes," in scores of
countries. In the US, Gülen schools[5] are the largest charter educational establishment in the country, with some 135 schools in
twenty-six states.[6] The schools are mainly aimed at preparing

students for university and civil exams. By all accounts, the Gülen dershanes are of high quality and successful—and cheaper than most of the competition—but according to US investigations they also serve as a recruiting ground for the Gülen movement. The schools are also a major source of funding for the Community, and the Erdoğan government's move to close them down is a serious threat to the movement's finances.[7]

The Gülenists favor wide-open free market capitalism and appear less conservative on social issues than the AKP. One needs to use the word "appear" because the Gülenists are secretive. They are considered more "pro-West," and more amenable to US policies in the region, particularly in relation to Israel. They also take a much harder nationalist line on the Kurds and have been less than supportive of peace talks between the Kurds and the AKP.

The Gülen Community also control food-service companies, construction firms, and several media outlets, including Samanyolu TV and the Turkish newspapers *Today's Zaman* and *Aksiyon Weekly*.

The Gülenists preach a moderate form of Islam that, at least on the surface, is ecumenical. A 1998 alliance between the Gülenists and Erdoğan's AKP successfully pushed the powerful Turkish military back to the barracks and elected an Islamist government in 2002. But in 2004 the former allies had a falling out that has now become a poisonous internal battle.

According to one cable on efforts by the Gülen Community to rally support for its schools and philosophy of religious cooperation, acting consul general Stuart Smith writes that the Gülen movement is prominent in the civil service and the Turkish National Police (TNP), "where they serve as the vanguard for the Ergenekon investigations." The latter, according to the embassy, relates to an "alleged vast underground network" of mainly military officers who were accused of plotting a coup in 2004. Hundreds of officers were tried and imprisoned [05ISTANBUL1336_a].

Recent revelations, however, suggest that some of the evidence was either tainted or manufactured. For instance, one incriminating document supposedly produced in 2004 used software that was not invented until 2007. "Ergenekon" is the name of a mythical Turkish empire in Central Asia—and, according to the authorities, the name of a secret group of officers. But the Turkish prosecution has never convincingly proved that the organization even existed. The Ergenekon investigation has deepened the divide between the Gülenists and the Turkish military. As one 2009 cable notes, "Not surprisingly, contacts close to the Turkish General Staff openly loathe Gülen, and contend that he and his legions of supporters are embarked on a ruthless quest not only to undermine the Turkish military but to transform Turkey into an Islamic republic similar to Iran" [09ANKARA1722].

Given the bitterness of the current infighting between Gülen and Erdoğan and its negative impact on the economy—the growth rate, which averaged 5 percent over the past decade, has dropped from a projected 3.7 percent to 1.7 percent—US contacts with the Turkish General Staff are worth watching.[8] Political infighting, coupled with an economic crisis, creates fertile ground for the kind of plots—real or imagined—that seem almost ingrained in Turkey's political life. It is no accident that Turkish soap operas are popular throughout the region.

A 2005 cable by acting consul general Stuart Smith reflects a deep suspicion about the Gülen Community:

```
Given the Gulenists' penetration of the National
Police … and many media outlets and their record
of going after anyone who criticizes Gulen,
others who are skeptical about Gulen's intentions
feel intimidated from expressing their views
publicly. Privately they note: (1) Gulen's
sharply radical past as a fiery Islamist preacher
in the 1970's-1980's [sic]; (2) his ruthlessness
in banishing people from his more inner circles
```

```
(Gulenists have admitted to us that they are
petrified of making a "mistake"); (3) his and
his inner circles' insistence that followers of
Gulen mediate their study of Islam solely through
his writings, i.e. no toleration of dissent
or critical thinking; and (4) the cult-like
obedience and conformity that he and the layers
of his movement insist on in his global network
of schools, his media outlets, and his business
associations. [05ISTANBUL1336_a]
```

The US embassy indicates that there are "deep and widespread doubts ... about his movement's ultimate intentions" and questions about the movement's transparency [05ISTANBUL1336_a]. According to Consul General Deborah K. Jones,

```
Fethullah Gulen sits at the center of a vast
and growing network encompassing more than 160
affiliated organizations in over 30 countries,
50 in the US. As a result, Gulen supporters
account for an increasing proportion of Mission
Turkey's nonimmigrant visa application pool.
As applicants, Gulenists are almost uniformly
evasive about their purpose of travel and their
relationships to Gulen, raising questions
among Consular officers. Our unease is also
shared by secular segments of Turkish society…
[06ISTANBUL832]
```

```
In short, the Gulenists' efforts to mold future
generations through their international schools
network (which exist throughout Turkey, Asia
[e.g., Afghanistan and Pakistan], and Africa, in
addition to the US) and their documented efforts
to infiltrate not just Turkish business circles
```

but government institutions as well have raised
questions about whether their moderation would
continue if they gained a preponderant voice in
Turkish Islam. [05ISTANBUL1336_a]

Despite all these alarm bells, the cable concludes that "the movement does not pose a clear and present danger to the state."

What goes unsaid is that the Gülenists are more supportive of many US policies than the more independent-minded AKP. Gülen, for instance, was sharply critical of Erdoğan's falling out with Israel over the 2010 Gaza flotilla that saw Israeli commandos kill eight Turks and one Turkish-American. The Gülenists have also been frostier to Iran. In short, as long as Gülen supports US policies in the region, Washington can live with a cult.

The cables suggest that the US may not be an entirely neutral bystander in the current fight over corruption (or power, depending on how one wants to look at it) between the Gülenists and Erdoğan. Has the US encouraged the Gülenists to go after Erdoğan? Are they quietly supporting President Gül—who is more pro-Israeli and closer to the Gülen Community—against the prime minister? One of the chief targets of the recent corruption probe is the Turkish Halkbank, which reportedly exported $6 billion in gold to Iran in 2012. The US has been trying to stop Halkbank from trading with Iran for several years. Did the US alert the Gülenists to Halkbank, or encourage prosecutors to go after the institution?

Many of the corruption charges directed at Erdoğan and his cabinet are undoubtedly valid. As numerous cables point out, the AKP is up to its elbows in malfeasance. But this is hardly breaking news to the Americans: the cables were reporting corruption in 2004. Ambassador Edelman writes in late December 2004 that the AKP

swept to power [in 2002] by promising to root
out corruption. However, in increasing numbers

```
AKPers from ministers on down, people close to
the party, are telling us of conflicts of interest
or serious corruption … We have heard from two
contacts that Erdogan has eight accounts in Swiss
banks; his explanation that his wealth comes from
the wedding presents guests gave his son and that
a Turkish businessman is paying the educational
expenses of all four Erdogan children in the US
purely altruistically are lame. [04ANKARA7211]
```

Even though the corruption scandal exploded on the eve of critical local elections in 2014, it apparently had little effect on the voters, a majority of whom voted for AKP candidates.

A major target of the Gülenist-dominated Turkish National Police is Hakan Fidan, an under secretary in the Turkish National Security agency. Prosecutors have charged him with carrying out secret talks with the Kurds aimed at settling that long-running war—charges that could derail the delicate negotiations between the AKP and the Kurds. It was, in fact, the attack on Fidan that sparked open warfare between the Gülenists and the Erdoğan government.[9]

Fidan was also accused by US newspapers of exposing Israeli agents in Iran—an accusation that was apparently fed to the American media by Gülen supporters in Turkey.

The attack on Fidan is consistent with the Gülenists' approach to the Kurds, Iran, and Israel. But did any of that information come via the Americans? The US is deeply concerned about almost anything involving Israel and Iran, and Washington is not happy about the current drift of the AKP on these two issues. Formally warm relations between Ankara and Tel Aviv have cooled considerably following the Israeli attack on Gaza in 2008–09 and the 2010 Israeli attack on the Turkish aid ship Mavi Marmara that killed several Turks. Turkey has also been negotiating with Iran over energy at a time when Washington is trying to isolate the Tehran regime.

For all their professed "concerns" about the Gülen Community, one cable outlines talking points for the media about how Gülen is promoting a secular Turkey:

Why is the US sheltering Fethullah Gulen and doesn't this mean that the US is promoting a non-secular Turkey?

A:

• The US is not "sheltering" Mr Gulen and his presence in the US is not based on any political decision. Mr Gulen applied for, and received, permanent residence in the US after a lengthy process that ended in 2008 when a Federal court ruled that he deserved to be viewed as an "alien of extraordinary ability" based on his extensive writings and his leadership of a worldwide religious organization.

• As a Green Card holder, Mr Gulen is entitled to all the privileges which that status entails. His presence in the US should not be viewed as a reflection of US policy toward Turkey.

[09ANKARA1722]

At the same time, the embassy reports that "our friends" say Gülen is working "on behalf of Islam in order to carry out a nationwide restoration."

The AKP does not come off particularly well, either. It is depicted as an organization, according to one cable, "compromised by its Islamist neo-Ottoman reflexes and single-party state spoils system." One cable is particularly critical of both Erdoğan and foreign secretary Davutoğlu: "According to a broad range of our contacts, Erdoğan reads minimally, mainly the Islamic-leaning press. According to others with broad and deep contacts throughout the establishment, Erdoğan refuses to draw on the analysis" of the military and national intelligence organization. "He never had a realistic world view ... instead he relies on his charisma, instincts, and the filtering of advisors who pull conspiracy theories off the web or who are lost in neo-Ottoman Islamist fantasies, e.g. Islamist foreign policy advisor and Gül ally Ahmet Davutoğlu" [05ANKARA1730_a].

It is sometimes difficult to figure out whether the cables are straightforward reportage or the writer is being ironic. In a 2004 cable speaking about the AKP, US ambassador Eric Edelman reports:

```
We have also run into the rarely openly-
spoken, but widespread belief among adherents
of the Turk-Islam synthesis that Turkey's role
is to spread Islam in Europe, "to take back
Andalusia and avenge the defeat of the siege
of Vienna in 1683," as one participant in a
recent meeting at AKP's main think tank put it.
This thinking parallels the logic behind the
approach of [Foreign Minister] Ahmet Davutoglu.
[04ANKARA7211]
```

*　　*　　*

The documents procured for the public by WikiLeaks not only give one a clear-eyed view of American foreign policy goals, but also help us think about what the future holds in this very pivotal region of the world. For all of Washington's focus on the "war on terrorism," American diplomats are comfortable talking about using organizations that the US officially considers "terrorist" to weaken, or even overthrow, their opponents.

There are certainly revelations: the role of Turkey in the odious rendition program, the lobbying in the interests of powerful aviation corporations, and the willingness to turn a blind eye to authoritarian practices in order to further foreign policy interests. But the diplomatic cables also serve as a guide to the future.

Turkey is currently involved in an intense political conflict between the Gülenists and the Erdoğan government—a conflict whose outcome the Americans have a stake in. A government like Erdoğan's—hostile to Israel, in conflict with the US-supported military regime in Egypt, and suspicious of the kind of freewheeling, wide-open market capitalism favored by the Americans—is not looked upon with great favor in Washington. In that sense, the Gülenists, whom the cables suggest are secretive and clandestine, are more in tune with US interests in the region.

The last Turkish elections demonstrated Erdoğan's hold over half the Turkish population, but the country is deeply polarized and the economy is shaky. Washington has been sharply critical of Erdoğan's attempts to suppress the media and the internet, and of his effort to increase his personal power. Turkey is preparing another flotilla to confront the Israelis over Gaza, and Ankara and Tehran are reviving the idea of a joint gas pipeline. Certainly Washington is not happy about more tensions between Turkey and Israel, and it is deeply opposed to any joint energy cooperation with Iran.

What the cables tell us is that the US will act in its interests regardless of what that might stir up in the Middle East. That should be a sobering thought for Turks and Americans.

9. Israel

Stephen Zunes and Peter Certo

In late 2010, as WikiLeaks prepared to release a treasure trove of stolen diplomatic cables issued from US embassies and consulates all over the world, Washington flew into a full panic. As law-enforcement agencies prepared a de facto embargo of WikiLeaks' finances, US diplomats scurried to warn their foreign counterparts about what revelations might lie ahead.[1]

One might have expected similar distress from Washington's clients in Israel, who after all were carrying on one of the most sensitive relationships with the United States in the world. Washington supplies Israel's military to the tune of $3 billion per year and uses its seat on the UN Security Council to shield Israel from diplomatic blowback over its policies in Palestine and Lebanon (even when they contradict Washington's own). The two countries' militaries are linked more closely than ever.

A number of exchanges revealed in these cables were potentially embarrassing to the US government, with US officials blithely accepting ongoing Israeli violations of international humanitarian law, UN Security Council resolutions, and a landmark ruling by the International Court of Justice against Israeli settlements in the Occupied Palestinian Territories. These were the kinds of violations that would almost inevitably have led to calls for sanctions if committed by a government less endeared to the United States than the right-wing coalition in Israel.

Poring through the documents, however, one gets a clear

sense that—rather than a case of "the tail wagging the dog," or of US diplomats cowering under pressure by the vaunted "Israel Lobby"—US support for Israeli policies appears to reflect the perception, however misguided, that US and Israeli interests almost always coincide. And sometimes, apparently, so do those of Washington's autocratic Arab allies. Instead of panicking along with their counterparts in Washington, Israeli officials homed in on early revelations that a laundry list of Sunni Arab autocrats had secretly appealed to Washington to launch strikes on Iran's nuclear infrastructure—or, in the words of King Abdullah of Saudi Arabia, to "cut off the head of the snake."[2]

"For the first time in modern history," Prime Minister Benjamin Netanyahu boasted in November 2010, "there is a not inconsequential agreement … in Israel and countries in the region that the main threat stems from Iran, its expansion plans, and its weaponization steps." Calling on Arab leaders "to say publicly what they say secretly," Netanyahu triumphantly declared "the bogus argument that it is Israel that is threatening peace and security in the region" debunked.[3] Summing up the Israeli establishment's apparent glee, Israeli columnist Sever Plocker quipped, "If WikiLeaks had not existed, Israel would have had to invent it."[4] (In the fever swamps of the internet, some conspiracy theorists apparently agreed. After the first cables were published, a handful of Arabic websites—and later some white nationalist publications in the United States—alleged that WikiLeaks was in fact part of a "Jewish conspiracy" to conceal damaging information about Israel while embarrassing its rivals.[5])

But the US-Israel alliance would not escape scrutiny after all. Thousands more cables related to Israel were released in the subsequent months, culminating in a drop of nearly 4,000 in August 2011. Although they contain only a few bombshells, they lend critical texture to some of the highest-profile issues in the US-Israeli relationship—namely Palestine and Iran—at a moment in which American civil society has become increasingly disillusioned with the US government's handling of both issues. These cables confirm the spaces between the stated policy preferences of the US and Israeli governments even as they illustrate how the spaces collapse in the execution of those policies. As historical documents, they may prove to be among the more valuable chronicles of a period in which both the limits and the extent of Washington's "special relationship" with Israel were laid bare.

PALESTINE

Since the 1993 Oslo Accords, Israeli-Palestinian relations have been locked into a framework that was never meant to be permanent. In an attempt to lighten the Israeli military's footprint in the Occupied Palestinian Territories, the accords created a putative Palestinian governing body—the Palestinian Authority (PA)—to administer parts of the Gaza Strip and the West Bank until a more legitimate Palestinian governing body could be established and a final status agreement reached between Israel and the Palestinian Liberation Organization (PLO). Since 2005, Fatah party leader Mahmoud Abbas—sometimes known as Abu Mazen—has led both the PA, charged with administering the Palestinian territories, and the PLO, charged with negotiating their release from Israel.

On paper, the Oslo system looked like a workable roadmap. But after years of stagnation, continued Israeli colonization of the occupied territories, a second and far more violent Intifada, the takeover by Hamas of the Gaza Strip, and all the violence—both spectacular and mundane—that has attended the ongoing Israeli occupation, the Oslo system has ossified into a hollow shell of what it was supposed to be. In the absence of a roadmap for the establishment of a viable Palestinian state alongside Israel, the PA remains dependent on the Israeli government, whose forces surround the scores of tiny West Bank enclaves under PA administration. In the meantime, in the hope of developing a model of self-reliance and self-empowerment—known as the "bottom-up approach"—Palestinian officials have tried to prove that they can provide good government, economic opportunity, the rule of law, and security for Israel. Their goal has been to convince Israel and the United States that they can govern a viable and responsible state if Israel withdraws its occupation forces from the West Bank and East Jerusalem.

The Israeli government, however, has no such intentions. After he was elected in 2009, Israeli prime minister Benjamin Netanyahu continued to go through the motions of (sometimes) showing up for US-sponsored peace talks. But, anchoring a coalition of right-wing parties largely hostile to Palestinian rights, from the beginning he evinced little interest in negotiating the creation of a real Palestinian state. Instead, the WikiLeaks cables reveal an Israeli prime minister more concerned with pacifying the West Bank through a combination of repression, economic development, and security cooperation with the PA, while blaming Abbas and his ministers—the same people Israel relies upon to keep a lid on Palestinian unrest—for the stalled peace process. All the while, illegal Israeli settlements continue to bloom throughout the West Bank and East Jerusalem, and the popular legitimacy of the PA grows ever weaker.

In Gaza, meanwhile, where Hamas wrested control from the PA in 2007, Israel relies on economic strangulation—punctuated by periodic air strikes and ground invasions—to prevent Hamas, which won a plurality of votes and the majority of seats in Palestinian parliamentary elections the previous year, from consolidating its power and normalizing life in the embattled enclave. Here there is no pretense at all at a plan to break the impasse—although Israeli and American officials complain bitterly about the diplomatic fallout over the Goldstone Report, the UN-sanctioned study that documented war crimes in Israel's 2008–09 invasion of Gaza.

That is where we find the "peace process" in much of the period documented by WikiLeaks. Significantly, while public statements from the Obama administration frequently blamed "both sides" for the failure of the peace process, the cables appear to indicate a growing consensus in private that the bulk of the blame lay on the Israeli side.

THE WEST BANK

Many of the cables come amid a US push for new peace talks early on in the Obama administration. In a November 2009 cable briefing US deputy secretary of state James Steinberg, US diplomats clearly sensed that the window for a two-state solution was closing, and with it the plausibility of using the PA to pacify the territories in lieu of one:

> The failure to re-launch Israeli-Palestinian
> negotiations and the political crisis in the
> Palestinian Authority is deeply disturbing
> to Israelis who still believe in a two-state
> solution. Even GOI [Government of Israel]
> skeptics are worried that the lack of a political
> dialogue and talk of a collapse of the PA are
> undermining the bottom-up approach they advocate
> as the alternative to a final-status agreement.
> [09TELAVIV2473]

When it comes to negotiations with the Palestinians, Netanyahu and his deputies feed US diplomats and visiting dignitaries many of the same complaints they make publicly. Israel's claims to good faith hinge on Netanyahu's June 2009 outline for a demilitarized Palestinian "state," if you can call it that, which would consist of a series of tiny non-contiguous cantons and would leave most of the sovereignty usually conceded to states—over borders, air space, airwaves, and security forces, among other things—to Israel. In his statements to a visiting US congressional delegation, the then newly elected Netanyahu painted these restrictions as a magnanimous concession unmatched by anything on the Palestinian side:

Netanyahu said he was prepared for "arrangements"
with the Palestinians that would entail
some limits on their sovereignty such as no
Palestinian army, and Israeli control over
borders, airspace, and the electromagnetic
spectrum. Netanyahu asserted that seventy to
eighty percent of Israelis are ready to make
concessions for peace but they do not believe
they have a Palestinian partner. [09TELAVIV1184]

In remarks the following year to US Representative Ike Skelton
(D-MO), Netanyahu added to his complaints:

Netanyahu stated that his government had removed
hundreds of obstacles and roadblocks in the West
Bank, helping the West Bank economy achieve a
seven percent growth rate, adding "and we can
kick it up to ten percent growth." Netanyahu said
his Bar Ilan address last June [where he outlined
his conditions for Palestinian statehood]
had been difficult for him, but it had united
Israelis in support of accepting a demilitarized
Palestinian state. The current GOI had also
restrained construction in settlements more than
its past several predecessors.

Netanyahu then contrasted his efforts with the
PA, which he said is maintaining a "political
and economic boycott" of Israel, setting
preconditions for negotiations, supporting the
Goldstone Report in the UN, and is now talking
about a unilateral declaration of independence.
Israel wants to engage, but the Palestinians do
not. [09TELAVIV2777]

Of course, Netanyahu repeatedly demonstrated the limits of his own willingness to engage core Palestinian demands. According to a 2007 cable, for example, when he was still opposition leader, Netanyahu told visiting US officials that he would judge the seriousness of Palestinian intentions by their willingness to relinquish the right of return for Palestinian refugees: "Netanyahu noted that he thought dropping the 'right of return' was the acid test of Arab intentions and insisted that he would never allow a single Palestinian refugee to return to Israel" [07TELAVIV1114]. Palestinian documents leaked to Al Jazeera noted that the Palestinian side had already dropped demands for a wholesale right of return, yet Netanyahu has never acknowledged this.[6]

Meanwhile, Netanyahu also splits hairs on the crucial issue of illegal Israeli settlement construction in the West Bank and East Jerusalem. Pressed by the Obama administration to agree to a freeze on settlement construction to make space for Israeli-Palestinian peace talks, Netanyahu argued that, while he could agree to slow the construction of new settlements, he had no problem building up older ones:

```
Regarding settlements, Netanyahu said he
wants to work with the US on the basis of
the understandings reached with the Bush
Administration, i.e. that Israel will not build
new settlements or seize more land, but if
families grow, they will still have the right
to build within existing settlement boundaries.
Now Israel is hearing that the US wants no
construction at all. Israelis consider this
position to be unfair, he said. The question
is whether the US is seeking a geographic
or a demographic restriction on settlements.
[09TELAVIV1184]
```

Palestinians have long considered the Israeli settlement project an attempt to create "facts on the ground" to force Palestine to cede more land to Israel proper in any agreement over a future Palestinian state. Indeed, in an apparent effort to encourage young Palestinians to leave Israeli-occupied lands, the Israeli government has routinely denied growing Palestinian families in occupied territories the right to build additional housing on their property or even expand existing homes, ruthlessly bull-dozing houses that violate such restrictions. But in remarks to a US congressional delegation, Netanyahu blithely insisted that the PA could be swayed: "[Settlements are] more of an issue with the US than with the Palestinians, Netanyahu asserted, arguing that the PA will go along if there is an understanding between Israel and the US" [09TELAVIV1184]. In fact, a leaked cable from Paris included a claim from Israeli defense minister Ehud Barak that the United States and Israel had reached just such an understanding: "MFA Middle East Director (Assistant Secretary-equivalent) Patrice Paoli informed POL Minister Counselor June 18 that Israeli Defense Minister Ehud Barak told French officials in Paris June 15 that the Israelis have a 'secret accord' with the USG to continue the 'natural growth' of Israeli settlements in the West Bank" [09PARIS827].

The expansion of Israeli settlements is illegal under the Fourth Geneva Convention, which forbids any country to transfer its civilian population onto lands seized by military force. Given that a landmark 2004 ruling by the International Court of Justice underscored the obligation of parties to the convention—such as the United States—to make a good-faith effort to enforce such international legal obligations on countries with which they have influence, this acknowledgment places the Obama administration in direct violation of this longstanding legal principle and of the World Court ruling. Similarly, continued Israeli settlement activity also violates UN Security Council resolutions 446, 452, 465, and 471, which underscored the illegality of Israel's coloni-zation of occupied territories. The "secret accord" would appear to place the United States in violation of Article 7 of UNSC resolution 465, which calls upon member states not to assist Israel in its settlement drive. Indeed, not long after this cable was written, the United States vetoed an otherwise unanimous UN Security Council resolution reiterating the illegality of Israeli settlements in the occupied territories and calling for a freeze on additional construction.[7]

At times, US diplomats seem to recognize the shell game that is being played here. In one cable, the writer acknowledges the limited appeal of Netanyahu's proposed Palestinian "state" to actual Palestinians: "Palestinian PM [Salam] Fayyad has recently termed Netanyahu's goal a 'Mickey Mouse state' due to all the limitations on Palestinian sovereignty that it would appear to entail" [09TELAVIV2473].

Despite claims by the Obama administration that it is trying to "bring the sides together" and Washington's insistence that attempting to impose a settlement based on international law is unnecessary, that same cable acknowledged: "[T]here is too wide a gap between the maximum offer any Israeli prime minister could make and the minimum terms any Palestinian leader could accept and [politically] survive" [09TELAVIV2473]. And in another, the author made a distinctly skeptical comment about Israeli assurances that IDF incursions into the West Bank were on the decline: "Israeli officials [cited] the decreased number of direct-action incursions, checkpoints and patrols, and seemingly drew a correlation between reduced IDF activity and increased PASF [Palestinian Authority Security Forces] authority" [09TELAVIV2482]. US officials were also skeptical of a claim by Netanyahu confidant (and later Israel's US ambassador) Ron Dermer that the settlement freeze was broadly unpopular in Israel: "[Dermer] claimed that 70 percent of the Israeli public opposes the moratorium (note: we think this is an exaggeration)" [09TELAVIV2734].

Nonetheless, Netanyahu's complaints seemed to suffice for many visiting US officials, who throughout the cables express more concerns about Palestinian governance than rights or state-hood. When US Representative Gary Ackerman (D-NY) did offer the rare nudge on Palestinian statehood, partly as a means to buoy Abbas and the PA, Netanyahu pivoted quickly back to economic issues:

> Ackerman commented that President Abbas and Prime Minister Fayyad are necessary for progress, and noted that both Israel and the US will be in trouble if they are replaced. Something needs to be done to help them stay in power. They need material support but also the promise of statehood. Foreign investment in the West Bank would give a real horizon as well. Netanyahu agreed, saying Gulf Arab investors had been successful in transforming their own societies and could make a great contribution to the Palestinians. He added that he wanted to bring Gulf investors into the West Bank since they would change reality for the Palestinians but also give Israelis confidence. Ackerman responded that this was a great idea, but it should come from Abbas, not Israel. The more credit Abbas can take for steps forward, the better.
> [09TELAVIV1184]

So, despite their lip service to the two-state solution, Israeli officials seem to suggest that conditions in the occupied West Bank are fine as they are, pointing to donor-fueled economic growth and often praising the "progress" made in the development of the Palestinian security forces, which—like the PA more generally—rely on international financing and an effective Israeli mandate. In November 2009, Israeli Major General Benny Gantz told Pentagon envoy Alexander Vershbow that he was quite pleased with the Palestinian security forces, although he made clear that

the IDF would always get the last word in the Palestinian territories: "MG Gantz cited Palestinian security sector reform as
a major accomplishment, stating that on-the-ground coordination between the PASF and IDF units has improved dramatically.
Despite these positive developments though, Israeli officials
repeatedly underscored the importance of retaining the right
to disrupt terrorist operations in the West Bank and Gaza"
[09TELAVIV2482].

In an earlier meeting, Israeli Security Agency (ISA) head Yuval
Diskin hinted at the extent of the cooperation between the ISA,
the elite Palestinian Preventative Security Organization (PSO),
and the Egyptian General Intelligence Organization (GIO):

```
In the West Bank, Diskin said that ISA has
established a very good working relationship
with the Preventive Security Organization (PSO)
and the General Intelligence Organization (GIO).
Diskin said that the PSO shares with ISA almost
all the intelligence that it collects. They
understand that Israel's security is central to
their survival in the struggle with Hamas in the
West Bank. [07TELAVIV1732]
```

In another cable, Israeli defense minister Ehud Barak effused
that he was "extremely impressed" [09TELAVIV1177] with US
efforts to train Palestinian security forces, who have been accused
by a number of human rights groups of committing human rights
violations alongside IDF troops.[8]

In effect, many of these cables suggest a degree of confidence among Israeli officials that they can create a version of
the neutered Palestinian "state" described by Netanyahu without
having to make the political concessions about land, refugees, or
borders that would accompany an actual, viable two-state solution. With economic conditions tolerable, if not flourishing, and
Palestinian security forces and civil authorities handling much of

the on-the-ground administration, Israeli officials seem to reckon that they can maintain a kind of status quo in the more populous Palestinian cities and towns, even as Israeli settlement building slowly erodes any prospect of a viable Palestinian state.

But even this plan requires a relatively stable partner in the PA, especially if, as Netanyahu told the delegation led by Ackerman, he has no wish to "rule" the Palestinians. And here, despite their supposed bearishness on the Palestinian economy—and despite Dermer's assertion that Abbas is not "as weak as he claims"— Israeli officials seem to have grave doubts.

In moments of candor, they even seem to admit that it is their own badgering of Abbas that has eroded his standing among Palestinians. Israeli Major General Amos Gilad admitted as much to Vershbow in 2009 when he acknowledged that Israeli pressure on Abbas to play down the Goldstone Report and compromise on Israeli settlements had proved politically devastating for the PA leader. And yet, when Gilad expressed his support for a new round of talks, it was clear that he supported them purely as a means to buy time for Abbas, not to negotiate peace or make concessions on substantive issues:

```
It was widely agreed that President Abbas is
currently in a weakened political state, and
Israeli officials generally cast a dour assessment
of Abbas's future. In one exchange, Amos Gilad
stated his opinion that Abbas will not survive
politically past the year 2011. Gilad further
stated that Abbas is facing unprecedented criticism
within the Palestinian Authority over his
handling of the Goldstone report, and that this,
coupled with a stubborn HAMAS, has weakened Abbas
considerably. The Israelis said the perception
in the Arab world was that the US had encouraged
Abbas to take difficult positions on Goldstone
and settlements only to walk away from him. ASD
```

Vershbow queried Gilad over measures that could be
taken to bolster Abbas. Gilad responded by stating
that Israeli-Palestinian peace discussions need to
be resumed immediately, but without preconditions,
and that both parties need to seek further
cooperation on a range of issues—specifically on
the security sector front. [09TELAVIV2482]

Neither US nor Israeli officials could deny the growing discontent
in the West Bank over ongoing Israeli repression and colonization. A February 2010 cable from the embassy in Tel Aviv frankly
discusses a premeditated effort by the Israeli army to increase its
use of force against peaceful demonstrators in the West Bank:

In meetings with US officials on February 4,
OC Central Command MG Avi Mizrachi expressed
frustration with on-going demonstrations in
the West Bank, which he believes are being
orchestrated to increase tensions. Mizrachi,
whose area of responsibility includes all of the
West Bank and Central Israel, warned that the IDF
will start to be more assertive in how it deals
with these demonstrations, even demonstrations
that appear peaceful … Mizrachi warned that he
will start sending his trucks with "dirty water"[9]
to break up these protests, even if they are not
violent, because they serve no purpose other than
creating friction …

On orders from Mizrachi, West Bank commander BG
Nitzan Alon and West Bank civil administrator BG
Poli Mordechi reportedly met with the Palestinian
security force commanders recently to deliver
a strong message that they must stop these
demonstrations or the IDF will. [10TELAVIV344]

In a revealing comment, the deputy chief of mission Luis G. Moreno noted the frustrations Israeli occupation forces had in dealing with the largely nonviolent protests: "Less violent demonstrations are likely to stymie the IDF. As MOD Pol-Mil chief Amos Gilad told USG [US Government] interlocutors recently, 'we don't do Gandhi very well'" [10TELAVIV344].

GAZA STRIP

For a hint at what could happen in the West Bank in the event of the PA's collapse, one need look no further than Gaza. In 2005, Israel unilaterally withdrew its remaining soldiers from parts of the Gaza Strip and dismantled its illegal settlements. Although Israel maintained control of Gaza's borders, waters, and air space—and thus remained both legally and practically the occupying power—the disengagement was part of a bid to turn the territory over to the full control of the PA. Following the Hamas victory in Palestinian legislative elections the following year and efforts by Fatah and Hamas to form a coalition government, the Bush administration pushed elements in Fatah's security apparatus to stage a coup that would expel Hamas from the PA. Learning of the incipient putsch in June 2007, Hamas attacked first. After several days of fighting, Fatah had rid the Palestine Authority and the West Bank of Hamas. But Hamas consolidated control in its stronghold in the Gaza Strip, where it subsequently functioned as the de facto government.

More than any other, this period revealed the depths of Israeli and US dependence on the Fatah-dominated PA to keep Palestinian resistance movements in check, as well as Fatah's own increasingly desperate reliance on Israel to bolster itself against its Palestinian rivals. In a particularly revealing June 2007 conversation shortly before Hamas routed Fatah's fighters in Gaza, ISA chief Diskin lamented Fatah's weakness and revealed to US ambassador Richard Jones that Fatah had urgently requested Israeli assistance in its battle against Hamas:

```
[Diskin] lamented what he characterized as a
crisis of leadership in Fatah, with PA President
Abbas already focusing on his retirement, and
his possible successors incapable of leading
the Palestinians in both the West Bank and the
Gaza Strip … Diskin said that Fatah is on its
"last legs," and that the situation bodes ill
for Israel … "We have received requests to train
their forces in Egypt and Yemen," [Diskin said] …
"They are approaching a zero-sum situation, and
yet they ask us to attack Hamas. This is a new
development. We have never seen this before. They
are desperate." [07TELAVIV1732]
```

Diskin also alluded to a plan by the US security coordinator for Israel, Lieutenant General Keith Dayton, to "equip security forces loyal to Palestinian Authority President Abbas and Fatah," though he said he personally opposed it out of concern that the weapons would find their way to Hamas.

By beating back what amounted to an armed US- and Israeli-backed coup, Hamas ejected Fatah and with it the entire Oslo framework from the Gaza Strip. In a meeting with Ambassador Jones that took place as Fatah's forces were crumbling, Israeli Defense Intelligence director Amos Yadlin presaged what would come next, musing that "Israel would be 'happy' if Hamas took over Gaza"—"as long as they have no (air or sea) port"—because "the IDF could then deal with Gaza as a hostile state" [07TELAVIV1733].

With Israel devoid of a proxy power to rule Gaza in its stead, that is exactly what happened. Israel had already imposed tight economic sanctions on Gaza in what amounted to a collective punishment for Hamas's electoral victory. Almost immediately following the battle for Gaza, the IDF scaled up its blockade of the tiny enclave by land, air, and sea, locking down the borders against any movement of human beings as well as virtually all consumer goods—civilian or military. Dov Weissglass, an adviser to then prime minister Ehud Olmert, famously said of this strategy, "The idea is to put the Palestinians on a diet, but not to make them die of hunger."[10]

In a number of leaked diplomatic cables, other officials piled on. The month after Fatah's expulsion, Israeli National Security Council (NSC) counter-terrorism head Danny Arditi held that the blockade would help Fatah regroup, but added an ominous note about a looming confrontation between Israel and Hamas:

```
Arditi said that the objective was to damage
the Hamas government in Gaza financially without
creating a humanitarian crisis, and to buy time
for Fatah to rebuild support. In Arditi's view,
the current closure of Gaza border crossings
is not sustainable, with several thousand
Palestinians currently waiting to enter Gaza
through the Rafah crossing. Arditi said that
sooner or later the GOI would have to deal with
Hamas … "This is not the first time we have tried
to help Fatah," [an aide] noted. [07TELAVIV2281]
```

But by late 2008, Israeli officials seemed to have determined that the blockade was sustainable after all: "As part of their overall embargo plan against Gaza, Israeli officials have confirmed to [US economic officers] on multiple occasions that they intend to keep the Gazan economy on the brink of collapse without quite pushing it over the edge" [08TELAVIV2447].

Interestingly, although the United States would vigorously defend the Gaza blockade in international bodies, US officials seemed to be wary of this plan. Early on, they urged Israel at least to release funds to pay PA civil-service employees who remained in Gaza:

```
A USG policy that encourages the GOI to review
its present policies (as requested by the
Office of the Quartet Representative and the PA)
while pressing the Israelis to approve as much
funding each month as possible under security
constraints, assisting the PA to improve its
regulatory regimes and due diligence procedures,
and continuing to foster direct dialogue between
officials of the GOI and PA on Gaza issues in the
monthly Joint Economic Commission meetings is our
best bet for minimizing economic/political gains
to Hamas in Gaza. [08TELAVIV2447]
```

But Gilad retorted: "They're not getting a dime."

The following months were marked by periodic exchanges of fire between Palestinian militants in Gaza and IDF forces, with militants shooting rockets and mortars into Israeli territory and Israel launching air strikes and occasional cross-border incursions into Gaza. The skirmishing was briefly stalled by a six-month ceasefire brokered by the Egyptians in June 2008. As late as May 2008, on the eve of the ceasefire, US officials apparently believed that a full-scale Israeli assault was unlikely, although they noted that Israel remained wary of the political ramifications of a ceasefire for Abbas. This cable was prepared specifically as a "scenesetter" for President Bush's May 2008 visit to Israel:

```
The [Israeli] political leadership is grappling
with whether an Egyptian-negotiated ceasefire in
Gaza would calm the situation or make it worse
by strengthening Hamas politically and militarily
while undermining Abbas. The only other options
on the table involve a broader armed conflict with
Hamas, but Israel is constrained by the potential
for high casualties, international condemnation,
```

```
and most of all, the lack of a good exit strategy
should it decide to invade Gaza to topple the
Hamas regime there. All of these calculations
could be upset at any time by a rocket from Gaza
that strikes a busy school or hospital, thus
forcing the Israeli leadership to order massive
retaliation. [08TELAVIV1005]
```

Yet despite a lull in the fighting, the ceasefire proved ineffectual. Israeli air strikes and incursions continued, Palestinian rocket and mortar attacks resumed, and in several instances Israeli forces killed Palestinian civilians near the Israel-Gaza border. By December the ceasefire was dead, and a final exchange of violence culminated in Operation Cast Lead—a massive Israeli air assault, naval bombardment, and ground invasion of the Gaza strip. By the time Israeli forces pulled back in mid January 2009, the United Nations estimated that some 1,400 Palestinians were dead—the majority of them civilians and non-military police officers. Even now, much of the strip remains unreconstructed—with even greater damage following seven weeks of bombardment during the summer of 2014—as Israel has continued to restrict the availability of construction materials. (Although the US government has downplayed the humanitarian crisis in Gaza, a leaked cable from Doha noted Senator John Kerry apparently acknowledging the extent of the humanitarian situation, telling Qatari prime minister Hamad Al Thani in 2010, "I was shocked by what I saw in Gaza.") [10DOHA71]

In one of the most explosive revelations from the entire tranche of cables about Israel, Defense Minister Ehud Barak confessed to visiting US members of Congress that Israel had approached both the PA and Egypt about taking control of Gaza prior to the Israeli invasion. But despite Fatah's evident entreaties for assistance, its leaders apparently understood that this was a bridge too far: "[Barak] explained that the GOI had consulted with Egypt and Fatah prior to Operation Cast Lead, asking if they were willing to assume control of Gaza once Israel defeated Hamas. Not surprisingly, Barak said, the GOI received negative answers from both" [09TELAVIV1177].

Following the assault, the "international opprobrium" that US officials apparently thought would prevent Israel from invading Gaza materialized in full force. The UN-commissioned Goldstone Report on the conflict, released in September 2009, documented evidence of potential war crimes on both sides of the fighting, including allegations that Israel had targeted civilians and civilian infrastructure, used shells laced with white phosphorus in populated areas (including on hospitals), and tortured detainees, among other charges. The report recommended that charges against both Israeli and Hamas officials be referred to the International Criminal Court if the two sides failed to investigate their own conduct during the war. The UN Human Rights Council subsequently passed a resolution endorsing the report's findings, and the General Assembly twice voted to urge the two sides to conduct independent investigations based on its allegations.

The Israeli government was furious. Netanyahu, who took office two and a half months after the cessation of hostilities, fiercely defended Israel's conduct in the war in a conversation with US Representative Ike Skelton. Netanyahu insinuated that he considered the Goldstone Report a threat to Israel on par with his other favored doomsday device—Iran's alleged nuclear weapons program: "Netanyahu commented that Israel currently faces three principal threats: Iran's nuclear program, missile proliferation and the Goldstone Report. Goldstone gave terrorists immunity to attack Israel if they fire from populated areas" [09TELAVIV2777].

In reality, the report said no such thing. Indeed, it underscored the threat faced by Israel from indiscriminate Hamas rocket attacks and acknowledged Israel's right to self-defense; it only raised concerns about disproportionate Israeli military operations impacting civilians. The committee's chair, Richard

Goldstone, enjoyed a longstanding reputation for fairness and objectivity, having previously led the war crimes prosecutions for Yugoslavia and Rwanda. Contrary to the Israeli government's protestations, Goldstone—a Jewish South African jurist whose daughter is an Israeli citizen—had agreed to accept the appointment by the UNHRC only if the commission's mandate were expanded to look at the actions of both sides of the conflict instead of just Israel's.[11] Indeed, it was the fact that Goldstone and his colleagues on the commission had such strong reputations for fairness that made the report so devastating. Furthermore, their findings closely paralleled similar detailed investigations by Amnesty International, Human Rights Watch, and other reputable human rights organizations.

Even Netanyahu seemed to admit that Israeli officials could be charged with war crimes for their role in the assault:

```
Netanyahu asked the [congressional delegation] to
imagine a situation in which Israeli Air Force
pilots must consult with lawyers before they can
travel abroad. Former PM Olmert, former FonMin
Livni and DefMin Barak could be hauled before
the International Criminal Court. Netanyahu
said he could not accept that IDF soldiers
could be charged with war crimes for protecting
their country from constant attack … Deliberate
targeting of civilians is a war crime, but what
should Israel do when terrorists deliberately
target Israeli civilians and then hide within
their civilian population? [09TELAVIV2777]
```

In reality, while the Goldstone Commission Report, Amnesty International, and Human Rights Watch criticized Hamas for stationing weapons and fighters in close proximity to civilian areas in the crowded enclave, they were unable to find any evidence for the oft-repeated Israeli charge that Hamas had used "human shields" or otherwise took deliberate steps to "hide within their civilian population."[12]

Nevertheless, the Obama administration sided with the right-wing Israeli government against the broad consensus of the international human rights community. Echoing Israel's complaints about the report, the US government vigorously lobbied its allies at the UN to vote against it in the General Assembly and, when that failed, prevented the UN Security Council (UNSC) from even considering it. In several cables, US officials reminded their Israeli counterparts of this fact, and in at least one case offered to advise Israel on how to conduct its own investigation to "deflect" damage from the report: "NSC Director for Israel and Palestinian Affairs Prem Kumar noted continued UNSC interest in the Goldstone Report, and asked Israel to inform the United States on any additional efforts or investigations the GOI was taking to help deflect any further damage from the report" [09TELAVIV2502].

In late 2009, in fact, Ron Dermer expressed his appreciation for Washington's backing on a host of diplomatic and military issues—including the Goldstone Report—and even suggested that the Obama administration's support for the Israeli government was underrated in Israel itself:

> Dermer said that President Obama does not
> get enough credit in Israel for weighing in
> helpfully on several issues affecting Israel's
> security, such as the Goldstone Report, problems
> in [Turkey-Israel] relations, and the recent
> EU Council statement on East Jerusalem [which
> described it as occupied territory]. He also
> cited the successful Juniper Cobra joint missile
> defense exercise hosted by Israel in November
> 2009. [09TELAVIV2734]

One cable seems to suggest that Washington's defense of Israeli war crimes was related to concerns about possible legal action over US violations of international law elsewhere. In a meeting with the Israeli Defense Ministry's director general, Alexander Vershbow offered to share ways in which the United States had engaged in damage control in response to allegations of war crimes in its own conflicts:

> [The Israeli director general] also compared
> Israeli operations in Gaza to US operations in
> Iraq and Afghanistan and stated that Israel
> would do whatever was necessary to protect its
> population. In response, ASD Vershbow recalled US
> support for Israel in handling of the Goldstone
> report, and offered to share US experience in
> investigating incidents in Iraq and Afghanistan
> as the GOI considered whether to conduct an
> additional investigation. [09TELAVIV2482]

The memos also reveal acknowledgement by the Israelis that their 2006 war on Lebanon and 2008–09 war on Gaza—both enthusiastically supported by the Bush administration and large bipartisan majorities in Congress—failed to reach any of their goals, and that both Hamas and Hezbollah had effectively re-armed. Rather than re-evaluating their failed strategies, however, Israeli officials were already beginning to think in terms of their next war on Gaza, which would be even more extreme in terms of civilian casualties: a cable quotes General Gabi Ashkanazi as saying, "In the next war Israel cannot accept any restrictions on warfare in urban areas." He also made clear that war could come soon, noting, "I'm preparing the Israeli army for a major war, since it is easier to scale down to a smaller operation than to do the opposite."[13]

Ironically, despite the hostility toward Hamas from the United States and Israel, in cables detailing the regular secret talks between US officials and Shin Bet head Yuval Diskin and other Israeli military officials, it was recognized that it would be unwise to weaken Hamas too much. Despite the United States and Israel blaming every rocket attack on Hamas, they acknowledged that even more extremist militias were emerging in Gaza, and only Hamas could control them. Major General Yoav Galant, responsible for security in Gaza and southern Israel, noted that Hamas needed to be "strong enough to enforce a ceasefire":

> Major General Yoav Galant recently commented
> to us that Israel's political leadership has
> not yet made the necessary policy choices among
> competing priorities: a short-term priority of
> wanting Hamas to be strong enough to enforce
> the de facto ceasefire and prevent the firing
> of rockets and mortars into Israel; a medium
> priority of preventing Hamas from consolidating
> its hold on Gaza; and a longer-term priority of
> avoiding a return of Israeli control of Gaza and
> full responsibility for the wellbeing of Gaza's
> civilian population. [09TELAVIV2473]

Though it remains a flashpoint for many of Israel's international critics, the Goldstone Report ultimately faded into near irrelevance as an instrument for mitigating the fallout from Cast Lead. Indeed, Israel exceeded its penchant for disproportionate violence in Operation Protective Edge in 2014, which killed an even greater number of Palestinians.

Israel still holds Gaza up as a cautionary tale for why it can never withdraw completely from the occupied West Bank. But in the absence of a plan for a viable Palestinian state with a legitimate government, it remains very much in doubt whether the chosen proxies of the United States and Israel can hold on there forever. These WikiLeaks cables offer some crucial texture and insight into what may turn out to be the last years of the Oslo process.

IRAN

Save for a crippling international and US sanctions regime on Iran, recent years have seen more sound than fury in the ongoing dustup over Iran's nuclear enrichment program—at least compared to the ghastly drama of Cast Lead and the slow-motion violence of settlement construction in the West Bank.

For years, Israeli politicians—especially Netanyahu and his deputies—have alleged, despite the lack of any credible evidence, that Iran is developing a nuclear weapon. Bolstered by their neoconservative supporters in the United States, they have urged the US government to take a hard line on Iran, constantly invoking alarmist timelines about Iran's purported progress toward a nuclear weapon and threatening to strike Iran on their own if Washington refuses—although few believe that Israel would be willing to go to war without an assurance of support from the United States (which bipartisan majorities of Congress have repeatedly sought to secure).[14]

Although US intelligence agencies concluded as far back as 2007 that Iran was not actively developing a nuclear weapon, the US government has played along with its Israeli allies, rallying the international community around sanctions, cooperating with Israel on covert actions against Iran, and forever maintaining that "all options are on the table," including during high-level negotiations between Iran and the P5+1 powers (the five members of the UN Security Council plus Germany) in 2013 and 2014.

Cables including Israeli warnings about Iran are too numerous to itemize. But a few are worthy of comment. For one thing, such warnings are often brought up in the context of Israeli-Palestinian negotiations, giving some credence to critics of Netanyahu who allege that his government hyped the Iran threat as a means to distract US and international attention from the stagnant peace process. The cable describing Netanyahu's 2009 meeting with a US congressional delegation, for example, links them explicitly: "If we could add a political process to the cooperation that currently exists, we could get security, economic development, and peace [between Israel and Palestine]. Netanyahu warned, however, that if Iran gets a nuclear bomb, the peace process would be 'washed away.'" Netanyahu went on to predict that Iran could have a bomb by 2012: "Representative [Steve] Israel asked Netanyahu about the timetable for Iran to achieve a nuclear weapon. Netanyahu responded that Iran has the capability now to make one bomb or they could wait and make several bombs in a year or two" [09TELAVIV2777].

But Netanyahu's was just one of a variety of do-or-die timelines offered by Israeli officials on the Iranian bomb. In 2009, Ehud Barak estimated that the window for air strikes could be closed within as little as six months: "Barak estimated a window between 6 and 18 months from now in which stopping Iran from acquiring nuclear weapons might still be viable. After that, he said, any military solution would result in unacceptable collateral damage" [09TELAVIV1177].

To their credit, US diplomats sometimes seemed to suspect that Israel was putting them on—an impression expressed beautifully in this 2009 cable stemming from a meeting with Israeli military intelligence officials:

```
Israel continues to offer a worst-case assessment
of the Iranian nuclear program, emphasizing that
the window for stopping the program (by military
means if necessary) is rapidly closing. General
Baidatz argued that it would take Iran one year
to obtain a nuclear weapon and two and a half
years to build an arsenal of three weapons. By
2012 Iran would be able to build one weapon
within weeks and an arsenal within six months.
(COMMENT: It is unclear if the Israelis firmly
believe this or are using worst-case estimates to
raise greater urgency from the United States).
[09TELAVIV2482]
```

Alluding to such skepticism, Barak insisted that the United States was being overly cautious just because the Bush administration's claims about WMDs in Iraq had turned out to be false. Despite the catastrophic fallout from the war in Iraq, Barak urged the US government to lower its standard of proof for Iran:

> When asked if the USG and GOI have fundamental
> differences of opinion when assessing Iran's
> nuclear program, Barak said we share the same
> intelligence, but acknowledged differences in
> analysis. He suggested that the USG view is
> similar to presenting evidence in a criminal
> court case in which a defendant is presumed
> innocent until proven guilty. As such, USG
> standards are tougher—especially following
> the failure to find WMD in Iraq—while end-
> products such as the 2007 [National Intelligence
> Estimate, which concluded that Iran's nuclear
> weapons research had been suspended for years]
> unintentionally take on a softer tone as a
> result. Barak said the fate of the region and the
> world rests on our ability to prevent Iran from
> gaining nuclear weapons—as such, the standards
> for determining guilt should be lower as the
> costs are higher. [09TELAVIV1177]

But Israeli leaders were peddling alarm about Iran long before Netanyahu and his coalition came to power in 2009. At times, in fact, Israeli officials themselves even admitted that their estimates should be taken with a grain of salt. This 2005 cable offered a brief history of past Israeli claims about Iran:

> GOI officials have given different timelines for
> when they believe Iran will have full enrichment
> capability. In February, PM [Ariel] Sharon told

the Secretary that he believes there is still
time remaining to pressure Iran, but that the
window of opportunity is closing quickly. DefMin
Mofaz cautioned that Iran is "less than one year
away," while the head of research in military
intelligence estimated that Iran would reach this
point by early 2007. Technical experts at the
[Israeli Atomic Energy Commission] predicted that
Iran would have enrichment capability within six
months of the end of the suspension agreement.
A few GOI officials admitted informally that
these estimates need to be taken with caution.
The head of the [Ministry of Foreign Affairs']
strategic affairs division recalled that GOI
assessments from 1993 predicted that Iran would
possess an atomic bomb by 1998 at the latest.
[05TELAVIV1593]

And despite the constant agitation for military action, some Israeli analysts—such as the former deputy director general of the Atomic Energy Agency, Ariel Levita—told US officials that it would be almost impossible for a military campaign to destroy Iran's nuclear program, given how widely dispersed Iran's various installations were.[15]

The absence of a political consensus on military force, however, has not prevented clandestine US and Israeli action against Iran. In recent years, for example, numerous Iranian nuclear scientists have been murdered in a program journalist Seymour Hersh linked to Israel, the United States, and the Iranian dissident group Mojahedin-e-Khalq (MEK), which was officially considered a terrorist organization by the US government at the time.[16]

In a 2007 meeting with the US undersecretary of state for political affairs, J. Nicholas Burns, Mossad head Meir Dagan—who would make headlines years later for calling the idea of a military assault on Iran "stupid"[17]—outlined a "five-pillared" Israeli plan to undermine Iran and prompt regime change, including implicitly through clandestine violence and agitation of Iranian minority groups:

Dagan described how the Israeli strategy consists of five pillars:

A) Political Approach: Dagan praised efforts to bring Iran before the UNSC, and signaled his agreement with the pursuit of a third sanctions resolution. He acknowledged that pressure on Iran is building up, but said this approach alone will not resolve the crisis. He stressed that the timetable for political action is different than the nuclear project's timetable.

B) Covert Measures: Dagan and the Under Secretary agreed not to discuss this approach in the larger group setting.

C) Counterproliferation: Dagan underscored the need to prevent know-how and technology from making their way to Iran, and said that more can be done in this area.

D) Sanctions: Dagan said that the biggest successes had so far been in this area. Three Iranian banks are on the verge of collapse. The financial sanctions are having a nationwide impact. Iran's regime can no longer just deal with the bankers themselves.

E) Force Regime Change: Dagan said that more should be done to foment regime change in Iran, possibly with the support of student democracy

```
movements, and ethnic groups (e.g., Azeris,
Kurds, Baluchs) opposed to the ruling regime.
```

[07TELAVIV2652]

In particular, Dagan emphasized the latter option:

```
Dagan urged more attention on regime change,
asserting that more could be done to develop the
identities of ethnic minorities in Iran. He said
he was sure that Israel and the US could "change
the ruling regime in Iran, and its attitude
towards backing terror regimes." He added,
"We could also get them to delay their nuclear
project. Iran could become a normal state."
[07TELAVIV 2652]
```

But when it comes to a truly comprehensive diplomatic agreement for a nuclear-free Middle East, Israel—the region's only actual nuclear power—has been steadfastly resistant. In 2004, for example, as the International Atomic Energy Agency (IAEA) was attempting to convene a conference to discuss a possible Nuclear-Weapons-Free Zone in the Middle East (MENWFZ)—one that would be comparable to already existing zones in Africa, Latin America, Southeast Asia, Central Asia, and the South Pacific—Israel consented to send a token delegation but balked at the participation of the Arab League. It also insisted that the conference be reduced to an "intellectual" exercise that produced no "concrete deliverables":

```
[Israeli Atomic Energy Commission deputy Eli]
Levite said that the ground rules and agenda for
the forum reflect understandings between Israel
and the IAEA. He said the Israeli view is that
the IAEA has no role to play in this area, but
```

that Israel wanted to make a "very modest gesture
of good will." The only outstanding issue is that
[IAEA director general Mohamed] El-Baradei wants
a more public platform that would include the
Arab League as an observer. The Israelis see Arab
League participation as "very difficult" and "not
consistent with the learning process" ... Israel
has urged the IAEA to view the forum as "a one-
time educational event." Levite said the outcome
should be "intellectual" without any concrete
deliverables. [04TELAVIV6547]

The proposal ultimately collapsed, but US officials revived it
in 2007 in a bid to preempt a possible IAEA resolution urging
Israel to join the Nonproliferation Treaty, which would require
Israel to declare its nuclear arsenal and submit to international
inspections. US negotiators apparently calculated that conven-
ing a toothless conference on the proposed MENWFZ would be
less embarrassing for Israel—and its supporters in Washington—
than an Israel-specific resolution by the same institution Israel
has called on to investigate Iran:

Israel Ambassador [Israel] Michaeli told [US
IAEA] Ambassador [Gregory] Schulte that he hopes
the EU can head off an Israel-specific agenda
item at the September General Conference (GC),
but he was not optimistic. Despite divisions
within the Arab group, Michaeli thought that an
Israeli threat resolution would likely be added
to the GC agenda. Israel was "reluctant" about
a US suggestion that the Director General revive
the Forum on a Middle East Nuclear Weapons Free
Zone (MENWFZ), but did not want to close the door
either, as long as it were based on the agreed
2004 agenda. [07UNVIEVIENNA435]

The forum was eventually held in 2011 and, true to Israel's demands, produced no binding "deliverables."

THE YEARS TO COME

The years following the release of the WikiLeaks cable tranche were tumultuous ones for the Middle East. But in Israel's neighborhood, familiar patterns played out, if more dramatically—and violently—than before. In yet another round of US-brokered Middle East peace talks in 2013–14, Israel again refused to budge on settlements or other controversial issues, leading Abbas and the PA to apply for membership in a score of international bodies and to seek a unity pact with Hamas that would see a technocratic PA government assume putative control of Gaza.

Although this latter development was exactly what Israel said it wanted—an end to Hamas's control of the Gaza strip—Netanyahu's government accused Abbas of consorting with terrorists and pulled out of the talks. When three teenaged Israeli settlers were kidnapped and murdered in the West Bank a short time later, Israeli security forces flooded the territory, ransacking Hamas offices, arresting elected officials, and demanding cooperation from the PA in a transparent effort to drive a wedge between the newly reunited Fatah and Hamas factions. As the situation spiraled out of control, air strikes and cross-border fire between Israel and Gaza gave way to Operation Protective Edge, an aggressive Israeli incursion into Gaza that claimed even more lives than Cast Lead, including those of hundreds of children. In the aftermath of the devastation, the future of the unity government appeared uncertain. But with many of the battered Palestinians in Gaza increasingly convinced that Israel would never make peace with them, Hamas's standing in the territory appeared all but assured. In a sense, this turn of events was a natural—if unremittingly tragic—evolution of the decaying Oslo process documented in the WikiLeaks cables.

If there was a silver lining to the sorry episode, it was that civil society groups in the United States—especially Jewish organizations like Jewish Voice for Peace, Americans for Peace Now, and J Street—had grown more willing than ever to speak out against Israel's policies in Palestine, and to call their own government to account for enabling them.[18] The US government itself, unfortunately, remained unmoved, with both the Senate and the House passing a series of resolutions by unanimous consent endorsing the campaign against Hamas.

News on the Iran front was more encouraging. In the years following the *Cablegate* revelations, Iran and the P5+1 powers broke fresh ground on an international understanding over Iran's nuclear enrichment program, with supporters of the talks beating back an aggressive push by Israel and its allies in the US Congress to scuttle them. Washington's nearly unprecedented decision to push forward on the talks over Israel's strident objections may have reflected the quiet US understanding, illustrated in a few of these cables, that the Iranian nuclear threat was never quite what Israel made it out to be.

Even prior to the diplomatic breakthrough with Iran, the White House—if not Congress—was keen to avoid giving any impression to Israel or the international community that the United States would sanction a unilateral Israeli military strike on Iran. A May 2009 cable detailing a meeting between US and Israeli defense officials, for example, noted that Washington would sell Israel "bunker buster" bombs that could penetrate underground—where some of Iran's nuclear installations are located—but took pains to ensure that the transfer would not be seen as a "green light" from Washington for Israel to attack: "Both sides then discussed the upcoming delivery of GBU-28 bunker busting bombs to Israel, noting that the transfer should be handled quietly to avoid any allegations that the USG is helping Israel prepare for a strike against Iran" [09TELAVIV2500].

The issue was especially salient in light of Israel's 2007 strike on an alleged nuclear reactor in Syria, a strike Meir Dagan had previously told US officials Israel had "no intention" of carrying out [07TELAVIV2280].

But by the same token, Washington's ongoing cooperation with Israel in clandestine operations against Iran—not to mention its covering for Israel's own undeclared nuclear arsenal, one of the giant elephants in the room in the entire nuclear saga with Tehran—indicates that Washington's big problem with Iran has never been nuclear weapons per se. Rather, it is the threat that a rival power might eclipse or challenge US and Israeli hegemony in the Middle East. Although negotiations over Tehran's nuclear program might yet pave the way for a broader understanding between the United States and Iran, Israel will not be put in a corner quietly.

It is worth remembering that, despite the deeply entrenched "special relationship" between Israel and the United States, there is nothing preventing Washington from charting a course independent of Israel's—if it can find the political will. Consider this 2009 cable in which Israeli officials complain that Washington's prodigious arms sales to the Gulf monarchies could undermine Israel's "qualitative military edge," or QME—the Israeli military advantage over its neighbors that Washington has pledged to uphold. Israeli major generals Amos Gilad and Benny Gantz make their concerns about the sales known, but then acknowledge that Washington has its own interests in the region and simply ask to be fairly apprised as developments unfold:

Amos Gilad acknowledged the sometimes difficult position the US finds itself in given its global interests, and conceded that Israel's security focus is so narrow that its QME concerns often clash with broader American security interests in the region ... While not explicitly saying it, [Gantz] seemed to acknowledge that Israel does not expect that all QME decisions will break in its favor, but that Israel only expects a fair

and equitable process that incorporates "intimate
dialogue." [09TELAVIV2482]

At the time of writing, "the US interest" in a viable two-state
solution and a stable truce with Iran has not yet received the
same accommodation as Washington's interest in plying its
autocratic Gulf allies with American-made weapons. But if the
WikiLeaks diplomatic cables illustrate nothing else, it is that even
the most formidable geopolitical forces must play out in the decisions made by individuals. Change will not likely come from the
characters who populate the cables—but it might yet come from
the people who read them.

10. Syria

Robert Naiman

On August 31, 2013, US president Barack Obama announced that he intended to launch a military attack on Syria in response to a chemical weapons attack in that country that the US blamed on the Syrian government. Obama assured the US public that this would be a limited action solely intended to punish the Assad government for using chemical weapons; the goal of US military action would not be to overthrow the Assad government, nor to change the balance of forces in Syria's sectarian civil war.

History shows that public understanding of US foreign policy depends crucially on assessing the motivations of US officials. It is likely inevitable as a result that US officials will present themselves to the public as having more noble motivations than they share with each other in private, and therefore that if members of the public had access to the motivations shared in private, they might make different assessments of US policy. This is a key reason why WikiLeaks' publishing of US diplomatic cables was so important.

The cables gave the public a recent window into the strategies and motivations of US officials as they expressed them to each other, not as they usually expressed them to the public. In the case of Syria, the cables show that regime change had been a long-standing goal of US policy; that the US promoted sectarianism in support of its regime-change policy, thus helping lay the foundation for the sectarian civil war and massive bloodshed that we see in Syria today; that key components of the Bush administration's regime-change policy remained in place even as the Obama administration moved publicly toward a policy of engagement; and that the US government was much more interested in the Syrian government's foreign policy, particularly its relationship with Iran, than in human rights inside Syria.

A December 13, 2006 cable, "Influencing the SARG [Syrian government] in the End of 2006,"[1] indicates that, as far back as 2006—five years before "Arab Spring" protests in Syria—destabilizing the Syrian government was a central motivation of US policy. The author of the cable was William Roebuck, at the time chargé d'affaires at the US embassy in Damascus. The cable outlines strategies for destabilizing the Syrian government. In his summary of the cable, Roebuck wrote:

```
We believe Bashar's weaknesses are in how
he chooses to react to looming issues, both
perceived and real, such as the conflict between
economic reform steps (however limited) and
entrenched, corrupt forces, the Kurdish question,
and the potential threat to the regime from
the increasing presence of transiting Islamist
extremists. This cable summarizes our assessment
of these vulnerabilities and suggests that there
may be actions, statements, and signals that the
USG can send that will improve the likelihood of
such opportunities arising.
```

This cable suggests that the US goal in December 2006 was to undermine the Syrian government by any available means, and that what mattered was whether US action would help destabilize the government, not what other impacts the action might have. In public the US was in favor of economic reform, but in private the US saw conflict between economic reform and "entrenched, corrupt forces" as an "opportunity." In public, the US was opposed to "Islamist extremists" everywhere; but in private it saw the "potential threat to the regime from the increasing presence of transiting Islamist extremists" as an "opportunity" that the US should take action to try to increase.

Roebuck lists Syria's relationship with Iran as a "vulnerability" that the US should try to "exploit." His suggested means of doing so are instructive:

```
Possible action:

PLAY ON SUNNI FEARS OF IRANIAN INFLUENCE: There
are fears in Syria that the Iranians are active
in both Shia proselytizing and conversion of,
mostly poor, Sunnis. Though often exaggerated,
such fears reflect an element of the Sunni
community in Syria that is increasingly upset by
and focused on the spread of Iranian influence in
their country through activities ranging from
mosque construction to business.

Both the local Egyptian and Saudi missions here
(as well as prominent Syrian Sunni religious
leaders) are giving increasing attention to the
matter and we should coordinate more closely with
their governments on ways to better publicize and
focus regional attention on the issue. [Emphasis
added.]
```

Roebuck thus argued that the US should try to destabilize the Syrian government by coordinating more closely with Egypt and Saudi Arabia to fan sectarian tensions between Sunni and Shia, including by the promotion of "exaggerated" fears of Shia proselytizing of Sunnis, and of concern about "the spread of Iranian influence" in Syria in the form of mosque construction and business activity.

By 2014, the sectarian Sunni-Shia character of the civil war in Syria was bemoaned in the United States as an unfortunate development. But in December 2006, the man heading the US embassy in Syria advocated in a cable to the secretary of state and the White House that the US government collaborate with Saudi Arabia and Egypt to promote sectarian conflict in Syria between Sunni and Shia as a means of destabilizing the Syrian government. At that time, no one in the US government could credibly have claimed innocence of the possible implications of such a policy. This cable was written at the height of the sectarian Sunni-Shia civil war in Iraq, which the US military was unsuccessfully trying to contain. US public disgust with the sectarian civil war in Iraq unleashed by the US invasion had just cost Republicans control of Congress in the November 2006 election. The election result immediately precipitated the resignation of Donald Rumsfeld as secretary of defense. No one working for the US government on foreign policy at the time could have been unaware of the implications of promoting Sunni-Shia sectarianism.

It was easy to predict then that, while a strategy of promoting sectarian conflict in Syria might indeed help undermine the Syrian government, it could also help destroy Syrian society. But this consideration does not appear in Roebuck's memo at all, as he recommends that the US government cooperate with Saudi Arabia and Egypt to promote sectarian tensions.

Note that, while Roebuck was serving in the George W. Bush administration, he was a career Foreign Service officer, a permanent senior member in good standing of the US government's foreign policy apparatus. He went on to serve in the US embassies in Iraq and Libya—in the latter as chargé d'affaires—in the Obama administration. There is no evidence that anyone in the US foreign policy apparatus found the views expressed by Roebuck in this cable particularly controversial; its publication did not cause scandal in US foreign policy circles.

So, while the sectarian character of the civil war in Syria is now publicly bemoaned in the West, it seems fair to say that in

2006 the US government foreign policy apparatus believed that promoting sectarianism in Syria was a good idea, which would foster "US interests" by destabilizing the Syrian government.

This view of US policy—happy to make common cause with Saudi Arabia in fostering Sunni-Shia sectarianism in Syria, and preoccupied with Syria's relationship with Iran above all else—is buttressed by a March 22, 2009 cable from the US embassy in Saudi Arabia, "Saudi Intelligence Chief Talks Regional Security with Brennan Delegation."[2] This cable summarizes a March 15 meeting including then US counter-terrorism adviser John Brennan and US ambassador to Saudi Arabia Ford Fraker with Prince Muqrin bin Abdulaziz al-Saud, the head of Saudi Arabia's external intelligence agency. Ambassador Fraker's summary recounted:

7. (C) PERSIAN MEDDLING: Prince Muqrin described Iran as "all over the place now." The "Shiite crescent is becoming a full moon," encompassing Lebanon, Syria, Iraq, Bahrain, Kuwait and Yemen among Iran's targets. In the Kingdom, he said "we have problems in Medina and Eastern Province." When asked if he saw Iran's hand in last month's Medina Riots (reftels), he strongly affirmed his belief that they were "definitely" Iranian supported. *(Comment: Muqrin's view was not necessarily supported by post's Saudi Shi'a sources.)* Muqrin bluntly stated "Iran is becoming a pain in the …" and he expressed hope the President "can get them straight, or straighten them out." [Emphasis added.]

Ambassador Fraker's comment that "Muqrin's view was not necessarily supported by post's Saudi Shi'a sources" was a severe understatement. Indeed, in a February 24, 2009 cable, "Saudi Shia Clash With Police In Medina,"[3] Ambassador Fraker had reported in detail on the February 20 clashes between Saudi security forces and Saudi Shia pilgrims in Medina, without any mention of Iran. Fraker's February 24 cable primarily attributed the clashes to, first, Saudi police having denied the Saudi Shia pilgrims access to the Baqi'a cemetery opposite the Prophet's Mosque, and second, the Saudi Shia community's long-simmering anger over historical grievances.

This indicates that the US government knows perfectly well that the Saudi government blames Iran for things that the Iranian government has nothing to do with, and is unconcerned about this. For the US government's own internal information, the ambassador wanted to make clear that, as far as the US embassy knew, the Medina clashes had nothing to do with Iran. But as the 2006 cable makes clear, the US was happy to make common cause with Saudi Arabia in blaming Iran for things happening in Syria with which Iran had no connection. The next paragraph in the cable is also instructive:

> 8. (C) WEANING SYRIA FROM IRAN: Brennan asked
> Muqrin if he believed the Syrians were interested
> in improving relations with the United States.
> "I can't say anything positive or negative," he
> replied, declining to give an opinion. Muqrin
> observed that the Syrians would not detach from
> Iran without "a supplement."

This suggests that, for the US government in March 2009, Syria's interest in "improving relations with the United States" was equivalent to its being "weaned" from Iran. Thus, the thing that the US really cared about in Syria was not, for example, the Syrian government's respect for human rights, but Syria's relationship with Iran.

Another theme that recurred in the 2006 cable focusing on Syria's "vulnerabilities" and how the US should try to exploit them was that the US should take actions to try to destabilize the

Syrian government by provoking it to "overreact," both internally and externally. One of the "vulnerabilities" of the Syrian government listed by Roebuck that the US should try to exploit was its "enormous irritation" with former Syrian vice president Abdul Halim Khaddam, leader of the opposition-in-exile National Salvation Front. Roebuck wrote:

```
Vulnerability:


THE KHADDAM FACTOR: Khaddam knows where the
regime skeletons are hidden, which provokes
enormous irritation from Bashar, vastly
disproportionate to any support Khaddam has
within Syria. Bashar Asad personally, and
his regime in general, follow every news item
involving Khaddam with tremendous emotional
interest. The regime reacts with self-defeating
anger whenever another Arab country hosts Khaddam
or allows him to make a public statement through
any of its media outlets.
```

Roebuck proposed a means of exploiting this vulnerability:

```
Possible Action:


We should continue to encourage the Saudis and
others to allow Khaddam access to their media
outlets, providing him with venues for airing the
SARG's dirty laundry. We should anticipate an
overreaction by the regime that will add to its
isolation and alienation from its Arab neighbors.
```

Note that the goal of encouraging the Saudis and others to "allow Khaddam access to their media outlets" was not to promote democracy and human rights in Syria, but to provoke the Syrian government to do things that would "add to its isolation" from its Arab neighbors. Of course, if the Syrian government acted in ways that would "add to its isolation," then the US could cite such actions as evidence that the Syrian government was a rogue government, unable or unwilling to conform to international norms, threatening to US allies in the region, and therefore that the US government had to take some action in response. But now we know that such actions by the Syrian government would not have been unfortunate developments to which the US would be reluctantly forced to respond, but the explicit goal of US policy.

For example, in August 2007—eight months after the above cable—Khaddam told the Saudi daily *Al-Watan* that reported remarks of Syrian vice president Faruq al-Sharaa criticizing Saudi Arabia were "part of the policy pursued by the ruling clique, which aims at severing Syrian links with the Arab world and tying it further to Iran's regional strategy," the Beirut *Daily Star* reported.[4] The newspaper noted that the Syrian government was actually trying to "calm the spat," saying that statements attributed to Sharaa had been "distorted." In the context of Roebuck's cable, these developments make sense: it was the US and its ally Khaddam that were trying to inflame tensions between Syria and Saudi Arabia, not the Syrian government.

Whatever one thinks of Khaddam or the Syrian government, it is not surprising that the latter would have been provoked in 2006 by countries like Saudi Arabia giving Khaddam a media platform, given what Khaddam had used such platforms to say in the past. Note that there is no question that the Saudi government controls the country's media for a purpose like this, exactly as Roebuck implied—indeed, the Riyadh embassy cable about the Medina clashes between Saudi police and Shia pilgrims noted that the Saudi government had successfully pressured Saudi media to suppress reports of the clashes.

Here is what Khaddam told the Saudi-owned newspaper *Asharq Al-Awsat* about his goals in an interview in Paris in January 2006:

```
Q: What are you[r] current priorities? Do you
want to reform the regime, reform it, or topple
it?
```

```
A: This regime cannot be reformed so there is
nothing left but to oust it.⁵
```

One imagines that if Iran had given a former Bahraini or Egyptian vice president a platform to say about the government of Bahrain or Egypt that "this regime cannot be reformed so there is nothing left but to oust it," the US government would not have responded well. This was eleven months before Roebuck's cable, and five years before the "Arab Spring" protests in Syria. We are told in the West that the current efforts to topple the Syrian government by force were a reaction to the Syrian government's repression of dissent in 2011, but now we know that "regime change" was the policy of the US and its allies five years earlier.

Indeed, another of Roebuck's proposed actions to exploit Syria's "vulnerabilities" carried the same message:

```
Possible Action:
```

```
ENCOURAGE RUMORS AND SIGNALS OF EXTERNAL
PLOTTING:
```

```
The regime is intensely sensitive to rumors about
coup-plotting and restlessness in the security
services and military. Regional allies like Egypt
and Saudi Arabia should be encouraged to meet
with figures like Khaddam and Rif'at Asad as a way
of sending such signals, with appropriate leaking
of the meetings afterwards. This again touches on
this insular regime's paranoia and increases the
possibility of a self-defeating over-reaction.
```

According to Roebuck, if Egypt and Saudi Arabia met with Khaddam and news of the meetings were "appropriately leaked," that would send a signal to the Syrian government that these countries were plotting against Syria, perhaps trying to organize a coup.

It is revealing that Roebuck described the regime as "paranoid" for having fears that appear to have been quite rational—fears based in significant measure on the actions of the United States and its allies. The most powerful government in the world and its allies in the region aspired to overthrow the Syrian government. The US has a long track record[6] of trying to overthrow governments around the world, including in the region—and, as Roebuck's cable makes clear, far from trying to allay such fears, the US wanted to exacerbate them. In 2014, the US was arming insurgents who were trying to kill Syrian government officials. Was the Syrian government's fear of the US government irrational, or was it rational?

Failure to acknowledge that US adversaries' fears of the US are rational suggests a world-view in which US threats are normal, unremarkable, an inevitable part of the landscape, which only mentally unstable people would object to, their fears serving as proof of their irrationality. During the US-organized Contra war against Nicaragua in the 1980s, Alexander Cockburn recounted the view of a visiting US congressman toward Nicaragua: "Nicaraguans tell stories about these US fact-finders with a certain wry incredulity. One congressman listened to a commandante outlining the murderous rampages of the contras and then burst out, 'Suppose 5,000 contras cross your border. Suppose you are invaded by the entire Honduran army, why should you worry. Are you *that* insecure?'"[7]

Listing resistance to economic reforms as a "vulnerability," Roebuck wrote:

Vulnerability:

REFORM FORCES VERSUS BAATHISTS—OTHER CORRUPT
ELITES:

Bashar keeps unveiling a steady stream of
initiatives on economic reform and it is
certainly possible he believes this issue is his
legacy to Syria. *While limited and ineffectual,
these steps have brought back Syrian expats to
invest* and have created at least the illusion of
increasing openness. Finding ways to publicly
call into question Bashar's reform efforts—
pointing, for example to the use of reform
to disguise cronyism—would embarrass Bashar
and *undercut these efforts to shore up his
legitimacy.* [Emphasis added.]

Presumably, a key goal of economic reforms would have been to "[bring] back Syrian expats to invest," so if they had that effect, then they were not ineffectual. This makes clear what Roebuck was and was not interested in. He was not interested in Syrian economic reforms succeeding in facilitating private investment, but in their failure. Even if they had some success, he wanted to present them as a failure and "undercut these efforts to shore up his legitimacy."

The notion of "legitimacy" is a key one in US foreign policy toward adversary governments in countries that the US does not fear militarily (for example, because they have nuclear weapons). In the context of US foreign policy, the term "legitimacy" is a term of art that has a specific meaning. The usual notion of government "legitimacy" in international law and diplomacy, which the US applies to its allies without question, has nothing to do with whether we like the policies of the government in question or consider them just. Either you are the recognized government of the country, holding its seat at the United Nations, or you are not. Hardly anyone in Washington would suggest that the governments of Saudi Arabia, Bahrain, Jordan, or Israel are not "legitimate" because they were not elected by all of their subjects or because they engage in gross violations of human rights. Nor would many in Washington suggest that the governments of Russia or China are not "legitimate," however one might dislike some of their policies, their lack of democracy, or their violations of human rights. These countries have nuclear weapons and a permanent seat and veto on the UN Security Council, so challenging their legitimacy could have dangerous consequences. The US may complain about their policies, but there is no chance that it will challenge their "legitimacy."

Countries like Syria, Iraq before the 2003 US invasion, and Libya before the 2011 US-NATO military campaign to overthrow Qaddafi, on the other hand, belong to a different category. If the US government thinks that their governments can be overthrown, then it may declare them to be "illegitimate." A US declaration that a government is "illegitimate" means that the United States is likely to try to overthrow it.

Roebuck underscored his point as follows:

DISCOURAGE FDI, ESPECIALLY FROM THE GULF: Syria
has enjoyed a considerable up-tick in foreign
direct investment (FDI) in the last two years
that appears to be picking up steam. The most
important new FDI is undoubtedly from the Gulf.

Again, the increase in investment would seem to suggest that economic reforms were working to encourage investment. But Roebuck saw this as bad. If the most important FDI was from the Gulf, that suggested that, contrary to the US and Khaddam's claims that Syria was trying to have bad relations with the Gulf countries, it was succeeding in projecting an image of a country that was trying to get along. But in Roebuck's view, this was not a good thing; this was a bad thing, which the US should try to counteract.

Roebuck spoke glowingly of *violent* protests against the Syrian government:

```
Vulnerability:


THE KURDS: The most organized and daring
political opposition and civil society groups are
among the ethnic minority Kurds, concentrated in
Syria's northeast, as well as in communities in
Damascus and Aleppo. This group has been willing
to protest violently in its home territory when
others would dare not. [Emphasis added.]
```

The word "daring" in English usually connotes exemplary courage. US newspapers, for example, do not generally describe the Palestinian use of violence against the Israeli occupation as "daring," because, while using violence in this instance obviously requires courage, it is not seen in the US as exemplary. This shows how US diplomats like Roebuck see the world: if you are protesting governments that are US allies, like Bahrain, Egypt, or Israel, then your protests should be nonviolent. But if you are protesting a government that the US would like to overthrow, then the use of violence demonstrates "daring." Roebuck suggested a means of taking advantage of this "vulnerability":

```
Possible Action:


HIGHLIGHT KURDISH COMPLAINTS: Highlighting
Kurdish complaints in public statements,
including publicizing human rights abuses will
exacerbate regime's concerns about the Kurdish
population.
```

There is no pretense here that the goal of this action would be to encourage greater respect by the Syrian government for the human rights of Kurds—the goal would be to destabilize the Syrian government. Roebuck also made clear his attitude toward terrorism in Syria:

```
Vulnerability:

Extremist elements increasingly use Syria as
a base, while the SARG has taken some actions
against groups stating links to Al-Qaeda. With
the killing of the al-Qaida [sic] leader on
the border with Lebanon in early December and
the increasing terrorist attacks inside Syria
culminating in the September 12 attack against
the US embassy, the SARG's policies in Iraq and
support for terrorists elsewhere as well can be
seen to be coming home to roost.

Possible Actions:

Publicize presence of transiting (or externally
focused) extremist groups in Syria, not limited
to mention of Hamas and PIJ. Publicize Syrian
efforts against extremist groups in a way that
suggests weakness, signs of instability, and
uncontrolled blowback. The SARG's argument
(usually used after terror attacks in Syria)
that it too is a victim of terrorism should be
used against it to give greater prominence to
increasing signs of instability within Syria.
[Emphasis added.]
```

Note that, in private correspondence, Roebuck has no problem acknowledging that Syria is the victim of terrorism and that the

Syrian government is trying to take action against terrorists. But if Syria is the victim of terrorism and is trying to do something about it, according to the view that Roebuck wants the US to present to the world, that is evidence that Syria is weak and unstable and is suffering "uncontrolled blowback" as its support for terrorists elsewhere "comes home to roost."

Imagine if a diplomat from a country perceived to be a US adversary suggested that the September 11, 2001 terrorist attacks against the World Trade Center and the Pentagon, and US efforts to prevent such attacks in the future, were evidence that the US is weak and unstable, suffering from "uncontrolled blowback" as past US support for terrorists elsewhere "came home to roost." How would this be perceived in the United States?

It is not hard to speculate. In May 2007, when Republican presidential candidate Ron Paul suggested that "blowback" from US foreign policy had helped cause the September 11 attacks,[8] Republican frontrunner Rudy Giuliani denounced him as a conspiracy theorist.[9] When in 2010, in a speech at the United Nations, the president of Iran noted the then widespread minority belief that the US government was behind the September 11 attacks, the US led a walkout and denounced the speech.[10] So it seems reasonable to conclude that, if the US put forward the view that terrorism in Syria were Syria's own fault, the Syrian government would be likely to perceive that as a very hostile act.

This cable shows that, in December 2006, the top US diplomat in Syria believed that the goal of US policy in Syria should be to destabilize the Syrian government by any means available; that the US should work to increase Sunni-Shia sectarianism in Syria, including by aiding the dissemination of false fears about Shia proselytizing and stoking resentment about Iranian business activity and mosque construction; that the US should press Arab allies to give access in the media they control to a former Syrian official calling for the ouster of the Syrian government; that the US should try to strain relations between the Syrian government and other Arab governments, and then blame Syria for the strain; that the US should seek to stoke Syrian government fears of coup plots in order to provoke the Syrian government to overreact; that if the Syrian government reacted to external provocations, it proved that the regime was paranoid; that the US should work to undermine Syrian economic reforms and discourage foreign investment; that the US should seek to foster the belief that the Syrian government was not legitimate; that violent protests in Syria were praiseworthy and exemplary; that if Syria is the victim of terrorism and tries to do something about it, the US should exploit that to say that the Syrian government is weak and unstable, and is experiencing blowback for its foreign policy.

We also know that, in the eyes of the US embassy in Riyadh, Syria was interested in improving relations with the United States if and only if it was interested in being "weaned" from Iran.

From other cables, we know that the US was funding Syrian opposition groups. The US government acknowledged this funding after the cables were published by WikiLeaks.[11] The US had previously announced funding to "promote democracy" in Syria, but what was not previously publicly known was the extent to which the US government was engaged in funding opposition groups and activities which it had internally conceded would be seen by the Syrian government as proof that the US was seeking to overthrow it. A February 21, 2006 cable noted:

```
Post contacts [i.e., US embassy contacts in
Syria] have been quick to condemn the USG's
public statement announcing the designation
of five million USD for support of the Syrian
opposition, calling it "na[i]ve" and "harmful."
Contacts insist that the statement has already
hurt the opposition, and that the SARG will use
it in the coming months to further discredit its
opponents as agents of the Americans.[12]
```

The cable also noted: "Several contacts insisted that the initiative indicated the US did not really care about the opposition, but merely wanted to use it as 'a chip in the game.'" Judging from the December, 2006 "vulnerabilities and actions" cable, it is hard to dispute this conclusion of the embassy's Syrian contacts.

The February 2006 cable elaborated:

> Bassam Ishak, a Syrian-American activist who ran
> as an independent candidate for the People's
> Assembly in 2003, said that the general consensus
> among his civil society and opposition colleagues
> had been that the USG is "not serious about us"
> and that the public announcement was "just to put
> pressure on the regime with no regard for the
> opposition." "We are just a chip in the game," he
> asserted.

Note that the view that there could be severe negative consequences from US funding of opposition groups, including by helping the government delegitimize opposition groups and individuals as agents of foreign powers, was shared by many of the embassy's own contacts in the Syrian opposition. Some of the people who were delegitimized in this way might otherwise have been credible interlocutors in negotiations toward more inclusive governance; thus, the strategy of funding opposition groups could have the effect of foreclosing diplomatic and political options. Some of the criticism expressed of the US announcement was that it was made publicly; but, as the cables demonstrate, it was likely that the Syrian government would find out what the US was doing in the long run, and therefore that the distinction between secret and public was not meaningful.

Another critic noted that the US was already secretly funding the Syrian opposition:

> MP Noumeir al-Ghanem, a nominal independent and
> chairman of the Foreign Affairs Committee of
> the Parliament, dismissed the funding plan as
> a stunt, saying the amount of money was small
> and that the US had already been funding the
> opposition secretly, without impact. The new
> initiative would make no real difference. In his
> view, the announcement angered most Syrians, who
> viewed it as interference in the internal affairs
> of Syria, something that the US always insisted
> that Syria should not do regarding Lebanon.
>
> Al-Ghanem said the US should engage in dialogue
> with the Syrian regime and work for a stable,
> slowly democratizing country that could further
> US interests in the region, instead of putting up
> obstacles to such dialogue.

An April 28, 2009 cable, "Behavior Reform: Next Steps for a Human Rights Strategy"—from a period of "policy review" in which the new Obama administration was exploring a less confrontational policy toward Syria—outlining US government–funded "ongoing civil society programming" in Syria, acknowledged that "[s]ome programs may be perceived, were they made public, as an attempt to undermine the Asad regime, as opposed to encouraging behavior reform." It also stated: "The SARG would undoubtedly view any US funds going to illegal political groups as tantamount to supporting regime change. This would inevitably include the various expatriate reform organizations operating in Europe and the US, most of which have little to no effect on civil society or human rights in Syria."[13] It noted that the State Department's US-Middle East Partnership Initiative (MEPI) had sponsored eight major Syria-specific initiatives, some dating back to 2005, that will have received approximately $12 million by September 2010.

One of those initiatives was described as follows: "Democracy Council of California, 'Civil Society Strengthening Initiative (CSSI)' (USD 6,300,562, September 1, 2006—September 30, 2010). 'CSSI is a discrete collaborative effort between the Democracy Council and local partners' that has produced a secure Damascus Declaration website (www.nidaasyria.org) and 'various broadcast concepts' set to air in April."

A February 7, 2010 cable, "Human Rights Updates—SARG Budges On TIP, But Little Else," indicates that "various broadcast concepts" referred to Barada TV, a London-based Syrian opposition satellite television network. The February 2010 cable referred to Barada TV as "MEPI-supported" and said: "If the SARG establishes firmly that the US was continuing to fund Barada TV, however, it would view USG involvement as a covert and hostile gesture toward the regime."[14]

But while the April 2009 cable had noted that the Syrian government "would undoubtedly view any US funds going to illegal political groups as tantamount to supporting regime change," the February 2010 cable shows that such funding continued, even though the April 2009 cable had identified "how to bring our US-sponsored civil society and human rights programming into line [with] a less confrontational bilateral relationship" as a "core issue" facing a US human rights strategy for Syria. The April 2009 cable had argued:

```
The majority of DRL [the State Department's
Bureau of Democracy, Human Rights and Labor
Affairs] and MEPI programs have focused on
activities and Syrians outside of Syria, which
has further fed regime suspicions about US
intentions. If our dialogue with Syria on human
rights is to succeed, we need to express the
desire to work in Syria to strengthen civil
society in a non-threatening manner.
```

It appears, however, that the shift argued for in the April 2009 cable never occurred. This apparently remained true even as the US embassy became increasingly aware of evidence that the Syrian government knew about the activities funded by the US that the April 2009 cable had warned that the Syrian government would see, if they became aware of them, as evidence of a regime-change policy, and would thus be likely to undermine US efforts to engage the Syrian government.

A July 8, 2009 cable on rifts in the Syrian opposition, "Murky Alliances: Muslim Brotherhood, the Movement for Justice and Democracy, and the Damascus Declaration," noted the "worrisome" fact of "recent information suggesting the SARG may already have penetrated the MJD [Movement for Justice and Development] and learned about sensitive USG programs in Syria."[15] The cable expanded on the issue as follows:

```
MJD: A Leaky Boat?

8. (C) [Damascus Declaration member Fawaz] Tello
had told us in the past that the MJD … had been
initially lax in its security, often speaking
about highly sensitive material on open lines …
The last point relates to a recent report from
lawyer/journalist and human rights activist Razan
Zeitunah (strictly protect) who met us separately
on July 1 to discuss having been called in for
questioning by security services on June 29.

9. (S/NF) Zeitunah told us security services
had asked whether she had met with anyone from
our "Foreign Ministry" and with anyone from the
Democracy Council [recipient of the US grant
for the MJD to run Barada TV]. (Comment: State
Department Foreign Affairs Officer Joseph Barghout
had recently been in Syria and met with Zeitunah;
we assume the SARG was fishing for information,
```

knowing Barghout had entered the country. Jim
Prince was in Damascus on February 25, and it
is our understanding he met with Zeitunah at
that time, or had done so on a separate trip.
End Comment.) She added that her interrogators
did not ask about Barghout by name, but they did
have Jim Prince's. [Jim Prince is the head of the
Democracy Council.]

...

11. (S/NF) Comment continued: Zeitunah's report
begs the question of how much and for how long
the SARG has known about Democracy Council
operations in Syria and, by extension, the
MJD's participation. Reporting in other channels
suggest the Syrian Muhabarat may already have
penetrated the MJD and is using MJD contacts to
track US democracy programming.

A September 23, 2009 cable, "Show Us the Money! SARG
Suspects 'Illegal' USG Funding," gave further evidence that the
Syrian authorities were increasingly aware of what the US was
funding:

1. (S/NF) Summary: Over the past six months, SARG
security agents have increasingly questioned
civil society and human rights activists about US
programming in Syria and the region, including
US Speaker and MEPI initiatives. In addition to
reported interrogations of the Director of the
Syrian Center for Media and Freedom of Expression
and employees of USG-supported Etana Press, new
criminal charges against detained human rights
lawyer Muhanad al-Hasani for illegally receiving
USG funding reflect the seriousness with which the
regime is pursuing these "investigations."

2. (S/NF) Over the past six months, civil
society and human rights activists questioned by
SARG security have told us interrogators asked
specifically about their connections to the US
Embassy and the State Department. As previously
reported, Razan Zeitunah (strictly protect)
recounted a June interrogation during which
she was questioned about MEPI-funded Democracy
Council activities as well as visiting State
Department officials. Kurdish Future Movement
activist Herveen Ose (strictly protect), brought
in for questioning in August, was also asked
about funding from "foreign embassies." MEPI
grantee Maan Abdul Salam (strictly protect)
recently reported one of his employees was
called in on September 4, at which time security
agents zeroed in on her participation in a MEPI-
funded People In Need (PIN) seminar in Prague
approximately eight months earlier.

...

4. (C) The ongoing case of human rights lawyer
Muhanad al-Hasani took a turn for the worse
on September 15 when, reportedly, the SARG
introduced a new charge against him. According
to a September 18 e-mail we received from his
colleague Catherine al-Tali (strictly protect),
the SARG accused Hasani of accepting USG funding
that was routed to him through the Cairo-based
Al-Andalus Center ... Embassy Cairo also informed
us that the Center was not currently receiving
funding from either the Embassy or MEPI, though
it had in the past.

...

8. (S/NF) Comment: It is unclear to what extent
SARG intelligence services understand how USG

money enters Syria and through which proxy organizations. What is clear, however, is that security agents are increasingly focused on this issue when they interrogate human rights and civil society activists. The information agents are able to frame their questions with more and more specific information and names. The charge that Hasani received USG funding vis-a-vis the Al-Andalus Center is especially worrying since it may suggest the SARG has keyed in on MEPI operations in particular.[16]

The February 7, 2010 cable cited earlier, "Human Rights Updates—SARG Budges On TIP, But Little Else," gave further evidence that the Syrian government was pursuing the funding of Barada TV:

Barada TV: The Opposition in Klieg Lights?

9. (C) Damascus-based director of MEPI-supported Barada TV Suheir Attasi outlined the many challenges facing the channel in a December 23 meeting.

...

10. (C) Attasi confirmed reports we had heard from other contacts about the SARG's interest in chasing down the financial and political support structure behind Barada. Security agents called her in for questioning in October and repeatedly asked her about her affiliations with the US Embassy and whether she knew Jim Prince … If the SARG establishes firmly that the US was continuing to fund Barada TV, however, it would view USG involvement as a covert and hostile gesture toward the regime. Just as SARG officials have

used the US position on Operation Cast Lead and
the Goldstone Report to shut down discussions
on human rights, it could similarly try to use
Barada TV to diminish our credibility on the
issue.[17]

Note that, although the July 2009, September 2009, and February 2010 cables address exactly the situation that the April 2009 cable had warned about—that the Syrian government would find out what the US was funding—there was no further discussion or concern expressed about what the April 2009 cable had warned would be the likely consequence: that the Syrian government would conclude that the US government was pursuing a regime-change policy in Syria, which would undermine US efforts to engage the Syrian government. Nor was there any further discussion of what the April 2009 cable had suggested: that this funding be reviewed to bring it in line with the policy of engagement.

What emerges from these cables is that, while there was undoubtedly a shift between the policy of the Bush administration after 2005 and the policy of the Obama administration in 2009–10 with respect to the question of regime change versus engagement, the shift was substantially less than publicly advertised. The US continued to fund opposition activities that it believed would, if known to the Syrian government, cause it to believe that the US was not serious about shifting to an engagement policy; the US continued to fund these activities as it came increasingly to believe that the Syrian government was becoming more aware of them. When they became public, the US denied that they amounted to a regime-change policy,[18] but we now know from the US government's internal communication that the US did not think that the Syrian government would give credence to such a denial.

This leads us to question the extent to which the Obama administration really shifted to a policy of engagement, or how much, when Saudi Arabia and others pushed it to adopt an explicit regime-change policy in 2011—a shift the administration eventually did make—these countries were pushing on an open door. The story that was presented to the US public was that its government had tried to engage Syria and failed, and that after the Syrian government cracked down on protests in 2011, the US had no choice but to abandon its efforts at engagement.

But reading the cables, it appears that the US was never really committed to a policy of engagement: it had one hand in the engagement policy, while keeping another hand in the regime-change policy. The Iranian government cracked down on protests in 2009, but the US did not completely abandon efforts to engage the Iranian government. Perhaps the danger of abandoning efforts at engagement with Iran were perceived to be higher, given Iran's nuclear enrichment program and the political pressure on the Obama administration to use force against Iran if diplomacy failed; perhaps the belief among the US and its allies that the Syrian government could be toppled by force, and the Iranian government could not, also played a role.

Knowing that the US never really abandoned a regime-change policy in Syria informs our understanding of the question of US military intervention in Syria today. It shows us that the US is not an innocent victim of circumstance, having to consider the use of force because diplomacy has been exhausted; rather, the US faces a situation that it helped create, by pursuing regime change for years and never fully switching to diplomacy.

11. Iran

Gareth Porter

The US diplomatic cables released by WikiLeaks represent a massive trove of documentation on US relations with key Middle Eastern regimes that would not have become available to journalists and scholars for decades but for the existence of the WikiLeaks channel. These cables cannot match the much more thorough and authoritative coverage provided by the declassified archival documents that are published by the US Department of State in its Foreign Relations of the United States volumes decades later. They are not top-secret documents and do not reveal the specifics of high-level policy decisions.

Nevertheless, the cables add an important dimension to our understanding of how the US national security state manages key interests in the Middle East. They provide glimpses of policy pursued by the State Department and by US and allied diplomats, and in particular of how other actors responded to signals from US administrations, and thus fit into the larger scheme of US policy. They also reveal contradictions between public rhetoric and the actual calculations and posture of the US and allied diplomats in pursuing US policy.

It is obviously impossible to discuss all the dimensions of US Middle East policy, much less all of the historical episodes on which cables can be found, within the scope of this chapter. The choice of issues covered here reflects the author's view that the triangular relationship involving the United States, Israel, and

Iran represents the central dynamic in US policy toward the region. The WikiLeaks cables provide many glimpses of how US diplomacy was conducted in relation to the Iran nuclear issue, which became a central US foreign policy concern in the Bush and Obama administrations. They also shed new light on how the United States accommodated the interests of Israel, and the extent to which that accommodation impinged on broader US diplomacy in the region. The cables shed important new light on how the US dealt with the role of the International Atomic Energy Agency (IAEA) in relation to the Iran nuclear issue.

Arms sales have long played a central role in shaping US policy toward client regimes in the Middle East and South Asia, from Iran to Pakistan to Saudi Arabia. The cables help to illuminate the connection between US policy toward Iran and the interest of the Pentagon and their contractors in military sales—especially missile-defense technology sales—to its Middle East allies.

The Israel factor pervades the formulation and implementation of US Middle East policy. The domestic political power of the Israeli lobby imposes obvious constraints on the ability of any US administration to carry out a fully independent policy in the region, whether the issue is Middle East peace or Iran's nuclear program. And US support for the continuation of Israeli military dominance in the Middle East is the primary nexus between that domestic interest group and US Israel policy. The heavy hand of domestic politics in US diplomacy is very much in evidence in the WikiLeaks diplomatic cables.

Three striking themes emerge from the diplomatic conversations revealed in the cables: first, the degree to which the US government is bound by past commitments to preserve Israel's military dominance in the region; second, the degree to which even the Obama administration ended up tilting in an obvious way toward the Israeli position in the Palestinian peace negotiations; and third, the Obama administration's semi-covert exploitation of the Israeli threat to attack Iran to build pressure on Iran.

The US government's longstanding commitment to giving Israel complete military dominance—not merely over any potential rival in the region but over any conceivable combination of rivals—is one of Israel's biggest advantages in pressuring Washington on virtually every policy issue in the region, as becomes clear from the diplomatic cable reporting the visit of the assistant secretary of state for political-military affairs, Andrew Shapiro, to Israel in July 2009 to discuss the maintenance of Israel's "qualitative military edge" (QME). In the meetings with Shapiro, Israel portrayed the situation in the region as threatening its QME, suggesting that it was the responsibility of the United States to ensure that even Arab regimes who were either strongly anti-Iran or in close cooperation with Israel in security matters could not grow any stronger militarily, because they might emerge as military adversaries of Israel in the future, and even insisted on seeing the classified intelligence on which US QME policy was based:

4. (S) GOI officials reiterated the importance of maintaining Israel's Qualitative Military Edge. They said that Israel understands US policy intentions to arm moderate Arab states in the region to counter the Iranian threat, and prefers such sales originate from the United States instead of other countries like Russia or China. However, Israel continues to stress the importance of identifying potential risks that may become future threats or adversaries, and for this reason maintains several objections as indicated in the official GOI response to the QME non-paper on potential US arms sales to the region (ref e-mail to PM/RSAT separately).

5. (S) GOI officials also expressed continued interest in reviewing the QME report prior to its

submission to Congress. A/S Shapiro reiterated
that the report was based on an assessment from
the intelligence community, and therefore not
releasable to the GOI. He referenced previous
points made to the Israeli embassy in Washington
regarding the report, and welcomed any comments
the GOI might have—although such comments
should be delivered as soon as possible as the
report is already overdue. Israeli interlocutors
appreciated the classified nature of the report,
but also made clear it was difficult to comment
on the report's results without reviewing its
content or intelligence assessment. In that
respect, Buchris and other GOI officials requested
that the QME process be reviewed in light of
future QME reports.

(S) GOI interlocutors attempted to make the
argument that moderate Arab countries could
in the future become adversaries—and that this
should be taken into account in the QME process.
During a roundtable discussion led by the MFA's
Deputy Director Policy Research gave intelligence
briefs on Saudi Arabia, Egypt, and Lebanon to
further support the argument that these countries
could become future foes.

...

A/S Shapiro cited a commonality of interests
with the Gulf States, which also view Iran as
the preeminent threat—we should take advantage
of this commonality, he said. During the
J5 roundtable discussion, IDF interlocutors
expressed skepticism that proposed military
assistance to the Gulf would help against Iran,
as some of the systems slated for delivery are

not designed to counter the threats, nuclear
and asymmetrical, posed by Iran. A/S Shapiro
agreed that assistance to Gulf states should not
diminish Israel's QME, but argued that it sends
a signal to those countries (as well as Iran)
that they have strong allies in the West. It
also helps convince these regimes that their best
interests lie with the moderate camp rather than
with Iran. [09TELAVIV1688]

These excerpts from the reporting cable of Shapiro's discussion with Israeli national security officials underline the reality that Israel's privileged legal and policy position ensconced in the QME assurance gives Tel Aviv leverage with which to challenge every aspect of US policy in the Middle East, and to argue against any enhanced military ties with any Arab regime—even if Israel itself was enjoying closer military and security ties with the regime, as was the case with both Egypt and Saudi Arabia.

The Obama administration's policies on Iran and on peace negotiations with the Palestinians were closely linked at the outset of his presidency. Obama intended to give priority to obtaining a freeze on Israeli settlements in order to push for agreement on a Palestinian state, and was prepared to subordinate his Iran policy to that interest. He had hoped to obtain Prime Minister Netanyahu's acquiescence in such a freeze in return for Obama's promise to take a tough line on Iran policy, implying that he would place more emphasis on pressure on Iran than on diplomacy with Tehran. But Netanyahu pushed back in the spring of 2009 through the American Israel Public Affairs Committee (AIPAC), getting three-fourths of the House of Representatives to sign a letter insisting that Obama avoid overt political pressure on Israel. That move made it clear that Netanyahu was refusing such a tradeoff, and Obama soon retreated from his advocacy of a freeze, making Dennis Ross his primary adviser on the Palestinian negotiations.[1]

Obama's retreat from pressing Netanyahu on the settlements issue meant that the United States was again in the position of tilting sharply, in effect, toward the Israeli side in the talks. Instead of insisting that Israel agree to the desired goal of a Palestinian state, which would have been the only role that encouraged a settlement, the Obama administration decided that it would not seek to change Netanyahu's well-known rejection of that objective. The reporting cable on Ross's meeting with the Chinese special Middle East envoy, Wu Sike, in October 2009 shows that Ross sought to conceal in his diplomatic contacts the administration's abject capitulation to Netanyahu's continued seizure of Palestinian land for Israeli settlements, undermining a central premise of the Oslo accords:

> Wu then asked whether the United States had a specific peace plan for the Middle East, and if so, when it would be made public. Ambassador Ross responded that such an action could have the unintended consequence of preempting instead of supporting a negotiation process and reiterated that the United States was focused on establishing terms of reference for negotiations, and if negotiations ensue, would be an active participant, providing bridging proposals as appropriate. [09BEIJING3001]

The real reason the Obama administration was not advancing any peace plan on the Israel-Palestine conflict was Obama's political decision to abandon any pressure on Netanyahu on the crucial issue of the continued expansion of Israeli settlements in the West Bank, which was supposed to be part of Palestinian territory in any settlement. The formulation of the US role as "providing bridging proposals as appropriate" was a roundabout way of describing a passive US diplomatic stance on the matter and was aimed primarily at avoiding political confrontation with Netanyahu on the Palestinian issue. In fact, just as Ross was meeting with the Chinese envoy, the Obama administration and the Netanyahu government were quietly reaching agreement, announced only a few days later, on a freeze for only ten months that would exempt Jerusalem and would allow the same level of settlements as had been planned earlier. That was a position that Ross and Obama knew was unacceptable to the Palestinians, and it doomed negotiations with the Palestinian Authority.[2]

Netanyahu's Iran policy was based on an ostensible threat to use military force as a last resort if the issue was not resolved to Israel's satisfaction by the United States and the permanent five members of the Security Council plus Germany (P5+1). A fully independent US Middle East policy would have rebuffed such an obviously destabilizing threat by a state that was heavily dependent on US political and economic support. But although the official stance of the Obama administration was to express its disapproval of any Israeli military action against Iran that was not undertaken in coordination with the United States, the administration's unacknowledged policy was to exploit that Israeli threat to enhance its diplomatic leverage over Iran and to get other states to support stronger pressure on Iran. Thus US officials sought to gain the support of its European allies, as well as Turkey, Russia, and China, for more severe sanctions against Iran partly by arguing that failure to place sufficient pressure on Iran would raise the risk of an Israeli attack on Iran, and of general war and instability in the region.

The idea of exploiting an Israeli threat to attack Iran for diplomatic advantage was first suggested publicly by former White House adviser on nonproliferation Gary Samore during the 2008 presidential election campaign.[3] Samore became President Obama's adviser on weapons of mass destruction in January 2009, and found a friendly reception for the tactic he advocated. On April 1, 2009, the very day that Benjamin Netanyahu took office as prime minister of Israel, Secretary of Defense Robert M. Gates and CENTCOM Commander General David Petraeus both suggested that Israel was likely to attack Iran if its nuclear program went too far.[4]

That idea was not repeated publicly after the Gates-Petraeus duo's comments, but WikiLeaks cables show that the administration exploited the ploy of hand-wringing about a possible Israeli attack in high-level meetings with foreign officials to influence various governments' policy on Iran. The cable on the meeting between Gates and the Italian foreign minister, Franco Frattini, in February 2010 shows how Gates used it to prod the Italian government to be more aggressive in supporting the US line on Iran:

```
(S/NF) SecDef emphasized that a UNSC resolution
was important because it would give the European
Union and nations a legal platform on which
to impose even harsher sanctions against Iran.
SecDef pointedly warned that urgent action
is required. Without progress in the next few
months, we risk nuclear proliferation in the
Middle East, war prompted by an Israeli strike,
or both. SecDef predicted "a different world"
in 4-5 years if Iran developed nuclear weapons.
SecDef stated that he recently delivered the
same warning to PM Erdogan, and he agreed with
Frattini's assessment on Saudi Arabia and China,
noting that Saudi Arabia is more important to
both Beijing and Moscow than Iran. [10ROME173]
```

Turkey was a particular target of the administration's argument about the danger of war with Israel, because the Erdoğan government was in close and frequent communication with Iran. The Obama administration wanted Turkish officials to discourage Iran from its defiance of the United States and the P5+1. Under Secretary of State William J. Burns brought up the Israeli attack threat in his meeting with his Turkish counterpart, Feridun H. Sinirlioğlu, when he resisted intensified sanctions:

```
2. (C) Burns strongly urged Sinirlioglu to
support action to convince the Iranian government
it is on the wrong course. Sinirliolgu reaffirmed
the GoT's opposition to a nuclear Iran; however,
he registered fear about the collateral impact
military action might have on Turkey and
contended sanctions would unite Iranians behind
the regime and harm the opposition. Burns
acknowledged Turkey's exposure to the economic
effects of sanctions as a neighbor to Iran, but
reminded Sinirlioglu Turkish interests would
suffer if Israel were to act militarily to
forestall Iran's acquisition of nuclear weapons
or if Egypt and Saudi Arabia were to seek nuclear
arsenals of their own. [10ANKARA302]
```

US policy toward Iran has long been shaped by unacknowledged political, bureaucratic, and economic interests. In the early 1990s, Iran was portrayed as posing a threat of the proliferation of nuclear weapons, in order to justify US military and intelligence programs that were threatened by the loss of the Soviet threat with the end of the Cold War. In the same period, missile-defense interests used the alleged threat from future Iranian ballistic missiles to the United States as their primary political lever to force the Clinton administration to agree in principle to establish a missile defense system. For the past several years, an alleged threat from future Iranian missiles to Europe and the Middle East has been a useful device to sell missile-defense and offensive weaponry to NATO allies and Persian Gulf regimes.

The political linkage between the US missile-defense program and the alleged military threat from an imagined future Iranian intercontinental Iranian ballistic missile had been firmly established during the Clinton administration. The missile-defense lobby waxed so powerful in the second half of the 1990s that the CIA came under intense pressure to revise a 1995 National Intelligence Estimate (NIE) that had dismissed the danger of an Iranian ICBM threat to the United States to bring it into line with the alarmist conclusions of the "Rumsfeld Commission" that such a threat was possible within fifteen years.[5] With the former Commission chairman, Donald Rumsfeld himself, as its defense secretary, the George W. Bush administration called in December 2002 for the beginning of deployment of missile defense by the end of 2004, and directed the Defense Department and the State Department to "promote international missile defense cooperation, including within bilateral and alliance structures such as NATO," and to "negotiate appropriate arrangements for this purpose."[6]

Robert M. Gates, who succeeded Rumsfeld as defense secretary in 2006, admitted, in effect, that there was no real evidence that Iran was working on an ICBM. He suggested in October 2007 that the United States would "complete the negotiations, we would develop the sites, build the sites, but perhaps would delay activating them *until there was concrete proof of the threat from Iran*"[7] (emphasis added). Gates continued to cater to the powerful bureaucratic-industrial alliance behind the missile policy as Barack Obama's secretary of defense. In September 2009, Obama approved a revised missile-defense program for Europe called the European Phased Adaptive Approach, which contemplated putting US missile defense technology into Europe roughly six or seven years earlier than the previous plan, now abandoned, because there was no intelligence to support the idea of a long-range Iranian missile.[8]

The Obama administration continued to embrace the accusation that Iran was working on a missile that would threaten European cities. In a cable conveying the "talking points" on the new European missile defense plan to be delivered to host governments around the world, the State Department portrayed Iran as an existing ballistic-missile threat to its neighbors in the Middle East, Turkey, and the Caucasus, and as "actively developing and testing ballistic missiles that can reach more of Europe" [09STATE96550].

The most important target of the administration's message of alarm about the alleged Iranian missile threat was Russia, with which the Bush administration had raised tensions after the crisis in Georgia in 2008. The Obama administration wanted to induce Russia to be part of the international coalition pressuring Iran to give up its enrichment program, as it had been during the period from 2005 to 2007.[9] Separate talking points to be used by national security adviser General James Jones in a meeting with Russian ambassador Sergei I. Kislyak included the far-reaching claim that Iranian missiles would threaten Moscow with nuclear warheads:

> Iran has made more progress on short-range and medium-range ballistic missiles, and less progress on ICBMs than anticipated. Now the threat is greater to the Middle East and to Europe, with a less immediate threat to the United States.
>
> ...
>
> There is no doubt that Iran is developing these missiles to arm them with a nuclear warhead. There is NO OTHER REASON to spend so much time and effort into [sic] developing these missiles. They are not useful weapons if only armed with a conventional warhead.
>
> The new plan for European missile defense is better designed to protect Europe from this Iranian threat that is emerging. We intend to deploy the SM-3 interceptor which is what we are deploying in the Middle East as well. SM-3s do not have the capability to threaten Russian ICBMs.

In the first stages of deployment, we also are
seeking to place these interceptors closer to
Iran (from what I understand, this is exactly
the idea that President Putin proposed to
President Bush during their July 2007 meeting at
Kennebunkport, Maine).

The new plan calls for radars and detection
systems to be deployed closer to Iran. These
radars will not have the capacity to track
Russian ICBMs.

With this decision behind us, we now want to move
aggressively to launch serious cooperation on
missile defense with Russia. [09STATE96550]

The *New York Times* reported that a WikiLeaks cable showed US intelligence had found evidence that Iran possessed a missile that would be able to reach European capitals.[10] But the diplomatic cable in question—from the secretary of state to diplomatic posts in February 2010—actually reveals that the Russian experts on Iran's missile program participating in a "Joint Threat Assessment" of the Iranian ballistic-missile program dismissed the US argument that any Iranian missile could pose such a threat for the foreseeable future, and that US officials were unable to back up their claims [10STATE17263]. Shockingly, the *Times* story provided no coverage of the meeting; in fact it made no mention of the fact that the WikiLeaks cable in question was a detailed report of a joint US-Russian assessment in which the US claims about the purported Iranian missile had been shown to be highly questionable.

The US delegation claimed that Iran possessed the "BM-25" missile, which it said North Korea had developed based on a long-obsolete Soviet submarine-launched ballistic missile that could reach ranges of up to 2,000 miles. When challenged by the

Russians on its evidence for the claim, however, the US delegation admitted it had no photographic or other hard evidence.
The US delegation asserted that the North Koreans had paraded
the BM-25 through the streets of Pyongyang, but the Russians
responded that they had watched videos of the parade, and that
the missile on display was an entirely different missile from the
BM-25.[11]

The State Department cable also shows that the Russians
dispatched the Obama administration's effort to introduce the
specter of nuclear weapons into the issue. "It is impossible from
the Russian point of view for Iran to put a nuclear device on
existing missiles with an improved range and throw weight,"
said a statement read on behalf of the deputy secretary of
Russia's National Security Council, adding: "Iran has no ballistic missiles capable of carrying nuclear weapons at this time"
[10STATE17263].

The Obama administration's line about the Iranian missile
threat to Europe and the Middle East also served the strong
interest of the Pentagon and its corporate allies in selling missile-defense and offensive technology to Saudi Arabia, the United
Arab Emirates, and Kuwait, and constructing a system for an
integrated missile defense system in the Gulf region. In December
2008, the United Arab Emirates (UAE) became the first Gulf state
to order the most advanced US missile defense system, purchasing
172 PAC-3 missiles, along with the launchers, ground equipment, software, training, and support for the entire system—all
of which was expected to generate about $5.1 billion in revenue
for Lockheed and Raytheon.[12]

The UAE sale was expected to be only the beginning of a new
wave of purchases of US anti-missile systems and offensive weaponry of staggering proportions. Negotiations with Saudi Arabia
on an arms deal worth $60 billion had begun in 2007, mainly for
new F-15 fighter planes and upgrades to the existing fleet of Saudi
F-15s, and the sale was all but officially announced in October
2010. The deal was expected to be worth as much as $150 billion

in total procurement and services contracts over two decades. US officials were also encouraging the Saudis to purchase the newest US missile-defense technology, known as THAAD.[13]

The *New York Times*'s lead story on the WikiLeaks cables focused heavily on the theme of the Gulf sheikdoms putting pressure on the United States to stop Iran's nuclear program—by force, if necessary. The story referred to the alleged urging by the Saudi king to "cut off the head of the snake," and the desire of crown prince Mohammed bin Zayed Al-Nayhan of the UAE that the US take action against Iran. Netanyahu gleefully cited the cables that had been highlighted by the *Times* as vindicating the Israeli assessment of Iran by showing that the Saudis and other Gulf states were in agreement with it.[14]

The strongly anti-Iran Sunni monarchies were certainly inclined to believe the narrative pushed aggressively by the Bush administration and Israel about Iran's ambitions to acquire nuclear weapons—and they wanted the United States to take care of the problem. But the WikiLeaks cables also reveal a more complex set of interactions between those Gulf regimes and the international crisis over the Iran nuclear issue, which helps to explain the upsurge of interest in missile-defense technology. They had long tied their security to the United States by offering military bases for US forces. Now that tensions were rising between the US and Israel, on one side, and Iran on the other, they had to consider the possibility that they could be caught in the middle. That combination of circumstances made them prime customers for US missile-defense sales and services.

A diplomatic cable from the US embassy in Abu Dhabi in early February 2007 reflects the complicated linkage between the Gulf regimes' interest in US anti-missile technology and the threat of war with Iran that was being increased by US and Israeli policies. In a meeting with US Air Force chief of staff General T. Michael Mosely, UAE crown prince Mohammed bin Zayed Al-Nayhan ("MbZ"), who was also deputy commander of UAE armed forces, expressed the desire to have the Iranian nuclear program "stopped by all means available." But the cable also revealed that the meeting had taken place in the context of ongoing discussions and negotiations over UAE interest in purchasing US missile-defense and other advanced military technologies, and that the leadership did not want to be caught in the middle between the US and Iran:

> MbZ warned Moseley of the growing threat
> from Iran, stating that they (Iran) "can't be
> allowed to have a nuclear program." MbZ further
> emphasized that Iran's nuclear program must be
> stopped "by all means available." As expected,
> MbZ inquired about Predator B. Moseley informed
> MbZ that the question of Predator B would require
> further discussion within the interagency [sic]
> and with our MTCR partners, while Ambassador
> noted that the USG looked forward to discussion
> of UAE defense requirements and our shared
> security objectives in the context of the Gulf
> Security Dialogue. MbZ expressed a desire to
> have a missile defense system in place by Summer
> 2009, and was looking to add ship-based launch
> platforms as a part of that system. He also noted
> that the UAE had identified a location on the
> northern border at an elevation of 6,000 feet
> that may be suitable for installation of an early
> warning radar system. End Summary.
>
> 6. (S) Moseley's meeting with MbZ immediately
> followed a Raytheon/Lockheed Martin briefing of
> MbZ on the ongoing development of THAAD/PAC-3
> and shared early warning systems. Speaking of a
> time frame for the first time, MbZ said he wants
> a complete missile defense system by summer
> 2009. MbZ expressed particular interest in the

possibility of mounting PAC-3 on Littoral Combat
Ships (LCS) …

7. (S) Comment: Although MbZ is increasingly
talking tough on Iran, i.e., stop Iran "by all
means possible" and "deal with Iran sooner rather
than later," his comments should also be taken in
the context of strong UAE interest in acquiring
advanced military technology and, specifically,
MbZ's repeated requests for Predator B. The UAEG
is clearly nervous about any US actions that
could upset their much larger and militarily
superior neighbor. The UAE's significant
trade relationship with Iran—approximately $4
billion—is another complicating factor in the
relationship. On more than one occasion, the UAE
leadership has expressed trepidation over the
prospect of being caught in the middle between
the US and Iran. End Comment. [07ABUDHABI187]

In early April 2009, as newly elected Israeli prime minister
Benjamin Netanyahu prepared to take office, senior Israeli and
Obama administration defense officials began, in an apparently
coordinated fashion, to put out to the news media, both publicly
and privately, the line that Israel might have to use military force
against Iran.[15] That line served the political-diplomatic interests
of both countries, and it was also a spur to the Gulf monarchies
to speed up their purchases of US missile defense systems. The
UAE military chief responded to those signals immediately in
a meeting between the crown prince and Ambassador Richard
Holbrooke, in which "MbZ" explicitly expressed concern about
the military option, as reported in a US diplomatic cable: "(S/NF)
Turning to his concerns about an armed confrontation, MbZ said
war with Iran would only harm the UAE. He is deeply concerned
that the current Israeli government will initiate military action

without consultation. An Israeli attack on Iran would have little impact on Iran's capabilities, but MbZ was certain Iran would respond" [09ABUDHABI1347].

In the context of the discussion of a possible military attack on Iran that both Israeli and American officials had mounted, the Gulf monarchies accelerated their installation of US missile-defense technology. At a conference at the conservative Institute for the Study of War in Washington, DC, in January 2010 CENTCOM commander General David Petraeus declared: "Iran is clearly seen as a very serious threat by those on the other side of the Gulf front," and said that the United States was installing "eight Patriot missile batteries, two in each of four countries."[16] A few days later, a US embassy cable from Kuwait reported that the *Times* article had heightened "Kuwaiti concerns" about an "armed confrontation" created by either the United States or Israel:

1. (C) Like some of its Arabian Gulf neighbors, the GoK was embarrassed and chagrined by discussion in a January 31 *New York Times* article linking plans to deploy defensive missile systems to Kuwait and a number of other Gulf countries to possible Iranian missile attacks. The article comes only days after a high-profile January 26-27 visit to Kuwait by Iranian Parliament Speaker Ali Larijani during which the Speaker pointedly and publicly warned GCC states not to allow US bases on their territories to be used for attacks on Iran. In tandem, the two events have served to heighten Kuwaiti concerns about the potential for an armed confrontation between Iran and the US (or between Iran and Israel), and increased fears that should such a contingency occur, Kuwait would be caught in the cross-fire. [10KUWAIT107]

The actual WIkiLeaks cables on the Gulf monarchies' attitude toward the Iran nuclear issue thus show clearly that the impression given by the *New York Times* story on the cables that those Gulf Arab regimes were effectively aligned with Israel's Iran policy was quite misleading. The UAE and Kuwaiti regimes, which were the leading purchasers of missile defense systems at the time, were strongly opposed to the Israeli threat of war, and were seeking missile-defense technology partly because of their fear of being caught in armed confrontation.

The core neoconservative group within the Bush administration conceived an Iran policy calling for regime change through military force, if necessary. The strategy for achieving that ultimate objective centered on making a case that Iran had conducted a covert nuclear weapons program involving a set of intelligence documents that purportedly came from within such a program. We now know that the documents were actually turned over to the German foreign intelligence agency by a member of the anti-regime Iranian exile organization Mojahedin-e-Khalq, which had carried out terrorist activities against US officials during the Shah's regime, then against the Islamic Republic; had served the Saddam Hussein regime in its war against Iran; then began working closely with Israeli intelligence in the 1990s. The documents themselves, moreover, were marred by both technical errors and contradictions with established facts that indicated that they had been fabricated.[17]

The Bush administration wanted the IAEA, which had the authority to determine whether a member state was abiding by its "Safeguards" agreement with the Agency, to give the "laptop documents" legitimacy as evidence of a covert nuclear weapons program. But the IAEA's director general, Mohamed ElBaradei, was skeptical about the documents' authenticity, and believed that they should not be used as evidence against Iran under the circumstances—especially since the United States refused to allow the Agency to share them with Iran.

Even worse for the Bush administration's efforts, ElBaradei reached an agreement with Iran on a "work plan" in August 2007 aimed at resolving several issues concerning Iranian experiments and other aspects of the history of its nuclear program that the Agency's Department of Safeguards had found suspicious. Under the plan, Iran agreed to provide a response to the "laptop documents," provided they were given copies of the documents to examine, but it made no commitment to resolve the issue to the satisfaction of the Agency.[18] The Bush administration and its European allies, the UK, France, and Germany ("P3+1" in US diplomatic cables), were very unhappy with the agreement, fearing that ElBaradei would find Iranian explanations credible, and that Iran would be seen as cooperative with the IAEA rather than hiding its nuclear weapons intentions from it.

A series of diplomatic cables from the US mission to the UN agencies in Vienna show how the United States and its allies sought to prevent ElBaradei and the IAEA from making any move toward "normalization" of Iran's file at the Agency unless Iran first made major concessions to Western demands to end enrichment and admitted to having had a nuclear weapons program. A cable describing a meeting a few months later recalled how the US and its three European allies had reacted to ElBaradei's announcement of the work plan with Iran with official diplomatic notes that sought to pressure him to back away from his plan. The cable reported that the French chargé d'affaires "recalled [that] the P3+1 demarches on the DG in August warned that the work plan could not result in the 'normalization' of the Iran file." He recounted that the IAEA's director of external policy, Vilmos Cserveny—an ally of ElBaradei—had interpreted the coordinated diplomatic notes as precisely such a threat, and had warned the French diplomat: "[Y]ou cannot challenge what we say, or you will break the machine" [08UNVIENNA31]. Cserveny was saying that, if the United States and its allies attacked ElBaradei's decisions on Iran, they would risk losing the IAEA as an effective international institution for dealing with the nuclear proliferation issue.

ElBaradei's November 2007 report on progress with the work plan indicated that Iran had provided information that satisfied the Agency's investigators on the issue of Iran's account of plutonium experiments in the late 1980s and early 1990s, and its work on P2 centrifuges and the contamination of equipment with highly enriched uranium, which turned out to be from centrifuge components that had been imported from Pakistan, rather than a product of secret Iranian enrichment for nuclear weapons, as some IAEA officials had suspected.[19]

That result of the first of two rounds of meetings between Iran and the IAEA in the work plan presented a serious political problem for the United States and its European allies. They had hoped to convince the Russians and Chinese to join in a new resolution by the IAEA Board of Governors that would pave the way for new UN Security Council sanctions against Iran. But that would depend on whether Iran appeared to be cooperating with the IAEA or not. When they met Russian and Chinese diplomats in Vienna immediately after ElBaradei's report was issued, a diplomatic cable reported, US and European diplomats tried to dismiss the first results of the work plan as insignificant. French ambassador Jean-François Deniau argued that ElBaradei's work plan "had not been much of a success," according to the cable—an assessment that contradicted the clear language of ElBaradei's report. Deniau went on to claim that "[o]nly the plutonium issue had been closed, and despite the DG's expectations in September, no other questions had been closed/resolved" [07UNVENNA705].

ElBaradei's moves to clear Iran on the first three issues on the work plan agenda had been followed by another setback for US and allied plans to increase pressure on Iran: in late November the US intelligence community released to the public the conclusion of a new National Intelligence Estimate that Iran had ceased all work on nuclear weapons research in 2003.[20] But the US permanent representative to the IAEA, Gregory L. Schulte, vowed in a cable to the State Department that the United States would

prevent ElBaradei from proceeding any further toward normalization of the Iran file:

> While the NIE has taken some wind out of our
> sails in Vienna, we plan to refocus the Vienna
> diplomatic community and the IAEA on the finding
> of "high confidence" that there was a nuclear
> weapon program in Iran up until 2003. This
> coincides with the inspectors' upcoming (week
> of December 10) trip to Tehran to hopefully
> receive Iran's answers to questions regarding
> "contamination," the Gachin mine, polonium 210,
> and, most importantly, the alleged studies. While
> we have little expectation that Iran will admit
> the military dimension of all those items, we
> need to ensure that the DG does not close these
> issues or even declare that Iran's information
> is "not inconsistent with" the Agency's findings
> as he has with the plutonium and centrifuge
> issues. Then we would be at odds not only with
> Iran, but with the DG and his many supporters.
> [07UNVIENNA705]

The United States met with the "likeminded" states in Vienna—the
Europeans, plus Canada, Japan, Australia, and New Zealand—
in early December. Diplomats of the US-led coalition expressed
their common consternation with ElBaradei for having closed
the files on the issues that had been resolved through Iranian
explanation and documentation. The cable shows the group's
determination to force him to avoid further agreement, regardless of what information the Iranians provided to the IAEA. The
"likeminded" diplomats were demanding in particular that the
Agency take a hard line on the highly questionable intelligence
documents that had been passed on to it by the Bush administration. The section of the cable reporting the petulant response of

the coalition, which bore the revealing headline "Secretariat Not Playing Ball," shows how the US and its allies believed ElBaradei and his staff were obliged to follow the line laid down by the dominant coalition on the Board in their handling of the Iran nuclear investigation:

> The IAEA's November correspondence with Iran
> on P1/2 issues and the U-metal document, the
> former of which the IAEA "removed from the list
> of outstanding issues," caused consternation
> among like-minded Ambassadors. Nuclear Counselor
> noted that while the IAEA cast the letters as a
> bureaucratic step necessitated by the sequential
> nature of the work plan, Iran had used them
> to declare the issues "closed." Smith was
> "singularly unimpressed" by the Secretariat's
> handling of the letters, and took issue with
> the use of language that differed from that
> used by the DG in reporting to the Board. He
> understood that the letters were not intended to
> be categorical and DDG Heinonen had told him that
> he could revert to P1/P2 issues in dealing with
> the uranium contamination issue. Deniau observed
> that the Secretariat's behavior demonstrated a
> lack of transparency and institutional difficulty;
> when asked for the letters, the Secretariat had
> claimed they were confidential and no different
> from the DG's report, only to have Jalili spring
> them on Solana in their November 30 meeting.
> (Note: The EU-3 will demarche the DG separately
> regarding the incident with Solana, and
> Ambassador Schulte has already raised the issue.
> End note).

9. (C) For the French, P1/P2 remained an
outstanding issue. French DCM Gross questioned
the Secretariat's methodology, and its apparent
lowering of standards in the context of the work
plan. He noted that Iran had not answered all
the questions and had not provided access to a
single individual outside AEOI, nor to archives
or facilities despite the numerous references
to military and other agency involvement in
nuclear activities. Gross worried that once it
confronted Iran with intelligence regarding
the alleged studies, the Secretariat would
accept Iran's responses without requiring
follow-up. He underlined that the Board must
give an independent judgment of the work plan.
Nuclear Counselor also expressed concern that
the Secretariat could deal with the remaining
outstanding issues in the same way as it
had plutonium and P1/P2 issues, and simply
declare Iran's non-answers to be "consistent."
[07UNVIENNA742]

When the same group of diplomats reconvened in mid January 2008, they were even more disturbed by evidence that ElBaradei intended to resolve the remaining issues, possibly even including the supposedly incriminating documents depicting a covert Iranian nuclear weapons project. Japan's permanent representative to the IAEA, Yukiya Amano, commented tartly that ElBaradei might conclude that Iran "confessed to being not guilty" at the conclusion of the work plan, and US ambassador Schulte insisted that "Iran must admit and explain the genesis and purpose of the studies; thus any pronouncement of 'not guilty' cannot be adequate" [08UNVIENNA31].

By February, the United States was ready to warn ElBaradei that failing to keep Iran under suspicion in regard to the intelligence documents would risk the loss of contributions to the IAEA from the United States and its allies, and wanted the message conveyed by the P3+1 in a demarche. As the reporting cable from Ambassador Schulte put it,

> In the coming weeks we must continue to set a
> high bar for the work plan and make clear in our
> public and private comments that the work plan
> is meaningless unless Iran admits weaponization
> activities and allows the IAEA to verify they
> have stopped. We must also warn the DG in very
> stark terms that the IAEA's integrity and his
> own credibility are at stake and that any
> hint of whitewash of Iran's weapons activities
> would cause irreparable harm to the Agency's
> relationship with major donors.

> (S) We recommend conveying these messages through
> a [P3+1] demarche in Vienna, an appropriately-
> timed phone call from the Secretary, ElBaradei's
> contacts in Paris and Munich in mid-February,
> and a possible stop by U/S Burns in Vienna next
> week. A [P3+1] demarche should take place prior
> to the issuance of the report, expected sometime
> between February 20-25. The French are not sure
> of joining such a demarche just after the DG's
> February 14 trip to Paris where he would have
> already heard a similar message from the GOF,
> but we have asked them to reconsider. A demarche
> prior to the DG report would also allow us to
> better assess where the DG stands on the work
> plan, and how to frame a Board resolution.

> (S) The [P3+1] will also work quietly on
> preparing a resolution, which could be tabled

> upon the issuance of the report. As to the
> content of that resolution, P3+1 Ambassadors
> considered options for a more critical vice
> consensual assessment of the Secretariat's
> efforts. If, as expected, the DG is not prepared
> to say Iran's cooperation on the work plan
> has been unsatisfactory, the UK is of the view
> that the Board will have to do so for him. A
> resolution would underline the Board/UNSC's basic
> requirements including suspension. The UK argued
> for a more critical resolution to "put an end to
> the work plan episode." Smith warned that in the
> face of an uncritical DG report, we will need to
> challenge the work plan, even if [it] means a
> vote. He said his vote counting gave us a bare
> majority in the Board even if the Russians and
> Chinese vote against. [08UNVIENNA64]

It was the second time in less than a year that the Bush administration had threatened that US and allied funding for the Agency would be cut if ElBaradei persisted in a course of action on Iran that was opposed to US policy. In mid 2007, Ambassador Schulte had passed on to ElBaradei a comment by Secretary of State Condoleezza Rice that "the Americans could treat the IAEA budget like that of the Universal Postal Union."[21]

In March 2008, however, the tone of US reporting on the IAEA and Iran shifted markedly to emphasize the need to support the IAEA push on the "weaponization studies," in particular. The reason for the new comfort level was that the head of the IAEA Department of Safeguards, Olli Heinonen, had emerged clearly as a firm ally of the US-led coalition on the IAEA's handling of the intelligence documents. Ambassador Schulte reported in late March on how that development played into US strategy:

We share UK Ambassador Smith's concern that
little public and private discussion of Iran
in Vienna will mean no progress on the Iran
file by the June Board. That would both feed
the perception that we are at a stalemate and
fuel pressure by ElBaradei and others that the
[P5+1]—and specifically the US—need to make a
concession to revive negotiations. The IAEA
Secretariat, meanwhile, appears divided between
those, like Heinonen, who want to press ahead on
the weaponization investigation, and others who
want to use passage of 1803 as an excuse to slow-
roll the Iran account for the rest of 2008. The
perception of a stalemate would feed into Iran's
strategy to delay and divide the international
community and make it more difficult to get
support if we decided to pursue a June Board
resolution that reaffirmed the role of the Board.
In the wake of the Majles elections and Iran's
declarations that the work plan is closed, this
drift could also give additional fuel to Iranian
hard-line arguments that non-cooperation and
aggressive diplomacy will be successful on the
nuclear issue and thus make Tehran's cooperation
even less likely. [08UNVIENNA185]

Reflecting the commitment of Heinonen to the US line implied
in the reporting cable, the IAEA reports of May and September
2008 presented the intelligence documents for the first time as
"credible," and even employed deceptive language to insinuate
falsely that Iran had acknowledged some of the activities portrayed in the documents, while suggesting that they were for
non-nuclear purposes. In fact, however, Iran had never acknowledged that anything in the laptop documents was real except for
the names of certain publicly known individuals, organizations,

and addresses, as the IAEA itself admitted in a report three years later.[22]

It was the start of a political campaign to indict Iran for refusing to cooperate with what was described as an IAEA investigation of the "possible military dimensions" of the Iranian nuclear program. What Iran had refused to do, however, was provide classified conventional military data that the IAEA was demanding as proof that Iran had not done what was portrayed in the documents.[23] But the IAEA's suggestion that Iran had admitted partial guilt and was refusing to cooperate with the investigation helped to propel the international crisis over the Iran nuclear issue for the next several years.

The diplomatic cables in the WikiLeaks files show the ebb and flow of State Department and embassy business, rather than the more exciting top-secret meetings of the administration's national security team. But among the tens of thousands in the collection are many cables that show how the official and media version of US policy in the Middle East concealed US motives and strategies, as well as objective political-diplomatic realities contradicting the approved narrative.

The WikiLeaks cables excerpted and quoted above show how the Bush and Obama administrations subordinated US diplomatic freedom and impartiality on the crucial issue of Israeli-Palestinian peace negotiations to its political imperative of support for Israeli interests. Secondly, they demonstrate that both administrations privately sought to exploit the threat of Israeli attack on Iran for diplomatic purposes. They pushed a public and private diplomatic line about a threat from Iranian ballistic missiles that was not based on objective fact, but reflected the bureaucratic and private economic interests of the Pentagon and its industrial allies. Finally, they used the threat to withdraw support from the IAEA to pressure the head of the Agency to come to conclusions about the Iranian nuclear program that were not consistent with the facts, but would be useful to US efforts to shut down Iran's nuclear program or punish it for refusing to do so.

The WikiLeaks collection of cables is an essential tool for unearthing the truth about US foreign policy. Unfortunately, the news media treatment of the cables, which focused overwhelmingly on Iran-related cables, obscured some of their important revelations and portrayed the cables as supporting the official line of the United States, Israel, and their European allies. The central lesson of the release of the cables is therefore that digging up the truth from leaked material is a job that can only be done by independent journalists and researchers—not by those whose search for truth is circumscribed by structures of interest and power.

12. Iraq

Dahr Jamail

On April 5, 2010, WikiLeaks released a classified US military video that showed in graphic, horrifying detail the murder of over a dozen people, including two Reuters news staff, in the Iraqi suburb of New Baghdad. The video quickly became known as "Collateral Murder."

The recording clearly captures one of the US helicopter crewmen exclaim: "Oh yeah, look at those dead bastards!" after multiple rounds of 30mm cannon fire left nearly a dozen bodies littering the street. To most people, the dehumanizing attitude toward murdering innocent civilians displayed in the video was shocking. But to journalists working in Iraq throughout the US-led occupation, this type of callous behavior was just another day at the office while reporting from the front lines of empire.[1]

The WikiLeaks cables from Iraq displayed the brutality of US policies in that country that were ongoing throughout the occupation. The home raids, creation and use of death squads, divide-and-conquer strategies exercised through the setting up of the proxy "Awakening Councils," and the use of torture are outlined here, and reveal just how important the WikiLeaks cables from Iraq were and continue to be in highlighting the US tactics of hegemony.

A cable published by WikiLeaks provides details of a home raid carried out by US forces on March 15, 2006, that led to the killing of ten people, including women and children. The cable, which included a letter by the UN Special Rapporteur on extra-judicial, summary, or arbitrary executions, Philip Alston, details what happened:

```
I have received various reports indicating that
at least 10 persons, namely Mr Faiz Hratt Khalaf
(aged 28), his wife Sumay'ya Abdul Razzaq Khuther
(aged 24), their three children Hawra'a (aged 5)
Aisha (aged 3) and Husam (5 months old), Faiz's
mother Ms Turkiya Majeed Ali (aged 74), Faiz's
sister (name unknown), Faiz's nieces Asma'a
Yousif Ma'arouf (aged 5 years old), and Usama
Yousif Ma'arouf (aged 3 years), and a visiting
relative Ms Iqtisad Hameed Mehdi (aged 23) were
killed during the raid. [06GENEVA763]
```

This particular raid had come after US air strikes had been carried out in the same area. The cable is evidence of a widespread US policy during the occupation of shooting first and asking questions later, as well as detaining anyone and everyone "suspected" of having any links to attacks on US forces. This writer interviewed dozens of US soldiers who served in Iraq who told of policies like "reconnaissance by fire," in which soldiers were literally ordered to shoot people first, then decide if the people killed were a threat or not. Several soldiers revealed that their officers would later cover for them, as long as they shot people if they perceived any kind of "threat." Given that the raids often ended in summary executions of innocent people, the US military in Iraq often took "suspected" to have the same meaning as "guilty." The cable goes on to remind the reader of the need for the US military to adhere to international and humanitarian law, in addition to alluding to the widespread pattern of excessive violence: "Other reports indicate that over the past five months, there have been a significant number of lethal incidents in which the [Multinational Force (MNF)] is alleged to have used excessive force to respond to perceived threats either at checkpoints or by using air bombing in civilian areas."

The WikiLeaks Iraq cables provide dozens of instances of admitted "excessive force" during the occupation. The aforementioned cable provides but one of tens of thousands of examples of violence carried out in Iraq by US forces that led to over one million deaths during the invasion and ten-year occupation.[2]

These documents, as much or even more than the others, pull back the veil on the tactics the US empire has used in Iraq and continues to use abroad to expand its reach. Several of the articulations of these doctrines are worth mentioning here, as they received little to no coverage in the corporate media.

Clear evidence is provided of a military strategy aimed at generating civilian casualties in order to turn the population against insurgents: "[T]he psychological effectiveness of the CSDF [paramilitary] concept starts by reversing the insurgent strategy of making the government the repressor. It forces the insurgents to cross a critical threshold—that of attacking and killing the very class of people they are supposed to be liberating." Another passage makes clear how detentions were encouraged: "The United States reserves the right to engage in nonconsensual [extraterritorial] abductions for three specific reasons ..."

The military was clear about the measures it used to control public dissent: "Checkpoints, searches, roadblocks; surveillance, censorship, and press control; and restriction of activity that applies to selected groups (labor unions, political groups and the like) are further PRC [Population and Resource Control] measures."

The next three passages provide examples of how the US used economic warfare against the people of Iraq as a means of battling insurgents—a policy that inevitably impacted the civilian population as well:

```
US policy states that the enemy's uniform may
be used for infiltration behind enemy lines.
```

However, Article 39 of Protocol I to the Geneva
Conventions prohibits this and other uses of
the enemy's uniform. "The agent controlling the
creation, flow, and access stores of value" wields
power. Although finance is generally an operation
of real and virtual currency, anything that can
serve as a "medium of exchange" provides those
who accept the medium with a method of financial
transaction. For both reasons, ARSOF understand
that they can and should exploit the active and
analytical capabilities existing in the financial
instrument of US power in the conduct of UW
[Unconventional Warfare].

In addition to intelligence and policy changes
that may provide active incentive or disincentive
leverage, the Office of Foreign Assets Control
(OFAC) has a long history of conducting economic
warfare valuable to any ARSOF UW campaign.

Like all other instruments of US national power,
the use and effects of economic "weapons" are
interrelated and they must be coordinated
carefully.[3]

All of the Iraq WikiLeaks cables provide vital information about
US policies that have left a US legacy of violence and political
instability that forms the basis of the failed state that is Iraq today.

DIVIDE AND CONQUER

History shows us that in Iraq, while there are clear differences in
the religious beliefs of the two sects of Islam—Sunni and Shia—
the kind of violent sectarianism that has become the norm today
did not exist in modern Iraq prior to the 2003 US-led invasion.

Several of the larger areas of Baghdad comprised equal numbers of Sunni and Shia, and this was common across many other cities, such as Baquba. Furthermore, one of the most important Shia shrines in the world, the Shrine of al-Askari, is located in the middle of Samarra, a primarily Sunni city in Iraq's al-Anbar province.

During the first six months of the occupation there was little violent resistance against the US military, but by late 2003 the Pentagon revealed that attacks had begun and were escalating. The US occupation of Iraq quickly devolved into chaos as the Iraqi resistance began to inflict ever-greater damage on occupation forces. At first, the armed resistance in Iraq was primarily Sunni, given that former Iraqi dictator Saddam Hussein was Sunni and that segment of the population had tended to benefit from his regime.

The resistance was then joined, in the spring of 2004, by an armed uprising by Shia cleric Muqtada al-Sadr's Mehdi Army militia. At this point the US was struggling to control not only much of Baghdad and the sprawling al-Anbar province, but also much of the south, including the Sadr City area of Baghdad, where Sadr's forces were located.

By April 2004, when the US siege of Fallujah was underway and simultaneously Sadr's forces were in open conflict with US forces, there were moments when the majority of US military supply lines in Iraq were cut off, indicating a massive slippage in US control over the country. The WikiLeaks cables, in both their content and timing, reveal what the US was orchestrating in order to attempt to control the events unfolding on the ground.

To regain control of the situation, on May 6, 2004, George W. Bush appointed John Negroponte as the first US ambassador to Iraq, where he served until 2005. Negroponte quickly brought in retired colonel James Steele, whom he had worked with closely when Negroponte was Ronald Reagan's ambassador to Honduras during the early 1980s. Negroponte's and Steele's covert actions in mobilizing death squads and conducting operations that resulted in tens of thousands of deaths across Central America are now well documented, including their extreme abuses of human rights.[4]

When it became clear to the Bush administration that it was rapidly losing control of Iraq, these two men were placed in Baghdad to resume their classic colonial strategy of divide and conquer, otherwise referred to as "counter-insurgency."[5] Less than two years after their implementation by Negroponte and Steele, death squads were ravaging and terrorizing Baghdad on a daily basis.[6] Iraqis living in the capital city were seeing the reality of sectarian-based civil war by the spring of 2006.[7]

As a result of the death squads, sectarian violence exploded. Many areas of Baghdad began to self-separate, as Sunni families began moving out of predominantly Shia areas, and vice versa. Ironically, as a result of their own policies, during 2006 and 2007 the US-military-backed separation of mixed Shia/Sunni neighborhoods in Baghdad became the norm.[8] Occupation forces erected massive concrete barriers spanning miles that separated families, further delineating the US-fomented Shia-Sunni divide in Iraq's capital city.[9] These actions were ironic given that the US was not an ally of Iran, and were augmented by the US backing of Iraqi prime minister Nouri al-Maliki, who has always maintained strong ties to Iran and is a member of the Shia Dawa Party, which has its origins in that country.

The US supported Maliki because he had agreed to keep Iraqi oil fields accessible to Western companies, as well as moving to begin the purchase of US military hardware and training. However, Maliki quickly began to be referred to by Iraqis as a "Shia Saddam," his overtly sectarian style of government being subject to widespread criticism.[10] The US backing of Maliki also caused political discord between Shia and Kurdish political parties from early on.[11] These facts, along with bombings of sacred Shia shrines, caused many Iraqis to become outraged about what was happening in their country, with many believing these were all attempts by the occupation forces to sow division between Iraqis.[12]

Many WikiLeaks cables and documents shed light the US policies that encouraged sectarianism. While documentation does
not reveal overt orders to foment violent sectarianism, it does
reveal US policies that led to sectarian tensions and violence. One
addressed a statement issued by a prominent Shia religious leader
who sharply criticized the US over a joint US-Iraqi raid in the Ur
neighborhood, calling the action a "heinous crime." The cable
accuses the US of siding with the Sunni minority of Iraq, and of
actively denying a sectarian war in the country. This was ironic,
given that US policies had provoked this sectarian war, which
by the time this cable was communicated was in full swing. It
is striking that this particular cable displays what appear to be
the retaliatory methods employed by the US military during the
occupation, as the Shia leaders' criticism of US tactics was then
followed by the violent raid mentioned above:

> On March 26 (before the Ur neighborhood raid) the
> office of Ayatalloh Muhammad al-Yaqubi (spiritual
> leader of the Fadhila party) criticized the
> [United States government] for denying the
> existence of a sectarian war in Iraq … Yacoubi
> pointed to the daily killings, attacks on holy
> shrines, and the displacement as evidence of
> this sectarian war. The statement called for
> political parties not to allow the participation
> of any side that does not renounce terrorism [a
> not-so-subtle reference to the Sunni Arabs]. It
> sharply criticized the new Iraqi National Security
> Council, the American Ambassador, and other Arab
> states. The statement concluded by demanding that
> the US change its Ambassador, that the Iraqi
> government confront the elements of this sectarian
> war, and that the Shia nation organize itself into
> "committees and groups to defend themselves and
> their holy places." [06BAGHDAD1050]

In a few years' time, Maliki had had time to solidify his power by marginalizing Sunni politicians in Baghdad, setting up the secret detention facilities for Sunnis that were later criticized by Human Rights Watch, and continuing his policies of home raids and detentions in primarily Sunni areas.[13]

Another cable reveals how sectarian tensions had increased so much that Fallujah leaders were complaining to the US military about how Iraqi Army (IA) units operating in the embattled city were stoking sectarian flames to such a degree that the Sunnis were requesting a continuance of the US presence:

```
Fallujah leaders echoed that ongoing sectarianism
would create trouble in Fallujah for IA units.
The current mood had increased tension among
residents; if sectarianism in Baghdad lessened,
IA units (dominantly Shia) would be better
received. If not, planned handover of security
responsibilities would become complicated and
be undermined. Abbas stressed that more Iraqi
Security Force units were needed in Fallujah
should Coalition Forces numbers be reduced, "two
or three times at least." City leaders registered
strong concerns about the growing power of
militias, which remained the main problem. Col.
Karim noted that the planned movement of a
special police battalion to Fallujah had been put
on hold, due to the volatile situation in the
capital. [06BAGHDAD4400]
```

Another cable reveals how leaders in Fallujah, along with some members of the Iraqi Army, had criticized the timing of the execution of Saddam Hussein, saying that it had been an act of "revenge" by the predominantly Shia government:

> Fallujah leaders told Al Anbar PolOff January 1
> that the city remained quiet following Saddam
> Hussein's December 30 execution. They criticized,
> however, the timing of the execution, which
> coincided with the start of the Eid al-Adha
> holiday. Fallujah's mayor said that the rush to
> execute Saddam appeared to be an act of "revenge"
> by the Shia-led government. An IA battalion
> executive officer (Shia), based in Fallujah,
> echoed the criticisms regarding the timing of the
> execution. He said that "the new year had been
> ushered in with a bad omen." Marines reported
> late January 2 that a pro-Saddam, anti-Moqtada
> Sadr demonstration had been held in Haditha.
> [07BAGHDAD29]

The cable quoted Fallujah City Council secretary Abbas Ali Hussein telling the US military that "the sacred nature of the Eid celebrations had been violated ... the same day we slay animals in celebration, the government slays Saddam." Indeed, the timing of the execution caused outrage among much of the Sunni population, both in Iraq and across the Middle East.[14]

Sectarian tensions and violence in Iraq began to increase in mid 2005, and by early 2006 were worsening dramatically. By that time, nearly every morning saw bodies on the streets of Baghdad after death-squad activities at night, and Shia cleric Muqtada al-Sadr's Mehdi Army militia had declared open war on Sunnis.

On April 3, 2006, at the height of the sectarian bloodletting in Iraq, a cable titled "Fallujah: Army-Police Friction and Perceived US 'Mixed Messages'" reveals the tensions on the ground, as articulated by Fallujah's mayor, that were created by the US policy of favoring the Shia over the Sunni through their backing of Maliki's government in Baghdad:

Reports of recent Iraqi Army (IA) and Iraqi
Police (IP) friction in Fallujah led to a
Marine-initiated meeting held March 20 to convey
Coalition Force (CF) concerns and implement
operational changes. The Shia-dominant army units
(two brigades) and Sunni-dominant city police
force (1,300 at present, locally recruited)
agreed to new procedures and improved liaison
activity. For now, the intra-ISF tension has
lessened, but army and police units in the still
volatile and symbolic city will require continued
close Marine oversight. Marine leaders made clear
that officers will be held personally accountable
for the actions of their forces. Fallujah's
mayor, Sheikh Dhari Abdel Hady Al-Zobaie, also
expressed frustration with US "mixed messages."
Fallujans remain concerned about perceived
coalition policy to stand aside should sectarian
violence worsen and extend beyond Baghdad.
They argue that the Coalition is responsible
for protecting Sunni Arabs against [Ministry
of Interior-run] militias, and have expressed
mounting anxiety over a premature US pullout.
[06BAGHDAD1087]

The cable provides further evidence of increasing sectarian
tensions:

Fallujan residents have regularly complained
to Marines and Poloff about IA behavior and
treatment … Sheikh Dhari also voiced concerns
over what he considered to be an unclear US
position regarding increased sectarianism and CF
reactions. Would US military forces stand aside,
as Secretary Rumsfeld implied in his recent

Senate testimony? He added "we are in a dilemma
and confusion. It is like Indian movies, which
all start with happiness but end with dilemmas."
Sheikh Dhari urged the US to be more clear on
these areas or risk exacerbating tension and
Sunni-Arab fears that they will be left to fend
for themselves against government-backed Shia
militias should the situation deteriorate.

The cable concludes with this prophetic note that perfectly summarizes why and how these sectarian tensions persist in Iraq today:

Sheikh Dhari's criticisms of US positions center
on the sustained fear, verging on fixation,
in Anbar of Iranian influence. This perception
of Tehran's meddling is widely shared. The
not unfounded anxiety over MOI militias will
likewise continue to drive the unsettled Sunni-
Arab mindset in Fallujah. One senior Fallujah
Imam recently told PolOff that while the Shia
and Kurds had their militias, the Badr Corp and
Pesh Merga respectively, the Sunnis only had the
resistance.

THE AWAKENING

As part of the so-called US military surge in 2006–07, the US reinvigorated a tactic used by Saddam Hussein in an effort to control armed resistance groups operating across Iraq's al-Anbar province.

The tactic involved finding key tribal leaders and dispensing tens of millions of dollars to them in order to entice them to order fighters under their control to "stand down" from their attacks against US occupation forces. The method was successful in causing many members of the Iraqi resistance, along with many outside it, to join the Sahwa forces that began to work directly with US forces. The Sahwa were promised jobs in the Iraqi Army and Iraqi security forces after the US withdrew, but the Maliki government never provided the vast majority of the nearly 100,000-strong Sahwa with the jobs they had been promised.[15]

A cable titled "Sunni Arab Insider Warns PM Maliki Will Reignite Insurgency" reads:

> Tens of thousands of Sunni Arab "Sons of Iraq" and Sahwa ("Awakening") fighters, who were instrumental in pushing Al-Qa'ida out of Anbar Province, and on the defensive elsewhere, will not be absorbed into the Iraqi Security Forces and vocational training programs as projected, a senior aide to (Sunni Arab) Vice President Hashimi predicted. Instead, he continued, the GOI, driven by an increasingly overconfident and sectarian-minded circle of advisors around Prime Minister Maliki, will likely arrest hundreds of Sunni Arab SOI and Sahwa commanders, and cast aside thousands of Sunni Arab Sahwa/SOI foot soldiers. This will result in a sharp backlash which will set back the national reconciliation process and could reignite Sunni Arab insurgency, he warned. [08BAGHDAD2781]

Hashimi's warnings would indeed prove prescient.

A separate cable provided yet another warning sign of how this policy of creating and supporting the Sahwa forces was exacerbating Sunni-Shia tensions:

> According to Sahwa leader Abu Azaam, the GOI and Shia have opposed Sahwa and the Sons of Iraq …

since its establishment, and transitioning the
Sahwa to GOI administration would lead to its
dissolution. This will increase the sense of
betrayal among Sunni Arabs, and could lead to
more anti-Coalition, anti-GOI actions. Abu Azaam
said that US forces must remain in Iraq, and
increase their presence rather than withdraw,
because a premature withdrawal of US forces would
directly serve Iranian goals. He stressed that
voters should throw out the current Iranian-
influenced leadership in upcoming elections,
although it will be difficult to elect new groups
because the current Shi'a political parties are
too strong and corrupt. [08BAGHDAD2831]

One of the primary goals for the creation the Sahwa was that of
self-protection, since the political cost of high numbers of dead
US soldiers in Iraq had become too high. By creating the Sahwa,
US soldiers were able to withdraw from the front lines fighting
al-Qaeda in Iraq and the insurgency. But after these new merce-
naries had done their job, the empire hung them out to dry.[16]

By 2009, it had become clear that Sahwa members were more
concerned with getting paid than they were with Baghdad's
overall security, or even with how other Sahwa members located
outside the capital were faring:

Contacts emphasized that Baghdad SOI are not
really connected with SOI groups in other
provinces. SOIs in the provinces are upset,
however, that the GOI has not yet established a
reliable mechanism to pay SOI salaries and honor
integration and new employment promises; they
question the GOI's commitment to the program.
Some SOI contacts also worry that SOI groups will
be abandoned as CF leaves Iraq. [09BAGHDAD899]

The controversial move of the US military to back Sunni Sahwa forces, as well as simultaneously backing the Shia-dominated government in Baghdad, drove another deep wedge between Sunni and Shia political groups. Following disputes between the tribal groups assembled into the Sahwa and the Iraqi government, the creation of these forces became a point of political friction between the Sunni and Shia that festers to this day.[17]

TORTURE

Ali Abbas lived in the Al-Amiriyah district of Baghdad. His story illustrates the scope and methodology of the US torture campaign used throughout Iraq. In a 2004 interview, he told me that so many of his neighbors had been detained that friends urged him to go to the nearby US base (in Amiriyah, Baghdad) to try to get answers as to why so many innocent people were being detained. He went three times. The fourth time—on September 13, 2003—he was detained himself, despite not having been charged with any crime. Within two days he was transferred from the military base to Abu Ghraib, where he was held for over three months.

"The minute I got there, the suffering began," he recalled. The treatment he described mirrors that contained in the *Iraq War Logs*, including evidence of torture in Abu Ghraib ignored by the US authorities.[18] Abbas's treatment included sexual humiliation, beatings, denial of food and water, mock executions, death threats, threats to his family, the use of dogs, and offenses against Islam. Abbas did not feel this was the work of a few individual soldiers: "This was organized, it wasn't just individuals, and every one of the troops in Abu Ghraib was responsible for it."

The *Iraq War Logs* revealed documents that directly implicated US General David Petraeus and Central American "dirty wars" veteran Colonel James Steele in Iraqi detainee abuse.[19] WikiLeaks added notes that

[t]he allegations made by both American
and Iraqi witnesses in the *Guardian*/BBC
documentary, for the first time implicates US
advisers in the human rights abuses committed
by the commandos. It is also the first time that
General David Petraeus—who last November was
forced to resign as director of the CIA after a
sex scandal—has been linked through an adviser
to this abuse.[20]

According to a Human Rights Watch report released on April 27, 2005, "Abu Ghraib was only the tip of the iceberg. It's now clear that abuse of detainees has happened all over—from Afghanistan to Guantánamo Bay to a lot of third-country dungeons where the United States has sent prisoners. And probably quite a few other places we don't even know about."[21]

The report added, "Harsh and coercive interrogation techniques such as subjecting detainees to painful stress positions and extended sleep deprivation have been routinely used in detention centers throughout Iraq." An earlier report by Major General Antonio Taguba had found "numerous incidents of sadistic, blatant, and wanton criminal abuses," constituting "systematic and illegal abuse of detainees" at Abu Ghraib. Another Pentagon report documented forty-four allegations of such war crimes at Abu Ghraib. An ICRC report concluded that, in military intelligence sections of Abu Ghraib, "methods of physical and psychological coercion used by the interrogators appeared to be part of the standard operating procedures by military intelligence personnel to obtain confessions and extract information." Amnesty International released similar findings.[22]

The majority of the WikiLeaks cables concerning torture in US military detention facilities were focused more on the media backlash against the release of the infamous photographs from Abu Ghraib than they were on bringing those responsible for the torture to justice.

A May 2004 cable titled "Special Media Reaction on Iraqi Prisoner Abuse" (note that the word "torture" is never used in the cables—only "abuse" or "mistreatment") simply shares information about how various Arab media outlets were covering the reaction to the demeaning photographs. [04AMMAN3388]

Another cable, titled "Public Reaction to Abuse of Iraqi Prisoners," revealed the primary concerns of the occupiers, and concluded with a suggestion of the "spin" to put on the story:

```
Negative and vehement public reactions to photos
and reports of Iraqi prisoner abuse continued.
Ever since it hit the press, the issue has been
dominating local and regional media as well as
public opinion in the UAE. Contacts commiserate
that public diplomacy efforts have become next
to impossible because the photos gave extremists
additional ammunition to criticize the US. A
senior contact noted that the good side of the
story reveals that there are good-hearted and
conscientious people involved with the issue.
[04ABUDHABI1508]
```

The US military was aware of secret prisons in various locations in Iraq, one of them being within Fallujah. This was confirmed by a memo dated February 2008, published by WikiLeaks.[23] It is a confidential memo from Major General Kelly, the commander of US forces in western Iraq. According to WikiLeaks, it was privately verified by WikiLeaks staff, and was neither denied nor contradicted by the Multinational Force West (MNF-W) when questioned by Shaun Waterman, the national security editor for UPI. The MNF-W commander's comments read:

```
I spent the entire day inspecting the Fallujah
city jail. I found the conditions there to be
exactly (unbelievable over crowding, total lack
```

of anything approaching even minimal levels of hygiene for human beings, no food, little water, no ventilation) to those described in the recent (18 February) FOX news article by Michael Totten entitled the "Dungeon of Fallujah." When queried the Iraqis and marines present throughout my inspection as to why these conditions existed, three conditions were universally cited as problems in Fallujah as well as the rest of Anbar.

First, there is zero support from the government for any of the jails in Anbar. No funds, food or medical support has been provided from any ministry. Second, the police that run Anbar's jails are the same personnel responsible for investigating crimes. These jailer/investigators are undermanned and more often than not spend most of their time out begging and scavenging for food than investigating crimes. (It is unlikely the prisoners will eat today.) Third, Anbar lacks trained Iraqi correctional officers (ICOS) to run the jails in Anbar. The development and employment of trained ICOS would enable the IP to focus on criminal investigation rather [than] jail supervision. I believe the Iraqi police are doing the best they can, and they literally begged me on humanitarian, moral and religious grounds to help them help the prisoners by somehow moving the government to action.

The MNF commander's comments show that even the US military was deeply concerned about the Iraqi government's treatment of detainees.

Meanwhile, Human Rights Watch reported in 2010 that US

military psychologists and psychiatrists were complicit in torture and other illegal procedures.[24]

Hence, while this kind of horrific torture and abuse of Iraqi detainees was common across US detention facilities throughout the occupation, it is telling that the majority of the cables and memos related to this issue were more focused on media damage control and on diplomatic fronts than they were of resolving the problem and bringing those responsible to account. The same priorities were in place when it came to the murder of Iraqis.

A document dated July 24, 2006, exposed a directive by a Lieutenant Colonel Nathaniel Johnson, Jr., requiring that, as posted by WikiLeaks, "No classified evidence be introduced into the Article 32 hearing of four soldiers. Private First Class Corey R. Clagett, Specialist William B. Hunsaker, Staff Sergeant Raymond L. Girouard, and Specialist Juston R. Graber executed three unarmed Iraqi detainees and attempted to make the incident look like an escape attempt, as reported in media coverage of the subsequent court martial."

WikiLeaks also published an appeal by Johnson against a report by Michael D. Steele in which Johnson is not selected for promotion. Steele was the commanding officer of the four accused soldiers, all of whom later testified that Steele had given the order to "kill all military-age men."[25]

These are just a few examples of how the US empire operated in Iraq, providing a clear display of how it operates on a regional level. In general, the Iraq cables show us the myriad methods the US used to bring its new subjects of empire to heel, along with the nefarious tactics employed to conceal, obfuscate, or "spin" the truth.

Never before has an empire had its inner workings so clearly revealed as when WikiLeaks decided to make these cables, memos, and other documents publicly available. As was revealed by WikiLeaks, US policies in Iraq were largely responsible for the disintegration of Iraq that we are witnessing today.

13. Afghanistan

Phyllis Bennis

The US war in Afghanistan was always an add-on war. Those in power in Washington—most especially the neoconservative warmongers who populated George W. Bush and Dick Cheney's White House, Pentagon, and beyond—saw the terror attacks of September 11, 2001, as an opportunity to justify a new era of global war. Their main international target would be Iraq, but Afghanistan, the temporary home of the al-Qaeda leadership who inspired the bombers, had to be attacked first.

The 9/11 attacks were shocking and terrifying for people in the US. There had not been such an attack on US soil, with so many killed in a single incident, in living memory. And the Bush administration provided only one choice in response: we either go to war, or we "let 'em get away with it." The option of recognizing the attacks as an enormous crime against humanity that demanded not war but a globally collaborative response, relying on international law and a strengthened system of international justice, was never on the table. As a result, almost no one was prepared to say no to an immediate war—90 percent of the US public supported attacking Afghanistan. In contrast, by March 2011, 64 percent of Americans said the Afghanistan war "was not worth fighting."

That does not mean there were no other options. In the WikiLeaks papers, a Congressional Research Service report describes the 9/11 attacks as

... the defining event that transformed the US
counter terror effort from law-enforcement
actions and limited military retaliation to a
global war on terror. In this context, 9/11
triggered a series of government actions—
to include the invasions and occupations of
Afghanistan and Iraq (despite the apparent lack
of direct connection between Iraq and the 9/11
attacks). [CRS-RS21937]

What remained unstated in that careful CRS document was that George W. Bush and his administration were only too happy to transform US "counter-terror" efforts into a global war. While its ideological foundations differed, the escalatory decision in some ways paralleled Bush's father's decision to go to war against Iraq in 1990–91. In that case, the George H. W. Bush administration decided to use a real (but hardly unprecedented) violation of international law—Iraq's invasion and occupation of Kuwait— as justification to lead "the world" (or at least a significant part of it) to war. The real reason for choosing to respond to the Iraqi move with full-scale war had far more to do with reasserting the US super-power identity as the Soviet Union collapsed and the Cold War ended than it did with punishing former US ally Saddam Hussein.

The war against Afghanistan was grounded in revenge, not justice. The 9/11 hijackers were not Afghans, but Egyptians and Saudis; they lived not in Afghanistan, but in Hamburg; they had not trained in Afghanistan, but in Florida; and they had attended flight school not in Afghanistan, but in Minnesota. So why the war? Largely because Afghanistan, where al-Qaeda's leadership core was headquartered, was the target that made public sense— at least in the first instance. Going after Iraq immediately, as some in the administration urged, would have been harder—Iraq had nothing to do with 9/11, there was no connection to al-Qaeda, and the false WMD argument would soon collapse. So they had to set the stage before going after the real target. Afghanistan was the overture.

The problem, of course, was that Afghanistan was not just the place where a radical government had allowed an even more radical movement to operate on its territory. Afghanistan was and is a real country where hundreds of thousands, millions of people with no connection to the 9/11 attacks, would be killed or see their lives and families destroyed because of a policy choice made half a world away. That was the part that too few people understood—and that was part of the reason why the WikiLeaks release of Afghanistan documents was so crucially important.

The war in Afghanistan, like the war in Iraq, was based on a host of lies. The WikiLeaks papers document what troops and commanders in the field report to other military officials—where they generally tell the truth. The realities of the wars in places like Afghanistan and Pakistan, like the realities and history of the Vietnam War, were hidden only from Americans. Neither the opposition fighters nor the countries' populations ever needed Pentagon documents to know what US/NATO forces were doing in their countries.

The US invasion and occupation set in motion a devastating destruction of much of the traditional social fabric of the country. Efforts to use modern Western military force and regime change to liberate Afghanistan's women or build new secular education systems largely failed. One might describe the US/NATO invasion and occupation as having

```
caused a diaspora of Afghanistan's small educated
and professional elite and the … collapse of
most vestiges of the old order. The Afghan
[government] attempted a number of social changes
that under other circumstances would have been
viewed as progressive, including measures to
promote secular education and liberate women, but
the … leaders, who came mainly from urban areas,
```

```
had little understanding of the countryside
or respect for rural traditions. Their clumsy
efforts to overturn the social and political
order in the tribal areas provoked widespread
rebellion.
```

Kept secret, though not classified, until it was released as part of WikiLeaks' *Afghan War Diary*, the passage reads like an intelligent and perhaps prescient description of the consequences of the still-new US occupation of Afghanistan. If its assessment had been acted upon, it might have led to a radically different set of decisions in a war that has now raged for more than thirteen years.

But, in fact, while that description came from a 2002 report prepared by the Congressional Research Service entitled "Afghanistan: Challenges and Options for Reconstructing a Stable and Moderate State" [CRS-RL31389], it referred to an entirely different era. The article retraced various periods of Afghan history, in this section critically examining the 1979–89 period of Soviet-influenced governments in Afghanistan, starting with the regime of Mohamed Daoud Khan, who had overthrown the Afghan king in 1973 and served as president until he was assassinated in 1978.

In full, the original paragraph reads:

```
Daoud's overthrow and the Soviet invasion caused
a diaspora of Afghanistan's small educated and
professional elite and the families associated
with the rule of Zahir Shah, leading to the
collapse of most vestiges of the old order. The
Afghan communists attempted a number of social
changes that under other circumstances would have
been viewed as progressive, including measures
to promote secular education and liberate women,
but the PDPA [People's Democratic Party of
Afghanistan] leaders, who came mainly from urban
```

> areas, had little understanding of the countryside
> or respect for rural traditions. Their clumsy
> efforts to overturn the social and political order
> in the tribal areas provoked widespread rebellion.

One might have hoped that access to such critical examination of the consequences of what were recognized as inappropriate efforts at modernization and Westernization might have helped lead to different decisions by US war strategists. But, instead, the United States and NATO installed pro-Western governments and schemes of social engineering in Afghanistan that, like those of their Soviet counterparts thirty years earlier, might "under other circumstances have been viewed as progressive, including measures to promote secular education and liberate women." The United States and its chosen government in Kabul, like its Soviet predecessors, "had little understanding of the countryside or respect for rural traditions. Their clumsy efforts to overturn the social and political order in the tribal areas provoked widespread rebellion."

It should not have been surprising to US planners that the Western-style "democratic" structures created and imposed by the terms of the international Bonn conference, set up in December 2001 to create an interim government in Afghanistan after the overthrow of the Taliban, never really worked. Unlike Iraq, where a similar model was imposed after the violent overthrow of the Iraqi regime in 2003, Afghanistan had no history of a dominant central government holding significant power over the whole territory. Traditional identity in Afghanistan was grounded far more in family, village, tribe, ethnic and linguistic affiliation, and religion, than it was in national identity—and power relationships were defined by these same categories. It was not accidental that one of numerous derogatory nicknames given to US-backed President Hamid Karzai was that of "mayor of Kabul"—reflecting the fact that his influence reached more or less to the city limits, but no further.

Once again, however, this historical reality was ignored. It is not that it was not known. In the same report on "Reconstructing a Stable and Moderate State" in Afghanistan, drafted in the very first months of the war, analysts recognized that one

> element in past periods of stability has
> been comparative harmony between the state,
> whose officials staffed the central government
> ministries and the provincial administrations,
> and the tribal leaders, Muslim clerics, and
> other notables who constituted the local power
> centers outside the capital. This relationship
> was aided by the fact that relatively few
> demands were imposed by the central government,
> which carried out limited functions. Relations
> between the state and local forces had become
> progressively more difficult with the increase
> of modernization and economic development.
> The complete breakdown of any semblance of a
> functioning administration, starting with the
> Marxist coup in 1978, including the destruction
> of the central bureaucracy and the complete
> disappearance of [Kabul's] involvement in
> provincial affairs, will make it very difficult
> to reestablish the structure of a functioning
> nation state. [CRS-RL31389]

*   *   *

The consequences that should have thus been expected immediately happened. Imposing a strong nationally centered government never really worked; ignoring "the social and political order in the tribal areas" did indeed "provoke widespread rebellion." The war to destroy whatever remnants of al-Qaeda had not already decamped to Pakistan and to overthrow the Taliban quickly became a full-scale counter-insurgency operation.

But this effort did not work either. Under the Bush administration, early claims about the war in Afghanistan centered on
bringing democracy, modernity, and women's rights to a country
about which most Americans knew virtually nothing, except
that a US-Soviet proxy war had been fought there in the 1980s
and that al-Qaeda had found a home there in the 1990s before
attacking the United States. Those heady claims of democracy
and beyond were never achieved. Instead, the real results of
the war in Afghanistan—aside from preparing the way for the
primary war to come in Iraq—had to do with killing everyone
the US deemed "terrorists." The fact that so many of the people
killed were not terrorists—very often they were farmers, wedding
guests, children—was less important than the body count of
those who could be identified as bad guys. But selling the enterprise required the construction of a mythology that this US war
of revenge would actually help the people of Afghanistan—make
them safer, bring modern medicine, educate the children, liberate
the women... A laundry list of justifications was there for the
choosing.

In the real world, the vast chasm of contradiction between
waging war and providing humanitarian assistance was obvious
in the first weeks and months of the war, and could not be reconciled with the pursuit of a lethal counter-insurgency strategy.
Even before the US invasion, Afghanistan already faced a humanitarian crisis driven by twenty-three years of war, abandonment
by Cold War–era sponsors who had left behind only weapons,
a continuing civil war, and five years of harsh Taliban rule and
international sanctions. Refugees were fleeing even before the
US attacks began, and hunger was endemic. International food
shipments stopped in anticipation of the US bombing, and aid
organizations withdrew their international staff.

Shortly after the bombing of Afghanistan began on October
7, 2001, the United States embarked on a major propaganda-
driven exercise, air-dropping individual food packets wrapped
in bright yellow (humanitarian daily rations, or HDRs) over

isolated parts of the country. Experts in humanitarian crisis assistance were unanimous that air drops of food were too expensive and logistically difficult, often did not reach their intended target population, and did virtually nothing to address even the most immediate consequences of the near-starvation conditions prevailing throughout much of the country. But they looked good on CNN—and, as the military well knew, were a great way to publicize the supposed humanitarianism of the US/NATO war in Afghanistan, thereby "winning the perception and information war." The problem was that the same bright-yellow plastic was used to wrap the bomblets contained in the cluster bombs that US war planes were dropping across Afghanistan.

A report prepared at the School of Advanced Military Studies of the US Army Command and General Staff College in Fort Leavenworth, dated December 2010 and released by WikiLeaks, provides a dry, clinical look at what happened next:

```
An element of the operation not considered by
planners was the risk of the HDRs falling into
areas containing unexploded ordinance. The yellow
color of the HDRs added to that risk. Sources at
Oxfam International, a multi-national aid and
human right [sic] organization, publicly stated
in an interview with CBS that there was a danger
that Afghans attempting to recover the food could
mistakenly enter one of the [country's] numerous
mined areas. Additionally, while MAF [Mobility
Air Forces] transports delivered yellow HDRs,
United States combat aircraft were delivering
another yellow package in Afghanistan, the BLU
92 cluster bomb. [This created] a potentially
hazardous situation for those that saw yellow
objects in open fields. To mitigate this risk,
United States forces transmitted messages
in Persian and Pashto warning Afghans of the
```

potential for confusion and how to identify whether … the yellow object is a bomb or food. The second order effect of the confusion between food and bombs was the reduced usage of the BLU 92 [cluster bombs] by order of the DoD. Additionally, a DoD press release covered by Reuters discussed the potential for confusion, resulting in producing negative strategic communications for the United States effort. In order to prevent this confusion in the future, the DoD directed that HDR packaging color changed from yellow to salmon.

…

The initial intent behind the airdrop was to feed Afghans located in hard to reach areas in northern areas of the country. Overall, MAF efforts were successful; people were fed and the local and global message of United States compassion for non-combatant Afghans was transmitted. This clearly occurred[,] with 2.5 million HDRs delivered during the initial days of the operation. MAF airdrop was not the desired delivery method for food and other vital supplies, but the nonexistent ground transportation systems and austere location of the people in need drove the requirement for airdrop[s]. However, having the capability to conduct those types of operations proved vital at the time to the overall United States strategy of defeating the support base for the terrorist organizations operating in Afghanistan. The hybrid power demonstrated by this operation ushered in an innovative way to combat an enemy while at the same time winning the perception and information war.[1]

The danger caused by confusion between yellow-wrapped ration packages and yellow-wrapped cluster bombs led to serious embarrassment for the Pentagon. The radio broadcasts announced:

> Attention people of Afghanistan! As you may have heard, the Partnership of Nations is dropping yellow Humanitarian Daily Rations … In areas far from where we are dropping food, we are dropping cluster bombs. Although it is unlikely, it is possible that not every bomb will explode on impact. These bombs are a yellow color … Please, please exercise caution when approaching unidentified yellow objects in areas that have been recently bombed.[2]

Another section of the same report even acknowledges:

> Unfortunately, the HDR missions were not as successful as planners had hoped. A report written by a retired Army Special Forces Lieutenant Colonel for the non-governmental agency Partners International Foundation, documented several shortcomings of the operation. Those shortcomings included an incomplete understanding of the long-term concerns of the Afghans, failure of numerous ration containers to maintain their integrity during airdrop operations, and the inclusion of non-edible moisture absorbent packets [in] the meals. The result was the consumption of both contaminated food and non-edible materials. The first shortcoming occurred because planners failed to understand how the Afghanis were going to use the materials. Food was scarce in Northern Afghanistan and winter was about to begin,

resulting in many Afghanis storing the food
for future consumption. According to Benjamin
Sklaver, a law and diplomacy graduate student
at Tufts University, [HDRs] are meant to feed
a population for a very short period—days to
weeks at most. They enhance food security simply
by putting a packet of food in the hands of
malnourished recipients. The meals were designed
to be consumed upon discovery, not as a food
store for future sustenance. Additionally,
Special Forces attached to the geographic area
discovered that many of the packages were damaged
during delivery and the food inside had spoiled.
Another shortcoming was the usage of desiccant
sachets, a material used to preserve freshness
and reduce moisture in food. These packages
were included in the packets with instructions
graphically depicted (circle with a line through
it) not to eat. The report cited that up to
thirty-five Afghans complained of being ill after
eating the substance.

On November 1, 2001, the Pentagon announced that it would change the food packets to blue. "It is unfortunate that the cluster bombs—the unexploded ones—are the same color as the food packets," said General Richard Myers, chairman of the Joint Chiefs of Staff. He admitted the possibility that Afghan civilians might confuse a desperately anticipated meal with an unexploded cluster bomb. "Unfortunately, they get used to running to yellow," he said. He did not, however, know how long it would take to change the colors. "That, obviously, will take some time, because there are many in the pipeline." In a press conference with Secretary of Defense Rumsfeld, General Myers also announced that the US did not intend to suspend the use of cluster bombs.

But for the Pentagon's PR image, the problem was far graver than the calm language of the report would later indicate. The United States is one of very few countries that has refused to sign the Ottawa Treaty banning anti-personnel land mines. Like the broad issue of the US using cluster bombs in Afghanistan, the refusal to sign the treaty was known—though resulting in remarkably low-key media coverage that sparked very little outrage—at the time it was happening.

But the *Afghan War Diary* provides information that goes even further. In a December 2008 cable, US officials bemoan the problems they faced following an internationally welcomed conference to impose an outright ban on cluster munitions—a gruesome anti-personnel weapon under any circumstances. Afghanistan had decided to sign the new Convention on Cluster Munitions (CCM). And since the convention banned the presence, as well as use, of cluster bombs, Washington suddenly faced the reality that it might have to deal with Afghan reluctance to continue allowing the Pentagon's deadly cache of cluster bombs to remain in their country, let alone their continued use:

Government of the Islamic Republic of Afghanistan joined 93 other states in signing the Convention on Cluster Munitions (CCM), December 3-4, 2008 in Oslo, Norway. The United States did not sign the treaty as cluster munitions continue to have military utility. The US Government believes Article 21 of the Convention provides the flexibility for signatories to continue to cooperate and conduct operations with US forces, and in turn for US forces to store, transfer, and use US cluster munitions in the territory of a State Party. The Department requests that Post approach appropriate interlocutors at the Afghan Ministries of Foreign Affairs and Defense to urge Kabul to interpret Article 21 in a

similar manner, minimizing any potential impact
of Afghanistan's signature of the Convention on
US operations and military cooperation. Given
the political sensitivities in Afghanistan
surrounding cluster munitions as well as air and
artillery strikes in general, the Department
believes that a low-profile approach will be
the best way to ensure a common understanding
that the CCM does not impede military planning
and operations between our two governments.
[08STATE134777]

Most of the cable refers to the claimed importance of cluster
bombs in protecting US and NATO troops. But in the discussion
points identified in the cable to be used in arguments with the
Afghan government, the US analysts make the astonishing claim
that using cluster bombs will actually prevent civilian casualties.
This claim appears in the last of the talking points, designated
"If Raised," apparently cautioning that these arguments only
be used if the contrary position has been expressed by Afghan
interlocutors:

IF RAISED: The United States currently has a
very small stockpile of cluster munitions in
Afghanistan. In certain circumstances, they are
the most effective system to use against light
armor, wheeled vehicles, materiel, and personnel,
while at the same time limiting collateral
damage. Not allowing the use of cluster munitions
will increase risk to coalition forces engaged
in combat from enemy counter-fire, reduce
responsiveness, decrease the number of different
targets that can be attacked within a specified
timeframe, and will substantially increase risks
of collateral damage by requiring usage of a

greater number of large, unitary warheads to accomplish the same mission.

Much of the cable's text expresses irritation at the Afghan government's decision to sign the cluster bomb treaty at all—particularly without the level of consultation with its US backers that Washington apparently deemed appropriate:

> Despite assurances to the contrary from President Karzai and Foreign Minister Spanta to Ambassador Wood in February 2008, the GIRoA [Government of the Islamic Republic of Afghanistan] joined 93 other states in signing the CCM, December 3-4, 2008 in Oslo, Norway. According to timely Post reporting, President Karzai decided at the last moment to overrule Spanta and sign the CCM without prior consultation with the USG or other key states engaged in operations in Afghanistan … Given the political sensitivities in Afghanistan surrounding cluster munitions as well as air and artillery strikes in general, the Department believes that a relatively low-profile dialogue at the sub-ministerial level will be the best way to ensure a common understanding between the USG and GIRoA that the CCM does not impede US and ISAF military planning and operations.

The fact that the United States remained an outlier, refusing to sign the cluster bomb ban, apparently did not prevent it from asserting the right to define what the convention did and did not prohibit for a country that had chosen to sign it.

Several years into the war, the longstanding debate inside the Bush administration over the nature of the war in Afghanistan shifted definitively away from the "winning hearts and minds" goals of counter-insurgency, in favor of counter-terrorism, eliminating any claim that the war had anything to do with protecting Afghans. Counter-terrorism essentially means that killing terrorists (with all the collateral damage that can result) is the only goal. In 2009–10, much was made of the new Obama administration's claim that its Afghanistan war policy would shift to counter-insurgency. In theory, counter-insurgency operations are supposed to win public support from the local population for the government and its foreign backers, by providing them with, among other things, protection from so-called insurgent forces.

In Afghanistan, that would mean protecting local Afghans from attacks by the Taliban and other anti-government and anti-US/NATO forces. Counter-terrorism, on the other hand, is all about killing "the enemy"—the bad guys, as defined in this case by the US military. The problem, of course, was that the Pentagon's bad guys were not necessarily bad guys in the local village or town. And protecting people from the Taliban did not provide any protection from becoming "collateral damage" in US/NATO air strikes and night raids.

The theoretical logic was clear: if your priority is to protect civilians, rather than to kill as many opponents as possible, you are much more likely to win support from the local population. But that theoretical logic leaves many questions unanswered when applied to the real world. The US counter-insurgency plan in Afghanistan, known as "clear, hold and build," remained grounded in targeting and killing insurgents, whether Taliban or other armed opposition groups. "Clear" referred directly to "clearing" an area of armed opponents of the US and its Afghan allies—in many cases without consultation with local Afghan community leaders—by killing them. But even if someone on the US "kill or capture list" was sometimes successfully targeted, far greater numbers of civilians were killed in most attacks. As part of a plan to win local support, the kill-based strategy was always doomed.

And it remained unclear who was on the White House's kill list, and why. Unlucky Afghans ratted out as "terrorists" to US soldiers were often just ordinary villagers struggling to make a living, who managed to get on somebody's bad side and were suddenly named as bad guys. The source often earned US bounty money as a result. Among the released papers is a document prepared just a few months into the war—an official report to Congress making clear that it was already known that "Afghan warlords have been accused of causing mistaken attacks on civilians or pro-Karzai groups by providing false intelligence to American forces" [CRS-RL31389]. (It is worth noting that the US attacks are referred to here as "mistakes"—only the intelligence provided by the warlords is deemed "false.")

Of course, while the Obama counter-insurgency plan was announced with great fanfare in spring 2009 as a plan to protect civilians, actual US operations on the ground continued to put civilians at enormous risk of attack by US airstrikes, crossfire between US and opposition forces, roadside bombs or other attacks meant for US or US-backed government troops, and Taliban and other insurgent forces punishing those believed to support the US and its allies.

In fact, the Obama administration's claimed shift from counter-terrorism to counter-insurgency was never real. The general appointed to lead it, Stanley McChrystal, was supposed to represent a new kind of military strategist, who would focus not on tracking down and killing the enemy but on this ostensibly new strategy of winning hearts and minds and protecting civilians. But McChrystal's own history belied that change. His earlier experience was in old-fashioned "get the bad guys" counter-terrorism, since his days in Vietnam. Before taking over the Afghanistan war in 2009, he spent most of five years commanding special forces units pursuing individual al-Qaeda and other insurgent leaders in Afghanistan, Iraq, and Pakistan. That meant primarily air strikes and targeted raids—the traditional methods of counter-terrorism.

Senior Pentagon officials admitted that McChrystal's approach would likely lead to "[e]scalating violence, an acceleration of targeted killings, and deniable attacks by US Special Forces on Taliban strong holds in Pakistan." According to Richard Sale, defense correspondent for the *Middle East Times*, those Pentagon sources warned that McChrystal's appointment "portends a much bloodier phase of the war ... 'McChrystal is an expert killer. That's what the teams he heads are good at,' said former senior DIA official Pat Lang."[3]

CIVILIANS IN THE WAR

There were a lot of expert killers in Afghanistan. The *Afghan War Diary* did not reveal a war different from what we knew, but they provided a level of corroborating detail, often in clinically detached language. The huge number of civilian casualties was a known feature of the US war in Afghanistan from the beginning. The attacks on civilians have remained a huge crisis in the Afghanistan war—but much of the detail remained hidden. Just three weeks after Barack Obama was sworn in as president, in February 2009, WikiLeaks released a confidential NATO report revealing that civilian deaths in Afghanistan had increased by 46 percent during 2008.[4]

According to the WikiLeaks introduction, the report "shows a dramatic escalation of the war and civil disorder." Attacks on US and NATO troops increased significantly, including a 27 percent rise in IED attacks, a 40 percent rise in rifle and rocket fire, and a 67 percent increase in surface-to-air fire against Coalition aircraft. All of that resulted in an increase in US/NATO military deaths of 35 percent, while kidnappings and assassinations rose by 50 percent, and attacks on the US-backed Afghan government more than doubled, rising by a massive 119 percent.

In the meantime, the report documents that only half of the families outside Kabul had access to even basic healthcare, and only half of the children had any access to a school.

But the report—drafted by the Pentagon's Central Command, officially as the "International Security Assistance Force for Afghanistan" (ISAF)—was kept secret, designated "For Official Use Only." One of the reasons it was kept secret may have been that the Pentagon's count of the rise in civilian deaths—46 percent higher than the year before—was significantly higher even than the 40 percent escalation calculated by the United Nations.

From its beginning, the US war in Afghanistan included official reliance on torture, official violations of human rights and international covenants, official disdain for human dignity, official contempt for Afghan cultural norms, and more. US troops and their local allies did not necessarily treat detainees or civilians worse than in earlier wars (the infamous tiger cages where the US-backed South Vietnamese government held prisoners offer one comparison), but the global war on terror certainly went further in justifying such treatment, in many cases virtually bragging about it.

In the summary of a 2008 report revealed in the *Afghan War Diary*, the analysis of congressional engagement with the issues of interrogation and torture, including the so-called "McCain Amendment," takes as a matter of course the category of "enemy combatants" and "terrorist suspects" detained by US troops, without any indication that the very terms were designed as part of a conscious strategy to disregard the obligations imposed by the Geneva Conventions regarding the treatment of prisoners:

```
Controversy has arisen regarding US treatment of
enemy combatants and terrorist suspects detained
in Iraq, Afghanistan, and other locations, and
whether such treatment complies with US statutes
and treaties such as the UN Convention Against
Torture and Other Forms of Cruel and Inhuman
or Degrading Treatment or Punishment (CAT) and
the 1949 Geneva Conventions. Congress approved
```

additional guidelines concerning the treatment of
detainees via the Detainee Treatment Act (DTA),
which was enacted pursuant to both the Department
of Defense, Emergency Supplemental Appropriations
to Address Hurricanes in the Gulf of Mexico, and
Pandemic Influenza Act, 2006 (PL 109-148, Title
X), and the National Defense Authorization Act
for FY2006 (PL 109-163, Title XIV). Among other
things, the DTA contains provisions that (1)
require Department of Defense (DOD) personnel to
employ United States Army Field Manual guidelines
while interrogating detainees, and (2) prohibit
the "cruel, inhuman and degrading treatment
or punishment of persons under the detention,
custody, or control of the United States
Government." These provisions of the DTA, which
were first introduced by Senator John McCain,
have popularly been referred to as the "McCain
Amendment." This report discusses the McCain
Amendment, as modified and subsequently enacted
into law. [CRS-RL33655]

In another section, the report provides a reminder of Bush's plan
to veto any congressional effort to hold the CIA accountable to
the same public standards that the Pentagon was supposed to
follow in the Army Field Manual. Those standards, however consistently they were violated, were at least officially designed to
meet the requirements of the Geneva Conventions. They were far
more restrictive than the official standards of the CIA's interrogation techniques, which blatantly included torture but insisted on
its denial:

Finally, this report briefly describes legislation
introduced in the 110th Congress that references
interrogation standards or requirements initially

established by the McCain Amendment. Discussed
legislation includes HR 2082, the Intelligence
Authorization Act for Fiscal Year 2008, which
was vetoed by President Bush on March 8, 2008,
and HR 4156, the Orderly and Responsible Iraq
Redeployment Appropriations Act, 2008, which was
passed by the House on November 14, 2007, but
has not been considered by the Senate due to the
failure to invoke cloture on the bill. Both bills
proposed to bar the CIA and other intelligence
agencies from employing any interrogation
tactic that is not authorized by the Army Field
Manual, effectively prohibiting these agencies
from employing certain harsh interrogation
techniques, including waterboarding, regardless
of whether those techniques had otherwise been
deemed legally permissible. The White House has
indicated that the President shall veto any
legislation requiring the CIA to use only those
interrogation techniques authorized under the
Army Field Manual.

THE COST OF WAR

Opposition to the war in Afghanistan grew—gradually at first,
then faster—from the first months of the US invasion and occupation. While casualties (US casualties, at least—unfortunately
Afghan casualties too rarely led to widespread opposition) played
a role in the rising public outrage about the war, but another
important reason was its cost. Since October 2001, US taxpayers
have paid about $715 billion for the war in Afghanistan alone.
That translates into more than $10 million every hour—every
day, every year since 2001.

And beyond the broad problem of paying for a war widely
understood to be failing at its expressed goals, there were

occasional bursts of indignation when it became clear that US taxpayer money—straight from the Pentagon's coffers—was helping to fund the Taliban insurgency. While that stark reality had been known in small circles before, WikiLeaks again provided detailed examples of how it worked.

In physical terms, Afghanistan is an extraordinarily isolated country. Landlocked and surrounded by mountains, half a world away from the United States, building up and supplying an occupying army of up to 150,000 US and NATO troops at any given moment was a logistical nightmare. With goods either trucked in over the Pakistani border to face long and dangerous drives to Kabul and beyond, or flown in at huge expense to Bagram Airbase outside of Kabul, provisioning and arming the hundreds of "Forward Operating Bases" scattered throughout the country required lots of local help. That meant hiring local transport companies, and it also meant paying for security. One 2007 cable describes just such a military contractor, a local Afghan trucking company with a striking name:

```
Four Horsemen International reported that they
were approached by Taliban personnel to talk
about payment for the safe passage of convoys
through their area. The current price for
passage is $500 US per truck from Kandahar to
Herat, $50US per truck from Kabul to Ghazni,
$100US per truck from Ghazni to Orgun-E, and
$200-300US per truck from Orgun-E to Wazi
Kwah. All negotiations are conducted outside
of Afghanistan with the Taliban POC located in
Quetta, Pakistan. This information has been
verified by other HNT companies and the other
companies state they are paying money for safe
passage. [CRS-RL33655]
```

The financial totals of up to $500 per truck paid to the Taliban (as well as other militias, some of them nominally supporters of the government) add up to hundreds of millions of dollars. Knowledge that these enormous sums were being paid to the Taliban, even as the ostensible justification for the US troops being in Afghanistan was the claimed need to wipe out the Taliban, played a significant role in reducing public support for the war.

Counter-insurgency wars waged far from the home country of the occupying soldiers are never easy. When the United States prepared to attack Afghanistan in 2001, the country's language and culture remained unknown to the vast majority of troops and commanders being sent. When the war in Afghanistan began, it was clear that the Bush administration had no concern for or interest in the people, religion, traditions, culture, or anything else there. The original claim from Bush's secretary of defense, Donald Rumsfeld, and others, was that the war would be quick and tidy: the Taliban government would be overthrown, the new government created at the Bonn Conference in November 2001 would be helicoptered into Kabul to take over, the population would be grateful, and the work would be over.

It did not turn out quite like that. The quick war rather swiftly morphed into a long-term counter-insurgency war, with US and other NATO troops facing conditions in which ignorance of the local people and culture put the troops themselves, as well as the evanescent goals of the war, at serious risk. Realizing that, several years into the war, the military began a project designed to embed academics—anthropologists, sociologists, and others—into military units in Afghanistan, to strengthen the capacity of the troops by providing cultural and social insight into Afghan society.

In August 2009, the *Washington Post* magazine documented the work of psychologists and anthropologists who joined the Pentagon's Human Terrain project. In the photos, the academics were dressed in camouflage and armed with standard weapons, indistinguishable from the regular soldiers. Their role in one "model" village, Pir Zadeh in southern Afghanistan, was described thus: "They would drive in MRAPs, heavy, armored vehicles designed to minimize the effects of makeshift bombs, then would get out and move west through the village. The soldiers would create a secure perimeter as they walked ... Any villager who wanted to pass the patrol would have to enter the perimeter and be frisked for weapons." The *Post* acknowledged that few social scientists were willing to participate, but never asked the critical question of why that might be. It never questioned just whose village the perimeter-establishing soldiers thought it was. Though tragic, it certainly should not have surprised anyone that an earlier Human Terrain recruit, described as a "soldier and aid worker," had been fatally attacked while she was on patrol in a neighboring village. The attacker was captured, and the Human Terrain social scientist's Army Ranger partner "pulled out his pistol and shot the man in the head." He pleaded guilty to manslaughter and was sentenced to probation and a fine.

It was left to WikiLeaks to bring to light the "Human Terrain Team Handbook"—unclassified but kept from the public—with its description of who makes up those teams and what they are tasked with in carrying out counter-insurgency war. Official members of the military or not, their task is clear: to strengthen the US army's military operations:

```
Human Terrain Teams (HTTs) are five- to nine-
person teams deployed by the Human Terrain
System (HTS) to support field commanders by filling
their cultural knowledge gap in the current
operating environment and providing cultural
interpretations of events occurring within their
area of operations. The team is composed of
individuals with social science and operational
backgrounds that are deployed with tactical
and operational military units to assist in
bringing knowledge about the local population
```

into a coherent analytic framework and build
relationships with the local power-brokers in
order to provide advice and opportunities to
Commanders and staffs in the field.

...

Each team is recruited and trained for a specific
region, then deployed and embedded with their
supported unit. The HTTs are comprised of a
mix of Soldiers and Department of the Army
Contractors that provide a mix of senior military
specialists and academicians with strong social
sciences credentials. An HTT integrates into the
unit staff, conducts unclassified open-source
and field research, and provides operationally-
relevant human terrain information in support
of the planning, preparation, execution and
assessment of operations.

A fundamental condition of irregular warfare
and counter-insurgency operations is that
the Commander and staff can no longer limit
their focus to the traditional Mission, Enemy,
Terrain and weather, friendly Troops and support
available, and Time.

...

In an irregular warfare environment "Commanders
and planners require insight into cultures,
perceptions, values, beliefs, interests, and
decision-making processes of individuals and
groups" and should be evaluated according to
their "society, social structure, culture,
language, power and authority, and interests."
The human dimension is the very essence of
irregular warfare environments. Understanding
local cultural, political, social, economic,

and religious factors is crucial to successful
counterinsurgency and stability operations, and
ultimately, to success in the war on terror. In
stability operations and irregular warfare, the
human aspect of the environment becomes central
to mission success.

Information on social groups and their interests,
beliefs, leaders, and the drivers of individual
and group behavior is needed to conduct effective
counterinsurgency operations. The expertise for
conducting research and analysis to provide
valid and objective information on these topics
are highly specialized in the social sciences.
Social science research of a host nation's
population produces a knowledge base that is
referred to as the Human Terrain, or "The element
of the operational environment encompassing the
cultural, sociological, political and economic
factors of the local population."[5]

The people of Afghanistan, then, had become an "element of the operational environment" of Washington's war.

THE MASSACRE OF DASHT-E-LEILI

The philosophy articulated in the Handbook saw massacres as an inevitable component of the US war. Of course, one of the most significant consequences of the release of the WikiLeaks papers was the detailed accounting of mass killing and other barbarities—actions that provide a shocking, though not surprising, prism for understanding the war. One such action, documented in excruciating detail, was the massacre, in just the first weeks after the US invasion of Afghanistan, of between 2,000 and 3,000 Taliban prisoners by US-backed Afghan soldiers. In many ways, the Dasht-e-Leili massacre would portend the continuing war crimes involving prisoners, torture, and attacks on civilians that would come to characterize the US "global war on terror" for at least the next twelve years.

While the cables are heavily redacted, they describe how "hundreds or perhaps thousands" of Taliban fighters had surrendered after brief fighting in Mazar-e Sharif and Konduz in November 2001, and were incarcerated in shipping containers to be transferred to US custody at Sheberghan Prison—a two-day journey from Dasht-e-Leili, where they had surrendered. But the metal shipping containers were sealed, and most of the prisoners suffocated before they arrived. Many were also shot through the walls of the sealed containers.

The killing of these prisoners represented a clear violation of the Geneva Conventions regarding protection of fighters who have surrendered. The kind of wanton disregard for human life shown in the killings should have led to immediate efforts to achieve accountability—including on the part of US forces. Instead, the atrocity is described coolly, with significant attention to the efforts (it remains unclear whether it refers to efforts by Afghans or US or other NATO forces) to keep the focus on Taliban atrocities, as if these somehow excused the horror of the atrocities committed by US-backed Afghan forces.

The documents regarding the massacre refer, without detail, to "Dostum," or occasionally "General Dostum." The reference is to General Ahmad Rashid Dostum, an ethnic Uzbek warlord who had fought in Afghanistan first with the pro-Soviet Afghan government in the 1980s against the anti-Soviet mujahideen, and then joined the mujahideen fighters of the US-backed Northern Alliance, until they were beaten by the Taliban in the mid 1990s, at which point Dostum fled to comfortable exile. Dostum returned to Afghanistan with the US invasion forces in 2001, and with US backing reclaimed leadership as chief of staff of the Afghan military installed by the US, as well as simultaneously reconstituting his Uzbek-based private militia.

Dostum had long been known for his brutality, alleged mass rapes of young girls by his militia, the brutal killing of individual soldiers and others who crossed him, and more. Dostum's Junbish militia allegedly dropped cluster bombs on residential areas of Kabul in January 1997 as the civil war wound down. According to another February 2008 WikiLeaks cable sent from the US ambassador in Kabul to the CIA, DIA, State Department, and beyond, "Dostum remains the quintessential warlord, an enduring symbol of Afghanistan's war-ravaged past whose bravado and violence earned for him the status of a respected, but deeply flawed national hero" [08KABUL491_a].

The WikiLeaks reports make clear the knowledge of US officials—military, intelligence, CIA, political, diplomatic, and beyond—about the Dasht-e-Leili massacre, and other examples of Dostum's culpability. The documents cite a reminder to recipients that they should "take every opportunity to remind observers that the Taliban were the primary abusers in the country and that any investigations into alleged Afghan military atrocities must be balanced with investigations into Taliban atrocities."

The Dasht-e-Leili massacre might have remained a horrific moment in the past, even with the details made available through WikiLeaks, were it not for the contemporary role of certain key players. In Afghanistan's presidential campaign in spring 2014, one of the leading candidates was Ashraf Ghani, a Western-oriented former World Bank official, who had in the past identified Dostum as a killer. But with ethnically based campaigning being central to Afghanistan's wartime election, Ghani suddenly welcomed General Dostum as his running mate, hoping to consolidate the Uzbek vote in Mazar-e Sharif and elsewhere in northern Afghanistan. After Ghani's hotly contested victory, the perpetrator of the Dasht-e-Leili massacre was sworn in as the new vice president of Afghanistan—with proud US and NATO backing for Afghanistan's new democracy.

Afghanistan's war continues.

14. East Asia

Tim Shorrock

When President Barack Obama was sworn into office in January 2009, important political transitions were underway in two of America's closest allies in Asia—South Korea and Japan. They involved ideological and political shifts over the role of US military forces in these countries that had been simmering for years, and greatly alarmed defense officials and policy-makers in both the Democratic and Republican parties. Beginning in the George W. Bush administration, Washington launched an intense lobbying campaign to realign the Korean and Japanese governments with US national security priorities in East Asia. The first to feel the pressure was the South Korean president Kim Dae Jung, who had brought about a deep change in the political climate in Asia by relaxing tensions with North Korea. But the campaign soon expanded to Japan, where a new political party repudiated many of the policies of the Liberal Democratic Party (LDP), which ruled Japan for most of the postwar period in close cooperation with the United States.

Given Obama's new openness to the world and his global reputation as the most liberal US president in generations, observers might have expected a more progressive, understanding approach than Bush's to these challenges. But the US diplomatic cables obtained by WikiLeaks instead show that the United States during the Obama years made a concerted effort to undermine the democratic left in Seoul and Tokyo, and to support conservative, pro-American parties like the LDP. These cables chronicle the close consensus between Democratic and Republican administrations in national security matters, and illustrate how little US policy toward Asia has changed since the dawn of the Cold War in the late 1940s.

In December 2007, a conservative former Hyundai executive named Lee Myung Bak was elected president of South Korea for a six-year term. His election marked a dramatic lurch to the right after twelve years of progressive rule under Kim Dae Jung, the longtime dissident leader who was president from 1998 to 2003, and Roh Moo-hyun, a 1980s-era human rights activist who succeeded him, serving from 2003 to 2008, who tragically committed suicide in 2009.

Kim and Roh had shattered decades of enmity with North Korea by introducing their "Sunshine policies," which embraced détente and dialogue with North Korea, and led to the first successful North-South summit meetings in history (in 2000 and 2007). The two presidents further deepened the process of national reconciliation by opening investigations into war crimes committed during the Korean War—an issue that had been off-limits during South Korea's long years of dictatorship. A Truth and Reconciliation Commission founded during the Roh administration (and modeled on South Africa's organization that had looked into crimes during the apartheid era) uncovered 1,222 instances of mass killings, including 215 episodes in which US war planes and ground forces had killed unarmed civilians.

The changes brought by Kim and Roh had caused deep fissures in the US-Korean relationship. They had come at a time when the United States was beginning to expand its military presence in East Asia for the first time since the Vietnam War and, under George W. Bush, taking a more muscular approach to foreign policy. When President Kim visited Bush at the White House in the spring of 2001, his host publicly repudiated his

Sunshine policy, declaring that Kim Jong Il, the North Korean dictator who died in 2011, was never to be trusted.

This and other actions by Bush's hardliners—which included identifying the North as part of an "axis of evil"—ended any chance for peace between the South and the North. They also deeply humiliated the South Korean leader, who had staked his presidency on changing the dynamics on the Korean Peninsula. Later, Roh's war crimes commission was given a cold shoulder by the Pentagon, which refused to comment on many of the reports from the commission. Then, when US crimes were finally acknowledged in relation to a 1950 massacre of civilians at Nogonri unearthed by the AP, US defense officials blamed them on "confusion" and "fear," and took no action to investigate further.

To the great relief of Washington, South Korea's divergence from US policies came to an end when Lee took over in February 2008. The new president immediately began to dismantle the Sunshine policies toward the North, along with the apparatus that had guided them. Like Bush, he also took a hardline approach to Pyongyang, and relations quickly deteriorated. In May 2009, just four months into Obama's presidency, Kim Jong Il tested a second nuclear device, leading the Obama administration to press the UN to expand economic sanctions. Pyongyang responded by expelling UN nuclear monitors, and vowed to conduct more tests. By the spring, the US-North Korea relationship was in cold storage. "The policy pursued by the Obama administration ... since its emergence made it clear that the [hostile US] policy toward the DPRK remains unchanged," the North Korean Foreign Ministry declared in a statement quoted by the *New York Times*; the situation remains virtually unchanged today. Over his period in office, President Obama developed a close friendship with Lee, and at one point even called him one of his "best buddies" and his "favorite president."[1]

Meanwhile, as South Korea moved from left to right, Japan was undergoing an unprecedented shift to the left in its foreign policy. In August 2009, just as Asian tensions were heating up with North Korea, Japanese voters cast out the ruling LDP for only the second time since the 1950s, handing a landslide victory to the newly formed Democratic Party of Japan (DPJ)—a coalition of former Socialists and LDP politicians led at the time by Yukio Hatoyama. He had campaigned on a platform of redefining Japan's Cold War relationship with Washington by negotiating a withdrawal of US Marines from Okinawa, as was widely demanded by the Japanese people, and taking a more independent stand toward Asia and the rest of the world. Worse from the Pentagon's perspective was the fact that the DPJ (much like the Korean ruling party under Roh) had also promised to investigate and make public secret and controversial agreements between the US government and the LDP during the Cold War— particularly those that allowed US nuclear-armed ships unfettered access to Japanese ports, in violation of the country's peace constitution and anti-nuclear principles. The DPJ had also publicly announced plans to terminate the Japanese role of refueling US ships en route to war zones in Iraq and Afghanistan.

Predictably, as in Korea during the Kim-Roh era, these reversals in policy greatly disturbed the Pentagon and the incoming Obama administration. For years, US military planners had been pushing Japan to become a "normal nation" and expand its military forces to buttress US power in the region. By the end of the Bush administration, they had nearly reached that goal. In July 2007, a *New York Times* reporter, writing from Guam, described Japan's unprecedented role in a US live-bombing exercise in the Western Pacific:

```
The exercise would have been unremarkable for
almost any other military, but it was highly
significant for Japan, a country still restrained
by a Constitution that renounces war and allows
forces only for its defense … In a little over
half a decade, Japan's military has carried out
```

changes considered unthinkable a few years back. In the Indian Ocean, Japanese destroyers and refueling ships are helping American and other militaries fight in Afghanistan. In Iraq, Japanese planes are transporting cargo and American troops to Baghdad from Kuwait.[2]

The *Times* emphasized the importance of the LDP to these developments, specifically mentioning then (and current) prime minister Shinzo Abe:

Abe used the parliamentary majority he inherited from his wildly popular predecessor, Junichiro Koizumi, to ram through a law that could lead to a revision of the pacifist Constitution. Japan's 241,000-member military, though smaller than those of its neighbors, is considered Asia's most sophisticated … Japan has also tapped nonmilitary budgets to launch spy satellites and strengthen its coast guard recently. Japanese politicians like Mr. Abe have justified the military's transformation by seizing on the threat from North Korea; the rise of China, whose annual military budget has been growing by double digits; and the Sept. 11 attacks—even fanning those threats, critics say. At the same time, Mr. Abe has tried to rehabilitate the reputation of Japan's imperial forces by whitewashing their crimes, including wartime sexual slavery.

Japanese critics say the changes under way—whose details the government has tried to hide from public view, especially the missions in Iraq— have already violated the Constitution and other defense restrictions. "The reality has already

moved ahead, so they will now talk about the need
to catch up and revise the Constitution," said
Yukio Hatoyama, the secretary general of the main
opposition Democratic Party.

Maintaining this status quo was a serious concern to Obama's
national security team, many of whom had come to the White
House and the Pentagon directly from the Center for a New
American Security (CNAS)—a think tank founded in 2008 by
veterans of the Clinton administration who had been seeking
to re-establish the Democratic Party as a major force in US
foreign policy. Its views on Asia were summarized early on by
Kurt Campbell, a former Clinton defense official in Asia who
co-founded CNAS and was now Obama's assistant secretary of
state for East Asia and the Pacific. In a study on US Asia policy
published in 2008, he had written a gloomy (and very US-centric)
take on the continent: "Asia is not a theatre at peace," it began,
according to an account in the *Weekend Australian* published on
September 9, 2009:

It is a cauldron of religious and ethnic
tension; a source of terror and extremism; an
accelerating driver of the insatiable global
appetite for energy; the place where the most
people will suffer the adverse effects of global
climate change; the primary source of nuclear
proliferation and the most likely theatre on
earth for a major conventional confrontation and
even a nuclear conflict.

As a postscript, the *Australian*'s editor added: "This is not just
rhetoric. For the first time, there are more warships in the US
Pacific fleet than in its Atlantic fleet. And a rarely acknowledged
truth is that Japan is Washington's most important ally anywhere
on the globe." The Obama administration wanted to keep it that

way. The WikiLeaks diplomatic cables examined in this chapter underscore the deep continuity in policy between the supposedly progressive Obama Democrats and the utterly reactionary neoconservatives of the Bush administration. In particular, they show that militarism and US imperial aims in Asia consistently trump any other factors when it comes to how American officials view their Asian allies.

This was ironic: after all, the Obama administration had come to power on an antiwar platform, vowing to usher in a period of peace and reconciliation with the rest of the world after the disasters of the Bush years. This new attitude had led Norway to award President Obama the Nobel Peace Prize. But the WikiLeaks cables show decisively that, from the start, Obama did all he could to support the pro-militarist right in both South Korea and Japan, and used the formidable economic and political power of the US to ensure that neither country deviated from its role as subservient ally. Most importantly, the incoming administration wanted to eliminate any barriers to the Pentagon's long-cherished goals to get Japan to step up its military role and establish closer strategic ties with South Korea, and then establish a three-way alliance with the United States directed against China.

The stakes for the United States were spelled out in a classified cable on February 21, 2006, to Secretary of State Condoleezza Rice from the US ambassador to Seoul at the time, J. Thomas Schaffer. This cable predicts much of the debate going on in 2014 over Japan's refusal to recognize its crimes during World War II and the LDP's consistent visits to the Yasukuni Shrine, where many of its war criminals are buried. The ambassador's main argument to Rice was that, recent reports of squabbling notwithstanding, Japan and South Korea were getting along just fine:

```
Despite headlines over the past year suggesting
dramatically deteriorating bilateral ties,
relations between Japan and the Republic of Korea
remain firmly rooted in common ground and are
```

thriving at most levels of society in the view
of leading Korean experts resident in Japan. The
country's foremost expert on Japan-Korea affairs,
a Japanese lawmaker of Korean ancestry, and
knowledgeable Japanese and South Korean diplomats
stationed in Tokyo all agree that while political
relations between Tokyo and Seoul have become
embittered at the highest level over persistent
historical issues, economic and cultural
interactions between the two countries are robust
and on the rise.

The most attention-grabbing feature of Japan-
ROK relations is the current dispute between
Prime Minister Koizumi and President Roh over
historical concerns, but now that South Korea has
become a fully-democratized country with a highly
developed economy, there is "no fundamental
regime friction" between the two countries …
[06TOKYO925]

But the one fly in the ointment, according to the ambassador, was
South Korea's left-wing government:

Diplomats from both countries observed that
the dramatic swing to the left in South Korean
politics, coincident with a definite swing to the
right in Japan, has exacerbated the ideological
divide between Tokyo and Seoul … [A Japanese
commentator] noted that the swing to the left in
South Korean politics has been so pronounced that
even members of his own opposition Democratic
Party of Japan have found it difficult to relate
to members of Korea's ruling Uri Party. Asked
whether the ROKG's left-leaning policy approach

will likely change when a new president takes
office at the end of Roh's term, [he] replied that
it is bound to swing back towards the center
"because they can't go any further left."

Also problematic was the possible rise to power of Japanese
politicians—such as Shinzo Abe, then the LDP's chief cabinet
secretary—who even rejected the verdict of the Tokyo War Crimes
Tribunals that had convicted many of Japan's wartime leaders:

At a lunch with the Ambassador in September,
ROK Ambassador Ra Jong-il said he has noticed a
"disturbing recent phenomena" [sic] in Japanese
political circles, including increasingly
frequent articles in the mainstream media
questioning the results of the "Tokyo Tribunal."
From the Korean perspective, Koizumi's visits to
Yasukuni imply that Japanese leaders are moving
in the direction of denying the validity of the
verdicts handed out by the war crimes tribunal.
Okonogi [a Japanese commentator] disagrees,
stating that Koizumi remains "within the post-war
consensus," but acknowledged that his visits to
Yasukuni have confused that message.

More disturbing for the ROK, Okonogi suggested,
is the fact that Chief Cabinet Secretary Shinzo
Abe has so far "obscured" his position on the
issue by saying the interpretation of history is
a job for historians. Abe, Okonogi added, may be
"outside the post-war consensus." According to
ROK Embassy First Secretary Chung, an even bigger
concern within the ROKG is that Foreign Minister
Taro Aso might become PM. That is because the
Aso family is well known for having used forced

Korean labor in its mines during the war, Chung
explained.

A year later, in a secret NOFORN cable [07SEOUL1670_a], a
political officer in the US Embassy assured Washington that, if
Lee Myung Bak was elected that year, normalcy would return
to US-South Korean ties. According to a Lee adviser, Kim Woo-
sang, Director of Yonsei University's Institute of East & West
Studies:

> Lee sees a stronger alliance relationship with
> the US as vital for the ROK's security in the
> region. *He assured us a Lee administration
> would handle US-ROK relations much better than
> President Roh or former President Kim Dae-jung,
> and the ROK "would be an entirely different
> country."* However, for public consumption, Lee
> would likely refer to the need for "pragmatic
> relations" with the US, staying away from
> referring to the "alliance." This would allow Lee
> to tighten the relationship after the election,
> without alienating those who chafe at too much
> American influence…

> Lee would change the tone of engagement policy
> to emphasize the reciprocity that President
> Kim Dae-jung's "Sunshine Policy" had initially
> envisioned. Lee's take on engagement would entail
> greater penetration of western values into the
> DPRK, which, Kim admitted, might be difficult
> for the DPRK to accept. *President Roh Moo-
> hyun's version of engagement policy was "simple
> appeasement," Kim scoffed.* [Emphasis added.]

With promises like this, President Lee established his bona fides with the Bush administration. But the US embrace of his "anti-appeasement" policies would deepen once Obama and his foreign policy team took over. With a pro-US right-winger in control in Seoul, they would try to keep the same status in Tokyo by encouraging the still-ruling LDP to stay the course. Their first chance came in February 2009, when Secretary of State Hillary Clinton came to Tokyo. The main purpose of her trip, as summarized by the *Times* on February 18, was to offer "reassurance" to the Japanese government by "calling its alliance with the United States a 'cornerstone' of American foreign policy."

But the overriding mission was to encourage Japan to remain on its militarized track. This is made clear in a secret cable to her from the US embassy in Tokyo [09TOKYO317]. It summarized the current state of US-Japan military ties and expresses strong hope that the right-wing LDP has managed to create a "new consensus" in the country in favor of a closer strategic relationship.

> Our bilateral security ties remain robust and in
> this area we have good news: our two countries
> recently reached an International Agreement
> on the realignment of US Forces, which you
> and Foreign Minister Nakasone will sign. This
> agreement, scheduled for Diet vote in March,
> will commit Japan to completing the relocation
> of Futenma Marine Corps Air Station on Okinawa
> and providing funds for USMC-related facilities
> on Guam. Japanese officials believe the agreement,
> and the allotment of over $900 million in
> realignment funding during the next fiscal year,
> will buttress Japan's commitment to the May 1,
> 2006, Alliance Transformation Agreement even if
> there is a change in government here.

In addition, Japan now hosts a forward-deployed nuclear-powered aircraft carrier, our missile defense cooperation is moving forward quickly and we are increasing bilateral planning coordination and intelligence sharing. *While pacifism remains deeply ingrained in Japan, there is a new consensus among the public and opinion makers—due in part to the DPRK threat and the PRC's growing power projection capabilities—that the US-Japan Alliance and US bases in Japan are vital to Japan's national security.* For example, the main opposition DPJ, while taking issue with some of the details of our basing arrangements, maintains as a basic policy platform the centrality of the alliance to Japan's security policy. We recommend that you inform your interlocutors we intend to hold an early 2 2 (Foreign and Defense Ministers) meeting given the importance of the Alliance. [Emphasis added.]

In April 2009, the Tokyo embassy sent another secret cable encouraging the Obama administration to deepen trilateral military ties between the United States, Japan, and South Korea, emphasizing the need for US officials to take the initiative [09TOKYO837]:

Trilateral security and defense dialogue with [Japan] and ROK will require close US supervision and proactive engagement with both governments. The US Government needs to use the opportunity provided by the current positive atmosphere between Tokyo and Seoul to help the two allies strengthen mutual trust, both in trilateral and bilateral settings. The close coordination demonstrated by the Japanese and ROK governments

```
in the events leading up to, and following the
recent Taepodong-II ballistic missile launch
by the DPRK is an indication that some of the
barrier between the two neighbors can be broken
down. Trilateral dialogue in all its various
forms—especially the trilateral J-5 strategy
talks—can be helpful in this process.
```

This cable also includes an astonishing admission. It notes that South Korean "participation in the November 2008 Defense Trilateral Talks (DTT) held in Washington was entirely due to strong US Government pressure." The writer adds that, according to a senior aide to President Lee, there is "nearly no public support for working with Japan on defense issues in South Korea." Yet, despite the obvious signs of public disapproval, the deepening of these ties is an absolute US priority.

A few days later, Timothy Keating, the commander of the US Pacific Command, visited Japan to meet with LDP defense minister Yasukazu Hamada, underscoring how deep US-Japan military cooperation has gone. Referring to the DPRK's missile test mentioned in the cable above, James P. Zumwalt, the chargé d'affaires at the Tokyo embassy, explained in a secret cable to the Office of the Secretary of Defense that the cooperation included the sharing of real-time intelligence:

```
Keating underscored that the level of bilateral
cooperation and information sharing in response
to the launch has never been higher. Being
able to share real-time information via Aegis
destroyers and respective command centers is
crucial for both countries' forces ability to
respond effectively to threats … The launch
allowed the Japanese side to gain valuable
experience coordinating with the United States,
with many lessons learned. [09TOKYO940]
```

In his meetings in Japan, Keating also spoke highly of the progress made in trilateral ties with South Korea, and said that "he had discussed pursuing expanded trilateral search and rescue exercises, small-scale humanitarian and disaster relief exercises, and other areas of cooperation for the three countries' forces."

By now, however, Japan's pesky voters were getting restive, and it was beginning to look like the LDP might be out of power. Suddenly, US diplomacy in Asia began to focus on "moderating" the views of the rising DPJ, which US embassy officials saw correctly was about to take over. The US arrogance toward the party—and the millions of Japanese citizens voting for the change it represented—is illustrated in a May 2009 cable from the US embassy to Deputy Secretary of State James Steinberg, a former analyst with the RAND Corporation. It includes an intriguing section entitled "DPJ: Friend or Foe?" The answer is clearly the latter:

Significant ideological differences within the party make it difficult to predict the impact on bilateral relations under a DPJ government. *Your meeting with DPJ President Hatoyama will continue the process begun by the Secretary of building stronger ties to the party and helping to moderate its views.* Despite its critical stance on a number of Alliance-related issues, the DPJ will seek positive relations with Washington and will likely steer clear [of] redlines we lay down on core issues. In this context, it will be useful to reiterate Secretary Clinton's message to former DPJ President Obama on our commitment to implement the realignment of US forces. [09TOKYO1162] [Emphasis added.]

The Obama administration's deep fondness for the right-wing LDP and its pro-militarist policies—and its concomitant dislike of the DPJ—was underscored a few weeks later, when Michelle Flourney, the under secretary of defense (and one of the co-founders of CNAS), visited Tokyo in June 2009. A secret memo prepared for Flourney by Zumwalt illustrates how badly the "progressive" Obama administration wanted Japanese voters to retain the LDP:

Building on Prime Minister Koizumi's and Prime Minister Abe's legacies, Prime Minister Aso has made progress in carving out a larger international role for Japan. Tokyo is playing a leading role in supporting stability in Pakistan and Afghanistan, most recently through hosting the Pakistan donors conference in April … In June, Japan deployed two P-3C patrol aircraft to Djibouti to join the two JMSDF destroyers already in the region conducting anti-piracy operations. Air Self-Defense Force and Ground Self Defense Force staff are also supporting Japan's anti-piracy mission, as are Japan Coast Guard personnel. Further political support for anti-piracy efforts are on the horizon as the Diet is on track to pass legislation that will broaden the SDF's ability to work with coalition forces and provide security to third country shipping vessels.

On the bilateral security front, the Aso administration has moved aggressively to implement the 2006 Alliance Transformation Roadmap, budgeting over one billion dollars this year for US base realignment and securing Diet ratification for the Guam International Agreement, signed by Secretary Clinton in February. Japan is also compiling its National

Defense Program Guidelines (NDPG) as we engage
in our own Quadrennial Review effort. Bilateral
consultations over these efforts should help
Japan focus its limited defense resources on
capabilities that will enhance the Alliance's
effectiveness. Close and effective coordination
in the lead-up to the North Korea Taepodong
launch in April has validated the trend towards
increased interoperability. Nevertheless, there
are still political and business interests
pressing the government to invest in expensive
and duplicative satellites and offensive weapons.

A defeat of the LDP in the upcoming Diet
elections will introduce an element of
uncertainty into our Alliance relations with
Japan. The opposition Democratic Party of Japan
(DPJ) has voiced strong support for the Alliance
per se, but many leading DPJ politicians oppose
funding the move to Guam, the Futenma Replacement
Facility (FRF) plan, and Japan's role in Indian
Ocean refueling and anti-piracy operations. It is
unclear at this point how much of their policy
pronouncements are campaign rhetoric and how much
are serious declarations of policy shifts under a
DPJ government. [09TOKYO1373]

And once again, the Pentagon's marching orders to a visiting US
delegation are to get the DPJ back in line:

Significant ideological differences within the
DPJ make it difficult to predict the impact
on bilateral relations of a DPJ government.
The party's "big tent" includes old-line
socialists on one side and pragmatic defense

*intellectuals who would be comfortable in the
LDP on the other. Your meeting with DPJ leaders
will be an opportunity to elicit their views
and to re-enforce with the DPJ importance of
implementing the transformation and realignment
agenda.*

The agenda, that is, of the LDP. Here we have an Obama official basically telling Japan's most important opposition party—and the millions of Japanese expected to vote for it in the next election—to abandon their principles and stick with the ruling party's pro-American agenda.

But the strategy backfired. In late August, Japanese voters threw out the LDP and, to the consternation of the Obama administration, ushered in a new era of real progressive rule in Japan. Here is how the *Times* reported the election and its implications:

Japan's voters cast out the Liberal Democratic
Party for only the second time in postwar history
on Sunday, handing a landslide victory to a
party that campaigned on a promise to reverse a
generation-long economic decline and to redefine
Tokyo's relationship with Washington. Many
Japanese saw the vote as the final blow to the
island nation's postwar order, which has been
slowly unraveling since the economy collapsed in
the early 1990s. In the powerful lower house,
the opposition Democrats virtually swapped places
with the governing Liberal Democratic Party,
winning 308 of the 480 seats, a 175 percent
increase that gives them control of the chamber,
according to the national broadcaster NHK. The
incumbents took just 119 seats, about a third of
their previous total. The remaining seats were
won by smaller parties.

"This has been a revolutionary election,"
Yukio Hatoyama, the party leader and presumptive
new prime minister, told reporters. "The people
have shown the courage to take politics into
their own hands." Mr. Hatoyama, who is expected
to assemble a government in two to three weeks,
has spoken of the end of American-dominated
globalization and of the need to reorient Japan
toward Asia. His party's campaign manifesto
calls for an "equal partnership" with the United
States and a "reconsidering" of the 50,000-strong
American military presence here … One change on
the horizon may be the renegotiation of a deal
with Washington to relocate the United States
Marine Corps' Futenma airfield, on the island of
Okinawa. Many island residents want to evict the
base altogether. The Democrats, who opposed the
American-led war in Iraq, have also said they may
end the Japanese Navy's refueling of American and
allied warships in the Indian Ocean.[3]

The Obama administration's response was to send Kurt Campbell
scurrying to Tokyo to repair the damage and impress on
Hatoyama that his attempts to "reorient" Japan's foreign policy
would be opposed on every front. This reflected a deep consensus within the US national security establishment: Campbell,
along with Flourney, had co-founded CNAS, and the Japanese
officials he spoke with must have been aware that their messages
to temper DPJ policies came not only from the Obama administration but from the broader spectrum of American political
power.

Another Zumwalt cable laid out the risks for the United
States, and described Campbell's response to a senior member of
the DPJ:

```
According to DPJ Diet Affairs Committee Chairman
Kenji Yamaoka, the new DPJ government's primary
goal will be to strengthen the US alliance
despite tactical differences with the previous
government. Japan will not extend Indian Ocean
refueling missions but is open to other ideas
for how Japan could contribute to US efforts in
Afghanistan and Pakistan. Base relocation efforts
in Okinawa should proceed from a dialogue with
the US on how Japan should fit into the overall US
strategic vision. Opposition to the bases from
local communities is real and the GOJ must make
the case for the US bases as playing an important
role in the defense of Japan. However, simply
defending the status quo will weaken rather
than strengthen the alliance. There must be
transparency concerning past "secret agreements"
on the introduction of nuclear weapons, but these
will not affect current practices regarding US
declaration of nuclear weapons introductions
or the kinds of propulsion systems allowed in
Japanese ports. [09TOKYO2196]
```

In his meeting with Yamaoka, Campbell made it clear that these choices were unpalatable. The United States, he said, would "listen," but wanted the incoming party to ameliorate its views and not get "bogged down" on these matters of principle:

```
Over dinner with DPJ Diet Affairs Committee
Chairman Kenji Yamaoka, Assistant Secretary Kurt
Campbell laid out the USG strategy for engaging
the new DPJ-led government and asked for advice
on how best to proceed. He stressed that the
USG would be in listening mode, was willing
to be flexible in a number of areas, but in a
```

limited number of areas, had less flexibility
requiring us to proceed with caution. Through
a series of high level engagements culminating
with the President's visit in November, our
overall goal will be to show that the alliance is
moving forward, focused on common interests and
cooperation, and not bogged down in disputes. In
public we will support the DPJ's stated goal of
an equal partnership with the US and encourage
a strong independent Japanese foreign policy
including better relations with the ROK and
China. We will also focus on preparations for
the 50th anniversary of the security alliance.
A/S Campbell flagged as areas of concern MOFA's
announced intention to pursue historical issues
related to the so-called secret agreement on
the introduction of nuclear weapons into Japan,
implementation of the base realignment agreement
in Okinawa/Guam, revisions to the SOFA agreement,
host nation support, and Japan's decision
to suspend the SDF's Indian Ocean refueling
missions.

On this same visit, Campbell also met with Naoto Kan, then the
DPJ's deputy prime minister, who would later be elected to lead
Japan. Kan, who was one of the most popular members of the
party, received an arrogant lecture from Campbell that sounds
very much like a parent berating a recalcitrant child:

Assistant Secretary of State for East Asian and
Pacific Affairs Kurt Campbell met with Deputy
Prime Minister and Minister for National Strategy
Bureau, Economic and Science and Technology
Policy Naoto Kan in Tokyo on September 18. The
officials spoke about the historic nature of the

DPJ's recent victory and ascension to power, the definition of an "equal relationship" between the US and Japan, security issues related to Okinawa, and upcoming high-level USG visits to Japan …

A/S Campbell advised that while the DPJ worked to bring about such historic changes, it keep in mind some lessons from the recent past. One such lesson was to not only take bold actions, but also take responsibility for those actions. Trying to justify unpopular actions by blaming foreign pressure was not helpful in building a strong and equal relationship between the US and Japan, Campbell said. Such a tactic may be politically expedient, but ultimately leaves a bad impression with the Japanese public, the A/S continued. Another lesson the DPJ could learn from the recent history of bilateral relations was that Japan's tendency to let the US take the initiative on security matters then simply responding was not indicative of an equal relationship. Campbell stated that the US also desires an equal relationship, but that a change in Japanese behavior was necessary. He said the DPJ victory represented a historic opportunity to bring about change in the relationship, and called on the two governments to work together to strengthen the alliance … Campbell said that the Futenma issue was extremely important, and pointed out that the maintenance of a strong US military presence in Asia during these difficult times was critical. The A/S pointed out that US troops in Japan were important for the Japanese as well, and implored Kan to move carefully on the Futenma issue. [09TOKYO2269_a]

Campbell continued his "listening tour" the next day in a meeting with Mitoji Yabunaka, Japan's new vice foreign minister. This meeting is notable for Campbell's direct warning to the DPJ that raising the issue of the secret US-Japan nuclear agreements from the Cold War would directly threaten US-Japan relations:

```
Touching on Foreign Minister Okada's plan to
investigate the so-called "secret" nuclear
agreement between the US and Japan, A/S Campbell
reiterated that the US had released all relevant
documents and did not plan to comment further.
He cautioned that focusing on the issue could
have operational implications for US forces.
[09TOKYO2277]
```

This comment is doubly hypocritical when you consider the fact that President Obama came into office pledging to lead the "most transparent" administration in US history. Yet here was his assistant secretary of state bluntly warning a sovereign government that exposing secret and undemocratic agreements from the Cold War past would jeopardize their current bilateral ties. Consider this rather bald warning:

```
Focusing on Japan's political transition with new
Prime Minister Hatoyama and the former opposition
Democratic Party of Japan (DPJ) taking power, A/S
Campbell said the US would publicly demonstrate
its confidence in the new government and express
strong support during Japan's political
transition. Publicly, the US would express
support for the tenets of the DPJ platform (e.g.,
a more independent Japanese foreign policy,
strong relations with China). At the same time,
the US would be intensely focused on reading
signals from the new administration …
```

Turning to Foreign Minister Okada's interest in
investigating the so-called "secret" agreements
between the US and Japan, A/S Campbell said
that the US had already released the relevant
documents through Freedom of Information Act
(FOIA) requests and that there would be little
the US could add to what was already available
publicly. While MOFA would conduct its own
document search, A/S Campbell said it would be
best if the US did not comment. *He stressed
that the US did not want this issue to create a
situation that would require the US to respond
in a way unhelpful to the alliance.* [Emphasis
added.]

A month later, Campbell was back in Tokyo, this time to lead a
combined State and DoD delegation to meet with the DPJ on its
plans for relocating the US Marine base in Futenma, Okinawa,
to Guam:

Members of the US delegation countered Ministry
of Defense (MOD) Bureau of Local Cooperation
Director General Motomi Inoue's suggestion that
US Marines presence in Guam alone would provide
sufficient deterrence capability in the region,
and the airstrips at Ie and Shimoji islands might
be a sufficient complement to Kadena's two runways
in a contingency. They stressed that relying
exclusively on Guam posed time, distance, and
other operational challenges for US Marines to
respond expeditiously enough to fulfill US treaty
obligations. [09TOKYO2378]

At one point in the meeting, Campbell told the DPJ that the
United States regarded the LDP era of US-military ties as the

standard by which all US relationships should be judged: "A/S Campbell pointed out that US allies regarded the US-Japan SOFA as the gold standard among basing agreements, and he counseled against moves to review simultaneously every aspect of the Alliance." Amazingly, the US delegation even told the DPJ that they had a better understanding of Japan's defense needs than the Japanese themselves, particularly with respect to China. The US side

```
elaborated that there might be contingencies
related not just to Situations in Areas
Surrounding Japan (SIASJ), but also to the
defense of Japan itself … [They] also related
this issue back to realignment, noting that the
redeployment of Marines in their entirety to Guam
would not give the US military the flexibility
and speed necessary to meet its Security Treaty
obligations to Japan … The dramatic increase in
China's military capabilities necessitated access
to at least three runways in a contingency, noted
A/S Campbell. In the 1990s, it had been possible
to implement contingency plans for South Korea
and China using only two runways in Okinawa,
Naha and Kadena. The most significant change
between 1995 (when the Special Action Committee
on Okinawa (SACO) plans for the relocation [of]
Futenma Air Base had been formulated) and 2009
was the build-up of Chinese military assets,
explained A/S Campbell.
```

In the final Japan cable in this series, Campbell is back in Japan to coordinate the US-Japanese message for President Obama's upcoming state visit to Tokyo. The message: yes, we can disagree, but please do not tell the public; all these discussions must remain secret:

In a November 5 meeting, EAP Assistant Secretary
Kurt Campbell, joined by the Ambassador, stressed
to Ministry of Foreign Affairs (MOFA) North
American Affairs Bureau Director General Umemoto
the importance of ensuring a successful visit to
Japan by the President and provided a five-point
suggestion from the White House (para. 2). A/S
Campbell and Umemoto agreed that both governments
should manage press reports depicting strains
in the US-Japan Alliance and instead steer the
press to cover broader aspects of the bilateral
relationship. Umemoto said he had persuaded
Foreign Minister Okada not to take up contentious
nuclear issues during the President's visit,
especially a no-first use policy …

A/S Campbell asserted that US and Japan public
affairs managers needed to work closely together
to address press reporting that the Alliance is
facing difficulties. These critical stories should
be addressed directly, using a message that
highlighted the process that had been put in place,
the deep respect the two nations had for each
other, the critical importance of the Alliance, and
our shared optimism of the future. [09TOKYO2614]

This charade would continue until DPJ prime minister Hashimoto resigned and was replaced by Naoto Kan. But, due to the US pressure on them not to change policy, both governments appeared weak in the eyes of Japanese voters, and—much to the Obama administration's relief—the LDP returned to power in 2012. Before describing that election and its implications, let us shift the scene back to South Korea, where pro-Americans were firmly in power.

*   *   *

In contrast to the Obama administration's disdain for Japan's liberal DPJ, by the fall of 2009 the president and his advisers were ecstatic about the conservative rule of President Lee in South Korea. This was particularly true as relations deteriorated with Pyongyang. In May, North Korea had announced that it had detonated a second nuclear test, "defying international warnings and drastically raising the stakes in a global effort to get the recalcitrant Communist state to give up its nuclear weapons program," the *New York Times* reported.[4] The test took place a few days after the shocking death by suicide of Roh Moo-hyun, Kim Dae Jung's successor, and the *Times* added this summary of North-South relations:

> Relations between the Koreas have plunged since Mr. Roh's successor, Mr. Lee, took office in February 2008, promising to reverse the "sunshine policy" of promoting political reconciliation with Pyongyang with economic aid. Agreements resulting from a 2007 summit meeting called for the South to spend billions of dollars to help rebuild the impoverished North's dilapidated infrastructure. Mr. Lee believed that such aid must be linked to improvements in the North's human rights record and the dismantling of its nuclear facilities. North Korea has viciously attacked Mr. Lee, calling him a "national traitor," cutting off official dialogue and reducing traffic across the countries' heavily armed border.

In September 2009, Deputy Secretary of State Steinberg paid another visit to Seoul, prompting a secret cable summarizing US-Korean relations in the Lee era from US ambassador D. Kathleen Stephens. The cable is remarkable in its open embrace of the right-wing Lee over his leftist predecessors:

Mr. Deputy Secretary, all of us at Embassy
Seoul warmly welcome you back to Korea. Your
visit comes as we are in a sweet spot in the
relationship, with a strongly pro-American
president who has largely recovered from last
year's debacle on the importation of American
beef and is committed to working with us. The
ROK has placed the DPRK nuclear issue firmly
at the center of North-South relations. More
broadly, President Lee's determination to build
a "Global Korea" will offer opportunities to
expand our strategic cooperation beyond the
Korean Peninsula, although we will have to be
sensitive to ROK concerns that such cooperation
is not a one-way relationship determined by the
US agenda …

At every level, ROK foreign policy is currently
dominated by experienced America hands who
believe deeply that the ROK must carefully
coordinate its policies with us. Seoul has
completely jettisoned the policy of the Roh Moo-
hyun years that attempted to separate the nuclear
issue from North-South relations, and President
Lee has firmly told the DPRK that the nuclear
issue is now central to relations with Pyongyang.
Your interlocutors will repeat this position;
in turn, they will want to be reassured that
the United States is committed to multilateral
talks on the nuclear issue and that we will not
enter into a bilateral negotiation with the DPRK.
[09SEOUL1529]

By the end of 2009, the US had got its way in South Korea, with
the conservative Lee—now Obama's "favorite president"—doing

America's bidding on every front of its foreign policy, including its own relations with the North.

The end result of these policies was a return to the hardline policies of the past and another series of crises for North and South Korea:

Relations across the DMZ took a nose-dive in March 2010, when Lee's government blamed the North for blowing up a South Korean warship off Korea's west coast, killing 46 sailors. The DPRK denied it, but a South Korean commission and an international team of investigators held the North responsible (many in the South still question those conclusions). That incident kicked off [a major] confrontation that had the Koreas and the United States talking of war. In November 2010, the United States and South Korea staged another major naval exercise on the west coast near where the Korean warship had gone down. The DPRK issued a series of warnings, saying that if any shells landed on their side of a disputed North-South maritime border, they would retaliate. Some did, and the North struck back ferociously by shelling the island of Yeonpyeong, killing several civilians.

South Korea, stung by this cruel attack on a non-military target, vowed to continue the exercises; the North issued more strong warnings. With several dozen US soldiers on Yeonpyeong as observers and thousands more participating in the exercises, any clash was bound to draw in the United States. For a few days the world held its breath to see if war would break out. Lights were on 24/7 at the crisis center at the

Pentagon … Then something unusual happened. At
the height of the crisis, on Dec. 16, 2010, Gen.
James Cartwright, the outspoken vice chairman
of the Joint Chiefs of Staff, told reporters
that he was deeply concerned about the situation
escalating out of control. In words designed
to be heard in Seoul, he made it clear that the
Pentagon wanted to ratchet down the situation.
If North Korea "misunderstood" or reacted "in
a negative way" by firing back, he said, "that
would start potentially a chain reaction of
firing and counter-firing. What you don't want to
have happen out of that is for the escalation to
be—for us to lose control of the escalation."
Cartwright, and the Pentagon, had no desire to
be drawn into a war that was not of their own
making … Cartwright's warning apparently worked.
The crisis ended. But a year later little had
changed—except that Kim Jong-un was now in charge
of the DPRK.[5]

Then, in December 2012, Kim's military defied global warnings
against his weapons program and successfully launched a rocket
that actually placed a satellite in orbit. The move was quickly
condemned by the United States and South Korea, but this time
criticism also came from China and Russia. In February 2013,
North Korea carried out its third test of a nuclear weapon, which
was nearly twice as large as its previous one. A few days later, the
UN Security Council imposed deeper sanctions on North Korea.
Its government lashed out again, but this time the rhetoric had
changed. In the past, the North had always blasted South Korea
as its primary antagonist, but early in January it began to frame
its problems in the context of its decades-long confrontation with
the United States. The North's primary enemy had shifted from
South Korea to the United States. Yet the Obama administration,

despite its pre-2009 pledge to negotiate even with unfriendly powers, still refuses to open direct lines of dialogue with the North that could lower tensions.

This was essentially the status quo with the DPRK in 2014 under the administration of Park Geun-hye, who succeeded Lee as president in 2013. Under her conservative rule, US military relations with South Korea have never been better. And as those relations have deepened, Obama's rhetoric on Korea has become increasingly shrill and warlike. In 2013, during celebrations marking the sixtieth anniversary of the armistice that ended the Korean War, the president had the audacity and arrogance to call the war a "victory," reviving a right-wing trope that has long been discredited by American historians of the war. In April 2014, during his state visit to Seoul, Obama stood side by side with President Park—the daughter of South Korea's former dictator—and praised the US-Korean relationship. "The US and South Korea stand shoulder to shoulder, both in face of Pyongyang's provocations and our refusal to accept a nuclear North Korea," he said. Here was another right-wing Korean leader with whom Obama could live—and, indeed, flourish.

And now it was Japan's turn to feel the American pressure: Tokyo was Washington's new problem child.

In late 2009, US diplomats and intelligence officials began to speak bitterly of the DPJ, comparing its independent policies to those of the former leftist government in Seoul. Here is how Martin Fackler, the *Times* reporter in Tokyo, put it in December 2009:

```
Two months after taking power, Japan's new
leadership is still raising alarms in the
United States with its continued scrutiny
of the countries' more than half-century-
old security alliance. But this reconsideration
```

is not a pulling away from the United States so much as part of a broader, mostly domestic effort to outgrow Japan's failed postwar order, say political experts here.

More important, the analysts say, these stirrings may also be the first signs of something that both Tokyo and Washington should have had years ago: a more open dialogue on a security relationship that has failed to keep up with the changing realities in Japan and, more broadly, in Asia.

Even after President Obama's feel-good visit to Tokyo last month, the government of Prime Minister Yukio Hatoyama has begun an inquiry to expose secret cold war-era agreements that allowed American nuclear weapons into Japan and has conducted a rare public review of its financial support for the 50,000 United States military workers based here. This continues the approach taken by Mr. Hatoyama since his Democratic Party scored a historic election victory in August on pledges to build a more equal partnership with Washington. A few political analysts in the United States have compared Mr. Hatoyama to Roh Moo-hyun, the former South Korean president who rode a wave of anti-Americanism to power in 2002.[6]

Over the next two years, the incessant US criticism of the DPJ (and the Obama administration's extraordinary intervention in Japan's internal affairs during the nuclear crisis at Fukushima in 2011) led to a crushing defeat at the polls for the party and the return to power of Japan's hard-right LDP. By 2010, Hatoyama's DPJ folded to the US pressure, backing away from his campaign pledge to force the US Marines out of Okinawa. Here is how the reversal was reported by the *Times*:

> Visiting Okinawa for the first time since
> becoming prime minister, Mr. Hatoyama asked
> residents to entertain a compromise that would
> keep some of the functions of the base on the
> island while the government explored moving
> some facilities elsewhere. "Realistically
> speaking, it is impossible" to move the
> entire base, called Futenma, off the island,
> he said. "We're facing a situation that is
> realistically difficult to move everything out
> of the prefecture [sic]. We must ask the people
> of Okinawa to share the burden." But Okinawans
> seemed in no mood for burden-sharing, heckling
> him after he met with local officials. "Shame on
> you!" one man shouted.
>
> Mr. Hatoyama's government could hang in the
> balance. He has pledged to come up with a plan
> by the end of this month to relocate the Marine
> air base and resolve a stubborn problem that has
> created months of discord with Washington. His
> delays and apparent flip-flopping on the issue have
> fed a growing feeling of disappointment in the
> prime minister's leadership, driving his approval
> ratings below 30 percent.[7]

The *Times* was correct. Within weeks, Hatoyama had quit, and his farewell statement made it clear how much it hurt. "This has proved impossible in my time," Hatoyama said in a "teary speech," the *Times* reported. "Someday, the time will come when Japan's peace will have to be ensured by the Japanese people themselves."[8] He was succeeded by Naoto Kan, the intense reformer who had cracked down on fraud and corruption within the Japanese Health Ministry in the 1990s.

In March 2011, Kan faced Japan's gravest crisis since World War II when a pair of nuclear reactors melted down following the Fukushima earthquake and tsunami of March 11. Kan had already given up on the idea of expelling the US Marines in Okinawa, but now the Obama administration began pressuring him in another way. After the Kan government asked the US Nuclear Regulatory Commission and the US Navy for support during the nuclear crisis, the US immediately began painting a picture of Kan's government as hopelessly out of touch with the reality of the crisis and unable to respond properly. Here is how I described the situation in a profile of Kan in *The Nation*:

On March 16, 2011, US Nuclear Regulatory Commission chair Gregory Jaczko openly contradicted the Japanese government by declaring that water in one of Tepco's reactors had boiled away, raising radiation in the area to "extremely high levels." He recommended evacuation to any Americans within fifty miles of the site—nearly double the evacuation zone announced by the Japanese government (which immediately denied Jaczko's assertions). The *New York Times* piled on the next day with a major article that pilloried the Kan government. "Never has postwar Japan needed strong, assertive leadership more—and never has its weak, rudderless system of governing been so clearly exposed," the reporters declared.

Among those the *Times* quoted was Japan expert Ronald Morse, who had worked in Washington in the Defense, Energy, and State Departments before taking a position with a government ministry in Japan. "There's a clear lack of command authority in the current government in Tokyo," he said. "The magnitude of it becomes obvious at a time like this."

Under pressure from both the Japanese public and the US government to act more assertively in the crisis, Kan eventually decided to step down and call new elections. This time, Japanese voters turned overwhelmingly to the LDP and Prime Minister Abe, the most conservative leader since the early 1950s. When he returned to power in 2012, Abe once again infuriated his neighbors by visiting the Yasukuni Shrine. But the Obama administration was willing to put up with that for the sake of maintaining the strong military ties between the two countries. It was back to business as usual.

With a willing Abe in command, the US stepped up its pressure to complete the 1996 agreement on returning Futenma that had been so rudely interrupted by the liberals of the DPJ. One of Abe's first acts, according to the Kyodo news service, was to create a new cabinet-level "minister in charge of alleviating Okinawa's base-hosting burden." By April 2013, the Abe and Obama administrations had agreed on basic terms: the US Marines' presence in Futenma would be substantially reduced by moving key units to the island of Guam.

But the bulk of the Marines—including the forward-based airborne elements considered so important by the United States— would move to a new site on Henoko Bay in the north of the island, near the existing US base known as Camp Schwab and close to the coastal city of Nago. In late 2013, the plan won the approval of Okinawa governor Hirokazu Nakaima, who had been elected in 2010 on a platform dedicated to relocating Futenma in five years. He signed on to the national government's plans for Henoko after Abe promised to spend over 300 billion yen—nearly $3 billion—every year until 2021 "to promote Okinawa's economy," according to the *Japan Times*.[9] The die seemed cast.

But, once again, democracy got in the way. In January 2014, Susumu Inamine, a fierce opponent of the new base at Henoko, was elected mayor of Nago City, easily defeating an LDP candidate who supported the Abe-Nakaima plan. His election reflected the strong feelings of Okinawans about US bases (75 percent of those questioned in recent polls want them removed), but also encompassed local views. Many in Nago are concerned that the landfill for the new runways to be built for the Marines will destroy precious coral reefs in Henoko Bay, and cause irreparable damage to the biodiversity of the coast.

In May 2014, Inamine led a small delegation of lawmakers and activists from Nago to Washington to plead for a change of policy. During their stay, they met with academics and NGOs who opposed the Henoko plan, as well as sympathetic groups and lawmakers closely following the debate about Okinawa. They included the Brookings Institution, the libertarian Cato Institute, and staffers for Senators Barbara Boxer (D-NY), Tom Coburn (R-OK), and Kirsten Gillibrand (D-NY). But the Pentagon—which has been at the forefront of the US demand for bases—haughtily refused to meet with Inamine; the only member of the Obama administration they encountered was a deputy at the State Department's Japan desk, members of the delegation told me.

The pain of the Okinawa struggle was clearly evident during a presentation by the Inamine delegation at an event at a Washington restaurant that I attended. Essentially, the mayor said, the US and Japanese government plans for Henoko Bay would make the area unfit for human habitation due to the danger posed by US war planes and helicopters taking off and landing, and the terrible noise from explosions of "out of use weapons and ammunition" only 300 meters from residential areas. He said that US planes at Futenma held, on average, fifty drills a day. "That's 20,000 takeoffs and landings in a year," he added. "This has a wide-scale impact on daily life. It's almost like being in a front line of a war." The construction of a new base in Henoko, he added, means "another 100 years of pain" for Okinawa.

Asked about the forces arrayed against the citizens of Okinawa,

Inamine was blunt. "In a nation like Japan, there's a monstrous power behind it—the huge corporations and their incentives. This national policy [of keeping US bases in Okinawa] doesn't benefit normal people." The opposition, he added, was "an expression of the people's will." Talking directly to President Obama, he said: "America is where human rights are respected. But this denial of democracy is a denial of human rights." He and many other Okinawans began planning to turn November's elections for governor into a plebiscite on the bases, and show once and for all that the island wants the US Marines moved somewhere else.

They succeeded beyond their wildest expectations. As summarized in January 2015 by the Australian historian Gavan McCormack, in November 2014

> the Okinawan electorate decisively rejected the
> Governor, Nakaima Hirokazu, who had reneged on
> his pledge to oppose base construction and issued
> the permit the government needed to commence
> reclamation of Oura Bay, electing in his stead
> a candidate [Takeshi Onaga] committed to doing
> "everything in my power" to stop construction
> at Henoko, close Futenma Air Base, and have the
> Marine Corps' controversial Osprey MV 22 aircraft
> withdrawn from the prefecture (and therefore
> stopping the construction of "Osprey Pads" for
> them in the Yambaru forest, also in Northern
> Okinawa); and in December all four Okinawan local
> constituencies elected anti-base construction
> candidates to the lower house in the National
> Diet.[10]

From top to bottom, the elections were a sweeping victory for Okinawa's anti-base forces, and a powerful expression of the prefecture's popular will.

In response, the Abe government—with the full support of the

Obama administration—has been moving decisively to make the Henoko base a permanent fixture. In April, shortly before Mayor Inamine came to Washington, Secretary of Defense Chuck Hagel declared in Tokyo that he was "looking forward" to the "facility's construction beginning soon," the *Times* reported. "A few weeks later at a news conference in Tokyo, President Obama and Prime Minister Shinzo Abe agreed that progress had been made."

For Okinawans, the "progress" was troublesome. Over the summer of 2014, construction crews began the first phase of land reclamation, drilling, and surveys of the coral reefs that are required before the new runways can be built. To keep protesters out, the Japanese government set up a "prohibited zone" around the reclamation area for the first time, and dispatched Coast Guard patrol vessels and boats "from across the nation" to enforce it, the *Yomiuri* reported in August. In a strongly worded editorial, the *Japan Times* pointed out that the moves

```
raised speculation that the [Abe] administration
was rushing to set the work in motion before
local voters have a chance to express their will
on the divisive relocation issue … It almost
looks as if the Abe administration is saying
it will not count popular will as a factor in
whether to proceed with the Futenma relocation
per the agreement with the US.
```

We do not have any WikiLeaks cables available from these recent events. But it is easy enough to imagine the glee contained in the cable traffic between Tokyo and Washington on Abe's forceful moves to meet the US demands to maintain its forward-based Marines on Okinawa. A hint of what might be in these communications came in the *Yomiuri*, which in August quoted a "US government source" on the situation. According to this source, "Japan and the United States agreed that to maintain deterrence while reducing the burden on Okinawa residents of hosting US military bases, there is no option to relocate Futenma's functions to the Henoko district."

There is no option. After seventy years of US military operations on Okinawa, that is an extremely revealing statement. Thus emerged the seemingly contradictory situation of a liberal Obama administration—one of the most left-leaning in history, some conservatives say—intervening in both South Korea and Japan to reverse progressive change and maintain right-wing, pro-militarist governments more to the liking of the United States. WikiLeaks' cables have shown us how this was done—and they underscore the critical importance of whistleblowers and a free, functioning press.[11]

15. Southeast Asia

Richard Heydarian

For the past seven decades, the United States—a continental, North American state—has stood as the preeminent power in East Asia, with a complex, evolving network of alliances, military bases, economic arrangements, and diplomatic entanglements underpinning American hegemony in the region. The decisive defeat of Imperial Japan, which sought to carve out its own sphere of influence across the Asia-Pacific region during World War II, solidified US ascendancy: largely unscathed, thanks to its geographical isolation from the main theaters of war in western Europe and East Asia, the United States emerged as the world's leading economic and military power by the mid twentieth century. Later, throughout the Cold War, not even the mighty Soviet Union—and its communist allies in North Korea, Vietnam, and China—could displace American hegemony in East Asia.

US dominance, however, was a combination of auspicious developments at home, on one hand, and a calculated (quasi-imperialist) approach to international affairs, on the other. Blessed with abundant natural resources and favorable demographics, the North American nation oversaw a dynamic process of industrialization and economic growth in the second half of the nineteenth century, allowing it to catch up rapidly with—and eventually eclipse—traditional European powers, including the United Kingdom. Confronted with colonial wars in the early twentieth century between status quo powers and revisionist

states, the US primarily acted as an offshore balancer: it reluctantly supported allied nations (Britain and France) against
emerging colonial powers such as Germany and Japan. Domestic
opposition to foreign interventions, amid a climate of quasi-iso-
lationism, encouraged the US to intervene, in a calibrated and
timely manner, only when, first, there was a clear and present
danger of regional domination by revisionist states on the
Eurasian landmass, and, second, its own interests (and territorial
integrity) were directly threatened, as when Japan attacked Pearl
Harbor.[1]

Historically, the US saw itself as an exceptional nation, founded
upon principles of liberal democracy and opposed to archaic,
oppressive forms of European colonialism. After all, the US itself
emerged out of a protracted struggle for independence, culminating in the American Revolutionary War against the British
monarchy (1775–83). But, as scholars such as John Mearsheimer
note,[2] hegemonic expansion was a recurring theme throughout
America's own uniquely successful state-building project:

> The United States is the only regional hegemon in
> modern history … the Founding Fathers and their
> successors consciously and deliberately sought
> to achieve hegemony in the Americas … To realize
> their so-called Manifest Destiny, they murdered
> large numbers of Native Americans and stole
> their land, bought Florida from Spain (1819)
> and what is now the center of the United States
> from France (1803). They annexed Texas in 1845
> and then went to war with Mexico in 1846, taking
> what is today the American southwest from their
> defeated foe. They cut a deal with Britain to
> gain the Pacific northwest in 1846 and finally, in
> 1853, acquired additional territory from Mexico
> with the Gadsden Purchase … The plain truth is
> that in the nineteenth century the supposedly

peace-loving United States compiled a record of
territorial aggrandizement that has few parallels
in recorded history … The bottom line is that
the United States worked hard for over a century
to gain hegemony in the Western Hemisphere, and
it did so for sound strategic reasons. After
achieving regional dominance, it has worked
equally hard to keep other great powers from
controlling either Asia or Europe.

Once the US consolidated its continental ambitions in North America, it began to venture outward, dominating the Caribbean waters and much of Latin America. By the late nineteenth century, it had acquired sufficient military and technological prowess to fully operationalize the Monroe Doctrine (1823), which underpinned Washington's long-term ambition of driving out European powers from the Western Hemisphere. Its victorious march against the crumbling Spanish Empire paved the way for American domination of not only Cuba *and* Puerto Rico, but also Pacific islands such as Guam.[3]

THE ASIAN HORIZON

The occupation of the Philippine Islands, however, marked a decisive moment in the US's burgeoning imperial ambitions, which by the early twentieth century extended far across the Pacific waters and right into the heart of East Asia.[4] Favorably located at the intersection of China and the Pacific, the Philippines represented an important geopolitical asset. By colonizing the Southeast Asian nation, the US became a credible "two oceans" naval power, fulfilling the dream of legendary American naval strategist Alfred Mahan, who played an important role in shaping Washington's global ambitions. For Mahan, in his groundbreaking book *The Influence of Sea Power Upon History: 1660–1783*, the domination of international waterways, crucial to trade, by a powerful naval and merchant fleet stood at the heart of Britain's hegemony in the seventeenth and eighteenth centuries; the US, he argued, should follow in the footsteps of its former colonial master if it wished to emerge as a global powerhouse. As two leading scholars in the field explain, the US, intent on consolidating its domination in the Western Hemisphere, gradually fell into expansionist dialectic:

> Capt. Alfred Thayer Mahan depicted overseas naval stations as one of three "pillars" on which sea power rested, beseeching would-be sea powers to obtain bases to support the voyages of steam-driven merchantmen and warships … Mahan had lobbied tirelessly for island outposts in the Caribbean and Gulf of Mexico and for the annexation of Hawaii … In Mahan's time, arguments that the Philippines furnished a steppingstone to the China market were a product of US power and purpose fulfilled through historical accident. The more territory the United States acquired and the more capable it became, the more expansive its vision of its purposes in the world. A "want" became a "need," even though objectively China never became an important market for American products until long after Mahan's day.[5]

Beyond gaining trading access to China, the world's largest consumer market at the time, the occupation of the Philippines, a centuries-old trading hub in the region, transformed the US into a major player in Asia—marking the arrival of a new Western power on the global stage. In 1853, Commodore Matthew Perry vaunted American naval prowess to bully Japan into opening its market to foreign trade. By 1898, the US had a strong foothold in Asia, with the infamous Treaty of Paris providing legal cover for Washington's takeover of Spanish colonies in the Western

Hemisphere and the Asia-Pacific region. The US occupation of the Philippines was primarily driven by geopolitical interests, with leading naval strategists justifying imperial expansion by invoking trade-related interests. By attaching an economic dimension to the issue—not to mention the thoroughly discredited notion of "Manifest Destiny," whereby the US (echoing the malicious justifications of other European powers) was supposedly engaged in "civilizing" what it saw as "savage" nations—the security establishment sought to create a gentler cover for what, by any standard, was sheer colonial expansionism. The US also tried to create a showcase colony out of the Philippines, hoping to project an aura of benign patronage; Washington, cognizant of domestic political sensitivities, tried to counter the perception that it was engaged in European-style colonial exploitation.[6] As Neil Sheehan succinctly explains:

> The United States did not seek colonies as such. Having overt colonies was not acceptable to the American political conscience. Americans were convinced that their imperial system did not victimize foreign peoples. "Enlightened self-interest" was the sole national egotism to which Americans would admit … Americans perceived their order as a new and benevolent form of international guidance. It was thought to be neither exploitative, like the [nineteenth-century-style] colonialism of the European empires, nor destructive of personal freedom and other worthy human values, like the totalitarianism of the Soviet Union and China and their Communist allies. Instead of formal colonies, the [US] sought local governments amenable to American wishes and, where possible, subject to indirect control from behind the scenes. Washington wanted native regimes that

would act as surrogates for American power. The
goals were to achieve the sway over allies and
dependencies which every imperial nation needs
to work its will in world affairs without the
structure of old-fashioned colonialism.[7]

During the American era, the Filipino political elite flourished as
never before, relishing the patronage of a foreign power. Detesting
the outright brutality and legendary indolence of the Spanish col-
onizers, the Filipino masses also welcomed Washington's more
benign form of colonization, marked by increasingly universal
basic education, improved welfare, and quasi-democratic elections. As Benedict Anderson notes,

Americans installed, by stages, a political
regime, modelled on their own, which turned out,
perhaps to their own surprise, to be perfectly
adapted to the crystallising oligarchy's needs
… the prominent collaborator oligarch Manuel
Roxas became in 1946 the independent Philippines'
first President. Before his death in 1948 he
had achieved the following triumphs: amnesty
for all 'political prisoners' (mainly those
held on charges of collaboration); an agreement
permitting the US to retain control of its bases
in the Philippines for 99 years, as well as a
US-Philippines Military Assistance Pact; and the
amending of the Commonwealth Constitution of 1935
to give Americans "parity" access to the economic
resources of the "independent" Philippines (and,
of course, the oligarchy's continuing access to
the protected American market).[8]

The US exercised full-spectrum colonization over a Southeast
Asian nation, which, ironically, launched the first modern

nationalist-independence movement in Asia.[9] The Filipino nationalists, who initially misperceived the US as a reliable ally against
the Spanish Empire, heroically fought for national independence,
culminating in the Philippine-American War (1899–1902).
But they stood no chance against America's industrial-military
complex, which allowed the North American power to rapidly
consolidate its control over much of the Philippine Islands despite
stiff resistance by various indigenous groups, from the Christians
in the north to the Muslims in the south.[10]

The US, however, could not hold on to its sole Asian colony
for long. With the likes of President Woodrow Wilson taking
up the cudgels (albeit only rhetorically) for the principle of
self-determination across colonized world,[11] and anticoloniza-
tion movements gaining pace across Asia in the early twentieth
century, the Philippines was bound to become a (formally) independent state. By 1946, the US had bequeathed independence to
the island nation. But the country, ruled by an oligarchy attached
both ideologically and commercially to Washington, struggled to
strike its own independent course. A culture of dependency had
defined the Southeast Asian nation's relationship with the US. As
James Fallows notes:

America prevented the Filipinos from consummating
their rebellion against Spain. In 1898 the
United States intervened to fight the Spanish
and then turned around and fought the Filipino
nationalists, too. It was a brutal guerrilla war,
in which some half million Filipino soldiers and
civilians died … But American rule seemed only
to intensify the Filipino sense of dependence
… in unmeasurable, intangible ways. [American
patronage] seems to have eroded confidence even
further, leaving Filipinos to believe that they
aren't really responsible for their country's
fate.[12]

As Antonio Gramsci observed, hegemony is not solely based on coercion. Instead, hegemony—understood as the institutionalized exercise of domination—is anchored by "consent"; it is about the ability of the dominant power to shape, through cultural and ideological instruments, the preferences and mindset of its subjects. In many ways, the Philippines reflected the potency of America's ideological hegemony over its sole Asian colony. The Philippines' national hero, Benigno Aquino, Jr., who led the fight against the Marcos dictatorship in the 1970s, captures this point dramatically:

Almost half a century of American rule bequeathed to the Asian Filipino a trauma by making him uncomfortably American in outlook, values and tastes. What was left was a people without soul … Filipinos are bewildered about their identity. They are an Asian people not Asian in the eyes of their fellow Asians and not Western in the eyes of the West … Under the Americans, while ostensibly we were being prepared for self-government, for self-reliance, actually we were being maneuvered by means of political and economic pressures to defer to American decisions [and] being conditioned by our American education to prefer American ways. The result is a people habituated to abdicating control over basic areas of their national life, unaccustomed to coming to grips with reality, prone to escape into fantasies … Filipinos in growing numbers now believe that the independence granted by the United States in 1946 had built-in strings designed to perpetuate American economic dominance—or "colonialism," as the ultra-nationalists call it.[13]

Under such conditions, the Philippines was seemingly bound to serve as the forward deployment base of the US in East Asia. The Philippines practically outsourced its national security and economic sovereignty to the US through a series of agreements such as the 1951 Mutual Defence Treaty and the 1947 Philippine Parity Rights; American military bases in the Philippines served as the primary deterrence against external aggression, while Americans enjoyed equal rights to exploitation of Philippine natural resources. The Philippines was effectively a client state.[14]

AMERICAN PRIMACY

After World War II, the US—now a dominant player in critical regions such as western Europe, the Middle East, and East Asia—became the world's first truly global hegemon.[15] The exact origins of America's drive for primacy—partly by design and partly contingent—are unclear, however. As Australian strategist Patrick Porter argues,

> Some strategists point to the thinking and
> calculations made during World War II … Its
> main principles were laid down in a Brookings
> Institution study of 1945, endorsed by the Joint
> Chiefs of Staff. This study argued for the
> prevention of any hostile powers or coalitions
> dominating the Eurasian landmass. Others argue
> that America's grand strategy under its new
> President, Harry Truman, was initially fluid, but
> between 1945-53 it solidified into an overarching
> project, with the Korean War acting as a
> catalyst. Others yet argue that … it was only
> with the [Kennedy] administration that America
> finally settled on uncontested primacy as its
> preferred status in the world.[16]

Up until the Cold War, US influence in Asia was largely limited to its strategic toehold in the Philippines. For much of the first half of the twentieth century, the British controlled present-day Malaysia, Brunei, and Singapore, while the Dutch controlled Indonesia. France was the main colonizer in Indochina, though Thailand was nominally independent, while Japan carved out a colony in the Korean Peninsula and Taiwan, before pushing further into mainland China after World War I. After World War II, however, European powers—devastated by the world wars and confronting determined indigenous independence movements—progressively retreated from East Asia, paving the way for the emergence of new postcolonial nation-states. The US was by now the leading Western power in the region—and beyond. To confront the communist bloc, America relied on allies in Australia, New Zealand, Thailand, the Philippines, Taiwan, South Korea, South Vietnam, and Japan, with the likes of Indonesia and Malaysia serving as important strategic partners. Southeast Asia served as the pivot around which America sought to "contain" what it saw as communist expansionism. Under the aegis of the Southeast Asia Treaty Organization (SEATO), a collective military alliance crudely patterned after NATO, Southeast Asian treaty allies such as the Philippines and Thailand played a crucial role in supporting—by sending military personnel and/or providing logistical support—America's anticommunist military operations in the Korean and Vietnam wars. The US gradually implemented what Zbigniew Brzezinski, the national security advisor during the Carter administration, identified as the essential elements of imperial geostrategy: maintaining the strategic dependence of allies on the imperial power, and preventing collusion between them; preventing enemies from uniting; and keeping protectorates as compliant as possible. At the height of the Vietnam War, Thailand hosted nearly 50,000 American servicemen on its soil, who supported coordinated air, naval, and ground assaults in Indochina; the Philippines, meanwhile, hosted America's biggest overseas bases in the coastal regions of Subic and Clark. Benedict

Anderson brilliantly encapsulates Southeast Asia's place in the US-led network of alliances during the Cold War:

> Nowhere else was it "hotter" in the third quarter of the century … The only two big wars the Americans fought were in this zone: on the Korean peninsula they were forced to accept a costly stand-off, while in Indochina they suffered a bitter and humiliating defeat. In every important country of South-East Asia, with the exception of Indonesia, there were major, sustained Communist insurrections, and Indonesia, in the early Sixties, had the largest legal Communist Party in the world outside the socialist bloc. In all these states, except Malaysia, which was still a colony, the Americans intervened politically, economically, militarily and culturally, on a massive scale. The notorious domino theory was invented specifically for South-East Asia. To shore up the line of teetering dominoes, Washington made every effort to create loyal, capitalistically prosperous, authoritarian and anti-Communist regimes—typically, but not invariably, dominated by the military. Many were tied to the US by security arrangements, and in some the Americans had a broad range of military installations. Each disaster only encouraged Washington to put more muscle and money behind its remaining political allies. No world region received more "aid."[17]

Driven by Cold War exigencies—that is, an obsession with the containment or rollback of communism at any cost—the US ended up supporting anticommunist Southeast Asian dictators such as Ferdinand Marcos (Philippines) and Suharto (Indonesia), who committed egregious human rights violations and stubbornly blocked any form of genuine democratization at home.[18]

THE UNIPOLAR MOMENT

By the 1980s, a wave of democratization was sweeping across East Asia, toppling authoritarian regimes in the Philippines, South Korea, and Taiwan. But "regime change" did not significantly alter these countries' strategic relationship with—and dependency on—the US. Meanwhile, post-Mao Beijing, under Deng Xiaoping, emerged as a major Western strategic partner, further isolating Moscow and post-unification Hanoi.[19] The decisive collapse of the Soviet Union in 1991 sparked a triumphalist celebration of American prowess, with conservative thinkers such as Francis Fukuyama prematurely declaring "The End of History." For Fukuyama, the apparent defeat of communism supposedly underscored the emergence of democratic capitalism as the ideological endpoint of human history, with US hegemony defining and underpinning the architecture of the post–Cold War global order.[20] America's wholesale embrace of its newfound role as the sole global superpower was starkly evident in key strategic documents such as the infamous 1992 Defence Planning Guidance, under the administration of George H. W. Bush, which stated the first objective of the US was

```
to prevent the re-emergence of a new rival,
either on the territory of the former Soviet
Union or elsewhere, that poses a threat on the
order of that posed formerly by the Soviet Union.
This is a dominant consideration underlying
the new regional defense strategy and requires
that we endeavor to prevent any hostile power
from dominating a region whose resources would,
under consolidated control, be sufficient to
generate global power … the US must show the
```

leadership necessary to establish and protect a
new order that holds the promise of convincing
potential competitors that they need not aspire
to a greater role or pursue a more aggressive
posture to protect their legitimate interests
... we must maintain the mechanisms for deterring
potential competitors from even aspiring to a
larger regional or global role. An effective
reconstitution capability is important here,
since it implies that a potential rival could
not hope to quickly or easily gain a predominant
military position in the world.[21]

While the Clinton administration relentlessly espoused further global economic integration (to the benefit of American multinational companies) and the eastward expansion of NATO into the post-Soviet space (to the consternation of post-Soviet Russia), the first administration of George W. Bush, early in his period of office and in response to the 9/11 attacks, dispensed with all pretentions to multilateralism, launching unilateral military interventions across the Middle East, pressuring allies to support his global war on terror, and vocally pursuing full-spectrum American hegemony, as explicitly reflected in the 2002 National Security Strategy.[22]

Under the Bush administration, Southeast Asia, home to decades-long Islamic insurgencies, was declared the second major front (after Afghanistan) in the "Global War on Terror" (GWOT), with Washington ramping up its military-intelligence support to allies such as the Philippines, which were caught in a protracted conflict with increasingly radicalized Islamist separatists in the southern Philippine island of Mindanao. In December 2001, Washington launched "Operation Enduring Freedom – Philippines," declaring the Southeast Asian country a major non-NATO ally in the GWOT. The following year, members of Special Operations Command Pacific were deployed to support counter-terror operations in the insurgency-hit areas of the Philippines, which the *New York Times* described as "the largest single deployment of American military might outside Afghanistan to fight terrorists since the Sept. 11 attack."[23] It effectively paved the way for the (re-)establishment of permanent US military bases in the country, with hundreds of US Special Forces offering intelligence and logistical support to the Armed Forces of the Philippines (AFP) against groups such as the Abu Sayyaf, Moro Islamic Liberation Front, and the al-Qaeda regional off-shoot, Jemaah Islamiya.[24] Across Southeast Asia, however, many countries, from Malaysia and Indonesia to Thailand and the Philippines, were disappointed with Washington's single-minded focus on counter-terrorism operations, which prevented the US and ASEAN from focusing on other strategic concerns, such as human development, trade, and investment.[25] The Bush administration's mindless assertion of American hegemony, particularly its destructive military interventions and failed nation-building projects in Iraq and Afghanistan, severely undermined Washington's fiscal health and economic well-being, and led to the diplomatic alienation of many allies and strategic partners, which opposed Bush's fiery brand of unilateralism.

Upon assuming power, the Obama administration swiftly made it clear that a cornerstone of its foreign-policy doctrine was to "rebalance" American strategic commitments abroad: in short, it promised to reduce US military commitments in the Middle East, while increasing its economic and military-related engagements in other critical regions, such as East Asia. Confronting what was by all means a classic case of "imperial overstretch," the new administration had to re-examine its foreign policy priorities, rationalize its defense spending and external commitments, and enhance existing alliances. This led to the emergence of the so-called "Pivot to Asia" strategy, which supposedly reflected the Obama administration's desire, first, to distance itself from the Bush-era strategic blunders in the Middle East, specifically the decade-long wars in Iraq and Afghanistan; and, second, to enhance its economic and military footprint in the increasingly more important Asia-Pacific theater. To demonstrate its commitment to and renewed interest in East Asia, the key Asian states of Japan, China, and South Korea were among President Obama's first official foreign trips. The strategic rationale behind the new policy had both economic and geopolitical dimensions. In economic terms, the Obama administration was eager to counter the impact of the 2007–08 Great Recession by enhancing US market access and exports to the booming economies of Asia—especially East Asian emerging markets, which have continued to rely on green-field investments and imports of high-end machinery and consumer products from Western multinational companies. In particular, Southeast Asian countries' decision to form a regional common market in 2015 presented a highly attractive opportunity for the US, which has traditionally been more focused on the larger economies of Northeast Asia and Australia. The Obama administration also progressively lobbied for the deeper liberalization of trading arrangements with the Asian economic giants of Japan, China, and South Korea.[26] The goal was to enhance the US balance of trade, deepen its market presence in major Asian markets, and accord its leading multinational corporations stronger protection of intellectual property rights (IPR).[27]

A more urgent strategic concern, however, was the rapid ascent of China as the preeminent economic power (top trading nation and biggest economy) in East Asia. From the mid 1990s to the early 2000s, Beijing managed to expand its sphere of influence dramatically across Southeast Asia, while accelerating its military modernization program. During this period, China rapidly upgraded its asymmetric military capabilities and enhanced the ability of the People's Liberation Army's Navy to project power on the high seas. For the Obama administration, the disproportionate focus of the Bush administration on the Eurasian theater—specifically the wars in Afghanistan and Iraq—allowed rising Asian powers such as China to undermine Washington's influence in other critical regions of the world, especially East Asia. Largely thanks to China's generous trade and investment offers, Indochinese states such as Cambodia and Laos were firmly placed within Beijing's orbit. (Since the Cold War period, these countries have been within China's strategic orbit, so it is more of a question of reinforcing an already-existing dependency.) Confronting isolation and Western sanctions, the military junta in Myanmar had little choice but to rely increasingly on Chinese patronage. Expanding economic linkages with China and the presence of a large Chinese business community at home encouraged Thailand, Singapore, and Malaysia to step up their political ties with Beijing. More worryingly for Washington, long-time allies such as the Philippines, despite bitter territorial disputes in the South China Sea, aggressively pursued greater strategic and economic ties with Beijing.[28] The Arroyo administration (2001–09) was intent on diversifying Manila's external relations, reducing the country's historical dependence on Washington.[29]

China's influence and self-confidence were boosted by the way in which Southeast Asian leaders enthusiastically embraced China's emergence as the primary economic force in East Asia. After all, throughout the post–Cold War era, the Southeast Asian region was largely ignored by Washington. While the Clinton administration was more concerned with integrating China into the global economic order, to accelerate economic integration and trade among the Asia-Pacific nations, the Bush administration, in turn, largely treated ASEAN as a pawn in its global war on terror. The proliferation of varying forms of extremist and al-Qaeda-affiliated organizations, such as Jemaah Islamiya and Abu Sayyaf in the Muslim-majority areas of the region—especially in areas hit by decades-long insurgency and ethnic strife such as the southern Philippine island of Mindanao—served as a pretext for Washington's designation of ASEAN as the second front of its global war on terror.[30]

One must, however, acknowledge that certain factors, such as the abrogation of the US Military Bases Agreement in the Philippines in 1991, played an important role in reducing Washington's post–Cold War footprint (and interest) in the region, encouraging the US increasingly to place a higher premium on its bilateral strategic ties with Northeast Asian partners such as Japan and South Korea and Pacific partners like Australia. China was able to fully exploit Washington's strategic neglect in Southeast Asia, first, by astutely leveraging its economic and cultural linkages with ASEAN and, second, by extending its territorial gains in the South China Sea, culminating in the capture of the Mischief Reef in 1995, which set off alarm bells in Manila and other claimant states, but solicited a minimal response from Washington. For both geopolitical and economic reasons, ASEAN and its individual member states served as a strategic battleground for Beijing and Washington. Engaging ASEAN became a pillar of the Obama administration's policy of pivoting toward Asia.[31]

No wonder there was huge concern over the WikiLeaks disclosure of US diplomatic cables in Southeast Asia, which could potentially have undermined Washington's efforts to enhance its influence in the region. To be fair, the Obama administration went the extra mile to win favor among the ASEAN countries. The Obama administration proactively engaged ASEAN, and impressed its members by considering a number of highly symbolic diplomatic maneuvers. Washington signed the Treaty of Amity and Cooperation—the cornerstone of Southeast Asia's drive to prevent conflict and great-power rivalry in the region—while opening a permanent US mission in ASEAN and reinvigorating the US-ASEAN Leaders' Meeting. Unlike the Bush administration, it supported ASEAN's constructive engagement with Myanmar. In an attempt to demonstrate its ecological and developmental concerns in Indochina, the Obama administration also conducted ministerial meetings with the Lower Mekong countries. The US also upgraded its strategic relations with ASEAN's informal leader, Indonesia. Eager to enhance strategic ties with Indonesia, Washington supported Jakarta's integration into the G-20, arguably the world's leading decision-making forum, and lavishly praised the Southeast Asian state's status as a booming emerging market and vibrant Muslim democracy.[32]

In light of growing territorial tensions between Beijing and its Southeast Asian neighbors, the Obama administration found an opportunity to enhance its regional influence among countries that had been rattled by China's rising territorial assertiveness. Washington formally supported a "regional" solution to the South China Sea disputes, and, crucially, announced that the "freedom of navigation" in international waters constituted an American national interest—signaling Washington's indispensable role in and commitment to ensuring regional stability. To demonstrate its solidarity with ASEAN, Washington encouraged the establishment of a binding code of conduct in the disputed areas, in accordance with the 2002 Declaration on the Conduct of Parties in the South China Sea and the relevant provisions of international law, specifically the United Nations Convention on the Law of the Sea (UNCLOS). Although not a direct party to the UNCLOS, the US nevertheless maintains that in practice it observes it and encourages signatories, particularly China, to behave within the boundaries of international law and related treaty obligations. Washington's critics, however, maintain that the US is using the maritime disputes as a pretext to isolate China, increase arms exports to allies, and justify as well as further expand its already significant military presence in the region. Chinese leaders argue vehemently that extra-regional actors such as the US should not intervene in what are essentially bilateral, regional disputes in Southeast Asia.

CHINA

With the disappearance of the Soviet Union, communist China represented a potential source of threat to US hegemony in Asia in the post–Cold War era. But the pragmatic leadership of Deng

Xiaoping—who built on the nascent rapprochement between Chairman Mao and President Nixon in the early 1970s—and of his successors, especially Jiang Zemin, paved the way for almost three decades of "strategic co-habitation" between Beijing and Washington.[33] For much of the post–Cold War period, Indonesia tried to balance its relations with China and the US equally, welcoming strategic cooperation and economic engagement with both powers. As China became a more dominant economic player in Asia, Jakarta progressively deepened its strategic ties with Beijing, while disagreements over the conduct of the global war on terror and concerns over Indonesia's human rights record prevented the full blossoming of US-Indonesian bilateral ties.[34] The cables released by WikiLeaks reveal continued US suspicion and misgivings with respect to China's designs in its own backyard. For instance, in Indonesia the cables reveal Washington's concerns with growing economic linkages between China, on one hand, and Indonesia and its leading oligarchs, on the other. In the cable "China Deepens Its Economic Influence in Indonesia," the American embassy in Jakarta reports:

```
China is deepening its economic influence in
Indonesia, through major deals in energy and
resources, as well as the impending entry into
force of the China-ASEAN Free Trade Agreement
on January 1. Bumi Resources, Indonesia's
largest coal miner and owned by the family of
Golkar chief Aburizal Bakrie, has entered into a
financial relationship with the China Investment
Corporation that will expand China's influence
in Indonesia's mining sector. This arrangement
represents a new approach to China's traditional
low-key investment in the mining sector.
[09JAKARTA2073]
```

The cable notes that "China's interest in resource extraction industries helps [Indonesian] officials with internal politics, despite a spike in Indonesian resource nationalism," allowing the Indonesian government to demonstrate that its increasingly pro-tectionist laws in extractive industries such as mining, specifically in terms of "mandatory in-country smelting and local provisions," are not as "onerous" and counterproductive as Western compa-nies assert. The cable also notes China's crucial role in helping Indonesia to weather the 2007–08 Great Recession by offering currency-swap schemes and other symbolic gestures, which rep-resent a "political show of support for Indonesia."

In Thailand, a critical American treaty ally, the cables reveal increasing annoyance with the supposed "naiveté" of Thai offi-cials and academics, who have largely embraced economic and sociopolitical linkages with China at the expense of American influence. In a cable titled "[China's] Sustained, Successful Efforts to Court Southeast Asia and Thailand—Perspectives and Implications," the American embassy in Bangkok provides a comprehensive account of Thailand's apparent drift into China's orbit:

Thai contacts from government to academia see a decade-long Chinese romance of Southeast Asia, both through ASEAN and bilaterally, to have been successful in increasing Chinese influence during a period in which many believe that US influence and prestige in the region has waned. The Chinese effort in Thailand in particular is multifaceted and deeply rooted, from diplomatic to economic, military to cultural. Chinese high-level visits to Thailand and reciprocal Thai visits to China by Prime Ministers, Foreign Ministers, Defense Ministers, and top-ranking military brass continued at a rapid pace in 2009, leading to a slew of new agreements … As part of the

```
Thai-specific charm offensive, the Chinese have
courted members of the Royal Family by supporting
lavish VIP trips to China. [10BANGKOK269]
```

The cables anxiously reveal Thai concerns with how the 2007–08 Great Recession "would severely limit the ability of the US to influence global economic affairs and to dedicate the budget necessary to maintain its military advantage in the [Southeast Asian] region," while other Thai sources "suggested that a fascination in Washington with Indonesia and Vietnam would likely lead to continued decreased interest/involvement in Thailand bilaterally." It also underscores the growing sophistication of Chinese diplomacy, with Chinese diplomats "fully fluent in Thai, led by the Chinese Ambassador, who has spent 17 years of his career posted here [Bangkok] and routinely makes local TV appearances." Alarmed by China's growing influence in Thailand, the cable calls for the US to take "more vigorous action to follow-up with sustained efforts to engage on issues that matter to the Thai [sic] and the region, not just what is perceived as the US's own agenda."

In the Philippines, arguably the closest US ally in the region, the cables reveal a careful and continuous survey of Beijing's courtship of Manila, especially under the Arroyo administration (2001–10). In a cable titled "More on Hu Jintao's Visit to the Philippines," the American embassy in Manila provides a thorough assessment, partly based on information provided by the Philippines' Department of Foreign Affairs, of the strategic implications of Chinese president Hu Jintao's visit to Manila:

```
President Hu's charm offensive in Manila does
not appear significantly different from that
in other ASEAN capitals. Better and broader
bilateral ties advance regional interests,
as other ASEAN members have also discovered.
However, the conservative Philippine defense
```

```
establishment—whose doctrine, equipment, and
training are all US-based—will be cautious so
as not to jeopardize its close relationship
with the United States military, especially
as it undertakes (with US help) fundamental
restructuring and continues to combat multiple
terrorist threats. [Philippine] Foreign
Secretary Romulo's upcoming visit to Washington
offers a timely opportunity further to discuss
the evolving PRC role in Asia and Philippine
perceptions of long-term Chinese goals.
[05MANILA2174]
```

In various cables, the US lost no opportunity to keep abreast of the latest developments in Philippine-China relations, as the two Asian countries moved into a "golden era" of bilateral relations in the mid 2000s. During this period, China offered multi-billion-dollar trade and investment deals, largely focused on infrastructural development, and pushed for "joint-development" schemes in the South China Sea's disputed geographical features, culminating in the tripartite Joint Maritime Seismic Undertaking agreement between the Philippines, China, and Vietnam. In a cable entitled "Joint Seismic Survey in South China Sea Makes Progress," the American Embassy in Manila cautiously welcomed the agreement as a timely confidence-building measure on the part of disputing parties:

```
The first phase of a joint seismic survey for
hydrocarbon deposits undertaken by the national
oil companies of the Philippines, China, and
Vietnam in an 143,000 square kilometer zone of
the South China Sea is near completion. After
its partners conducted a "reconnaissance" survey
of the entire zone, the Philippine National Oil
Corporation is now interpreting the initial
```

survey data, which it expects to finish by the
end of the year. Promising areas identified in the
first phase will be surveyed again more closely
in the second phase. If viable deposits are
ultimately found, a new agreement would be needed
to cover any joint development, which Philippine
sources predicted would be reserved for the three
national oil companies. The joint seismic survey
offers a good model for potential subsequent
cooperation on exploration and exploitation, and
fits neatly with Philippine goals of increased
interaction between ASEAN and China and the
promotion of confidence building measures. The
true test of the cooperative spirit, however,
will come when the parties may contemplate
extraction.

During the Bush administration (2001–09), China was able to
enhance its geopolitical and economic influence in Southeast Asia
dramatically. But the entry of the Obama administration, with its
more calibrated and proactive diplomatic strategy, coincided with
growing territorial tensions between China and its neighbors.
The more recent cables reflect growing regional anxiety over the
emergence of a more assertive and callous China in the post–Great
Recession period. In a diplomatic cable entitled "Stomp Around
and Carry a Small Stick: China's New 'Global Assertiveness,'"
the American embassy in Beijing explains growing international
criticisms of China's increasingly more aggressive diplomacy:

The harsh (per usual) PRC [People's Republic of
China] reaction to the recent US announcement
of arms sales to Taiwan and President Obama's
intention to meet with the Dalai Lama has focused
Chinese domestic attention on a phenomenon
already observed (and criticized) abroad: China's

```
muscle-flexing, triumphalism and assertiveness in
its diplomacy. Foreign diplomats note that China
is making no friends with its newly pugnacious
attitude, but the popular assessment of China's
stance, personified by the nationalistic,
jingoistic and Chinese Communist Party-affiliated
newspaper Global Times (Huanqiu Shibao), is "it's
about time." [10BEIJING383]
```

The cable explains that "numerous third-country diplomats, in their conversations with the US embassy staff in Beijing, have complained that dealing with China has become more difficult in the past year." More specifically, it notes that "Europeans have been the most vocal in their criticism," while "Indian and Japanese ambassadors voiced similar complaints." The cable analyzes the emergence of "ultra-nationalism" and jingoistic media in the country, exacerbating territorial tensions with neighboring countries.

In the Philippines, meanwhile, blossoming relations with China hit a snag, as maritime disputes and corruption scandals related to Chinese investments in the country undermined bilateral relations. In a cable titled "Limits of Chinese Soft Power in the Philippines," the US embassy in Manila examined the seeming unsustainability of Philippine-China rapprochement, while reiterating the firmly established American influence in the country:

```
China's soft-power diplomacy has recently
stumbled in the Philippines under a months-
long media barrage of corruption allegations and
scandal investigations. This has occurred against
the backdrop of a tenfold increase in bilateral
trade since 2000, increased security cooperation,
and the signing of dozens of bilateral agreements
in recent years. In spite of the influence wielded
by Filipinos of Chinese ancestry, recent scandals
```

```
have reawakened long-held views among Filipinos
that link ethnic Chinese to corrupt practices.
[08MANILA998]
```

Interestingly, the cable notes Washington's confidence that its supposed popularity among the Filipino populace and its self-proclaimed consistent commitment to good governance in the Philippines will ensure revitalized Philippine-China ties "do not imply a weakening of our strong bonds with the Philippines," and that the latent prejudice against China has been reinforced by Beijing's recent mishaps—significantly limiting the impact of China's soft power.[35]

A crucial indication of rising worries over China's renewed assertiveness was Singapore's decision to share its growing concerns with the American diplomats. For decades, Singapore sought a perfect balance between its relations with the US and China, serving as diplomatic intermediary between the two great powers. Singapore's paramount leader, Lee Kuan Yew, always maintained strong ties with the upper echelons of the Chinese Communist Party, even serving as a trusted advisor to luminaries such as Mao Zedong and Deng Xiaoping. Singapore also played a crucial role in facilitating China's efforts to improve relations with ASEAN countries, with Singaporean leaders repeatedly emphasizing the benign aspects of China's rise and downplaying concerns with its opaque political system and rapid military modernization program.[36] In a diplomatic cable titled "Singapore Takes Notice as China Becomes More Assertive," the American embassy in Singapore, after extensive discussions with leading local academics and journalists, aptly reflects the shifting regional attitude toward China in recent years:

```
Singapore hopes the United States will not back
down in the face of Chinese pressure because that
would encourage China to become increasingly
assertive in its dealings with other countries
```

on issues such as its claims in the South China
Sea. However, Singapore also fears a continued
escalation of tensions between the United States
and China, which Singapore believes would only
be bad for the region ... Singapore is concerned
that if China's new assertiveness causes the
United States to back down, China might take a
harder edge in its dealings with individual ASEAN
countries, especially in its effort to press its
claims in the South China Sea. [10SINGAPORE166]

Over the succeeding years, as the Obama administration's policy
of pivoting toward Asia gained pace, other Southeast Asian
states such as Malaysia, Indonesia, Vietnam, and even Thailand,
expressed their growing concerns—both in confidence and
publicly—with China's territorial assertiveness and diplomatic
inflexibility, despite Beijing's continued economic engagement
with the region.[37]

CONCERTED COORDINATION ON "ROGUE STATES"

In addition to China, the cables also reveal constant US efforts to
coax and cajole its Southeast Asian allies and strategic partners
into pressuring "rogue states" such as North Korea, Myanmar,
Sudan, and Iran.

While recognizing Indonesia's long history of non-aligned
foreign policy, and its efforts to serve as a diplomatic intermediary between the West and the Islamic world, the cables show
how Washington constantly sought Jakarta's support against
Iran's nuclear program. In the run-up to the imposition of puni-
tive Western sanctions against Tehran in late 2011, a cable
entitled "Iran—Mobilizing Pressure on the Nuclear Issue," the
US embassy in Jakarta, in conversations with Indonesian diplomat Andy Rachmianto, deputy director for international security
and disarmament affairs at the department of foreign affairs,

underlines the close degree of coordination between the two countries over Iran:

> [Rachmianto] welcomed [Washington's] continued
> consultation with Indonesia on Iran's nuclear
> program, [since] Indonesia was becoming
> frustrated with Iran's refusal to accept the
> IAEA and [P5+1] offers regarding nuclear fuel
> for peaceful uses, including the Tehran Research
> reactor. He promised that Indonesian officials
> would consider [Washington's] views about the
> need for new UNSC action. He expressed caution,
> however, that increased pressure on Iran could be
> counterproductive and make continued engagement
> more difficult. On a related note, Rachmianto
> told [the embassy] that Indonesia planned to seek
> election to the IAEA Board of Governors for 2011-
> 2012. [10JAKARTA152]

With respect to the Philippines, the cables reveal a greater level of bilateral coordination over the Iranian nuclear program. In a cable titled "Philippine Government Finds Iran Not Complying," the US embassy in Manila noted that Washington strongly encouraged the Philippines to question the supposedly peaceful nature of the Iranian nuclear program:

> [The embassy met with] Leah Ruiz, Director of the
> DFA's Office of United Nations and International
> Organizations, as part of an ongoing effort to
> encourage the Philippine government, as a member
> of the International Atomic Energy Agency Board
> of Governors, to pressure Iran to comply with its
> international obligations. Ruiz said the report
> from IAEA Director General ElBaradei demonstrated
> that Iran's cooperation in the implementation of

the Work Plan was inadequate … Ruiz assured [the
embassy] that the Philippine government believed
the report showed Iran had neither suspended
its proliferation-sensitive nuclear activities,
nor implemented the Additional Protocol.
[07MANILA3770]

In another cable, "Philippines Looks Ahead to Chairing NPT Review," the US embassy in Manila expresses its support for the Philippines' bid to chair the 2009 Nonproliferation Treaty Review Conference in New York, with Philippine foreign secretary Alberto Romulo underscoring his government's desire "to be helpful in furthering the two nations' shared non-proliferation agenda." Annoyed by the Non-Aligned Movement's diplomatic confrontation with Washington over the issue of nonproliferation, the cable gladly notes that "senior Philippine officials have expressed a clear desire to work with the US in achieving substantive NPT goals, including full compliance with Treaty provisions by all 190 Parties." Numerous cables suggest that Filipino officials consistently consulted with the US embassy in Manila over the Philippines' positions on the NPT issues in multiple international forums, from the NAM to the UN General Assembly and the IAEA. A similar level of coordination was extended to NPT- and humanitarian-related issues in such places as North Korea and Sudan. For instance, in a cable titled "Pressing Philippines on Sudan Special Rapporteur," the US embassy in Manila noted that it had urged the Philippine government to "support a one-year extension of the Special Rapporteur position for Sudan, without any watering down of the Special Rapporteur's mandate," with top Filipino diplomats "fully understanding our deep concern and pledg[ing] to raise the issue with other senior officials at DFA, including the Assistant Secretary for the UN and International Organizations (UNIO)."

On Myanmar, also known as Burma, the cables also reveal Washington's efforts to encourage ASEAN countries, especially treaty allies such as the Philippines and Thailand, to lobby for political reform. While the Bush administration was largely focused on isolating and punishing the military junta, the Obama administration, in contrast, showed greater appreciation for ASEAN's preference for a more gradualist advocacy of democratization in the country. In a cable entitled "Urging Asean to Press Burma: Philippines Response," the US embassy in Manila reflects Washington's satisfaction with the Philippines' position on Burma, top Filipino diplomats stating that "the Philippines would remain solidly with the US on Burma and was ready to help in any way possible." It also reflects ASEAN's satisfaction with the Burma policy review, which underscored the Obama administration's more collaborative approach with regional partners in pushing for political reform in the country [09MANILA2230].

With respect to Thailand, in a cable titled "Thailand to Push for Dialogue in Burma," the US embassy in Bangkok reports:

> During a meeting with MFA Permanent Secretary
> Theerakun Niyom, the Ambassador reviewed
> US policy towards Rangoon and emphasized
> the important role [Thailand] could play in
> encouraging broad and inclusive political
> dialogue in Burma. The Permanent Secretary
> expressed agreement, and signaled that [his
> government] would work closely with the US to
> press for inclusive, free, and fair elections in
> Burma this year. [10BANGKOK86]

As the cables reveal, US engagement with the region was not confined to individual nation-state partners, but extended to the secretary general of the ASEAN organization itself. In a cable entitled "ASEAN Sec-Gen Surin Discusses ASEAN, Burma," the US embassy in Bangkok explained its direct engagements with the ASEAN secretary general, Surin Pitsuwan, a Thai national, on critical issues concerning, among other things, Myanmar.

The cable covered discussions on the humanitarian crisis in the aftermath of Cyclone Nargis in Myanmar in 2008, which eventually prompted the military regime to seek external assistance and agree to special mechanisms such as the post–Cyclone Nargis Tripartite Core Group (TCG), composed of the government of Myanmar, the UN, and ASEAN. In the cable, Surin told the American embassy that he "hoped that the ASEAN-brokered presence [in Myanmar] and [humanitarian] activities would remain meaningful, not just diplomatic cover [merely a public relations maneuver for ASEAN]," and sought to "expand the TCG mechanism beyond the cyclone-affected Delta and to broaden its mandate to include policy issues to make assistance sustainable." The ASEAN general secretary also "stressed that an ASEAN-led mechanism like the TCG had advantages for Burma as chair, and he expected the Burmese to be pragmatic in relation to deliverables. He added that several other new ASEAN members [a reference to Laos, Cambodia, and Vietnam] remained reluctant to allow ASEAN a sustained role in Burma for fear of the precedent it would set." There were also discussions on the plight of the Rohingya Muslim minority group in Myanmar, which has been heavily marginalized in recent years. Surin urged his American counterparts not to regard the issue in religious terms (and by extension fear the possibility of a new Muslim insurgency), but instead treat it as a "humanitarian issue." In response, the US embassy stated: "if ASEAN wanted to be taken seriously," it needed to play a more decisive role to address such humanitarian issues [09BANGKOK454]. In short, the US partly tried to place the blame on ASEAN's institutional deficiencies for any shortfall in humanitarian-related activities, implying that the success of any future coordination between the US and ASEAN would depend largely on the political will of Southeast Asian leaders to enhance the capabilities of the regional body.

COUNTER-TERRORISM OPERATIONS

With the global war on terror (GWOT) representing a top priority of the Bush administration, it comes as no surprise that the cables reveal a high degree of coordination between Washington and its regional allies, especially the Philippines, on counter-terrorism operations. Washington consistently pushed other Southeast Asian countries, such as Malaysia and Indonesia, to cooperate closely on counter-terrorism operations, stepping up joint exercises, sharing intelligence, and more vigorously cracking down on extremist groups in the region. But the highly unpopular wars in Afghanistan and Iraq consistently undermined bilateral relations between Washington and Muslim-majority countries such as Malaysia and Indonesia, the leaders of which openly opposed the Bush administration's unilateral interventions in the Middle East. Among Southeast Asian states, the Philippines had the deepest level of strategic and tactical cooperation with the Bush administration, and subsequently with the Obama administration.

The cables reveal American participation in directing and facilitating the Philippines' counter-terrorism operations, specifically in the southern island of Mindanao, which experienced an uptick in insurgency-related violence as well as an upsurge of activity by extremist groups in the first decade of the twenty-first century. In a cable titled "Fighting the GWOT in the Philippines," the US embassy in Manila provided a gloomy assessment of the security situation in Mindanao:

```
Terrorism is a disturbingly ordinary, ongoing
reality here. The southern Philippines lies along
a strategic fault line in the global campaign
against terrorism, with its porous borders,
weak rule of law, long-standing and unaddressed
grievances of Muslim minorities, and high levels
of poverty and corruption offering a fertile
field for nurturing terrorist groups. Only
```

Afghanistan in the Nineties had a mix of elements
more conducive to the spread of radical Islamic
movements and the safeguarding of terrorists.
[05MANILA1614]

The cable argues that terrorism in the Philippines is "arguably
more dangerous in the long-term in the [country] than anywhere [else] in East Asia," the southern island of Mindanao
hosting four groups on the US Foreign Terrorist Organizations
list, namely the New People's Army (the armed wing of the
Philippine communist insurgency), the Abu Sayyaf Group (ASG),
the Pentagon Gang, and Jemaah Islamiya. Noting the inefficacy
of the Philippine government in dealing with the crisis, the cable
essentially recommended that the US government overhaul the
Philippine counter-terror state apparatus by conducting the following projects:

Comprehensive "Management Assessment of the
Philippine Police" … development of a fusion
model involving [Royal Military Academy
Sandhurst], other relevant Embassy offices, and
concerned USG [US Government] elements to provide
embedded USG analysts at a single GRP [Government
of the Repiblic of the Philippines] counterpart
agency, to be selected from among the current
proliferation of GRP Task Forces and Centers;
USG assistance to redress inefficiencies in the
Philippine judicial system that make prosecution
of terrorist suspects at best a long-term
struggle; technical assistance to develop high-
security jail facilities for holding terrorist
suspects, some of whom have, notoriously, escaped
Philippine prisons; an expanded ATA [Anti-
Terrorism Assistance] program focused on the
Philippines' Anti-terrorism Task Force (ATTF)

under Malacanang Palace (the President's Office).
[05MANILA1614]

In another cable, titled "Staying Engaged with Counterterrorism Cooperation," the US embassy in Manila argued that "US counterterrorism assistance, ranging from operations/intelligence fusion support for the Armed Forces of the Philippines (AFP) to RMAS' involvement with the Philippine National Police (PNP), has helped the Philippines register some counterterrorism successes in 2004 and 2005." Noting the US government's "tremendous access" to counter-terror operations, the cable insisted that "continued, sustained engagement is needed if we want to ensure that the [Philippine government] turns the corner on terrorism" [05MANILA2590].

Perhaps most controversial of all—given the Philippines' constitutional restrictions on the establishment of permanent US bases and the activities of foreign troops in the country—were multiple cables suggesting direct US involvement in combat operations against terrorist groups in Mindanao. In a cable titled "AFP Anti-Terrorism Operations Advance on Jolo," the US embassy admits that, during an offensive by the Armed Forces of the Philippines (AFP) against Jemaah Islamiya and ASG leaders in Jolo, Mindanao, US Special Forces troops and vessels provided "intelligence, surveillance, and reconnaissance support to the 87-plus maritime interdictions" conducted in the operation area. This was all possible, the cable shows, due to the full integration of combat units from US Navy's Joint Venture and Joint Special Operations Task Force—Philippines (JSOTF-P) into the Philippine Navy. The cable also suggested that US officials deny direct American participation in combat operations by insisting that they were only in a "support role" to "advise, train, and share information with AFP forces" [06MANILA3401].

In another cable, titled "October 20 Update on Jolo Operations," the US embassy noted the close collaboration between Philippine and US forces in hunting down a leading terrorist suspect, Umar Patek, in a 2006 combat operation in Jolo:

> Significantly, on the night of October 17, US and Philippine forces worked seamlessly to intercept two vessels (one of them high-speed) attempting to flee Jolo for Basilan. Following reports that Umar Patek may have been trying to escape, US P-3 aircraft; Joint Task Force 515 helicopters and unmanned aerial vehicles; and Joint Special Operations Task Force-Philippines (JSOTF-P) MK-V vessels shadowed the two boats and vectored an intercept by Philippine Navy and Philippine National Police Maritime Group units. Although Patek was not on board, the speedboat was found to belong to a known ASG logistician, and was piloted by his brother. [06MANILA4439]

In a cable titled "AFP/DND Talks Produce Progress on Counterterrorism," the US embassy in Manila discussed the extensive consultation between the two governments to ensure the optimal participation of US forces in combat operations without explicitly violating constitutional restrictions on foreign troops' activities on Philippine soil:

> Norman Daanoy, Chief of the [Department of National Defense] Office of Legal Affairs, in a January 13 legal brief to Secretary Cruz, argued that, while prohibited from engaging in combat except in self-defense, US forces in the Philippines could engage in a range of "combat-related activities," to include providing intelligence, surveillance, and reconnaissance support to the AFP … DND staff separately said they recognized the need to build backing for

```
the initiative, and planned to launch a public
communications effort entitled "Freedom from
Fear" that would demonstrate the benefits of
enhanced US-RP counterterrorism cooperation.
[05MANILA286]
```

*   *   *

A key pillar of the Obama administration's policy of pivoting toward Asia was the introduction of the Trans-Pacific Partnership (TPP) free trade agreement, covering twelve Pacific Rim countries, and about 40 percent of the world's economy.[38] According to the cables, this initiative may have been inspired by earlier proposals by Singapore's long-time leader Lee Kuan Yew. In late 2007, in a cable titled "Lee Kuan Yew on Burma's 'Stupid' Generals and the 'Gambler' Chen Shui-bian" [07SINGAPORE1932_a], the Singaporean minister mentor "urged the United States to pursue more Free Trade Agreements to give the region options besides China," lest Beijing leverage its economic prowess to displace American influence in Southeast Asia altogether.

By excluding China, Asia's biggest economy, the TPP represented a thinly veiled attempt by the Obama administration to regain Washington's economic centrality in the Pacific theater, containing Beijing's economic dominance in East Asia. Of the ASEAN members, Singapore, Malaysia, Brunei, and Vietnam were among the parties involved in the TPP negotiations. But much of the negotiation and the content of the proposed trading agreement were shrouded in mystery. Thanks to WikiLeaks, however, it soon became clear that the TPP was a free-trade agreement designed to empower (American) multinational corporations at the expense of the welfare of consumers, especially those in the developing world. On November 13, 2013, WikiLeaks released the TPP's secret negotiated draft text of the chapter on intellectual property rights. Interestingly, the draft even shows the negotiating position of individual countries on specific provisions of the proposed deal. For instance, US opposition to the inclusion of certain diseases subject to protection by national health and safety considerations is stated in Article QQ.A.5: "The obligations of this Chapter do not and should not prevent a Party from taking measures to protect public health by promoting access to medicines for all, in particular concerning cases such as HIV/AIDS, tuberculosis, malaria ... and other epidemics as well as circumstances of extreme urgency or national emergency."[39]

Taken together, the leaks show that the US and Japan are among the most isolated parties in the negotiations, often failing to garner support from other parties on varying provisions, while the Southeast Asian states of Singapore and Malaysia enjoyed the highest degree of support on many of their negotiating positions.[40] The TPP negotiations, which missed their late 2013 deadline for conclusion, have entered a protracted stalemate, with the two leading negotiating parties locked in major disagreements: Japan and the US have squabbled over the former's trade barriers on agricultural imports (rice, wheat, and sugar), restrictions on the import of pork and beef, and the opening of Japanese markets to American automobile manufacturers. Bilateral trade talks virtually collapsed in late September 2014, with Akira Amari, Japan's economy minister, storming out of talks in Washington with his American counterpart.[41]

The leaked documents revealed the aggressive US pursuit of its aims of privatizing public services in the Asian markets, protecting the intellectual property rights of multinational firms at the expense of consumer welfare, and enhancing the legal power of private firms to sue individual governments, further undermining support for the TPP among ASEAN countries such as Malaysia and Vietnam. It is little wonder that the TPP failed to meet its finalization target in late 2013, with the Obama administration still struggling to gain both domestic and international support to fast-track the negotiations.

The cables also show Washington's efforts at soliciting regional support on non-traditional security issues, such as the environment, especially with the international community calling for greater American commitment to climate change–related mitigation and adaptation measures. For instance, in a cable titled "Philippines Concurs with US Views Regarding UN," the US embassy in Manila noted:

> Officials at the Philippine Department of Foreign Affairs (DFA) Office of United Nations and Other International Organizations (UNIO) welcomed our thoughts on the Pacific Small Island Developing States (PSIDS) proposed resolution on Climate Change that would call for a UN Security Council resolution on the subject … UNIO Assistant Director G. Marie Concha for the Environment, Science and Technology said on August 20 that the DFA had not reached a final position but "was moving in the direction" of the US position. [08MANILA1981]

In another cable, "Philippines Appears to Moderate Pre-Copenhagen Climate Change Stance," the embassy in Manila reported the Philippines' decision to adopt a more "pragmatic position" on greenhouse gas emissions, "calling for mandatory cuts for 'all the big boys, including China,' instead of its earlier calls [for] 'deep and early cuts' by developed countries." Relishing the Philippines' shift in its negotiating position ahead of the historic 2009 Climate Conference in Copenhagen, the cable described a unique opportunity for Washington to "engage a moderate and influential G77 member in substantive discussions on global actions" [09MANILA2483].

By evincing the most intimate (and cynical) exchanges among the members of the US diplomatic core, and revealing the extent of quasi-espionage conducted by American diplomats, who were instructed to gather confidential information from their counterparts in the United Nations,[42] the WikiLeaks documents caused unprecedented embarrassment for Washington. Among Southeast Asian leaders, Indonesian president Susilo Bambang Yudhoyono was angered by US diplomatic cables—which implicated his wife in corruption schemes and suggested the president had abused his power—dismissing them as "character assassination."[43]

Nevertheless, the leaked cables have not dramatically altered Washington's position in the region. A combination of rising concerns over China's territorial assertiveness and a continued belief (among some allies and strategic partners, such as the Philippines and Vietnam) in the US role in supposedly ensuring regional stability has allowed the Obama administration to push ahead with its policy of pivoting toward Asia without much resistance among ASEAN states. In fact, many ASEAN countries have stepped up their strategic cooperation with Washington, including non-treaty allies such as Myanmar, Malaysia, and Vietnam, due to their desire to diversify their foreign relations and reduce their dependence on China.[44] If anything, many ASEAN countries, from the Philippines to Singapore, have sought even greater American commitment to the region.[45] It seems that considerations of national interest have tempered regional responses to and anger at the WikiLeaks revelations, with many Southeast Asian countries still willing to push the envelope and welcome a greater American strategic footprint in the region.

16. South Africa

Francis Njubi Nesbitt

The WikiLeaks cables that were published in 2010 provide evidence of a consistent and aggressive effort by diplomats to promote US security and corporate interests in southern Africa. For decades, colonial and white-minority regimes were portrayed as natural allies of the United States because they were staunch anticommunists at a time when black African states were forging stronger ties with the Soviet Union, China, and Cuba. This policy agenda is evident in Republican and Democratic administrations, and cuts across ideological lines.

In fact, the policy dates back to the early years of the Cold War, when the Truman administration cast its lot with odious but useful allies in countries such as Iran, Chile, Portugal, Guatemala, and South Africa. The overarching goal was to promote US business and security interests; human rights concerns were lesser considerations in the making of foreign policy.

During the Eisenhower administration, Richard Nixon himself toured Africa and recommended that the US support pro-business nationalists in newly independent African countries. He also argued that the US corporations in South Africa should be allowed to set policies on discrimination and inequality without government intervention. A leaked National Security Study Memorandum (NSSM 39) from the early Nixon years revealed the details of his policy toward southern Africa: publicly deplore apartheid while secretly facilitating corporate and security ties.

White-minority regimes were considered natural allies in the Cold War.

The series of cables under review covers the ensuing media firestorm, and documents the State Department's efforts to counter the international blowback. The cables feature State Department officials seeking direction on how to respond to questions about US foreign policy during the Kissinger years. An October 1974 cable, for instance, covers a State Department briefing about a *Washington Post* article tiled "Kissinger's First Big Tilt." The Jack Anderson article, published on October 11, 1974, argued that Kissinger had convinced President Nixon to adopt a "secret tilt" toward white supremacist nations in southern Africa. According to Anderson, "Henry Kissinger guided president Nixon, in January 1970, along a tightrope between black and white Africa, with a secret tilt toward the white supremacist nations" [1974STATE225811_b].

The August 1969 NSC report argued that US interests in the region were not vital, but pointed out the need to contain the growing influence of the Soviet Union and China in independent Africa. "Racial oppression by minority regimes and black African opposition to it" posed two problems for US interests in the area: first, US interests in the white states affected its credibility in Africa; and, second, the prospect of increased violence, "growing out of black insurgency," could jeopardize US interests.

It listed five foreign-policy options for the United States, ranging from disengagement to an alliance with white-minority regimes. Kissinger advocated "option two" which suggested the United States "balance its economic, scientific, and strategic interests in the white states with the political interests dissociating the US from white regimes and their repressive racial policies." The report concluded: "The whites are here to stay and the only way that constructive change can come about is through them." The policy option suggested that the US relax sanctions against white regimes to "encourage some modification of their racial and colonial policies."

During the October 12, 1974 briefing, officials acknowledged the existence of NSSM 39 but denied that the administration had adopted "Option Two" in a "secret tilt" toward the colonial and white-minority regimes.

Questions during the briefing focused on two main issues raised by anti-apartheid activists: relations with Rhodesia and arms shipments to Portuguese Africa. Reporters grilled US officials about the implementation of United Nations–imposed sanctions on Rhodesia after its white-minority regime, led by Ian Smith, had issued a unilateral declaration of independence (UDI) from Britain in 1965. The mandatory sanctions required member states to cut diplomatic, military, and business ties with the regime. US officials argued that the US cut diplomatic relations with the white-minority regime in accordance with UN sanctions, but were unable to explain why the consulate in Salisbury remained open between 1965 and 1970.

By 1970, it had become clear that the Nixon administration would maintain the status quo in southern Africa. In line with NSSM 39's recommendations, Nixon relaxed sanctions against Rhodesia and approved legislation allowing the importation of Rhodesian chrome.[1] This policy violated UN sanctions against the UDI regime and angered both African Americans and African states.[2]

Nixon also continued to provide military assistance to Portugal, despite African opposition. The Africans argued that US aid would release Portuguese resources for use against liberation movements in Angola and Mozambique. They also argued that Portugal had used NATO airplanes to bombard civilians in southern Africa. The Africans argued that the US had sacrificed the principle of self-determination for the sake of maintaining its rights to the Azores base, which was no longer necessary for refueling airplanes.[3]

At the United Nations, the US shifted to openly supporting South Africa in Security Council deliberations. During the Kennedy-Johnson years, the US frequently abstained on votes about colonial issues. After 1969, however, the US often aligned itself with South Africa and Portugal in votes against decoloniza-tion. On November 22, 1969, for instance, the *New York Times* reported that the United States had voted against a resolution condemning apartheid "for the first time in years." In a change of rhetoric and policy, the US suddenly insisted that South Africa was not a threat to international peace and did not warrant sanc-tions. In the 1972 General Assembly, the US voted negatively on seven out of eight resolutions on southern Africa. On October 30, 1974, the US, France, and Britain vetoed a Security Council resolution to expel South Africa from the United Nations. A month later, the US cast the only vote against a more stringent arms embargo.

The South African regime was grateful for the support. A 1973 cable, for instance, quotes an interview with South African prime minister John Vorster praising the Nixon administration in striking Cold War language:

```
During interview with South African journalist
March 8, PM Vorster said SAG had cordial
relations with United States and Britain. He said
that notwithstanding statements which were made
about these countries' use of their influence with
SA, ambassadors concerned had not meddled in
South African affairs. He expressed admiration
for president Nixon who, he said, deserved
cooperation of all non-communist nations. He said
president Nixon "has a terrific job to do," for he
carries great responsibility "on behalf of all of
us in the free world." [1973CAPET00187_b]
```

THE CARTER YEARS

The Carter years brought a new emphasis on human rights in US foreign policy. Carter opposed the Nixon administration's policy of overlooking human rights abuses in countries ruled by US allies. He rejected the Nixon administration's policy of fighting fire with fire, equating it with adopting "the flawed and erroneous principles and tactics of our adversaries, sometimes abandoning our own values for theirs." He argued that this was a failed policy, "with Vietnam the best example of its intellectual and moral poverty."

Carter argued that his foreign policy was based on an historical vision of the US role in a changing world: "Our policy is rooted in our moral values, which never change. Our policy is reinforced by our material wealth and by our military power. Our policy is designed to serve mankind."

These policies were reflected in Carter's Foreign Service appointments. Secretary of State Cyrus Vance practiced affirmative action, increasing the proportion of minorities from 6 to 11 percent and of women from 10 to 14 percent in the Foreign Service. Black ambassadors, a rarity during the Nixon years, were appointed to serve all over the world, not just in black states. By the end of his term, Carter had appointed a record fourteen black ambassadors.

These changes were epitomized by the appointment of civil rights leader Andrew Young as the country's ambassador to the United Nations in 1977.[4] Diplomats at the State Department seemed to take a particular interest in Ambassador Young's stormy career. In January 1977, Kissinger himself forwarded a summary of then-Congressman Young's interview on *Meet the Press* [1977STATE000828_c].

During the interview, Young signaled strong support for "majority rule" in Rhodesia and Namibia, and in South Africa itself. According to Young, this new policy favoring majority rule was a departure from the Nixon years that he hoped would lead to a new era of cooperation with African states at the United Nations. But he rejected African calls for sanctions against South Africa, claiming that they had "seldom worked."[5]

During his tenure, he was criticized for meeting with leaders of the Palestinian Liberation Organization, supporting Robert Mugabe of Zimbabwe, and making undiplomatic comments about South Africa.[6] Young was eventually forced to resign, in 1979, after he defied protocol and met with PLO officials despite US assurances to Israel.[7]

This new focus on human rights and majority rule was deeply resented in South Africa. Just six months into Carter's tenure, South African prime minister Vorster wrote Carter a letter filled with threats, innuendo, and resentment: "Over the last six months we have become convinced that your administration is determined to impose upon South Africa prescriptions for the arrangement of her internal structure which you have found to be most appropriate for the United States" [1977PRETOR06374_c]. Vorster warned that pressure for majority rule from the United States would be counterproductive and increase violence in the region. The letter alluded repeatedly to the threat of destabilization from "outside the region."

The cables from the Carter years include a series of accounts of the administration's support for a corporate responsibility agenda. Diplomats went out of their way to provide support to voluntary efforts by US-based companies to reduce inequality in the workplace. UN ambassador Andrew Young captured the Carter doctrine early on when he signaled that corporations would play a major role in the campaign against apartheid. The cables highlight the Polaroid Experiment, one of the earliest attempts to implement the corporate responsibility agenda [1977JOHANN03086_c]. The diplomats followed the experiment closely through media and firsthand reports. Although the Polaroid Experiment failed to improve conditions for black workers, it became a model for corporate responsibility. In one of the cables, an official named Johnson criticizes his boss, Secretary of State Vance, for expressing his support for corporate responsibility in South Africa.

There is also a particular focus on the activities of corporate responsibility advocate and General Motors director Rev. Leon

Sullivan [1977STATE045121_c]. Like the Carter administration, Sullivan was opposed to economic sanctions. Instead, he advocated a series of reforms that included higher pay and training for black workers. The cables indicate open State Department support for Sullivan, a civilian who was not associated with the diplomatic service. This reformist agenda enraged an increasingly radical anti-apartheid movement that refused to accept half-measures.[8]

"CONSTRUCTIVE" ENGAGEMENT

The 1980s were crucial years for the anti-apartheid movement, when South Africa was embroiled in an all-out civil war. July 1985 saw the introduction of broad government powers to arrest and detain suspects indefinitely without trial, censor media organizations, put civilians under surveillance, and move populations at will. The death rate from such incidents increased fivefold, from 100 in 1984 to 500 in 1985. In 1985, the State Security Council (SSC), the most powerful security body in the country, called on the troops to gun down leaders of demonstrations.[9] The South African Defense Force also conducted frequent military incursions into neighboring states that it accused of harboring dissidents and "terrorists."

By the 1980s, most countries at the United Nations had imposed political, economic, and military sanctions on the South African regime. The exceptions were the Western countries of Britain, France, and the United States, all of which argued that sanctions would hurt black Africans most. The Reagan administration reverted to Nixon's "tilt" toward white-minority regimes in southern Africa. Reagan's "constructive engagement" policy was very similar to Nixon's policy of "communication" with the white-minority regimes in southern Africa. The policy provided incentives, such as foreign investment and diplomatic support, rather than sanctions. The cables document diplomats' efforts to defend these policies. A January 1985 cable, for instance, defends the Reagan administration's "constructive engagement" policy [1985GABORONE97_a]. It was written in response to reports in the African press that the US was supporting South Africa's military incursions into neighboring states.

By the mid 1980s the system of apartheid was under siege. Internally, the country was becoming ungovernable, while international pressure was relentless. In the United States, a vigorous anti-apartheid movement demanded that cities, states, pension funds, banks, and universities divest themselves of shares in companies doing business in South Africa. In 1985, Citibank announced that it would no longer provide South Africa with loans.[10] Later that year, Chase Manhattan refused to roll over short-term credit, demanding that South Africa repay its debts in full. Other banks followed suit. This was a major blow to the South African economy. The country's business community, which bore the brunt of international sanctions, was also demanding reforms. By the mid 1980s, negotiations had become inevitable. The beginning of the end came in October 1986, when the US Congress passed the Comprehensive Anti-Apartheid Act (CAA) over President Reagan's veto.[11]

As the campaign for majority rule gained momentum, a confidential November 1987 cable praised the South African government for releasing Govan Mbeki, a former Communist Party leader, from prison, speculating that the freeing of political prisoners was designed to create space for dialogue with moderate black leaders, and partly also an attempt to avoid the deaths of aged ANC patriarchs in prison [1987PRETORIA17012_a].

The cable stressed that the South African government was aware that the "situation was stumbling head over heels toward some sort of catastrophe," and that a gesture of some kind was needed to "break up the momentum." The cable concludes that the prisoner release was designed to set the stage for dialogue with "credible black leaders" such as Buthelezi, the leader of Inkatha, a Zulu nationalist organization.

A subsequent secret cable discussing a November 1989 meeting between the ANC's International Department director, Thabo Mbeki, and Assistant Secretary Warren Clark highlights the differences between the US and the ANC [1989STATE368870_a]. In a contentious meeting, Mbeki made it clear that the ANC did not consider Buthelezi a "credible black leader," partly because of his refusal to denounce attacks on ANC activists in Natal province. Mbeki also refused to give credit to the South African president at the time, F. W. de Klerk, for ongoing reforms including the release of political prisoners. Mbeki argued that de Klerk was responding to local and international pressure.

Clark made it clear that the US would not accept language that designated the ANC as the sole representative of the South African people. He also insisted that language referring to sanctions was "unacceptable," despite the Comprehensive Anti-Apartheid Act that had become law in 1986. Mbeki appeared to acquiesce to both US demands.

By the early 1990s, internal unrest and international sanctions brought the apartheid regime to the brink of collapse. In response, the de Klerk regime was forced to release political prisoners and legalize opposition movements such as the African National Congress. The release in February 1990 of ANC leader Nelson Mandela epitomized this momentum toward majority rule. The growing unrest and clamor for change are reflected in a March 1990 cable, for instance, that transcribes a speech delivered in Durban by the US ambassador, which vividly reflects the contentious relations between the African nationalists led by Mandela and the Bush administration. The ambassador emphasized that the US continued to oppose apartheid but vowed that the US would reject any settlement that was not acceptable to all parties [90CAPETOWN623_a]. The ambassador noted that President Bush had invited both F. W. de Klerk and Nelson Mandela to the White House. He took time to praise de Klerk for releasing political prisoners, and called on US allies in Europe to support the South African prime minister. The speech underscores the Bush administration's tilt toward the white-minority regime. The ambassador clearly signaled the Bush administration's ambivalence about the US sanctions mandated by the Comprehensive Anti-Apartheid Act of 1986 and 1988. His boss, George Bush, had opposed both pieces of legislation as vice president in the Reagan administration.

The Clinton administration established a closer relationship with South Africa. This is reflected in the diplomats' unusual interest in Thabo Mbeki, the presumed successor to Nelson Mandela. In March 1995, for example, in a confidential intelligence assessment, the INR posited that Thabo Mbeki would probably succeed Mandela as ANC leader and thus as the next South African president [1995STATE51417_a].

The report describes Mbeki as a "moderate" but warns that "growing rifts within the ANC will increasingly test Mbeki's leadership." One of these rifts is between moderates, led by Mbeki and Mandela, and "party militants." The report attributes the rise of the militants to widespread frustration over the pace of reforms. Among the "populists" named are Winnie Mandela, Peter Makoba, Bantu Holomisa, and Rocky Malebane-Metsing, who argue for a radical redistribution of resources. This message reportedly appealed to the poorest South Africans, including squatters, peasants, the unemployed, and marginalized youth.

Another confidential assessment titled "Thabo Mbeki: The Man Who Would Be President," took an in-depth look at Mbeki's character [1995PRETORIA5893_a]. It argued that, though Mbeki's image "appear[ed] a bit tarnished" by his handling of scandals involving Winnie Mandela and Allan Boesak, he nonetheless remained the most likely successor to Mandela. Mbeki is described as "self-assured, articulate and charismatic," but inefficient and ill-advised. The generally positive evaluation of Mbeki's administration reflects the close relations between South Africa and the United States during the Clinton years. Mbeki was considered a key asset in the implementation of US foreign policy in southern Africa.

RELATIONS SOUR

The administration of George W. Bush had a less sanguine relationship with South Africa's leadership. A 2001 cable referred to Mbeki as "thin skinned" and questioned his judgment on the HIV/AIDS issue [2001PRETORIA1173_a]. The cable also criticizes Mbeki for failing to "speak out on human rights and rule of law violations taking place in Mugabe's Zimbabwe." The cable reflects a growing resentment toward Mbeki's administration, questioning his loyalty to cabinet ministers—who are described variously as "AIDS denier," "petulant," and "truculent." Mbeki himself is described as inclined to "shrillness" and "defensiveness," despite his "widely acknowledged" intelligence. The cable nonetheless recommends that Washington accommodate this "brilliant, prickly leader of Africa's most important state."

The Mugabe issue was a particular sticking point. By 2000, Mugabe had become the bogeyman of the Western media establishment because he stood accused of encouraging former liberation fighters to invade white-owned farms. In 2008, at the behest of the United States, Thabo Mbeki was asked to mediate, but Mbeki proved a huge disappointment to the Bush administration. He supported the African Union's position that Mugabe was the legitimate leader of Zimbabwe and refused to throw Mugabe under the bus. These tensions are evident in Mbeki's recent statements accusing British prime minister Tony Blair of plotting an invasion of Zimbabwe.

Another confidential cable titled "The End of the ANC Intellectual?" blames Mbeki for killing intellectualism in the African National Congress [2008PRETORIA2715_a]. According to analysts contacted by the embassy, the ANC was no longer a standard-bearer for intellectualism: "The days of Sisulu, Tambo, Mandela, Mbeki, Slovo, and Hani are over, and they have been over for a long time," the author noted. The cable argued that many intellectuals had left party politics because of Mbeki's "top down leadership style"—an authoritarianism seen as a threat to the ANC's history of intellectual excellence.

This portrait of a declining ANC includes a damning assessment of a new generation of leaders, such as Jacob Zuma and Julius Malema. In an assessment of Mbeki's successor, for instance, analysts judged that Zuma's poor judgment in his personal and professional life raised questions about his leadership skills and effectiveness in promoting South Africa's future foreign policy agenda. The cables argued that the ascendancy of leaders such as Malema raised questions about the party's reputation as a fount of ideas, depicting Malema as "uneducated" and "unpolished." Several assessments of the newly elected President Zuma depicted him as a "country bumpkin," whose appeal was the "dumbing down of the ANC's intellectual traditions even more than what happened under Mbeki." They identify the emergence of a "cult of personality" surrounding Zuma as a sure indicator of anti-intellectualism in the ANC. A second risk factor identified was the struggle over "who should have access to state patronage mechanisms."

This concern with the democratization process has continued into the Obama era. A January 2010 cable, for instance, asked whether the ANC was as "democratic" as it claimed to be [2010DURBAN3_a]. The cable examines the ruling party's forceful ejection of slum-dwellers, in a policy eerily reminiscent of the apartheid regime. In a cable designated "unclassified, for official use only," analysts suggested that the ANC was using tactics deployed by the apartheid regime—though conceding that the realities of development would have forced the South African government to relocate the slum-dwellers to the "rural periphery."

In the final analysis, the cables confirm suspicions of a consistent US policy in southern Africa that cuts across ideological lines. Both Democratic and Republican governments have emphasized security and corporate interests at the expense of human rights. Even the Carter and Clinton administrations continued to prioritize corporatism, despite their attention to human rights. So far, the same can be said of the Obama years.

17. Latin America and the Caribbean

Alexander Main, Jake Johnston, and Dan Beeton

In a speech at the Organization of American States (OAS) in 2013, US secretary of state John Kerry declared: "the era of the Monroe Doctrine is over." A nearly 200-year-old hemispheric policy conceived in theory to protect Latin America from foreign intervention but in practice used to justify countless US military invasions and deep internal meddling was, according to Kerry, a thing of the past. "The relationship that we seek," Kerry said, "and that we have worked hard to foster is not about a United States declaration about how and when it will intervene in the affairs of other American states. It's about all of our countries viewing one another as equals..."[1]

Much of the major English-language media coverage of the WikiLeaks cables on Latin America and the Caribbean support the thesis that the Monroe Doctrine has gone out of style, and that US diplomacy in the region is, nowadays, largely benign and non-interventionist. Many of the "revelations" highlighted in news outlets have focused on US foreign service officers' colorful and potentially embarrassing descriptions of heads of state or senior government officials. As a DC analyst told the *Washington Post*, the cables show "a strange preoccupation with the personal and mental health of leaders, but [do not] fit the stereotype of

America plotting coups and caring only about business interests and consorting with only the right wing."[2]

As this chapter will demonstrate, even a limited examination of the WikiLeaks cables on Latin America confirms that US interference in Latin American countries' internal political affairs remains, in fact, alive and well in the twenty-first century. The arch-enemy has changed—the Soviet Union has to some degree been replaced by the specter of Venezuelan Bolivarianism—but the goal remains the same: to use every means available to support Washington's friends and subvert its (perceived) foes.

What has evolved since the Cold War era are the mechanisms of US intervention, as the cables attest. From the early 1950s, when the CIA organized a military coup in Guatemala, to the 1980s, when the Reagan administration supported repressive military regimes with security assistance and counter-insurgency training, an alleged communist threat served to justify direct support for brutal dictatorships and the unconstitutional ousting of left-leaning governments. Starting in the late 1980s, as William I. Robinson,[3] Greg Grandin,[4] and other scholars have shown, Central America—particularly Nicaragua—served as a testing ground for new, softer methods of political intervention that, by the 1990s, had become standard practice.[5] As democratic regimes became the rule rather than the exception in the region, the US began organizing, funding, and training political organizations and networks of "civil society" entities generally aligned with US interests through the US Agency for International Development (USAID) and para-governmental organizations like the National Endowment for Democracy (NED).

WikiLeaks' cables for Latin America and the Caribbean show how US diplomatic missions coordinate closely with USAID country offices to pursue a desired course of political change. In some cases, senior US diplomats even provide direct guidance to political allies on how to cultivate a network of US-funded NGOs that can help them consolidate "civil society" support. The cables also provide evidence of the manner in which US embassies try to leverage unilateral and multilateral development aid so as to affect electoral outcomes and pressure governments into adopting acceptable policy agendas.

The cables show how US diplomats, in violation of Article 41 of the Vienna Convention on Diplomatic Relations, have worked to unify divided political groups opposed to governments the United States does not like, sought to mobilize campaign funding in favor of political allies, and even engaged in smear campaigns against candidates they oppose. As will be seen, the language used in these cables to characterize political figures and movements—for example, "democratic" and "anti-democratic," "good" and "bad" economic policies, and so on—reveal much more about the ideological framework within which US diplomats operate than about the actual characteristics of the people and organizations described.

As is the case with other parts of the world, the leaked cables for the region are mostly from the period between 2004 and 2009—a moment of profound political change for many Latin American countries. While soft US methods of intervention helped maintain right-wing, Washington-friendly political parties in power during the period of democratization of the 1990s, beginning in 1998 a tide of left-leaning candidates began winning elections, from the southern tip of South America to El Salvador. By 2009, the vast majority of Latin Americans—who had experienced an unprecedented economic growth failure for more than two decades[6] under governments that adhered to the neoliberal "Washington Consensus"—were living under governments that explicitly rejected many of these policies.

This chapter will examine the actions, recommendations, and observations of US diplomats in five countries, four of which saw left-wing political governments elected to power, and one of which experienced a US-backed coup that was followed by political violence and repression. The methods of intervention described above are all apparent in El Salvador, Nicaragua, Bolivia, and Ecuador, where US diplomatic missions sought to undermine left-leaning candidates and governments. In Haiti, the fifth country in our study, the strategies of intervention promoted and applied by the US embassy in Port-au-Prince appear to go far beyond what we see in other countries in the region.

This study is far from exhaustive. Though many of the cables cited here have not been previously referenced in the media, several were first noticed by researchers and journalists whom we acknowledge below.

Readers may ask why the two countries of the region that have had the most antagonistic relations with the US in recent years are absent from this survey. In Cuba, unlike other countries in the region, US policies of intervention and regime change, though opaque in their implementation, are a matter of lengthy public record. In the limited space reserved for Latin America and the Caribbean in this book, we focus here on countries for which the cables help reveal less overt and less publicized interventions.

Internal intervention in Venezuela—another country that experienced a US-backed coup in 2002—will be examined in detail in the following chapter, where we will also analyze cables that show how a policy of containment toward a supposed Venezuelan "threat" shaped US relations with other countries.

EL SALVADOR

From 1979 until 1992, El Salvador experienced a bloody civil war, pitting a repressive military regime against a broad-based insurrectionary movement called the Farabundo Martí National Liberation Front (FMLN, by its Spanish initials). The US government provided the Salvadoran army with training and hundreds of millions of dollars of assistance, despite abundant evidence of military involvement in death squads that murdered tens of thousands of unarmed civilians.

Cables from the US embassy in El Salvador show that in recent years US policy toward that country has focused on bolstering support for the Nationalist Republican Alliance (ARENA), a far-right party linked to the former military regime and death squads, and undermining the FMLN, which demobilized and became a political party after the war, eventually winning the presidency in 2009 and 2014.

In 2004, Antonio Saca, the fourth consecutive ARENA president, was elected. The Bush administration made no secret of its support for his candidacy and its intense opposition to FMLN candidate Schafik Handal. In a call with the Salvadoran press just days before the election, the assistant secretary of state for the Western Hemisphere, Otto Reich, could not have been clearer: "We are concerned about the impact that an FMLN victory would have on the commercial, economic and migration-related relations that the United States has with El Salvador."[7] Given the country's enormous economic dependence on the US—with 50 percent of the country's exports going to the US and remittances from Salvadoran emigrants reaching 18 percent of GDP—these statements were bound to have an impact on voters.

Saca's government would go on to be a key regional ally of the US, even sending troops to Iraq (the only Latin American government to do so). As the embassy cables show, to maintain this relationship, and to try to prevent the FMLN from taking office, the US would leverage its influence using aid programs and other mechanisms to support ARENA's candidates in the 2006 legislative elections.

Six months before the 2006 national legislative elections, Michael Butler, the US chargé d'affaires in San Salvador, laid out the embassy's strategy for supporting ARENA in a cable. He first noted:

```
The close US-El Salvador bilateral relationship
tends to further strengthen ARENA's hand in next
spring's elections. Newspapers have frequently
publicized USAID-funded projects in housing
construction for 2001 earthquake victims, potable
water supplies for poor rural communities, new
```

```
clinics and schools, agricultural and rural-sector
development finance through USDA, and other much-
needed social investment, and US assistance is
widely perceived to be a benefit of postwar ARENA
governments' close relationships with the US.

...

All of these projects and the close personal
relationship between Presidents Saca and Bush
provide the US with multiple opportunities
to continue to showcase the benefits of the
relationship, and to contrast El Salvador's
democratic parties with the FMLN's radicalism.
[05SANSALVADOR2507]
```

In the same cable, Butler states that everything indicates that the FMLN "has little money at this time to mount a robust national campaign, and clearly cannot match ARENA's resources," while "Saca and his ARENA team are impressive political operatives who know how to use the power and resources of the presidency to run an effective national campaign." Nevertheless, Butler suggests that the US provide additional support to ARENA's campaign by moving forward with a Millennium Challenge Corporation (MCC) compact, or aid grant: "Signing a compact with the MCC would also help legitimize ARENA's economic program by showing it carries concrete benefits." Two months after Butler wrote this cable, the US administration selected El Salvador as eligible for MCC assistance.[8]

In the years that followed, the Salvadoran economy performed badly, with poverty increasing from 34.6 percent to 40 percent between 2007 and 2008.[9] In 2009, presidential elections were held in the midst of a sharp economic downturn resulting from El Salvador's acute exposure to the US recession. Six months before-hand, the US embassy had outlined a plan to bolster the ailing incumbent government. The strategy again involved deploy-ing banner projects from the development-assistance arsenal, and also deliberate, if discreet, proactive measures to support ARENA. In its initial assessment of ARENA's beleaguered campaign, a cable from US ambassador Charles Glazer to the secretary of state noted, despite the recession and prior sluggish growth:

> Simply playing on the fear of economic
> catastrophe in the event of an FMLN victory will
> not win the election for ARENA, which must play
> up its own positive record. The country has made
> remarkable economic progress and ARENA should be
> trumpeting those advances. ARENA needs to draw a
> direct link between the economic ideology of FMLN
> and the economic freefall in Venezuela, Nicaraua
> [sic], Bolivia, etc. and contrast that with
> concret [sic] examples of successful free market
> economies.

Under the title "Demonstrating the Benefits of a Good Relationship," Glazer offered an eleven-point plan designed to mobilize US assistance and clout in favor of the ARENA campaign. The points included:

- Embassy believes a well-timed editorial by
  the Secretary published in regional, not just
  Salvadoran, media, extolling our views on
  core principles of open markets, liberalized
  trade, accountable and accessible government
  (including judicial systems) would have *a
  positive impact in focusing voters' minds.*

- Washington could prepare a fact sheet comparing
  the relative performance of the economies of
  Venezuela, Nicaragua, and Bolivia against
  that of Chile, Brazil, and others, in order to

```
highlight the benefits of the core principles to
be described in the above op-ed.
...
```

• MCC: As part of a public dipomacy [sic] push,
the Embassy will highlight the large pending
infrastructure investment represented b
[sic] the MCC compact, though ribbon-cutting
ceremonie [sic] will not be possible until
early 2009, perhaps ven [sic] after the first
round of presidential elections March 15.
[08SANSALVADOR1133] [Emphasis added.]

As in many other cables that touch on Latin America's new left governments, the manner in which ideology trumps basic facts in the analysis of US diplomats is readily apparent. Glazer and many of his colleagues appear oblivious to the reality that the economies of Venezuela and Bolivia had actually performed at par with or better than the more moderate governments of Brazil and Chile over the previous three years.[10]

Ultimately, the FMLN candidate, Mauricio Funes, won the second round of the 2009 elections by a nearly three-point margin. Before the elections even took place, embassy cables made it clear that the US strategy would consist in trying to distance Funes, a popular journalist who had only recently become an FMLN member, from the left-wing leadership of the party. On March 11, two days before the first round of elections, the embassy sent an "action request" to Secretary of State Clinton regarding next steps in the event of a Funes victory:

```
A concerted effort by the USG, perhaps allied
with the Brazilian government, could conceivably
hold Funes to a responsible center-left approach
to governing, giving him the strength necessary
to push back against the radical elements of the
FMLN. If high-level USG attention is required, we
```

will not hesitate to request it, starting with
a post-election congratulatory call from the
President. [09SANSALVADOR206]

At Funes's inauguration, the State Department decided to deploy its biggest gun in pursuit of this strategy. Rarely do US secretaries of state attend presidential inaugurations in small developing countries, but for the historic Salvadoran inauguration of 2009—marking the first time a left-wing party had occupied the country's presidency—the Obama administration made an exception. The reasons for Hillary Clinton's visit are abundantly clear in the "scene-setting" cable that the embassy sent her beforehand. The cable is permeated by the fear of a Chávez-and-Castro ideological takeover:

President-Elect Mauricio Funes, who ran as a
US-friendly moderate, has stated his desire
to make the US and Brazil his closest allies.
But he is also being pulled towards radicalism
by elements in the left-wing FMLN, the party
he joined in 2008 to propel his presidential
candidacy. While Funes has cultivated some
FMLN members to take a pragmatic approach to
governing, the party's center of gravity is still
radical left, and linked to Chavez and the Castro
brothers. Your very presence at his inauguration,
and your comments to the new president and to the
public regarding the broad and deep commitment of
the USG to support El Salvador will reinforce to
him: (1) that his own instincts toward pragmatism
are correct; and (2) that the USG is as good
as its word when we say that we don't judge a
government on its ideology, but rather on its
respect for democratic values. [09SANSALVADOR445]

Later cables discuss US diplomats' efforts to "engage and support moderates in the GOES" at the expense of "hard-line" FMLN elements "seeking to carry out the Bolivarian, Chavista game-plan [10SANSALVADOR37]. Tensions between Funes and the FMLN leadership reached a head in late 2011 and early 2012, when the Salvadoran president removed FMLN leaders from key security posts and replaced them with military officers—a controversial and arguably unconstitutional move that a senior FMLN official attributed to US government pressure.[11]

Five years later, when longtime FMLN leader Salvador Sánchez Cerén won the 2014 presidential elections, the Obama administration displayed no optimism about its ability to co-opt the new president, and sent a particularly low-level delegation to Cerén's inauguration led by Maria Contreras-Sweet, administrator of the US Small Business Administration.

NICARAGUA

The last century has seen near-continuous direct intervention in Nicaragua's affairs on the part of the United States, notably including opposition to the Sandinista government that overthrew the decades-long US-backed dictatorship in 1979. This intervention included arming and training an insurrectionary force, the "Contras," that became infamous for its atrocities but received continued US support even after a Sandinista government was democratically elected in 1984. Opposition to this intervention within the US led Congress to cut off aid to the Contras in 1985, leading to the Iran-Contra scandal when it was revealed that the White House had continued to fund the insurgency through extra-legal means.[12]

Fifteen years later, with Daniel Ortega and the Sandinista National Liberation Front (FSLN) poised for a political comeback at the ballot box, how would the US react? Had US policy in Nicaragua truly changed? While the language may be more diplomatic, the cables reveal a US government still working against the Sandinistas.

In November 2003, Secretary of State Colin Powell dined with Nicaraguan president Enrique Bolaños in Managua, telling the press that, while the "history between the United States and Nicaragua has been mixed over the years, and I was part of an earlier era," it was now a "brighter era" full of democracy and the rule of law that would "allow Nicaragua to play an important role, its rightful role, in Central America and in the Americas."[13]

Three years later, just days before the election that would return Ortega and the FSLN to the presidency, State Department spokesperson Sean McCormack told the press: "We do not ... we are not trying to shade opinion or to try to take a position. This is a democratic election. If you look around the globe, we do not take positions. We do not try to influence these elections."[14]

But, as the cables reveal, the US embassy in Nicaragua had long been working to prevent an FSLN victory by channeling funds to opposition parties, warning of the possible impact on US relations, and developing "rap sheets" on leading candidates whom the US did not want to see come to power. The election was a five-way race, and it is clear from the cables that the United States backed Eduardo Montealegre of the Nicaraguan Liberal Alliance (ALN), and especially opposed former president Daniel Ortega of the FSLN and José Rizo of the Constitutionalist Liberal Party (PLC).

In May 2006, six months ahead of the elections, US ambassador to Nicaragua Paul Trivelli sent a cable to the State Department with an update on the US government's "democracy promotion strategy":

```
The USG should encourage support of democratic
candidates by encouraging funds to flow in
the right direction; promoting defections of
salvageable individuals from the PLC camp;
granting Montealegre high-profile meetings in
```

```
the United States; bringing internationally
recognized speakers to discuss successful
reform campaigns; and countering direct partisan
support to the FSLN from external forces (notably
Venezuela and Cuba). [06MANAGUA1105]
```

Trivelli continued by noting that the embassy had been a part of "numerous discreet meetings" with Nicaraguan financiers and others on the issue of directing election funds: "We should continue to encourage Pellas and other Nicaraguan and international financiers to 'do the right thing' by supporting Montealegre."

Beyond these direct mechanisms for influencing the elections, the embassy sought to highlight past abuses allegedly perpetrated by FSLN members and Arnoldo Alemán, as evidenced by another May 2006 cable Trivelli sent to the CIA, the DIA, and relevant State Department bureaus:

```
In preparation for the November 2006 national
elections in Nicaragua, post has developed three
"rap sheets" on the records of Daniel Ortega,
the Sandinista party (FSLN) and Arnoldo Aleman,
highlighting their systematic crimes and abuses.
...
Post intends to use the information from
these rap sheets in discussions with domestic
and international interlocutors as a means
of reminding Nicaraguan voters and others of
the true character of Aleman, Ortega, and the
Sandinistas. [06MANAGUA1002]
```

The embassy even went so far as to bring a State Department employee to Nicaragua to "work on several high-profile human rights issues that have considerable election year significance," as Trivelli had explained in an earlier cable [06MANAGUA599].

As the elections approached, the embassy continued to signal its preference for a non-FSLN presidency. With Ortega leading in the polls, Trivelli wrote in late September 2006:

```
Ambassador and other senior USG officials have
made clear statements to the Nicaraguan public
that, while they are of course free to chose
[sic] their political leaders, their choice will
have a positive or negative impact on relations
with the US. Specifically, we have been clear that
an administration lead [sic] by FSLN candidate
Daniel Ortega could damage Nicaragua's economy if
Ortega, as he has stated, attempts to manipulate
the market economy, the system of remittances,
and the DR-CAFTA framework. [06MANAGUA2116]
```

Trivelli's statements made it into the Nicaraguan and international press,[15] and in response the OAS issued a press release "lamenting the active intervention of authorities and representatives of other nations in the Nicaraguan electoral debate."[16]

Despite the embassy's efforts, Daniel Ortega went on to win the November 2006 election. With Ortega in office, the embassy prioritized strengthening the opposition through indirect funding and organizing.

The US acts to unite the opposition

In February 2007, the embassy's deputy chief of mission, Peter Brennan, wrote:

```
The Nicaraguan Liberal Alliance (ALN) is in debt
from its campaign commitments and urgently needs
funding to maintain its momentum, enable leader
Eduardo Montealegre to emerge as the uncontested
leader of the opposition, and prepare for the
2008 municipal elections. [07MANAGUA493]
```

In a meeting with Kitty Monterrey, the ALN planning coordinator, the embassy explained that the US did "not provide direct assistance to political parties," but—as a means of bypassing this restriction—suggested that the ALN coordinate more closely with friendly NGOs that would be able to receive US funding. Monterrey, according to the cable, "offered to forward a comprehensive list of NGOs that indeed support ALN efforts." Brennan concluded: "Monterrey will next meet with IRI [International Republican Institute] and NDI [National Democratic Institute for International Affairs] country directors. We will also follow up on capacity building for fundraisers and continue to engage the local private sector."

Just one month later, in a cable to the secretary of state, intelligence agencies, and aid agencies, the ambassador bluntly stated: "We need to take decisive action and well-funded measures to bolster the elements of Nicaraguan society that can best stop him [Ortega] ... Without our support, our democratic-minded friends may well falter" [07MANAGUA583)]. The cable requests "additional funds over the next four years to keep our place at the table and help Nicaraguans keep their country on a democratic path—approximately $65 million above our recent past base levels over the next four years." This should continue "through the next Presidential elections to make this work." Among the activities to be funded were the strengthening of political parties, "democratic" NGOs, and "rapid response" funds in order to "advance our interests, and counter those who rail against us."

Beyond simply supporting opposition parties, the embassy actively engaged in organizing a united opposition. In March 2007, Trivelli, under a section titled "Embassy Jump Starts Liberal Unity Discussions," reported: "After splintering under the weight of mutual suspicion and recriminations, DCM hosted a cocktail to bring together members of the Nicaraguan Liberal Alliance (ALN) and Liberal Constitutional Party (PLC) to reactivate discussions on the need to forge a unified opposition to confront President Ortega's totalitarian ambitions" [07MANAGUA616].

The US embassy appears to have wanted the Nicaraguan opposition to learn from the defeats of their Venezuelan counterparts. At the end of the meeting, the US ambassador and his staff "set the meeting back on course" by relaying the claim that a fractured Venezuelan opposition had allowed Chávez "to gain absolute control." When members of the Nicaraguan opposition asked for the embassy to help continue negotiations between the opposition parties, a USAID democracy and governance officer offered to "assist if/as needed."

Despite US efforts to counter Ortega's re-emergence and unify the opposition, Ortega went on to win the 2011 election with over 60 percent of the vote.

ECUADOR

In April 2005, President Lucio Gutiérrez of Ecuador resigned from the presidency under popular pressure, fleeing to Brazil to seek asylum; his departure was the latest event in a nine-year period of turmoil that saw six different presidents come and go. Though the US became more critical of Gutiérrez near the end of his presidency, Ambassador Kristie Kenney outlined the US view of Gutiérrez as an "ally" in a September 2004 cable: "Despite his political vulnerability (and perhaps contributing to it), Gutiérrez is a US ally on many key issues ... His growing weakness make [sic] him increasingly ineffective implementing this shared agenda. But any scenario providing for his departure is unlikely to produce a more amenable ally or a noticeably stronger (lame duck) president" [04QUITO2497].

After Gutiérrez's departure, the US embassy "established several working groups to review US policy toward and assistance to Ecuador." In an October 2005 cable titled "Transforming Ecuador: Action Plan for Democracy," new ambassador Linda Jewell outlined actions to encourage "desirable political and economic change in Ecuador." The primary objective was to "[b]ring together Ecuadorians committed to change, [and to] motivate and activate them," in order to "[d]evelop leaders for the future" [05QUITO2416].

But soon another, more pressing issue would emerge: the rising popularity of Rafael Correa—a popular former finance minister who opposed signing a "free trade" agreement with the US and called for the closure of a US military base in the west of Ecuador: the only permanent US military outpost in South America. As the country prepared for presidential elections in late 2006, the US embassy became more concerned about a possible Correa victory. In late August 2006, Ambassador Jewell sent a cable to the secretary of state and regional embassies, warning: "While none of the candidates will return the bilateral relationship to the halcyon days when then-president-elect Lucio Gutiérrez declared himself our 'strongest ally in Latin America,' none of the top contenders would affect USG interests as thoroughly as Rafael Correa."

Jewell added, bluntly, that Correa's election would "derail any hope for more harmonious commercial relations with the United States," and that the embassy would expect Correa "to eagerly seek to join the Chávez-Morales-Kirchner group of nationalist-populist South American leaders." While acknowledging that "overt attempts to influence voter decisions is [sic] fraught with risk," Jewell added: "Privately, however, we have warned our political, economic, and media contacts of the threat Correa represents to Ecuador's future, and have actively discouraged potential alliances which could balance Correa's perceived radicalism" [06QUITO2150].

Without an alliance to temper Correa's "radicalism," the US believed his chances of success were severely limited. However, as had happened in other countries that saw historic shifts to the left in the last decade, the US vastly underestimated the appeal of Correa's message. After finishing second in the first round, Correa easily won the run-off election, with nearly 57 percent of the vote.

Despite the embassy's fears of a Correa presidency moving Ecuador closer to Venezuela, and the negative implications that would entail for their bilateral relationship, US officials' public statements portray a drastically different picture.[17] For example, Jewell sent the following "press guidance" to the State Department in the days before the second-round vote:

```
Q: Will the apparent win by Correa/Noboa hurt or
help US-Ecuador relations?

A: The United States has traditionally enjoyed
good relations with the government of Ecuador.
We look forward to maintaining a positive,
cooperative bilateral relationship with the
next Ecuadorian government, consistent with our
commitment to Ecuador's democratic institutions
and the peace and security of its people.

Q: (If Correa wins) Are you concerned about
Correa's ties to Venezuelan President Hugo
Chavez?

A: We respect the sovereign right of the
government of Ecuador to build relations with any
government it chooses.

[06QUITO2894]
```

Acting to limit progressive change

In December 2006, before Correa had even taken office, Jewell wrote:

```
We are under no illusions that USG efforts alone
will shape the direction of the new government
or Congress, but hope to maximize our influence
by working in concert with other Ecuadorians
```

and groups who share our views. Correa's reform
proposals and attitude toward Congress and
traditional political parties, if unchecked,
could extend the current period of political
conflict and instability. [06QUITO2991][18]

It is worth noting that the eight years since Correa was elected
have been one of the most politically stable periods in Ecuador's
modern history, with Correa still enjoying very high approval
ratings. Here, as elsewhere in many diplomatic cables, "political
conflict and instability" are code for "a government that we do
not want."

In the same cable, Jewell identifies "redlines" that "if crossed,
should trigger an appropriate USG response." A primary concern
was Correa's proposed Constituent Assembly, which could dissolve congress as part of its mandate. To counteract this, the
embassy decided to "offer limited technical assistance to boost
the professionalism of the new Congress," in order to increase
its favorability ratings and decrease chances that Correa could
move forward with the Constituent Assembly.

In early 2007, Jewell met with banker Guillermo Lasso, who
"briefed [her] on a systematic effort he is coordinating to develop
a cohesive private sector response to the Correa administration's
policy." The embassy told their contacts that they needed to reach
a consensus and offer a responsible alternative to Correa as "a
necessary pre-condition before any international engagement can
be truly effective." Days later, in another meeting Jewell describes,
the embassy's economic counselor met with the president of the
Guayaquil Chamber of Commerce, María Gloria Alarcón, who
outlined "how the business sector plans to address Correa's call
for a Constituent Assembly." Alarcón stated that "whomever the
business community decides to support will 'have a lot of money'
to support their campaign." This cable reveals that the embassy
saw business support as a potential way to "balance" the "competing interests" behind the Constituent Assembly [07QUITO768].

Despite the efforts of the US embassy, voters approved the proposal for a Constituent Assembly with 80 percent of the vote, and gave Correa's party a majority of the seats in the assembly. The new constitution—which contained numerous progressive initiatives, such as enshrining the rights of nature, treating drug abuse as a health issue, and food sovereignty—was approved with 64 percent of the vote.[19] While the US ultimately proved unsuccessful in preventing Correa's rise, the cables reveal the embassy's clear intention to thwart the public's will.

The concerns of the United States about Correa, and its activities against Ecuador's progressive movement, did not end with the election of President Obama, however. In January 2009, Ambassador Heather Hodges wrote: "Over the past two months, Correa has taken an increasingly leftist, anti-American posture, apparently unconcerned that his actions would result in frayed ties with the United States." Hodges discussed the leveraging of US aid funds in order to influence Correa:

```
[W]e are conveying the message in private that
Correa's actions will have consequences for his
relationship with the new Obama Administration,
while avoiding public comments that would
be counterproductive. We do not recommend
terminating any USG programs that serve our
interests since that would only weaken the
incentive for Correa to move back into a more
pragmatic mode. [09QUITO15]
```

The Obama administration proved no more hesitant than its predecessor to intervene in Ecuador's internal affairs when it decided that such intervention would advance their goals for Ecuador or the region. In March 2009, the Ecuadorian government expelled US official Mark Sullivan, accused by Correa and others of being the CIA station chief in Quito, following Sullivan's alleged role in suspending US assistance to a special investigative police unit after rejecting the Ecuadorian government's choice of chief for the unit. Correa also accused Sullivan and other embassy officials of seizing computers belonging to the unit that contained valuable national security information. Surprisingly, the State Department failed to carry out any retaliatory measures, a fact that—for many Ecuadorians—seemed to confirm that Sullivan was indeed a CIA agent. Embassy memos from this period registered frustration and dismay with the situation:

```
9. (C) The public relations dynamic in Ecuador
is not working in our favor. Correa's continued
condemnation of US Embassy actions, combined
with our lack of response since the Department
statement on February 19, have led many
Ecuadorians to conclude that US Embassy officials
were caught doing wrong and deserved expulsion.
[09QUITO176]
```

In late 2009, embassy staff met with local representatives of large US pharmaceutical companies to discuss Correa's plans to enact compulsory licensing laws—which are legal and legitimate under the rules of the World Trade Organization—and encourage local production of pharmaceutical drugs [09QUITO998]. The companies worked in concert with the embassy and some dissident Ecuadorian ministers to thwart the plans. Hodges wrote: "Local representatives of US and other international R&D pharmaceutical companies have identified and been in contact with potentially sympathetic ministries ... these ministers have tried to explain to Correa the potential negative implications for economic development and the health system of issuing wholesale compulsory licenses" [09QUITO893].

The cable notes that the health minister was even "looking into financial irregularities and business dealings of some of the local producers in an attempt to gain some leverage..." Despite the fact that Ecuador's proposed changes were compliant with

World Trade Organization rules, the US warned that trade preferences under the Andean Trade Promotion and Drug Eradication Act (ATPDEA) and the Generalized System of Preferences would be jeopardized if the government went ahead with its plans, and that the proposal represented "a serious problem" for bilateral relations.

In April of 2010, Ecuador granted its first compulsory license for an HIV/AIDS drug.[20] By 2011, 54 percent of people with advanced HIV infection had received antiretroviral therapy coverage, up from just 30 percent in 2009, according to the World Bank.[21]

Relations between Ecuador and the US grew increasingly tense in the years that followed. In September 2010, an attempted coup took place when hundreds of national police kidnapped President Correa for ten hours, then shot repeatedly at the vehicle transporting him as he was being rescued by an elite military unit. An investigative commission created by the government asserted that "foreign actors" had played a role in the coup, and one of the three commissioners told the press that he believed the US Department of State and Central Intelligence Agency were involved.[22]

In April 2011, Correa expelled US ambassador Heather Hodges when the Ecuadorian press broke the story of a WikiLeaks cable signed by Hodges stating that Correa tolerated corruption in the national police force.

BOLIVIA

Cables show that, among South American leaders, Evo Morales—after Chávez—has probably been the most strongly opposed by the US government since his election in 2005. Morales's electoral victory represented a seismic shift in Bolivia's history—he is the country's first indigenous president—and cables show that some foreign governments perceived him as "Bolivia's Mandela." His triumph at the ballot box by an unprecedented margin[23] came after a string of unpopular predecessors (one, Gonzalo Sánchez de Lozada, notoriously spoke Spanish with an American accent).

As embassy cables reveal, the US government was antagonistic toward Morales from the beginning, referring to him derisively in a State Department background note in 2005, for example, as an "illegal-coca agitator."[24] This attitude continued even after Morales took office.

On January 3, 2006, just two days after Morales's inauguration as president, the US ambassador made clear that multilateral assistance to Bolivia would hinge on what the embassy would subsequently refer to as the "good behavior" of the Morales government:

> [The ambassador] also showed the crucial
> importance of US contributions to key
> international financial [*sic*] on which
> Bolivia depended for assistance, such as the
> International Development Bank (IDB), the World
> Bank and the International Monetary Fund. *"When*
> *you think of the IDB, you should think of the*
> *US,"* the Ambassador said. *"This is not blackmail,*
> *it is simple reality."*
>
> …
>
> *"I hope you as the next president of Bolivia*
> *understand the importance of this,"* he said,
> *"because a parting of the ways would not be good*
> *for the region, for Bolivia or for the United*
> *States."* [06LAPAZ6] [Emphasis added.]

Unfortunately for the US Department of State, the Morales government would quickly show that it was not interested in a new IMF agreement[25]—an unprecedented stance from a country that had been under IMF agreements for virtually all of the preceding twenty years, and a clear signal to Washington that this was a government determined to be more independent than its predecessors.

A few weeks later, Ambassador David Greenlee explicitly laid out a "carrots and sticks" approach to the Morales administration. Many of these related to Bolivia's relationship with the IDB or to the existing preferential trade arrangement with the US, the ATPDEA:

> 4. (C) Dealing with the MAS-led government will require a careful application of carrots and sticks to encourage good, and to discourage bad, behavior and policy.
>
> ...
>
> [I]t may be important to send clear signals early on, shots over the bow, that it will not be business as usual. A menu of options that could be used depending on circumstances and that would resonate clearly include:
>
> • Use USG's veto authority within the IDB's Fund for Special Operations (from which Bolivia currently receives all its IDB funding) to withhold IDB funding for Bolivia, estimated by the IDB Resrep in Bolivia to total $200 million in 2006.
>
> • Postpone decision on the forgiveness of IDB debt (approximately $800 million under the Fund for Special Operations and $800 million under the IDB's regular program) pending clarification of the new GOB's economic policies.
>
> • Pursue a postponement of the World Bank's vote on debt relief for Bolivia. Request a 6-month delay, pending a review of the GOB's economic policies.

- Disinvite GOB participation as observers at
  future Andean FTA events, pending clarification
  of the new GOB's interest in participating in
  the FTA.

- Discourage GOB interest in pursuing dialogue on
  a possible MCC compact.

- Deny GOB requests for logistical support by
  NAS aircraft and equipment, except in cases of
  humanitarian disasters.

- Stop material support (tear gas, anti-riot
  gear, and other assistance) for Bolivia's
  security services.

- Announce USG intention to not extend the ATPDEA
  trade benefits beyond the December 31, 2006
  expiry date.

[06LAPAZ93]

"Many USAID-administered economic programs run counter to the direction the GOB wishes to move the country," the cable also noted.

Supporting a violent opposition

Cables and much other evidence reveal that the US government supported a violent opposition movement in Bolivia. The US sought to redefine power relations in Bolivia—to the advantage of regional governments and the detriment of the central government—and used USAID to further this goal: "US assistance via USAID continues at previous levels, but *the focus of assistance has shifted from the central government to Bolivia's prefects and other decentralized players*"[26] [06LAPAZ1952] [Emphasis added.]

Significant support was allocated to the opposition-based departments of the "Media Luna," an eastern "crescent" comprised of Beni, Pando, Santa Cruz, and Tarija, where the majority of Bolivia's important natural gas deposits lie.[27] A cable from April 2007 describes "USAID's larger effort to strengthen regional governments as a counter-balance to the central government" [07LAPAZ1167]. A USAID report from 2007 stated that "OTI has approved 101 grants for $4,066,131 to help departmental governments operate more strategically."[28] A year later, the Media Luna departments would feel sufficiently emboldened to hold referenda on autonomy—despite these having been ruled illegal by the national judiciary.

As this later cable shows, the US embassy in La Paz shared a common political strategy with opposition groups—some of which were pursuing an actual separatist goal—versus the Morales government:

> In a March 27-28 outreach trip to Santa Cruz, A/
> DCM met briefly with the Prefect (Governor), new
> Civic Committee President, business leaders,
> leaders in the forestry sector, a media owner,
> and the Cardenal. *While they understand there are*
> *limits to what the US can do to reverse anti-*
> *democratic trends in Bolivia, they are grateful*
> *for continued US engagement.* [09LAPAZ501]
> [Emphasis added.]

Support for departmental governments became, whether intended or not, wrapped up with support for a violent, destructive campaign against the Morales government in the later months of 2008.[29]

When a full-blown political crisis emerged in August and September 2008, there was no public indication that the US government attempted to temper the opposition, and at no point did the US denounce the opposition violence as did, for example, the Union of South American Nations.[30]

Following weeks of violence (in the worst incident, over a dozen indigenous Morales supporters were killed in Porvenir, in Pando province, apparently by a far-right militant group), property destruction (including the ransacking of government offices and the sabotage of a gas pipeline), and road blockades, there was hope that dialogue between the Morales government and the opposition would resolve the crisis. But this cable from September 18, 2008, shows that the opposition preferred a hard line that they did not expect the Morales government to accept, and opposition prefects and the central democratic opposition coalition (CONALDE) "were in agreement" that the "next stage" would be "to blow up gas lines." The cable does not describe US officials attempting to dissuade the opposition figures from this strategy:

> 7. (C) Opposition Strategist Javier Flores told Emboff the morning of September 17 that the dialogue will break down, "it's only a question of when." Flores and opposition civic leader Branko Marinkovic predict more violence after the dialogue fails. Some radicals in the Santa Cruz prefecture and Santa Cruz civic committee reportedly wanted to stop the process yesterday and begin blowing up gas lines, but Flores and Marinkovic advocated playing out the dialogue option first. Once dialogue breaks down, however, the opposition group CONALDE is generally in agreement that the next stage is to blow up gas lines. [08LAPAZ2004]

Similarly, a cable from September 9 shows that "both [Pando prefect Leopoldo Fernández] and also Tarija's opposition Prefect,

Mario Cossio see violence as a probability to force the government to admit to the divisions in the country and take seriously any dialog" [08LAPAZ1931]. Fernández was arrested a week later in connection with the Porvenir massacre two days after this cable, on September 11.[31]

Despite a lack of public commentary from US officials to this effect at the time, cables reveal that internally the State Department took seriously the possibility of Morales's ouster or assassination in 2008. "Sources report that both sides are armed with personal weapons and ready to fight, with the opposition-aligned Santa Cruz Youth Union and university students reportedly preparing a trap for the government forces which could lead to a bloodbath," noted a secret cable of September 24, 2008, describing how the Emergency Action Committee would "develop, with [US Southern Command Situational Assessment Team], a plan for immediate response in the event of a sudden emergency, i.e. a coup attempt or President Morales' death" [08LAPAZ2083].[32]

Fed up with US support for people and groups working to violently overthrow it, the Morales government declared US ambassador Philip Goldberg persona non grata on September 10, 2008, and expelled him. USAID's lack of transparency regarding whom it was funding in Bolivia had contributed to the breakdown in relations; Bolivian officials had repeatedly requested the information, to no avail. Cables from 2007 describe the anger of the minister of the presidency, Juan Ramón Quintana, at the secretive nature of USAID's programs [07LAPAZ2387]. US researchers also sought the release of USAID and related documents; by the time of the September 2008 events, three-and-a-half-year-old Freedom of Information Act requests remained unanswered. The US continued to send hundreds of millions of dollars to unnamed recipients in Bolivia via USAID after 2009.[33] Ultimately, in 2013, Bolivia expelled USAID as well.

HAITI

In 2004, the US flew democratically elected president Jean-Bertrand Aristide out of Haiti in what, for all practical purposes, was a rendition flight enacting a coup d'état. US marines were dispatched to Haiti for "peacekeeping" purposes, even though it was paramilitary death squads—some of them former CIA assets who had participated in the 1991 coup and subsequent murders—who were responsible for the great majority of the violence at the time.[34] A "peacekeeping" force under the UN Stabilization Mission in Haiti (MINUSTAH) would replace the marines a few months later.

Embassy cables shed light on how committed the US has been to opposing popular movements in Haiti and ensuring a strong military presence in the country to keep the populace in check.[35] Although the interests of foreign investors may be part of this commitment,[36] as shown by US opposition to minimum-wage increases, it appears that US intervention in Haiti is more driven by the aim of incorporating Haiti into its strategic plan for the hemisphere. Unlike in other countries, US efforts in Haiti have been aided in recent years by a "coalition of the willing" of other countries.

The cables illuminate the value that the US government sees in MINUSTAH, and why it has been a priority for US policy toward Haiti. In turn, they also offer insight into why UN "peacekeepers" remain in Haiti despite the lack of a civil war or other ongoing armed conflict. An October 2008 cable by then ambassador Janet Sanderson explains:

> The UN Stabilization Mission in Haiti is an indispensable tool in realizing core USG policy interests in Haiti. Security vulnerabilities and fundamental institutional weaknesses mean that Haiti will require a continuing—albeit eventually shrinking—MINUSTAH presence for at least three and more likely five years.

...

MINUSTAH is a remarkable product and symbol of
hemispheric cooperation in a country with little
going for it. There is no feasible substitute for
this UN presence. *It is a financial and regional
security bargain for the USG. USG civilian and
military assistance under current domestic and
international conditions, alone or in combination
with our closest partners, could never fill the
gap left by a premature MINUSTAH pullout.*

[08PORTAUPRINCE1381] [Emphasis added.]

The cable goes on to emphasize the role MINUSTAH plays in
the US "management" of Haiti, and in getting Latin American
countries to participate:

In the current context of our military
commitments elsewhere, the US alone could
not replace this mission. *This regionally-
coordinated Latin American commitment to Haiti
would not be possible without the UN umbrella.*
That same umbrella helps other major donors—led
by Canada and followed up by the EU, France,
Spain, Japan and others—justify their bilateral
assistance domestically. *Without a UN-sanctioned
peacekeeping and stabilization force, we would be
getting far less help from our hemispheric and
European partners in managing Haiti.* [Emphasis
added.]

MINUSTAH, the cable reveals, also helps the US to address
other Haiti priorities, such as preventing Haitian "boat people"
from coming to the US, and holding back "populist" groups:
"A premature departure of MINUSTAH would leave the Preval

government or his successor vulnerable to resurgent kidnapping and international drug trafficking, revived gangs, greater political violence, *an exodus of seaborne migrants*, a sharp drop in foreign and domestic investment, and *resurgent populist and anti-market economy political forces*—reversing gains of the last two years" (emphasis added).[37]

Other cables provide a more chilling look at the role MINUSTAH troops have played at the urging of the US government and Haiti's elite. As has been well documented,[38] MINUSTAH assisted in targeting members of the Fanmi Lavalas political party (headed by Aristide) and its base of support in impoverished communities. Thousands of people were killed in the two years following the 2004 coup, many targeted for political reasons.[39] One cable from January 2006 describes a business leaders' meeting with then US chargé d'affaires Tim Carney, in which the business group requested additional ammunition for police (who were gunning down civilians at the time) and for MINUSTAH to "take back" the Cité Soleil neighborhood (a stronghold of Aristide support). Carney, according to the cable, acceded to these elites' requests even though he recognized it would "inevitably cause unintended civilian casualties"—something human rights attorney Dan Kovalik says "would be a knowing and premeditated violation of the Geneva Conventions," as well as a "war crime" and a "crime against humanity":[40]

> Leaders of the Haitian business community told
> Charge that they would call a general strike for
> Monday, January 9 to protest MINUSTAH,s [sic]
> ineffectiveness in countering the recent upswing
> of violence and kidnappings. Representatives
> will also meet with [special representative to
> the UN secretary general] Juan Gabriel Valdez to
> pressure him to take action against the criminal
> gangs. *They also pleaded with the Charge for more*

ammunition for the police. Charge told the group to be ready to assist Cite Soleil immediately after a MINUSTAH operation, if it were to take place, and countered that the problem of the police was not [a] lack of ammunition, but a lack of skills and training. Clearly, the private sector is worried about the recent upsurge in violence.

5. ... Representatives of the private sector will also meet one-on-one with UNSRSG Juan Gabriel Valdez to pressure him personally to take action against the criminal gangs in Cite Soleil. [President of the Haitian Chamber of Commerce and Industry Reginald] *Boulos argued that MINUSTAH could take back the slum if it were to work systematically, section by section, in securing the area. Immediately after MINUSTAH secured Cite Soleil, Boulos said that he and other groups were prepared to go in immediately with social programs and social spending.* NOTE: Boulos has been active in providing social programs in Cite Soleil for many years. END NOTE.

6. (SBU) *The Charge cautioned that such an operation would inevitably cause unintended civilian casualties given the crowded conditions and flimsy construction of tightly packed housing in Cite Soleil. Therefore, the private sector associations must be willing to quickly assist in the aftermath of such an operation, including providing financial support to families of potential victims. Boulos agreed.*

[06PORTAUPRINCE29][41] [Emphasis added.]

As journalist Kim Ives has noted, one cable from June 2005 about a meeting between US and Brazilian officials states that then US secretary of state Condoleezza Rice had called "for firm Minustah action and the possibility that the US may be asked to send troops at some point." Ives writes: "Less than a month after these meetings, on 5 July 2005, a browbeaten [MINUSTAH military commander Brazilian General Augusto] Heleno would lead Minustah's first deadly assault on the armed groups resisting the coup and occupation in Cité Soleil."[42] A State Department cable (released in response to a Freedom of Information Act request) describes MINUSTAH firing 22,000 shots in just seven hours in this raid.[43] Dozens of people, including several small children, were killed.[44] Similar raids on Cité Soleil were carried out in the following months.[45]

Cables also reveal that MINUSTAH participated in other political activities, such as spying on student groups,[46] and that it sought to keep Aristide from returning from his exile in South Africa. The US government did as well: "Ambassador and PolCouns also stressed continued USG insistence that *all efforts must be made to keep Aristide from returning to Haiti or influencing the political process*, and asked whether the GOB also remains firm on that point" [05BRASILIA1578] (emphasis added).

In the *Nation*, Ives and Herz have dissected a 2005 cable that describes US efforts to enlist other countries (in this case, France) in pressuring the South African government to block Aristide's attempt to leave South Africa and return to Haiti.[47] The Haiti policies of the Bush era have continued into the Obama era, with Obama calling South African president Jacob Zuma in a last-ditch attempt to stop Aristide's return to Haiti,[48] and MINUSTAH remaining in Haiti with US support, despite growing popular opposition to its presence.

18. Venezuela

Dan Beeton, Jake Johnston, and Alexander Main

A major theme recurring in WikiLeaks' US diplomatic cables from Latin America and the Caribbean is an obsession with the government of the late Venezuelan president Hugo Chávez Frías, and with Chávez as a political actor. Chávez's regional influence was a central concern for the State Department in the years after he was elected, and especially in the years following a tumultuous period in which the Venezuelan opposition (with varying degrees of US support) attempted to remove him from power by various extra-constitutional means.

US relations with Chávez would be tense from early on. Chávez broadly rejected neoliberal economic policies, developed a close relationship with Cuba's Fidel Castro, and loudly criticized the Bush administration's assault on Afghanistan following the 9/11 attacks (the US pulled its ambassador from Caracas after Chávez proclaimed: "You can't fight terrorism with terrorism"). Chávez—through public diplomacy—successfully lobbied OPEC members to raise oil prices, and would increase state control over Venezuela's oil resources. These were moves that displeased Washington.[1]

Nevertheless, Chávez was popular and democratically elected. As the cables show, the US worked to bolster the Venezuelan opposition, which would engage in a series of attempts—some constitutional, some not—to oust Chávez: a military coup d'état

(2002—overturned by mass public opposition just two days later); an economically damaging oil strike (2002–03); and a recall referendum (2004). US support for these efforts—especially for the coup—would poison relations between the two countries. The US provided funds to groups and individuals involved in the coup, and after the coup had occurred encouraged other countries to recognize the coup government. It was later revealed that the CIA had known of the coup plans in advance but did nothing to warn Venezuela's elected government; and, perhaps most tellingly, despite Washington's knowledge of the coup, US officials tried to convince the world when it was happening that it was not a coup, but that President Chávez had resigned.[2] The US provided significant funding to Súmate, the main organization involved in organizing the 2004 recall effort;[3] the cables also show near-constant communication between the State Department, Súmate, and other opposition leaders in the period leading to the vote.

Chávez would emerge from each attempt to remove him stronger than before. Other leaders who challenged Washington also began to emerge in the region: Evo Morales, who won Bolivia's elections in 2005, Rafael Correa of Ecuador and Daniel Ortega of Nicaragua (both elected in 2006), and Cristina Fernández de Kirchner of Argentina (who would succeed her husband Néstor Kirchner—both often showing public support for Chávez), among others. Increasingly, "center left" leaders such as Brazil's Lula da Silva and Chile's Michelle Bachelet publicly defended Chávez against US criticism. The cables show that, disconcerted by this "pink tide," the US saw Chávez as trying to establish his "dominion" [07ASUNCION396] in Latin America and—ironically, given the record of the United States itself in the region—expressed concern that he was trying to interfere in the internal politics of his neighbors. Containing the "Chávez threat" became a priority for Washington's Latin America policy.

This chapter will examine the US strategy to oppose the "Bolivarian Revolution" in Venezuela, and beyond. Inside Venezuela, the cables reveal constant coordination between the

US embassy and the Venezuelan opposition, and clear efforts to undermine the government by various means. These included the funding and training of students (some of them known to be violent, as cables show), support for NGOs and other civil society groups in their protests, propaganda campaigns, and other efforts against Venezuela's elected government. Throughout years of cables, the embassy has shown concern over perennial splits within the opposition, and has attempted to foster unity while simultaneously attempting to co-opt and divide Chavistas. The embassy has aided opposition politicians in their campaigns as it has worked to isolate Venezuela diplomatically, politically, and economically on the world stage.

Pursuing its obsession with the idea of Chávez's powerful influence abroad, US efforts to contain and isolate Venezuela became a central focus of its strategy in the Western Hemisphere. The United States pressured countries in the Caribbean and Central America to steer clear of Venezuela's Petrocaribe program (which offers discounted oil on credit), often in vain; and it pursued efforts to keep Venezuela out of the South American trade bloc Mercosur—also without success. The United States attempted to enlist the support of Argentina, Brazil, and other countries in "containing" Venezuela. Finally, US diplomats expressed great concern over close relations between the Venezuelan government and emerging left-leaning presidents in the region, whom they also sought to undermine. In the post-Chávez era, but with the Bolivarian government still in place in Venezuela, there is little reason to think that the strategies the United States has pursued both inside Venezuela and internationally have been abandoned.

UNDERMINING THE VENEZUELAN GOVERNMENT FROM WITHIN VENEZUELA

Following the abortive military coup against Chávez in 2002, the US launched a USAID/Office of Transition Initiatives (OTI) operation in Venezuela. While publicly the US embassy would say that "the United States seeks the best possible relations with all governments" [07CARACAS766], the cables reveal that it was actively working to undermine the Chávez government.

This cable from November 2006, written by Ambassador William Brownfield and classified "secret," explains the USAID/OTI strategy and lays out a point-by-point plan to undermine Venezuela's elected government:

In August of 2004, Ambassador outlined the
country team's 5 point strategy to guide
embassy activities in Venezuela for the period
[2004-2006] (specifically, from the referendum
to the 2006 presidential elections). The
strategy's focus is: 1) Strengthening Democratic
Institutions, 2) Penetrating Chavez' Political
Base, 3) Dividing Chavismo, 4) Protecting
Vital US business, and 5) Isolating Chavez
internationally. [06CARACAS3356]

We will examine several of these strategy components in turn.

"Strengthening democratic institutions"

When diplomatic cables discuss the promotion or strengthening of democracy, it is usually in reference to various forms of support for US allies. US support for—if not outright coordination of—a 2004 referendum to recall Chávez, and other efforts to see Chávez replaced by an opposition government, are apparent throughout numerous cables. One cable from Brownfield even links Súmate—an opposition NGO that organized the recall and played a central role in other opposition campaigns—to "our interests in Venezuela" [06CARACAS339]. Another describes coordination with Súmate: "Embassy will continue seeking ways to be helpful to Sumate, and will ensure that any efforts are carefully coordinated with Sumate and will help the cause of this valiant pro-democracy NGO" [06CARACAS2478]. Other cables reveal that the State Department has lobbied for international support for Súmate [05MADRID2557; 06CARACAS340] and encouraged US financial [05CARACAS1805], political, legal [06CARACAS3547], and other support for the organization, including via the National Endowment for Democracy (NED).

Nor has such support and close coordination been limited to NGOs. A December 2006 funding request for USAID/OTI activities to implement the strategy outlined above and help to "counter [Chávez's] anti-American axis" describes areas in which additional funding might assist the National Democratic Institute (NDI) and the International Republican Institute (IRI) to "expand their party-building efforts toward 2008 local and state races" [06CARACAS3547]. Other NDI and IRI activities included:

```
Training the Next Generation of Political
Leaders[:] IRI and NDI continue to work on
political party renovation, primarily with
young(er) leadership, primarily outside of
Caracas. They are also identifying potential
future political leaders who are not affiliated
with a political party. Those identified will
participate in a program to prepare them for a
run at local council seats and/or mayorships in
2008. [06CARACAS2374_a]
```

While the NED, IRI, and NDI often claim that such political training and party support is purely non-partisan, the same cable notes that "target populations continue to be political parties and civil society" that "can counterbalance—even in a minor way—the billions of dollars that Chavez has at his disposal." Political parties are, by definition, partisan; and in a polarized society like Venezuela during this time, there were few—if any—"civil society" organizations for Washington to fund that were "non-partisan."

A 2004 cable notes that IRI did approach parties affiliated to the Bolivarian Republic of Venezuela (BRV), but these declined participation in electoral party training "despite IRI/HD[4] offering to hold separate courses for government-affiliated parties" [04CARACAS2224]. Considering that senior IRI staff had openly applauded the coup just two years before,[5] the BRV parties' reticence must have been expected by the IRI. It is likely that this approach was simply a formality.

So cozy has the embassy relationship with the opposition been that opposition leader Manuel Rosales asked the State Department for "help in arranging meetings" abroad. "The Ambassador advised that it would be better if [Rosales's] own people took the lead, but said if approached by his international coordinator for help on specific appointments, we probably could help behind the scenes" [07CARACAS569]. The IRI also provided "technical specialists to assist the Rosales [presidential] campaign" in the weeks before the 2006 elections [06CARACAS3532].

Promoting international support for Venezuela's opposition is another frequently described activity in the cables:

14. (S) An important component of the OTI program
is providing information internationally regarding
the true revolutionary state of affairs. OTI's
support for human rights organizations has
provided ample opportunity to do so … *[USAID/
OTI contractor Development Alternatives, Inc.]
has brought dozens of international leaders to
Venezuela, university professors, NGO members, and
political leaders to participate in workshops and
seminars, who then return to their countries with
a better understanding of the Venezuelan reality
and as stronger advocates for the Venezuelan
opposition.* [Emphasis addded.]

Throughout numerous cables, the embassy expresses concern with divisions within the opposition[6] and discusses its efforts to foster opposition unity. For example, in a section of a 2007 cable titled "The Opposition?—Divided, Of Course," deputy chief of mission Philip French writes, "there is no unified opposition effort to oppose Chavez' constitutional plans. Quiet efforts to coordinate opposition positions have so far been unsuccessful" [07CARACAS1611]. Encouraging opposition groups to unify behind a single national agenda was a key objective for the USAID/OTI program from the start [04CARACAS2224]. Embassy frustration with the opposition's failures to unite around strategies in response to elections—whether to participate or boycott, claiming "fraud"[7]—are a recurring theme.[8] (The opposition's boycott of the 2005 legislative elections was a notorious strategic failure, leaving pro-government parties in complete control of the National Assembly.) "Encouraging voter turn-out" has been another priority for USAID/OTI activities in Venezuela [06CARACAS3532]. Election results over the past fifteen years in which the Chavistas have prevailed, coupled with the US government's proven close coordination with the opposition, should leave little doubt as to which political sectors USAID and OTI wanted to see showing up in greater numbers to vote.

This 2009 cable from John Caulfield, the top-ranking US diplomat in Venezuela at the time, shows the degree of reliance on the US of some opposition organizations:

```
We risk losing these efforts as Chavez
radicalizes his revolution. Without our continued
assistance it is possible that the organizations
we helped create, which arguably represent the
best hope for a more open democratic system in
Venezuela, could be forced to close as local
funding options dry up for fear of possible
government retaliation. As reftels indicate, the
Chavez government is constantly attacking those
```

```
who call for dialogue and consensus. Our funding
will provide those organizations a much-needed
lifeline. [09CARACAS404] [Emphasis added.]
```

Another cable, for example, notes that "USAID ... is the major international funder of civil society" in Venezuela [06CARACAS2104]. For US diplomats in Venezuela and elsewhere, the term "civil society" typically refers to NGOs with strong international connections but limited local or national representation, rather than more broad-based community groups or indigenous and peasant social movements.

"Penetrating Chávez's political base"

The importance of penetrating the Chavista base is highlighted again and again in cables from Caracas. Considering the wide margins by which Chávez won elections in 1998, 2000, and 2004—among others—the State Department understands that this task is central if the opposition ever hopes to regain the presidency, or even control of the legislature.

Crucial for this strategy, and related to the objective of "dividing Chavismo" (examined below), are efforts to highlight "failures" of the Chávez government, as this "secret" cable mentions:

```
When we have concrete intelligence on an issue
about which our friends in the region share our
concern—e.g., Venezuela's relationship with Iran—
we should share it to the extent we can. And
when Chavez's programs feed local elite appetites
for corruption or otherwise fail to deliver
on their promises, we need to make it known.
[07SANTIAGO983] [Emphasis added.]
```

Another cable by Brownfield from January 2007 describes a USAID/OTI-funded program through the Pan-American

Development Foundation (PADF) that seeks to highlight the Chávez government's alleged failings:

> PADF has funded 9 NGOs to support projects
> focusing on documenting and reporting on the
> BRV's failures, namely: judicial independence,
> the right of association, violent crime, the
> prison situation, self-censorship of the media,
> harassment of journalists, women's political
> rights, human rights, and BRV support to micro-
> entrepreneurs. [07CARACAS175]

Brownfield explicitly lays out the purpose: "This project seeks to shine a flashlight into the dark corners of the revolution, to collect and document information and make it public, domestically and internationally. This will help deconstruct some of the mythology around Chavez and his revolution, and demonstrate that the lives of the Venezuelans really aren't better." Some of these organizations would also "add value to the Rosales debate" during the 2006 election campaign, Brownfield noted in a separate cable [06CARACAS3532].

Deputy chief of mission Kevin Whitaker highlighted an example of Venezuelan government failings in August 2006: "[T]he Observatorio Venezolano de Prisiones, regularly infuriates the Minister of Justice with bursts of non-partisan public criticism regarding prison-related issues. This leads to constant unkept promises to fix things and highlights the generalized incompetence of the government" [06CARACAS2374].

Here the priority is highlighting the BRV failure to improve deplorable prison conditions—a serious problem that long predates the Chávez government—rather than actually seeking to improve prison conditions. Indeed, such improvements would prove inconvenient to the USAID/OTI programs, as indicated by their stated objectives.

"Dividing Chavismo"

Related to penetrating Chávez's base was the task of dividing it, as Brownfield's secret November strategy cable explains:

> 9. (S) Another key Chavez strategy is his
> attempt to divide and polarize Venezuelan
> society using rhetoric of hate and violence.
> OTI supports local NGOs who work in Chavista
> strongholds and with Chavista leaders, using
> those spaces to counter this rhetoric and promote
> alliances through working together on issues
> of importance to the entire community. OTI has
> directly reached approximately 238,000 adults
> through over 3000 forums, workshops and training
> sessions delivering alternative values and
> *providing opportunities for opposition activists*
> *to interact with hard-core Chavistas, with the*
> *desired effect of pulling them slowly away from*
> *Chavismo.* We have supported this initiative
> with 50 grants totaling over $1.1 million.
> [06CARACAS3356] [Emphasis added.]

Another cable notes that "a local USAID partner has capitalized on the splits in Chavismo, incorporating government and pro-Chávez party leaders into democracy promotion programs" [06CARACAS3462].

THE RELEVANCE OF THE CABLES TO POST-CHÁVEZ VENEZUELA

it is worth examining cables that have some relevance for more recent events in Venezuela, such as the violent street blockades and protests carried out in 2014 in connection with the "Salida" ("exit") campaign calling for the ouster of president Nicolás Maduro, elected following Chávez's death in early 2013. While the US government has supported the whole spectrum of opposition groups and political tendencies in Venezuela, it has at times shown preference for some of the more "radical" actors within the opposition, such as Súmate, which Ambassador Brownfield characterized as "the most viable Chavez opponent in Venezuela's political landscape" [07CARACAS1368; 05CARACAS93]. Súmate co-founder María Corina Machado—along with Leopoldo López—helped to launch the "Salida" campaign at the end of January 2014.[9] Both Corina Machado and López supported the 2002 coup: Corina Machado supported the infamous "Carmona decree" of the coup regime, which abolished the elected National Assembly, the Constitution, and the Supreme Court [04CARACAS3219]; López—as mayor of Chacao—oversaw the violent arrest of the minister of the interior of the deposed Chávez government during the short-lived coup.[10]

Waves of violent student protests also rocked Venezuela several times during the Chávez administration. One secret cable from August 2009, well after President Obama took office, cites USAID/OTI contractor DAI referring to "all" the people protesting Chávez at the time as "our grantees": "[DAI chief of party] Fernandez said that 'the streets are hot,' referring to growing protests against Chavez's efforts to consolidate power, and *all these people (organizing the protests) are our grantees.*' Fernandez has been leading non-partisan training and grant programs since 2004 for DAI in Venezuela" [09CARACAS1132] (emphasis added).

Sometimes the protesters that the US has supported have been known to have violent histories. The cables reveal that the US Department of State provided training and support to a student leader it acknowledged had led crowds with the intention "to lynch" a Chavista governor: "During the coup of April 2002, [Nixon] Moreno participated in the demonstrations in Merida state, leading crowds who marched on the state capital to lynch MVR governor Florencio Porras" [06CARACAS1627]. Yet, a few years after this, "Moreno participated in [a State Department]

International Visitor Program in 2004" [07CARACAS591]. Moreno would later be wanted (in 2007) for attempted murder and threatening a female police officer, among other charges.

Cables from 2007 to 2009 describe growing ties between López and the student movement. A June 2007 cable noted that López "is actively advising [students] behind-the-scenes" and another cable from later the same year noted: "The government sees Lopez as the best channel to the student movement" [07CARACAS1128; 07CARACAS2290]. By 2009, the embassy observed that "disgruntled figures like Leopoldo Lopez may be preparing to launch their own self-serving 'movement,'" which it later described as a "movement of movements" [09CARACAS724; 09CARACAS1145]. López would indeed emerge on the world stage in early 2014 in conjunction with the "Salida" campaign and a violent and disruptive youth movement.

CONTAINING THE VENEZUELAN REGIONAL "THREAT"

A quick search for "Venezuela" on the *Cablegate* search engine reveals that the South American country is mentioned in no less than 9,424 of the US diplomatic cables published by WikiLeaks. This is more than any other country in Latin America and the Caribbean except Brazil (9,633 cables)—a country with seven times the population of Venezuela—and four times the total number of cables sent from the US embassy in Caracas. Mexico, the biggest US trading partner in Latin America, is less frequently mentioned (8,966), and Argentina, the second-biggest economy in South America, is referenced in just 5,653 cables. Why does Venezuela receive so much attention?

A partial examination of the thousands of "Venezuela" cables produced by US diplomatic missions outside of Venezuela shows that, along with trying to remove Chávez from power, the US government has made enormous efforts to isolate the Venezuelan government internationally and counter its perceived influence throughout the region. During the Cold War, the US strategies of containment and rollback—targeting the alleged Soviet and Cuban "threat"—had a major influence on US policy toward all the countries of Latin America and the Caribbean, and served to justify countless interventions to remove left-leaning governments and prop up right-wing military regimes. Similarly, the WikiLeaks cables show that a new set of strategies seeking to contain and isolate the new regional "bad guy" has had a major impact on US policy toward a number of governments in Latin America and beyond.

Cables show the heads of US diplomatic missions in the region developing coordinated strategies to counter the Venezuelan regional "threat" in joint meetings—for example, at a conference in Rio de Janeiro in May 2007 with the chiefs of mission of Argentina, Bolivia, Brazil, Chile, Paraguay, and Uruguay. As WikiLeaks first revealed in December 2010,[11] following the Rio conference a cable was sent to the secretary of state and to President Bush's national security advisor with a detailed report on President Chávez's alleged "aggressive plans ... to create a unified Bolivarian movement throughout Latin America," and what to do about it. Ominously, the "areas of action" include enhancing ties with the region's military leaders:

> Venezuelan President Hugo Chavez is aggressively seeking to divide Latin America between those who buy into his populist, anti-American policies and authoritarian message and those who seek to establish and strengthen free-market, democratic based policies and institutions.
>
> ...
>
> Septel will offer our posts' collective views about how to best address the threat this campaign represents to US interests, but it is clear we need more (and more flexible) resources and tools to counter Chavez's efforts to assume

greater dominion over Latin America at the
expense of US leadership and interests.

1. … From posts' perspectives, there are six main
areas of action for the USG as it seeks to limit
Chavez's influence:

• Know the enemy: We have to better understand
  how Chavez thinks and what he intends;

• Directly engage: We must reassert our presence
  in the region, and engage broadly, especially
  with the "non-elites";

• Change the political landscape: We should
  offer a vision of hope and back it up with
  adequately-funded programs;

• Enhance military relationships: We should
  continue to strengthen ties to those military
  leaders in the region who share our concern
  over Chavez;

• Play to our strength: We must emphasize that
  democracy, and a free trade approach that
  includes corporate social responsibility,
  provides lasting solutions;

• Get the message out: Public diplomacy is key;
  this is a battle of ideas and visions. Septel
  provides detailed suggestions.

[07ASUNCION396]

A second follow-up cable goes further into the specifics of how to keep Venezuela from deepening its relations with the countries of South America's southern cone. The cable discusses pressuring governments belonging to the regional trade organization Mercosur in an effort to block Venezuela's entry into the group:

> 9. (C) With regard to Mercosur, we should not
> be timid in stating that Venezuela's membership
> will torpedo US interest in even considering
> direct negotiations with the trading bloc, and
> in questioning when and how Mercosur plans to
> apply its democracy clause strictures to Chavez's
> regime. Without voicing hostility to Mercosur per
> se, we can continue to pursue FTA's [sic] with
> interested countries, and encourage alternative
> arrangements, such as Chile,s [sic] "Arco del
> Pacifico" initiative. [07SANTIAGO983]

Though Paraguay's right-wing legislature refused to approve Venezuela's membership in Mercosur, Venezuela finally succeeded in becoming a full member in July 2012, after Paraguay was briefly suspended from the group following a "technical coup" against the country's elected president. Meanwhile, US government officials—in particular Vice President Joe Biden[12]—have been increasingly active promoters of the Pacific Alliance, a "free trade" initiative that succeeded the "Arco del Pacifico." Made up of some of the closest US allies in the region—Colombia, Mexico, Peru, and Chile—the Pacific Alliance is seen by former Brazilian president Lula,[13] Bolivian president Evo Morales, and others as a US-backed attempt to divide the region.

As the cables show, the US government also aggressively opposed Venezuela's efforts to build strong relations with the countries of the Caribbean and Central America. US diplomats in those countries focused in particular on trying to prevent their host governments from becoming members of the Venezuelan regional energy agreement, Petrocaribe.

Halting the expansion of Petrocaribe

Petrocaribe provides oil to member countries on a concessionary basis, with only a portion of the bill paid upfront and the remainder financed by Venezuela with extremely low long-term interest rates. In this way, Petrocaribe is conceived to eliminate the middlemen—the multinational oil companies that have long dominated the market—and allows for the formation of state-run companies and joint ventures to handle the import, distribution, and other infrastructure of the oil market. Petrocaribe also generated additional available funds for member governments which, according to the agreement's terms, are prioritized for social programs and other development projects.

Leaked cables show that, while US diplomats privately acknowledged clear economic benefits for countries joining Petrocaribe, behind the scenes they sought to prevent governments from becoming members—in some cases working with multinational oil firms in an effort to counter Venezuela in the region.

US authorities were concerned about Petrocaribe from the beginning. In July 2004, US deputy chief of mission in Venezuela, Stephen G. McFarland, warned: "We believe Venezuela is aggressively pushing its plans for the integration of energy companies throughout the Hemisphere to gain political strength" [04CARACAS2255].

For the US government, this was not about economic development, or increasing the sovereignty of countries beholden to the whims of the oil market and monopolistic multinationals; it was a political game, and one that has continued under the Obama administration. In June 2009, John Caulfield, the top-ranking US diplomat in Venezuela at the time, explained clearly why the US had invested so much in trying to counteract Petrocaribe: "Chavez's outsized ambition backed by petrodollars makes

Venezuela an active and intractable US competitor in the region" [09CARACAS750].

The US was worried that these new regional alliances would further erode US influence in the region. In January 2010, the US ambassador to Venezuela, Patrick Duddy, wrote that Chávez's "vision" for the hemisphere was "almost the mirror image of what the United States seeks," and that: "To the extent that Chavez succeeds in creating 'Bolivarian' regional institutions, he may be able to secure his own role in the region even if elections in other countries remove his political allies from office" [10CARACAS15].

The US apparently feared that Petrocaribe would succeed and traditional allies in the Caribbean would be less reliant on Washington, and therefore less beholden to US interests, no matter whom they elected as their leaders.

The US pushes back in Jamaica and Haiti

In August 2005, Chávez traveled to Jamaica to finalize the Petrocaribe cooperation agreement between the two countries. While the US could not block Jamaica's ascension, its displeasure was quickly revealed during a meeting on August 25:

```
Rattray [bilateral affairs director] then
asked the USG's perspective on PetroCaribe
arrangements. Pol/Econ Chief acknowledged the
seeming attractiveness of the agreement but
observed that it seemed highly unlikely that the
GOV would offer such favorable terms with no
expectation of quid pro quo. He then outlined USG
concerns about Chavez's destabilizing activities
in neighboring states, and his undermining of
democratic institutions at home.
```

Though Prime Minister P. J. Patterson signed the agreement, the chargé d'affaires, Thomas Tighe, noted in the same cable:

"Patterson is well aware of current difficulties between the USG and the GOV, and of potential downsides to concluding the agreement" [05KINGSTON2026].

But the potential downsides did not concern the impact of Petrocaribe on the Jamaican economy. Just a few months later, Tighe noted that, while "some quarters are beginning to fear a backlash from the US," in fact, "PetroCaribe could have a transforming effect on the Jamaican Economy." Later in 2008, as the world economic crisis spread, the embassy acknowledged: "Petrocaribe benefits have helped Jamaica avert economic disaster."

Another powerful set of actors opposed to Petrocaribe were international oil companies operating in Jamaica. In the months after Jamaica joined, the embassy had multiple meetings with officials from these companies who expressed concern about competing with the new state-owned companies. Texaco's country manager emailed an embassy official: "It is clear, that the present Government wants to vertically integrate into the [retail] petroleum sector. This is a significant policy shift which will have serious implications for the market" [05KINGSTON2495].

While the embassy officers had "repeatedly" engaged GOJ officials on Petrocaribe, they became frustrated that they had little to offer as an alternative. Consul General Ronald Robinson wrote in June 2006: "[I]n the absence of a clear USG alternative, traction is proving difficult" [06KINGSTON1298]. In August, Ambassador Brenda LaGrange Johnson suggested one such alternative, writing: "there are ways in which the USG can counter an over-reliance on the GOV," for example through a Millennium Challenge Corporation (MCC) agreement [06KINGSTON1687]. In this way, US efforts were similar to what was seen in Chapter 17, above: leveraging aid to influence and counter perceived shifts toward Venezuela. In the end, however, Jamaica failed to qualify for an MCC agreement. Since 2005, Jamaica has received funding support in excess of $2.4 billion through Petrocaribe—quite a large sum, amounting to more than 2 percent of the country's GDP from 2005 to 2013.[14]

In Haiti, the embassy worked hand-in-hand with big oil companies to try to prevent the country from joining Petrocaribe, despite acknowledging that it "would save USD 100 million per year," as was first reported by Dan Coughlin and Kim Ives in *The Nation*.[15] In April 2006, Ambassador Janet Sanderson wrote: "Post will continue to pressure [Haitian president René] Preval against joining PetroCaribe. Ambassador will see Preval's senior advisor Bob Manuel today. In previous meetings, he has acknowledged our concerns and is aware that a deal with Chavez would cause problems with us" [06PORTAUPRINCE692].

Leading multinational oil companies also expressed reservations. In October 2006, the embassy encouraged the companies to express their concerns regarding Petrocaribe to the government [06PORTAUPRINCE1960], and later, in January 2007, chargé d'affaires Thomas C. Tighe reported: "Chevron country manager Patryck Peru Dumesnil confirmed his company's anti-Petrocaribe position and said that ExxonMobil, the only other US oil company operating in Haiti, has told the GoH that it will not import Petrocaribe products" [07PORTAUPRINCE78].

The Haitian government eventually warned the oil companies that if they did not agree to the terms of the deal, "the companies may have to leave Haiti." Though Chevron eventually agreed to the terms, their opposition to Petrocaribe was made clear in a cable from February 2008: "Chevron management in the US does not want to make a lot of 'noise' about the agreement because they do not want to appear to support PetroCaribe" [08PORTAUPRINCE234].

Like Jamaica before it, Haiti ended up joining Petrocaribe, and has received over 30 million barrels of oil, amounting to well over $3 billion. The resources have become a key source of reconstruction financing following the January 12, 2010 earthquake, accounting for around 25 percent of all investment expenditures in 2013. Haitian president Michel Martelly has consistently praised the agreement, noting: "The cooperation with Venezuela is the most important in Haiti right now in terms of impact, direct impact."[16]

The Caribbean as a battlefield—against Chávez

In March 2006, SOUTHCOM, the US military's regional command, planned a "Partnership of the Americas" maritime exercise in the Caribbean. The US ambassador to Venezuela at the time, William Brownfield, wrote to regional embassies, SOUTHCOM, and the State Department in support of the plan:

Post supports Southcom's planned "Partnership of the Americas" maritime surge to the Caribbean to be led by the aircraft carrier USS George Washington. The deployment will help us to counter President Hugo Chavez' courtship of Caribbean countries and his attempts to pit them against the United States. The ship visit will provide benefits to participating nations that offer a stark contrast to the Venezuelan Government's failures to provide concrete help against drug trafficking and to promote sustainable economic development. Finally, the deployment advances US interests by feeding into Chavez' increasingly paranoid behavior and by creating conditions in which the Venezuelan leader could make a mistake.

Brownfield elaborated on what this "mistake" might be:

Post will promote the visit of the carrier group as a routine US military and humanitarian outreach to the region. Nonetheless, the BRV's portrayal of the deployment as evidence of US imperialism will likely be the fallout. If the

```
BRV does not allege the visit as proof of US
plans to invade, it will certainly bemoan it as
a show of power aimed at intimidating Venezuela.
Any Chavez attempts to portray regional states
as "colonies" of the empire will further
undermine the Bolivarian President's credibility.
[06CARACAS776]
```

The USS George Washington would go on to dock not just in a number of Caribbean countries, but also in Honduras and Nicaragua. But if the US believed this show of force would prevent Caribbean countries from developing closer relations with Venezuela, they turned out to be mistaken. Despite intense lobbying from US embassies and the direct involvement of President Bush and other high-ranking officials, countries throughout the region continued to sign up for Petrocaribe.

Petrocaribe moves into Central America

In 2008, as Guatemala prepared to join Petrocaribe, US ambassador James Derham acknowledged:

```
Embassy officers have repeatedly urged the
GOG to weigh carefully the pros and cons of
a PetroCaribe deal, and suggested that the
[Ministry of Foreign Affairs] ask current
PetroCaribe members about their experiences
with Venezuelan compliance with the terms of
agreements. The influential private sector and
some media have also urged the GOG not to sign.
[08GUATEMALA600]
```

President Álvaro Colom backed out of the agreement after a visit to Washington, DC. Derham wrote in June 2008: "When President Colom returned from Washington after meeting with President Bush in Washington in late April, he instructed Meany [minister of energy and mines] to back off negotiations with Venezuela" [08GUATEMALA783]. In case that was still not enough, Derham then told Meany: "[T]he decision to sign a Petrocaribe agreement would be an unpleasant surprise to Washington."

President Bush also became involved when the Honduran government began to give serious consideration to joining Petrocaribe. Ambassador Charles Ford wrote to the CIA, the secretary of state, and various other agencies in May 2006 in a secret cable: "A suggested POTUS warning to [President of Honduras Manuel] Zelaya that does not challenge his option for making a deal, but leaves him anxious about USG reactions to closer ties to Chavez, could prove a crucial bulwark against the spread of Chavez's influence in the region." Ford added that, "since the deal cannot likely be stopped, we should use it to extract maximum advantage in other areas of bilateral importance," concluding: "Zelaya is no Chavez, but if left unchanged, circumstances could make him complicit in advancing Chavez's influence in the region" [06TEGUCIGALPA985].

After the meeting with Bush, Zelaya actually portrayed it as a "green light" for Honduras to move forward with Petrocaribe—an interpretation that caused the embassy much grief. Chargé d'affaires James Williard wrote:

> Despite very clear warnings from Post and from POTUS about the risks of a deal with Chavez, it seems clear from his remarks that Zelaya remains intent on pushing forward with his plan. It is unclear if his is a case of hearing only what he wants to hear, or of grossly misrepresenting POTUS' remarks for political motives. In either case, it seems clear to Post that Zelaya seeks to convince his domestic audience that the USG would be comfortable with a GOH/GOV deal. This has two

```
immediate, sharp repercussions: first, it makes
the inking of such a deal more likely (with all
the negative consequences that implies for warmer
GOH relations with Chavez), and second, this
public spin could be used to undermine Post's
credibility, by implying (as El Heraldo has done)
that Post's tough stance on this issue is not
supported by Washington. [06TEGUCIGALPA1026]
```

The next year, in March 2007, Ford bragged in a cable: "Over the last year, USG action stopped a PetroCaribe deal with Venezuela" [07TEGUCIGALPA493]. Yet this victory was short-lived, as Honduras would go on to join Petrocaribe in December 2007. Relations would further deteriorate after this point between Honduras and the US, culminating in the June 2009 coup d'état, as will be discussed in more detail below.

Lasting impact

The diplomatic cables provide clear evidence that the US was both concerned about Petrocaribe and actively seeking to convince countries not to join—not because the deal did not make sense, but because of a perceived political battle for the region. For the US, however, it has been a losing battle. With El Salvador's decision to join in May 2014 following the election of President Salvador Sánchez Cerén, there are at the time of writing nineteen countries participating in Petrocaribe.

According to PDVSA, the Venezuelan state oil company, the program is providing over 40 percent of the energy needs of member countries.[17] It has become so important to these economies that SOUTHCOM commander General John F. Kelly told the press in March 2014 that, without Petrocaribe, "[t]heir economies would, I think, collapse."[18] More recently, the agreement has allowed for countries to pay back debt with in-kind goods, such as agricultural products, which now account for an estimated 21 percent of all payments.

Lobbying other governments in efforts to isolate Venezuela

In many instances, cables show US officials lobbying other governments to assist the US in its attempts to isolate the Venezuelan government. In November of 2007, for instance, Secretary of State Condoleezza Rice sent a cable to eleven US embassies in Latin America, its embassy in Canada, and the US mission to the European Union, asking them to urge their hosts to criticize Venezuela publicly:

```
Department requests action addressees demarche
host governments, at the highest appropriate
level, to: 1) share our concerns about the anti-
democratic changes in the proposed constitutional
reform package; 2) highlight growing dissension
within Venezuela and the increasingly repressive
methods employed by the GoV; and 3) request that
host governments join the voices of international
concern regarding GoV lack of adherence to its
commitments under the Inter-American Democratic
Charter. [07STATE154674_a]
```

The constitutional reform package may not have been to the US government's liking but, given that it was to be voted on in a national referendum, as required by the constitution, it would be difficult to label it "anti-democratic." Unsurprisingly, with the exception of staunch US allies El Salvador (at the time) and Canada, no other governments in the region complied with the secretary of state's request. "This is an internal Venezuelan matter," a Chilean diplomat told a US political counselor who delivered the demarche.[19]

A key component of the US strategy for "containing" Chávez regionally was to encourage Argentina and Brazil—the two largest economies in South America—to act as a mitigating force. The governments of Néstor Kirchner and Lula da Silva were seen in Washington policy circles as "center left" administrations when they first entered office; both would move farther to the left in their foreign policies as time went on.

After years of encouraging the government of Argentina (GOA) to act as a moderating influence on Chávez, US diplomats appeared frustrated when, later on, Argentina seemed to move closer to Venezuela. In a May 2006 cable describing Kirchner's remarks to the press, Kirchner reportedly denies that the US (or Brazil) has "pressured him" to limit Chávez's influence; but the US embassy in Buenos Aires appears to disagree:

> President Kirchner said that the US and Brazil
> had not pressured him "to limit the influence of
> Chavez in the region," although he acknowledged
> that US officials had expressed their concern
> about Chavez to him. (Comment: US officials, from
> President Bush to the Ambassador and leading
> Embassy officials have all repeatedly stated
> our concerns to President Kirchner and his top
> advisors about Chavez and his policies at home
> and in the region. *While we have not enlisted
> the GOA's support in "limiting the influence of
> Chavez" per se, we have repeatedly sought the
> GOA's help in moderating Chavez and his policies
> in Venezuela and the region.* [06BUENOSAIRES1176]
> [Emphasis added.]

However, during a February 2007 trip to Venezuela, Kirchner publicly repudiated the pressure to "contain" Chávez:

> During the agreements signing ceremony, Kirchner
> commented "we are and will be absolutely
> respectful, both of us, of the relations and
> internal situations in our countries … *It is
> said that some countries should 'contain' others,*

> that *Lula and I should 'contain' Chavez. That*
> *is absolutely wrong. Together with our brother,*
> *President Chavez, we are building integration in*
> *South America for the dignity of our peoples." ...*
> In response to Kirchner's comments, local media
> reports that Chavez said "they have failed and
> will fail—the travelers from the North who are
> coming to the South to try to divide us, to sow
> discord." [07BUENOSAIRES360] [Emphasis added.]

The US also attempted to enlist Brazil in its effort to "contain" Chávez. As with Argentina, this has achieved little success. In a March 2005 cable, Brazilian foreign minister Celso Amorim pushes back hard when the US ambassador says that Chávez is a "threat to the region":

> 2. (S) Ambassador outlined points ... on the USG's
> growing concern about Chavez's rhetoric and
> actions, and stressed that *the USG increasingly*
> *sees Chavez as a threat to the region. Per*
> *refs, he asked that FM Amorim consider*
> *institutionalizing a more intensive political*
> *engagement between the USG and GOB on Chavez,*
> *and standing up a dedicated intelligence-sharing*
> *arrangement. FM Amorim was clear in his response:*
> *"We do not see Chavez as a threat."* Amorim said
> that Chavez has been democratically elected
> (in a general election that was reaffirmed by a
> referendum), enjoys substantial domestic support,
> is a popular figure on the international left and
> is leader of a major power on the continent. For
> those reasons, "we have to work with him and do
> not want to do anything that would jeopardize
> our relationship with him," Amorim affirmed.
> [05BRASILIA715] [Emphasis added.]

Instead, Brazil would support Venezuela's entry into Mercosur [06BRASILIA206]—strongly opposed by the US government—and, in September 2009, privately urged the US government to re-establish diplomatic relations with Venezuela:

> 7. (C) While insisting they did not want to engage in mediation between the USG and GOV, both Garcia and Amorim used the opportunity to encourage the United States to establish "a direct channel of communication with President Chavez." Amorim suggested that a good USG-GOV dialogue would have an impact on the domestic situation in Venezuela, as well, because much of the opposition to Chavez has ties to the United States. [09BRASILIA1113]

Opposing the rise of Venezuela's "radical populist" allies

The cables clearly show that the US government opposed some political leaders in the region who it considered to be too close to Venezuela. US diplomats portray these leaders as agents of Chávez simply because they had warm relations with the Venezuelan president and supported a similar anti-neoliberal or nationalist agenda. For example, soon after Evo Morales was elected president of Bolivia, US ambassador David Greenlee commented that Bolivia's government had "fallen openly into Venezuela's embrace" [06LAPAZ1418]. In Ecuador, a US diplomat labeled Rafael Correa a "stalking-horse for Chavez" months before he was first elected president, in 2006.[20] "Were he to be elected," the same diplomat later wrote, "we would expect Correa to eagerly seek to join the Chávez-Morales-Kirchner group of nationalist-populist South American leaders."[21]

While commander of SOUTHCOM in 2004, General James Hill announced that the region's "radical populist" leaders were an emerging national security threat for the US.[22] The State

Department shared a similar view and, as we saw in Chapter 17, opposed these left-leaning leaders through various forms of internal intervention. Part of the justification for this intervention was based on the supposition that Chávez effectively controlled these leaders thanks to his political charisma and to Venezuela's petrodollars.

In March 2006, the US ambassadors from Central America held a strategy and coordination meeting with the assistant secretary of state for the Western Hemisphere, Thomas Shannon. The first issue on their agenda was "Populist Politics," and they focused on the upcoming Nicaraguan elections that Sandinista leader Daniel Ortega was widely expected to win. His victory, according to US ambassador to Nicaragua Paul Trivelli, would signal the expansion of Chávez's influence in the region:

```
2. (SBU) Ambassador Trivelli made it clear
that Ortega is the same populist Mafioso who
drove Nicaragua into the ground under previous
Sandanista [sic] rule. An Ortega victory in
upcoming presidential elections would give Chavez
a foothold in the region and trigger another
round of human and capital flight. A/S Shannon
said it is important that neither Ortega nor
Aleman win, given Ortega's influence over Aleman.
Leaders in the region must focus on how important
these elections are, he added. [06SANSALVADOR963]
[Emphasis added.]
```

The ambassadors also expressed concern about the potential rise of pro-Chávez "leftist demagogues" in Panama and Guatemala, the latter being where "the election of Morales in Bolivia [had been] a welcome event in the indigenous population." But the US ambassador to Guatemala, James Derham, assured his colleagues that the indigenous in Guatemala were "still reeling from the war years" (during which a US-backed counter-insurrection campaign had killed an estimated 200,000 civilians) and, as a result, were "not yet organized enough to put together a political campaign." Going forward, the diplomats agreed to "continue to monitor populist political activities in the region and share experiences on best practices to support democracies in the region."

At the time of this meeting, the ambassadors did not yet consider Honduran president Manuel Zelaya to be a Chávez-aligned "radical populist." But this perception gradually changed after Zelaya's government joined Petrocaribe in 2007, and then the left-wing Bolivarian Alliance for the Peoples of Our America group of nations in 2008. A February 2008 cable shows that the US embassy believed that Chávez had an influence on bilateral talks regarding the possible commercialization of Honduras's Soto Cano airbase—the US military's main platform in Central America:

```
12. (C) Under this administration, we can
expect to continue to receive requests for
"re-examining" the issue, especially as Zelaya
creeps closer and closer to Venezuela's Hugo
Chavez. We believe that Chavez and other left-
leaning friends might question Zelaya as to
why Honduras has a US base within its borders,
and press him to demand more "benefits."
[08TEGUCIGALPA165]
```

By September 2008, it was clear that the embassy had given up on Zelaya and was focused on the prospect of a political transition with the elections of November 2009:

```
10. (C) With only 16 months before he leaves
office, our goal is to get Zelaya through his
term without causing any irreparable damage
to bilateral relations or to Honduras, [sic]
future development possibilities, and to
```

minimize further expansion of relations with
Chavez. Successful elections that lead to a
successor will play a key role. We intend
to work with the other donor nations and
international organizations to support this end.
[08TEGUCIGALPA863]

Zelaya was ejected from office in June 2009 through a military coup d'état executed by General Romeo Vásquez Velásquez— "friend of the USG and the Embassy" according to a 2007 cable.[23] Though the Obama administration eventually made statements against the coup, they balked at efforts by member countries of the Organization of American States to achieve the quick return of Zelaya to power.[24] Instead, State Department officials first hinted, then announced, that they would support and recognize the November 2009 elections regardless of whether Zelaya was reinstated beforehand, thereby removing pressure on the coup government to restore democracy.

Cables show that, in the weeks before and following the elections, US embassy officials in a number of Latin American countries attempted to persuade host governments to recognize the Honduran elections,[25] as did Arturo Valenzuela, assistant secretary of state for Western Hemisphere affairs, when he traveled to Argentina, Brazil, Paraguay, and Uruguay.[26] Despite this campaign by Washington, nearly every country in the region considered the vote—held under an illegal coup regime—to be illegitimate.

There is a great deal of consistent evidence in the cables, from within Venezuela and elsewhere, as well as declassified CIA and other government documents, suggesting that the US has generally followed the strategy laid out in cable 06CARACAS3356. The stated objective of "isolating Chavez internationally" has been pursued with particular zeal in the Latin American and Caribbean region, where the US has attempted to sway or pressure countries to avoid close relationships with the Venezuelan government, and has attempted to undercut Venezuelan initiatives (such as Petrocaribe), to isolate Venezuela from international fora (such as Mercosur), and tried, without success, to use other left-leaning countries—most notably Argentina and Brazil—to "manage" Venezuela and limit its influence. Within Venezuela, other components of the strategy have clearly been followed, such as efforts to "penetrate Chavez's base" and "divide Chavismo." Throughout the Chávez era, the US coordinated closely with various elements of Venezuela's opposition, from law-abiding political parties to violent student protesters, coup-supporters, and others.

There is evidence that these strategies were not abandoned after Chávez's death, and that in fact the US government may be pursuing them even more assiduously in the post-Chávez era. Only when more evidence emerges, through leaked or declassified State Department cables or other government documents, will we be able to judge to what extent many of their more aggressive actions were part of an overall strategy—for example, Washington's refusal to recognize the legitimacy of Maduro's 2013 election to the presidency.[27] (The opposition took advantage of Maduro's relatively narrow margin of victory to cry fraud, even as audits of the ballot showed clearly that Maduro had won fairly.[28] The Obama administration alone refused to recognize Maduro's victory—a clear signal encouraging the opposition to continue to claim the new president lacked legitimacy—and only later reversed its position, under pressure from South American governments.) Embassy cables rarely offer any glimpse into some of the most subversive activities being carried out by the US government abroad, so what they reveal may only be the tip of the iceberg in terms of US efforts to undermine and de-legitimize Venezuela's government and counter its influence in the region.

Notes

INTRODUCTION

1   For a fascinating account of the communications used in historical empires, see Harold Innis, *Empire and Communications* (Oxford: Clarendon, 1950).

2   In 2002, US writer Charles Krauthammer observed that people were "now coming out of the closet on the word 'empire,'" reflecting the unrivaled dominance of the United States 'culturally, economically, technologically and militarily.'" Google statistics for words in books published in English over the thirty-year period to 2008 show a 450 percent increase in the use of the phrase "US empire" between 2000 and 2008, without any corresponding increase in the left-wing phrase "US imperialism" (Google Books Ngram Viewer, at books.google.com). On January 5, 2003, the Sunday magazine for the *New York Times* ran with a cover declaring: "American Empire: Get Used To It." Even military operations are starting to adopt the word. For example, the yearly combined Anglophone space, air, and ground intelligence and targeting fusion exercise led by the United States, which posits an insurgent challenge to occupying Anglophone forces, is called "Operation Empire Challenge." (**https://wikileaks.org/wiki/Anglo_spy_fusion:_Operation_Empire_Challenge_-_87_documents,_2008**).

3   "The United States may conduct some ARSOF [Army Special Operations Forces] UW [Unconventional Warfare] operations in states that are not belligerents. The US Ambassador and his Country Team may in fact have complete or significant control over ARSOF inside the ambassador's host country of responsibility. In such cases, the relationship between ARSOF conducting UW and the Country Team requires the best possible coordination to be effective and appropriate." This quote is from what is probably the single most important book for understanding the current US approach to bringing all elements of US national power (diplomatic, media, financial, law enforcement, intelligence, commercial, and military) to bear in order to coerce smaller states into submission. The range of possible

outcomes ascends to and includes covertly overthrowing the state's government through the use of surrogate forces controlled by US Special Operations Command. The handbook, which is active policy, was not for public release, but was released by WikiLeaks. "Army Special Operations Forces Unconventional Warfare, FM 3-05.130, 30 Sep 2008," Chapter 2-2: "Diplomatic Instrument of United States National Power and Unconventional Warfare," at **https://wikileaks. org/wiki/US_Army_Special_Operations_Forces_Unconventional_ Warfare,_FM3-05.130,_30_Sep_2008**. It should be read together with the counter-revolution equivalent, also released by WikiLeaks, "US Special Forces Foreign Internal Defense Operations, FM 3-05.202, Feb 2007, at **https://wikileaks.org/wiki/US_Special_Forces_Foreign_ Internal_Defense_Operations,_FM_3-05.202,_Feb_2007**, and the 2003 version of "Unconventional Warfare," at **https://wikileaks. org/wiki/US_Special_Forces_Unconventional_Warfare_Operations:_ overthrowing_governments%2C_sabotage%2C_subversion%2C_ intelligence_and_abduction%2C_FM_3-05.201%2C_Apr_2003**.

4 "Strategic Plan, FY 2014–2017," at **http://www.state.gov/documents/ organization/223997.pdf**.

5 Brian Fung, "5.1 Million Americans Have Security Clearances. That's More than the Entire Population of Norway," *Washington Post*, March 24, 2014.

6 "US Air Force Blocked Websites," at muckrock.com.

7 Defense Security Service, "Notice to Contractors Cleared under the National Industrial Security Program on Protecting Classified Information and the Integrity of Government Data on Cleared Contractor Information Technology (IT) Systems," February 11, 2011, at muckrock.s3.amazonaws.com; "1-24-14_MR9321_RES_ ID2014-095.pdf," pp. 36–46, at muckrock.s3.amazonaws.com.

8 Rachel Slajda, "Library of Congress Blocks Access to Wikileaks," TPM, December 3, 2010, at talkingpointsmemo.com; Matt Raymond, "Why the Library of Congress Is Blocking Wikileaks," December 3, 2010, Library of Congress, at blogs.loc-gov.

9 Subsequently reversed. Kevin Gosztola, "US National Archives Has Blocked Searches for 'WikiLeaks,'" *The Dissenter*, November 3, 2012, at dissenter.firedoglake.com.

10 Chelsea (formerly Bradley) Manning was detained without trial for 1,103 days, an infringement of her right to speedy justice. The United Nations special rapporteur for torture, Juan Méndez, formally found that Manning had been treated in a manner that was cruel and inhuman, and that possibly amounted to torture. See Ed Pilkington, "Bradley Manning's Treatment Was Cruel and Inhuman, UN Torture Chief Rules," *Guardian*, March 12, 2012. The government charged Manning—accused of being a journalistic source for WikiLeaks— with thirty-four individual counts of violations of the Uniform Code of Military Justice, including parts of the Espionage Act, the combined maximum sentence for which was over one hundred years in prison.

See Kim Zetter, "Bradley Manning Charged with 22 New Counts, Including Capital Offense," *Wired*, February 3, 2011, at wired.com. Manning was prohibited by the court from making defense arguments as to public interest, motive, or the lack of actual harm resulting from her alleged actions (see Ed Pilkington, "Bradley Manning Denied Chance to Make Whistleblower Defence," *Guardian*, January 17, 2013), and she offered a limited guilty plea (see Alexa O'Brien, "Pfc. Manning's Statement for the Providence Inquiry," Alexaobrien.com, February 28, 2013). This plea was refused by the government, which sought to convict Manning on the full charge sheet. The case went to trial in June 2013 under conditions of unprecedented secrecy, against which WikiLeaks and the Center for Constitutional Rights litigated. In August 2013 Manning was found guilty on seventeen counts and sentenced to thirty-five years in prison. See Tom McCarthy, "Bradley Manning Tells Lawyer After Sentencing: 'I'm Going to Be OK'—as it happened," *Guardian*, August 21, 2013. At the time of publication, she is appealing her case to the United States Army Court of Criminal Appeals, and a hearing is expected in mid 2015. See "Chelsea Manning's 35-Year Prison Sentence Upheld by US Army General," *Guardian*, April 14, 2014.

11 Josh Gerstein, "Blocking WikiLeaks Emails Trips Up Bradley Manning Prosecution," *Politico*, March 15, 2012, at www.politico.com.

12 Simon DeDeo, Robert X. D. Hawkins, Sara Klingenstein, and Tim Hitchcock, "Bootstrap Methods for the Empirical Study of Decision-Making and Information Flows in Social Systems," Cornell University Library website, February 5, 2013, at arxiv.org. "Scholars in other disciplines have been more willing to make use of leaked information. In fields as varied as informatics, applied mathematics, geography, and economics, researchers have enthusiastically turned to the leaked information of the Afghan War Diary and the Iraq War Logs as invaluable data sources for modeling and predicting conflict (O'Loughlin et al., 2010; Linke et al., 2012; Zammit-Mangion et al., 2012; Cseke et al., 2013; Rusch et al., 2013; Zammit-Mangion et al., 2013). Indeed, DeDeo et al. say that the Afghan War Diary 'is likely to become a standard set for both the analysis of human conflict and the study of empirical methods for the analysis of complex, multi-modal data' (p. 2,257). Legal scholars have also begun to discover the value of the *Cablegate* corpus as a data source. Khoo and Smith (2011) and Mendis (2012) both cite WikiLeaks cables to support their analyses of international relations in Asia. More recently, El Said (2012) quotes extensively from leaked diplomatic cables to elucidate the bilateral free trade agreement negotiations between the United States and Jordan." Gabriel J. Michael, "Who's Afraid of Wikileaks? Missed Opportunities in Political Science Research," *Review of Policy Research*, December 22, 2014 (forthcoming).

13 An example of political censorship by the *New York Times* involved the cable 10STATE17263. The cable, which is lengthy, covers discus-

sions between Russian and American diplomats about the rumor that Iran had acquired ballistic missiles from North Korea. The *New York Times* claimed the cable showed that the North Korean missiles would let Iran's "warheads reach targets as far away as Western Europe, including Berlin." However, the overwhelming majority of the cable's 11,150 words present the view that the shipment, if it occurred at all, was for research or part salvage, and was of little consequence, as North Korea had not even successfully tested the design. The *New York Times* actively misrepresented the content of the cable "on the request of the Obama administration," gutting the document almost in its entirety, using only the twenty-six words that supported its stance on Iran, and censoring the other 99.97 percent of the original cable. William J. Broad, James Glanz, and David E. Sanger, "Iran Fortifies Its Arsenal with the Aid of North Korea," *New York Times*, November 28, 2010. See also Peter Hart, "NYT Oversells WikiLeaks/Iranian Missiles Story," FAIR, November 29, 2010, at fair.org.

Most of our media partners engaged in similar kinds of selective censorship of our materials. Among the more prolific of the censors were the *New York Times*, the *Guardian* and *El País*. The website Cabledrum has assembled statistics on the instances of censorship by some of our major partners. See Cabledrum, "Short Analysis of Cablegate Redactions," Cabledrum, October 3, 2011 (see also Cabledrum, "Cable Publications by Mainstream Media," Cabledrum, October 2011). Cabledrum has also assembled a list of particularly serious instances of political censorship. See Cabledrum, "Cablegate Redactions Abused for Censorship," Cabledrum, October 3, 2011. See also Cabledrum, "Redacted Company Names," Cabledrum, October 2011. All of the above references are available at cabledrum.net.

The topic of censorship among our media partners is discussed at length in my other work. See Julian Assange, *Cypherpunks* (New York: OR Books, 2012), pp. 121–4, and endnotes 104–12; Julian Assange, *When Google Met WikiLeaks* (New York: OR Books, 2014), pp. 167–70, and footnotes 259–63.

14 Hillary Rodham Clinton, "America's Engagement in the Asia-Pacific," US Department of State, October 28, 2010, at state.gov.

15 Daniel Ellsberg to Henry Kissinger, 1969, quoted in *Secrets: A Memoir of Vietnam and the Pentagon Papers* (London: Penguin, 2013), p. 238.

CHAPTER 1: AMERICA AND THE DICTATORS

1 https://www.wikileaks.org/plusd/cables/09ASHGABAT1633_a.html.

2 Justin Elliott, "What Other Dictators Does the US Support?," *Salon*, February 2, 2011.

3 Domenico Losurdo, *Liberalism: A Counter-History* (London/New York: Verso, 2011).

4   See Antony Anghie, *Imperialism, Sovereignty and the Making of International Law* (Cambridge/New York: Cambridge University Press, 2004).

5   On this background, see Erez Manela, *The Wilsonian Moment: Self-Determination and the International Origins of Anticolonial Nationalism* (Oxford/New York: Oxford University Press, 2007). On the colonial and racist aspects of Wilson's policy, see Richard Seymour, *The Liberal Defence of Murder* (London/New York: Verso, 2008), pp. 97–104.

6   William J. Foltz, "Building the Newest Nations: Short Run Strategies and Long Run Problems," in Karl Wolfgang Deutsch and William J. Foltz, eds, *Nation Building in Comparative Contexts* (New Brunswick, NJ: Transaction, 1966), p. 118.

7   On the racist rationale for supporting right-wing dictatorships, see David F. Schmitz, *The United States and Right-Wing Dictatorships, 1965–1989* (Cambridge/New York: Cambridge University Press, 2006), pp. 10–18. On the colonial assumptions of "modernization theory," see Nils Gilman, *Mandarins of the Future: Modernization Theory in Cold War America* (Baltimore/London: Johns Hopkins University Press, 2003). As Gilman puts it: "The categorical construction of enlightened modernity ... emerged from the simultaneous construction of its malformed twin: a non-European, or non-Western Other. Although modernization theory eschewed the racism of earlier colonialist discourses, it still defined modernity in contrast to an implicitly inferior 'traditional' other" (p. 28).

8   Jeane J. Kirkpatrick, "Dictatorship and Double Standards," *Commentary*, November 1, 1979; Jeane J. Kirkpatrick, "The Hobbes Problem," AEI Public Policy Papers, Washington, DC, 1981.

9   On the rise of human rights discourse in US foreign policy, see Nicolas Guilhot, *The Democracy Makers: Human Rights and the Politics of Global Order* (New York: Columbia University Press, 2012).

10 Thomas Carothers, *In the Name of Democracy: US Policy Toward Latin America in the Reagan Years* (Berkeley, CA/Oxford: University of California Press, 1991), p. 242.

11 Weinstein quoted in David Ignatius, "Innocence Abroad: The New World of Spyless Coups," *Washington Post*, September 22, 1991.

12 Greg Grandin, *Empire's Workshop: Latin America, the United States and the Rise of the New Imperialism* (New York: Metropolitan, 2006), pp. 100–6; William I. Robinson, *Promoting Polyarchy: Globalization, US Intervention, and Hegemony* (Cambridge: Cambridge University Press, 1996); Noam Chomsky, *The Culture of Terrorism* (London: Pluto Press, 1989); William I. Robinson, "What to Expect from US 'Democracy Promotion' in Iraq," *New Political Science* 26: 3 (September 2004).

13 The IRI, an affiliated institute of the NED, was directly involved in the Bush administration's intervention in Haiti. See Walt Bogdanich and Jenny Norderberg, "Mixed US Signals Helped Tilt Haiti Toward

Chaos," *New York Times*, January 29, 2006. On Venezuela, see Christopher Marquis, "US Bankrolling Is Under Scrutiny for Ties to Chávez Ouster," *New York Times*, April 25, 2002. On Egypt, see Eric A. Snider and David M. Faris, "The Arab Spring: US Democracy Promotion in Egypt," *Middle East Policy* 18: 3 (Fall 2011), pp. 49–62.

14 https://wikileaks.org/cable/2004/12/04ANKARA7211.html.

15 Ibrahim Saleh, "WikiLeaks and the Arab Spring: The Twists and Turns of Media, Culture and Power," in Benedetta Brevini, Arne Hintz, and Patrick McCurdy, eds, *Beyond WikiLeaks: Implications for the Future of Communications, Journalism and Society* (London: Palgrave Macmillan, 2013), p. 241.

16 https://wikileaks.org/cable/2008/06/08TUNIS679.html.

17 http://www.wikileaks.ch/cable/2009/07/09TUNIS492.html.

18 "Fact Sheet on US Military and Political Assistance for Tunisia," Embassy of the United States, Tunisia, April 2012, at tunisia.usembassy. gov.

19 For some useful background on this, see L. B. Ware, "The Role of the Tunisian Military in the Post-Bourgiba Era," *Middle East Journal* 39: 1 (Winter 1985), pp. 27–47.

20 https://wikileaks.org/cable/2006/01/06TUNIS55.html.

21 Ian Black, "WikiLeaks Cables: Tunisia Blocks Site Reporting 'Hatred' of First Lady," *Guardian*, December 7, 2010.

22 Sean Yom, "Authoritarian State Building in the Middle East: From Durability to Revolution," Centre for Democracy, Development and the Rule of Law, Working Papers No. 121, February 2011.

23 Milan Sanina, "WikiLeaks Cables Help Uncover What Made Tunisians Revolt," *PBS Newshour*, January 25, 2011; David Kirkpatrick, "Protests Spread to Tunisia's Capital, and a Curfew Is Decreed," *New York Times*, January 12, 2011. On the wider issue of WikiLeaks' role in the Arab Spring, see Ibrahim Saleh, "WikiLeaks and the Arab Spring: The Twists and Turns of Media, Culture and Power," in Brevini, Hintz, and McCurdy, eds, *Beyond WikiLeaks*.

24 Pro-American slogans reported in Anouar Majid, *Islam and America: Building a Future Without Prejudice* (Lanham, MA: Rowman & Littlefield, 2012), p. 6. See also "Statement by the President on Events in Tunisia," White House Office of the Press Secretary, January 4, 2011, at whitehouse.gov. Amazingly, the Obama administration began to complain that it had not foreseen the revolt, and had been let down by intelligence and diplomatic staff. In fact, as the WikiLeaks documents attest, US diplomats told their bosses all they needed to know about Tunisia. Mark Mazetti, "Obama Faults Spy Agencies' Performance in Gauging Mideast Unrest, Officials Say," *New York Times*, February 4, 2011.

25 https://wikileaks.org/cable/2009/07/09CAIRO1468.html.

26 Ibid.

27 http://www.wikileaks.ch/cable/2008/09/08CAIRO2091.html.

28 https://www.wikileaks.org/cable/2009/05/09CAIRO874.html.

29 Christian Fuchs, *Social Media: A Critical Introduction* (London: Sage, 2014), p. 193.

30 Simon Mabon, "Aiding Revolution? Wikileaks, Communication and the 'Arab Spring' in Egypt," *Third World Quarterly* 34: 10 (2013).

31 "Egypt Braces for Nationwide Protests," *Agence France-Presse*, January 25, 2011.

32 Susanna Kim, "Egypt's Mubarak Likely to Retain Vast Wealth," *ABC News*, February 2, 2011.

33 Heba Afify, "Activists Hope 25 January Protest Will Be Start of 'Something Big,'" *Almasry Alyoum*, January 24, 2011; "Egyptians Report Poor Communication Services on Day of Anger," *Almasry Alyoum*, January 25, 2011; Elizabeth Bumiller, "Calling for Restraint, Pentagon Faces Test of Influence with Ally," *New York Times*, January 29, 2011.

34 Dan Murphy, "Joe Biden says Egypt's Mubarak No Dictator, He Shouldn't Step Down..." *Christian Science Monitor*, January 27, 2011.

35 "Blair Says Leak of Palestine Papers 'Destabilising' for Peace Process," *Ulster Television News*, January 28, 2011.

36 Quoted in Maria do Céu de Pinho Ferreira Pinto, "Mapping the Obama Administration's Response to the Arab Spring," *Revista Brasileira de Política Internacional* 55: 2 (July–December 2012).

37 For an insight into the growing coordination between the Egyptian left and Islamists, see Hossam el-Hamalawy, "Comrades and Brothers," *Middle East Report* 37: 242 (Spring 2007).

38 Hossam el-Hamalawy and Joel Beinin, "Egyptian Textile Workers Confront the New Economic Order," Middle East Research and Information Project, March 25, 2007.

39 https://wikileaks.org/plusd/cables/08CAIRO2572_a.html; https://cablegatesearch.wikileaks.org/cable.php?id=07CAIRO3001.

40 Nicholas Kitchen, "The Contradictions of Hegemony: The United States and the Arab Spring," in *After the Arab Spring: Power Shift in the Middle East?* (London: LSE Ideas, 2012).

41 Eric A. Snyder and David M. Faris, "The Arab Spring: US Democracy Promotion in Egypt," *Middle East Policy* XVIII: 3 (Fall 2011).

42 https://wikileaks.org/plusd/cables/08CAIRO2572_a.html. The April 6 movement was named after a wildcat labor strike that had turned into a violent conflict with state authorities. A Facebook group in support of the workers had gained 77,000 supporters by early 2009, at a time when only 500,000 Egyptians had Facebook access.

43 Ron Nixon, "US Groups Helped Nurture Arab Uprisings," *New York Times*, April 14, 2011.

44 Kirit Radia and Alex Marquardt, "Young Leaders of Egypt's Revolt Snub Clinton in Cairo," *ABC News*, March 15, 2011.

45 Anne-Marie Slaughter, "Interests vs. Values? Misunderstanding

Obama's Libya Strategy," *New York Review of Books Blog*, March 30, 2011, at nybooks.com.

46 https://wikileaks.org/plusd/cables/09SANAA1669_a.html. On the strikes in the Abyan province, see Hakim Almasmari, "US Makes a Drone Attack a Day in Yemen," *The National*, June 15, 2011. On the broad-based opposition, see Ahmed Al-Haj, "100,000 Protesters Hit the Streets in Yemen," *NBC News*, June 10, 2011.

47 Adam Entous and Julian E. Barnes, "US Wavers on 'Regime Change,'" *Wall Street Journal*, March 5, 2011; Kevin Baron, "Gates: Protracted Bahrain Negotiations Allowing Greater Iran Influence," *Stars and Stripes*, March 12, 2011; Nick Turse, "How the Tiny Kingdom of Bahrain Strong-Armed the President of the United States," *TomDispatch.com*, March 15, 2011.

48 https://wikileaks.org/gifiles/docs/85/85406_-alpha-fwd-private-police-advisor-to-moi-update-.html.

49 The suppression of the Yemen opposition began well before the Arab Spring. See, for example, Dana Priest, "US Military Teams, Intelligence Deeply Involved in Aiding Yemen on Strikes," *Washington Post*, January 27, 2010. On the agreement with Saudi Arabia, see Pepe Escobar, "Exposed: The US–Saudi Libya Deal," *Asia Times*, April 2, 2011. On the Obama administration's close relationship with Egyptian dictator General Sisi, see "Egypt Army 'Restoring Democracy,' says John Kerry," *BBC News*, August 1, 2014; and Jay Solomon, "John Kerry Voices Strong Support for Egyptian President Sisi," *Wall Street Journal*, June 22, 2014. On the massacres, see Patrick Kingsley, "Egypt Massacre Was Premeditated, Says Human Rights Watch," *Guardian*, August 12, 2014.

50 On the largely overlooked intervention in Bahrain, see Amy Austin Holmes, "The Military Intervention that the World Forgot," Al Jazeera America, March 29, 2014. On the wider Saudi-led offensive, see Mehran Kamrava, "The Arab Spring and the Saudi-Led Counterrevolution," *Orbis* 56: 1 (2012), pp. 96–104.

51 Quoted in Adam Hanieh, *Lineages of Revolt: Issues of Contemporary Capitalism in the Middle East* (Chicago: Haymarket, 2013), p. 21. On the origins of modern Saudi Arabia, see Robert Vitalis, *America's Kingdom: Mythmaking on the Saudi Oil Frontier* (London/New York: Verso, 2009).

52 Leo Panitch and Sam Gindin, *The Making of Global Capitalism: The Political Economy of American Empire* (London/New York: Verso, 2012), pp. 104–5.

53 On the Lebanon crisis, see Douglas Little, *American Orientalism: The United States and the Middle East since 1945* (Chapel Hill, NC: University of North Carolina Press, 2002).

54 George H. W. Bush, "Address Before a Joint Session of the Congress on the Persian Gulf Crisis and the Federal Budget Deficit," US Congress, September 11, 1990.

55 Hanieh, *Lineages of Revolt*, p. 36.

56 US trade representative Robert Zoellick made exactly this case in June 2003 at the World Economic Forum. See Hanieh, *Lineages of Revolt*, p. 38.

57 Barack Obama, "Middle East Speech," Washington, DC, May 19, 2011, available at newstatesman.com.

58 David Cameron, "Prime Minister's Speech to the National Assembly Kuwait," February 22, 2011, available at gov.uk.

59 Quoted in Hanieh, *Lineages of Revolt*, p. 166.

60 G8, "Declaration of the G8 on the Arab Springs," Deauville, May 26–27, 2011.

61 On Tunisia's stilted progress in implementing Deauville, see International Monetary Fund, "Arab Countries in Transition: Economic Outlook and Key Challenges," Deauville Partnership Ministerial Meeting, October 10, 2013, Washington, DC.

62 On the IMF loan issue and its divisiveness within Egyptian politics, see Tarek Amr, "Egypt: The IMF Loan," Open Democracy, August 20, 2012.

63 "Egypt: Security Forces Used Excessive Lethal Force," Human Rights Watch, August 19, 2013, at hrw.org.

64 Maggie Fick, Stephen Kalin, and Sophie Sassed, "Egypt Turns to Western Economic Advisers, Signalling Possible Reforms under Sisi—Sources," *Reuters*, June 7, 2014; Asa Fitch, "IMF Cozies Up to Egypt Amid Economic Reform," *Wall Street Journal*, October 7, 2014.

65 On this process, see Jenny Pearce, *Under the Eagle: US Intervention in Central America and the Caribbean* (London: Latin American Bureau, 1982); and Edward Kaplan, *US Imperialism in Latin America: Bryan's Challenges and Contributions, 1900–1920* (Westport, CT: Greenwood, 1998).

66 See Mary A. Renda, *Taking Haiti: Military Occupation and the Culture of US Imperialism, 1915–1940* (Chapel Hill, NC/London: University of North Carolina Press, 2001); Brenda Gayle Plummer, *Haiti and the United States: The Psychological Moment* (Athens, GA: University of Georgia Press, 1992); Hans Schmidt, *The United States Occupation of Haiti, 1915–1934* (New Brunswick, NJ: University of Rutgers Press, 1995).

67 The best account of this revolution is Michael J. Gonzales, *The Mexican Revolution, 1910–1940* (Albuquerque, NM: University of New Mexico Press, 2002).

68 Sidney Lens, *The Forging of the American Empire: From the Revolution to Vietnam: A History of US Imperialism* (London: Pluto/ Haymarket, 2003), pp. 220–32; John A. Britton, *Revolution and Ideology: Images of the Mexican Revolution in the United States* (Lexington, KY: University of Kentucky Press, 2006), pp. 5, 30–2.

69 On the background to this shift, see Neil Smith, *American Empire: Roosevelt's Geographer and the Prelude to Globalization* (Oakland, CA: University of California Press, 2004); Walter LaFeber, *Inevitable*

Revolutions: The United States in Central America (New York: W.W. Norton, 1993), p. 67.

70 Greg Grandin, *The Last Colonial Massacre: Latin America in the Cold War* (Chicago/London: University of Chicago Press, 2004); Greg Grandin, *The Blood of Guatemala: A History of Race and Nation* (Durham, NC/London: Duke University Press, 2000).

71 Pearce, *Under the Eagle*, pp. 61–6.

72 Grandin, *Empire's Workshop*, pp. 48–9, 94–6; Pearce, *Under the Eagle*, pp. 53–6.

73 Tamar Jacoby, "The Reagan Turnaround on Human Rights," *Foreign Affairs*, Summer 1986.

74 Amy Wilentz, *Rainy Season: Haiti—Then and Now* (New York: Simon & Schuster, 2010), p. 272.

75 Eva Golinger reports that the US distributed $100 million to Venezuelan anti-Chávez opposition groups in the 2000s. See Golinger, "The Dirty Hand of the National Endowment for Democracy in Venezuela," *Postcards from the Revolution*, April 23, 2014, at chavez-code.com.

76 On this quote, see David F. Schmitz, *Thank God They're on Our Side: The United States and Right-Wing Dictatorships* (Chapel Hill, NC: University of North Carolina Press, 1999), pp. 3, 313.

77 By far the best history of this coup is Peter Hallward, *Damming the Flood: Haiti and the Politics of Containment* (London/New York: Verso, 2011).

78 Kim Ives and Ansel Herz, "WikiLeaks Haiti: The Aristide Files," *Nation*, August 5, 2011.

79 Dan Coughlin and Kim Ives, "WikiLeaks Haiti: Let Them Live on $3 a Day," *Nation*, June 1, 2011.

80 Dan Coughlin and Kim Ives, "WikiLeaks Haiti: Country's Elite Used Police as Private Army," *Nation*, June 22, 2011.

81 Wien Weibert Arthus, "The Omnipresence of Communism in the US-Haitian Relations under Eisenhower and Duvalier," Institute for Russian, European and Eurasian Studies, George Washington University, April 23, 2010, available at gwu.edu; William Blum, *Killing Hope: US Military and CIA Interventions since World War II* (London: Zed Books, 2004), pp. 145–6.

82 Quoted in Timothy Naftali, ed., *The Presidential Recordings: John F. Kennedy: The Great Crises, Volume I, July 30–August 1962* (New York/London: W.W. Norton, 2001), p. 295.

83 "Anti-Duvalier Activity and Projected Plan of Action by Louis Dejoie," memorandum for Mr. McGeorge Bundy, Special Assistant to the President, Central Intelligence Agency, April 12, 1963, available at archives.gov.

84 Hallward, *Damming the Flood*; Peter Hallward, "Option Zero in Haiti," *New Left Review* II/27 (May–June 2004).

85 Noam Chomsky, *Year 501: The Conquest Continues* (London/New York: Verso, 2002), pp. 210–11; Hallward, "Option Zero in Haiti."

86 These cables are included in the Public Library of US Diplomacy: https://search.wikileaks.org/plusd.

87 https://wikileaks.org/plusd/cables/P860114-1573_MC_b.html.

88 For some compelling reporting on this, see Brendan O'Malley and Ian Craig, *The Cyprus Conspiracy: America, Espionage and the Turkish Invasion* (London: I.B. Tauris, 2001); and Christopher Hitchens, *Hostage to History: Cyprus, from the Ottomans to Kissinger* (London/New York: Verso, 1997). For later documentary evidence, see Larisa Alexandrovna and Muriel Kane, "New Documents Link Kissinger to Two 1970s Coups," *Raw Story*, June 26, 2007, at rawstory.com.

89 Available at www2.gwu.edu/~nsarchiv.

90 US Department of State, "Hinchey Report on CIA Activities in Chile," September 18, 2000, available in full at tni.org.

91 Quoted in Christopher Hitchens, *The Trial of Henry Kissinger* (London/New York: Verso, 2002), p. 56. On the coup prospecting, see "Memorandum of Conversation," Dr. Kissinger, Mr. Karamessines, General Haig, White House, October 15, 1970, available at www2.gwu.edu.

92 Hitchens, *Trial of Henry Kissinger*, pp. 56–62.

93 Telegram, Davis to SecState, "Gen. Pinochet's Request For Meeting With MILGP Officer," September 12, 1973.

94 REQUEST FOR CHILEAN ARMED FORCES FOR SPECIAL FORCES TRAINING, 1973 September 25, 22:19 (Tuesday), available at https://www.wikileaks.org/plusd/cables/1973STATE182051_b.html.

95 Ibid.

96 https://www.wikileaks.org/plusd/cables/1973SANTIA04909_b.html.

97 Discussed in Hitchens, *Trial of Henry Kissinger*, p. 68. See also O'Malley and Craig, *The Cyprus Conspiracy*.

98 PINOCHET REACTS TO UN HUMAN RIGHTS COMMISSION CABLE, 1974 March 7, 21:15 (Thursday), availalbe at https://wikileaks.org/plusd/cables/1976SANTIA01734_b.html.

99 Quoted in Mark Ensalaco, *Chile Under Pinochet: Recovering the Truth* (Philadelphia, PA: University of Pennsylvania Press, 2011), p. 160.

100 DOD Intelligence Information Report, number 6 804 0334 76, cited in Cecilia Menjívar and Néstor Rodríguez, eds, *When States Kill: Latin America, the US, and Technologies of Terror* (Austin, TX: University of Texas Press, 2005), p. 30.

101 For detailed background, see J. Patrice McSherry, "The Undead Ghost of Operation Condor," *Logos*, Spring 2005.

102 For a brief summary, see David Harvey, *A Brief History of Neoliberalism*, Oxford/New York: Oxford University Press, 2005), pp. 7–9.

103 Panitch and Gindin, *Making of Global Capitalism*, pp. 215–17.

104 "Is the Milgov Bearing Perceptibly Leftward?" Bureau of Inter-American Affairs, November 3, 1973, available at aad.archives.gov.

105 Dana Frank, "In Honduras, a Mess Made in the US," *New York Times*, January 26, 2012.

106 https://www.wikileaks.org/plusd/cables/09TEGUCIGALPA645_a.html.

107 Arshad Mohammed and David Alexander, "Obama Says Coup in Honduras Is Illegal," *Reuters*, June 29, 2009.

108 US Department of State, "Senior State Department Officials on Honduras," Special Briefing, US Department of State, August 25, 2009, available at state.gov.

109 Lauren Carasik, "Honduras: When Will the US Stop Funding Death Squads?," Al Jazeera, June 4, 2013; Mark Weisbrot, "Top Ten Ways You Can Tell Which Side the United States Government Is On With Regard to the Military Coup in Honduras," *Common Dreams*, December 16, 2009, at cepr.net; Dana Frank, "WikiLeaks Honduras: US Linked to Brutal Businessman," *Nation*, October 21, 2011.

110 Weisbrot, "Top Ten Ways."

111 Ismael Moreno, "Honduras: Behind the Crisis," *Open Democracy*, July 3, 2009; Eva Golinger, "Obama's First Coup d'État: Honduran President has been Kidnapped," *Venezuelanalysis*, June 28, 2009, at venezuelanalysis.com.

CHAPTER 2: DICTATORS AND HUMAN RIGHTS

1 Quoted in Global Policy Forum, "War and Occupation in Iraq," June 2007, www.globalpolicy.org/security/issues/iraq/occupation/report/full.pdf.

2 Talal Asad, *On Suicide Bombing* (New York: Columbia University Press, 2007); Talal Asad, "Thinking About Terrorism and Just War," *Cambridge Review of International Affairs* 23: 1 (2010).

3 Matthew Schofield, "WikiLeaks: Iraqi Children in US Raid Shot in Head, UN Says," *McClatchy*, August 31, 2011.

4 "Leaked US Video Shows Deaths of Reuters' Iraqi staffers," *Reuters*, April 5, 2010.

5 Nick Davies, "Afghanistan War Logs: Task Force 373—Special Forces Hunting Top Taliban," *Guardian*, July 25, 2010.

6 Rob Evans and David Leigh, "WikiLeaks cables: Secret Deal Let Americans Sidestep Cluster Bomb Ban," *Guardian*, December 1, 2010.

7 John Goetz and Matthias Gebauer, "CIA Rendition Case: US Pressured Italy to Influence Judiciary," *Spiegel Online*, December 17, 2010, at spiegel.de.

8 Jeremy Scahill, "The (Not So) Secret (Anymore) US War in Pakistan," *Nation*, December 1, 2010.

9 See https://wikileaks.org/gitmo.

10 Jeremy Scahill, "WikiLeaks and War Crimes," *Nation*, August 12, 2010.

11 Philippe Sands, *Lawless World: Making and Breaking Global Rules* (London: Penguin, 2006); Philippe Sands, *Torture Team: Deception, Cruelty and the Compromise of Law* (London: Allen Lane, 2008).

12 Available at **https://wikileaks.org/gitmo**.

13 **wikileaks.org/gitmo/pdf/ym/us9ym-000027dp.pdf**; Joel Campagna, "Sami al-Haj: The Enemy?," Committee to Protect Journalists, October 3, 2006, at cpj.org.

14 IZ ON IZ DETAINEE ABUSE INCIDENTS IVO ISKANDARIYAH: 4 CIV INJ, 0 CF INJ/DAMAGE, June 19, 2005, available at **http://warlogs.wikileaks.org**.

15 Geraldine Sealey, "Hersh: Children Sodomized at Abu Ghraib, on Tape," *Salon*, July 15, 2004.

16 Caitlin MacNeal, "Cheney Seems Unfazed by Question About Innocent Detainee Who Died," *Talking Points Memo*, December 14, 2014, at talkingpointsmemo.com.

17 George W. Bush, "President George W. Bush's Address to the Nation Regarding Iraq," September 7, 2003, at whitehouse.gov.

18 Walter Pincus, "CIA Studies Provide Glimpse of Insurgents in Iraq," *Washington Post*, February 6, 2005; Loretta Napoleoni, *Insurgent Iraq: Al-Zarqawi and the New Generation* (London: Constable & Robinson, 2005); Nick Davies, *Flat Earth News* (London: Chatto & Windus, 2008), pp. 205–57; E. Knickmeyer and J. Finer, "Iraqi Sunnis Battle to Defend Shiites," *Washington Post*, August 14, 2005.

19 Department of Defense, "Measuring Stability and Security in Iraq," June 2007, Report to Congress, at defense.gov; Fred Kaplan, "Western Targets: The Iraqi Insurgency Is Still Primarily an Anti-Occupation Effort," *Slate*, February 9, 2006.

20 International Council on Security and Development, "Eight Years after 9/11 Taliban Now Has a Permanent Presence in 80% of Afghanistan," press release, September 10, 2009, available at uruknet. info; Antonio Giustozzi, *Koran, Kalashnikov, and Laptop: The Neo-Taliban Insurgency in Afghanistan* (New York: Columbia University Press, 2007), pp. 108–9.

21 "Leverage Xenophobia," *Washington Post*, April 10, 2006.

22 General Sir Richard Dannatt, "Address to the International Institute for Strategic Studies," September 21, 2007, at mod.uk.

23 "King: WikiLeaks Release 'Worse than Military Attack,'" CBS New York, November 28, 2010, at newyork.cbslocal.com.

24 Chris McGreal, "Is WikiLeaks Hi-Tech Terrorism or Hype? Washington can't decide," *Guardian*, February 5, 2011.

25 K. T. McFarland, "Yes, WikiLeaks Is a Terrorist Organization and the Time to Act Is NOW," Fox News, November 30, 2011, at foxnews. com.

26 David Leigh and Luke Harding, *WikiLeaks: Inside Julian Assange's War on Secrecy* (London: Guardian, 2011).

27 This phrase is from a chat with Assange, discovered by US authorities. Kim Zetter, "Jolt in WikiLeaks Case: Feds Found Manning-Assange Chat Logs on Laptop," *Wired*, December 19, 2011.

28 Ed Pilkington, "Bradley Manning Treated More Harshly than a Terrorist, Lawyer Argues," *Guardian*, July 12, 2012; Ed Pilkington, "Bradley Manning's Treatment Was Cruel and Inhuman, UN Torture Chief Rules," *Guardian*, March 12, 2012.

29 See Richard Jackson, Marie Breen Smyth, and Jeroen Gunning, eds, *Critical Terrorism Studies: A New Research Agenda* (Oxford: Routledge, 2009); and Marie Breen-Smyth, ed., *The Ashgate Research Companion to Political Violence* (Farnham: Ashgate, 2012).

30 Steve Inskeep, "State Department Defends America's Image Abroad," National Public Radio, March 27, 2006.

31 George W. Bush, in Presidential Debate with John Kerry, University of Miami, MSNBC, October 1, 2004.

32 "22 US Code § 2656f—Annual Country Reports on Terrorism," available from the Legal Information Institute, Cornell University Law School, at law.cornell.edu.

33 Quoted in Alex P. Schmid, *The Routledge Handbook of Terrorism Research* (Abingdon/New York: Routledge, 2011), p. 46.

34 Quoted in Steve Best and Anthony J. Nocella II, "Defining Terrorism," *Animal Liberation Philosophy & Policy Journal* 2: 1 (2004).

35 https://www.wikileaks.org/irq.

36 Iraq Body Count estimates an additional 15,000 unreported deaths from a survey of the war logs. "Iraq War Logs: What the Numbers Reveal," *Iraq Body Count*, October 23, 2010.

37 An example in the files is the case of soldiers firing 200 bullets into a single vehicle, killing two children, and their mother and father: https://wikileaks.org/irq/report/2005/09/IRQ20050923n2490.html. Another incident involved troops firing up to fifteen rounds of bullets into a vehicle, killing the two children inside: https://wikileaks.org/irq/report/2005/10/IRQ20051026n2733.html.

38 The lawyer at the airbase told the soldiers that killing them would be fine, as one cannot surrender to an aircraft: http://wardiaries.wikileaks.org/id/E8DE9B9F-E468-B587-E4B332C09FF48BE2.

39 The US decision to overlook the continued practice of torture is contained in the infamous directive "Frago 242": http://warlogs.wikileaks.org/id/88029AA5-6833-404A-826A-BD586F829FE0. As will be discussed later in this chapter, there is evidence that a significant reason for this is that the US was involved in organizing torture by Iraqi forces, under the rubric of "Iraqization." An example of the type of torture that was deliberately overlooked included the case of a prisoner, said to have committed suicide, who had bruises and burns all over his body, and visible injuries to his head, arms, torso, leg, and neck: http://wardiaries.wikileaks.org/id/5D554D29-AA6A-1679-3B0EDB9A4357473F/.

40 "Afghan War Diary, 2004–2010," July 25, 2010, at wikileaks.org.

41 http://wardiaries.wikileaks.org/id/080e0000011e1f38da79160d271 eb9ae.

42 https://www.wikileaks.org/afg/event/2007/08/AFG20070816n891. html.

43 https://www.wikileaks.org/afg/event/2007/03/AFG20070321n586. html.

44 In fact, the cable shows that the US military suppressed the killings—which were subsequently exposed by human rights organizations—instead clinically recording an IED attack and escape: https://www. wikileaks.org/afg/event/2007/03/AFG20070304n586.html.

45 Naomi Klein, "Iraq is not America's to sell," *Guardian*, November 7, 2003.

46 Ahmed Janabi, "Iraqi Unemployment Reaches 70%," Al Jazeera, August 1, 2004.

47 George Packer, *The Assassin's Gate* (New York: Farrar, Straus & Giroux, 2006), pp. 66–8, 77–97.

48 Aram Roston, *The Man Who Pushed America to War: The Extraordinary Life, Adventures, and Obsessions of Ahmad Chalabi* (New York: Nation Books, 2009), p. 222.

49 Eric Herring and Glen Rangwala, *Iraq in Fragments: The Occupation and Its Legacy* (London: Hurst, 2006), pp. 16, 53, 126; Faleh A. Jabar, *The Shi'ite Movement in Iraq* (London: Saqi, 2002), pp. 253–63.

50 "Torture in Iraq 'Worse than Under Saddam,'" *Guardian*, September 21, 2006.

51 Federal News Service, "Department of Defense Bloggers Roundtable with Brigadier General David Phillips, Deputy Commanding General, Civilian Police Assistance Training Team," September 21, 2007, at defense.gov; T. Christian Miller, "Soldier's Journey Ends in Anguish," *Los Angeles Times*, December 4, 2005; Peter Maass, "The Way of the Commandos," *New York Times*, May 1, 2005; General David Petraeus, "Gangs of Iraq: Interview with General David Petraeus," *PBS*, October 11, 2006; Todd Clark, "Forging the Sword: Conventional US Army Forces Advising Host Nation (HN) Forces," *Armor*, September 1, 2006.

52 Michael Hirsch and John Barry, "'The Salvador Option': The Pentagon May Put Special-Forces-Led Assassination or Kidnapping Teams in Iraq," *Newsweek*, January 9, 2005.

53 Andrew Buncombe and Patrick Cockburn, "Iraq's Death Squads: On the Brink of Civil War," *Independent*, February 26, 2006; Neil Macdonald, "Iraqi Reality-TV Hit Takes Fear Factor to Another Level," *Christian Science Monitor*, June 7, 2005; Jim Krane, "Pentagon Funds Pro-US Network in Iraq," Associated Press, November 28, 2003; Peter Beaumont, "Revealed: Grim World of New Iraqi Torture Camps," *Guardian*, July 3, 2005.

54 Kim Sengupta, "Operation Enduring Chaos: The Retreat of the Coalition and Rise of the Militias," *Independent on Sunday*, October 29, 2006.

55 See "15,000 Previously Unknown Civilian Deaths Contained in the Iraq War Logs Released by WikiLeaks," *Iraq Body Count*, October 22, 2010, at iraqbodycount.org.

56 Prof. Gilbert Burnham, Riyadh Lafta, Shannon Doocy, Les Roberts, "Mortality After the 2003 Invasion of Iraq: A Cross-Sectional Cluster Sample Survey," *Lancet* 368: 9,545 (October 12, 2006).

57 Mark Benjamin, "When Is an Accidental Civilian Death Not an Accident?," *Salon*, July 30, 2007.

58 Michael Mann, *Incoherent Empire* (London/New York: Verso, 2003), p. 138.

59 Data can be found at collateralmurder.com.

60 "Investigation into Civilian Casualties Resulting from an Engagement on 12 July 2007 in the New Baghdad District of Baghdad, Iraq," Department of the Army, available at i2.cdn.turner.com. Quoted in Tom Cohen, "Leaked Video Reveals Chaos of Baghdad Attack," *CNN*, April 7, 2010.

61 David Leigh, "Iraq War Logs Reveal 15,000 Previously Unlisted Civilian Deaths," *Guardian*, October 22, 2010.

62 Justin Podur, "The First Battle of Fallujah 2004 in the Iraq War Diary," November 16, 2010, at killingtrain.com.

63 "No Longer Unknowable: Falluja's April Civilian Toll is 600," *Iraq Body Count*, October 26, 2004, at iraqbodycount.org. IBC's total estimate of civilian deaths was and remains far lower than that of the Lancet. "Red Cross Estimates 800 Iraqi Civilians Killed in Fallujah," *Democracy Now*, November 17, 2004, at democracynow.org. An Iraqi NGO put the estimate at between 4,000 and 6,000. Brian K. Lamphear, "2. Media Coverage Fails on Iraq: Fallujah and the Civilian Deathtoll," *Project Censored*, April 29, 2010, at projectcensored.org. The estimate comes from the Iraqi NGO group Monitoring Net of Human Rights in Iraq.

64 Michael Hirsh, "Hirsh: How US Makes Enemies," *Newsweek*, July 26, 2006; Robert F. Worth, "Sergeant Tells of Plot to Kill Iraqi Detainees," *New York Times*, July 28, 2006; "US Won't Let Men Flee Fallujah," Associated Press, November 13, 2004.

65 Jo Becker and Scott Shane, "Secret 'Kill List' Proves a Test of Obama's Principles and Will," *New York Times*, May 29, 2012. See also Chris Woods, "Analysis: Obama Embraced Redefinition of 'Civilian' in Drone Wars," Bureau of Investigative Journalism, May 29, 2012, at thebureauinvestigates.com; and Glenn Greenwald, "'Militants': Media Propaganda," *Salon*, May 29, 2012, at salon.com.

66 Spencer Ackerman, "41 Men Targeted but 1,147 People Killed: US Drone Strikes—The Facts on the Ground," *Guardian*, November 24, 2014; "US Drone Strikes Kill 28 Unknown People for Every Intended Target, New Reprieve Report Reveals," Reprieve press release, November 24, 2014.

67 Madelyn Hsiao-Rei Hicks, Hamit Dardagan, Gabriela Guerrero Serdán, Peter M. Bagnall, John A. Sloboda, and Michael Spagat, "The

Weapons That Kill Civilians—Deaths of Children and Noncombatants in Iraq, 2003–2008," *New England Journal of Medicine* 360: 1,585–1,588 (April 16, 2009).

68 Quoted in Mohammad-Mahmoud Ould Mohamedou, *Understanding Al Qaeda: The Transformation of War* (London/Ann Arbor, MI: Pluto Press, 2007), p. 43.

69 **https://wikileaks.org/wiki/Classified_U.S_report_into_the_Fallujah_ assult;** https://wikileaks.org/wiki/Complex_Environments:_Battle_of _Fallujah_I,_April_2004.

70 Global Policy Forum, "War and Occupation in Iraq," June 2007, at globalpolicy.org.

71 Martin Shaw, *The New Western Way of War* (Cambridge: Polity Press, 2005).

72 For example, the prison's oldest detainee, Mohammed Sadiq, was eighty-nine when detained. He was unwell, was diagnosed with prostate cancer, and suffered from dementia and depression (**wikileaks. org/gitmo/pdf/af/us9af-000349dp.pdf**). Haji Faiz Mohammed was seventy. His file stated that "there [was] no reason on the record" for him to have been taken to Guantánamo (**https://wikileaks.org/gitmo/ prisoner/657.html**). Naqib Ullah, a child when he was captured, was acknowledged on his record to have been abducted, abused, and conscripted to fight for the Taliban. Even though he possessed a weapon, he had never fired it (**wikileaks.org/gitmo/pdf/af/us9 af-000909dp.pdf**).

73 Pilkington, "Bradley Manning's Treatment Was Cruel and Inhuman"; Ryan Creed, "Comments on Prisoner Treatment Cause State Department Spokesman to Lose His Job," *ABC News*, March 13, 2011; Paula Reid, "DOJ Not Expected to Initiate Charges Against CIA Officers over Torture Report," *CBS News*, December 9, 2014.

74 "US Does Not Torture, Bush Insists," *BBC News*, November 7, 2005.

75 "White Paper on the Law of Torture and Holding Accountable Those Who Are Complicit in Approving Torture of Persons in US Custody," available at prisonlegalnews.org.

76 Greg Grandin, "Secrecy and Spectacle: Why Only Americans Are Worthy of Being Called 'Torturable,'" *Nation*, December 17, 2014.

77 Colin Freeman, "CIA Torture Report: How Waterboarding Reduced Even Interrogators to Tears," *Daily Telegraph*, December 9, 2014.

78 On this view of legal interpretation, see Martti Koskenniemi, *From Apology to Utopia: The Structure of International Legal Argument* (Cambridge/New York: Cambridge University Press, 2005); and China Miéville, *Between Equal Rights: A Marxist Theory of International Law* (Leiden/Boston, MA: Brill, 2005).

79 Alfred W. McCoy, *A Question of Torture: CIA Interrogation, from the Cold War to the War on Terror* (New York: Metropolitan, 2010); Alfred W. McCoy, *The CIA's Secret Research on Torture: How Psychologists*

Helped Washington Crack the Code of Human Consciousness, Now and Then Reader, 2014; Alfred W. McCoy, *Torture and Impunity: The US Doctrine of Coercive Interrogation* (Madison, WI: University of Wisconsin Press, 2012).

80 Many critics of the American empire, even the most radical, assume that it is contemptuous of the international legal system to whose creation it made such a large contribution. As Alfred W. McCoy puts it: "At the UN and other international forums, Washington opposed torture and advocated a universal standard for human rights. But, in contravention of these diplomatic conventions, the CIA propagated torture during those same decades." This is a mistake: the US government obsessively legalized its torture program, providing rafts of interpretation to justify its stance. McCoy, *A Question of Torture*, p. 4.

81 Louis Pérez, Jr, *The War of 1898: The United States and Cuba in History and Historiography* (Chapel Hill, NC: University of North Carolina Press, 1998), pp. 13–14.

82 On this, see David F. Schmitz, *Thank God They're on Our Side: United States and Right-Wing Dictatorships, 1921–65* (Chapel Hill, NC: University of North Carolina Press, 1999); and Greg Grandin, *Empire's Workshop: Latin America, the United States, and the Rise of the New Imperialism* (New York: Metropolitan Books, 2010).

83 A detailed historical background is provided by Scott Packard, "How Guantánamo Bay Became the Place the US Keeps Detainees," *Atlantic*, September 4, 2014.

84 "Bush Defends Guantánamo Prison," Al Jazeera, July 6, 2005.

85 Paul Harris, "Soldier Lifts Lid on Camp Delta," *Guardian*, May 8, 2005; Josh White, "Abu Ghraib Tactics Were First Used at Guantánamo," *Washington Post*, July 14, 2005.

86 "Bush State of the Union address," CNN, June 29, 2002.

87 "Cheney: Gitmo Holds 'Worst of the Worst,'" Associated Press, June 1, 2009.

88 See https://wikileaks.org/gitmo.

89 https://wikileaks.org/The-Unknown-Prisoners-of.html; "WikiLeaks Documents Reveal US Knowingly Imprisoned 150 Innocent Men at Guantánamo," Democracy Now!, April 24, 2011, at democracynow. org. Worthington himself had already accumulated extensive experience in analyzing the cases of prisoners at Guantánamo, documenting the process of extraordinary rendition, false imprisonment, and torture visited on hundreds of detainees. See Andy Worthington, *The Guantánamo Files: The Stories of the 774 Detainees in America's Illegal Prison* (London/Ann Arbor, MI: Pluto Press, 2007).

90 Chase Madar, *The Passion of Bradley Manning* (New York/London: Verso, 2013), p. 132.

91 "WikiLeaks Documents Reveal US Knowingly Imprisoned 150 Innocent Men at Guantánamo," Democracy Now!, April 25, 2011, at democracynow.org.

92   Andy Worthington, "WikiLeaks Reveals Secret Files on All Guantánamo Prisoners," wikileaks.org. There are also those whose situation is simply unclear. For example, Abd Al Rahim Abd Al Razzaq Janko was captured in Afghanistan in May 2002, and has been in the prison ever since, but his captors do not seem to have any idea whether he is a jihadi or an intelligence operative working for the United Arab Emirates. Nonetheless, he is listed as "medium" risk and held without any judicial process. **wikileaks.ch/gitmo/pdf/sy/us9sy-000489dp.pdf.**

93   "President Obama Issues Executive Order Institutionalizing Indefinite Detention," ACLU, March 7, 2011, at aclu.org.

94   See Glenn Greenwald, "Newly Leaked Documents Show the Ongoing Travesty of Guantánamo," *Salon*, April 25, 2011, at salon.com.

95   McCoy, *CIA's Secret Research on Torture.*

96   McCoy, *Torture and Impunity*, Kindle loc. 2049–2280.

97   Ibid., Kindle loc. 2345–2455.

98   See the gruesome case of Manadel al-Jamadi, tortured to death during a CIA interrogation at Abu Ghraib. This case became notorious for the pictures of Specialists Charles Graner and Sabrina Harmon posing with the corpse. Seth Hettena, "Reports Detail Abu Ghraib Prison Death; Was It Torture?," Associated Press, February 17, 2005; McCoy, *Torture and Impunity*, Kindle loc. 2545, 2584, 2599; ACLU, "Department of Defense Memoranda Released Under the Freedom of Information Act," 2005, at aclu.org; Human Rights Watch, "Leadership Failure: Firsthand Accounts of Torture of Iraqi Detainees by the US Army's 82nd Airborne Division," *Human Rights Watch* 17: 3 (September 2005), available at hrw.org.

99   Referenced in **http://warlogs.wikileaks.org/id/88029AA5-6833-404A-826A-BD586F829FE0.**

100   Nick Davies, "Iraq War Logs: Secret Order that Let US Ignore Abuse," *Guardian*, October 22, 2010.

101   McCoy, *Torture and Impunity*, Kindle loc. 2627.

102   For discussion and extensive referencing on the Special Police Commandos, see Richard Seymour, *The Liberal Defence of Murder* (London/New York: Verso, 2008), p. 227. The *Guardian* newspaper later alighted on this story with an in-depth account of the activities of Colonel James Steele, sent by Donald Rumsfeld to help organize the death squads. See Mona Mahmood, Maggie O'Kane, Chavala Madlena, and Teresa Smith, "Revealed: Pentagon's Link to Iraqi Torture Centres," *Guardian*, March 6, 2013.

103   Senate Select Committee on Intelligence, "Committee Study of the Central Intelligence Agency's Detention and Interrogation Program," December 3, 2014, at intelligence.senate.gov.

104   Guantánamo Detainee US9GZ-010016DP: Abu Zubaydah.

105   Reed Brody, "Prisoners Who Disappear," *International Herald Tribune*, October 12, 2004.

106 Sam Masters, "CIA Torture Report: The Doctors Who Were the Unlikely Architects of the CIA's Programme," *Independent*, December 9, 2014.

107 "Former CIA Director: 'We Don't Torture People,'" CBS News, December 9, 2014.

108 https://wikileaks.org/wiki/CIA_logbook_of_Congressional_member_torture_briefings,_2009.

109 Scott Shane, "Political Divide About CIA Torture Remains After Senate Report's Release," *New York Times*, December 9, 2014.

110 "Memorandum for Alberto R. Gonzales, Counsel to the President," US Department of Justice, Office of Legal Counsel, August 1, 2002, available at resourcelists.ed.ac.uk.

111 Carl Schmitt, the German legal scholar and prominent Nazi, was cited by constitutional law professor Sanford Levinson as the "true éminence grise" of the Bush administration. Quoted in Noam Chomsky, *Failed States: The Abuse of Power and the Assault on Democracy* (London: Penguin, 2007).

112 "White Paper on the Law of Torture and Holding Accountable Those Who Are Complicit in Approving Torture of Persons in US Custody," National Lawyers Guild, at prisonlegalnews.org.

113 McCoy, *A Question of Torture*, p. 113.

114 Steven Donald Smith, "Guantánamo Detainees Being Held Legally, Official Says," American Forces Press Service, February 15, 2006, at defense.gov.

115 Lars Erik Aspaas, "The Power of Definition: How the Bush Administration Created 'Enemy Combatants' and Redefined Presidential Power and Torture," University of Oslo, MA thesis, Spring 2009, available at duo.uio.no.

116 Peter Forster, "CIA Tortured Terror Suspects 'to Point of Death,' US Senate Report Will Say: Source," *National Post*, September 8, 2014.

117 Anthony D'Amato, "True Confessions? The Amazing Tale of Khalid Shaikh Mohammed," *Jurist*, March 16, 2007. For the list of confessions, see "Khalid Sheikh Mohammed's '31 Plots,'" BBC News, March 15, 2007.

118 Rebecca Gordon, "US Torture Didn't End When Bush Left Office," *Nation*, December 15, 2014.

CHAPTER 3: WAR AND TERRORISM

1 Thomas Friedman, "A Manifesto for the Fast World," *New York Times Magazine*, March 28, 1999.

2 "Business and WikiLeaks: Be Afraid," *Economist*, December 9, 2010.

3 Andy Greenberg, "WikiLeaks' Julian Assange Wants To Spill Your Corporate Secrets," *Forbes*, November 29, 2010.

4 https://wikileaks.org/wiki/Minton_report:_Trafigura_toxic_

dumping_along_the_Ivory_Coast_broke_EU_regulations,_14_
Sep_2006.

5   David Leigh, "Trafigura Hoped to Make a Fortune. Instead They
    Caused a Tragedy," *Guardian*, September 16, 2009.

6   "A Gag Too Far," *Index on Censorship*, October 14, 2009.

7   Mark Sweney, "Bank Drops Lawsuit against Wikileaks," *Guardian*,
    March 6, 2008; "Wikileaks Given Data on Swiss Bank Accounts," *BBC
    News*, January 17, 2011; "WikiLeaks to Target Wealthy Individuals,"
    Daily Telegraph, January 17, 2011.

8   Yochai Benkler, "A Free Irresponsible Press: Wikileaks and the Battle
    over the Soul of the Networked Fourth Estate," *Harvard Civil Rights-
    Civil Liberties Law Review* 46 (2011); Lisa Lynch, "'We're Going to
    Crack the World Open': Wikileaks and the Future of Investigative
    Reporting," *Journalism Practice* 4: 3 (2010)—Special Issue: The
    Future of Journalism.

9   John Vidal, "WikiLeaks: US Targets EU over GM Crops," *Guardian*,
    January 3, 2011.

10 See Mariana Mazzucato, *The Entrepreneurial State: Debunking
    Public vs Private Sector Myths* (London/New York/Delhi: Anthem
    Press, 2013), Kindle loc. 2302–2320; and Leo Panitch and Sam
    Gindin, *The Making of Global Capitalism: The Political Economy of
    the American Empire* (London/New York: Verso, 2013), p. 288.

11 https://wikileaks.org/tpp-ip2/pressrelease.

12 Peter Gowan, *The Global Gamble: Washington's Faustian Bid for
    World Dominance* (London/New York: Verso, 1999).

13 Quoted in Leo Panitch and Sam Gindin, "Global Capitalism and the
    American Empire," *Socialist Register* 40 (2004).

14 Figure cited in Andrew G. Terborgh, "The Post-War Rise of World
    Trade: Does the Bretton Woods System Deserve Credit?" London
    School of Economics, Working Paper No 78/03, September 2003,
    available at lse.ac.uk.

15 On the breakdown of Bretton Woods, see Fred L. Block, *The Origins
    of International Economic Disorder: A Study of United States
    International Monetary Policy from World War II to the Present*
    (Berkeley/Los Angeles: University of California Press, 1977). On the
    political significance of Washington's adaptation to this trend, see
    Gowan, *Global Gamble*.

16 On the convergence of austerity policies and financial interests, see
    Robert W. Bailey, *The Crisis Regime: The Mac, the ECFB, and the
    Political Impact of the New York City Financial Crisis* (New York:
    State University of New York Press, 1984); William K. Tabb, *The
    Long Default: New York City and the Urban Fiscal Crisis* (New
    York: Monthly Review Press, 1982); Eric Lichten, *Class, Power and
    Austerity: The New York City Financial Crisis* (Westport, CT: Bergin
    & Garvey, 1986).

17 Dianna Melrose, *Nicaragua: The Threat of a Good Example?*
    (London: Oxfam, 1989).

18 https://wikileaks.org/plusd/cables/01HANOI686_a.html; "Vietnam: Progress on Reform under World Bank and IMF Poverty Reduction Loans," November 20, 2000, [01HANOI3054_a]; https://www. wikileaks.org/plusd/cables/04HANOI898_a.html; https://www. wikileaks.org/plusd/cables/04HANOI3331_a.html.

19 Thomas Oatley and Jason Yackee, "American Interests and IMF Lending," *International Politics* 41 (2004), pp. 415–29.

20 The best overall guide to postwar Vietnam and its economic policies is Gabriel Kolko, *Anatomy of a Peace* (London/New York: Routledge, 1997).

21 https://www.wikileaks.org/plusd/cables/06QUITO1157_a.html.

22 On "dollar diplomacy," see Eric Helleiner, "Dollarization Diplomacy: US Policy Toward Latin America Coming Full Circle?," *Review of International Political Economy* 10: 3 (August 2003). On the uses of different currencies to support a Jim Crow pay system, see Robert Vitalis, "The Graceful and Generous Liberal Gesture: Making Racism Invisible in American International Relations," *Millennium—Journal of International Studies* 29 (2000). On the reaction to dollarization in Ecuador, see Sean Healy, "Latin America: Trend toward Dollarisation Accelerates," *Green Left Weekly*, January 24, 2001.

23 https://cablegatesearch.wikileaks.org/cable.php?id=05 QUITO882&q=ecuador.

24 https://www.wikileaks.org/plusd/cables/05QUITO895_a.html.

25 https://www.wikileaks.org/plusd/cables/05QUITO897_a.html.

26 https://wikileaks.org/plusd/cables/05QUITO900_a.html.

27 https://www.wikileaks.org/plusd/cables/05QUITO945_a.html.

28 https://www.wikileaks.org/plusd/cables/05QUITO898_a.html.

29 https://wikileaks.org/plusd/cables/05QUITO2699_a.html; https:// wikileaks.org/cable/2006/08/06QUITO2150.html; https://wikileaks. org/cable/2006/04/06QUITO995.html. On NED funding, the fact is advertised on its own web page—see information on Ecuador at ned. org.

30 https://www.wikileaks.org/plusd/cables/08QUITO35_a.html.

31 https://wikileaks.org/plusd/cables/08QUITO75_a.html. This program entailed using state control of strategic sectors of the economy, such as oil, to benefit the poor, and to shift power from capital to labor. At the same time, a peculiar irony of Correa's development model was that it actually required the state to produce less oil, leaving some 20 percent of the confirmed oil reserve unexploited in order to protect the environment and promote the rights of the indigenous: the "good life" and sustainability took precedence over economic growth. This was a product of his relationship to popular social movements to which, within the limits of his powers, he sought to give some expression in government. More generally, his government argued that it would subordinate economic growth to the needs of the people, and would seek to update and democratize the old constitution, consistent with the participatory aspect of "twenty-first-century social-

ism." Cristina Espinosa, "The Riddle of Leaving the Oil in the Soil: Ecuador's Yasuní-ITT Project from a Discourse Perspective," *Forest Policy and Economics*, 2012, published on academia.edu. The limits of Correa's environmental commitments, which took second place to development, led to a series of conflicts with indigenous movements. See Paul Dosh and Nicole Kligerman, "Correa vs. Social Movements: Showdown in Ecuador," *NACLA: Report on the Americas* 42: 5 (2009).

32   A constitutional referendum in Ecuador passed with just over 80 percent popular support and became the supreme law of the land in 2008. Previous constitutional settlements had mainly been imposed by dictatorial regimes more concerned with the interests of economic elites than the popular classes. Like similar referenda in Venezuela and Honduras, this reform combined a series of progressive measures, long overdue democratic reforms, and the bolstering of the executive branch of government as a locus of strength for the populist left. The key measures established a series of popular rights, including sexual and gender rights, as well as ecosystem rights protecting the environment, the right to food self-sufficiency, and the legalization of drugs for personal consumption. It also promised an end to the neoliberal development model; overturned the independence of the central bank, making it part of the executive branch; and proposed the expansion of popular and solidarity-based financial systems—such as co-ops and credit unions—to compete with the for-profit sector. On the relationship between the constitutional change and the social movements, see Marc Becker, "Correa, Indigenous Movements, and the Writing of a New Constitution in Ecuador," *Latin American Perspectives* 38: 1 (January 2011).

33   https://www.wikileaks.org/plusd/cables/07QUITO2604_a.html.
34   https://www.wikileaks.org/plusd/cables/07QUITO2575_a.html.
35   https://www.wikileaks.org/plusd/cables/08QUITO36_a.html.
36   https://cablegatesearch.wikileaks.org/cable.php?id=07QUITO2659.
37   Judith Ugwumadu, "Ecuador Urged to Moderate Public Spending," *Public Finance International*, August 22, 2004.
38   https://wikileaks.org/cable/2009/10/09QUITO905.html; https://wikileaks.org/cable/2009/11/09QUITO973.html.
39   https://www.wikileaks.org/plusd/cables/09QUITO579_a.html. The purpose of the court was to "depoliticize" such disputes by deciding them in a formally neutral setting. Ibrahim Shihata, "Towards a Greater Depoliticisation of Investment Disputes: The Roles of ICSID and MIGA," *ICSID Review: Foreign Investment and Law Journal* I (1986). By agreement, the court took precedence over Ecuadoran national sovereignty. This was both unacceptable to Correa and arguably inconsistent with the new constitution.
40   https://wikileaks.org/plusd/cables/10QUITO53_a.html.
41   https://wikileaks.org/cable/2009/10/09QUITO893.html; https://www.wikileaks.org/plusd/cables/10QUITO75_a.html.

42 https://wikileaks.org/plusd/cables/10QUITO53_a.html.

43 https://www.wikileaks.org/plusd/cables/08QUITO191_a.html.

44 Karl Polanyi, *The Great Transformation: The Political and Economic Origins of Our Time* (Boston, MA: Beacon Press, 2001).

45 https://wikileaks.org/tisa-financial.

46 https://wikileaks.org/tpp-ip2.

47 An insightful critique of intellectual property is Christopher May, *The Global Political Economy of Intellectual Property Rights: The New Enclosures?* (London/New York: Routledge, 2000). See also Debora J. Halpert, *Resisting Intellectual Property* (London/New York: Routledge, 2003).

48 https://wikileaks.org/tpp-ip2/attack-on-affordable-cancer-treatments.html.

49 Ibid.

50 "No Party may prevent a service supplier of another Party from transferring, accessing, processing or storing information, including personal information, within or outside the Party's territory, where such activity is carried out in connection with the conduct of the service supplier's business." This passage from TISA was released through the WikiLeaks-like organization the Associated Whistleblowing Press. "Proposal of New Provisions Applicable to All Services of the Secret TISA Negotiations," Associated Whistleblowing Press, December 17, 2014, at data.iwp.is.

51 "Trade in Services Agreement," US Chamber of Commerce, February 7, 2014, at uschamber.com.

52 Parker Higgins and Maira Sutton, "How the US Trade Rep Ratchets Up Worldwide Copyright Laws that Could Keep Your Devices Locked Forever," Electronic Frontier Foundation, March 26, 2013, at eff.org.

53 For example, Apple invoked this Act in 2008 to threaten a nonprofit website that discussed how to make the iPod interact with other software, claiming that this constituted circumvention of its DRM technology. Fred von Lohmann, "Apple Confuses Speech with a DMCA Violation," Electronic Frontier Foundation, November 25, 2008, at eff.org.

54 This is pointed out by Canadian lawyer Michael Geist in "New TPP Leak: Canada Emerges as Leading Opponent of US Intellectual Property Demands," October 16, 2004, at michaelgeist.ca.

55 Edmund T. Pratt, chair of Pfizer Plc, attended GATT negotiations as the official advisor to the US trade representative, and he remarked: "Our combined strength enabled us to establish a global private sector government network which laid the groundwork for what became TRIPs." Edmund J. Pratt, "Intellectual Property Rights and International Trade," Pfizer Forum, 1996, quoted in "WTO Millennium Bug: TNC Control Over Global Trade Politics," *Corporate Europe Observer* 4 (July 1999).

56 See "Remarks by Ralph G. Neas on Trans Pacific Partnership," *Pharmacy Times*, December 17, 2014.

57 Simon Lester, "The WTO vs. the TPP," *Huffington Post*, May 2, 2014, at huffingtonpost.com.

58 "WikiLeaks Reveals True Intent of Secret TiSA Trade Talks," ITUC, June 26, 2014, at ituc-csi.org.

59 **http://wikileaks.org/tisa-financial/Analysis-of-secret-tisa-financial-annex.pdf.** In the 1999 agreement, it was the Financial Leaders Group, comprising the likes of Barclays, Chase Manhattan, and Goldman Sachs, that led the charge to liberalization. A significant lobby in today's TISA negotiations, meanwhile, is the business coalition named Team Tisa, chaired by Citigroup, IBM, UPS, and Walmart, among others. See teamtisa.org.

60 It is worth noting that most financial activity has little to do with supporting productive investment. In 2001, the total daily turnover of international financial markets was $40 trillion, well above the $800 billion that would be needed to support transactions and investment flows in the "real" economy. David Harvey, *A Brief History of Neoliberalism* (Oxford/New York: Oxford University Press, 2005), p. 161. On the pitfalls of "innovation" and its role in the great financial crash, see Ewald Engelen, Ismail Ertürk, Julie Froud, Sukhdev Johal, Adam Leaver, Mick Moran, Adriana Nilsson, and Karel Williams, *After the Great Complacence: Financial Crisis and the Politics of Reform* (Oxford/New York: Oxford University Press, 2011), Kindle loc. 979–1063. On the drawbacks of financialization for productive investment, see Costas Lapavitsas, *Profiting Without Producing: How Finance Exploits Us All* (London/New York: Verso, 2013).

61 Panitch and Gindin, *Making of Global Capitalism*, pp. 216–19.

62 "Conclusion," in "The Financial Crisis Inquiry Report: Final Report of the National Commission on the Causes of the Financial and Economic Crisis in the United States," February 2011, at gpo.gov.

63 David McNally, *Global Slump: The Economics and Politics of Crisis and Resistance* (Oakland, CA: PM Press, 2011), p. 86.

64 Panitch and Gindin, *Making of Global Capitalism*, pp. 236–7.

65 Ibid., pp. 310–30. See also Leo Panitch, Sam Gindin, and Greg Albo, *In and Out of Crisis: The Global Financial Meltdown and Left Alternatives* (Oakland, CA: PM Press, 2010); Philip Mirowski, *Never Let a Serious Crisis Go to Waste: How Neoliberalism Survived the Financial Meltdown* (London/New York: Verso, 2013).

66 Tony Wood, "Good Riddance to New Labour," *New Left Review* II/62 (March–April 2010).

CHAPTER 5: US WAR CRIMES AND THE ICC

1 Lesley Wroughton, "US, Afghans Agree Most of Pact, Elders to Make Final Decision," *Reuters*, October 13, 2013, at reuters.com.

2 Josh Dougherty, "When Victimless Crimes Matter and Victims Don't:

The Trial of Bradley Manning," Iraq Body Count, August 2, 2013, at iraqbodycount.org.

3 Glen Greenwald, *With Liberty and Justice for Some: How the Law Is Used to Destroy Equality and Protect the Powerful* (New York: Metropolitan, 2011).

4 White House, "Statement of President Barack Obama on Release of OLC Memos," April 16, 2009, at whitehouse.gov.

5 White House, "Statement by the President Report of the Senate Select Committee on Intelligence," December 9, 2014, at whitehouse.gov.

6 John R. Bolton, "'Legitimacy' in International Affairs: The American Perspective in Theory and Operation," November 13, 2003, at 2001-2009.state.gov, cited in Erna Paris, *The Sun Climbs Slow: The International Criminal Court and the Struggle for Justice* (New York: Seven Stories Press, 2009), p. 79.

7 http://wikileaks.org/cable/2002/12/02TEGUCIGALPA3350.html.

8 http://wikileaks.org/cable/2002/10/02COLOMBO2003.html.

9 http://wikileaks.org/cable/2002/12/02COLOMBO2323.html.

10 http://wikileaks.org/cable/2006/06/06MASERU261.html.

11 Ian Traynor, "East Europeans Torn on the Rack by International Court Row," *Guardian*, August 17, 2002, cited in Paris, *The Sun Climbs Slow*, p. 70.

12 Institute for the Study of Human Rights, "US & ICC: Bilateral Immunity Agreement Campaign: Reaction to BIAs," n.d., at amicc. org.

13 http://wikileaks.org/cable/2003/04/03ZAGREB798.html.

14 http://wikileaks.org/cable/2008/03/08CHISINAU314.html.

15 http://wikileaks.org/cable/2004/06/04GUATEMALA1361.html.

16 http://wikileaks.org/cable/2003/12/03SANAA3010.html.

17 http://wikileaks.org/cable/2004/07/04SANAA1733.html.

18 http://wikileaks.org/cable/2004/05/04MANAMA676.html.

19 http://wikileaks.org/cable/2004/06/04MANAMA831.html.

20 http://wikileaks.org/cable/2005/02/05MANAMA158.html.

21 http://wikileaks.org/cable/2004/03/04MANAMA368.html.

22 http://wikileaks.org/cable/2004/03/04MANAMA368.html.

23 http://wikileaks.org/cable/2004/06/04MANAMA831.html.

24 Anna Fifield and Camilla Hall, "US and Bahrain Secretly Extend Defence Deal," *Financial Times*, September 1, 2011.

25 http://wikileaks.org/cable/2007/04/07KUWAIT487.html.

26 http://wikileaks.org/cable/2005/07/05AMMAN5624.html.

27 http://wikileaks.org/cable/2005/08/05AMMAN6612.html.

28 http://wikileaks.org/cable/2006/11/06MANAMA1925.html.

29 http://wikileaks.org/cable/2005/07/05ASUNCION869.html.

30 http://wikileaks.org/cable/2005/07/05ASUNCION860.html.

31 http://wikileaks.org/cable/2006/07/06ASUNCION750.html.

32 http://wikileaks.org/cable/2005/07/05ASUNCION860.html.

33 Elise Keppler, "The United States and the International Criminal Court: The Bush Administration's Approach and a Way Forward

Under the Obama Adm," Human Rights Watch, August 2, 2009, at hrw.org.

34 http://wikileaks.org/wiki/CRS:_Article_98_Agreements_ and_Sanctions_on_U.S._Foreign_Aid_to_Latin_America,_ March_22,_2007.

35 http://wikileaks.org/cable/2005/11/05SANJOSE2717.html.

36 Council on Hemispheric Affairs, "Costa Rica's Fateful Move: San José Expands Its Role in US-Led Counter-Narcotics Efforts," August 4, 2010, at coha.org.

37 http://wikileaks.org/cable/2004/03/04BRASILIA745.html.

38 http://wikileaks.org/cable/2004/12/04BRASILIA3154.html.

39 http://wikileaks.org/cable/2005/12/05SANTIAGO2573.html.

40 http://wikileaks.org/cable/2005/12/05SANTIAGO2573.html.

41 http://wikileaks.org/cable/2006/01/06SANTIAGO130.html.

42 http://wikileaks.org/cable/2004/11/04QUITO3028.html.

43 http://wikileaks.org/cable/2004/11/04QUITO3103.html.

44 http://wikileaks.org/cable/2005/03/05QUITO590.html.

45 http://wikileaks.org/cable/2005/04/05QUITO773.html.

46 http://wikileaks.org/cable/2005/05/05QUITO1048.html.

47 http://wikileaks.org/cable/2005/05/05QUITO1169.html.

48 http://wikileaks.org/cable/2005/09/05QUITO2235.html.

49 http://wikileaks.org/cable/2006/05/06QUITO1157.html.

50 http://wikileaks.org/wiki/CRS:_Article_98_Agreements_ and_Sanctions_on_U.S._Foreign_Aid_to_Latin_America,_ March_22,_2007.

51 Glenn Greenwald, "US Continues Bush Policy of Opposing ICC Prosecutions," *Salon*, February 28, 2011, at salon.com.

52 Colum Lynch, "Exclusive: US to Support ICC War Crimes Prosecution in Syria," *Foreign Policy*, May 7, 2011, at foreignpolicy.com.

53 https://wikileaks.org/cable/2010/02/10TELAVIV417.html.

54 Clayton Swisher, "Spy Cables: Abbas and Israel Ally Against 2009 UN Probe," Al Jazeera, February 23, 2015, at aljazeera.com.

55 Jeff Rathke, "Statement on ICC Prosecutor's Decision," Press Statement, US Department of State, January 16, 2015, at state.gov.

56 Allyn Fisher-Ilan, "US Senator Threatens Aid Cut to Palestinians Over ICC Move," *Reuters*, January 19, 2015, at reuters.com.

CHAPTER 6: EUROPE

1 For a full rundown of American assessments of Sarkozy's personality and leadership style, see Angelique Chrisafis, "Nicolas Sarkozy Thin-skinned and Authoritarian," *Guardian*, November 30, 2010.

2 "Internal Source Kept US Informed of Merkel Coalition Negotiations," *Der Spiegel*, November 28, 2010.

3 Annalisa Piras, "WikiLeaks Cables Portrait of Silvio Berlusconi Is a Worry Beyond Italy," *Guardian*, December 3, 2010.

4 Eric Lipton, Nicola Clark, and Andrew Lehren, "Diplomats Help Push

Sales of Jetliners on the Global Market," *New York Times*, January 2, 2011.

5 Ivan Dikov, "The Bulgaria 2011 Review: Defense," Novinite.com, January 6, 2012.

6 Mark Adomanis, "Defense Spending in 'New Europe' Is Collapsing," *Forbes*, July 31, 2013.

7 Food and Water Watch, *Biotech Ambassadors* (Washington, DC: Food and Water Watch, 2013), p. 16.

8 Geoff Pugh, "Food Minister Owen Paterson Backs GM Crops," *Daily Telegraph,* December 12, 2012.

9 Belén Fernández, "Monsanto and the Other Chemical Weapon," *Warscapes*, April 25, 2014.

10 Vlad Odobescu, "Romania Bowing to US Pressure to Rethink GMO Ban," *Black Sea*, October 30, 2013.

11 On September 22, 2003, the European Commission passed Regulation 1829/2003 which established a single authorization for the sale and use of GM food and feed products. The full text of the Regulation on genetically modified food and feed, "Regulation (EC) No 1829/2003 of the European Parliament and of the Council of 22 September 2003," can be found at ec.europa.eu.

12 According to the European Union, "Under European Commission regulation No. 1829/2003 GM food and feed may only be placed on the market when, after an extensive risk assessment by EPSA, it has been authorized following a single authorization procedure. Poland did not respect the harmonized procedures foreseen in this Regulation neither for the authorization of GM feed nor for the adoption of safeguard measures ... Therefore, the Commission considers that, by introducing a ban in 2013, Poland is creating legal uncertainty and is in breach of its obligations under EU law." For more information and documents related to the dispute, see europa.eu/rapid/press-release_IP-11-292_en.htm.

13 Dave Keating, "French Court Annuls GMO Ban," *European Voice*, August 2, 2013.

14 Frederic Bozo, *Histoire secrète de la crise irakienne* (Paris: Perrin, 2013).

15 "Rumsfeld: France, Germany Are 'Problems' in Iraqi Conflict," CNN.com, January 23, 2003.

16 Jean-Marie Colombani, "Nous Sommes Tous Américains," *Le Monde*, September 12, 2001.

17 Matthias Gebauer and Marcel Rosenbach, "Skimming Off the TOP: US Army Charged Germany Fees for Afghanistan Donations," *Der Spiegel*, December 2, 2010.

18 For more on the continuing public protests at Shannon Airport, see "Protests at Shannon Airport Increase Despite Two-Thirds Fall in US Military Flights," *Irish Times*, February 19, 2014.

19 "Italians 'Cannot Try US Soldier,'" BBC, October 27, 2007.

20 Khaled El-Masri, "I am not a state secret," *Los Angeles Times*, March 3, 2007.

21 Nicholas Kulish, "Court Finds Rights Violation in CIA Rendition Case," *New York Times*, December 13, 2012.

22 John Goetz and Matthias Gebauer, "US Pressured Italy to Influence Judiciary," *Der Spiegel*, December 17, 2010.

23 Gaia Pianigiani, "Italy Jails Ex-Officials for Rendition," *New York Times*, February 12, 2013.

24 "Spanish Jurist Garzon at Forefront of WikiLeaks Fight," *EuroNews*, August 17, 2012.

CHAPTER 7: RUSSIA

1 David Remnick, "Watching the Eclipse," *New Yorker*, August 11, 2014.

2 Fred Weir, "Wikileaks Release: In Russia, Fear of Damage to Future US Relations," *Christian Science Monitor*, November 26, 2010.

3 Heather Hurlburt, "Why WikiLeaks is Bad for Progressive US Foreign Policy," *New Republic*, November 30, 2010.

4 Michael Barker, "Elite 'Democratic' Planning at the Council on Foreign Relations," ZNet, February 27, 2008, at zcomm.org.

5 Keir A. Lieber and Darryl G. Press, "The Rise of US Nuclear Primacy," *Foreign Affairs*, March/April 2006.

6 Charles King, "The Five Day War," *Foreign Affairs*, November/December 2008.

7 "How the Rose Revolution Happened," BBC News, May 10, 2005.

8 Niall Green, "WikiLeaks Exposes US Cover-Up of Georgian Attack on South Ossetia," World Socialist Web Site, December 6, 2010, at wsws.org.

9 C. J. Chivers, "Embracing Georgia, US Misread Signs of Rifts," *New York Times*, December 1, 2010.

10 Jonathan Masters and Greg Bruno, "Ballistic Missile Defense," Council on Foreign Relations, May 1, 2013, at cfr.org; James E. Goodby, "Looking Back: The 1986 Reykjavik Summit," *Arms Control Today*, September 2006.

11 "US Missile Defense Programs at a Glance," Arms Control Association Fact Sheet, June 2013, at armscontrol.org.

12 Ibid.

13 David M. Herszenhorn and Michael Gordon, "US Cancels Part of Missile Defense that Russia Opposed," *New York Times*, March 16, 2013.

14 Eric Auner, "Missile Defense Budget Holds Steady," Arms Control Association, April 2014, at armscontrol.org.

15 Jeffrey Lewis, "Bar Nunn," *Foreign Policy*, October 17, 2012.

16 SBLMs are submarine-launched ballistic missiles, as opposed to ICBMs, which are land-based intercontinental ballistic missiles. CBMs are conventional ballistic missiles, which are not armed with nuclear warheads.

17 The United States Department of Defense, "National Security and Nuclear Weapons in the 21st Century," September 2008, at defense.gov.

18 Streltsov was referring to Secretary of State Clinton, who was in Moscow to meet with Minister of Foreign Affairs Lavrov.

19 Interview by email with Jeffrey Lewis of the James Martin Center for Nonproliferation Studies, March 10, 2014.

20 "Russia Warns of Nuclear Response to US Global Strike Program," *RIA Novosti*, November 11, 2013.

CHAPTER 8: TURKEY

1 Michael Kelly, "Former Ambassador: NATO Needs to Help 'Contain and Isolate' the Chaos in Syria," *Business Insider*, October 5, 2012, p. 2.

2 "Turkish Experts Not Surprised by WikiLeaks Revelations," *Today's Zaman*, November 30, 2010, pp. 1–2.

3 Eric Draitser, "Russia, Europe, and the Geopolitics of Energy," *New Eastern Outlook*, February 25, 2014, p. 2.

4 Ibid.

5 Okan Al Tiparmak and Claire Berlinski, "The Wikileaks Cables on Turkey: 20/20 Tunnel Vision," *Meria Journal* 15: 1 (March 2011).

6 Valerie Strauss and Sharon Higgins, "Largest Charter Network in US: Schools Tied to Turkey," *Post Local*, March 27, 2012.

7 Fabio Vicini, "The Irrepressible Charm of the State: Dershane Closures and the Domestic War for Power in Turkey," *Jadaliyya*, March 24, 2014.

8 David P. Goldman, "Turkish Financial Crisis Adds to Region's Chaos," *Asia Times*, February 5, 2014.

9 Murat Yetkin, "Kurdish and German Angles of Erdoğan-Gülen Rift," *Daily News*, February 4, 2014.

CHAPTER 9: ISRAEL

1 Jill Lawless/Associated Press, "WikiLeaks Release: US Briefs Allies About Upcoming Revelations," *Huffington Post*, November 26, 2010, at huffingtonpost.com.

2 Ross Colvin, "'Cut Off Head of Snake' Saudis Told US on Iran," *Reuters*, November 29, 2010, at reuters.com.

3 Allyn Fisher-Ilan, "Israel Says WikiLeaks Vindicates Its Iran Focus," *Reuters*, November 29, 2010, at reuters.com.

4 Sever Plocker, "The World Thinks Like Us," *Ynetnews*, November 29, 2010, at ynetnews.com.

5 Anti-Defamation League, "Conspiracy Theories Linking Israel to WikiLeaks Circulate on the Internet," January 18, 2011, at archive.adl.org.

6 Amira Howeidy, "PA Relinquished Right of Return," Al Jazeera, January 24, 2011, at aljazeera.com.

7 Ed Pilkington, "US Vetoes UN Condemnation of Israeli Settlements," *Guardian*, February 18, 2011.

8 See, for example, Human Rights Watch, "Israel/Palestine: Growing Abuse in West Bank," January 21, 2014, at hrw.org.

9 "Dirty water" is a reference to the IDF's chemically treated water that duplicates the effects of skunk spray.

10 Conal Urquhart, "Gaza on Brink of Implosion as Aid Cut-Off Starts to Bite," *Guardian*, April 15, 2006.

11 Following Israel's granting of access to Goldstone of documents to which the commission had previously been denied access, Goldstone expressed his belief that one short segment of the 575-page report accusing Israel of certain crimes against humanity should not have been written as definitively as it had. Some analysts have erroneously claimed subsequently that he renounced the entire report.

12 See Stephen Zunes, "Gaza and the Bipartisan War on Human Rights," *Foreign Policy In Focus*, October 17, 2014, at fpif.org.

13 See Juan Cole, "Wikileaks: Israel Plans Total War on Lebanon, Gaza," Informed Comment, January 2, 2011, at juancole.com.

14 "US Senate Committee Passes Resolution to Back Israel in Conflict with Iran," *Haaretz*, April 17, 2013.

15 See *Jewish Chronicle Online*, "WikiLeaks: Extent of US-Israel Ties Laid Bare," April 14, 2011, at thejc.com.

16 Seymour Hersh, "Our Men in Iran," *New Yorker*, April 6, 2012.

17 Isabel Kersher, "Israeli Strike on Iran Would Be 'Stupid,' Ex-Spy Chief Says," *New York Times*, May 8, 2011.

18 Noah Habeeb, "A US Shift Away from Israel?," *Foreign Policy in Focus*, August 8, 2014, at fpif.org.

CHAPTER 10: SYRIA

1 "Influencing the SARG in the End of 2006," December 13, 2006, https://wikileaks.org/cable/2006/12/06DAMASCUS5399.html.

2 "Saudi Intelligence Chief Talks Regional Security with Brennan Delegation," March 22, 2009, https://wikileaks.org/plusd/cables/09RIYADH445_a.html.

3 "Saudi Shia Clash with Police in Medina," February 24, 2009, http://www.wikileaks.org/plusd/cables/09RIYADH346_a.html.

4 "Khaddam Slams Syria over Row with Saudi Arabia," *Beirut Daily Star*, August 20, 2007, at dailystar.com.lb.

5 "Interview with Former Syrian Vice-President Abdul Halim Khaddam," *Asharq Al-Awsat*, January 6, 2006, at aawsat.net.

6 See, for example, Stephen Kinzer, *Overthrow: America's Century of Regime Change from Hawaii to Iraq* (New York: Times Books, 2006).

7   Alexander Cockburn, "Fact Finding," *Village Voice*, December 27, 1983, republished in Alexander Cockburn, *Corruptions of Empire* (London: Verso, 1987), p. 349.

8   Andy Sullivan, "Candidate Paul assigns reading to Giuliani," *Reuters*, May 24, 2007, at reuters.com.

9   Nitya Venkataraman, "Ron Paul Recruits Anonymous to Attack Rudy's Foreign Policy," ABC News, May 22, 2007, at abcnews. go.com.

10 "US Walks Out on Ahmadinejad's 9/11 Comment," CBS News, September 23, 2010, at cbsnews.com.

11 "US admits funding Syrian opposition," CBC News, April 18, 2011, at cbc.ca.

12 "Announcement to Fund Opposition Harshly Criticized by Anti-Regime Elements, Others," February 21, 2006, **https://wikileaks.org/ plusd/cables/06DAMASCUS701_a.html**.

13 "Behavior Reform: Next Steps for a Human Rights Strategy," April 28, 2009, **https://wikileaks.org/plusd/cables/09DAMASCUS306_a. html**.

14 "Human Rights Updates—SARG Budges on TIP, but Little Else," February 7, 2010, **https://wikileaks.org/plusd/cables/10DAMASCUS 106_a.html**.

15 "Murky Alliances: Muslim Brotherhood, the Movement for Justice and Democracy, and the Damascus Declaration," July 8, 2009, **https://wikileaks.org/plusd/cables/09DAMASCUS477_a.html**.

16 "Show Us the Money! SARG Suspects 'Illegal' USG Funding," September 23, 2009, **https://wikileaks.org/plusd/cables/09DAMA SCUS692_a.html**.

17 "Human Rights Updates—SARG Budges On TIP, But Little Else."

18 Elise Labott, Brian Todd, and Dugald McConnell, "US Denies Support for Syrian Opposition Tantamount to Regime Change," CNN, April 19, 2011, at cnn.com.

CHAPTER 11: IRAN

1   Gareth Porter, *Manufactured Crisis: The Untold Story of the Iran Nuclear Scare* (Charlottesville, VA: Just World Books, 2014), pp. 275–7.

2   Glenn Kessler, "US Hails Israeli Plan on West Bank Settlement Building," *Washington Post*, November 26, 2009.

3   Gary Samore, remarks at a Council on Foreign Relations Symposium on "Iran and Policy Options for the Next Administration, Session Two, The Nuclear Dimension and Iranian Foreign Policy," Harvard University, September 8, 2008. The transcript of the session has been taken down from the CFR website, but the author has a copy of the transcript in his possession. See also Gareth Porter, "US Nuclear Option on Iran Linked to Israeli Attack Threat," Inter Press Service, April 23, 2010.

4   Gareth Porter and Jim Lobe, "Obama Team Debates Stance on Israel Attack Threat," Inter Press Service, April 8, 2009.

5   On the CIA's retreat from its 1995 NIE on ballistic missile threats under political pressure from the missile defense interests in Congress, see Michael Dobbs, "How Politics Helped Redefine Threat," *Washington Post*, January 14, 2002.

6   See National Security Presidential Directive/NSPD-23, December 16, 2002, at fas.org.

7   Michael Abramowitz and Walter Pincus, "Administration Diverges on Missile Defense," *Washington Post*, October 24, 2007.

8   DOD News Briefing with Secretary Robert Gates and Vice-Chairman of the JCS Gen. James Cartwright, September 17, 2009.

9   On the previous Russian cooperation with the US in putting pressure on Iran to cease enrichment, see Gareth Porter, "Russian Manipulation of Reactor Fuel Belies US Iran Argument," Inter Press Service, May 19, 2014.

10 William Broad, James Glanz, and David E. Sanger, "Iran Fortifies Its Arsenal with the Aid of North Korea," *New York Times*, November 28, 2010.

11 The most authoritative analysis of the North Korean missile program confirmed that it was only in October 2010—ten months *after* the joint assessment meeting—that North Korea first displayed what appeared to be a B-25 or "Musadan" missile in a military parade. And a close examination of the photographs of the missile showed clearly that it had been a crudely constructed mock-up rather than a real missile. Markus Schiller, *Characterizing the North Korea Nuclear Missile Threat* (Santa Monica, CA: RAND Corporation, 2012), p. 87.

12 Reuters, "UAE First Mideast Buyer of PAC-3 missile—Lockheed," December 23, 2008; Antonie Boessenkool, "UAE to Buy Raytheon's Patriot Missiles," *Defense News*, December 18, 2008.

13 Adam Entous, "Saudi Arms Deal Advances," *Wall Street Journal*, September 12, 2012; Michael Knights, *Rising to Iran's Challenge: GCC Military Capability and US Security Cooperation*, Washington Institute for Near East Policy, Policy Forum 177, June 2013, p. 9; Arthur Bright, "Eyeing Iran US Details $60b. Arms Sale to Saudi Arabia," *Christian Science Monitor*, October 21, 2010.

14 David E. Sanger, James Glanz, and Jo Becker, "Around the World, Distress Over Iran," *New York Times*, November 28, 2010; Barak Ravid, "Netanyahu: WikiLeaks Cables Show Israel Is Right on Iran," *Haaretz*, November 29, 2010.

15 Porter, *Manufactured Crisis*, pp. 272, 277–8.

16 David E. Sanger and Eric Schmitt, "US Speeding Up Missile Defenses in Persian Gulf," *New York Times*, January 31, 2010.

17 Porter, *Manufactured Crisis*, pp. 135–9, 191–208.

18 Ibid., pp. 178–87.

19 IAEA Report GOV/2007/58, November 15, 2007, pp. 4–5.

20 *Iran: Nuclear Intentions and Capabilities*, National Intelligence Estimate, November 2007, at graphics8.nytimes.com.

21 Mohamed ElBaradei, *The Age of Deception: Nuclear Diplomacy in Treacherous Times* (New York: Metropolitan, 2011), p. 253.

22 GOV/2011/65, November 8, 2011, annex, p. 2.

23 Porter, *Manufactured Crisis*, pp. 212–16.

CHAPTER 12: IRAQ

1 Dahr Jamail, "Iraq War Vet: 'We Were Told to Just Shoot People, and the Officers Would Take Care of Us,'" Truthout, April 7, 2010, truth-out.org.

2 Just Foreign Policy estimates 1,455,590 Iraqi deaths as a result of the US-led invasion and occupation, as of April 26, 2014.

3 FM 3-05.130.

4 FM 3-05.130.

5 Dahr Jamail, "The Dirty War," Truthout, July 9, 2009, truth-out.org.

6 Dahr Jamail, "Govt. Death Squads Ravaging Baghdad," Inter Press Service, October 19, 2006.

7 Dahr Jamail, "Baghdad Slipping into Civil War," Inter Press Service, April 19, 2006.

8 Dahr Jamail, "Partition Fears Begin to Rise," Inter Press Service, July 16, 2007.

9 Dahr Jamail, "A Tale of One City, Now Two," Inter Press Service, November 12, 2007.

10 Dahr Jamail, "Iran Ties Weaken Government Further," Inter Press Service, August 13, 2007.

11 Dahr Jamail, "Kurds and Shia Fight for Power in Baghdad," Inter Press Service, May 29, 2007.

12 Dahr Jamail, "Skeptical After Second Shrine Attack," Inter Press Service, June 20, 2007.

13 Human Rights Watch, "Iraq: Detainees Describe Torture in Secret Jail," April 27, 2010, at hrw.org.

14 Dahr Jamail, "'Illegal' Execution Enrages Arabs," Inter Press Service, January 2, 2007.

15 Philip Dermer, "The 'Sons of Iraq,' Abandoned by Their American Allies," *Wall Street Journal*, 1 July 2014.

16 Ibid.

17 Dahr Jamail, "'Awakening' Forces Arouse New Conflicts," Inter Press Service, December 26, 2007.

18 "WikiLeaks: Iraq War Logs 'Reveal Truth about Conflict,'" BBC, October 23, 2010.

19 WikiLeaks, "Revealed: Pentagon's Link to Iraqi Torture Centres," March 6, 2013, at wikileaks-press.org.

20 Ibid.

21 Human Rights Watch, "US: Abu Ghraib Only the 'Tip of the Iceberg,'" April 28, 2005, at hrw.org.

22   Amnesty International, "Iraq: A Decade of Abuses," March 11, 2013, at amnesty.org.
23   WikiLeaks, "Classified Memo from US Maj. Gen. Kelly Confirms Fallujah Gulag," March 26, 2008, at wikileaks.org.
24   Human Rights Watch, World Report 2010, at hrw.org.
25   WikiLeaks, "Murder in Iraq: US Army Protective Order for Article 32 Investigation, Jul 24, 2006," February 9, 2009.

CHAPTER 13: AFGHANISTAN

1   Russell O. Davis, "Hybrid Power: Mobility Air Forces and Foreign Policy," Army Command and General Staff Coll., Fort Leavenworth KS School of Advanced Military Studies, May 21, 2010, at dtic.mil.
2   Deborah Zabarenko, "US Offers Lesson on How to Tell Cluster Bombs from Food Packs," Washington Post, October 30, 2001.
3   Richard Sale, "A New Kind of War Part 1," Sic Semper Tyrannis, May 25, 2009, at turcopolier.typepad.com.
4   ISAF, "Metrics Brief, 2007–2008," at wlstorage.net.
5   Cpt Nathan Finney, "Human Terrain Team Handbook," September 2008, at wlstorage.net.

CHAPTER 14: EAST ASIA

1   Foreign Policy, January 19, 2012.
2   Normitsu Onishi, "Bomb by Bomb, Japan Sheds Military Restraints," New York Times, July 23, 2007.
3   Martin Fackler, "With Bold Stand, Japan Opposition Wins a Landslide," New York Times, August 31, 2009.
4   Choe Sang-Hun, "North Korea Claims to Conduct 2nd Nuclear Test," New York Times, May 25, 2009.
5   I summarized the impact of the Lee-Obama collaboration in Tim Shorrock, "North Korea: What's Really Happening," Salon.com, April 5, 2013.
6   Martin Fackler, "Memo From Japan: Japan's Relationship with US Gets a Closer Look," New York Times, December 1, 2009.
7   Martin Fackler and Hiroko Tabuchi, "Japanese Leader Backtracks on Revising Base Agreement," New York Times, May 10, 2009.
8   The article's title, too, was sadly revealing: Martin Fackler and Mark Landler, "US Relations Played Major Role in Downfall of Japanese Prime Minister," New York Times, June 3, 2010.
9   If this comes to fruition, Okinawa will receive over $24 billion in subsidies over the next eight years.
10   Gavan McCormack, "Storm Ahead: Okinawa's Outlook for 2015," Asia Pacific Journal 13: 2 (3) (January 12, 2015), available at japanfocus.org.
11   Readers interested in following events in Okinawa since the dramatic

November 2014 election should follow the *Japan Times* dispatches of Jon Mitchell, a Welsh reporter based in Tokyo, at japantimes.co.jp.

CHAPTER 15: SOUTHEAST ASIA

1   Patrick Porter, "Sharing Power? Prospects for a US Concert-Balance Strategy," Strategic Studies Institute, 2013, at strategicstudiesinstitute. army.mil.
2   John Mearshimer, "Can China Rise Peacefully?," *National Interest*, October 25, 2014, at nationalinterest.org.
3   Ibid.
4   Walden Bello, "From American Lake to People's Pacific in the Twenty-First Century," in Setsu Shihematsu and Keith Camacho, eds, *Militarized Currents: Toward a Decolonized Future in Asia and the Pacific* (Minneapolis: University of Minnesota Press, 2010).
5   James Holmes and Toshi Yoshihara, "Is China Planning String of Pearls?" *The Diplomat*, February 21, 2011, at thediplomat.com.
6   Bello, "From American Lake to People's Pacific."
7   Neil Sheehan, *A Bright Shining Lie: John Paul Vann and America in Vietnam* (New York: Vintage, 1989), p. 131.
8   Benedict Anderson, "Old Corruption," *London Review of Books*, February 5, 1987.
9   Pankaj Mishra, *From the Ruins of Empire: The Revolt Against the West and the Remaking of Asia* (New York: Picador, 2013); Benedict Anderson, "First Filipino," *London Review of Books*, October 16, 1997.
10 James Fallows, "A Damaged Culture: A New Philippines?," *The Atlantic*, November 1, 1987; Anderson, *First Filipino*.
11 Mishra, *From the Ruins of Empire*.
12 Fallows, "A Damaged Culture."
13 Benigno Aquino, "What's Wrong with the Philippines," *Foreign Affairs*, July 1968.
14 Walden Bello and David Kinley, *Development Debacle: The World Bank in the Philippines* (California: Institute for Food and Development Policy, 1982).
15 Mearsheimer, "Can China Rise Peacefully?"
16 Porter, "Sharing Power?," p. 16.
17 Benedict Anderson, "From Miracle to Crash," *London Review of Books*, April 16, 1998.
18 Walden Bello, *Dilemmas of Domination: The Unmaking of the American Empire* (New York: Holt, 2006); Benedict Anderson, "Exit Suharto: Obituary for a Mediocre Tyrant," *New Left Review* II/50 (March 2008).
19 Henry Kissinger, *On China* (New York: Penguin, 2011).
20 Francis Fukuyama, "The End of History?," *National Interest*, Summer 1989.

21 "Excerpts From Pentagon's Plan: 'Prevent the Re-Emergence of a New Rival,'" *New York Times*, March 8, 1992.

22 Bello, *Dilemmas of Domination*.

23 Eric Schmitt, "US-Philippine Command May Signal War's Next Phase," *New York Times*, January 16, 2002.

24 Richard Javad Heydarian, "The China-Philippines-US Triangle," *Foreign Policy in Focus*, Institute for Policy Studies, Washington, DC, December 16, 2010.

25 Ibid; Achariya and Arabinda Achariya, "The Myth of the Second Front: Localizing the 'War on Terror' in Southeast Asia," *Washington Quarterly*, Fall 2007.

26 It was common knowledge, reflected in Washington's statements in Obama's trips to these countries, that the US has been irked by the supposedly protectionist policies of these countries, which had affected American companies' ability to increase their exports.

27 Richard Javad Heydarian, "Obama's Free Trade Strategy Falters in Asia," Inter Press Service, June 14, 2014, at ipsnews.net; "Japan, America and the Trans-Pacific Partnership: Stalemate," *The Economist*, October 4, 2014.

28 Joshua Kurlantzick, *Charm Offensive: How China's Soft Power Is Transforming the World* (New York: Yale University Press, 2007).

29 Amado Mendoza and Richard Javad Heydarian, "Member Country: Philippines," *ASEAN-CHINA Free Trade Area: Challenges, Opportunities, and the Road Ahead*, Monograph No. 22, National University of Singapore, 2012.

30 Heydarian, "China-Philippines-US Triangle."

31 Kurlantzick, *Charm Offensive*.

32 Kurt Campbell and Ely Ratner, "Far Eastern Promises," *Foreign Affairs*, May/June 2014.

33 Kissinger, *On China*.

34 Kurlantzick, *Charm Offensive*.

35 American popularity in the Philippines is in fact consistently reflected in surveys by Gallup and Pew. See, for example, Pew Research Center, "Chapter 1. Attitudes toward the United States," July 18, 2013, at pewglobal.org; and Zachary Keck, "Obama's Approval Rating Rises in Asia," *The Diplomat*, April 12, 2014, at thediplomat.com.

36 Robert Kaplan, *Asia's Cauldron*.

37 See Kaplan, *Asia's Cauldron*.

38 Heydarian, "Obama's Free Trade Strategy Falters in Asia."

39 **https://wikileaks.org/tpp.**

40 Henry Farrell, "US Isolated in the Trans-Pacific Partnership Negotiations," *Washington Post*, November 18, 2013.

41 Heydarian, "Obama's Free Trade Strategy Falters in Asia"; "Japan, America and the Trans-Pacific Partnership: Stalemate."

42 Toby Harnden, "WikiLeaks: US diplomats 'have been spying on UN leadership," *Daily Telegraph*, November 28, 2010.

43 "Cables 'Character Assassination': SBY," *Sydney Morning Herald*, March 14, 2011.

44 Kaplan, *Asia's Cauldron.*

45 Critics of the policy of pivoting toward Asia, such as Robert Ross, however, contend that Washington has exacerbated the maritime disputes by encouraging hardliners both in Beijing and in rival claimant states to push the boundaries of their territorial posturing in order to test American commitment to its allies amid China's expanding maritime ambitions. See Robert Ross, "The Problem with the Pivot," *Foreign Affairs*, November/December 2012.

CHAPTER 16: SOUTH AFRICA

1 Francis Njubi Nesbitt, *Race for Sanctions: African Americans Against Apartheid, 1946–1994* (Bloomington, IN: Indiana University Press, 2004).

2 Charles C. Diggs and Lester L. Wolff, *Report of Special Study Mission to Southern Africa, August 10–30, 1969* (Washington, DC: Government Printing Office, 1969).

3 Nesbitt, *Race for Sanctions*, pp. 73–4.

4 Ibid., p. 105.

5 Ibid., p. 105.

6 "Group Decries Rhodesia Elections, Urges Sanctions," *Washington Post*, March 21, 1979, p. A17.

7 "Is There Life After Andy?," *Washington Post*, September 16, 1979, p. A4.

8 Nesbitt, *Race for Sanctions*, pp. 92, 129.

9 Truth and Reconciliation Commission of South Africa (1998, 2003). *Report* (Volumes 1-7). Cape Town: The Truth and Reconciliation Commission. TRC, 1998, vol. 2, p. 176.

10 Francis Njubi Nesbitt, "The rise and fall of apartheid," in Patrick Mason, ed., *Encyclopedia of Race and Racism*, Vol. 2 (New York: Macmillan Reference, 2013), p. 159.

11 Ibid., p. 160.

CHAPTER 17: LATIN AMERICA AND THE CARIBBEAN

1 John Kerry, "Remarks on US Policy in the Western Hemisphere," November 18, 2013, at state.gov.

2 Juan Forero, "Cables Released by WikiLeaks Reveal US Concerns over South America," *Washington Post*, December 2, 2010.

3 William I. Robinson, *A Faustian Bargain: US Intervention in the Nicaraguan Elections and American Foreign Policy in the Post–Cold War Era* (Boulder, CO: Westview, 1992).

4 Greg Grandin, *Empire's Workshop: Latin America, the United States, and the Rise of the New Imperialism* (New York: Holt, 2007).

5   This is not to underplay US interference in foreign elections, bribery, and the cooptation of foreign officials, politicians, civil society and other groups, and other forms of foreign interference, which the US had carried out for decades, through the CIA and other agencies—and which it still does. See, for example, Tim Weiner, *Legacy of Ashes: The History of the CIA* (New York: Anchor: 2008).

6   This was between 1980 and 2000. See Mark Weisbrot and Rebecca Ray, "The Scorecard on Development, 1960–2010: Closing the Gap?," Center for Economic and Policy Research, April 2011, at cepr.net.

7   Joe Rubin, "El Salvador: Payback," *Frontline* (PBS), October 12, 2004, at pbs.org.

8   Millennium Challenge Corporation, "El Salvador Compact," at www.mcc.gov.

9   World Bank, "El Salvador Overview," at worldbank.org.

10 World Economic Outlook Database, April 2014 Edition, International Monetary Fund, at imf.org.

11 See "EUA ya eligió a Munguía Payés para el cargo, dice vocero del FMLN," La Prensa Grafica, November 15, 2011, at laprensa grafica.com.

12 Robinson, *Faustian Bargain*.

13 Colin Powell, "Remarks with Nicaraguan President Enrique Bolaños before Their Working Dinner," State Department, November 3, 2003, at 2001-2009.state.gov.

14 Sean McCormack, "Daily Press Briefing," State Department, November 2, 2006, at 2001-2009.state.gov.

15 Adam Thompson, "Interview: Paul Trivelli, US Ambassador to Managua," *Financial Times*, September 14, 2006.

16 Organization of American States, "Declaracion de Prensa Mision de Observacion Electoral en Nicaragua," September 25, 2006, at oas.org.

17 "La retórica ocultaba las reales intenciones de la embajada," *El Telégrafo*, May 15, 2012, at www.telegrafo.com.ec.

18 "La base de Manta, la 'joya' por la que EE.UU. se jugó todo," *El Telégrafo*, May 16, 2012, at telegrafo.com.ec.

19 *Constitution of the Republic of Ecuador*, October 20, 2008, at pdba. georgetown.edu.

20 Public Citizen, "Timeline on Ecuador's Compulsory Licensing," at citizen.org.

21 World Bank, World Development Indicators, "Antiretroviral Therapy Coverage (% of People Living with HIV)," at data.worldbank.org.

22 ULAN, "Confirman participación de agentes externos en intento de golpe de Estado en Ecuador en 2010," June 12, 2014, at agenciasulan. org.

23 See Richard Lapper and Hal Weitzman, "Morales Poised for Win in Bolivia," *Financial Times*, December 19, 2005.

24 US Department of State, "Bolivia (06/05)" (background note), June 2005, at state.gov.

25 See Mark Weisbrot, "Bolivia's Economy: The First Year," Center for Economic and Policy Research, January 2007, at cepr.net.

26 See also [08LAPAZ1426].

27 Mark Weisbrot and Luis Sandoval, "The Distribution of Bolivia's Most Important Natural Resources and the Autonomy Conflicts," Center for Economic and Policy Research, July 2008, at cepr.net.

28 USAID, "USAID/OTI Bolivia Field Report Jan.–Mar. 2007," archived at web.archive.org.

29 See, for example, Eduardo Garcia, "Foes of Morales Stage General Strike in Bolivia," Reuters, August 19, 2008; Franz Chávez, "Bolivia: Divisions Emerge in Opposition Strategy," Inter Press Service, September 4, 2008, at ipsnews.net; Dan Beeton, "The Fun House Mirror: Distortions and Omissions in the News on Bolivia," *NACLA Report on the Americas*, May 4, 2009, at nacla.org.

30 Senator Richard Lugar (R-IN), the ranking minority member of the Foreign Relations Committee at the time, would subsequently issue a statement acknowledging that the US had made a mistake in not condemning the violence. See Beeton, "Fun House Mirror."

31 See Franz Chávez, "BOLIVIA: Governor Arrested for 'Porvenir Massacre,'" Inter Press Service, September 16, 2008, at www.ipsnews.net.

32 See also [08LAPAZ2000], which states: "There is increasing chatter about threats to President Evo Morales. EAC will form a working group to review consequences should Morales be removed from power either by assassination or coup."

33 Jake Johnston, "Bolivia Expels USAID: Not Why, but Why Not Sooner," Americas Blog (CEPR), May 1, 2013, at cepr.net.

34 Jeb Sprague has done important original research on this subject through interviews with many of the paramilitary leaders, their financiers, and others involved in these events, as well as numerous declassified US government documents. See Jeb Sprague, *Paramilitarism and the Assault on Democracy in Haiti* (New York: Monthly Review, 2012). See also Peter Hallward, *Damming the Flood: Haiti and the Politics of Containment* (London: Verso, 2010); Randall Robinson, *An Unbroken Agony: Haiti, From Revolution to the Kidnapping of a President* (New York: Basic Civitas, 2007); Justin Podur, *Haiti's New Dictatorship: The Coup, the Earthquake and the UN Occupation* (London: Pluto, 2012).

35 Podur includes many cable excerpts and analyses of cables in *Haiti's New Dictatorship*.

36 Dan Coughlin and Kim Ives, "WikiLeaks Haiti: Let Them Live on $3 a Day," *Nation*, June 1, 2011.

37 For more analysis of this cable, see CEPR, "US Embassy: 'Without a UN-Sanctioned ... Force, We Would Be Getting Far Less Help ... in Managing Haiti,'" Haiti Relief and Reconstruction Watch Blog, August 24, 2011, at cepr.net.

38 See, for example, Hallward, *Damming the Flood*, pp. 281–6; Athena

Kolbe and Royce Hutson, "Human Rights Abuse and Other Criminal Violations in Port-au-Prince, Haiti: A Random Survey of Households," *Lancet* 368 (September 2006), pp. 6–9.

39 Kolbe and Hutson, "Human Rights Abuse."

40 Dan Kovalik, email communication with Dan Beeton, June 11, 2014: "… this would be a knowing and premeditated violation of the Geneva Conventions which requires the protection of civilians during an armed conflict, including one of a non-international character, and which prevents the indiscriminate killing of civilians. In this instance, it is being acknowledged in advance that there would be civilian casualties in this operation, and no one, including the [chargé], is saying anything about trying to protect the lives of the civilians in advance or even trying to limit civilian casualties; they are only saying that they will try to provide some aid after the inevitable slaughter has already happened. Indeed, one could argue that this amounted to a premeditated mass murder or massacre (of 4 individuals at a time or more) which would certainly be a war crime and violation of international humanitarian law. This would also amount to a crime against humanity as defined by Article 7 of the Rome Statute of the International Criminal Court which forbids the act of murder 'when committed as part of a widespread or systematic attack directed against any civilian population, with knowledge of the attack.' This would also amount to a war crime as defined by Article 8 of the Rome Statute of the ICC which prohibits 'willful killing' as well as '[i]ntentionally directing attacks against the civilian population as such or against individual civilians not taking direct part in hostilities … when committed as part of a plan or policy …'"

41 For additional analysis, see CEPR, "As US Chargé D'Affaires, Clinton Bush Haiti Fund VP Green Lighted Assault on Slum Despite 'Inevitable …civilian casualties,'" Haiti Relief and Reconstruction Watch, August 31, 2011, at cepr.net.

42 Kim Ives, "WikiLeaks points to US meddling in Haiti," *Guardian*, January 21, 2011.

43 Haiti Information Project, "US Embassy in Haiti Acknowledges Excessive Force by UN," January 24, 2007, at haitiaction.net.

44 See "Haiti's UN Occupation Forces Carry Out Massacre of Poor in Port-au-Prince," July 8, 2005; and "Evidence Mounts of a UN Massacre in Haiti," July 12, 2005, both available at haitiaction.net. Some video footage from the incident is included in Pina's documentary *Haiti: We Must Kill the Bandits* (Haiti Information Project, 2007).

45 Podur provides a summary accounting of many, if not all, of these raids in *Haiti's New Dictatorship*.

46 Dan Coughlin, "WikiLeaks Haiti: US Cables Paint Portrait of Brutal, Ineffectual and Polluting UN Force," *Nation*, October 6, 2011.

47 Kim Ives and Ansel Herz, "WikiLeaks Haiti: The Aristide Files," *Nation*, August 5, 2011.

48 Reported in ibid., among other articles.

CHAPTER 18: VENEZUELA

1 Chávez's "lack of support for the war on terrorism" and "involvement in the affairs of the Venezuelan oil company and the potential impact of that on oil prices" were cited as policies that "irrita[ted]" the US government in a report by the Office of the Inspector General of the United States Department of State and the Broadcasting Board of Governors. See "A Review of US Policy Toward Venezuela: November 2001 April 2002," Report 02-OIG-003, July 2002, at oig.state.gov, pp. 37–9.

2 For additional details, see Mark Weisbrot, "Venezuela's Election Provides Opportunity for Washington to Change Course," McClatchy-Tribune Information Services, December 6, 2006, at cepr.net; Eva Golinger, *The Chávez Code: Cracking US Intervention in Venezuela* (London: Pluto, 2006); *South of the Border*, dir. Oliver Stone (Cinema Libre, 2010).

3 Golinger, *Chávez Code*.

4 Hagamos Democracia, a beneficiary of IRI grants.

5 International Republican Institute, "IRI President Folsom Praises Venezuelan Civil Society's Defense of Democracy," press release, April 12, 2002, at thefreelibrary.com.

6 See, for example, [06CARACAS1262] and [06CARACAS2478].

7 See, for example, [04CARACAS3291].

8 See, for example, [05CARACAS1011], [04CARACAS3342], and [04CARACAS3013].

9 See the excerpt from López and Corina Machado's press conference in the video "What's Really Going on in Venezuela," March 14, 2014, youtube.com.

10 Footage of this incident can be seen in the video "Heroes of Human Rights," available at vimeo.com.

11 https://WikiLeaks.org/U-S-secret-blueprint-to-undermine.html.

12 White House, Office of the Press Secretary, "Remarks to the Press by Vice President Biden and Colombian President Santos, Bogota, Colombia," May 27, 2013, at whitehouse.gov.

13 "Lula advierte sobre interés geopolítico de la Alianza del Pacífico," at youtube.com.

14 Jamaica Information Service, "US$2.4 Billion Provided Under Petrocaribe," March 18, 2013, at jis.gov.jm.

15 Dan Coughlin and Kim Ives, "WikiLeaks Haiti: The PetroCaribe Files," *Nation*, June 1, 2011.

16 Ian James, "AP Interview: Haiti Leader Says Venezuela Aid Key," Associated Press, December 4, 2011, at news.yahoo.com.

17 Ernesto J. Tover, "Pdvsa provee 43% de la energía de 17 países en Petrocaribe," *El Universal*, March 16, 2014, at eluniversal.com.

18 John F. Kelly, "Department of Defense Press Briefing by Gen. Kelly in the Pentagon Briefing Room," US Department of Defense, March 13, 2014, at defense.gov.

19 https://www.WikiLeaks.org/plusd/cables/07SANTIAGO1828_a. html.

20 https://WikiLeaks.org/cable/2006/02/06QUITO407.html.

21 https://WikiLeaks.org/cable/2006/08/06QUITO2150.html.

22 Rudi Williams, "SOUTHCOM Faces Threats to Peace in Latin America, Caribbean," US Department of Defense, American Forces Press Service, March 31, 2004, at defense.gov.

23 https://www.WikiLeaks.org/plusd/cables/07TEGUCIGALPA 1828_a.htm.

24 Tim Padgett, "Is US Opposition to the Honduran Coup Lessening?," *Time*, October 16, 2009.

25 See, for example, [09GUATEMALA977] and [09MEXICO3387].

26 See, for example, [09MONTEVIDEO641] and [10BUENOSAIRES11].

27 Mark Weisbrot, "The United States shows its contempt for Venezuelan democracy," *Guardian*, April 22, 2013.

28 See David Rosnick and Mark Weisbrot, "A Statistical Note on the April 14 Venezuelan Presidential Election and Audit of Results," Center for Economic and Policy Research, May 2013, at cepr.net.

About the Contributors

Foreign Policy in Focus (FPIF) is a "Think Tank Without Walls" connecting the research and action of more than one thousand scholars, advocates, and activists seeking to make the United States a more responsible global partner. It is a project of the Institute for Policy Studies. It is on the web at www.fpif.org.

Dan Beeton has more than a dozen years of experience working on international policy issues with organizations including the Center for Economic Justice, Haiti Reborn, and the US Campaign for Burma. He was associate director for Citizens Trade Campaign. His writings on Haiti, Latin America, trade, and other topics have been published in the *Los Angeles Times* and the *NACLA Report on the Americas*. He is currently the international communications director at CEPR

Phyllis Benn is a fellow of the Institute for Policy Studies and the Transnational Institute in Amsterdam. Her books include *Before and After: US Foreign Policy and the War on Terror*, *Ending the US War in Afghanistan: A Primer*, and the forthcoming *Understanding ISIS and the New Global War on Terror*.

Michael Busch is senior editor at *Warscapes* magazine and contributor to *Foreign Policy in Focus*. He teaches international relations at the City College of New York, and is a doctoral candidate in political science at the Graduate Center, City University of New York.

Peter Certo is a writer and editor based at the Institute for Policy Studies in Washington, DC, where he edits the institute's *Foreign Policy in Focus* website and serves as deputy editor of the nonprofit editorial syndicate *OtherWords*. He is also a former editor and researcher for Right Web, a project that monitors the efforts of foreign policy hawks and neoconservatives to influence US foreign policy, and before that he helped coordinate the first annual Global Day of Action on Military Spending. His writings for *Foreign Policy in Focus* have been syndicated in the *Nation, Common Dreams, Truthout,* and *AlterNet,* among many other progressive outlets, as well as in regionally focused publications like the *Asia Times* and *Informed Comment.*

Conn Hallinan can be read at dispatchesfromtheedgeblog.word press.com.

Sarah Harrison is a journalist, and WikiLeaks' investigations editor. In June 2013, Harrison accompanied Edward Snowden when he left Hong Kong to seek asylum, ensuring he could leave Hong Kong safely and receive asylum from the Russian Federation. She is the acting director of the Courage Foundation, which manages the legal defense of Edward Snowden, among others, and fights for the protection of truth-tellers worldwide. Harrison was a senior coordinator in the *Cablegate* publication, and in the creation of the PlusD archive.

Richard Heydarian is an assistant professor in political science at De La Salle University, Philippines, where he teaches graduate and undergraduate courses on international relations. He has authored more than 400 articles, policy papers, and op-eds on Asian geopolitical and economic affairs, writing for and/or interviewed by *Foreign Affairs*, the BBC, Bloomberg, Al Jazeera, the *Huffington Post*, the *New York Times*, the *Wall Street Journal*, the *National Interest*, and the *Nation*, among other publications. As a specialist on foreign policy and economic development issues, he has served as a consultant to a number of local and international institutions, and written for various leading think tanks across the Asia-Pacific region and beyond. He is the author of *How Capitalism Failed the Arab World: The Economic Roots and Precarious Future of the Arab Uprisings* and *The Philippines: The US, China and the Struggle for Asia's Pivot State* (forthcoming).

Dahr Jamail is an award-winning independent journalist who reported from within US-occupied Iraq for over a year. He is the author of three books about the US invasion and occupation of Iraq, and is a staff reporter for Truthout.org.

Jake Johnston is the lead author for CEPR's Haiti: Relief and Reconstruction Watch blog, and has authored papers on Haiti concerning the ongoing cholera epidemic, aid accountability and transparency, and the US foreign aid system. His articles have been published in outlets such as the *Hill*, *AlterNet*, *Truthout*, and the *Caribbean Journal*.

Alexander Main is the senior associate for international policy at CEPR. His areas of expertise include Latin American integration and regionalism, US security and counternarcotics policy in Central America, US development assistance to Haiti, and US relations with Bolivia, Ecuador, Honduras, and Venezuela. He has written for *Foreign Policy*, the *Los Angeles Times*, *NACLA*, *Dissent* and *Le Monde diplomatique*. He is regularly interviewed by international media such as CNN en español, Telemundo, Al Jazeera English, and the Canadian Broadcasting Corporation.

Robert Naiman is policy director at Just Foreign Policy (just-foreignpolicy.org), a non-partisan, nonprofit membership organization dedicated to reforming US foreign policy so that it reflects the values and interests of the majority of Americans. He writes on US policy reform issues for the *Huffington Post* and other publications. He is president of the board of *Truthout*.

Francis Njubi Nesbitt is an associate professor of Africana studies at San Diego State University. He is the author of *Race for Sanctions* and *Politics of African Diasporas* (2012). He was a visiting scholar and professor at the University of California, Los Angeles (2004–05) and at the United States International University in Nairobi, Kenya (2013). He has published numerous book chapters and articles in journals such as *African Affairs*, *Critical Arts*, *Journal of American History*, *International Journal of Southern African Studies*, *African Issues*, *Mots Pluriels*, *Loccumer Protokolle*, *KulturAustausch*, *African World*, and *Africa World Review*. He is a regular contributor to *Foreign Policy in Focus*. His articles on Africa and foreign affairs are published in numerous newspapers and magazines around the world.

Linda Pearson is a Sydney-based activist and writer. She has covered Cablegate for *Green Left Weekly* on a range of topics, from Australian foreign policy to US interference in Ecuador. She has also documented the US criminal investigation into WikiLeaks and the Australian government's treatment of Julian Assange since 2010. She has been actively involved in campaigning to support WikiLeaks and defend the rights of Julian Assange and Chelsea Manning.

Gareth Porter is an independent investigative journalist and historian who specializes in covering issues related to the US national security state. Since 2004, he has written on US policy and operations in Iraq, Afghanistan, and Pakistan, as well as toward Iran. Porter was the winner of the 2012 Gellhorn Prize for Journalism. He was Saigon bureau chief of Dispatch News Service International in 1971. He was co-director of the Indochina

Resource Center in Washington, DC, an antiwar education and lobbying organization, from 1973 to 1975. Porter is the author of five books. His latest book is *Manufactured Crisis: The Untold Story of the Iran Nuclear Scare*.

Tim Shorrock is a writer based in Washington, DC, and the author of *Spies for Hire*, the first book about the mass privatization of US intelligence. He grew up in Japan and South Korea during the Cold War, and has been covering the East Asia region since the late 1970s. In 1996, he broke a major story about the previously hidden role of the US government in a violent 1980 military coup in South Korea. Shorrock's writings have appeared in many publications, including the *New York Times*, the *Nation*, *Salon*, the *Daily Beast* and *Foreign Policy in Focus*. He currently writes a weekly blog for the *Nation* on national security, media, and the business of war. Much of his writing, as well as many documents from his stories, can be found on his blog Money Doesn't Talk, It Swears, at www.timshorrock.com. He also posts frequently on Twitter using @TimothyS.

Russ Wellen edits the *Foreign Policy in Focus* blog Focal Points for the Institute of Policy Studies. His interests include Russia and nuclear weapons, and he is a disarmament activist. He has written for the *Bulletin of the Atomic Scientists* and the *Journal of Psychohistory*. Currently, he is writing a book with the working title *Nuclear Ghoul*.

Stephen Zunes is a professor of politics and international studies at the University of San Francisco. Recognized as one the country's leading scholars of US Middle East policy and of strategic nonviolent action, he serves as a senior policy analyst for the Foreign Policy in Focus project of the Institute for Policy Studies, is an associate editor of *Peace Review*, a contributing editor of Tikkun, and a co-chair of the academic advisory committee for the International Center on Nonviolent Conflict.

Index

On the Typeface

This book is set in Sabon, a narrow Garamond-style book face designed in 1968 by the German typographer Jan Tschichold. Tschichold had been a leading voice of sans-serif modernist typography, particularly after the publication of his *Die neue Typographie* in 1928. As a result, the Nazis charged him with "cultural Bolshevism" and forced him to flee Germany for Switzerland.

Tschichold soon renounced modernism—comparing its stringent tenets to the "teachings of National Socialism and fascism"—and extolled the qualities of classical typography, exemplified in his design for Sabon, which he based on the Romain S. Augustin de Garamond in the 1592 Egenolff-Berner specimen sheet.

Sabon is named after the sixteenth-century French typefounder Jacques Sabon, a pupil of Claude Garamond and proprietor of the Egenolff foundry.